Religion and Culture

Religion and Culture

An Anthropological Focus

Raymond Scupin, Editor
Lindenwood University

Prentice Hall, Upper Saddle River, New Jersey 07458

Library of Congress Cataloging-in-Publication Data

Religion and culture: an anthropological focus / RAYMOND SCUPIN,
   editor.
      p. cm.
    Includes index.
    ISBN 0-13-938235-6
    1. Religion and culture.   2. Religions   I. Scupin, Raymond.
  BL65.C8.R427   2000
  306.6—dc21   99-30916

Editorial director: *Charlyce Jones Owen*
Editor in chief: *Nancy Roberts*
Managing editor: *Sharon Chambliss*
Editorial/production supervision: *Edie Riker*
Buyer: *Benjamin D. Smith*
Cover director: *Jayne Conte*
Cover design: *Kiwi Design*
Cover photo: *Tungwai Chau/Stock Illustration Source*
Marketing manager: *Christopher DeJohn*

This book was set in 10/12 New Baskerville by East End Publishing Services, Inc.,
and was printed and bound by RR Donnelly & Sons Company. The cover was
printed by Phoenix Color Corp.

© 2000 by Prentice-Hall, Inc.
Upper Saddle River, New Jersey 07458

Printed in the United States of America

10 9 8 7 6 5 4 3 2

ISBN   0-13-938235-6

Prentice-Hall International (UK) Limited, *London*
Prentice-Hall of Australia Pty. Limited, *Sydney*
Prentice-Hall Canada Inc., *Toronto*
Prentice-Hall Hispanoamericana, S.A., *Mexico*
Prentice-Hall of India Private Limited, *New Delhi*
Prentice-Hall of Japan, Inc., *Tokyo*
Pearson Education Asia Pte. Ltd., *Singapore*
Editora Prentice-Hall do Brasil, Ltda., *Rio de Janeiro*

Contents

Preface

This textbook is designed for the undergraduate student who may never have taken an anthropology or religion course. It is intended as an introduction to the anthropology of religion for the general student who is not majoring in anthropology, and who may be taking only one anthropology course during his or her entire undergraduate experience. At the same time, each chapter includes endnotes with references to classic and current anthropological research for anthropology majors or those students who want to pursue studies in the anthropology of religion. However, the textbook does not emphasize minor theoretical debates among specialists within the discipline of anthropology that may deflect attention away from the major insights that have been gained within the anthropology of religion. We try to cover the basic issues that need to be addressed in order to understand the anthropological perspective on religion. In other words, we intend this textbook to be extremely readable for a general student population

In the first chapter, we introduce the field of anthropology and the research methods used within this field. In addition, we introduce a definition of religion by Clifford Geertz that has been widely influential within the discipline of anthropology so that students can understand the anthropological perspective on religion. The second chapter presents an overview of the early classical theories in the anthropology of religion based on the grand narratives of Tylor, Frazer, Durkheim, Marx, Weber, and Freud. The third chapter introduces the twentieth-century theories within the anthropology of religion based on ethnographic research including the fieldwork orientation of Boas, Malinowski, and Evans-Pritchard and the more recent symbolic approaches of Turner, Douglas, and Geertz. These three chapters provide both a theoretical and evaluative aspect for the classical and contemporary approaches in the anthropology of religion

The rest of the textbook explores the various religious traditions and topics investigated by contemporary anthropologists. Chapters are written by specialists on myth and folklore, ritual, shamanism, sorcery and witchcraft, aboriginal religions, African religions, classical Old World religions, (Mesopotamia, Egypt, Persian, Greek, Roman), and classical New World religions (Olmec, Mayan, Aztec.), Vedic-Hindu, Buddhist, Chinese and Japanese religions, Judaism, Catholicism, Protestantism, Islam, New Age religious trends, and a concluding chapter on prospects for future religious developments. Each of these chapters was written by authors who are currently involved in doing research in these different traditions. We have attempted to produce state-of-the-art readable essays that introduce students from many different backgrounds to the fascinating contemporary research in the anthropology of religion

The textbook is unique when compared with most of the textbooks available for the anthropology of religion in that it deals with the traditions that most anthropologists are currently doing research on. This book will cover some of the basic ethnographic research and findings on traditional aboriginal religions, shamanism past and present, sorcery and witchcraft past and present, and some of the work done by archaeologists on early literate religious traditions. However, many anthropologists are doing research on what are referred to as the world religions or great religious traditions such as Buddhism, Hinduism, Islam, Christianity, and Judaism, and the various transformations occurring today within these traditions. One of the important findings within the anthropology of religion that needs to be communicated to undergraduate students is that these world religions or great religious traditions are not uniform throughout the world. There is a tremendous amount of diversity based on variant interpretations of these religious traditions dependent on specific culture circumstances. These religious traditions do not exhibit universal features or characteristics regarding belief, ritual, or practice. This textbook will emphasize the variations of these religious traditions in different regions of the world. In addition, in contrast to the approach used in religious studies or comparative religion that covers this material in their textbooks, this text will emphasize how anthropologists focus on the interrelationship between religious traditions and particular cultural contexts, which includes the political economy and institutional framework of various societies. Many of these essays demonstrate how anthropologists focus on the interconnections between the political economy, social structure, class, caste, gender, ethnicity, and religion.

Currently, many ethnographers are doing research on the world religions, partly because many of the so-called traditional or aboriginal peoples are converting to these traditions. The text deals with some of the complexities of the conversion process, revitalization movements, and with what has traditionally been referred to as syncretism. The world religious traditions are increasingly important in geographical regions where most anthropologists are based for ethnographic research. For example, many, if not most, ethnographers are currently working on Islam in the Middle East, Africa, or Asia, or Catholicism and Protestantism in Europe, North, Central, and South America, and developments in Buddhism, Taoism, Confucianism, or Hinduism in Asia. These ethnographers find that older indigenous types of spiritualism such as shamanism, sorcery, and witchcraft practices are reshaped and absorbed into the world religions, which makes the traditions significantly different from one world area to another. Presently, most of the research within the anthropology of religion is focused on understanding both the aboriginal-indigenous religions and the world religious traditions, and how they are being transformed by globalization processes within specific cultural contexts. Additionally, as indicated within the chapter on New Age religions, some individuals in Western societies are seeking out new forms of religious experience by combining some of the traditional forms of spiritualism with novel innovative spiritual practices. The last chapter briefly hints at the major changes in contemporary religion throughout the world, and what humanity may anticipate in the future development of religion in the twenty-first century.

Although this textbook is not intended to be comprehensive, it could be used by itself for a general course in the anthropology of religion. However, it could easily be supplemented with another textbook in religion or the anthropology of religion. For anthropology majors it could be complemented with a more theoretically oriented text or more in-depth ethnographic case studies.

As with all other textbook projects, an enormous amount of teamwork and assistance needs to be coordinated. I would like to thank Nancy Roberts, Editor in Chief for the social sciences at Prentice Hall, for her interest and support of this project. Managing editor Sharon Chambliss helped me organize the process of reviewing the chapters.

I would like to thank reviewers of various portions of the prospectus and manuscript. Robert Hefner of Boston University reviewed the prospectus, and offered helpful suggestions. James Provinzano, University of Wisconsin, reviewed the entire manuscript and assisted with suggestive comments. Paul (Jim) Roscoe, University of Maine, reviewed the chapter on aboriginal religions and made useful suggestions. Henry Munson, University of Maine, and Mary Elaine Hegland at Santa Clara University reviewed the Islam chapter and offered valuable advice. An archaeologist specializing in religion, Deborah J. Shephard of University of Minnesota, contributed much to the chapters on old world and new world traditions. George Saunders of Lawrence University made useful comments on the Catholicism chapter. Misty Bastian of Harvard University reviewed several chapters on myth and folklore, sorcery, and witchcraft and made helpful recommendations. Doug Dalton of Longwood College assisted in reviewing the chapter on shamanism.

I would also like to express my greatest appreciation to all the authors who contributed chapters for this textbook, supported the general theme of the text, and made considerable efforts to make deadlines and revise manuscripts whenever appropriate. Many of the contributors made extensive recommendations and suggestions regarding the content and organization of this textbook. Without their help this project would have not been worthwhile.

LIST OF CONTRIBUTORS

Michael F. Brown, Williams College, United States
Andrew Buckser, Purdue University, United States
Marcia Calkowski, Regina University, Canada
Jeffrey Carter, Davidson College, United States
Michael and Neathery Fuller, St. Louis Community College, United States
Jack Glazier, Oberlin College, United States
David Kozak, Fort Lewis College, United States
Scott Littleton, Occidental College, United States
John McCreery, Sophia University, Japan
Michael Murphy, University of Alabama, United States
Kristin Norget, McGill University, Canada
Mary Patterson, Melbourne University, Australia
Raymond Scupin, Lindenwood University, United States
Wade Tarzia, Naugatuck Valley Community-Technical College, United States
Maxine Weisgrau, Barnard College, United States

Religion and Culture

One

The Anthropological Perspective on Religion

Raymond Scupin
Lindenwood University

In the period of hectic social and cultural change that transpired during the 1960s in the United States and most European societies, religion was being reexamined on a number of different fronts. On its April 8, 1966 cover, *Time* magazine stated in bold red type on a black background: "IS GOD DEAD?" The United States during the 1960s was fraught with turbulent internal conflicts stemming from the civil rights movement, the Vietnam war, campus rebellions, and political assassinations. Many young people were engaged in mass demonstrations and experimentations with sex, drugs, and rock and roll culture, which usually resulted in disillusionment. Many were also dissatisfied with the established religious denominations and institutions in U.S. society. Weekly attendance was declining at Catholic, Protestant, and Jewish services. U.S. culture seemed to be saturated with an antireligious atmosphere. Religion appeared to be waning in U.S. society. Most of the Western European societies were also experiencing a similar decline in traditional religiosity.

The 1966 essay in *Time* magazine on the death of God drew on the perspective of different social scientists who attributed the diminishing influence of religion to the rapid evolution of modern society. Many social scientists were predicting that religion was going to disappear with the development of more scientific and secular attitudes within society. Some of these theorists predicted that science would displace religion, and scientific explanations would provide alternative views as to the origins of the universe, humans, and the purpose and meaning of life. Other social scientists were predicting that if religion did not disappear, it was becoming a very personal and "private" affair for individuals. However, several decades later, as we approach the beginning of the twenty-first century, in what some have termed the "postmodern age," religion appears to play an even more significant and public role in societies throughout the world. The popularity of television ministries, the rapid growth of religious movements such as fundamentalist Christianity, Islam, or Hinduism, the expanding interest in the West in spiritual traditions emanating from Asia, the evolution of political movements based on religious beliefs and practices, and the continuing adherence of millions of people in advanced modern societies to various religious traditions demonstrate that most of the prophecies and predictions of the social theorists of the

1950s and 1960s were wrong. In contrast to the antireligious atmosphere of U.S. culture in the 1960s, more people report a belief in the afterlife, the existence of heaven, the intervention of angels, the evidence of miracles including the power of prayer to heal, and other spiritual phenomena. Books on spiritual experiences top the best seller lists in U.S. society, as well as in many other countries throughout the world. It appears that in all probability, religion in the twenty-first century will continue to resonate deeply with the basic existential problems faced by humankind. As the future change and the rapid development of scientific and technological advances persist and confront humanity with vexing economic, political, social, and moral problems, many people will undoubtedly rely on religious faith and various spiritual traditions for assurance and hope.

Against this backdrop of rapid global change producing uncertainty, institutional changes, and the firm persistence and relevance of religion and spirituality in the twentieth-first century, anthropologists have been committed more than ever to a more comprehensive understanding of religious phenomena. This text demonstrates this fundamental commitment to examining religion in its many forms and practices by anthropologists. However, before proceeding to an introduction to the anthropology of religion and culture, and the anthropological methods relied upon to understand these phenomena, we need to clarify some issues. First, many religious people with strong faith view with considerable suspicion any attempt by a social scientist, such as an anthropologist, to examine their religious faith. Yet, anthropologists are not in a position to make judgments or to disprove or verify any particular set of religious beliefs or practices. Religion is based on faith, which is not subject to falsification or verification through empirical findings or scientific practices. Religious faith is anchored on subjective convictions (internal beliefs) that are not provable through objective, sensory experience. Thus, anthropologists cannot possibly verify or disprove anyone's religious beliefs. In addition, anthropologists cannot act as umpires deciding which religious beliefs and practices are true or false based on their cross-cultural studies. Just as anthropologists cannot pass judgment on the final truth or falsity of any religion, they cannot offer any absolute comments on the basic questions about the meaning and purpose of human existence. One of the implications of these conclusions is that it doesn't matter whether the anthropologist is deeply committed to a particular religious tradition or not. As we will see in this text, many anthropologists in the past and present have been capable of having broad, global perspectives on religion, without giving up their specific religious faith.

If the anthropologist cannot prove or disprove religious beliefs or expound on the meaning and purpose of life, what is the role of the anthropologist in the study of religion? Though religion is highly subjective, and is linked with the internal beliefs, moods, and motivations of religious believers, it does have an external dimension. In other words, religion is manifested in various rituals, prayers, hymns, and other external practices that can be observed by the anthropologist. These are public behaviors that are shared within communities that are observable. In addition, as we will see below, anthropologists reside with the people in the communities participating in their daily lives, asking in-depth questions to query people about their internal subjective beliefs. Generally, people answer the questions that anthropologists have about religion through narratives or stories that they have learned in their society. Anthropologists rely on these narratives to gain an understanding of both the external and internal aspects of the religious beliefs and practices within a community.

If anthropologists study religion based on this type of research, how does anthropology of religion differ from that of the field of religious studies? After all, the field of religious studies is interested in religious beliefs, rituals, and practices, and religious studies scholars often do research on the different religions of the world. However, traditionally, the religious scholar was engaged in the study of religious doctrines (usually represented in texts), and compared these doctrines cross-culturally to comprehend the meaning of these doctrines and to explicate the difference between various religious traditions. Generally, anthropologists, unlike religious studies scholars, were more concerned about the relationship and interconnections between people's religious traditions and doctrines (represented in both texts and nontextual materials) and other aspects of their society. The anthropologist tries to explore the linkages between religious beliefs and practices to other institutions within the society such as the economy, social life, politics, and media. Presently, there is some convergence of approaches within anthropology and religious studies. There are wholesome indications that anthropologists and religious studies scholars are collaborating on research, and the rigid boundaries between the fields are being replaced by interdisciplinary research. Many of the findings within the anthropology of religion and religious studies are illuminating and enhancing our understanding of religious phenomena throughout the world.

THE DISCIPLINE OF ANTHROPOLOGY

The word anthropology is derived from the Greek words *anthropo*, meaning "human beings" or "humankind," and *logos*, which has a large range of related meanings, including "speech," "word," "reason" but is often popularly translated as "knowledge of" or "the study of." Thus, we can define anthropology as the systematic study of humankind. This definition in itself, however, does not distinguish anthropology from other disciplines. After all, historians, psychologists, economists, sociologists, and scholars in many other fields systematically study humankind in one way or another. Anthropology stands apart because it combines four subdisciplines, or subfields, that bridge the natural sciences, the social sciences, and the humanities. These four subdisciplines—physical anthropology, archaeology, linguistic anthropology, and ethnology—give anthropologists a broad approach to the study of humanity the world over, both past and present. Physical anthropology includes the study of human evolution and genetics by focusing on changes in the biological characteristics of humanity from the past to the present. These scientists study fossils of early humans as well as the genetics of modern humans to gain an understanding of the past evolution and the biological variation within humans today. Some of these biological anthropologists concentrate on understanding the biochemical and neurophysiological mechanisms of contemporary humans. In some cases, these biological studies are applied to the study of various religious experiences. For example, a number of anthropologists are trying to identify what types of neurophysiological processes are operating during various types of religious experiences. Archaeology is the field that focuses on the study of artifacts left behind by past societies to help explain and understand the cultures of the past. Artifacts include countless types of material items ranging from jewelry, monuments, tools, pottery, musical instruments, and any other physical thing discovered by the archaeologist to help interpret and explain past societies. As will be seen in this textbook, archaeologists have contributed to the understanding of religious traditions of the past such as the ancient Egyptians, Mesopotamians, Greeks, Romans, Mayans, and Aztecs through the intensive examination of artifacts and the interpretation of the written texts of these cultures.

Linguistic anthropology concentrates on the study of the languages throughout the world. The linguistic anthropologists investigate the historical development of different languages, tracing the evolution and interconnections among these languages. They also compare the similarities and differences among the world's languages to determine the variation of sound, meaning, and grammatical structures in language. In addition, they attempt to understand the relationship between language and culture. For example, the linguistic anthropologist might try to comprehend the relationship between the grammatical patterns within a language with the thought processes of people that share a culture. Do learning and speaking a particular language influence how people perceive time, space, or other aspects of life? Linguistic constructions may have a relationship to specific concepts within a particular religious tradition. Or how does the use of language affect everyday interactions among people within a society? What are the various patterns of linguistic use that appear in sermons, chants, prayers, and other religious discourse? These are the types of issues and problems taken up by linguistic anthropologists.

The most well-known subfield within the anthropology of religion is "ethnology," more popularly known as "cultural anthropology." Cultural anthropology is the subfield that is devoted to the examination of contemporary societies throughout the world. Cultural anthropologists or ethnologists do research in all parts of the world, from the tropical rainforests of Zaire and Brazil to the arctic regions of Canada, from the deserts of the Middle East to the urban areas of China. Until recently, most ethnologists conducted research on non-Western or remote cultures in Africa, Asia, the Middle East, Latin America, and the Pacific Islands, and on the native American populations in the United States. Presently, however, many anthropologists have turned to research on their own cultures to gain a better understanding of its institutions and cultural values. Cultural anthropologists or ethnologists (sometimes the term ethnographer is used interchangeably for ethnologist) use a unique research strategy in conducting their fieldwork in the different settings in which they work. This research strategy is referred to as "participant observation," which involves learning the language and culture of the group being studied by participating in the group's daily activities. Through this intensive participation, the ethnologist becomes deeply familiar with the group and can understand and explain the society and culture of the group as an insider. The results of the fieldwork of the ethnologist or cultural anthropologist are written up as an ethnography, a description of a society. A typical ethnography reports on the environmental setting, economic patterns, social organization, political system, and religious rituals and beliefs of the society under study. This description of a society is based on what anthropologists call ethnographic data. The gathering of ethnographic data in a systematic manner is the specific research goal of the ethnologist or cultural anthropologist.

The majority of the studies that will be cited within this textbook on the anthropology of religion are based on the methods of participant observation by cultural anthropologists. These cultural anthropologists are involved in the study of religious phenomena from many different societies throughout the world. This participant observation method involves learning the language and culture of the group being studied and participating in its daily activities. Language skills are the most important asset that an ethnologist has in the field. One of the means of learning about religion and culture is through direct observation. This direct observation consists of making accurate descriptions and reliable records of the religious activities of the people within the society.

In addition to direct observations, typically, the ethnologist learns about the society through trusted "key informants," who give the ethnologist insights into the society's religious culture. These informants become the initial source of information and help the ethnologist identify major sources of data. Long-term collaboration with key informants is an integral part of quality ethnological research on religious traditions. The ethnologist tries to choose key informants who have a deep knowledge of the myths, folklore, rituals, beliefs, and practices within the community. These informants are usually "native ethnologists" who are interested in their own religious beliefs and practices. They serve as tutors or guides, answering general questions or identifying topics about religious phenomena that are of interest to the ethnologist. They often help the ethnologist establish rapport with the people in the community. In many situations, the people may not understand why the ethnologist is interested in the religious traditions of their society. The key informant can help explain the ethnologist's role. In some cases, the key informant may become involved in interviewing other people in the community to assist the ethnologist in collecting data about religious phenomena. The relationship between the key informant and the ethnologist is a close personal and professional one that usually produces lifelong friendship and collaboration.

When examining the religious culture of a society the ethnologist relies heavily upon the use of interviews, which may involve open-ended conversations with informants, to gain insights into a culture. These interviews may include the collecting of religious narratives, myths, folklore, and explanations about rituals. The strength of this type of interviewing is that it gives informants tremendous freedom of expression in attempting to explain their culture. The informant is not confined to answering a specific question that is designed by the ethnologist. The informant may, for example, elaborate on connections between certain beliefs and political power in the community. For example, Fredrik Barth discovered through his informant among the Baktaman people of New Guinea that when young males go through their initiation ceremonies they are introduced to the secret lore and sacred knowledge of the males who are in authority. Thus, religious and cultural beliefs are transmitted along with political authority. Without his informant's help, Barth might not have paid attention to this relationship between religious belief and the transmission of political authority.[1]

The ethnologist tries to record as much qualitative data from interviewing and questioning informants and other people within the society about their religious culture and practices. Ethnologists have a number of different methods for recording qualitative data. The best-known method is the writing of *field notes*, which is the systematic documentation of observations or interviews into a field notebook. Ethnologists should have some training in how to take useful field notes and how to manage them for more effective coding and recording of data. An increasing number of ethnologists now use the computer as a means of constructing databases to manage their field notes. They select appropriate categories for classifying their findings on religious beliefs, practices, myth, or folklore. These data can then easily be retrieved for analysis. Some ethnologists rely on tape recorders for interviews, though at the same time they recognize the problems that such devices present for producing valid accounts. Sometimes recording interviews can influence the manner is which the people respond to the ethnologist's questions. Most ethnological field workers utilize photography to record and help document their findings. Ethnologists must use extreme caution when using these technologies, however, since in some societies people are very sensitive about being recorded or photographed. Today, many anthropologists use video cameras when gathering primary data. Video recording is one of the most exciting recent developments in the anthropological studies of religion. One drawback to video recording, however, is that people who know they are being filmed frequently behave differently from the way they would normally. This may distort the ethnologist's conclusions. On the other hand, the video can be used to present playbacks to informants for comments on the recorded behaviors. William Rittenberg, who did studies of Buddhist rituals in villages in central Thailand, often played back his video recordings of rituals to members of the community. The informants, including the Buddhist monks, would view the recordings and offer more elaborate explanations of the meanings of the ritual. These strategies frequently help the ethnologist gain a more comprehensive understanding of the culture.

THE CHARACTERISTICS OF CULTURE

Culture is a fundamental concept within the discipline of anthropology. In everyday use, many people use the word culture to refer to "high culture"—Shakespeare's works, Beethoven's symphonies, Michelangelo's sculptures, gourmet cooking, imported wines, and so on. Anthropologists, however, use the term in a much broader sense to refer to all of the learned and shared ideas and products of a society. E. B. Tylor, the first professional anthropologist, proposed a definition of culture that includes all of human experience:

> Culture . . . is that complex whole which includes knowledge, belief, arts, morals, law, custom, and any other capabilities and habits acquired by man as a member of society.[2]

This view suggests that culture includes tools, weapons, fire, agriculture, animal domestication, metallurgy, writing, the steam engine, glasses, airplanes, computers, penicillin, nuclear power, rock-and-roll, video games, designer jeans, religion, political systems, subsistence patterns, science, sports, and social organizations. In Tylor's view, culture includes all aspects of human activity from the fine arts to popular entertainment, from everyday behavior to the development of sophisticated technology. It contains the plans, rules, techniques, designs, recipes, and policies for living.

This nineteenth-century definition of culture has some terminology that would not be acceptable to modern anthropologists. For example, it relies on the word "man" to refer to what we presently would refer to as humanity. Presently, most anthropologists would accept a broad conception of culture as a shared way of life that includes values, beliefs, and norms transmitted within a particular society from generation to generation.

Notice that this definition includes the term society. In the past, anthropologists attempted to make a simple distinction between culture and society. Society was said to consist of the patterns of relationships among people within a specified territory, and culture was viewed as the byproducts of those relationships. This view of society as distinguishable from culture was derived from ethnographic studies of small-scale societies. In such societies, people within a specific territory usually share a common culture. However, in most countries where modern anthropologists conduct ethnographic research, the societies are extremely complex and consist of distinctive groups that maintain different cultural traditions. Thus, this simple distinction between society and culture is too artificial for modern anthropologists. Some anthropologists have adopted the hybrid term sociocultural system—a combination of the terms society (or social) and culture—to refer to what used to be called "society" or "culture."

When anthropologists refer to the concept of culture, they are emphasizing a nonbiological property. We do not inherit our culture through our genes in the way we inherit our physical characteristics such as eye color or body build. Instead, we obtain our culture through the process of what is called *enculturation*. Enculturation is the process of social interaction through which people learn and acquire their culture. Humans acquire their culture both consciously through formal learning and unconsciously through informal social interaction. Anthropologists distinguish among several types of learning. One type is known as situational learning, or trial-and-error learning, in which a person adjusts behavior on the basis of direct experience. In other words, a stimulus is presented in the environment, and the person responds and receives reinforcement or feedback from the response, either in the form of a reward (pleasure) or punishment (pain). Psychologists refer to this type of learning as conditioning.

Another form of learning important to enculturation is called social learning, which occurs when one person observes another person or other people responding to a circumstance and then adds that response to their own collection of behaviors. Obviously, humans learn by observing classmates, teachers, parents, friends, and the media. However, the form of learning that is most important for humans and provides for the capacity for culture is known as *symbolic learning*. Symbolic learning is based on our linguistic capacity and ability to use and understand symbols, arbitrary meaningful units, or models that humans use to represent reality. They are the conceptual devices that we use to communicate abstract ideas to each other. We communicate these symbols with each other through our language. Humans learn most of their behaviors and concepts through symbolic learning. We do not have to depend on situational learning or observations of others to perceive and understand the world and one another. We have the uniquely human ability to abstract the essence of complex events and patterns, creating images through symbols and bestowing meaning on them. Symbolic learning has almost infinite possibilities in terms of absorbing and using information in creative ways. Most of our learning as humans is based on this symbolic learning process.

The human capacity for culture is based on our linguistic and cognitive ability to symbolize. Culture is transmitted from generation to generation through symbolic learning and language. Culture is the historical accumulation of symbolic knowledge that is shared by a society. This symbolic knowledge is transmitted through learning, and it can change rapidly from parents to children and from one generation to the next. Culture consists of the shared practices and understandings within a society. To some degree culture is based on shared meanings that are to some extent "public" and thus beyond the mind of any individual. Culture exists before the birth of an individual into the society, and it will generally continue (in some form) beyond the death of any particular individual. These publicly shared meanings provide designs or recipes for surviving and contributing to the society. However, anthropologists have discovered that cultural understandings are not shared equally by all members of a society. The degree to which a culture is shared within a group is an empirical question. Even in small-scale societies, culture is shared differently by males and females or by young and old. For example, some individuals in these societies have a great deal of knowledge about religious beliefs and practices. But those beliefs, practices, and knowledge are not equally distributed. The same thing is true for more complex societies such as the United States. Priests, ministers, rabbis, or other religious leaders are generally more knowledgeable about religious beliefs and practices than other people. Thus, culture, to some extent, varies from person to person, from subgroup to subgroup, from region to region, from age group to age group, and from gender to gender. Yet, despite this variation, common cultural understandings allow members of society to adapt, to communicate, and to interact with one another. Without these common understandings, a society could not exist.

When discussing the concept of culture, anthropologists have tried to isolate the key elements that constitute culture. Two of the most basic components are material and nonmaterial culture. Material culture consists of the physical products of human society (ranging from jewelry, houses, weapons, clothing styles, to temples or churches), whereas nonmaterial culture refers to the intangible products of human society (values, beliefs, and norms). When studying religions of different societies, anthropologists analyze the material culture related to religious phenomena. For example, they describe the design of religious buildings such as temples or churches, or sacred sites where rituals may occur, or the characteristics of other religious paraphernalia such as rosaries, prayer wheels, printed texts, bells, incense, or specialized ritual garments. However, it is obvious that these material aspects of culture cannot be understood separately from the symbolic, nonmaterial aspects of culture. These material objects are intricately bound to symbolic abstract ideas, values, beliefs, and norms which are shared by the people within the society. Material objects do not stand as "things" separate from the symbolic, nonmaterial aspect of culture.

Generally when anthropologists use the term *values*, they are referring to the explicit standards by which members of a society define what is good or bad, holy or unholy, beautiful or ugly. They are well-known assumptions that are widely shared within the society. Values are a central aspect of the culture of a society and they are important because they influence the behavior of the members of a society. For example, in U.S. society individual freedom and equality are values that are emphasized within the economic, political, and other institutions. Though these values may not be fully expressed in actual situations and circumstances, most members of U.S. society would assent that these values are fundamentally important. Values are found to be a central feature of every religious tradition and culture throughout the world.

However, as we will see in this text, religious values may differ radically from one society to another. Beliefs held by the members of a society are another aspect of nonmaterial culture. Beliefs are cultural conventions that concern true or false assumptions, specific descriptions of the nature of the universe and humanity's place in it. Whereas values are generalized notions of what is good and bad, beliefs are more specific and, in form at least, have more content. In reference to religious phenomena, anthropologists find widely divergent beliefs in different areas of the world. For example, in some societies, people believe in multiple spirits or gods, while in other societies the belief in one god is predominant. In addition, many anthropologists refer to the *worldview* of a particular society. A worldview consists of interrelated beliefs and assumptions about the nature of reality. It provides people with a more or less consistent orientation toward the physical, social, and metaphysical world. Various religious traditions have worldviews, which usually help people interpret and understand the reality surrounding them. We will return to this concept of worldview when we discuss the definition of religion below. In addition, all societies and religious traditions have *cosmologies*, various beliefs and assumptions regarding how humans are interconnected with the universe. Most of these cosmologies try to provide an orderly explanation of the origins of humans, animals, plants, and the rest of the universe. All humans have profound questions regarding existence that perplex us the most. Who are we? Where did we come from? Why are we here? What is our place in the universe? Cosmologies are conceptual frameworks that attempt to answer these questions.

Another important component of culture described by anthropologists are *norms*—a society's rules of right and wrong behavior. Norms are shared rules or guidelines that define how people "ought" to behave under certain circumstances. These rules are generally connected to the values, beliefs, and worldviews within a society. Norms guiding ordinary usages and conventions of everyday life are sometimes known as folkways or patterns of etiquette. Members of a society frequently conform to folkways so readily that they are hardly aware these norms exist. Folkways or etiquette norms help ensure that social life proceeds smoothly by providing both guidelines for an individual's behavior and expectations of other people's behavior. In the study of religion anthropologists discern patterns of etiquette that are related to how religious phenomena are encountered within a society. For example, in many societies religious leaders are treated in distinctive ways as an acknowledgment of their symbolically and ritually important status. In the Roman Catholic tradition, when the Pope is greeted, people bow and kiss his ring. In Thailand or Tibet, Buddhists greet the monks with deferential bowing demonstrating norms of respect. Other norms of etiquette are used and shared within different societies when people interact with religious leaders.

Other types of norms known as *mores* (pronounced "MOR-ays") are much stronger norms than are folkways. Members of society believe that their mores are crucial for the maintenance of a decent and orderly way of life. People who violate mores are usually punished severely, though punishment for the violation of mores varies from society to society. It may take the form of ostracism, vicious gossip, public ridicule, exile, losing one's job, physical beating, imprisonment, commitment to a mental asylum, or even execution. As we will see in this text, all religious traditions have mores, ranging from the ten commandments of the Judeo-Christian tradition, to the laws of *dharma* in Hinduism and Buddhism, to the Confucian ethics of the Chinese religion, to the oral ethical codes of the native American Indians. Not all norms can be neatly categorized as either folkway-etiquette norms or mores. Distinguishing between the two is especially difficult when dealing with societies other than our own. In reality, norms fall at various points on a continuum, depending on the particular circumstances and the society under consideration. For example, as we will see later in the text, in some Islamic societies such as Iran and Saudi Arabia, the manner in which women dress in public is considered morally significant. If a woman violates the dress code in these societies, she may be arrested and imprisoned. Thus, within a society, rules of etiquette may come to have moral significance. The proper form of dress for women in some societies is not just a matter of etiquette but it also has moral or religious connotations.

Values, beliefs, norms, and worldviews are terms used by many anthropologists when referring to aspects of culture. However, not all anthropologists agree with concise, clear-cut distinctions among these linguistic terms. This language is used as a starting point to help understand the complex symbolic aspects of another culture. We need to remember that these terms represent a vocabulary that is used by the anthropologist to describe culture and religious phenomena. This vocabulary may not be consistently used in a rigorous manner by all anthropologists. Again, anthropologists emphasize that the degree in which people share values, beliefs, norms, or worldviews is an open empirical question. And, in many cases the anthropologists find that these terms are not used or even considered by other people in different cultures. Yet, in interpreting different religions and cultures, this vocabulary serves as an initial analytical device for an understanding of these phenomena.

One additional cautionary note must be emphasized before leaving the discussion of the concept of culture. When anthropologists emphasize the enculturation process or socialization, students are often confronted with this question: Are humans only robots, who respond rigidly to the demands of their values, beliefs, worldviews, and norms of their culture? If our behavior depends so much on the enculturation process, what becomes of human concepts such as freedom and free will? Do people in our society or other societies have any personal choice over their behavior, or are all behavior and thought shaped and determined by the culture of these societies? Most anthropological research has demonstrated conclusively that although enculturation plays a major role in producing personality and behavioral strategies within society, there are a number of reasons why enculturation is not completely determinative. First, people are born with different innate tendencies for responding to the environment in a variety of ways. Our individual behavior is partially a result of our biological constitution, which influences our hormones, metabolism, and other aspects of our physiology. All societies have people who differ with respect to temperament because of these innate tendencies. Enculturation cannot produce people who respond only to environmental or cultural pressures in a uniform manner. In addition, enculturation is never a completely uniform process. The experiences of past enculturation are blended in unique ways by each individual. Even in the most isolated, small-scale societies, young people behave differently from their parents. Furthermore, not all people in a particular society are socialized or enculturated in exactly the same manner. The vast amounts of information transmitted through enculturation often lead to variations in what children are taught in different families and institutions. Also, norms and culture do not dictate behavior in any rigid manner. People within any society are always confronted with contradictory norms, and society is always changing, affecting the process of enculturation. Enculturation rarely provides people with a precise blueprint for the behavioral responses needed in the many situations they face.

Thus, enculturation is an imprecise process. People may internalize the general program for behavior—a series of ideal values, beliefs, worldviews, norms, rules, and cultural guidelines for action—but how these general principles apply in any specific set of concrete circumstances is difficult or impossible to specify. In some cases, people may subscribe to the social and cultural rules completely, whereas in others they violate or ignore them. Enculturation provides the historically developed cultural forms through which the members of society share meanings and symbols and relate to one another. But in actuality anthropologists find that people do maneuver within these cultural forms, choosing their actions to fulfill both their own needs and the demands of their society.

One of the reactions that many students have when first confronting other cultures and religions than their own is known as *ethnocentrism*. Ethnocentrism is the practice of judging another society by the values and standards of one's own society. Ethnocentrism usually involves the belief that one's own culture is superior to that of other cultures. To some degree, ethnocentrism is a universal phenomenon. As humans learn the basic values, beliefs, and norms of their society, they tend to think of their own culture as the most preferable, ranking other cultures as less desirable. In fact, members of a society become so committed to particular cultural traditions that they cannot conceive of any other way of life. They often view other cultural traditions as strange, alien, inferior, crazy, or immoral. As we will see in Chapter Two, many early anthropologists viewed other cultures and religions in an ethnocentric manner. But, anthropologists now recognize that ethnocentrism inhibits an understanding of other cultures and religions. To combat the problem of ethnocentrism, twentieth-century anthropologists developed the concept of *cultural relativism*. Cultural relativism is the view that any cultural tradition must be understood within the context of a particular society's solutions to problems and opportunities. Because cultural traditions represent somewhat unique adaptations and symbolic systems for different societies, these traditions must be understood as objectively as possible. Cultural relativism offered anthropologists a means of investigating other societies without imposing ethnocentric assumptions. At the same time, anthropologists, as other humans, are sometimes confronted with values and practices that may harm individuals or society as a whole. Therefore, anthropologists do not suggest that any set of values, norms, and practices are equally permissible. Extreme forms of relativism are not acceptable within the field of anthropology.

RELIGION: AN ANTHROPOLOGICAL DEFINITION

As will be seen in Chapter Two, many nineteenth-century scholars tried to offer precise, analytical definitions of religion. Some scholars defined religion as a belief in supernatural deities, whereas others tried to define religion as a more basic belief in the sacredness of certain phenomena experienced by humans. Religious studies scholars offered definitions of religion that emphasized the ultimate existential concerns of humans everywhere. The scholarly concern with defining religion in a precise manner extended into the twentieth century; however, there has been no general consensus on any single definition satisfactory to all scholars. Within the field of anthropology, a well-known scholar, Clifford Geertz, offered a definition of religion that helped set the stage for the anthropology of religion. Geertz admitted that any definition of religion will not establish anything by itself but will provide a useful orientation and effective way to develop the investigation of religion. Additionally, he admits that any definition of religion will be flawed.[3] But, in this text, we will use Geertz's formulation of a framework to understand religion as a baseline definition for our purposes in introducing the anthropology of religion. Since his well-known definition of religion has assisted so many anthropologists in refining their studies of religion, it will serve here as an introduction to the anthropology of religion. Geertz offers his definition of religion in his 1966 landmark essay "Religion as a Cultural System," where he says: "A religion is a (1) *system of symbols which acts to* (2) *establish powerful, pervasive, and long-lasting moods and motivations in men by* (3) *formulating conceptions of a general order of existence and* (4) *clothing these conceptions with such an aura of factuality that* (5) *the moods and motivations seem uniquely realistic.*"[4]

Let us examine this definition more closely. Geertz suggests that central to any religion is a "system of symbols" that includes all sacred objects, ranging from Christian crucifixes, the Catholic mass, a medicine pouch of a native American tribe, Buddhist mandalas or prayer wheels, Hindu statues of Shiva, the layout of a Jewish temple, to sacred myths such as Genesis or the Ramayana of Hinduism. A symbol is an external source of information publically shared within the society. In the essay Geertz goes on to say that the symbols play a double role. They simultaneously express a "model of" reality and a "model for" reality. Thus, religious symbols provide a representation of the way things are (the "model of") as well as guides and programs directing human activity (the "model for"). The "model of" reality articulates a description of natural and cultural phenomena, whereas the "model for" reality shapes how one "ought" to behave and act in the natural and cultural world.

Various religious symbols have produced fundamental metaphors and meanings in different religious traditions. For example, the symbols associated with the Virgin Mary in Roman Catholicism have developed into national symbols of unity for some countries. In Mexico, the symbolism associated with the Virgin of Guadalupe has served to unify various ethnic communities.[5] After Spain had colonized the indigenous Indian communities of Mexico beginning in the sixteenth century, many of the Indians such as the Aztecs were converted to Roman Catholicism. According to Mexican tradition, the Virgin Mary appeared before a Christianized Indian, Juan Diego, in 1531, in the form of a brown-skinned Indian woman. Tepeyac, the place where the apparition occurred, was the sacred site of an Aztec fertility goddess, Tonantzin, known as Our Lady Mother. Aztec cosmology contained many notions regarding the virgin births of deities. For example, Huitzilopochtli, the deity believed to have led the Aztecs to their home in the city of Tenochtitlan, had been miraculously conceived by the Aztec mother goddess. Thus, Aztec religious conceptions regarding Tonantzin somewhat paralleled Catholic teachings about Mary and made it easy to incorporate these teachings with traditional beliefs.

During the Virgin's appearance, she commanded Juan Diego to inform the bishop of Mexico that a shrine should be built at the spot. The Shrine of the Virgin of Guadalupe is today a huge church, or basilica. Over the altar, Juan Diego's cloak hangs embossed with the image of a young, dark-skinned woman, wearing an open crown and flowing gown, standing on a half-moon that symbolizes the Immaculate Conception. The Virgin of Guadalupe became a potent symbol that has endured for generations, assuming different meanings for different social groups. To the Indians of Mexico, the Virgin embodies both Tonantzin and the newer Catholic beliefs and aspirations concerning eternal salvation. To the mestizos, people with mixed Spanish and Indian ancestry, she represents the supernatural mother who gave them a place in both the indigenous and colonial worlds. To Mexicans in general, the Virgin represents the symbolic resolution of the many conflicts and problems that resulted from violent encounters between the Europeans and the local population The Guadalupe shrine has become one of the most important pilgrimage sites in Mexico.

The Virgin Mary has also played an important symbolic role in a European country that has undergone major political and social transformations. Until recently Poland was a socialist country under the indirect control of the former Soviet Union. Beginning in the 1980s, however, the Polish people, who were organized through a union-based political party known as Solidarity, began to challenge the Communist party that ruled Poland. During Communist party rule in Poland, religious symbolism and Roman Catholicism, deeply rooted in Polish history and culture, were to some degree repressed by the government. One of the most important symbols of Polish Catholicism is a famous picture of the Virgin Mary located in a Paulite monastery. According to Polish tradition, the picture, known as the Black Madonna of Czestochowa, was painted by St. Luke the Evangelist, one of the authors of the Christian New Testament, on a piece of Cypress wood from the table used by Mary. After the picture was placed in the monastery, where it was revered by many Polish Catholics, a party of robbers raided the monastery for treasures in 1430 and slashed the image of the Madonna with a sword. Although painstakingly restored, the picture still bears the scars of that destruction, with sword slashes on the cheek of the Black Madonna. As Poland was divided among different countries such as Sweden, Germany, Turkey, and Russia during various periods, the image of the Black Madonna served as a symbol of Polish religious and national unity. It became one of the most important pilgrimage sites for Polish Catholicism. Millions of pilgrims from Poland and other European countries made their way to the Czestochowa shrine every year to take part in religious rites. When the Solidarity movement in Poland challenged the Communist party during the 1980s, leaders such as Lech Walesa wore an image of the Black Madonna on their suit lapels. Pope John Paul II visited the Black Madonna shrine and placed a Golden Rose there to help resuscitate religiosity in Poland. Thus, the Black Madonna image served to unify Polish Catholics in their struggle against the antireligious stance of the Communist authorities. In the cases of these two countries, the system of symbols related to the Virgin Mary provided "models of" and "models for" reality as Geertz emphasizes. The symbols represent the reality it stands for providing a way of looking at the world and encourage certain forms of social action.

Geertz goes on to say that these symbols act to produce powerful, pervasive, and long-lasting "moods." He suggests that these moods such as happiness, elation, awe, sadness, or grief have no end point and no beginning point, they just come on us varying in intensity and lack direction. As Geertz notes, moods are like fogs that just settle and lift. Moods come and go with different frequencies. Think of the moods that are induced when a Christian thinks about the crucifixion and suffering of Jesus Christ, or when a Buddhist reflects on the general suffering experienced in life generally. Various beliefs, rituals, and practices in Christianity and Buddhism incorporate symbols that provide the context for inducing these moods, as do all religious traditions. Geertz indicates that these moods are "made meaningful" by the symbols that refer to the conditions which we believe brought them on. In other words, the crucifixion of Jesus for the Christian, or the life of constant suffering for the Buddhist furnish the symbolic background that brings about these moods. In contrast to "moods," Geertz describes how the religious symbols establish "motivations" that do have end points, or goals for people. And, religions sustain specific means for attaining certain types of directed goals and ethical orientations for people. For example, goals such as the attainment of eternal salvation for Christians or spiritual enlightenment for Buddhists are available for individuals who follow a particular moral code. In other words, when one is religiously motivated, one is directed toward specific ends. Motivations are "made meaningful" in relation to the end goals they are to produce.

Geertz highlights how religious symbols also engender and reaffirm a particular worldview by "formulating conceptions of a general order of existence." This worldview, sometimes referred to as the *theodicy* of a religious tradition, provides a "meaning" or "purpose" to life and the universe. A religious worldview helps humans comprehend the meaning of pain and suffering, or evil in the world. Throughout our lives we are confronted with situations and circumstances that are not understandable within our analytical or "scientific" capacities. We may experience or witness an event that defies a scientific explanation, no matter how much investigation we undertake. In addition, when we witness the suffering of others, we may not be able to explain these phenomena satisfactorily. The problem of suffering in the world is difficult for anyone to comprehend. Also, all humans confront and experience the problem of evil. All religious traditions address these basic problems through worldviews or theodicies. Typically, theodicies assert that humans cannot escape ignorance, pain, injustice, and suffering in the world. Yet, religious worldviews try to provide humans with meaningful ways of how to endure ignorance, pain, injustice, loss, or worldly suffering.

The final portion of Geertz's definition—that these systems of symbols act to cloth those conceptions in "such an aura of factuality that the moods and motivations seem uniquely realistic"—attempts to deal with the questions sometimes asked about religious believers. How do humans come to believe in metaphysical ideas regarding spirits, souls, revelations, and many untestable and unobservable conceptions? Geertz's answer to this question is that religious rituals in which humans participate create that "aura of factuality," and it is through ritual that deeper realities are reached. Religious rituals such as the Catholic Mass, Jewish Passover rites, and the native American sweat-lodge rites, which include prayer, meditation, and other spiritual communication shape religious experience. Religious experience is nonempirical and nonrational in its search for truth. It is not based on conclusions from scientific experience but is "prior" to experience. Religious truth is not "inductive," providing evidence for metaphysical explanations. In other words, religion is not a product of our human experience that is based on common sense or scientific understandings. It transcends our everyday experiences and moves us to an underlying spiritual reality that fulfills a purpose or meaning in our lives. Unlike a scientific view, religion is not based on any sense of objectivity or detachment, it is based on religious faith and commitment.

The strength of Geertz's definition of religion is that it attempts to bring together a range of questions dealing with the intellectual, emotional, cognitive, and social aspects of religious traditions. He sees the anthropology of religion as a two-stage process: first, an analysis of the system of symbols, which constitute the religious tradition, and second, the investigation of the relationship between the symbols and the social and psychological processes within the society. Though Geertz's conception of religion is not without challenges within the anthropological community, it allows us to begin exploring the various dimensions of religious phenomena that have been studied by anthropologists. Following the next two chapters that focus on some of the early and contemporary theories that have informed the research on religion by anthropologists, we will be considering the results and findings of anthropological research on religion throughout the world.

The various authors who have contributed to this textbook share the general perspective that a course in the anthropology of religion enhances global awareness and an appreciation for religions and cultures other than our own. In this age of rapid communication, worldwide travel, increasing economic interconnections, and the expanding cultural and religious diversity within our own societies, young people preparing for careers in the twenty-first century must recognize and show sensitivity toward the religious and cultural differences that exist among people, while at the same time understand the fundamental similarities that make us all distinctly human. Sustaining this dual perception—of underlying similar human characteristics in the face of outward religious and cultural differences—has both practical and moral benefits. Nationalism, ethnic and racial bigotry, and religious ethnocentrism are rife today in many parts of the world, yet our continuing survival and prosperity depend on greater mutual understanding. Anthropology promotes a cross-cultural perspective that allows us to see ourselves as part of one human family in the midst of tremendous religious and cultural diversity. In learning about religious traditions and cultural values in distant societies, students both question and acquire new insights into their own religious traditions and cultures. Thus, the anthropology of religion helps nurture personal enlightenment, one of the fundamental goals of education.

NOTES

1. This point regarding Fredrik Barth's research is from his book *Ritual and Knowledge Among the Baktaman of New Guinea* (Oslo: Universitets Forlaget; and New Haven: Yale University Press, 1975).
2. This definition of culture was first produced in Edward B. Tylor's book *Primitive Culture* (London: J. Murray, 1871).
3. One book by Talal Asad, *Genealogies of Religion: Discipline and Reasons of Power in Christianity and Islam* (Baltimore, MD: John Hopkins Press, 1993), is a sustained critique of Geertz's conception of religion.
4. Geertz's essay "Religion as a Cultural System" appeared in Michael Banton, ed., *Anthropological Approaches to the*

Study of Religion (London: Tavistock Publications Ltd., 1966). The essay was reprinted in Clifford Geertz, *The Interpretation of Cultures* (New York: Basic Books, 1973).
5. Anthropological analyses of the Virgin of Guadalupe have been authored by Eric Wolf in "The Virgin of Guadalupe: A Mexican National Symbol," *Journal of American Folklore* 72: 34–39, 1958; John Ingham in *Mary, Michael, and Lucifer: Folk Catholicism in Central Mexico* (Austin: University of Texas Press, 1986); and Donald Kurtz "The Virgin of Guadalupe and the Politics of Becoming Human," *Journal of Anthropological Research* 38: 194–210, 1982.

Two

Early Anthropological Perspectives on Religion

Raymond Scupin

Lindenwood University

The early development of the anthropology of religion was an intellectual project stemming from the European Enlightenment (1600–1900 C.E.) in Western history. Prior to the Enlightenment period there were very few critical or analytical approaches in the study of religion. In ancient Greece some writers such as Herodotus (484–425 B.C.E.) compared the deities of Egypt and Greece, implying that these deities were human self-created projections. Later, Euhemerus (330–260 B.C.E.) relied on critical thinking to refer to Greek mythical beings as representing various forces of nature, and ancestors of powerful people. However, it was only after the Protestant Reformation in the 1500s that challenged the dominant religious authorities in Europe, the confrontation of the Western world with non-Western religious traditions, and the new intellectual and scientific developments during the European Enlightenment which eventually resulted in critical approaches that led toward an anthropology of religion. The new intellectual and scientific developments included the social evolutionary ideas suggested by Locke, Rousseau, and Hegel, and the biological evolutionary ideas of Charles Darwin. All these developments led some Western thinkers toward more 'scientific' or critical views of religion.

Aside from the intellectual and scientific developments of the Enlightenment, there were earlier historical processes that led to analytical and more scientific approaches to the study of religion. The Protestant Reformation beginning in the 1500s that convulsed Western Christendom opened up new ways of viewing Biblical truth as it had been accepted for over a thousand years in European society. Some Western Christians became less certain regarding the religious practices and beliefs that had been transmitted for generations. In addition, at about the same time, the exploration of non-European areas of the world exposed Westerners with other religious traditions such as Hinduism, Buddhism, or native American Indian religions. These experiences opened alternative ways of approaching the supernatural world which had an influence on some thinkers. The fact that a society such as China could develop a complex civilization with a highly ethical religion such as Confucianism without having the revelations of the Judeo-Christian civilization introduced novel ideas concerning the understanding of religion. These historical developments set the stage for a more critical perspective and a scholarly framework for explaining religious traditions.

RATIONALIST APPROACHES

Two major streams of Enlightenment thought influenced the early anthropologists of religion. The first stream emphasized the use of the scientific method or "reason" and "rationality" as the mechanism to explain and understand human life and history. The second stream of thought embedded within the Enlightenment project was that through the use of rationality and reason, humans were improving and modifying their institutions and values, resulting in progress and unilineal evolution. Thus, societies and cultures were becoming more refined and progressive through the systematic use of reason and the scientific method. These twin concepts of "reason" and "progress" were accepted by most European thinkers during the Enlightenment. These rationalist approaches were relied upon to comprehend all human life including institutions and values, and religious beliefs and practices. These evolutionary-rationalist views provided a metaphorical framework for explaining and understanding religious beliefs and practices and were eventually promoted by the first anthropologists such as Edward B. Tylor and James G. Frazer.

Edward Burnett Tylor (1832–1917) was a self-educated Englishman who was brought up in a family of prosperous Quakers. For health reasons, in the 1850s Tylor traveled to Central America, which stimulated his interest in different customs and cultures. He took extensive notes on his travels and upon returning to England, Tylor began to devote his full time to writing about different societies throughout the world. After publishing his first book based on his travels to Mexico, he turned his attention to the study of prehistoric and "primitive" societies.[1] Eventually, he published a two-volume work entitled *Primitive Culture* (1871), based on data collected by missionaries, travelers, soldiers, and traders from around the world. This book was one of the earliest text of anthropological science and led to the appointment of Tylor as the first professor of anthropology at Oxford University.

Influenced by the evolutionary views of Charles Darwin and others, Tylor's work reflected the nineteenth-century anthropological perspective now known as unilineal evolution. This perspective suggested that all societies were in the process of evolving from earlier primitive stages referred to as "savagery" through a more advanced stage called "barbarianism" up toward the stage of "civilization." The unilineal theory of social and cultural evolution was established by collating data from many different societies and using those data to rank various societies according to the level of technological, economic, social, political, and cultural developments. According to Tylor, all humans were using rational thought to bring about this unilineal evolution toward civilization by refining and improving their technologies, economic, and other social institutions. He believed that each generation of people stood on the shoulders of earlier generations, and this resulted in the progress of humanity toward civilization. However, Tylor believed that not all societies evolved at the same pace. Some societies lagged behind others in evolutionary development, and some folklore, superstitions, magic, and earlier customs survive and remain within the most highly developed civilizations such as England.

Tylor applied the rationalist and unilineal evolutionary perspective to the development of religious beliefs and practices. He speculated that in the early stages of prehistory, humans, using their rational thought to explain mysterious experiences such as sleep, dreams, trances, hallucinations, or shadows, originated the idea of humans as having a soul or spirit. Eventually as an outgrowth of the idea of the soul, other spirits were posited. These early humans reasoned that other aspects of nature such as the sky, wind, rain, stars, trees, and other animals were animated by spirits or souls. Tylor referred to these early religious beliefs as animism (from the Latin term "anima" translated as soul). Eventually, according to Tylor, animism gave way to the evolution of polytheism, as the spirits begin to acquire their own personal identities and character. For example, in the civilizations of the Mesopotamia, India, Greece, Rome, and the Aztecs various deities that represented aspects of nature such as the sun, stars, the sea and wind were worshiped. Finally, as religious evolution progressed, humans constructed the "highest" stage of religious development, monotheism, the belief in one supreme divinity. Tylor believed that Judaism and Christianity were the dominant traditions that represented the logical end of religious evolution. Yet, he maintained all religious evolution was interconnected to the earliest stages of animism and believed that this early form of spiritualism persisted in the form of concepts of reincarnation or the resurrection and immortality of the soul in many religions.

Another important unilineal theorist who studied Tylor's work carefully was James George Frazer (1854–1941) who studied at Cambridge University. Although raised by Scottish Calvinist parents, Frazer as a young man rejected his parent's religious heritage but was throughout his life intellectually fascinated by the topic of religion. Like most other educated people of his generation in Victorian England, Frazer studied the classical languages of Latin and Greek and became a devoted scholar of the mythologies, folklore, and customs of the classical civilizations. Later, he was introduced to Tylor's text *Primitive Culture* and was captivated by the theory of animism, and the anthropological perspective. Leaving his classical studies behind, Frazer devoted himself to the production of an immense research project resulting in a 12-volume set of texts entitled the *Golden Bough.* The first installations of the *Golden Bough* were published in 1890, and the last of the 12 volumes were finished in 1915. This encyclopedic work was abridged as a single volume by Frazer in 1922.[2]

In the *Golden Bough* Frazer elaborates on the unilineal evolution perspective by imagining that some of the early forms of religion were based on magical practices. He proposed that the early "savage" philosophers and scientists were engaged in solving various practical problems such as producing more food and resources. Hunters demanded more animals and farmers needed rain and sun to grow their crops. To sustain their livelihood, these early people developed what Frazer called "sympathetic magic." Sympathetic magical thinking was based on the observation that nature works by sympathies or influences. There were two forms of sympathetic magic that Frazer wrote about: imitative magic and contagious magic. Imitative magic involved practices such as sprinkling water in a ceremony, which would hopefully result in rain falling on the crops. In other words, as Frazer put it, "like affects like." Contagious magic is based on how "part affects part," such as sticking pins in a doll that has the hair of an enemy, which will bring harm to that enemy. Frazer collected an enormous amount of data from diverse societies around the world where these magical practices were in evidence and suggested that these practices represented the survivals of early human innovations.

In the *Golden Bough* Frazer presents the view that religion displaces these early magical practices as societies evolve. Religion evolves as early people begin to suspect that deities control the natural world, and they begin to pray and sacrifice to gods or goddesses in order to help them cope and survive. Frazer suggests that religious explanations and development represent a progressive evolution in human thought. Magic is based on rules of imitation and contagion, and sometimes it does not work. The "savage philosophers" saw that magic was not always effective. Religion, however, based on the notion that deities controlled nature, was more rational because it was a more fruitful explanation. Sometimes the gods and goddesses do produce for humans, sometimes they do not. Thus, Frazer reasoned that religion is a more advanced stage of thought because it coincided with the experiences of early humans. At times the prayers and sacrifices are answered by the deities and sometimes they are not. In this sense, Frazer acknowledges that early humans began to recognize that they alone could not control the natural world. Magician kings give way to religious specialists and eventually to the development of priest kings, who have an ability to communicate with the gods, and often were believed to be divine themselves. Yet, Frazer, like Tylor, finds that magic survives in most of the world's cultures and is combined with religious beliefs and practices.

Other rationalist approaches to understanding religious beliefs and practices were produced by the well-known German social philosopher Karl Marx (1818–1883) and German sociologist Max Weber (1864–1920). These German thinkers have had some influence on anthropological interpretations of religion. Karl Marx was born into a German family descended from Jewish rabbis on both his mother's and father's sides. However, because of anti-Semitic laws in Germany at that time, Marx's father had converted to Christianity before Karl was born. Marx studied philosophy and law at the University of Bonn and eventually transferred to the University of Berlin. As part of his education as a German university student, he was introduced to the works of Georg W.F. Hegel (1770–1831). Eventually, Marx became a critic of Hegel's idealist philosophy, which emphasized how mental ideas, or concepts, are fundamental determinants of human behavior, and that material things are secondary. Marx, as many scholars have put it, 'turned Hegel on his head,' arguing that the material things of life were primary, and ideas and concepts were secondary. Later, Marx wrote many tracts such as *Toward the Critique of Hegel's Philosophy of Right: Introduction* (1843), *Economic and Philosophic Manuscripts* (1844), and *Das Kapital* (in English, *Capital*) (1867), which emphasized his philosophy of materialism, sometimes referred to as historical materialism.

In his historical materialist thesis, Marx argued that economic realities, or what he termed the mode of production, which included the way a society organized its economy and technology, were the primary determinant of human behavior and thought. A second ingredient in Marx's historical materialist thesis was that all human history was driven by class struggle, perpetual conflicts between the groups who owned resources and had political power and those who owned very little and had very little political power. Marx and his close collaborator Friedrich Engels developed a sweeping unilineal evolutionary scheme based on the different modes of production that societies had developed since early prehistory.[3] The earliest mode of production was hunting and gathering followed by the development of agriculture, succeeded by feudalism, which evolved into industrial capitalism. Each of these different modes of production was transformed by class conflicts and struggles resulting in the successive stages of societal evolution. In their lifetimes, Marx and Engels believed that a struggle was emerging between the bourgeoisie (owners of factories, mines, and other industries) and the proletariat (the working class) in industrial capitalist societies such as England, Germany, and the United States. They maintained that through this class conflict new modes of production would develop, first socialism, and eventually communism, which represented the end of class conflict, private property, poverty, economic exploitation, warfare, and power struggles.

As an aspect of the historical materialist thesis, Marx criticized the various religious traditions that had developed throughout the world. He was convinced that a particular mode of production, referred to as the "base" of a society, significantly shapes other spheres of society such as religion. Religion, along with philosophy, ethics, and the arts, was called the "superstructure" of society and represented ideologies, which reflected the inner tensions and interests of the class struggles and conflicts within any type of society. Specific ideologies become the dominant ruling ideas in a society organized by a particular mode of production. Marx argued that the original basis of religion was produced by humans themselves who began to create spirits, gods, and other supernatural beings and attribute powers to these spiritual beings. According to Marx, this represented the first stages of human "alienation," giving control and power to spirits or deities over humans. In other words, in Marx's view religion robs humans of their own merit and gives them to a supernatural source.

After the origins of religion, from Marx's standpoint, religion has had an extremely powerful effect on human society. In his view, in primitive society religion arose because of human helplessness in the struggle against nature, but as class society develops, religion becomes rooted in the struggle of upper-class humans against lower-class humans. In one of his best-known statements, Marx says: "Religion is the sigh of the oppressed creature, the heart of a heartless world, just as it is the spirit of a spiritless situation. It is the *opium* of the people." In other words, Marx saw religion as a type of narcotic, easing pain as it created fantasies for people. He referred to how the upper classes in society controlled the minds and thoughts of the working classes through religion. Emphasizing how life in the next world, in heaven with streets paved with gold, or a world where one would be released from suffering, religion provided a comforting escape from the travails of daily life. Marx wrote about how religion was used by the upper classes as an ideology to justify slavery, inequality, and political oppression in many societies throughout history. In his view religion becomes a "dominant ideology" that serves ruling elites by legitimizing the status quo and diverting people's attention from the economic and political inequities of society.

Max Weber (1864–1920) was a prolific German scholar and sociologist who produced what many regard as the most important rationalist contribution to the sociology of religion. His views on religion have influenced many anthropological interpretations. Weber was born to a prosperous German family and received a typical Germanic education, which included the study of Hegel and Marx. Though Weber shared many of Marx's ideas of social conflict and the power of technology, he departed from Marx's materialist conception of history. Weber became convinced that societies differ primarily in the ways in which their members "think" about the world. In other words, for Weber, ideas, beliefs, and values have transforming effects on society. Societies are not just products of technology and a particular mode of production, but also of culture, the modes of thinking within a society.

In Weber's analysis of different societies he relied on ideal types, an abstract statement, or model, of the essential characteristics of any social phenomena. For example, in his comparisons of religion, he contrasted the ideal "Catholic," with the ideal "Protestant," "Jew," "Hindu," or "Buddhist" knowing that these models do not refer to any specific individual or actual behavior or action. Like other nineteenth-century theorists, Weber developed his own unilineal evolutionary framework of society. However, unlike Marx, Weber highlighted the differences in the worldview of a society rather than just the technological or productive systems. He maintained that preindustrial societies were "traditional" in their worldview, whereas people in modern industrial capitalist society endorsed "rationality." Traditional societies were guided by sentiments and beliefs passed from generation to generation, while modern societies embraced "rationality," deliberate strategies, including scientific methods, to pursue efficient means to obtain particular goals. According to Weber, traditional sentiments and beliefs are swept away by the process of "rationalization" as a society modernizes. Weber views the "rationalization of society" as the historical change from a traditional world view to rationality as the dominant mode of human thought and action.

In his study of religion Weber took a comprehensive cross-cultural approach with broad comparisons of Judaism, Protestantism, Catholicism, Islam, Hinduism, Buddhism, and the Confucian and Taoist traditions of China.[4] He focused on the primacy of religious views to determine whether these worldviews promoted or hindered the process of rationalization in their respective societies. Weber, writing within the unilineal evolutionary framework, speculated that animism represented the early stages of religious development in small-scale societies. He contended that the next stage of religious development took place in agricultural state societies where polytheistic pantheons emerged with a hierarchy of priests. Eventually, the traditions of Hinduism, Buddhism, Confucianism, and Taoism develop in Asian societies and are intertwined with the political economy in these societies. According to Weber, these Eastern religious traditions have "exemplary prophets," who encourage contemplative methods for their followers. In contrast, Weber views the emergence of Judaism, Christianity, and Islam as revolutionary philosophical worldviews emphasizing what he refers to as "ethical prophecy." These traditions of ethical prophecy demand obedience to God, which leads to tension between the individual (sinner) and salvation. These tensions that are emphasized by the ethical prophetic traditions result in "transformative" rather than a "contemplative" attitude toward the world. In other words, within these traditions, as Weber understands them, the tensions between the imperfections of the world and the perfections of God resulted in people refashioning the world in accordance with God's purposes.

Weber, like the other nineteenth-century unilineal evolutionists, argued that the emergence of the prophetic religions, or what he called the world historical religions, of Hinduism, Buddhism, Confucianism, Taoism, Judaism, Christianity, and Islam represented both an ethical revolution as well as a "cognitive" or "intellectual" revolution.. In contrast to "traditional" religions, these "world religions" had highly complex spiritual doctrines that were more "rational." In other words, as religion evolved from more primitive or traditional stages, the doctrines and practices became rationalized. Instead of relying on magicians to control the supernatural world as in the traditional religions, the world historical religions developed a hierarchy of specialized religious officials and clerics, who interpreted abstract religious concepts and doctrines. These religious clerics attempt to suppress earlier magical practices and provide for spiritual needs through the elaboration of more abstract philosophical and religious doctrines. Both doctrines and rituals become more authoritative, standardized, and codified in these world historical religions. Weber proposed that this early rationalization of religion evolved in response to the new historical circumstances and conditions of complex agricultural societies.

The major transformative development of world history in Weber's account came with the Protestant Reformation, which he perceived as the key to the development of a comprehensive "rationalization" and subsequent technological and economic change in the West. In an influential book on religion titled *The Protestant Ethic and the Spirit of Capitalism* (1904), Weber contended that rationalization and modern industrial capitalism were the byproducts of Calvinism, a Christian religious movement fathered by the Protestant Reformation in the 1500s. The central doctrine associated with early Calvinism was predestination, the view that an all-knowing and omnipotent God has preordained some people for salvation and others for damnation. This doctrine suggested that a person's fate was set before birth, and people could do nothing to alter their destiny. Individuals could not even know what their future destiny would be. Thus, the lives of Calvinists were shaped by hopeful visions of salvation and anxious fears of unending damnation. Weber believed that this worldview of the Calvinists made for a continuous anxiety and restlessness for individuals as they went about their daily lives.

Weber argued that the Calvinists gradually came to a resolution regarding their unknowable destiny. They began to believe that those chosen for salvation in the next world ought to be able to see signs of divine favor in this world. This conclusion prompted Calvinists to interpret worldly prosperity and success as a sign of God's grace. In order to obtain this prosperity Calvinists emphasized the ethics of hard work, discipline, and thrift as a means of acquiring salvation. They threw themselves into this quest for material success for religious reasons. The quest for material success itself was considered to be self-indulgent and sinful. Thus, spending money foolishly and lavishly was frowned upon. The ever-present duty of these early Calvinists was to pursue material success in what they held to be their personal "calling" or "vocation" from God. As they emphasized a form of asceticism, not indulging in worldly sensual pleasures, these early Calvinists reinvested their profits from their businesses for greater material success, and in doing so they built the foundations for the economic system of capitalism. They used their wealth to generate more wealth and eagerly adopted scientific and technological advances that bolstered their efforts. Weber linked this early Protestant ethic as the revolutionary key for the development of rationalization and modern industrial capitalism.

Pinpointing the areas where capitalist economies initially developed in Northwest Europe, Weber believed that Calvinism had characteristics that distinguished it from other religions such as Catholicism. He held that the Catholic worldview was "otherworldly," which resulted in the hope of a greater reward in the life to come. For Catholics, material success did not have the spiritual significance that motivated Calvinists. Thus, Catholicism did not give rise to industrial capitalism and rationalization as did the Protestant ethos of Calvinism. Weber's concentration on religious views and beliefs contrasted with the Marxist focus on material factors. He believed that the continuous restlessness and systematic work among these early Calvinists, as they pursued their means of salvation, became the powerful lever for the expansion of capitalism. Weber's study of Calvinism and its relationship to modern industrial capitalism provided a striking example of how religious ideas had the power to shape society. One of the major purposes of his study was to counter the narrow explanation of emergence of industrial capitalism as espoused by Marx.[5]

At the end of *The Protestant Ethic and the Spirit of Capitalism*, Weber reflects on what happened to the early Calvinist worldview in modern industrial society. He concludes that rationalization resulted in the development of large-scale bureaucratic organizations, a specialized division of labor in society, cultural values such as achievement, success, and efficiency, and an emphasis on technical competence and skills and abilities. Weber thought all of these aspects of modern society were consequences of the original Protestant ethic. However, he believed that there were some negative aspects of the Protestant ethic of modern society. As the religious fervor of the Calvinists diminished among later generations, success seeking and personal discipline remained strong, but the religious ethic became simply a "work ethic." And industrial capitalism developed as what Weber termed a "disenchanted" religion, with wealth and material success now valued for its own sake. In addition, as rationalization proceeded in modern industrial society, Weber believed that people devalued personal feelings and emotions and concentrated on their rational and technical abilities. In his words, these early Calvinist formulations were transformed into modern industrial capitalist societies as values that produced "specialists without spirit, and sensualists without hearts."

ANTIRATIONALIST APPROACHES

As seen above, the Enlightenment in Europe produced a number of rationalist or intellectualist approaches to the understanding of religion in the 1800s. However, there were other scholars who were developing what could be referred to as antirationalist perspectives in explaining and interpreting religion. For example, a German scholar, Friedrich Max Müller, who had studied ancient Indian languages and religion, argued in the mid-1800s that the "emotions" rather than the intellect, led to the origins of religion.[6] Müller speculated that "primitive" humans were overwhelmed and dwarfed by the powerful forces of nature and the fragilities of life. He referred to his theory of the origin of religion as "naturism." Early humans were so awed by the forces of nature such as thunderstorms, earthquakes, and hurricanes that they created deities representing these powerful forces. According to Müller, religious ideas and mythologies develop from deep emotional feelings and early peoples attributed personal characteristics to the forces of nature. Thus, the gods and goddesses of various religions are linked to the sun, moon, stars, and other aspects of nature. Thus, to Müller "emotional" factors play a more important role in the origins and development of religions than do rational or intellectual capacities.

One prominent French sociologist who also fostered an antirationalist approach to religion was Emile Durkheim (1858–1917). Durkheim was born in northeastern France in the small rural town of Epinal. His father was a rabbi, and as a young student Durkheim was exposed to the teachings of Judaism and Catholicism. These experiences may have contributed to his interest in religion, but by the time he was a young man he declared himself an avowed agnostic. Durkheim studied at the most elite schools and universities in France and was introduced to the early scholarly writings of sociology and anthropology. For some time he taught at a secondary high school near Paris, but eventually he was able to obtain a position as a researcher and professor at the University of Bordeaux, in 1887. While at the University of Bordeaux he produced a voluminous amount of writing including his first major text *The Division of Labor* (1893), followed by *The Rules of the Sociological Method* (1895), and a classic sociological study entitled *Suicide* (1897). Through this prolific scholarship he was able to obtain a professorship at the University of Paris in 1903 and was recognized as the most important sociologist of France. In his later years in Paris he turned to the sociological study of religion and produced his masterwork, *The Elementary Forms of the Religious Life,* in 1912.

In his first book, *The Division of Labor,* Durkheim provided the basic principles of his sociological explanations, which informed all of his thinking throughout his scholarly life.[7] In that text he challenged the rationalist views of the anthropologists such as E.B. Tylor and James Frazer who assumed that society was based on the rational calculations and self-interest and social contracts of individuals. Instead, Durkheim argued that individuals were embedded within a social context and framework, which determined and influenced the thinking and actions of individuals. Emphasizing the sociological approach, Durkheim conceived that individual decision-making and social contracts were regulated and shaped by the social conditions of any particular society. First and foremost, Durkheim argued that the "social" or "society" exists beyond the individual. He argued that society is more than the sum of individuals who compose it and is established long before an individual is born, and it stretches beyond anyone's personal experience. Patterns of human behavior established *social facts,* which have an objective reality beyond the lives and perceptions of specific individuals and have the power to shape thoughts, emotions, and actions.

Like other nineteenth-century thinkers, Durkheim witnessed the rapid changes of the Industrial Revolution in Europe. He developed his own unilineal evolutionary framework to explain these developments. In *The Division of Labor* he referred to two different forms of society: the mechanical and the organic. The mechanical form of society was developed in prehistoric times by early humans and was constituted by people who were born into groups—families, clans, tribes that shaped their thought and behavior. In this form of society, social solidarity was brought about through the strong traditional sentiments that were developed through kinship ties and a shared culture. By "mechanical solidarity" Durkheim referred to the simple, general division of labor, or occupations of these societies, as well as to the shared traditional morality and sentiments that united the members of these societies. The "organic" form of society was modern industrial society wherein the division of labor was more specialized, consisting of many different occupations. And, yet, in Durkheim's view the "organic" modern society resulted in a new type of social solidarity through the interdependence of various occupations and specialization. In the organic industrial society people had to rely on each other's work and count on the efforts of thousands of strangers to survive. Thus, organic modern society rests less on morality and sentiments of kinship, and more on the "functional" interdependence of specialized occupations. According to Durkheim, in modern society humans have to become dependent on people that they do not know personally, and sometimes trust less, in order to secure the basic necessities of life.

In his final classic work, *The Elementary Forms of Religious Life*, Durkheim concentrated on the sociological study of religion. In that text, Durkheim relied upon the description of some early scholars who studied the aboriginal peoples of Australia.[8] He wanted to explore what he thought to be the most elementary types of religion, which he believed would cast light on basic features and characteristics of *all* religions. Durkheim emphasized that as human beings we organize our surroundings by classifying most objects, events, or experiences as profane, that which is an ordinary element of practical, routine, everyday life. However, other aspects of life that surpass the limits of human understanding and knowledge are designated as sacred, that which is defined as extraordinary, inspiring a sense of awe, reverence, and even fear or submission. The "sacred" represents the essence of religious symbols, beliefs, and practices. Instead of defining religion in terms of the beliefs of supernatural beings or gods, he defines religion as a socially shared system of beliefs and practices based upon a conception of the sacred. Shared socially, symbols and practices associated with sacred phenomena are set apart from everyday experience and are regarded with reverence, awe, and suspense. Durkheim maintained that all sacred phenomenon such as religious symbols like the "Star of David" for Judaism, the "cross" for Christianity, the "crescent" for Islam, or the "lotus" for Buddhism, or religious rituals, such as prayer, chanting, and singing hymns, have significant consequences for society.

In his analysis of Australian aborigine religion, Durkheim noted that these people transformed certain everyday experiences and objects into sacred symbols of their collective life, or society. He described the Australian aborigine religious traditions as totemism, wherein an animal or plant is transformed into an important sacred symbol of their society. The basic social unit of aborigine society was the clan, a group of families linked together through descent. The totemic plant or animal is linked inextricably with the clan. The totem becomes the centerpiece of ritual, symbolizing the clan, the aborigine's basic unit of collective social life. Aboriginal clans are represented by totems such as kangaroos, wallabies, or other plants and animals. These totems provide a strong unifying effect for the clan through shared symbols and rituals. For example, most of the time, the aborigines would not eat the meat or vegetation of the animal or plant that symbolically represented their clan. The consumption of the totemic animal or plant was tabooed and forbidden, as they were classified as sacred phenomenon. However, at designated times of the year, the clans would sacrifice the animal or plant and have a communion ceremony and the totem would be consumed in a ritual meal. According to Durkheim, this communion ritual would have a powerful cohesive and emotional effect, which consolidated the clan. He describes these rituals as exuberant ecstatic rituals in which individuals lose their sense of self and merge their identities with the clan. And, the clan itself becomes sacred, as it is considered symbolically to be one with the totem. During these types of ceremonies and rituals the worshipers endorse their commitment to the totem, and likewise to the clan. In doing so, the individual becomes emotionally bonded to the social collective life of the totemic clan.

Through his analysis of the religious life of Australian aborigines, Durkheim concluded that all religions have basic "functions" for society. Religion unites societies and communities through shared sacred symbols, values, and practices. Religious rituals function to underscore both moral and emotional ties to each other within the community. Sacred religious imagery, beliefs, and mores also promote individual conformity, supporting social control within society. Many cultural norms are given religious justification and are imbued with sacred symbolic ideas. Most religious traditions have ethical prescripts such as the "Ten Commandments" of the Judeo-Christian tradition that are used to enforce social control within society. In addition, Durkheim emphasizes, all religions offer the comforting sense that the vulnerable human condition serves some greater purpose. When confronted by life's calamities and insecurities, religious beliefs and rituals provide a source of emotional comfort and security within society. Though Durkheim focused on totemism, which he believed was the most elementary form of religion, he did not believe that totemic religions were different in kind from the religions in more complex, organic societies. He asserted that all religions were fundamentally equal in providing these basic functions for society. In his view all religions were true in their own fashion, and all provide answers in their own ways to the difficulties of human existence.

Durkheim highlights the power of religion to influence human ideas and motivations. He asserted that religion molds our basic categories of understanding such as time, space, and causes through its symbols and representations of reality. As religion is primarily a social affair based on shared beliefs and practices within a community, the categories of understanding reality and the world are determined by social processes. Thus, religion ultimately defines the totality of our experiences of both the natural and supernatural world. The spiritual and the natural world are all modes of a single reality. Thus, in his last book, Durkheim suggests that all of culture, and all of human reason and thought are based on religious sources that stem from shared beliefs and rituals.

FREUD

Another antirationalist approach to explaining and examining religion was developed by the father of psychoanalysis, Sigmund Freud (1856–1939).[9] Freud was born in Moravia, in what was then part of the Austro-Hungarian empire. As a young boy his family moved to Vienna, the capital of the empire. Although the empire was primarily populated by Catholic families, Freud's family was Jewish, but they had a fairly comfortable and prosperous life in the city of Vienna. Freud was a gifted student who took courses in Greek, Latin, and Hebrew, and eventually became fluent in French, English, Italian, and Spanish, as well as his native German. At the age of 17 he became a medical student and began to do research in subjects such as the physiology of the brain. After completing his medical studies, he continued doing research on the brain at the Vienna General Hospital. Eventually, Freud turned his attention to the study of mental illnesses such as neurosis, and problems that were then referred to as "hysteria." By using techniques such as hypnotism, conversation, and dream interpretation with patients, Freud reported that he had success in curing problems such as neurosis. He referred to these new methods of treatment as "psychoanalysis." Throughout his professional life Freud produced a number of books explaining and understanding the human personality that led to a revolution in twentieth-century modern thought. Though, for the most part, his work concentrated on the individual mind and personality, he also turned to more general topics such as the origins of religion, and its effects on society. He wrote three major books on religion including *Totem and Taboo* (1913), *The Future of an Illusion* (1927), and *Moses and Monotheism* (1938).

Based on his experiences in psychoanalysis Freud viewed human behavior as a reflection of innate emotional factors. His theory of human behavior emphasizes the importance of emotions in the development of an individual's personality. He tried to demonstrate that a great deal of emotional life is unconscious; that is, people are often unaware of the real reasons for their feelings and actions. Freud postulated that the personality is made up of three aspects: the id, ego, and superego.

Freud believed that all humans are born with a number of unconscious, innate drives including the drives for sex and aggression. These unconscious drives are contained as a bundle of emotional needs within the id. He referred to the sex drive as the unconscious motive for "life" or *eros* (Greek for "love"), whereas the aggressive drive was an unconscious wish for "death" or *thanatos* (Greek for "death"). According to Freud, these drives promote the seeking of immediate pleasure and the avoidance of pain. The id represents the basic needs of humans, emotional needs that exist in the unconscious. The id is the storehouse of these deeply rooted unconscious urges to eat, kill, or to engage in sex. It is the earliest and most basic stage of the development of the human mind or personality. The id is rooted in the biological organism and is present at birth as a bundle of needs.

Freud thought that these sexual and aggressive drives are often frustrated by society and culture, which produces the superego of the personality. The superego is the presence of culture within the individual. The superego is based on the internalized values and norms of society which through the process of enculturation form the individual's conscience. Thus, in Freud's view, the id, the unconscious desires of the individual, motivates specific behaviors, while at the other extreme, at 'the top of the personality,' the superego tries to curb these behaviors. This sets up a dynamic conflict between the id and the superego within the individual. The superego develops first in response to parental demands, but gradually the child learns that he or she has to respond to the society and culture at large. For example, Freud hypothesized that within the id, all male children are driven by an unconscious desire to have an affectionate and sexual relationship with their mother. This unconscious desire leads to hostility toward their natural father, the authority figure within the family. Freud called this the Oedipus complex. This desire is frustrated by the morality and norms of society, which produce the superego. These emotional feelings become repressed, and the mature ego of the individual emerges to intervene between these desires and the dictates of society. Repression takes place when the energy based on these sexual and aggressive drives of the id is unconsciously redirected into socially approved forms of expression.

Eventually, the part of the personality Freud called the ego develops as a result of the conflict between the id and the superego. The ego represents the conscious attempt to balance the innate pleasure-seeking drives of the human organism with the demands and realities of the society. The ego is the "conscious' part of the personality and Freud sometimes referred to the ego as the "reality part' of the personality. Freud's hypotheses were highly controversial within his own lifetime and remain so today. Although his theories are based on limited examples from his European medical and psychoanalytic practice, he extended his conclusions to all of humanity. However, his emphasis on emotional development and the role of the unconscious in personality represented a revolutionary approach in explaining the human mind.

Freud applied this threefold schematic of the human personality to an explanation of the origins and functions of religion. In his earliest work on religion, *Totem and Taboo* (1913), he was influenced by early theorists such as J.G. Frazer and Emile Durkheim who wrote about the early "primitive" religions known as totemism. Freud relied on some of their descriptions combined with early Darwinian concepts, along with discussions of primate behavior, to develop his notions regarding the origins of religion. In *Totem and Taboo* Freud describes the earliest primitive families residing together as groups who were randomly mating with one another. The older males of these groups were monopolizing the females to satisfy their own sexual appetites. Eventually, the younger males within these early families began to resent their father's exclusive access to sexuality with the females and became rivals to the older males.

According to Freud, the younger males revolted against the older males, the fathers, and killed them. After this "primal patricide," the young males ate the older males in an act of savage cannibalism. Afterwards, these brothers felt tremendous guilt and remorse. From these feelings of guilt and remorse, the young males developed the earliest religion, totemism, wherein ancestral animal spirits representing the dead fathers were worshiped. For example, the totemic animals are consumed in a ritual communion feast as a memorial to their fathers, who had become more powerful in death than in life. In addition, at the same time, the young males initiated the incest taboo, which prohibited sexual relationships within their own family group. Young males would be able to marry and have sex only with women outside their own families. Although Freud equivocates on whether this early episode was an actual event or a fantasy, in his conclusion to this book he argues that the psychic reality of modern people is shaped by these events within these early human groups. For example, the Oedipal complex is developed and retained within the id of the male personality of modern humans as a result of this primal patricide, regardless of whether it was a reality or a fantasy.

In his later work on religion, *The Future of an Illusion* (1927), Freud focuses on how religion functions to satisfy our emotional needs. He begins his analysis from the standpoint of an evolutionary perspective as he perceives humans confronting a natural world that constantly threatens destruction. The natural world is filled with predators, disasters, diseases, and eventually physical decline and death. In Freud's view, human nature, especially the "id," drives us toward satisfying our sexual desires and aggressive impulses, but we learn that we cannot do this through our enculturation. Our culture teaches us through norms and values to behave in "civilized" ways to restrain our "id." Yet, humans still feel helpless as they confront the dangers of nature, disease, predators, and ultimately death. According to Freud, this extreme helplessness makes humans very childlike and they project religious beliefs and worship a powerful, paternalistic God, who allays the fears of nature, and bestows comfort and security to them. This cultural creation, religion, which Freud refers to as an "illusion," also helps humans understand how they have to obey the norms of their culture in order to survive. Thus, being obedient to a powerful God and the eternal laws such as the Ten Commandments will enable humans to fulfill both their earthly lives and gain immortal life in an afterworld. Freud uses the specific term "illusion" to refer to religion. Illusions are not the same as "delusions." He contends that religious beliefs are illusions that humans strongly wish to be true. However, Freud did maintain that modern people who have religious beliefs are like neurotic children. Like many of the other nineteen-century thinkers such as Tylor or Frazer, Freud believed that healthy mature modern people ought to be guided by reason and science, and not by religious beliefs and illusions.

Freud's last major book on religion, *Moses and Monotheism* (1939), was an unusual view of the history of the Biblical traditions of Judaism. Freud interpreted the narrative about Moses and the children of Israel in a highly speculative manner based on his psychoanalytic thesis. First, Freud questions the idea that Moses was really a true Israelite. Based on his reading of the Bible, Freud suggests that Moses was really an Egyptian prince who had been influenced by the Pharaoh Akhenaton. Akhenaton had tried to establish a religious tradition based on a pure monotheism in Egyptian society. Following Akhenaton's death, the tradition of monotheism was overruled by the Egyptian priests. However, according to Freud, Moses attempted to keep this tradition of monotheism alive. Moses embraced the Israelite people and led them out of Egypt from the yoke of slavery as described in the story of Exodus. But, in Freud's interpretation, the ancient Israelites later rebelled against Moses' leadership, renounced his monotheistic God, and killed him. Later, in Freud's narrative, the Israelites developed their own monotheistic cult of Yahweh, as they struggled to win the Promised Land. Subsequently, in the history of Judaism, Freud asserts that the Hebrew prophets such as Amos, Isaiah, and Jeremiah demand the worship of the one universal God announced by Moses. In Freud's interpretation a revival of Jewish monotheism took place, which became the basis of both the Judaic and Christian religious traditions.

Of course, Freud provided a psychoanalytic interpretation for this speculative narrative. He believed that narrative of Exodus followed basic unconscious psychic processes. Just as the primal patricide described in *Totem and Taboo* resulted in the initial origins of religion, the murder of Moses by the ancient Israelites led to the development of the Judaic-Christian religious tradition. After the murder of the powerful father-figure Moses, the ancient Israelites were filled with remorse and guilt. This ancient murder lay within the unconscious collective mind of the ancient Israelites, which was repressed for many years. Yet, Freud argued that this repression of the feelings of guilt and remorse found release as the Israelites restored the Mosaic religion, and Moses himself was idealized as a loving monotheistic God. In later sections of *Moses and Monotheism* Freud theorizes on how the development of Christianity also reflected basic unconscious psychic processes. He asserts that the same type of guilt and remorse over the death of Christ, who had atoned for the original sin (interpreted by Freud as the sin committed by the first sons of the "primal horde") led to the rise of Christianity. Christ was eventually believed to be the "Son of God" and became the center of worship within the Christian tradition, in Freud's view, as a loving deity who brings about salvation for humanity. This loving deity represents the yearnings of the Christian community to release the pent-up guilt and remorse of original sin. Thus, Freud views both the Jewish and Christian religious traditions arising from emotional conflicts that lie deep within the unconscious mind, below the more rational, normal surfaces of the personality.

CONCLUSIONS ON CLASSICAL THEORY

These nineteenth-century (and early twentieth-century) theories on religion, both rationalist and antirationalist, were influential ideas that have had some consequences for later anthropological analyses of religion. However, as we will emphasize in the next chapter on contemporary theory in the anthropology of religion, these early theories were largely speculative theories without solid evidence based on ethnographic research. This is particularly clear with respect to the rationalist, unilineal evolutionary ideas of Tylor, Frazer, Marx, and Weber. The sources that these thinkers drew from were based on various descriptions of so-called "primitive" people around the world who were depicted by traders, missionaries, or government officials, without regard for a social and cultural context for the religious traditions. Tylor, Frazer, Marx, and Weber erected their unilineal schemes of evolution and pigeonholed the data from various peoples throughout the world to fit within their framework. They associated beliefs and practices from widely divergent societies with one another and ranked them according to their fixed evolutionary categories or stages of development. These reconstructions of the evolution of animism, magic, and religion were highly speculative endeavors that were, as one later anthropologist remarked, "just so stories." As we will see in later chapters, some preliterate societies in the world maintain monotheistic traditions, which contradict the unilineal evolutionary frameworks assumed by these early theorists.

The antirationalist theories of Durkheim and Freud were based on some early scholarly descriptions of the Australian aborigines. Although these early scholarly studies provided a more firm foundation for analysis than the speculative ideas about the origins of religion of the rationalists, eventually these studies on Australian aborigine religion have been widely criticized and have been rejected by more contemporary anthropologists. In addition, it appears that both Durkheim and Freud arranged their theoretical schemes before assessing the evidence from these early ethnographic studies. In other words, their theoretical schemes were constructed before they considered the anthropological evidence. Furthermore, the most serious criticism of both Durkheim and Freud is known as reductionism, that is, reducing religious phenomena to either social or psychological functions. As we will see in the next chapter, contemporary anthropologists agree that religion does provide some basic social functions as Durkheim proposes in his work. Psychological factors, as Freud emphasized, are also an important aspect of religious belief and motivation. However, both of these theorists tended to reduce religion to nothing but "social functions" in the case of Durkheim, and "psychological functions" in the case of Freud. This aggressive type of reductionism is eschewed by contemporary anthropologists. Though both psychological and social factors are important in understanding and explaining religion, religion cannot be reduced to simplistic, single causal explanations.

Though these early rationalist and antirationalist explanations and speculations had internal theoretical weaknesses, they served later anthropologists as a starting point in their analysis and understanding of religion. These early thinkers set the stage for a more informed, comprehensive approach for the anthropology of religion. We will take up these contemporary approaches in the next chapter.

NOTES

1. See Tylor's book *Anahuac: Or Mexico and the Mexicans, Ancient and Modern* (London: Longman, Green, Longman, and Roberts, 1861) for a description of Mexican culture based on a four-month trip on horseback. For a full-length biography of Tylor, see R.R. Marett, *Tylor* (London: Chapman and Hall, 1936). Marett was one of Tylor's devoted students and a religious theorist himself. Tylor's major anthropological and theoretical works are *Primitive Culture*, 2 volumes [Volume 2 is titled *Religion in Primitive Culture* (London: Harper Torchbooks 1871/(1958)]; *Researches into the Early History of Mankind and the Development of Civilization* (John Murray, 1881); and *Anthropology: An Introduction to the Study of Man* [New York: D. Appleton & Co., 1881/(1898)].

2. The abridged edition of *The Golden Bough: A Study in Magic and Religion* was published by Macmillan in 1924. For a good assessment of the sources used by Frazer in *The Golden Bough*, see Robert Fraser, *The Making of the Golden Bough: The Origins and Growth of an Argument* (New York: St. Martins Press, 1990). Robert Ackerman has written a thorough biography of Frazer in *J.G. Frazer: His Life and Work* (Cambridge: Cambridge University Press., 1987).

3. Marx and Engels derived many of their ideas about the unilineal development of society from the American anthropologist Lewis Morgan who wrote a major treatise called *Ancient Society* (1877, recently reissued by University of Arizona Press, 1985). For the best overview of Marx's analysis of religion see David McLellan, *Marxism and Religion*, (New York: Harper and Row, 1987). Also, McLellan has the best biographical account of Marx in *Karl Marx: His Life and Thought* (New York: Harper and Row, 1973).

4. One of the classics of social theory written by Max Weber is *Economy and Society* [New York: Bedminster Press, 1968 (orig. 1922)]. Aside from *The Protestant Ethic and the Spirit of Capitalism* (1904), Weber's other works on religion include *The Religion of China* (New York: The Free Press, 1951); *Ancient Judaism* (New York: The Free Press, 1952); and *The Religion of India* (New York: The Free Press, 1958). Weber began a study of Islam but did not complete it. However, Bryan Turner's book *Weber and Islam* (London: Routledge, 1974) analyzes the notes of Weber's understanding of Islam. A thorough biographical sketch of Weber is in H.H. Gerth and C. Wright Mills, eds., *From Max Weber* (London: Routledge, 1948). A recent overview of the life of Weber and his work is Randall Collins, *Max Weber: A Skeleton Key* (Beverly Hills, CA: Sage, 1986).

   One of the intellectual influences on Weber's research projects was the German idealist traditions that emphasized what has been referred to as hermeneutical, or intepretive, understandings of human behavior. Hermeneutical approaches are associated with the German school of philosophy begun by Wilthem Dilthey (1833–1911) who was influenced by Hegel and Immanuel Kant. Dilthey argued that human behavior and culture, including religion, could not be understood in the same manner as one understood the natural world. He divided the sciences between Naturwissenschaften, which was the study of the natural world, and Geistewissenschaften, which was the study of the human world, including culture, history, religion, and symbolism. According to Dilthey in order to understand human culture, or religion, one had to use a special method known as *Verstehen* (sympathetic imagination), or a comprehension of the internal ideas, meanings, and symbols of the culture. Weber used this method in his research projects, along with a more scientific, objective approach. He attempted to synthesize the hermeneutical, interpretive methods with more postivistic objective methods. As we will see in later chapters, this attempted synthesis of Weber is still influential among many contemporary anthropologists.

5. Although Weber's hypothesis regarding the Protestant ethic and its relationship with capitalism became widespread, it has been challenged by many contemporary scholars. In his later works such as *General Economic History* (1927) Weber paid more attention to institutional factors and political economy, and the Protestant ethic was relegated to a less significant role in the evolution of capitalism. Weber, in the Protestant Ethic, stated that he did not intend to put forward a one-sided spiritual explanation to contrast with the one-sided materialist explanation of Marx. He says that he simply wanted to accentuate one process by subjecting it to a close examination.

6. A book that provides an overview of Müller's life and work is Nirad Chaudhuri, *Scholar Extraordinary: The Life of Professor of the Rt. Hon. Friedrich Max Müller* (London: Chatto & Windus, 1974).

7. Two books that provide a good summary of Durkheim's theoretical approach are Steven Lukes *Emile Durkheim: His Life and Work: A Historical and Critical Study* (New York: Harper and Row, 1972) and Anthony Giddens, *Emile Durkheim* (New York: Viking Press, 1978).

8. A number of early ethnographic studies informed Durkheim's analysis of Australian aborigine religion. B. Spencer and F.J. Gillen, *Native Tribes of Central Australia* (New York: Macmillan, 1899); was a principle source for Durkheim's analysis. However, B. Spencer and Gillen were not anthropologists. For a good critique of early studies of Australian aborigine religion, see W.E. H. Stanner, "Reflections on Durkheim and Aboriginal Religion," in W.S.F. Pickering, ed., *Durkheim on Religion* (London: Routledge and Kegan, 1975).

9. An old biography of Freud written by one of his followers is Ernest Jones, *The Life and Work of Sigmund Freud*, 3 vols. (New York: Basic Books, 1953–1957). A more recent biography by an intellectual historian is Peter Gay's *Freud: A Life for our Times* (New York: Norton, 1988).

Three

Contemporary Anthropological Perspectives on Religion

Raymond Scupin

Lindenwood University

The major contrast between the classical theories of religion that were described in Chapter 2 and the anthropological theories to be described in this chapter is that contemporary theory is based on descriptions of religious traditions from systematic ethnographic research. The early classical theories were based on speculative ideas regarding the origins and functions of religion without much reference to actual ethnographic research. Even Emile Durkheim's citations of some early scholarly accounts of Australian aborigine religions (also cited by Freud) were not based on the systematic studies of professional anthropologists. These early theories were based primarily on the tales of travelers, colonial officials, and missionaries. Though some of these reports were somewhat accurate, most of the reports were based on superficial observations, which led, in many cases, to exaggerated stereotypes and misconceptions regarding religious phenomena in other societies. Beginning in the twentieth century, a number of anthropologists began to criticize these nineteenth-century unilineal schemes of religious evolution, characterizing them as "just so stories," and wild speculations. In addition, these early theorists focused on the origins of religious traditions and tended to view the early stages of "primitive religions" as the childlike (or savage) forms of thought and ritual. As a twentieth-century anthropology emerged, these characterizations of "primitive peoples" were also criticized leading to a more nuanced understanding of these religious traditions. Two of the leading anthropologists who developed these critiques of the classical approaches to religion were the U.S. anthropologist Franz Boas and the British-trained anthropologist Bronislaw Malinowski.

INTO THE FIELD

Franz Boas

Franz Boas (1858–1942) received his early education in Germany as a natural scientist but eventually became interested in geography. His studies in geography took him to the arctic for research among the Eskimo peoples in northern Canada.

Through this research and contact with a non-Western culture, Boas gravitated toward the study of culture and the field of anthropology. Eventually he conducted fieldwork among a group of native American Indians known as the Kwakiutl, who lived on the northwest coast of Canada. Like many other Germans of his generation, he immigrated to the United States and became a U.S. citizen. Through his scholarly and scientific efforts Boas became the nation's foremost leader and scholar in anthropology at Columbia University in New York, where he trained many pioneers in the field until his retirement in 1937. Boas had a tremendous impact on the development of anthropology both in the United States and internationally. Boas became a vigorous opponent of the nineteenth-century unilineal evolutionists. He criticized their attempts to propose stages of evolution through which all societies evolve. Boas critiqued the way they used the comparative method and the haphazard manner in which they organized the data to fit their theories of evolutionary stages. He maintained that these nineteenth-century schemes of evolution were based on insufficient empirical evidence. Boas called for an end to "armchair anthropology" in which scholars took data uncritically from travelers, traders, and missionaries and plugged these data into a speculative model of evolution. He proposed that all anthropologists do rigorous, scientifically based fieldwork to collect basic ethnographic data. Boas urged his students to do intensive ethnological fieldwork to investigate the different cultures throughout the world, while shedding one's own ethnocentric biases.

Boas' fieldwork experience and his intellectual training in Germany led him to conclude that each society has its own unique historical development. This perspective, known as historical particularism, maintains that each society must be understood as a product of its own history. This view led Boas to adopt the notion of *cultural relativism*, the belief that each society should be understood in terms of its own cultural practices and values.[1] One aspect of this view is that no society evolved higher or lower than another. Thus, we cannot rank any particular society above another in terms of degree of savagery, barbarity, or civility. Boas called for an end to the use of these derogatory ethnocentric terms. The so-called "primitive" or "savage" people had cultures that were different, but not inferior to those of modern humans in industrial societies. These people who had been classified as "childlike" savages had their own forms of religious thought and cosmologies that were in many ways just as complex as so-called "civilized" peoples. Boas criticized the notion that "primitive religion" was based on distinctive modes of reasoning or prelogical forms of thought.

Boas worked in all four subfields of anthropology: physical anthropology, archaeology, ethnology, and linguistics. Some of his most important work involved taking precise assessments of the physical characteristics, including brain size and cranial capacity, of people in different societies. Boas was one of the first scientists in the United States to demonstrate that brain size and cranial capacities of modern humans are not linked directly to intelligence. His research indicated that a wide range of differences in brain size and cranial capacity occur within all groups of people. Boas's findings challenged the racist and ethnocentric assumptions put forward by the unilineal evolutionists. He was adamantly opposed to any racialistic or biological explanation of human behavior. Racial and biological characteristics were determined by genetics or heredity, whereas culture and behavior were learned through the process of enculturation. He and his students saw the individual thoughts, feelings, and behaviors as shaped by cultural factors. They focused on the enculturation process and its effects on humans.

The Boasian view became the dominant theoretical view in anthropology during the first half of the twentieth century. Anthropologists began to do ethnographic fieldwork in different societies to gather sound empirical evidence. Boas instituted the participant-observer method as a basic research strategy within ethnographic fieldwork (see Chapter 1). This strategy enabled ethnologists to gather valid empirical data to help explain and understand human behavior. Boas also encouraged his students to develop their linguistic skills so they could learn the languages of the people they studied. In particular Boas emphasized that one had to understand the language of other societies in order to understand and interpret the culture. This was particularly important in understanding the religious concepts, symbolic meanings, and cosmologies of other cultures.

Boas trained many U.S. anthropologists who did a massive amount of ethnographic research on cultural and religious traditions throughout the world. His students included Ruth Benedict, Margaret Mead, Edward Sapir, Alfred Kroeber, Paul Radin, and many others who developed the concepts of cultural relativism and historical particularism in their understanding of various societies. For example, Paul Radin's major book *Primitive Man as Philosopher* (1927), based upon the accumulating findings of ethnographic research, demonstrated how native Americans and other so-called primitive or "childlike savage" people have sophisticated and profound cosmologies that compare with any other groups of humans. Radin translated the folklore of many of these native peoples and showed how they represented highly abstract thought and ethical codes that are based on logical and rational foundations. He studied the Winnebago native American Indians for over 50 years, a lifelong field research project which underscored how these people who had been characterized as "savages" or "primitives" had developed their own cosmologies and religious forms of thought that were as philosophically complex as modern humans. Under Boas's immense influence and the studies of many of his students, such as Radin, Benedict, and Mead, the terms such as "savage" or "primitive" became pejorative and were no longer used to describe people in small-scale societies. Boas and his students created a better awareness and appreciation of these native peoples in small-scale societies as having distinctive, yet, in no way, inferior cultures.

Bronislaw Malinowski

At approximately the same time that Boas and his U.S. students were questioning the claims of the nineteenth-century unilineal evolutionists, British anthropologists were developing their own criticisms of these early theorists. One important British-trained anthropologist pursuing a critique of the early unilineal evolutionary views was Bronislaw Malinowski (1884–1942). Malinowski was born and educated in Cracow, Poland. Like Boas, he received his first training as a natural scientist, attaining his doctorate in physics and mathematics in 1908. However, during a prolonged illness, his mother read to him from Frazer's *Golden Bough,* and he became so fascinated with this work that he decided to migrate to England to do postgraduate studies in anthropology. Malinowski received his doctorate of science in anthropology from the London School of Economics in 1910. In 1914 he went to the Trobriand Islands in Melanesia to do fieldwork. Since Malinowski was from an area of Poland controlled by Austria at that time, he was declared an enemy alien of England in World War I and could not return to the London School of Economics. Therefore, he stayed in the region of the Pacific and Melanesia for the duration of World War I from 1914–1918 and set high standards for "participant observation" research in anthropology.

After his return from the Trobriand Islands, Malinowski wrote a number of monographs in English describing Trobriand society and culture. In doing so he challenged many of the assumptions of the nineteenth-century unilineal evolutionists regarding their characterization of "primitive" or "savage society." Malinowski used his data on economic, social, and political institutions to criticize theorists such as Marx or Freud. In addition, in his studies of religion and magic used by the Trobriand peoples, he refuted many of the speculations of Tylor and Frazer regarding "primitive societies." Like Boas, Malinowski believed that you had to understand the language and culture of the native people as they understood it themselves. One had to adopt the "insider's perspective" to explain and understand the culture and symbols of people. As a consequence of his long stay in the field, Malinowski perceived how the culture of the Trobriander people was integrated. He argued that each aspect of culture had to be understood within the wide context of economic, social, political, and religious institutions. Thus, as did Boas, Malinowski emphasized the idea of "cultural relativism." Each culture had its own unique cultural heritage and traditions. In order to get this understanding of a culture, one had to know the native language and become immersed within the lifeways of the society.[2] Malinowski chided the nineteenth-century "armchair anthropologists" for not understanding the context of the customs and beliefs that they had described based on superficial observations.

Malinowski's theoretical perspective emphasized how society functions to serve the *individual's* interests or needs. This view is sometimes known as *psychological functionalism.* He tried to demonstrate how individuals use cultural norms and beliefs to satisfy certain needs. In contrast to Durkheim, who argued that religious values and institutions satisfied the demands of society, Malinowski suggested that culture, including religion and magic, satisfied the needs of *individuals.*[3] He asserted that individuals have biological and psychological needs, as well as social and cultural needs. The basic biological needs of the individual include the desire for satisfying hunger and bodily comfort or safety from physical harm and reproduction. In his view, cultural systems including the organization of food production, the technology of housing construction, and family organization are developed to serve these basic needs. In addition, individuals also have psychological needs. These psychological needs demand the production of various cultural responses. It was these psychological needs that Malinowski featured in his analyses of magic and religious concepts and institutions.

Malinowski argued that magic and religion were not merely abstract doctrines or philosophies but instead were modes of behavior that were used in a pragmatic sense to serve the interests of individuals. He saw Trobriand Islanders as individuals who were as rational and pragmatic as any other humans in any part of the world including Europe. In particular, Malinowski viewed magic as a basic set of mechanisms in societies that did not maintain formal scientific methods. For example, according to Malinowski, societies that did not have a good understanding of the germ theory of illnesses often invoked supernatural causes to explain these illnesses. Consequently, various magical practices were utilized to help cure individuals of sickness and reduce anxiety and discomfort for individuals. In his most classic description of magical practices Malinowski studied fishing practices. He observed that when the islanders went fishing in enclosed lagoons where fishing was reliable and safe, they depended on their technical knowledge and skill alone. However, when they went fishing on the open sea, which was more dangerous and highly unpredictable, they employed an extensive number of magical beliefs and techniques. Thus, Malinowski argued that the use of magic and ritual arises in situations where humans have no control over circumstances, such as weather conditions. Magical practices and rituals are used to reduce internal anxieties and tensions for these individuals. Thus, magic and ritual function to exert control over dimensions of life that are outside human control.

In addition to magic, the Trobrianders have an elaborate system of religious beliefs concerning death, the afterlife, and other spiritual concerns. In his book *Magic, Science, and Religion, and Other Essays* (1954) he criticizes the Durkheimian approach to religion, which highlighted the group functions of religious belief. Malinowski contended that religion was based on individual experiences, especially the individual crisis of death faced by all humans. Although Malinowski acknowledged that death rituals were always important public and group events, the final crisis of life—death—is of the greatest importance to the individual. Malinowski believed that the desire for immortality was a universal psychological need for individuals. Thus, religious inspirations arose from deep emotional needs of the individual. However, Malinowski contended that religion had fundamentally different characteristics than magic or ritual. Whereas magic was always related to a utilitarian end or purpose, religion must be viewed as an end it itself. Religion also had a moral aspect, while magic was primarily amoral.

As Boas did in the United States, Malinowski trained a whole generation of anthropologists in Great Britain that had an enormous influence on the discipline. His intensive systematic fieldwork became a model for ethnographers around the world.[4] Like some of the other early developments within anthropology, Malinowski's psychological functionalism has its theoretical weaknesses. It failed to explain why religious traditions are different or similar. If all individuals have the same basic physical and psychological needs, why do some societies have different types of magical and religious traditions when similar ones might be able to fill the same functions? This weakness arose from the tendency of Malinowski and other functionalists to ignore historical processes. Unlike Boas, he did not pay much attention to the historical development of differing spiritual traditions but rather focused exclusively on how these traditions served the individual. However, Malinowski set the stage for an emphasis on intensive ethnographic investigations of religious traditions. One anthropologist influenced by Malinowski's example of intensive fieldwork was Edward Evans-Pritchard who cultivated an interest in the anthropology of religion through his ethnographic research in East Africa. Yet, in contrast to Malinowski, E. Evans-Pritchard highlighted the importance of a historical perspective in understanding another culture.

Edward Evan Evans-Pritchard

Edward Evan Evans-Pritchard (1902–1973) was a student of history at Oxford University in the 1920s when he became interested in anthropological studies. After obtaining his M.A. degree at Oxford, he decided to study at the London School of

Economics with several anthropologists including Malinowski. Malinowski encouraged Evans-Pritchard to do long-term intensive field work, to immerse himself in a tribal society, and study the culture in great depth. Eventually, Evans-Pritchard decided to do his ethnographic research in Africa.[5] He traveled to the region of Sudan in East Africa where the Nile and Congo rivers find their source. In that area he first conducted research from 1926 and 1931 among an ethnic group known as the Azande, with whom he lived with for some 20 months and he became fluent in their language. The most important ethnography based on this research was titled *Witchcraft, Oracles, and Magic among the Azande* (1937). Later, between 1931 and 1936, he conducted intensive field work among the Nuer tribe of the Sudan region. The Nuer are a pastoralist tribal people who maintain cattle as their basic subsistence activity. This field work resulted in a number of important monographs including *The Nuer: A Description of the Modes of Livelihood and Political Institutions of a Nilotic People* (1940). During World War II Evans-Pritchard served in the British army, leading the Azande in raids against the Italian defense forces in East Africa. In addition, during the war he was posted as a political officer in Libya where he did further ethnographic research on a Muslim Sufi group known as the Sanusi. Following the war, Evans-Pritchard joined the faculty at Oxford University where he became professor of social anthropology until he resigned in 1970. Much to his dismay and dislike of aristocratic pretensions, this ethnographer was knighted by the British queen in 1971 and was subsequently known as Sir Edward Evans-Pritchard.

Evans-Pritchard changed his intellectual and theoretical orientation late in his career in anthropology, anticipating some of major contemporary theories within the anthropology of religion. In his early work Evans-Pritchard was influenced by the functionalist approach of Emile Durkheim. In his early work on Nuer society, this Durkheimian influence is evident. He describes Nuer social and political structure in precise technical, and scientific terms to focus on how these structures had provided functions for the society. Evans-Pritchard's aim in this early work was to analyze these social and political structures and determine how they functioned with respect to the ecological and economic conditions of the Nuer. By concentrating on the different social segments known as lineages of Nuer society, he believed he could perceive how these segments linked institutions and individuals maintaining the stability of a tribal society.[6] However, later in his career Evans-Pritchard rejected this scientific form of functionalism. It became clear to him that he had neglected the historical processes that led to the development of various types of social structures of the people he studied. In the 1950s Evans-Pritchard turned to a more historically informed type of anthropology and disavowed some of his early work that relied too heavily on a scientific, functional, and reductionist analysis. He asserted in his famous Marett lecture in 1951 that "social anthropology is best regarded as an art and not as a social science." In addition, his understanding of religion moved from functional analysis to a more nuanced comprehension of the "meaning" of religious beliefs and practices within a society. He declared that religion needs to be understood, not as a natural system, but as a moral and symbolic system. This movement from a scientific platform for understanding religion to a more historical and humanistic perspective portended a new direction in the anthropology of religion.

This change of direction in Evans-Pritchard's theoretical orientation is explicit in his book *Nuer Religion* (1956). In this work Evans-Pritchard focuses on how Nuer religion is a legitimate form of explanation of the mysteries of the world. He strives to present how the various beliefs and practices of the Nuer provide a coherent worldview when one begins to understand the meanings of this religious phenomenon. In order to grasp the meaning of these beliefs and practices the ethnographer has to understand how the various symbols and concepts interrelate. This implies an understanding of not only the objective aspects of the religious tradition, but also an appreciation of the subjective dimension of religious beliefs and practices. In other words, the anthropologist must strive to get an insider's view and understanding of the religion. Evans-Pritchard encouraged ethnographers to seek out the connections and shades of differences in meaning or emphasis in the meaning of beliefs and practices. In this important ethnography of Nuer religion, he indicates how from an outsider's perspective a tribal people's religion appears to have no formal dogmas, liturgies, organized rituals, sacraments, or mythology. However, he demonstrated Nuer religion actually has all these features when the ethnographer eventually unlocks the meaning of the religious traditions as understood by the people themselves.

In a later work *Theories of Primitive Religion* (1965) Evans-Pritchard emphasized that earlier theories of small-scale societies such as Tylor, Frazer, Durkheim, Freud, or Malinowski were based on naive psychological or sociological reductionist arguments. He stressed how ethnographers must understand the subjective meanings of religious beliefs and practices in order to discover the internal logic and coherence of these religious phenomena. By exploring the logic and symbolic associations of the religious traditions of the culture from the insider's perspective, the researcher could begin to discern the meanings of the spiritual concepts and related practices of the people. In this nonscientific humanistic vein, Evans-Pritchard concluded that religion is ultimately an "interior state of mind." Spiritual experiences are based on intuitive apprehensions that can only be understood through an insider's perspective.[7] At the same time, Evans-Pritchard asserted that the anthropologist should not just concentrate on the study of theological doctrines and beliefs of the people, but also on how these doctrines and beliefs interconnect with the other institutions in a particular society. He rejected the broad generalities of religious evolution or functionalism of his predecessors in anthropology. Evans-Pritchard's work provided an example of how anthropologists can provide deep and rich explanations of religious phenomena when they are rooted in close, meticulously detailed studies of a particular culture.

SYMBOLIC ANTHROPOLOGY

Mary Douglas

One scholar deeply influenced by Evans-Pritchard is Mary Douglas who is one of the most creative contemporary anthropologists of the twentieth century. Mary Douglas was born in Italy in 1921 and was brought up and educated in Great Britain in a Catholic convent. During World War II she served as a civil servant in what was known then as the Belgian Congo. This experience pulled her toward the field of anthropology, and she returned to Oxford to study with Evans-Pritchard in 1946. For her doctoral research she did an ethnographic study of the Lele people of Zaire (formerly part of the Belgian Congo). She received her doctorate from Oxford in social anthropology in 1951. Douglas lectured at Oxford University for a brief period but eventually launched her teaching and research career at University College, London. Later she moved to the United States as research director of the Russell Sage Foundation, and as Avalon professor of humanities at Northwestern University. Finally after two years at Princeton University, Douglas returned to England in 1988.

After writing several ethnographic studies focused on the Lele of Zaire, Douglas turned to more theoretical and cross-cultural research on religion, symbolism, ritual, and cosmology. However, unlike the early cross-cultural research of scholars such as Tylor, her work drew primarily on the systematic fieldwork of other ethnographers such as Evans-Pritchard. On the other hand, in order to illustrate her theoretical points, Douglas refers to religious textual sources from Judaism, Christianity, or Hinduism. Her first major theoretical work that drew worldwide attention from scholars in religion was *Purity and Danger: An Analysis of Pollution and Taboo* (1963). In this work Douglas draws extensively from her mentor Evans-Pritchard's work. Her next book *Natural Symbols* (1970) remains one of the most innovative works in the anthropology of religion. Throughout her work , Douglas, like Evans-Pritchard, emphasizes that both preliterate and literate peoples have rituals and symbols that create a symbolically meaningful and consistent worldview that can be understood only through an in-depth understanding of the entire culture. She emphasizes that what appears to be irrational and inconsistent by an outsider's superficial observation of a society can be understood and explained by the ethnographer after she or he penetrates the levels of meaning of the beliefs and practices of the society.

In her first theoretical book *Purity and Danger*, Douglas compared various beliefs about purity and pollution, which she contended is found in all societies throughout the world. In particular she suggests that many of the beliefs about pollution and purity—for example, what is considered dirty or clean—is found in all human societies, even though the symbols of these phenomena may vary from culture to culture. Earlier theorists such as Tylor, Frazer, and Durkheim had discussed taboos and prohibitions in different societies. Douglas advances their queries by suggesting that all societies have classifications of certain objects that are unclean, tabooed, polluted, or dirty, as well as what is clean, pure, or undefiled. She finds that many ethnographers have discovered that the human body is associated with what is polluting or dirty in various societies. Blood, excreta such as urine or feces, breast milk, or saliva are often associated with polluting substances within different societies. For example, she found that among the Lele of Zaire human secretions such as blood and excrement were believed to be highly polluting substances. These substances were classified as dirt and pollution and were symbolically associated with the emotions of shame. These polluting substances are also connected with other unclean aspects of life, including corpses and death.

Douglas compares these ideas of pollution with those among Hindus in India. She draws on Hindu texts and ethnography to show how the human body provides a symbolic metaphor for society, and its classifications of what is pure and impure. Within the tradition of Hinduism, the myth of Purusha in the ancient Vedas describes how humans were created in a hierarchical order. According to the creation myth, the deity Purusha is sacrificed by other gods and from his mouth came the priests, from his arms the warriors, from his thighs the merchants, and from his feet the laborers. This resulted in the division of society into a hierarchical order of castes, with the highest caste, the priests, as the most pure, whereas those who are the lowest castes are the menial laborers and are most polluted, have the tasks of disposing of human wastes, corpses, and refuse. Thus, the human body becomes a symbolic expression of the ordering of society. In her discussions of purity and pollution, Douglas suggests that all societies attempt to classify matter and substance into these different domains. Dirt and pollution are considered dangerous, and out of place, and lead to disorder, while purity and cleanliness are associated with order and harmony.

To further illustrate her ideas regarding the classification of matter in *Purity and Danger,* Douglas examined the ancient Israelite's classification of animals and taboos against eating certain animals such as pigs and shellfish as described in Leviticus in the Bible. Douglas argues that like other humans the ancient Israelites classify reality by placing things into distinguishable "mental boxes." However, some things don't fit neatly into distinguishable mental boxes. Some items are anomalous and ambiguous and fall between the basic categories that are used to define cultural reality. These anomalous items are usually treated as unclean, impure, unholy, polluting, or defiling. Douglas refers to how these processes influenced the classification of animals among the ancient Israelites. She alludes to the descriptions in the first chapter of the Bible, Genesis where God creates the animals with specific characteristics. Birds with feathers are soaring in the sky, fish with scales and fins are swimming in the water, and creatures with four feet are walking, hopping, or jumping on the land. However, some animals did not easily fit into the cultural categories used for the classification of animals. Animals that combined elements of different realms were considered ambiguous, and therefore unclean or unholy. For example, terrestrial animals that moved by "swarming upon the earth" were declared unclean and were prohibited from being eaten. Pigs were also unclean and prohibited in the ancient Israelite diet. Clean edible animals such as sheep, goats, and cattle had cloven hoofs and chewed cud. However, pigs had cloven hoofs but did not chew cud. Consequently, the pig was unclean, polluting, and tabooed because it failed to fit into the cultural classification of reality accepted by the ancient Israelites. Shellfish and eels are also unclean animals because they swim in the water but lack fins and scales. These anomalous creatures fall outside the systematic classification of animals. Douglas maintains that the dietary laws of Leviticus represented an ideal construction of reality that represented God's plan of creation, which was based on perfection, order, and holiness.

Douglas's focus on the interrelationship between symbolic classification and social structure led her to the development of a cross-cultural theoretical schematic based on what she referred to as the "group-grid axis." First proposed in *Natural Symbols,* different societies are classified by Douglas as having various types of "group-grid axis." "Group" refers to the degree in which the individual is controlled by social relationships. A tightly controlled society where the individual has very little independence would constitute a strong "group." "Grid" refers to the symbolic system and rules of the culture, and the degree in which the symbolic system classifies reality in a systematic, coherent worldview. Some societies have strong group and weak grid symbolic systems, whereas other societies have weak group ties and strongly developed grid symbolic systems. Societies that have both weak group and weak grid symbolic systems generally are fluid and flexible with very few elaborate rituals and symbols. For example, in societies, such as the Mbuti hunting and gathering society of the Ituri rain forest in Central Africa, religion is based primarily on internal feelings and emotions, without much external symbolism and formalized ritual. Nomadic societies such as the Mbuti allow for tremendous flexibility in behavior and belief. However, generally, in agricultural societies where people are settled down, there are elaborate symbolic classifications and strong controls over individuals— "high group and high grid"—behavior is rigidly ordered, there is little personal freedom, and religion is highly symbolic and ritualized. In these agricultural societies people are more concerned about group boundaries and authority. Thus, group boundaries and hierarchical control are much more developed in the religious traditions of these agricultural societies. Douglas has applied this group-grid model to many different forms of religious experience throughout the world.

Victor Turner

Another anthropologist who pioneered in the area of symbolic anthropology was Victor Turner. Victor Turner (1920–1983) was born in Glasgow, Scotland. He studied at the University College, London, and received his doctorate in anthropology at the University of Manchester. Turner was influenced by Monica Wilson and Max Gluckman, anthropologists who had done field work in Africa. Turner became a research anthropologist at the Rhodes-Livingston Institute in Zambia, where he carried out in-depth ethnographic research among the Ndembu people. He taught at the University of Manchester until 1963. Turner moved to the United States and taught at the University of Chicago, Cornell University, and later at the University of Virginia until the time of his death. Turner married Edith Davis in 1943. She accompanied him on his field work projects, and is an accomplished contemporary anthropologist in her own right who continues to contribute to the theoretical work in the anthropology of religion.

One early book by Turner, *The Forest of Symbols: Aspects of Ndembu Ritual* (1967), focused on the role of symbols in ritual and thought among the Ndembu. In this work Turner illustrates how symbols operate within any society. He notes how symbols are "storage units" of meaning that represent something that has analogous qualities or is associated with some abstract thought. He distinguishes between two different types of symbols: referential symbols and condensation symbols. Referential symbols are those symbols that are used in ordinary speech or writing that have a relationship with some concrete item or fact. For example, referential symbols include flags with their various meanings used to identify countries and the collective values of those countries. Referential symbols are primarily cognitive and related to thinking processes. Condensation symbols are those symbols that synthesize a variety of meanings within one single form and tend to be associated with emotional rather than cognitive processes. Condensed symbols stir the deep emotions of the unconscious within individuals.[8] But Turner asserts that all symbols have *multivocality*, that is, they are subject to different interpretations by different individuals and groups. Symbols speak to different people representing many different meanings. In addition, each symbol has what he refers to as a *polarization of meaning*. Symbols have two different axes or poles of meaning. At one pole a symbol may refer to some physiological characteristic such as blood or breast milk, but at the other pole it may refer to some aspect of the social structure of the society.

One example of Turner's symbolic analysis is the Ndembu villagers' conceptions of the "mudyi tree." The mudyi tree is one of the most important key symbols of Ndembu society. It is where female puberty rituals are carried out. When a young girl reaches puberty she is wrapped in a blanket and placed at the foot of the mudyi. To the Ndembu the mudyi tree symbolizes the most important dominant ritual center. The mudyi tree seeps a milky latex substance that symbolizes human breast milk and is thus associated with the color white, and also with mother and children. Ndembu social structure is based on matrilineal groups, where mother and child are the center of the society. Thus, the mudyi tree represents both physiological aspects of females, breast milk, as well as the social aspects of matrilineal society. The mudyi tree is a powerful symbol representing both multivocal, condensed, and polarized meanings reflecting both cognitive and emotional processes. The mudyi tree is the symbolic flag of the Ndembu, embodying the claims of both females and males from their matrilineal ancestresses.

Though Turner began his career when the functionalist approach of British anthropology was at its height, he moved toward a more in-depth analysis and interpretation of symbolism. Acknowledging that symbols had a very personal, and sometimes unconscious meaning to individuals, he asserted that ethnographers could penetrate the social and ideological meanings of symbols. Turner combined the insider's perspective with that of the ethnographer's view. He encouraged ethnographers to view the external forms and observable characteristics of symbols and to pay attention to the native religious specialist's and layperson's interpretations of these symbols. But, in addition, the ethnographer was obligated to explore the hidden levels of meaning below the surface of the external symbols. Turner argued that this could only be done by understanding the total social and cultural context of the society, which is sometimes beyond the grasp of the insider's perspective. It was up to the ethnographer to penetrate these different levels of meaning by examining the intricate details of the rituals, symbols, and culture.

Clifford Geertz

The most prominent symbolic anthropologist within North American anthropology is Clifford Geertz. In Chapter 1, we discussed Geertz's contributions toward a definition of religion. In that discussion, we emphasized how he views religion as a system of symbols. Geertz has had a major influence on the anthropology of religion and symbolic anthropology. Clifford Geertz was born in San Francisco in 1926. After serving in the Navy during World War II, he attended Antioch College in Ohio where he received his B.A. degree in philosophy. Geertz went on to Harvard University where he entered the department of social relations, then headed by the internationally known sociologist Talcott Parsons. The department of social relations was an interdisciplinary department that recruited professors of psychology, sociology, and anthropology in order to offer broad theoretical examinations of social phenomena. Students would emphasize one of these programs, but they had to take examinations in all of these fields. While a graduate student Geertz focused on anthropological studies and decided to do fieldwork in Indonesia. In 1952, he and

his wife Hildred traveled to the island of Java and stayed there with a team of other social scientists for two years. Upon returning from the field he wrote his Ph.D. thesis
based on his fieldwork and received his degree from the department of social relations in 1956. After receiving his degree, he and Hildred returned to Indonesia to do
research on the island of Bali. After completing fieldwork in Bali, he joined the faculty at the University of California at Berkeley in 1958, but eventually moved to the University of Chicago in 1960, where he taught and did research for ten years. During his
years at Chicago, Geertz did more ethnographic field work in Morocco in North Africa.
In 1970 Geertz became the only anthropologist, in fact the only social scientist, named
as professor at the famed Institute for Advanced Study in Princeton, the think tank
where Einstein once worked. He was nominated for this position because of his enormous influence on many scholars within both the social sciences and humanities.

Geertz's first major book, *The Religion of Java* (1960), was a classic ethnography
based on his field work in Indonesia. This ethnography is a detailed analysis of the
complexities of religion in Indonesia, which is a mix of Islam, Hinduism, and animist
spiritual traditions. His next major work, *Agricultural Involution* (1963), is an ecological and economic analysis of Indonesia, focusing on how Dutch colonialism had an
impact on the prospects of economic development in this Asian country. In another ethnography of the same year, *Peddlars and Princes* (1963), Geertz compared the
Javanese town of Modjokuto with the Balinese town of Tabanan to illustrate how cultural and religious traditions of various peoples effected economic development. In
1965 in *The Social History of an Indonesian Town*, he continued his examination of
Modjokuto to explore the connections between politics, economics, social life, and
religion. After his field trips to Morocco, Geertz published an influential book *Islam
Observed* (1968) where he compares the Islamic tradition in Morocco with that of Indonesia. However, his most influential work, which has had a wide impact beyond the
field of anthropology, is the collection of essays in *The Interpretation of Culture* (1973).
In these critical essays, Geertz reflects on the enormous difficulties of understanding
culture, religion, and society. In doing so, he initiated a whole new style of doing
and thinking about ethnographic research. This work was followed by another widely commended set of critical essays, *Local Knowledge* (1983), which resumed his discussions of the difficulties of interpreting culture.

In *The Interpretation of Culture,* Geertz advocates a method of ethnographic inquiry that he refers to as "thick description." Drawing on a famous statement of Max
Weber, Geertz describes the most important aspect of culture as the "webs of significance," that is, symbols that have meaning that humans have spun. Thick description focuses on the collection of data—especially the symbolic meanings or the webs
of significance reflecting the point of view of the members of the society studied—
on social structure, the economy, ritual, myth, symbols, and cultural values. Geertz
advances the view that culture is shared intersubjectively by people. Culture is therefore objective rather than subjective. It is not something just stored within the mind,
but rather it is publicly shared by individuals through their everyday language and
behavior. As ethnographers use the methods of thick description, they can observe,
discern, and understand the interconnected patterns of meanings, motives, moods,
intentions, and activities of people. To do this they must interpret the meanings of
the symbolic concepts and metaphors from the point of view of the people in a specific society using what Weber refers to as *verstehen* (sympathetic understanding).[9]

The aim of the symbolic anthropologist is to make other people's values, beliefs, and worldviews meaningful and intelligible to others. Geertz acknowledges that when the anthropologist is writing her or his ethnographic text, they are interpreting other peoples symbolic worlds. But, rather than reducing religion or symbolic culture to some social function or scientific explanation, Geertz advocates the search for the "symbolic meaning" or significance of culture, rather than trying to seek out the "causes" or "laws" of culture.

In Chapter Nineteen we will discuss Geertz's important comparative analysis of the Islamic tradition in Indonesia and Morocco which has had a considerable impact on the study of the Islam and religion. The other major area of Geertz's ethnographic research, the island of Bali in Indonesia, illustrates the intellectual affinity that he has had with Max Weber and his concern with symbolic interpretation. In a widely cited essay "'Internal Conversion' in Bali" published in 1964, Geertz begins with the scheme proposed by Weber regarding the "rationalization" of modern society. As discussed in Chapter Two, Weber distinguishes between two different forms of religion found throughout the world: the "traditional" and the "rationalized." So-called primitive people have "traditional" religions imbued with polytheistic concepts and a multiplicity of spirits. According to Weber, primitive religions also tend to be concretely associated with the everyday details of life, and various magical rituals are in abundance. Conversely, in the worldview of "rationalized religions" such as Judaism, Christianity, Islam, Hinduism, and Buddhism, the divine is conceptualized in terms of one or two or just a few great spiritual principles. In addition, rationalized religions are more abstract, logically coherent, and disassociated from the regular aspects of daily life. Also, Weber suggested that the problem of evil in the world is addressed differently in traditional and rationalized religions. Traditional religions tended to associate evil with specific actions of a difficult spirit or a witch. Rationalized religions attempt to answer the question regarding evil in the world by relying on broad comprehensive worldviews or "theodicies." Though Geertz criticizes Weber's simplistic dichotomy between traditional and rationalized religion, he uses it as a starting point in his analysis of Balinese religion.

Using his ethnographic research as a basis, Geertz describes the tradition of Hinduism that exists in Bali as different than what exists in the classical religious texts. It is not the intellectually based form of mysticism of a rationalized religion. Instead, though the Balinese refer to themselves as Hindus, they practice a religion based on concrete spiritual ideas that is interwoven with everyday actions and is consequently more like a traditional religion. He describes how the Balinese are involved in ceremonies such as offering palm leaves to deities, preparing elaborate ritual meals, falling into spontaneous trances, and sustaining large-scale religious festivals requiring much time and labor. The thousands of Balinese temples have a complex social structure managed by local priests who belong to the Brahmin caste. These priests rely on a network of client-followers, who believe in the divine status of the priests to work on the spectacular rituals that are organized around life cycle rituals such as tooth filing, cremation upon death, agricultural fertility rituals, and other family and political rituals. Geertz explains how the rituals organized by the Brahmins symbolically inform the hierarchical ranking of the royalty, princes, and peasants in Balinese society, reinforcing the differences between the high born and low born.

To emphasize the traditional type of worldview or theodicy of Balinese religion, Geertz writes about the cult of death and witches. On certain occasions such as the "birthday" ceremony of a particular temple, an extravagant ritual performance of a battle between two characters from Balinese mythology takes place. One character named Rangda represents the queen of the witches, symbolizing an ancient widow, a used-up prostitute, and a child-murdering incarnation of death. Rangda is the symbol of unqualified evil. The other mythological figure, Barong, is a benign, comical monster, who is described by Geertz as a cross between a clumsy bear, a foolish puppy, and a Chinese dragon. Both of these beings are saturated with powerful spiritual energy. One villager dances the role of Barong, while another dances the role of Rangda. During the dance the audience becomes involved in the performance by taking the parts of the characters, falling into trancelike states, and using their krisses (small swords) to stab themselves, (which is ineffective while they are in trance). This is not just a performance to be watched: individuals must also participate in this cosmic battle. Though Rangda is evil, she is also irresistibly attractive and tempting. At the height of the battle the ritual performance becomes an intense emotional drama, which brings the crowd into an almost chaotic state of frenzy. The struggle between Barong and Rangda ends without a clear winner. However, the ritual symbolizes the constant and uncertain struggle between life and death, and good and evil. Geertz interprets this mythology and its accompanying ritual as an illustration of the concrete worldview and theodicy of the traditional characteristics of Balinese religion.

Yet Geertz discusses how major social changes such as urbanization, population growth, modern education, and contact with the outside world through improved communication were having an effect on these traditional forms of Balinese religion. He describes how the Balinese through a process of "internal conversion" were developing more "rationalized" forms of religion. New social changes were creating turmoil within traditional Balinese society. Young people were beginning to question the basis of the traditional basis of Balinese religion. For example, Geertz noticed how a philosophical discussion broke out at a funeral regarding ritual and practice. These discussions prompted various questions regarding the purpose and meaning of rituals and religious beliefs. These types of questions represented a whole new way of approaching religion and were the hallmark of a society moving toward a "rationalized" form of religion. Religious literacy and interpretations were spreading beyond the realm of the priestly caste. According to Geertz, Bali in 1964 appeared to be where Greece or China was during the fifth century B.C.E. People were becoming "disenchanted" with traditional forms of religion that relied upon multiple spirits and concrete ritualism. And, the priests were beginning to become more "rational" providing reasons and doctrines, and they began to reorganize their religious institutions in more formalized ways as a means of justifying their ritual status. Geertz closes the essay by stating that if we look carefully at how religion changes in Balinese contemporary society, we may be able to better understand how the world's religions have developed.

Like the other symbolic anthropologists such as Douglas, Turner, and including Evans-Pritchard, Geertz embraces the idea that religion can only be explained and understood by interpreting the systems of meanings. In contrast to some of the early twentieth-century anthropologists such as Malinowski, or other theorists such as

Freud or Durkheim, Geertz stresses that religion cannot be reduced to psychological or social needs. On the other hand, in Geertz's ethnographies he constantly illustrates how religion does interconnect with both individual and social concerns. The other major issue that Geertz is concerned with in his approach to understanding religion is cultural comparison. He does not think that one can produce generalizations about religion based on cross-cultural comparisons. The emphasis on "thick description" as a method for understanding another religious culture involves the notion that no two cultures can be the same. Each religion develops its own unique configuration of symbols, rituals, beliefs, values, worldviews, and theodicies within a particular historical, social, and cultural setting. No two religions are going to be the same. Humans create their own "webs of significance" in incomparable ways. Geertz maintains that all human affairs, all human knowledge, including religious knowledge, is "local knowledge." By focusing on the local knowledge and closely reading and interpreting the key symbols, the ethnographer can gain insights into the religious traditions of different societies.

CONCLUSION

The twentieth-century anthropologists have provided the anthropology of religion with its empirical and theoretical foundations. The early ethnographers such as Boas and Malinowski criticized the nineteenth-century theorists as speculative, armchair anthropologists. They advocated a fieldwork approach to understanding culture and society. The ethnographer had to comprehend the language and remain with the people for some time before understanding the culture and religion of the society. In addition, through their empirical field work with non-Western small-scale societies they disparaged the early attempts at portraying these native peoples as having a primitive mentality, or prelogical, irrational forms of thought. They adopted what has been termed cultural relativism, arguing that one society cannot be ranked above another based on criteria such as religious belief or practices. All societies have developed cultural and religious traditions based on their own unique historical circumstances. The traditions of thorough empirically based participant observation and fieldwork, along with cultural relativism, have remained as the key components of the anthropology of religion in this transition toward the twentieth-first century.

Building on the foundations of ethnographers such as Boas and Malinowski, later ethnographers generated more theoretical insights within the anthropology of religion. The British-trained ethnographers such as E. Evans-Pritchard, Mary Douglas, and Victor Turner provided valuable frameworks for the analysis of religion in different societies. Evans-Pritchard turned away from a scientific, reductionist analysis of religion toward a more humanistic understanding of symbolism and religious language. Following in his footsteps, Douglas and Turner initiated more in-depth analyses of the interrelationship between symbolism, society, and religious objects, processes such as rituals, and other events. They developed what has been referred to as symbolic anthropology. The American ethnographer Clifford Geertz enhanced the field of symbolic anthropology with his espousal of "thick description" in the analysis of culture and religion. This interpretive approach has had immense influence in both the social sciences and humanities. His critical essays and ethnographic-based studies of religion have been widely read throughout the world.

A number of criticisms have been directed at symbolic anthropology. One major charge is that symbolic anthropologists focus exclusively on cultural symbols at the expense of other factors that may influence human thought and behavior. These critics emphasize that symbolic anthropologists may neglect the economic or political conditions and processes that lead to the making of culture.[10] For example, socioeconomic conditions and political power may be important factors in the development of religious rituals and symbolism. Critics of symbolic anthropology, or interpretive anthropology, emphasize that culture cannot be treated as an autonomous phenomenon separate from historical, political, and economic processes and conditions that affect a society. Another criticism is that symbolic anthropology substitutes one form of determinism for another. Instead of emphasizing technological or economic or political variables, symbolic anthropologists stress the meaning of cultural symbols. Despite their rejection of causal explanations, they have been accused of reducing explanations of society and human activity to the "meanings" of cultural symbols.

Despite these criticisms these symbolic anthropologists furnished the theoretical foundations that have inspired the ethnographers in the field struggling to understand different religious traditions in the world. Many of the studies that you will be reading about in this text were directly or indirectly a result of the theoretical foundations produced by the twentieth-century ethnographers discussed in this chapter.

NOTES

1. Boas, like the German sociologist Max Weber, was influenced by the German idealist philosophers such as Wilthem Dilthey who used the hermeneutical or interpretive approach in understanding culture and symbols (see endnote 4 in Chapter 2). In addition, Boas was influenced by Johann Gottfried Herder (1744–1803) who stressed the diversity of cultures throughout the world. Unlike most of the Enlightenment thinkers, Herder argued that different cultures and languages were incomparable with each other. Herder was what was known as a German romantic who believed that every known society—Chinese, Indian, Egyptian, Greek, Roman, German, French—had developed in its own unique time and place and could not be compared with each other. He thought that each culture should respect others but be true to their own particular culture. Because of this view, he is also known as the father of nationalism.

2. One interesting book on Malinowski edited by Robert Thornton and Peter Skalník, *The Early Writings of Bronislaw Malinowski* (Cambridge: Cambridge University Press, 1993) emphasizes his early intellectual influences in Cracow, Poland that led him in the direction of cultural relativism. In particular these authors cite the influence of the German philosopher Friedrich Nietsche and the Austrian scientist Ernst Mach who both promoted notions of relativism. Another book that looks at these early influences on Malinowski is edited by Roy Ellen, G. Kubica, and J. Mucha, *Malinowski Between Two Worlds: The Polish Roots of an Anthropological Tradition*

(Cambridge: Cambridge University Press, 1988). The American historian of anthropology George Stocking, Jr., has an in-depth account of Malinowski's activities as an ethnographer in *The Ethnographer's Magic and Other Essays in the History of Anthropology* (Madison: University of Wisconsin Press, 1992).

The major monographs of Malinowski include *Argonauts of the Western Pacific* (London: Routledge & Sons, 1922); *A Scientific Theory of Culture and Other Essays* (Chapel Hill: University of North Carolina Press, 1944); *Coral Gardens and Their Magic* (London: Kegan Paul, 1935); *Sex and Repression in Savage Society* (New York: Noonday Press, 1955); *Magic, Science and Religion, and Other Essays* [London: Souvenir Press. 1974 (1925)]. After Malinowski's death, his fieldwork diary that recorded his personal notes while he was in the Trobriand Islands was published with the permission of his widow. The diary titled *A Diary in the Strict Sense of the Term* (New York: Harcourt, 1967) created a controversy because it revealed some of Malinowski's ethnocentric biases, which were not evident within his monographs.

3. Another British anthropologist, A.R. Radcliffe-Brown (1881–1955) upheld the tradition of functionalism associated with Emile Durkheim and introduced what he referred to as "structural-functionalism to the English-speaking British and American anthropological community. Radcliffe-Brown taught in England, Australia, South Africa, and the United States. He relied upon the Durkheimian tradition in his ethnographic

studies among Australian aborigines and Andaman Islanders in which he viewed religion and its related institutions as serving the needs of society. In other words, religious beliefs and practices served to hold society and groups together in harmony and creating community stability.

4. Malinowski was the professor who taught anthropology to Jomo Kenyatta, a native of East Africa who later led the independence and nationalist movement against the British in Kenya and became the first president of Kenya. In the later stages of his career Malinowski turned to issues related to international problems such as the conditions of native peoples in areas such as South Africa. He began to speak out in favor of human rights and economic development for all people throughout the world.

5. Evans-Pritchard's choice of Africa was not made in a random manner. The British government controlled areas of East Africa, and funded an ethnographic survey project of the tribes of that region. Evans-Pritchard's field work was financed by the British in order to better understand the tribal societies in their colonial region.

6. Evans-Pritchard had been exposed and influenced by A.R. Radcliffe-Brown, who had brought Durkheim's functionalism into British anthropology. See endnote 3 above.

7. Evans-Pritchard was the son of an Anglican clergyman. However, in 1944 Evans-Pritchard converted to Catholicism. Many anthropologists have acknowledged that this conversion was partially responsible for his turn from scientific, functionalist analysis of religion to a more humanistic orientation.

8. Turner did agree that symbols are partly influenced by unconscious motivations and ideas, but he emphasized that anthropologists should focus on the ideological or social aspects of symbolism and through this type of analysis may be able to assist the psychoanalyst.

9. Geertz's education at Harvard's department of social relations had a formative influence on his work. Talcott Parsons, the major sociologist who headed the department, had introduced the work of Max Weber into U.S. society. He had translated some of Weber's most important texts, including *The Protestant Ethic and the Spirit of Capitalism*. Geertz's works reflected Parson's and Weber's influence. He cites Weber's concepts and methods more than any other social theorist in his theoretical essays.

10. One critic of symbolic anthropology as espoused by Geertz in the anthropology of religion is Talal Asad. Asad's major book *Genealogies of Religion: Discipline and Reasons of Power in Christianity and Islam* (Baltimore, MD: John Hopkins Press, 1993) is a sustained attack on the Geertzian form of symbolic analysis. Another more indirect critique of symbolic anthropology is to be found in the work of Maurice Bloch. One of Bloch's set of essays on religion is *Ritual, History and Power: Selected Papers in Anthropology* (London School of Economics. 1989).

Four

Myth and Folklore

Wade Tarzia

Naugatuck Valley Community-Technical College

The following statement is said thousands of times daily: "Oh, that's just a myth!" This utterance is so common that we might believe that myths are all around us, and that whatever a myth is, its survival is well assured. Actually, myths *are* all around us, and the survival of myths is not in question. However, the term "myth" has, in popular usage, shifted in meaning until it has nearly become worthless from the anthropological point of view. What used to mean "a sacred story" is now more likely to imply "lie, falsehood, unexamined belief, silly superstition, story told by uneducated people." The goal of this chapter is to restore the meaning of the term "myth" for use in studying anthropological approaches to religion. This is not to say that the meaning of a term should remain static through the years—language is in the possession of the people of a society, and no one can or should stop the shift in meanings of words. However, to avoid the thorny process of suggesting an entirely new term, the author of this chapter will use the term "myth" in its formerly academic, anthropological sense and hope that readers will agree with this decision during the time it takes to read this chapter.

Time will be spent here on what myths are, but let us begin with what they are *not*. As hinted above, a myth, as considered by an anthropologist, should *not* connote a falsehood (although you may not believe in the myths from another society, just as they may not believe in your own myths). A myth is *not* simply the stories of the gods of the classical Greeks and Romans (although these are also myths). In fact, a *myth* is not simply a story from long ago (we have records of many ancient myths, but myths still exist and are continually renewed and created). A myth is *not* simply the belief of tribal people living in far-away jungles (although they do have their myths, just as do people living within industrialized societies). And myth is *not* necessarily an early and erroneous form of science and now replaced by science. Science and myth/religion are counterposed often enough to warrant some separate thoughts at the conclusion

Acknowledgment: The author would like to thank the following people for their ideas and reference suggestions: John R. Cole, Liz Locke, John McCreery, and Steven Olbrys. Others too numerous to mention also contributed to discussions about myth on the Internet listserv groups Ansax-L, Anthro-L, and Folklore-L.

of this chapter. Let us understand now, though, that science and religion function similarly in some ways, and yet are in other ways very different.

A myth is a "sacred story," and this deceptively simple term will lead to many interesting ideas. This chapter will detail some of the major theories of myth studies (also called *mythography*). We begin with a brief definition of the possible aspects of a sacred story, situate myths in the larger category of folklore, and then review some of the major scholars and approaches seen in the history of myth studies.

The Issues of Myths

The study of something as important as myth cannot be without complexity and controversy, a fact that has made and continues to make this field an exciting one to investigate. Just consider the following characteristics of mythography. Myths are sacred stories about a society's gods, spirits, and monsters; the origins of the cosmos; the origins of important human institutions; the reasons of common events such as death; and examples for behavior that the society deems fundamentally important. Mythic narratives have been interpreted in several ways: as allegories, distorted memories of actual events, primitive science, functional systems, and so forth.[1] The following discussion of features suggests some topics particularly interesting in anthropological study. However, understand that the types and functions of myths vary widely across the years and miles, and no single, academic model of myth will fit every society.

Myth as Memory and Performance. Myths are part of religion but do not exist only within an actual religious space or ritual. A myth exists in the human mind before being spoken, and resides in a book before being read. It is therefore always a "potential" public act (performance). When it is left unperformed and alone in an individual human mind, the anthropologist has little to say about myth; we can only speculate how the memory of myth influences a person (when we gaze at the stars, are we awe-inspired and reminded of creation myths? Do we create artistic works inspired by myth?). Of course, the myth *can* be performed and so made a public act involving others: A myth can be read to children at home or at a religious study group or during a literature or anthropology class. And of course a myth can be performed during the physical movements and within the ritual spaces that make a formal religion: read in a place of worship, acted in a drama, told in stained-glass scenes, or sung. A sacred story has a well-rounded life.

Myth is both past and present. Myths are often perceived by the people who believe in them to be a record of events that took place in a special, far distant time—a record of events that formed the physical and social world in which we exist today. Yet myths also may represent divine "ideals" of events— events that once transpired or were enacted by gods and spirits, but which can be replicated in the present during ritual to ensure the continued well-being of the world.[2]

Myths can serve personal and social functions. Myths serve many important functions for people, from psychological support for individual people (myths may answer such questions as, "What is our purpose? Why must we die?") to the ideological support of a specific way of life (myths often provide a model, in the form of an entertaining story, about successful ways of living, or are the basis of shared beliefs that help communities cohere). Myths can be narrated in group rituals when society is experiencing a crisis (famine, war, succession of a new leader); the crisis period is disorderly to society, and the cosmic and social models preserved in myths help legitimize political succession, while group participation in ritual can help restore social order.[3] Various approaches have been used to study the functions of myth. Some of these theories are mutually exclusive: A theory that states that all myths arose to explain a religious ritual is not compatible with a theory stating that rituals arose from existing myths. Yet, one scholar can think that myths depict psychological motivations of repressed desires (a Freudian approach) without disagreeing necessarily with a scholar who feels that myths are adapted to local environments and social systems (a structural approach, functionalist approach, etc.). A particular myth may not serve all such functions, but we ought to think about the various roles a cultural product can serve. Automobiles can be a method of transportation, a symbol of the owner's wealth, a symbol of ideology (the different assumptions we make about lifestyles believed to be associated with a practical family automobile versus a powerful, expensive sportscar), or a combination of all of these functions. A myth, too, can ply more than one trade in its society.[4]

Myths and Geography. Myths are found around the world, and some seem very similar to each other; this fact has suggested to scholars both (1) diffusion of stories from certain times and locations and (2) independent generation at many times and locations (myth arising out of the similar workings of human minds around the world). Yet, some myths also seem to have arisen only in strict localities, have small geographical distribution, and are adapted to local life-ways and historical trajectories, making us need to be cautious about theorizing on the general distribution of myths.[5] Some scholars have seen a generic myth or a small number of myth types underlying all the world's sacred stories, while others find such comparisons too loose or ill-conceived.[6]

Myths on Our/Their Terms. The terms for a variety of story telling covering the sacred and secular—terms such as myth, legend, folktale—are terms used in scholarly tradition. Terms have their uses, but they have caused confusion because native people do not always agree with the anthropologist's terminology. Some societies, for example, use one term to cover *our* genres of myth and legend. In one society, myth may tell about cosmological origins, and in another the origins of natural features or animal/human traits or of fundamental cultural institutions (such as kingship), or a combination of all of the above. In fact, not all scholars will agree on what a myth is and what it should include. Many anthropologists and literary scholars have blurred the differences between myth, folktale, and legend (terms to be discussed below). When you hear the term "myth," immediately request a full definition of terms!

FOLKLORE AND MYTH

Definition of Folklore

To begin to place the genre of myth in context it is useful to begin with a discussion about folklore. In both ancient and modern societies (especially nonliterate ones) where traditional oral story telling is the primary method of preserving and communicating important cultural information, myths are a part of folklore. Now, "folklore" is another term that, like "myth," is often given a negative connotation in popular usage. Folklore does *not* mean "falsehood" or "opinion held only by uneducated or credulous people." Folklore is many other fascinating things, though, and you experience them every day—such as customs, beliefs, short sayings, and narration shared by people who belong to a common social group. As have myths, folklore has existed in the past (perhaps is nearly as old as humankind) and still thrives today. More specific to the topic of this chapter: Much of the communication of religion and myth has propagated (and still does in many areas) through the folklore process. Folklore, like myth, is the knowledge of "the people"; folklore, myth, and religion are closely entwined.

Folklore (the lore/knowledge of "folk") is a body of common knowledge, performed in certain social contexts according to certain methods of performance. Folklore exists in the minds of groups of people and takes shape when uttered or otherwise communicated. It is *not* the property of any single individual but is rather commonly "owned" passed on (often by hearing it told), and able to be used by anyone who belongs to the group that shares a folklore tradition (the terms "tradition" and "traditional" will be considered here as being synonymous with "folklore"). This fact may limit the membership of certain myths in the realm of folklore because some myths exist in religious texts such as the Bible and the Quran, which have been for centuries set down in print. After a story has been recorded, it is under the predominant control of a small number of the elite class of a society (including political leaders, priests, scholars, and editors). When knowledge is controlled by the few as opposed to large numbers of the "folk," a social group has fewer opportunities to contribute to shared knowledge, a situation that is "anti-folk," so to speak. Yet most myths, even when they exist in books, began as traditional narratives; they still carry some of the marks of those traditions, so we are justified in relating myths to the wider category of folklore. In addition, some scholars do not draw strict lines between folklore and written texts, for good reasons: Both can be related by defining the people who use folklore—the folk group, the consideration of which helps us understand what folklore is and why it is important.

The idea of the "folk group" unites both oral and textual narratives under the folklore category. The basic premise that underlies folk groups is that *folklore is a function of shared identity.* As defined by Alan Dundes, the folk group is that group of people using a tradition that is built around at least one common factor such as occupation or religion. The folk group might then be a regional complex of tribal villages in the mountains of New Guinea, or the students on the third floor of a college dormitory, or a group of people meeting weekly to sew quilts and converse, or a company's softball team, or subcontractors (carpenters, roofers, plumbers, electricians) who meet periodically to build houses, as well as just the plumbers, just the roofers, and so on. The important point, here, is that we all belong to folk groups of one kind or another. When some number of people share a belief or way of life and communicate about it (have a shared identity), a folk group is formed, and folklore—the group's shared property consisting of beliefs, sayings, jokes, anecdotes, stories, songs, rituals, and material artifacts—is born.[7] Religious groups obviously fulfill the minimum requirement of a folk group. Indeed, they make perfect folk groups in some ways to the extent that the members meet fairly regularly to share the religion during religious holidays and may live in a locale where the group members may meet regularly outside of religious holidays. Religious folklore itself can form a specialized genre (although keep in mind that the division between religious and secular ideas is not distinct in some societies).[8]

Once, the definition of folklore was restricted to "orally transmitted beliefs, sayings, and stories within small groups" especially traditional agricultural societies.[9] This definition still describes well much folklore around the world. However most folklorists now broaden the definition to include many kinds of communities, from farming villages to factory and office workers. Similarly, many kinds of texts are now admitted into folklore study, such as printed texts and broadcast media.[10] Thus the range of potential folklore materials is huge. In any case, the most important common aspect of all folklore is that the beliefs, sayings, stories, and art are the property of the folk group and can be transmitted by any member of the group, usually with only minor variations acceptable for the specific folk group and genre.

Jokes, which are one of the most common forms of folklore in modern Western societies, are a good example of folklore. Although the individual number of jokes is countless, they actually follow a much smaller number of forms. The names and characters may change, but jokes follow a somewhat predictable structure. The "light bulb" jokes follow the formula, "How many [certain category of people] does it take to screw in a light bulb?" The answers and characters change but the essential form and function (casting derision on a certain category of person) remain largely unchanged. And anyone is "allowed" to tell such a joke; it is common property.

But with that common property come unwritten "rules" of use. Indeed, if folklore is to represent the important ideas of a group of people, then individuals must *not* be free to change the lore idiosyncratically or drastically. Changes in a folklore item are possible because of a combination of the story teller's creative impulse (usually restrained within the "traditional rules" of performance) and the existence of an audience that has certain expectations of how performance within their tradition ought to proceed. The audience listens and often judges and makes their judgments known, and the teller is affected by the comments and attitude of the audience (think of someone laughing or frowning when you tell a joke). The teller has some latitude to change a story or its dramatic presentation if she sees that the audience is bored, interested, or puzzled.

For example, if you take a familiar joke and change a few surface details, it will still be recognized as a certain kind of joke. But if you change too many details, the joke will no longer be understood as a joke, and your audience will not laugh. They may not, in fact, be aware that you have made them your "audience" and so may not have been listening very well—for "proper" folklore performance marks out a ritual moment that people recognize as deserving more than ordinary attention.[11] This is what is meant by the inability of changing folk materials too much—the public likely to understand a folklore item will penalize the radical innovator by saying, "That's not funny," or "I don't understand it." In many other ways, this is the process that restricts too much change within a folklore tradition, whether the lore be jokes, riddles, melodies, folktales, or myths.[12] Yet the ability of individual performers in a tradition to vary their performance within certain limits means that, yes, change does occur, and no single telling of a folklore item is exactly the same as any other (short genres such as proverbs and riddles can be exceptions). Still, most tellings of a certain folklore type in a given locale (say, the light bulb joke, or a dragon slayer legend) will have a common "core" of structure and theme from telling to telling. The conservative tendency in folklore acts as a normative force in society—ensures that a stable core of common understanding exists in a community. Yet folk tradition does in fact change, usually slowly, but inevitably. Consider the advantages of both conservatism and innovation in any culture, and know that societies can use both to advantage, and do, and have always done so.

Folkloristics—the modern study of folklore (including myth)—concerns the fund of ideas that a folk group uses (what is said, made, and acted in a tradition); and it concerns the settings where things are said, made, and acted, into which shared ideas are funneled during performance. Because folklore is a set of ideas held in common by human groups, it is a living system, and seldom can we point to one original story or one fixed form of a story (think of a joke you heard recently; how would you trace its origin? Where and what is its "original"?). Instead, as mentioned above, there are literally endless numbers of stories told by individuals over the years. Most of them will resemble one another closely, but because folklore is told in specific settings—for family, at a gathering of neighbors, on ritual occasions—the purposes and specific character of any one telling are never quite the same. For these reasons, modern approaches to folklore attempt not just a passive collection and publication of the words or movements of a traditional performance, but also try to record the social context: who was present at the performance (family, adults only, children, friends, dignitaries, etc.), in what kind of physical space (indoors/outdoors, ritual space, etc.), when the story was told (season, time of day, holiday), and what dramatic gestures accompanied the story (Did the performer make gestures, or sing, or use prose, poetry, or a mixture of all? Did the audience speak refrains, or make other interjections or participation?). Unfortunately, after folklore is made static as print, photograph, video, or sound recording, the contextual details surrounding the folklore are gone, and the item becomes "frozen" in form and may become viewed as a "typical" piece of folklore by readers, viewers, or listeners when in fact the performance may not have been typical. However, the modern folklorist provides as much of this background as possible, as well as clues in the text about how the story was told. Special symbols can be inserted in a printed text to indicate when the narrator smiled or gestured or raised the pitch of her voice; annotation of the text can provide other information about the context of the performance.[13]

Contextual details are important when we want to speculate about the reasons for change in performances, and when we want to consider function. Folklore can have many functions, and the same kind of story can have different functions in different societies (the dragon slayer story can be a myth in one society and a legend or folktale in another). Sometimes folklore can have very direct roles in "getting things done" in society. The use of proverbs is a perfect example. Traditional proverbs can be told to get a point across by avoiding direct mention of a potentially upsetting subject. If you dislike getting up early to go to work, someone might say, "The early bird catches the worm," sending you a message without having to say directly, "You're lazy! Go to work!" Even when folklore is not aimed at obtaining some direct action, the stories serve as models of behavior that can generally educate the audience in social values. Audiences of folk traditions may go on to emulate the good behavior of heroes and avoid or criticize aberrant behaviors of antiheroes. Especially in an oral/aural setting, individuals can observe the reactions of others to the events in folk narrative and learn how certain behaviors are valued in the community. (You learn the same thing by listening to ordinary conversations, but folklore offers the advantage of condensing and enhancing social information and presenting it in a focused medium.)[14]

What is important to note is that none of these possibilities can be explored without including contextual information in the study of folklore. We need answers to such questions as: Does the audience emulate or avoid (or value or devalue) patterns of behavior portrayed in the lore? Does the performance "get something done" in the society? What stories are told to whom, and when? What relevant events were occurring in the community at the time the story was told, and was the story told as a symbolic comment about those events? With this kind of information, we can learn much about the role of folklore in living society.[15]

Legend versus Myth

Several categories under the term folklore have already been mentioned—songs, proverbs, anecdotes, folktales, legends, myths. Folklore indeed exists in many forms. The short list below is meant to provide some idea of these forms but is not a complete listing; nor do all forms appear in all societies.

- Short sayings (either as relatively formless beliefs—those that can be communicated in a variety of ways—or certain forms such as jokes and proverbs, which are recognized only when appropriately structured and told at certain occasions).
- Anecdotes (generally factual personal stories that nevertheless can mix in exaggeration or even fantasy).
- Full narratives (stories), sometimes called fables or folktales, and are taken to be fiction (can include narrative songs, sagas, and epics, although scholars often see these as separate narrative genres).
- Myths: sacred stories taken to be true.
- Legends, usually taken to have an element of local history (known characters, events, and landmarks) but may involve supernatural elements. Legends can invite different positions of belief—they can be believed, partly believed, or not believed, yet passed along as an interesting story (a house in your neighborhood reputed to be haunted is a good example; some people may believe in a ghost, others may keep back their opinion but agree that something there is strange, others may laugh at the whole idea). Religious folklore makes frequent use of legend style. Modern reports of sightings of the Virgin Mary show signs of the legend form and process.

The built-in ambiguities of legends (especially contemporary legends) make this genre fascinating yet difficult as a category because it can use anecdotal narration (personal story told as true), story telling (narrator is distanced from the legend), supernatural events, and local characters. Also, legends can be divided into more than one kind. Two broad divisions are legends of the distant past involving important folk heroes (the exploits of King Charlemagne, St. Patrick, or George Washington can be analyzed as legends), and local legends involving the near-past of one's community (the author's neighborhood recounted stories about his cousin's adventures on motorcycle and horseback, some of which involved supernatural motifs, such as stretches of country road terrorized by strange people living in the woods).

- Nonverbal behaviors are also included in folklore, such as dance and handicrafts. The general fund of shared folk ideas can affect behaviors as diverse as telling a story, dancing a dance, or building a bench or sewing a quilt in ways that can be identified with a certain tradition and folk group.

The three genres of most importance in this chapter are legend, folktale, and myth. These are the genres that most often seem to be confused with each other. Myths concern primarily a history of the distant past with its supernatural beings and events. However, gods and other supernatural events may appear in legends; the Norse sagas illustrate this problem splendidly. In the Old Norse saga-cycle of the Rhine Gold, the Norse gods appear in one part of the cycle and commit an accidental murder. As compensation they must pay the victim's family—a family of other supernatural folk—a "blood fine." This payment is a method of compensating kinship groups who have suffered a crime and is used in many societies to avoid the cycle of vengeance typical of disputes in tribal and chiefly societies (those characterized by little central authority). The mortal (and fictional, as far as we can tell) hero Sigurth appears later in this story cycle, as well as characters having a historical basis. The entire story cycle contains secular legends that focus on heroic characters and how they deal with their relations cemented by exchanging status goods and engaging in blood-feud. These stories are not concerned with cosmology despite the occasional appearance of a god or dragon.[16] Similarly, legends can deal in institutional origins, as myths sometimes do, but without involving the gods or the depths of mythic time. Consider in this light the legendary tales of the traditional kings of Ireland, which dealt with the origins of dynasties and customs.[17] Yet in other ways legends and sagas bear little resemblance to myths because they are not concerned with the creation of the cosmos, detailed doings of gods, or fundamental social relations (such as gender definition) that we expect from myths.

Myth and Story

The problem of differentiating myth from folktale has caused some confusion because the same story patterns can appear in narratives used differently in different societies. Myths, as discussed above, are concerned with the very ancient (mythical) past. Legends deal with more recent past. In both cases the "past" is believed to be actual, and the locale can be identified by the people who tell the story. But folktales are generally defined as narratives considered by the society to be fictitious. The characters and settings of folktales are usually generic: The setting may be in a castle or near a mountain, but not usually ones that the local people can point to and see; and the story is about a girl, or a king, or a widow, but not anyone the community knows. And folktales deal with the fantastic elements (monsters, magic) without being about cosmology.[18]

Given these considerations, you might think there is little room to argue, and differentiating myth from folktale would seem easy. In practice, differentiation can be hard work. Also, not all scholars have been aware of the above-mentioned distinctions or have agreed with them. Then it becomes easier to understand the confusion that has arisen over defining myth/folktale/legend. The confusion is enhanced when a story pattern is widely distributed. The story tradition of northern

Europe again provides telling examples. The pattern of the hero who slays a dragon and then dies appears in a myth of the Norse god Thor slaying the World Serpent. Yet the same basic pattern appears in the epic *Beowulf*, where the mortal hero acts within supernatural, legendary, and historical events. The pattern of the dragon slayer appears also in prose sagas and folktales across Europe.[19]

The ability, then, of similar narrative patterns to co-exist in different genres and regions is a general trait of folklore, making one story pattern a myth in one society, a legend in another, and a folktale in yet another. Such transfers are made possible because folkloric ideas exist as a general fund of knowledge across regions, and individual societies use these ideas for various purposes, but not always for the same purposes.[20] These transfers tell us that narrative genres are fluid: The form taken by narrative can be independent from its context. Not only narrative form but also what people *do* with that form are important.[21] This does not mean that genre carries no meaning; but it does mean that the social context of a story is indeed critical to analyze the form and function of traditional narrative. When we encounter stories with similar patterns, we must not be quick to label them without first engaging in some careful thought about their use and status in the society that tells the tale.

Not only do myths blend with other genres because folklore uses a common fund of ideas, but also because myths are usually structured as *stories* and affect our emotions and expectations the way stories do. However, myths are not *only* stories. They are *not* taken to be fictions by the people who believe in them. Indeed, most societies make a distinction between stories believed as truth and stories for which the audience is expected to suspend disbelief for the duration of the story. So myths are stories but with this qualifier: They are sacred narratives, and they are believed to be true. Myths may have story structure but are distinguished from other stories that are told but *not* used as true stories of cosmology or as part of religion (keep in mind that some societies do not distinguish clearly between fiction and nonfiction the way we do).

The "truth" of myth is bound up in its relation to history and its function as a divine "model" that organizes society in the present. When a myth is performed in ritual, it has an aspect of timelessness: People can in effect reexperience the events of the myth (our ability to "lose" ourselves in a good book or movie may be related to this phenomenon). In this sense the myth is not only a story about a people's cosmological history but is also their *present*. This can be a difficult concept to understand, so it deserves some explanation, being an idea central to the difference between myth and story.

Myth is the depiction of a worldview through expression in an idealized pattern (such as stories about the acts of the gods) based on a specific society. Myth is a model (example: the story of Christ's birth as told in the Bible), and religious ritual acted out in the present becomes a version born from the mythic model (example: a Christmas play presenting the birth of Christ in the manger). Religious ritual makes myth actual and material in the form of actors (priests, worshippers), objects (bull-roarers, mosques, Nativity scenes), and ideas (performance of sacred stories; explanations of the meaning of a sacred story). Similarly, a tribal god can epitomize a community by representing the community's values. The god performs acts and lives in a world that resembles the world of the living in an idealized fashion. All this happened in the deep past, but the stories of the god—myth—is an expression of the community's values, which can be reflected in an actual ritual in which the tribal king participates. Even historical events can be conceived as divine elements of mythic history: A battle fought between people in the present might be conceived as a continuation of battles fought by gods and heroes in the sacred past as preserved in myths.

Myth, story, and ritual are, then, interconnected. In a story a mortal king may be depicted as slaying a dragon for the good of his people. In a myth, the god slays the dragon for the benefit of humankind or the cosmos. In a ritual, the living king may act out the god's slaying of a dragon to ensure the continued benefits of monster slaying for the present world (for example, to ensure that the sun will return after the winter solstice in a society where the myth involves the devouring of the sun by a monster). The relation of an idealized past with the present is still a common event. Frequently, people of political, religious, and cultural importance visit historic sites of significance to their movements for making speeches and other ritual acts—the drive to associate the crises of the present with those of the past is a general one and can be studied as an impulse similar to myth-ritual.

In an integrated myth-ritual, the narrative of a myth becomes real to the society believing the myth and will become real again when the myth-ritual is performed in the future. This then is one difference between story and myth.[22]

REVIEW OF MYTH THEORIES

The study of myth can be said to have begun when the first person looked upon myth as something besides sacred truth. Perhaps this may occur when someone within the society becomes critical or detached toward his or her own culture or when someone from *outside* the society, one who has not been raised within that religious system, comes to record the myth, such as a missionary or anthropologist. When myths become objects of study, they can become appropriated for various uses. The traveler, colonial administrator, or missionary may observe and record myths as exotic curiosities, as examples of the natives' "primitive" and "erroneous ways" (obviously *not* the way an anthropologist would approach the beliefs of others, as discussed in Chapter 3), or as enigmas worthy of study. Many outsiders were sincerely curious about the beliefs of other people even when these outsiders were untrained in cultural study; from such respectful curiosity anthropology/ethnography was born. What early researchers often lacked was the realization that all people have myth and ritual that can seem strange to outsiders—that the religion of the researcher is just as "strange" as the religion of the society under study when the tables are turned and the student becomes the studied! So even sincere, educated scholars had difficulty, at first, in avoiding posing "our advanced society" against the "interesting but primitive and childlike culture of others" (or non-Western peoples).

When recording of myth leads to analysis, outsiders often perform "demythologization": a way of seeing myths in any way except as true, sacred stories. The myth may be rejected as false and worthless babbling, especially when the ideas seem so foreign to the observer. Or some people may grant that myths are a necessary point in human intellectual evolution but see science or philosophy as better replacements (or "more evolved"). Or myths can be used so that they are preserved in future generations but are "filtered" through modern interpreters, who explain how a sacred story need not be taken literally; then a myth is seen to have symbolic or artistic value (writers sometimes rewrite myths and folktales for contemporary readers). An interpreter can say, for instance, that Christ's resurrection was not a historical event but can symbolize a human's ability to endure suffering for a worthy goal and to "rise up" after apparent failure or crisis. Then, the New Testament has become "rescued" or "salvaged" for a set of readers who may have become disengaged from fundamentalist belief but do not wish to abandon uplifting ideas with such a long and significant history.

In the ensuing historical review we will encounter several approaches to myth. The important point is that only one all-embracing theory *cannot* explain a phenomenon as complex as mythology. We need many theories, and not all of them (few, in fact!) have been invented recently. Past theories do not mean erroneous theories. Some ideas about myths stemming from earlier scholars are still of value. One element of a person's explanation may be useful even if another element may have been found to be weak years later. And, in general, we need to be wary of any claim that one theory is the most powerful (or only!) explanation of myths. No single theory of myth will suffice, and parts of most theories will be applicable to certain myths under certain circumstances. True: Some approaches led to dead ends or were severe oversimplifications. In such cases, we have to strive to analyze the evidence, be true to modern scholarly methods, yet acknowledge that all theories have helped us get to where we are today. All scholars stand on the shoulders of others and are products of the advantages and limitations of the societies in which they are born.[23]

The Ancients

Myths have been critically viewed since early times. Unfortunately, the written records that survived or became easily available to us because of cultural bias have favored the Mediterranean world, especially Classical Greece. Still, the case of Greece is an instructive one in understanding the process of traditional ways of thinking (myth and folklore) meeting an emerging new intellectualism (philosophy) struggling to deal with the old and the new. The dilemmas of the Greek intellectuals may remind us of our own society, itself dealing with contradictions in a time when spacecraft of awesome sophistication are launched monthly while millions of people remain undernourished and beyond advanced medical attention, or where belief in the occult continually crosses paths with scientific belief.

The case of Classical Greece shows us that studying myth as an analyst rather than a believer is not a modern innovation. The Greek intellectuals engaged in the critique and reuse of myths during the Greek enlightenment (beginning around the fifth century B.C.E.). The early Greek historian Herodotus felt that Greek myths had been borrowed from other cultures in the Mediterranean, an idea that implicitly questions the basis of one's own religion. The Greek philosopher Plato thought that people invented gods by watching the movement of the stars (explaining the basis of religion in natural phenomenon), and as he worked on his philosophy of the ideal state, he decided that he would not admit religion into it because of its irrationality.[24] Some philosophers began questioning the received mythological and religious *traditions*; Plato was especially critical of the value of received myths.

Yet these philosophers did not abandon myths entirely: These sacred narratives had much authority in society where beliefs had been ingrained for centuries. The sophists (philosophers often bent on using logic for political ends rather than as a pursuit of truth) decided to interpret the myths to salvage them and reuse their traditional authority for pragmatic purposes. The stories were to be considered allegories containing moral and naturalistic truths. In contrast, Epicurean philosophers (they did not believe in the influence of the gods on human affairs) were suspicious of myths, thinking they were devices used by the elite rulers (priests and statesmen) to fool and control the population. Euhemerus (third century B.C.E.) favored the theory that all myths stemmed from natural and historical events that became distorted over time. So the various Greek philosophical traditions did not approach myths in a literal sense but the aims of each tradition varied: Some saw myths as useful allegories; Some as historical distortions; and others saw them as pure fictions invented for cynical purposes of social control.

Medieval, Renaissance, and Enlightenment Periods

The Classical Greek period of mythological critique merged into the early Christian period, in which the ideas of the Epicureans helped Christians negate pagan religions; thinkers such as St. Augustine (died 430 C.E.) could rationalize the Old Testament stories as a mixture of literal truth and allegory, while disavowing any usefulness of pagan myths. From these times we have inherited the tendency to view "our" Judeo-Christian myths as "truths" and non-Judeo-Christian myths as "myths" in the negative sense of the term (i.e., falsehood, delusion, childlike philosophy).[25]

The medieval era in Europe also witnessed alternative views of myth: Saxo Grammaticus, (died ca. 1220) a Danish historian, wrote that northern peoples had worshipped "wizards" (appearing as giants, gods, and offspring of the two in Norse folklore), all still believed by the "foolish." He collected and recorded his people's folklore but divided himself from belief of it. Snorri Sturluson, an Icelandic chieftain and historian (died 1241) wrote that people after the Biblical Flood forgot the nature of God, but reinvented a name for a creator, that is, Odin, the chief of the pagan Norse gods. Snorri saw these beliefs as paths toward the divine truth, and so he did not condemn the people for their beliefs. He also developed the theory that the Norse gods were actually heroic humans of the past whom, because of their great deeds, the story tellers had associated with divine attributes; this was a common theory of the times and reminds us of the historicizing theories of the Epicureans and of some later scholars.

Mythology was revived in the European Renaissance (fourteenth through sixteenth centuries C.E.) as Greek and Roman culture became a topic of interest. Christians tolerated classical themes, including mythology, as allegories—as long as *belief* in the old pagan gods was not involved, stories and art about them could be enjoyed as poetry or allegorical expression of human existence. Yet, a growing phenomenon of *rationalism* during the Enlightenment (eighteenth-century intellectual movement in Europe) once again made mythology the target of suspicion by some thinkers, such as the French philosopher Voltaire (died 1778), who was concerned with promoting reason and had little use for belief based in faith. The growth of rationalism was generally associated with an urge to challenge ancient authorities. Additionally, the growth of ethnography was starting to influence social theorizing. European so-cieties were coming into frequent contact with other cultures after the age of great seafaring explorations around the globe, which increased familiarization with other ways of life (comparison with a student's college experience comes to mind). Be-ginnings in the fields that would become ethnography, anthropology, and folklore were furnishing the eighteenth-century rationalist thinkers with new ideas beside those of the ancient and classical eras of the Mediterranean region.

Falling in line with the rationalist outlook was Bernard de Fontenelle (1657–1757), a scholar who published an important book in 1724 called *On the Ori-gin of Fable.* In his rationalist approach, Fontenelle admitted the apparent absurdity of Greek myths but lay the origin of myths in the mental framework of the early hu-mans who produced them. "Primitive" people (Fontenelle drew comparisons with the "savages" of his times: Laplanders, Iroquois, etc.) encountered a strange natural world. They sought to explain nature empirically, Fontenelle felt, but their lack of modern knowledge led them to make odd conclusions about the events of nature, and so odd myths were born. Despite the unhelpful aspects of some of Fontenelle's ideas, his explanation of myth through historical origins and theorizing about "prim-itive" mentality predated similar theories that would arise much later; he represent-ed an advance for his times.

Some important founders of myth studies during the age of rationalism were from Germany. Christian Gottlob Heyne (1729–1812) was a philologist (they com-bine study of literature and linguistics) and professor of Greek who took myths se-riously because so many of the texts of the ancient world referred to them. To Heyne, myths arose from a "childlike" phase of humankind and were explanations of awe-inspiring natural events. The mentality of "primitive people," he reasoned, gave rise to myths, worship of inanimate things, and the association of great people (a famous hunter, for instance) with both myths and the worship of gods and heroes. He turned to the so-called "primitive" people of his day to draw analogies between these mod-ern day "child-like" peoples and those of the distant past.

Johann Gottfried Herder (1744–1803) and Heyne exchanged their ideas and so influenced each other in many ways. Herder also saw in modern "savages" a model of the way of thinking that had given rise to classical myths (although Herder broad-ened his definition of "savage" to include the "coarse" sailors among whom he had traveled to learn the proper frame of mind to study Homer's *Odyssey*!). Unlike Heyne, Herder thought that myth was the early humans' response to the environment to express a religious emotion rather than to explain the environment. Both scholars represent an advance over previous theories because they helped begin the trend of viewing myths with respect, as stories that could be understood beneath an apparent, not actual, absurdity.

The rationalist era in Europe gave birth to another cycle of myth valuation, this time, however in the form of the Romantic Movement. The movement grew in the eighteenth and nineteenth centuries as a reaction against rationalism; it gained inspiration from the egalitarian ideals of the French Revolution and, eventually, from the Industrial Revolution with its sometimes tragic influences on society. Romantics typically comprised writers and artists who promoted a naturalistic philosophy. In this way of thinking, the emotions and senses (artistic imagination and personality) were exalted over reason or abstraction (i.e., scientific and technological modes of thought) and over the increasing urbanization and mechanization of their society (in contrast, today the term "naturalistic philosophy" usually refers to a scientific, materialistic ontology). Romantics extolled the natural life, which was usually an idealized vision of rural, agricultural peasant ways in which the innate goodness of humans could be fostered. Each nation had its own form of romantic movement, but in many cases it involved an idealized and revived vision of nationalistic culture based in an idealized history of the nation. That is to say, Germans might revive an interest in their pagan past as seen in the operas of Wagner; the Irish, long under the control of England, could rally around their Celtic past by reviving through translation and study their native Gaelic literature; and wealthy English might build sham medieval-styled buildings on their estates in homage to their own idealized past. Naturalistic paintings, music, landscape design, literature, and poetry were all influenced by the Romantic Movement.

The effects of the Romantic Movement did not always result in purely aesthetic responses to the past. Sometimes its effect was to kindle an interest in a nation's past for scholars who were capable of rigorous investigation. In Europe, two such scholars were the brothers Grimm, Jakob (1785–1863) and Wilhelm (1786–1859), who are among the key founders of folklore and philology. The Grimms' work was in many ways advanced, and some of their conclusions can still seem fresh (their definition of the legend genre seems particularly modern)—this, despite their situation in the Romantic Movement and their active roles in seeking information to promote their vision of a national German culture.

The Grimms are popularly known as the collectors of "fairytales" from Germany published as *Kinder- und Hausmarchen, Nursery and Household Tales,* in 1812. At first they produced relatively faithful translations of the tales they collected from folk narrators, but soon they found that some elements of these stories could be confusing or distressing to their modern readers, so they began editing or "cleaning up" their collections (such pressure to edit a national folklore collection was common in this early period of folklore but is now deemed to be an unfortunate act that destroys much of the information that an anthropologist needs to understand other societies). What is important to us is that the Grimms saw these folktales as the decaying record of myths and customs from ancient Europe, even if they were now being told as entertainment in their nineteenth-century German folktales. Few of the Grimms' folktales are what we might call myth or a record of actual custom, but their early formulations led to their continued thinking about myths in general and Jakob Grimm's *Deutsche Mythologie, German Mythology* (1825), in particular: a compendium of information and folklore collection that is still useful.

The Nineteenth and Early Twentieth Centuries

In the history of mythography, the training of Western scholars almost exclusively in Classical languages, history, and literature became a restricting mold that made it difficult for them to analyze myths that were different from Classical myths. The myths of the ancient Celts and Germans were comparatively easy to relate to those of the Greeks (all share a heritage in Indo-European culture), and such relations were frequently made. Meanwhile, the myths of other people around the world, which seemed so different from the tales of the Indo-Europeans, were rarely understood in any positive way. But this situation began to change slowly beginning in the late nineteenth century as myths began to be related to the ethnography of non-Western cultures.

Nature Mythology

Nature themes came to predominate mythography, partly as a heritage from romanticism, and partly arising from demonstrable themes of nature to be found in many myths. Some theorists made certain phenomena the focus of their theories. Thus, the thunderbolt associated with sky gods could be viewed as a central principle behind a people's myth: The thunderbolt presages rain, which is important for agriculturists especially, and so lightning could be understood as a central motif in myth, in a theory of myth grounded in natural phenomena.

One of the most important of the nature mythologists was Max Müller (1823–1900). Müller published a long essay on comparative mythology in 1856 that changed the direction of folklore studies. Until his death in 1900, Müller and his scholarly adversary Andrew Lang used each other as intellectual punching bags, refining their ideas through vigorous offense and defense. Müller's ideas were influenced by the Romantic Movement. His romantic worldview was founded on the pantheistic religions of the Classical world, which the romantics associated with natural themes (Classical mythology supplied the romantics with plenty of such themes through mythological creatures such as the half-human, half-animal satyr, and gods associated with natural elements, such as Poseidon and Apollo). Müller's theory that myths were allegories about natural phenomena had a great affect on myth studies.

Müller focused on the motif of "daybreak", which he thought to be one of nature's most elevating blessings and so must have had—he reasoned—a major force in forming myths. A typifying analysis went like this: The Greek goddess Athena was an incarnation of the dawn since she was born from the forehead of Zeus, just as the morning light is born in the east. Müller also worked by comparing Indo-European gods. He found support for his Zeus-Athena theory because the "east" in Sanskrit (an ancient language of India) meant "the forehead of Heaven." This kind of reasoning can have potential for forming hypotheses for investigation but by itself is rather weak.

Müller was led to make these cross-cultural comparisons because he borrowed his methods from the field of comparative philology. In this method, a scholar may find similarities between words from two different societies, separated perhaps by time, cultural and geographical distance, or both. So if the names of a god of ancient Greece and ancient India can be shown to have similar philological origins, then we might speculate about their connection. Perhaps, once, the names of certain gods had a common ancestor, stemming from times before a group of people (or their language and culture) had spread elsewhere and changed. Thus Müller saw philological links between Greek and Vedic (Indian) gods and heroes and hypothesized about links to other European gods. He rightly saw, for instance, a similarity between the name of the Roman god *Jupiter* and of the Indic god *Dyaus pita*; he traced both back to a supposed Indo-European prototype word, "dyeus pater", meaning "father sky." (The Indo-European root /deiw-/ means "to shine" and is the basis for other ideas such as god, heaven, and sky. The root for sun is, however, /sawel-/.)

Müller felt that his theory of nature myth could solve some enigmas. For nineteenth- century scholars (Müller especially) one enigma was the grotesque, inexplicable acts of the Greek gods. Think of it: Here was an ancient society that had produced some of Western civilization's most enduring ideas in art and philosophy, had produced in addition pristine, gleaming white marble statues and temples (we now know them to have been painted in gaudy colors!) yet how do the Greek gods act in their myths? In one case, Cronos castrates his father (at his mother's request) and then marries his own sister and swallows their children as they are born. Zeus escapes this fate and rescues his siblings by inducing Cronos to vomit. Clearly some explanations were long overdue. Müller began to supply them in his theory of "solar" myth, in which, for instance, Cronos and his odd diet are symbols of the sky devouring and then releasing the clouds. The sun and the sky, and their profound effect on primitive people, became Müller's central principle in explaining Indo-European myth.[26]

Another important theorist working in the times of Müller and Lang was Sir Edward Burnett Tylor (1832–1917), one of the fathers of English anthropology whose major contribution is his *Primitive Culture* (1871) (Tylor is discussed in greater detail in Chapter Two of this book). A theme that runs through Tylor's mythography is his attempt to dig down to the foundation of the mental process that gives rise to myths. He thought that reality was transformed into myth by the mechanism of the "animation of nature": the attribution of human personality to inanimate objects such as celestial objects, rivers, mountains, rocks, trees, weather phenomena, and so forth. The reason Tylor gives anticipates later psychological approaches to myth. Children, he thought, learn first to understand themselves and so attribute familiar motives behind other things in the world, which must be understood and treated as other humans are. Tylor surmised that the "lower tribes"—whether of the present or the past—were characterized by such mental processes as well. He believed that evidence of this childlike phase of mythology existed as "survivals" of past customs existed among contemporary peasant communities, which could be used as a window on the past of cultural evolution. These assumptions led Tylor into thinking that myths followed stages of development: The "rough" nature myths of contemporary tribal people engaging in "childlike" contemplation of the world were analogous to the early phase of myth in ancient human history.

The animation of nature is related to the more general process of *analogy*. We make analogies when we suggest an underlying similarity between two things that seem, on the surface, dissimilar. If a poet says that a waterfall is sighing, the poem makes an analogy between the waterfall and a melancholy person. Tylor theorized that analogies were once real to past humans, and even poetic metaphors were treated cautiously and consistently because early people believed a metaphor's literal truth. The sighing waterfall of the example above would indeed be a spirit or deity and not just a metaphor, as would have been the "rosy-fingered dawn" of Homer's epics. (But do not forget that other modes of thought use analogy and metaphor; analogy may be the beginning of scientific hypotheses, for instance.)[27]

Tylor pointed out some worldwide comparisons of analogies to suggest the general existence of the analogy mechanism; one such example is the motif of the rainbow that is a bridge, which is an analogy between nature and architecture that has appeared in various folklore traditions. Tylor wrote that the comparison of object with object is a deep mental process that evolved in myths over the ages. Early myths were "sensible analogies" with fairly direct comparisons between the humanlike attributes and nature, whereas the myths of later societies, as those of the classical Greeks, represented "verbal myth," the product of "higher" civilization wherein the links between two concepts was highly metaphorical.

This scheme is problematic, as the reader may guess. One can test this notion by observing the products of complex society—ourselves—engaging in some "animation of nature": Boat owners usually name their boats, and sometimes even car owners and truck drivers name their vehicles, as did the crews of World War II combat planes. The naming—or suggesting of a human personality—of boats and combat planes suggests the potential function of animation: That which has a personality seems human and therefore may be properly cared for and expected to be helpful. The belief would seem useful and comforting for people (boat crews and combat air crews) in highly dangerous professions. Extrapolate, then, to peoples of all ages who might suffer in the coming months after a flood, or insect infestation, or unusually harsh winter, for whom the analogy between the human and the nonhuman world (making some aspect of the world into a god that could be addressed in prayer) might have offered some comfort. There is something of use in Tylor's theory of animation, although his evolutionary scheme does not work well. Also a problem is his theory of cultural "survivals." The premise of this theory is that certain practices of the past were the only "true" or "real" practices, leaving present-day people only the role of acting out mechanically the customs they have inherited from the past. To be brief about an important issue: All behaviors that exist in the present are "modern." They are always affected by the past yet are not dead "fossils" but rather behaviors serving some function in the present.

Early Modern Theorists

Myth and Ritual

Sir James Frazer (1854–1941), writing near the end of the nineteenth-century, strongly influenced the comparative study of folklore and religion in the early twentieth-century. His monumental series of volumes published as *The Golden Bough* (starting in 1890) reflected his beginnings in classical scholarship, which he went beyond to theorize about how human societies adapted to local environmental and social conditions by applying a common human inheritance to them. His theories are characterized by the "myth and ritual" school of thought. In the moderate form of the theory, myths and rituals are seen to depend on each other equally for their respective operation in society (i.e., the myth needs the ritual in order to have effective public exposure, and the ritual needs the myth to supply beliefs and dramatic structure). The theory can also be expressed in an extreme form, in which myths are seen to be explanations of pre-existing rituals and have no existence apart from the rituals they explain.[28] Frazer favored the extreme theory.

Frazer's focus was the ritual of the sacrifice of a king, for which he saw evidence from cultures worldwide, in both actual practice and mythology. "Primitive" people, he wrote, believe that their well-being resides in the health of their king because tribal kings are associated with the tribal gods; they care for the king in his life but will not let him become too sick or aged to ensure that his ill-health will not result in general bad health of the society (or of the entire world). The solution that many societies invented, said Frazer, was the ritual killing of the king when his strength began to fail. Frazer thought that many myths preserved evidence of these practices. Remnants of these ancient rites might also survive to the present day as "survivals" of beliefs and customs that could be observed in communities of rural folk (an idea that has problems, as was discussed for Tylor, above).

Frazer was a cultural evolutionist, having developed a three-stage scheme of mythic development. (1) People first began believing that natural events represented magical power, which could be manipulated in rites; (2) then they developed religion and the belief in gods, from whose will all natural events arose; (3) people saw nature as an area able to be studied scientifically. He viewed myth as an early phase of human's understanding of nature, especially that of farming people. Myth was to be viewed as a misguided groping toward truth and control over nature (with people attempting the use of magical control over life) for which science (Frazer thought) had become a better replacement as societies advanced. Myth was also a reflection of human belief in the magic that was in natural forces. Magic, in turn, was a misunderstanding of causality. That is to say, Frazer felt that the seeking of causality is itself a sound process of analysis—the cause of disease, for instance, once isolated, might be dealt with—but he thought early humans were misguided in their theories of causality.

Frazer's work is plagued by several problems. His belief that myths were statements about nature made by farming people seems to ignore the fact that non-farming hunter-gatherers have myths: What theory explains them? Frazer did not say. His theory stating that remnants of ancient rituals and beliefs existed as "survivals" in present-day rural communities is problematic for the same reasons that Tylor's similar theory was: This idea can make present-day behaviors seem like mere vestiges of the past, giving us modern folk literally nothing to do except act out past customs![29]

Frazer was a rampant comparativist. Comparison is useful, and sometimes critical, in anthropological studies, but the method has its dangers. Cultural customs from different times and places may have surface similarity and seem good choices for comparison, but we may find after deeper investigation that the customs have different consequences for each respective culture. Consider as a case in point the wearing of clothing such as blue jeans, which began as simple, rugged workclothing before becoming a kind of uniform for young people and others, and still later was produced in "designer" styles considered very fashionable. And in other countries American blue jeans sometimes held high status and could be sold for extravagant prices on both legal and black markets. So how would we as anthropologists compare the function of blue jeans in general? Very carefully, with an eye toward the complexity of the subject! Frazer was not always so careful about comparing myths and customs: He compared wildly different sources—from literature to folktales—with little discrimination. In a sense he was a sophisticated and wide-ranging collector of customs but not a sophisticated analyst of them.

Another problem is that Frazer's approach to cultures other than his own elite Western class of society was usually condescending. As many people do, Frazer believed his own society to be the pinnacle of human development, whereas other peoples, whether the farmer in the village near his home or a tribal people far away, were "savage," "childlike" in their beliefs, and "primitive" (remember how useless these terms are in anthropology). Such an attitude would not help his study of world religions. To be fair, we must judge Frazer to be a man of his times in this; these attitudes were not unusual for educated people of his day and unfortunately are still with us in various forms.

The drawbacks to Frazer's theories are also due to some of the general weakness of the extreme form of the myth and ritual theory. By positing that ritual is the precedent of myth, myth becomes relegated to explanation-after-the-fact. Stated differently, we can ask the question, "If ritual precedes myth, were there no stories about the gods when the ritual was developing? Why would a society have no stories about the gods and cosmological creation during or even previous to the development and performance of a certain religious ritual?" Simple questions, but they help check the plausibility of a theory; they reveal some weak assumptions of the extreme form of the myth and ritual theory. Further, by relegating myth to a secondary role to ritual, this approach cannot deal well with societies in which myth is important and rituals associated with the myth are uncommon or nonexistent. We ought not abandon the possibility that some rituals did indeed spawn myths, and vice versa. Better for us to concede many possibilities of interdependence between myth and ritual. However, Frazer can be credited with bringing this theory before a wide public and making available reams of literary and ethnographic material for consideration by both anthropologists and literary scholars. His charming writing style, besides, helped ensure his adoption by a wide readership.

Modern Theorists

The Psychoanalytical Approach

Sigmund Freud (1856–1939), discussed in Chapter 2, developed an interest in myth that continues to influence some contemporary anthropologists. In *The Interpretation of Dreams*, Freud declares that myths contain psychological projections cast into the world beyond the individual human mind. In other words, ideas and impulses that we vaguely understand or do not acknowledge nevertheless arise in our daily lives, become a part of our traditions, and influence the stories we tell, including mythology. This idea followed from Freud's belief that some of our dreams are "typical"—that is, most people seem to have experienced similar kinds of dreams, and the shared dreamtypes of humanity arise from our shared humanity. This idea is a powerful one because it provides a universal method to approach the myths of all societies. We live in many different ways on this planet, yet we all have gone through similar experiences, says Freud, such as being born, having parents of two sexes, and developing through infancy, from a state of no knowledge or goal beyond that of basic biological impulses, to a gradual awakening to the world (social and physical) beyond these impulses. Therefore Freud saw good reason to extend the study of dreaming (we might call this a tradition of dreaming) to themes in myths, some of which seem to share the themes of dreaming and reflect processes of the unconscious mind, especially those processes related to the child's development.

Freud's conception of the relation of anthropology to psychology are made clear in his book *Totem and Taboo* (discussed in Chapter 2). As with others we have reviewed, Freud believed contemporary people living a simple tribal or hunter-gatherer life-way represent the kind of life led by our own ancient forbears; for Freud the psychoanalyst they represented "in their psychic life a well-preserved, early stage of our own development." The folklore of contemporary "savages" was to be seen as a record of their psychology. Their folklore/psychology could, in turn, be compared to "the psychology of the neurotic as it has become known through the psycho-analysis. . . ." For Freud, the neurotic person has a minor disturbance of the mind stemming from repressed desires. Humans acclimated to the restrictions of a social world cannot do whatever pleases them, so they repress their desires. Most people can deal with these conflicts, of course. But when they cannot, these hidden psychological drives arise again and transfer into neurotic behavior (one of the ways is through "transference" of the urges or ideas into other beliefs and behaviors, as a kind of safety valve for the repressed desires). Still, the conflicts (or unconscious memory of them) do not disappear and can arise to be projected. Freud observed these desires in neurotic individuals and theorized that myths (and other aspects of religion in general) were a projection not of an individual but rather of an entire society. The well-known Oedipus complex can arise in individuals and be expressed in a group tradition, which it did, in the traditional story of Oedipus. By now you will be starting to understand that Freud's theory of religion rests in pathology—religion is a symptom of a social problem, in a strict form of Freudian approach.[30]

Another psychological approach developed in a different way. Carl Jung was a psychologist who studied dreams and symbols arising in them. Jung saw relations between archetypal dream symbols and symbols arising in myth and legend. He saw dream symbols as a common human psychological inheritance (and so was not much concerned with the influence of specific societies and their histories on myths). Mircea Eliade was also concerned with archetypal symbols. Further, both scholars promoted the use of myth studies to help guide human life by helping us find parallel symbols in other myths and religions. This kind of study would, in turn, help revive and strengthen contemporary religions (Jung and Eliade favored Christianity) and make them more meaningful by showing the parallels with other religions. In this, these two scholars had a very different view of religion compared to Freud; in addition, they seemed willing to become part of religion instead of just observers of it. Jung's and Eliade's theories are difficult to reconcile with some of the aims of anthropology (Jung especially, for his ideas, so reliant on Indo-European culture and history, go against cultural relativism, which is important in anthropology). Freud has had greater success in anthropology because his theories are based in observable, universal aspects of human development.[31]

Alan Dundes is one of the contemporary folklorists who has used a Freudian approach to culture. He is a proponent of multimethodological approaches to folklore study, having witnessed too many mono-cultural, mono-methodological studies of traditions that ignore the complexities behind any traditional text. He critiques functionalism that ignores studies of the history of a piece of folklore—where it came from and how it developed—and uses his psychological approach to develop a cross-cultural comparison that fills in some of the gaps in the functionalist method. In contrast to Boas and Malinowski (discussed next), Dundes saw that folklore data can contradict as well as reflect reality, making problematic any theory of functionalism that insists that folklore must reflect social systems directly. Dundes does not apply a Freudian way of thinking without some modifications. While Dundes admits the possibility of finding universal psychological symbolism in a folktale or myth, he does not take "possibility" to mean that we will always find such universals. Through empirical observation we might find that some myth symbols appear in nearly every society, whereas other symbols are restricted to certain traditions or certain regions. Not all symbols in a myth need reflect unconscious ideas but rather conscious ones (as Freud himself insisted: Sometimes in a dream a cigar is just a cigar [not a phallic symbol]). Dundes and others' post-Freudian studies keep Freudian approaches alive but do not overapply them to the exclusion of other useful ways of study.

Dundes' article "Earth-Diver: Creation of the Mythopeic Male" is a classic work representative of his psychoanalytical approach to folklore. He first outlines some problems with viewing myths as representations of either the ancient past of a society or purely its present social system. Myths preserve much information from the past history of a society, but they also can change slowly over the years (as does the broader category of folklore), thereby adjusting to the local culture by modifying ancient and widespread folklore patterns. Yet, we cannot automatically take a myth and use it as an example of a culture's current "personality" because basic mythic and folkloric patterns and tale types exist in a variety of times and geographical locations. We can analyze how a myth *differs* from similar myths in other societies—the differences between two similar myths will highlight how each society has adapted a basic tale type to its own needs. We can also analyze many myths from many societies to see how they show some of the *same* patterns. This case is where a Freudian method is most powerful. Freud believed in the existence of "typical dreams"—those that occur throughout humanity. He reasoned that myths were an expression of the same tendencies; that is, some dream patterns that occurred in many individuals would become projected into our myths. Such a process, Dundes suggests, would explain why similar tale types can be found around the world. And this is Dundes' goal in his "Earth-Diver" analysis: To suggest how a Freudian approach can help us seek potential universal themes in folklore and myth.

The "earth-diver" myth is common among the North American native Americans. The typical story pattern involves an animal such as a turtle, otter, or muskrat (all animals accustomed to watery environments but also able to live on land) that desires dry land to be created, dives under the water, and comes up with a little mud, usually lodged under a claw. The mud expands until the world has dry land as well as water.[32] The theory used to analyze this myth derives from Freud's observations of child psychology. Very young children do not understand the exact process of childbirth and are usually not allowed to witness an actual birth. They understand only that the mother produces a child out of her body. The child, is however, experienced in one form of production from the body: excrement from the anus. It is no surprise that children often think that infants are produced from the anus, a logical deduction based on what they know of anatomy! A second theory called in is based on both psychological and ethnographic observations of fantasies and rituals in which males express an envy of women's ability to produce valuable material from their bodies. In a "couvade" ritual a man simulates childbirth when his wife is giving birth; and in some puberty rituals, the symbolic message is that the young boys are "born" (i.e., born into manhood) through the participation of the adult males at the puberty ritual.

With this theory, we can see how the same theme is expressed in myth. The theme need not be overtly expressed, and in fact may often be sublimated, or transformed into a symbol for male anal birth. The myth of human creation in Genesis may portray a remnant of the sublimated theme: Note that Adam gives birth to Eve, albeit from his rib; still, the ability to produce "valuable material" from a body is successfully possessed by a male in Genesis. In other myths, such as "earth-diver," the theme is more apparent: The mud that the creature has found at the bottom of the primeval waters takes the place of fecal material (mud and feces having roughly the same consistency); and like an infant's growth after birth, or like a pregnant woman's belly, the mud expands to create dry land and subsequent creations. Note that sublimation need not occur: Some myths simply portray the creation of humans or of the world from the excrement of a supernatural being (why shouldn't a supernatural being use fertilizer for creating?).

In summary, Dundes's analysis of the myth of the earth-diver suggests that we may be able to find universal themes in world myths, and that Freudian analysis allows us to make such a search. Psychological themes as those mentioned above have been and can be observed both clinically and ethnographically, so such a theory can be tested empirically unlike some other psychological approaches to myth. This kind of exploration, says Dundes, does not preclude the important idea of cultural relativism in anthropological work—surely we must continue to analyze societies in their own contexts. Even so, cultural relativism should not make us so obsessed with differences between social groups that we become blind to the potential for universals in human culture.[33]

Functionalist Interpretation of Myth

Bronislaw Malinowski, discussed in Chapter Three in some detail, was one of the founders, with others such as Franz Boas, of the functionalist approach to myth. In functionalism as formulated by the French sociologist Emile Durkheim (1858–1917), social values are seen as the most important of human concepts. These concepts become translated via religion into religious ideas (i.e., the character and actions of a god evinces a society's values). Religion marks and emphasizes social values so that they can become models of socially approved behavior; myth and ritual become the media that make society's values visible through belief and action, which make society cohesive. In this sense, religion is functional because some of its effects on society can be observed and even may be discovered to be practical.[34]

Malinowski's version of functionalism arose from his intense fieldwork among Melanesian tribes. He was not specifically a mythologist but rather a field anthropologist developing and promoting the field-work method of anthropological research. From his observations he concluded that myth was a reflection of actual lifeways and had observable roles to play in a community: Myth worked as a mechanism that helped continuity of culture by strengthening tradition, ritual, and knowledge by lending tradition prestige through tracing it back to ideal supernatural origins. Providing a social charter and codification of belief was another important function in his view; myth did not explain belief or history but rather offered evidence, in its story, for the success of traditional ways.

Malinowski did not prefer to think of myth as symbolic but rather as a direct expression of its subject matter. It was a lived reality, a narrative that resurrects, when told, the reality of primeval times. When a ceremony or rule requires justification, the myth relating to the practice is narrated, associating the lived practice with the sanctity of antiquity. Malinowski therefore reacted strongly against the idea that myths were entertainment—myths were rather to be considered functional, hard-working mechanisms in culture. This view made him suspicious of the psychoanalytical approach, whose practitioners, he felt, could supply an endless series of explanations to suit any theory by citing unconscious psychological material and hidden meanings, which would go against the one-to-one relation of myth and life that he had observed.

Malinowski's great contribution to anthropology and myth was his promotion of the important idea of cultural relativism—of visiting societies in their native locale and analyzing them according to intimate participation in their life way and the native"s own frame of reference. However, his conception of "myth as social model" was an oversimplification. Nowadays the anthropologist differentiates between two kinds of models in stories—those that reflect social realities and those that pose ideals of society, in other words, models that the story-telling tradition (through priests, story tellers, etc.) suggest are the proper ways of behaving or believing (refer back to the folklore section where the topic of "emulation and avoidance' was mentioned.) Malinowski's theory of "myth as social charter" needs, then, to be considered among these other possibilities: Myths may reflect and support social realities but also may prescribe behaviors and set up ideals in the belief that the ideals are good and will be followed by society. Myth also has a history, not just a life in the present, and functionalism in general has failed to adequately incorporate the influence of the past on present social systems.[35]

The Structuralist Study of Myth: Claude Lévi-Strauss

The work of Claude Lévi-Strauss (1908–), a French anthropologist, has dominated the study of mythology in recent times both because of his position and because his approach, structuralism, was a radically new way to compare certain kinds of myths in a universal way. Structuralism approaches cultural studies by assuming that human behavior is largely determined by communication, and that communication has underlying patterns, or relationships between individual elements of a cultural system. The cultural system may be any sort of communication; for our purposes it is verbal narrative. Different kinds of structures exist. One kind suggested by Vladimir Propp, a Russian folklorist, concerns the *sequence* of actions in folktales (or "syntagmatic" structure, as in the syntax of a sentence). In a sequence, one structure follows another in a related chain, usually in a certain order. A hero leaves his home to go on a quest, meets someone who needs help, and after being helped, offers the hero important advice or confers a gift that will later be important. Each structure (or subplot, or theme) follows another and may occur in many different kinds of stories. In another kind of structuralism, the elements of the system may be less obviously sequential but rather balanced against each other in binary relationships (oppositions). For example, nature can be opposed to culture. A monster, such as the ogre Grendel in the Anglo-Saxon epic *Beowulf,* lives in a cave under water, while the humans whom Grendel attacks live in houses on land. The oppositions are wild lands versus settled lands (or nature versus culture), and under versus over. The *Beowulf* poet mentions a hideous tree overhanging Grendel's lake (wild nature), and at the end of the adventure, Beowulf, having defeated the monsters of the wilds, carries home Grendel's head on a spearshaft, or hewn wood (tamed nature shaped by humans, or culture). This is the binary type of structuralism that Lévi-Strauss emphasizes.[36]

The strength of structuralism is that it offers a method to compare aspects of culture across different cultures. Just as linguistics has offered some general rules of language to explain human language in general, structuralism has sought to provide a "language of culture" and particularly for our concerns, a language of traditional narratives such as myths. In literary studies, structuralists suggested that not just so-called "high" literature has structure, but so do a variety of other forms and genres that language can take, a reminder that has helped promote a more balanced study of language in general.[37]

Lévi-Strauss's important contribution was not only in teaching us about the basic structures in myth (polarities, parallelisms, reversals) but also in teaching that so-called "primitive" peoples have a sophisticated process of thought. As we have seen, failure to evaluate other societies even-handedly was (and unfortunately often still is) a problem in earlier mythography, which often saw myths as being told by simple, "childlike people" who occupied a lower evolutionary scale than we moderns. Lévi-Strauss is a strong proponent of this idea of "cultural relativity", an idea that continues to be important in anthropological thinking.

Lévi-Strauss's most developed arguments for structuralism appear in the four volumes of his *Introduction to a Science of Mythology.* However, we can gain a grounding in his ideas by considering a shorter, earlier work typical of his theories, "The Story of Asdiwal." This is a story from the pacific coast of Canada where native Americans called the Tsimshian lived. Several of their myths were collected by Franz Boas at the turn of the century, and Lévi-Strauss chose the story of Asdiwal to apply his theory. It is a story of the birth, life, and death of Asdiwal, whose mother is impregnated by a stranger from the sky world. He gives her several gifts for his son to be born (bow, arrows, snowshoes, basket, lance, bark raincoat, etc.), all with magical properties that are of great benefit. Asdiwal marries a woman from the sky, lives there for a time, eventually leaves her, and marries a woman back on earth. He travels with her brothers and proves he is a great hunter, in both the hills and on the sea. His death occurs when he goes hunting in the forest and forgets his snow shoes, and he is turned to stone halfway up a mountainside.

The way the details of the story balanced against each other and meshed with the actual life-way of the Tsimshian were what fascinated Lévi-Strauss. The Tsimshian lived a transhumant (seminomadic) life as fishers, hunters, and wild-plant food gatherers. In the summer, they relied on salmon caught from the Skeena river, which they smoked for winter storage. The families would move inland to hunt and gather but return to permanent villages for the winter. They would endure famine at the end of winter when the stored food was depleted as they awaited the candlefish to come up the Naas river in March. They took boats to the fishing grounds to catch and process these fish. They would return to the

Skeena for summer fishing. The story of Asdiwal takes place in these locations and cultural settings.

Lévi-Strauss analyzed this myth through different frameworks. In the geographical framework, the binary structures concerned direction. Asdiwal in his journeys traveled in East-West then South-North directions. The binary oppositions are interesting because they parallel the geographical environment and transhumant life ways of the Tsimshian between inland (East) and coastal (West) settlement and the two fishing seasons at the rivers Skeena (South) and Naas (North). In the economic framework, Asdiwal (a land-hunter) and other peoples he meets (sea-hunters) form a binary unit. The sociological framework concerns the matrilineal and patrilocal nature of Tsimshian society (inheritance is reckoned through the female side, although the wife moves to join her husband's family; a son will inherit his mother's family's titles). Although these features are suggested in the story, a reversal of known custom is also emphasized: The marriages portrayed in the story are all matrilocal, which are *reversals* of Tsimshian social values![38]

The previous discussion suggests what structures this method seeks out, but structuralism in general and Lévi-Strauss in particular are not content to merely reveal structure. Structure must *mean* something, it must be decoded, and then shown why it is significant to the society that evolved the conceptual structures. The sociological dimension of the Asdiwal story is most revealing: Here the story does not reflect social reality but rather reverses it by emphasizing an unreal matrilocal residence pattern. Lévi-Strauss suggests that the story tradition functions as a "thought experiment"—a way of justifying reality, however disagreeable it may sometimes be, by showing its extreme opposite (a binary polarity), an imaginary situation that would not work in real life. For Asdiwal's unusual marriage settlement-patterns are *not* successful in this story, and his final state is one of patrilocality (he resides in the village of his birth), which is normal to the Tsimshian. Why is this "lesson" significant? Lévi-Strauss suggests that the story functioned to comment on social reality but to do so required the reversal of that reality. The marriage and settlement system in Tsimshian life offered complications as the maternal and paternal sides of one's family competed for influence during marriage and inheritance. These problematic residence patterns of real life could be brought to the attention and manipulated in the *story*—reversed to show that another social system (matrilocality) would not work. Therefore the story justifies reality, and, perhaps, soothes some of the tensions of life. The details of the story reflect social particulars of Tsimshian life, while the binary structures of the story reflect universals in the human mind state—a way of thinking about life and of presenting it in narrative.

Lévi-Strauss has invigorated the discussion of myth but he has also attracted criticism. Critics have noted that he has considered large areas of study in ethnography, making many overgeneralizations as he sought to make comparative statements about the narratives of many societies; he has based his pronouncements on intuitive judgments, seldom offering solid, detailed evidence. Critique also centers on his reduction of human thinking to binary oppositions while ignoring *syntagmatic* structures (such as the narrative sequences discussed by Vladimir Propp). Although binary logic does seem to be an aspect of human thinking, it is not the only aspect, and different kinds of logic may be operational in the human mind at any given moment. Edmund Leach, a cautious supporter of Lévi-Strauss, sees him as a useful visionary whose specific results may not always add up. Yet Lévi-Strauss's critics agree that he has brought justified attention to binary structuralism even if it will be of more use to anthropology when scholars begin to show how structure affects behavior, as based on empirical evidence.[39] Finally, it has been noted that Lévi-Strauss lumped together myths and folktales in his researches ("Asdiwal" in fact has more of the folktale about it than the myth), which has been a common act even among anthropologists. Furthermore, it must be noted that binary oppositions exist in all folk genres.

Similarly, structuralism itself has been criticized, as most theories eventually are. Structuralism looks at the underlying set of laws that govern symbols—how symbols combine to provide meaning—even while it ignores (in its extreme application) what the symbols mean. So a major criticism of the method is that it isolates a text from its background: its social context and the history of the society that produced the text. The text becomes a closed-loop object in which the relations between structures in the text take precedence over the analysis of meaning and the material world beyond the text. And structuralism's abolition of the creative subject (author, narrator, builder, artist) worries scholars who think that the humans and their intentions that are behind the structures remain important parts of the analysis of culture. The field of discourse analysis has, for some, improved some of the weaknesses of structuralism since discourse studies combine structure, language, meaning, and social context.[40] Of course, structuralism is a legitimate approach when it is applied while recognizing all of its consequences.[41]

MYTH AND SCIENCE

Myth and religion cross paths with scientific modes of thought, and the interplay between them spawns much debate (for the sake of broad argument, the fields of applied science are included here: engineering and medicine). The debate is not entirely new: As mentioned earlier, the Greek philosophers crossed paths with traditional ways of thinking over 2,000 years ago.[42] Although the physical sciences are often involved in this subject, the social sciences such as anthropology and folklore also enter into the issue.[43] At a superficial level of the debate, science is often posed as a modern way of thinking opposed to traditional ways of thinking (religion, myth, and folklore). Sometimes science is seen as a replacement for traditional modes of thought, a welcome "evolution" of human cognition out of the "darkness" of less rigorous methods. This evolutionary concept is rather curious in one sense: Science may have existed for as long as traditional knowledge—not specific scientific fields of, for instance, antibiotics and lasers, but rather the scientific *method* of examining the material world.

Carl Sagan makes the suggestion that hunter-gatherers, in making the observations and deductions required in tracking an animal across the desert, use a method nearly identical to that of planetary astronomers studying the "footprints" (craters) left behind by meteorites. He calls the thinking of the !Kung hunters "science in action"—and says that this scientific, problem-solving thinking has probably been with humans from the beginning. Science has been much refined since the Enlightenment, but it may always have been part of the human's mental "tool box" in the form of both empiricism and hypothesis testing. Now then, since folklore may well be an equally ancient human way of knowing, one that has existed next to analytical thinking, any supposed replacement of folklore by science or clash of scientific versus traditional modes of thought needs to be carefully reconsidered: Humans have evidently used both ways of thinking for a long time. This could suggest a hypothesis: That humans have needed both ways of thinking.[44]

There is nothing in science as a *method* (this distinction is important) that has to be based in modern times: As a method science uses reasons for conclusions and empirical evidence to support those conclusions. And those conclusions must change when better evidence arises and forces us to revise our thinking. This is a method open to a chemist, a hunter, an astronaut, a plant gatherer, an engineer, or a blacksmith. Yet science can also be considered broadly, not as only a method of investigation, but as (1) a community (or "folk-group"!) of scientists and science enthusiasts (not necessarily trained as scientists), (2) socially valued knowledge (industrial society especially values the science that produces means to design technological ideas and products), and (3) a body of knowledge produced by all of the above and able to be used in various ways: politically, socially, and, yes, mythologically and religiously. Much misunderstanding might be avoided if discussants of the field of science first make clear what aspect of science is being discussed!

Critics of science often make the statement that it is merely another form of religion. It is true that both religion and science make statements about the world. Also true: Knowledge produced by the scientific method can be used in spiritual ways, just as patterns of thought in religious thinking may coincide with the general view of a scientific theory. For example, many religions have ideas about the end of the world, as do scientific fields (physics and astronomy) about the end—or "death"—of the universe as it expands and cools to lifelessness or contracts again to an infinitely hot and massive point. At any point the knowledge produced by scientific methods can be selected to serve many of the same functions as religion. One can imagine (and science fiction writers have often done so) how a scientific theory could be appropriated for religious purposes. Yet science is also worked into religious thinking: The Catholic Church recently endorsed the theory of evolution, with the proviso that God had set the machinery of evolution in motion. Many scientists and those who apply science in practical uses have been deeply religious, and some have seen science and technology as being useful in attaining religious goals.[45] Science and religion have always "negotiated," and the dividing line between the two is not always sharp. Yet, this is also true: Scientific theory may change in accordance with new methods or data, which is unlike typical religions. Religions can and do change, but science is *designed* to change, as rapidly as possible, when new information is discovered. Science as a *method* is not similar to a religion, even if scientific *knowledge* is sometimes used for religious goals, as the creationism movement sometimes attempts,[46] and as technologists and scientists have so often done.

Just as science is unfairly compared with religion, so can religion and myth be unfairly judged against the model of science. As discussed above, many early scholars saw myth as "false science" and legend as "false history"—ideas that persist today among many people. To say that myth is false science is to miss the point that myth and the religious system in which it may be planted have a purpose different from that of science. Unlike the scientific method, we are not asked or required to test the truths of religion (and in fact many religious ideas are untestable because they transcend the physical world). We are expected to *believe* in truths communicated within our individual societies if we want to be considered as members of a certain religion or social group.

Stated another way: The knowledge produced by science and technology has consequences in the physical world—we learn to manipulate materials and energy to produce radios, medicine, spacecraft, refrigerators. What science does not usually do—and what most scientists avoid—is explain the "ultimate truths" of human existence (Are there good and evil? Is there a grand plan for the universe?). They may not answer why a universe should exist, and why it should have been created, and why it should end. The answer from a scientist may be, "Because that is the way it is; I can say no more because the question is beyond the boundary of the method of science." And that would be a fair answer.

This is where religion and myth have their place. Myth involves belief not necessarily (or even usually) based on evidence. Even so, we need to ponder how humans from the earliest times have observed the world at work and drawn from it analogies on how it works and have woven these observations into their sacred stories—so nonscientific thinking is certainly not devoid of "reality." Yet for myth, at any rate, *belief* is more important than empirical reasoning because we do not synthesize antibiotics from myths but rather define and hold societies together with sacred stories. Once you believe in the myth, you are part of the culture in which the myth is known, and you can interact with the people of that culture.

Even if science and religion can be used toward the same ends—both can provide a way of knowing that gives the individual a philosophical and social home in the world—science and myth are not the same. Science will not explain the meaning of death. A myth will not explain the action of antibiotics. They do *not* have to do each other's work. Science attempts a universal explanation of phenomena in the natural world for people of *any* social identity, although scientists sometimes speak and write in "narratives" akin to myths. Myth explains the origins and meaning of the world to a *certain* cultural group by using terms of more psychological function than precision and consistency with detailed physical phenomena (although a myth may include observations about the material and social world). The terms of myth may be said to be *socially appropriate* to the society using the myth, as are the terms of science proper for its own uses.

Yet we can think of science and myth as related in one sense because both are truths invented by humans. Science excels at consistency of results in the application of its method (it can predict many effects in the physical world). Science can provide both benefits (medicine) and horrors (nuclear weapons), as well as other results and concepts that need not be thrust within these two opposing categories. Myth excels at presenting ideas otherwise unexplainable by idealizing society to suggest behaviors deemed most important in a society, by providing ideas that people can share (enabling them to identify each other as members of one common group), and by providing an artful presentation (in narrative, ceremony, and material art) that itself is important in social rituals and personal pleasure. Myth like science provides—besides a host of interesting ideas—benefits and horrors (racist attitudes are one of the ideologies sometimes communicated in folkloric modes of thought.[47]) Science and myth are different truths that share some goals and attributes. Too strict a comparison between myth and science in order to evaluate them in a contest is not a fair or productive venture.

NOTES

1. J. W. Rogerson sketches the various approaches to mythology: "Slippery Words: Myth," *Expository Times* 90:10–14, 1978–1979.
2. Mircea Eliade theorized about "mythic time". A discussion of his theories is beyond the scope of this chapter, but you can consult: "Cosmogonic Myth and Sacred History," in *The Quest: History and Meaning in Religion* (Chicago: U. of Chicago Press, 1969), 72–87; *Patterns in Comparative Religion* (New York: Harper & Row, 1963): *Myth and Reality* (New York, Harper & Row, 1968).
3. On rituals used to help society cohere during crises, see Edward Shils, "Ritual and Crisis," *The Religious Situation*, ed. Donald R. Cutler (Boston: Beacon Press, 1968). See also discussion of Victor Turner in Chapter Three of this book as well as his *The Ritual Process: Structure and Anti-Structure* (Ithaca, NY: Cornell University Press, 1969).
4. For a detailed and wide-ranging review of the various approaches to myth, see William G. Doty, *Mythography: The Study of Myths and Rituals* (Tuscaloosa: University of Alabama Press, 1986). Alan Dundes has collected a series of important articles covering a range of approaches to myth, and he introduces each article with very helpful commentary: *Sacred Narrative*, ed. Alan Dundes, (Berkeley: University of California Press, 1984). In this volume, see G.S. Kirk. "On Defining Myths," 53–61. See also Kirk's *Myth: Its meaning and Functions in Ancient and Other Cultures* (Berkeley: University of California, 1970). Fritz Graf focuses on Greek mythology in his book, but his introductory chapters present succinct reviews of the history of myth studies and modern approaches to myth: *Greek Mythology: An Introduction*, trans. Thomas Marier (Baltimore, MD: Johns Hopkins University Press, 1987/translated 1993).
5. On geographic tendencies of myths, see Anna Birgitta Booth, "The Creation Myths of the North American Indians," *Anthropos* 52:497–508, 1957. Her approach is applicable to the distribution of folklore in general.
6. Joseph Campbell's theories have not been well received in anthropology because of his overgeneralizations, as well as other problems. See Robert A. Segal, "Joseph Campbell's Theory of Myth: An Essay Review of his Oeuvre," *Journal of the American Academy of Religion* 44:97–114, 1978; also collected in Dundes' *Sacred Narrative*, cited above.
7. Richard Bauman, "Differential Identity and the Social Base of Folklore," in *Toward New Perspectives in Folklore*, ed. A. Paredes and R. Bauman (Austin: University of Texas Press, 1972), 31–41. See Alan Dundes' works on the folk group and folk idea: "Folk Ideas as Units of World View," in *Toward New Perspectives in Folklore*, ed. A. Paredes and R. Bauman (Austin: University of Texas Press, 1972), 93–103, and *Interpreting Folklore* (Bloomington: Indiana University Press, 1980).
8. On religious folklore see: Larry Danielson, "Religious Folklore," in *Folk Groups and Folklore Genres: An Introduction*, ed. Elliott Oring (Logan: Utah State University Press, 1986).
9. Concerning definitions of folklore centering around the size and nature of groups, see Ben-Amos, "Toward a Definition of Folklore in Context," *Toward New Perspectives in Folklore*, A. Paredes and R. Bauman, eds., Austin: University of Texas Press, 3–15, 1972; and Alan Dundes, "Folk Ideas as Units of World View," cited above.
10. See Linda Dégh, *American Folklore and the Mass Media*, (Bloomington: Indiana University Press, 1994); and Catherine Lynn Preston and Michael Preston, eds., *The Other Print Tradition: Essays on Chapbooks, Broadsides, and Related Ephemera* (New York: Garland Press, 1997).
11. Consult the review article of Richard Bauman and Charles L. Briggs to learn more about the function of performance in society: "Poetics and Performance as Critical Perspectives on Language and Social Life," *Annual Review of Anthropology* 19:59–88, 1990.
12. Excellent introductory texts to folklore will serve the student well to gain a general background in folklore studies. Elliott Oring, ed., *Folk Groups and Folklore Genres: An Introduction* (Logan: Utah State University Press, 1986/8th printing 1996); Barre Toelken, *The Dynamics of Folklore* (rev. and expanded edition) (Logan: Utah State University Press, 1996); Robert A. Georges and Michael Owen Jones, *Folkloristics: An Introduction* (Blommington: Indiana University Press, 1995). Collections of classic folklore studies can be found in Alan Dundes' *The Study of Folklore* (Englewood Cliffs, NJ: Prentice-Hall, 1965), and *Interpreting Folklore*, (Bloomington: Indiana University Press, 1980). The classic work on oral epic traditions is Albert Lord's *The Singer of Tales* (Cambridge: Harvard University Press, 1960). See also John Miles Foley, *The Theory of Oral Composition*)Bloomington: Indiana University Press, 1988). On the general concept of tradition, see Henry Glassie, "Tradition," *Journal of American Folklore* 108/430:395–412, 1995. J.E. Limon and M.J. Young review recent theories in "Frontiers, Settlements, and Developments in Folklore Studies, 1972–1985," *Annual Review of Anthropology*, Vol. 15, Bernard J. Siegal, ed. (Palo Alto, CA: Annual Reviews, Inc., 1986).
13. For examples and discussion of such methods see Henry Glassie's *Passing the Time in Ballymenone* (Philadelphia: University of Philadelphia Press, 1982); and Dell Hymes, "Ethno-Poetics, Oral Theory, and Editing Texts," *Oral Tradition* 9/2: 330–370, 1994.
14. For discussion of ways in which folk traditions served as emulative or avoidance models of behavior, see: Joseph J. Duggan, "Social Functions of the Medieval Epic in the Romance Literatures," *Oral Tradition* 1:3. 728–766, 1986; Roger D.

Abrahms, "Personal Power and Social Restraint in the Definition of Folklore," *Toward New Perspectives in Folklore*, ed. A. Paredes and R. Bauman (Austin: University of Texas Press, 1972), 16–300.

15. On the ways in which context influences and frames performances in a group, see Mary Hufford, "Context," *Journal of American Folklore* 108/430: 528–549, 1995. The following works consider the function of folklore: William R. Bascom, "Four Functions of Folklore," *Journal of American Folklore* 67:333–349, 1954; Richard Bauman and Charles L. Briggs (1990, cited above); Charles L. Briggs, "The Pragmatics of Proverb Performances in New Mexican Spanish," *American Anthropologist*, 87/4:793–810, 1985; Luisa Del Giudice, "Oral Theory and the Northern Italian Ballad Traditions: An Ethnographic Approach to the Ballad Formula," *The Journal of Folklore Research* 31:1–3: 97–126, 1994; see also Duggan (1986, cited above); John C. Messenger, Jr., "The Role of Proverbs in a Nigerian Judicial System," *Southwest Journal of Anthropology* 15: 64–73, 1959.

16. Hollander, cited above, collects the stories of the Norse sagas. On the system of feuding among the Norse, see William Ian Miller, *Bloodtaking and Peacemaking: Feud, Law, and Society in Saga Iceland* (Chicago: University of Chicago Press, 1990).

17. Gerard Murphy, *Saga and Myth in Ancient Ireland* (Dublin: Colm O'Lochlainn, 1961), discusses the medieval Irish king tales. Examples are also accessible in T.P. Cross and C. H. Slover, eds. and trans., *Ancient Irish Tales* (New York: Henry Holt, (1969 rpt./1936)), who present translations of Irish myths, legends, and sagas.

18. On the folktale, see Dan Ben-Amos, "Folktale," in *Folklore, Cultural Performances, and Popular Entertainments*, ed. R. Bauman (New York: Oxford University Press, 1992), 101–118.

19. Lee. M. Hollander, trans., *The Poetic Edda*, 2nd ed., rev. (Austin: University of Texas Press, 1986 rpt./1962.); Burton Raffel, trans., *Beowulf* (New York: New American Library, 1963.); Jesse L. Byock, trans., *The Saga of the Volsungs* (Berkeley: University of California Press, 1990).

20. On genre variance among myth, folktale, and legend, see William Hansen, "Homer and the Folktale,"in *A New Companion to Homer*, ed. I. Morris and B. Powell (New York: Brill, 1997), 442–462.

21. For a definition of genre, see Richard Bauman, "Genre,"in *Folklore, Cultural Performances, and Popular Entertainments*, ed. R. Bauman (New York: Oxford University Press,1992), 53–59. The challenges posed by the idea of genre are discussed in Trudier Harris, "Genre," in *Journal of American Folklore* 108:509–527, 1995.

22. For other details, see Theodor H. Gaster, "Myth and Story," *Numen* 1/3:184–212, 1954; also collected in Dundes' *Sacred Narrative*, cited above.

23. Stith Thompson humorously but bitingly puts single-theory pretensions in perspective in his "Myth and Folktale," in *Myth: A Symposium* edited by Thomas Sebeok, (Bloomington: Indiana University Press, 1958), 169–180, cited above. As a complement to Thompson's caution, highly recommended is Elli Köngäs Maranda's article showing how various approaches can be applied to one myth: "Five Interpretations of a Melanesian Myth," *Journal of American Folklore* 86/339:3–13, 1973. In addition, consider that scholars have devised theories out of their specific social and historical environments; this fact does not negate the value of their work obviously (we are all products of our homelands!) but emphasizes that no theory arises out of a position of objectivity; theorizing in fact is a very subjective business, making it necessary to include a range of theories to help us refine our methods. See Ivan Strenski on the social and historical environments of some major scholars of myth: *Four Theories of Myth in Twentieth Century History: Cassirer, Eliade, Lévi-Strauss and Malinowski* (London: Macmillan, 1987).

24. Lauri Honko, "The Problem of Defining Myth," in Dundes' *Sacred Narrative*, 41–52, cited above. See also Rogerson, cited above.

25. On Greek philosophical approaches to myth, see Fritz Graf, "VIII. Philosophers, Allegorists, and Mythologists," in *Greek Mythology*, trans., Thomas Marier (Baltimore, MD: Johns Hopkins University Press, 1993).

26. An excellent discussion and bibliography for Müller's and Lang"s theories are to be found in Richard M. Dorson's, "The Eclipse of Solar Mythology," *Journal of American Folklore* 68: 393–416, 1955; also collected in Dundes' *The Study of Folklore*, cited above.

27. Analogy is not restricted to myths and poetic language but is rather a general characteristic of human thought and is important in science, which is sometimes (mistakenly) thought of as the opposite of myth and art. See W.H. Leatherdale, *The Role of Analogy, Model and Metaphor in Science* (New York: American Elsevier Publishing, Inc., 1974).

28. Other supporters of the myth-and-ritual school are Jane Ellen Harrison, who supports a ritual-dominant theory in her *Themis: A Study of the Social Origins of Greek Religion* (Cleveland: World Press, 1957/rpt.1927); Lord Raglan, who modified the ritual-dominant theory by admitting that myths could survive once their rituals had died in, "Myth and Ritual" in Sebeok cited above; see also his *The Hero: A Study in Tradition, Myth, and Drama* (New York: Vintage Books, 1956/rpt.1935). Clyde Kluckhohn also favored a theory of interdependence in "Myth and Rituals: A General Theory," *Harvard Theological Review* 35: 45–79, 1942.

29. Sir James Frazer, *The Golden Bough: A Study in Magic and Religion*, abridged ed. (New York: Macmillan, 1963/rpt.1922). For a critique of Frazer, see Edmund Leach, "Golden Bough or Gilded Twig," *Daedalus* 90/2:371–387, 1961. Theodor H. Gaster, *Thespis: Ritual, Myth, and Drama in the Ancient Near East* (New York: Anchor/Doubleday, 1961) saw myth and ritual as parallel events in

society rather than as their existing in an evolutionary relationship.

30. A.A. Brill, ed. and trans., *The Basic Writings of Sigmund Freud: Psychopathology of Everyday Life, The Interpretation of Dreams, Three Contributions to the Theory of Sex, Wit and Its relations to the Unconscious, Totem and Taboo, The History of the Psychoanalytic Movement* (New York: The Modern Library, 1995).

31. Mircea Eliade, *Patterns in Comparative Religion*, trans. Rosemary Sheed (New York: World Press, 1958); and *Myth and Reality*, trans. William R. Trask (New York: Harper and Row, 1963). Carl. G. Jung and Karl Kerényi, *Essays on a Science of Mythology: The Myth of the Divine Child and the Mysteries of Eleusis*, trans. R. Hull (Princeton, NJ: Princeton University Press, 1963).

32. One earth-diver myth and other myths can be found in Stith Thompson's *Tales of the North American Indians* (Bloomington: University of Indiana Press, 1929/rpt. 1966); see "VIII. The Creation (Maidu)."

33. Alan Dundes, "Earth-Diver: Creation of the Mythopeic Male," *American Anthropologist* 64: 1032–50, 1962. Also collected in his *Sacred Narrative*, cited above. For more of his psychoanalytic studies, see his *From Game to War, and Other Psychoanalytic Essays on Folklore* (University Press of Kentucky, 1997). Michael Carrol critiques Dundes in his "The Rolling Head: Towards a Revitalized Psychoanalytic Perspective on Myth," *Journal of Psychoanalytic Anthropology* /1:29–56, 1982; and in Elliott Oring, "Book Review: Interpreting Folklore," *Journal of American Folklore* 96: 84–88, 1983. On other psychological approaches see D. Hufford, "Psychology, Psychoanalysis, and Folklore," *Southern Folklore Quarterly* 38: 187–197, 1974.

34. Emile Durkheim, *The Elementary Forms of Religious Life* (New York: The Free Press, 1915/rpt. 1965).

35. Bronislaw Malinowski, *Magic, Science, and Religion and Other Essays* (Garden City, NY: Anchor Press, 1948). For a review of Malinowski, see William Bascom's, "Malinowski's Contributions to the Study of Folklore," *Folklore* 94: 163–172, 1983. See a critique of functionalism in Roy A. Rappaport, *Ecology, Meaning, and Religion* (Richmond, CA: North Atlantic, 1979).

36. For sequential structuralism, see Vladimir Propp, *Morphology of the Folktale*, trans. Laurence Scott (Austin: University of Texas Press, 1968). David Bynum details the structure of the "two trees" in oral tradition in his *The Daemon in the Wood* (Cambridge: Harvard University Press, 1978).

37. Terry Eagleton in Chapter 3 of his *Literary Theory: An Introduction* (Minneapolis: University of Minneapolis Press, 1983), reviews the effect of structuralism on literary studies.

38. Lévi-Strauss's analysis of Asdiwal is to be found in Edmund Leach, ed., *The Structural Study of Myth and Totemism* (London: Tavistock, 1967). For in-depth study, see Lévi-Strauss's *Introduction to a Science of Mythology*, 4 vols.: *The Raw and the Cooked*, Vol. 1 (New York, 1969); *From Honey to Ashes*, Vol. 2 (New York, 1973); *The Origin of Table Manners*, Vol. 3 (New York, 1978); *The Naked Man*, Vol. 4 (New York, 1978). For other applications of structuralism to folklore, see Pierre Maranda and Elli Köngäs Maranda, eds., *Structural Analysis of Oral Tradition* (Philadelphia: University of Pennsylvania Press, 1971).

39. Edmund Leach, *Claude Lévi-Strauss*, rev. (New York: Viking, 1976)

40. Mikhail Bakhtin is an important scholar in discourse studies; see his *Rabelais and His World*, trans., Helene Iswolski, (Bloomington: Indiana University Press, 1988).

41. For critiques of structuralism in folklore, see Alan Dundes, "Structuralism and Folklore," *Studia Fennica* 20: 75–93, 1976. For critiques specific to Lévi-Strauss, see Alan Dundes, "Binary Opposition in Myth: The Propp/Lévi-Strauss Debate in Retrospect," *Western Folklore* 56: 39–50, 1997; and David G. Mandelbaum, "Myths and Myth Maker: Some Anthropological Appraisals of the Mythological Studies of Lévi-Strauss," *Ethnology* 26:31–36, 1987.

42. Fritz Graf's book *Greek Mythology*, cited above, can be consulted to learn the details of Greek myths and subsequent treatment of myths by the classical philosophers.

43. Gregory Schrempp, "Folklore and Science: Inflections of "Folk' in Cognitive Research," *Journal of Folklore Research* 33/3:191–206, 1996, proposes four theoretical relations of science and folklore, which can be extrapolated to the relation of science and religion.

44. Carl Sagan, "The Wind Makes Dust," in *The Demon Haunted World: Science as Candle in the Dark* (New York: Random House, 1995).

45. The historian David F. Noble in his *The Religion of Technology: The Divinity of Man and the Spirit of Invention* (New York: Alfred A. Knopf, 1998), documents the history of the hand-in-hand development of religion and science/technology. He sees no opposition between science/technology and religion (nor do they necessarily complement each other), but rather they represent enterprises that have been merged, with technological endeavors being suffused by religious beliefs, as evidenced in the lives of many scientific or technological practitioners.

46. "Scientific creationism" is an extreme case of scientific ideas being selected to coincide with religious goals, as Eugenie C. Scott details: "Antievolutionism and Creationism in the United States," *Annual review of Anthropology* 26: 263–289, 1997. See also Francis B. Harrold and Raymond A. Eve, eds., *Cult Archaeology and Creationism*, rev. and expanded edition (Iowa City: University of Iowa Press, 1995), and M. Ruse, *But is it Science? The Philosophical Question in the Creation/Evolution Controversy* (Buffalo, NY: Prometheus, 1988).

47. The chilling possibilities of horrors perpetuated in folklore are evident from the research of Alan Dundes and Thomas Hauschild, "Auschwitz Jokes," *Western Folklore* 42: 249–260, 1983.

Five

Ritual

Kristin Norget
McGill University

INTRODUCTION: DEFINING RITUAL

> "In ritual, the world as lived and the world as imagined . . .
> turn out to be the same world."
>
> *Clifford Geertz*

The word "ritual " for many of us evokes images of stodgey tradition, or of exotic ceremonies of far away "primitive' peoples. Defining ritual is a difficult task; attempts within anthropology have been numerous, and sometimes contradictory.[1] What constitutes ritual behavior? What are its boundaries? Is it important to distinguish between religious and secular ritual, ritual and ceremonial? What does ritual activity do that other modes of human action or behavior cannot?

There is an infinite diversity not only in types of rituals, but also in ways of interpreting them. Ritual is often something we associate with "other', nonsecularized societies, seeing it as a phenomenon typically bound up with folklore and superstition. But this view neglects to acknowledge the way very similar rites and ceremonies structure and give significance to people's lives on a cross-cultural basis.

Typically, rituals are viewed as public events performed in special (sacred) places or at designated times. Many anthropologists are firm in the more classic association of ritual to religion, and to "preliterate" societies. Yet there are also conceptions that understand ritual in broader terms, seeing it as a genre of human activity which may be either religious (i.e., relating to the supernatural), or secular (i.e., non-religious), including different types of ceremonial, festivals, sports events, or dramatic performances. While this kind of approach runs the risk of overgeneralizing the understanding of what constitutes a "ritual," at the same time it allows for a broader understanding of how a range of collective events or kinds of cultural performances share certain communicative properties in any cultural context.

Contemporary anthropologists generally see ritual as referring to any kind of formalized (structured, repetitive, and stereotyped sequence of activities), socially prescribed symbolic behavior. The minimal definition of ritual would see it as a category or an aspect of behavior which is stereotyped, predictable, prescribed, and communicative, which differs from the more classic anthropological uses of the term. Nevertheless this skeletal, still somewhat ambiguous set of ritual's defining features fails to convey the richness of various anthropological approaches to the understanding of ritual.

Theories may present the relationship between religion, society, and culture in different ways. As Catherine Bell has pointed out, regardless of the approach, ritual is still regarded as the definitive component of the various processes that are deemed to constitute religion, or society, or culture. Bell sees that most theories of ritual belong to one of two schools of thought: Some stress the *distinctiveness* of ritual—that is, how it is clearly different from other kinds of activity; others stress the parallels between ritual and *other forms of human action*, underlining its general expressive and communicative qualities.[2]

Yet here again we are faced with the same uncertainties: What is the difference between ritual, rite, ceremony, festival, carnival, or public performance such as a dramatic play or opera? While certain features may link some of the above kinds of events as one genre, there are clearly important differences between them, especially with regard to the relationship between participants (performers) and audience, their overt purposes, the relative regularity of their occurence, and so on. Is a deeper kind of understanding afforded when we relate all of these under the common term "ritual"? What action may be considered as "ritual" even if it has no apparent relation to religion? When is it important to distinguish between religious ritual and "secular" ritual? Further, how does ritual, as a clearly bounded event, communicate what it does?

Early anthropology associated ritual with religious practice. Implied herein was a strong contrast between "primitive" and "modern" societies. In the nineteenth and early twentieth centuries, ritual as related to simple, "primitive" cultures was regarded as symbolic action which produced no practical result, to be distinguished from rational, nonritual thought and instrumental action which was found in "modern" Western society. Contemporary anthropology goes far beyond those divisions, focusing instead on the importance of ritual in all societies, and the differences but common features among them.

Certain anthropologists reject the original sacred association with the term "ritual", and focus exclusively on the stylized, repetitive sequence of ritual elements, a perspective that highlights the *communicative* nature of ritual. British social anthropologist Edmund Leach shows, for example, that rituals may be seasonal, marking a culturally defined moment of change in the seasonal round or an activity such as planting, harvesting; or they may be to commemorate important moments in an individual's life cycle or in collective, social existence. For Leach, ritual is customary behavior which makes statements about the hierarchical relations among people. In the same vein, another well-known theorist of ritual, Victor Turner, sees that seasonal rituals and festivals owe their persistence to their link with recurrent communal experiences and needs. He argues that while individual life-cycle rituals underline fundamental values of the society exhibited to participants as sacred, cyclical rituals are more occasions for social commentary and "plural reflexivity": They are frames, "within which members of a certain group create a language, both verbal and nonverbal, for talking about their reality."[3]

Other thinkers, such as Max Gluckman, feel it important to distinguish between religious and secular rituallike behavior or events on the basis of a presence or absence of a connection with a supernatural power. In such a perspective, then, ritual is necessarily sacred and is important as a facet of religion.

However we can see underlying both the above views of ritual is a concern with power (here defined as a kind of coercive authority) from some kind of transcendent, external source, whether that is defined explicitly as "sacred" (i.e., supernatural) or not. We can therefore see ritual as affording a special kind of space and occasion for special social experience, underlining, yet potentially altering, social life. Performed at regular intervals, "generation after generation," rituals may convey timeless cultural messages, collectively held values and beliefs, and senses of identity. Though participants in ritual can be seen to be concerned with representation for the sake of representation, many rituals have a concrete purpose and are aimed at accomplishing some socially defined goal.

Thus we may concern ourselves with the question of why ritual is declared to be, as Roy Rappaport calls it, "*the* basic social act," a means essential in the organization and integration of the social fabric. But it is also important to consider the special *ways* in which ritual communicates its message and is able to bring out its desired effect. In other words, what are the special properties of ritual that make it such an extraordinary form of human action?

RITUAL AND SOCIAL LIFE

Early twentieth-century anthropological understandings of religion drew from the work of theologian *William Robertson-Smith* (1846–1894) (1899), and Victorian ethnologists *E.B. Tylor* (1871) and *Sir James Frazer* (1890).

Following the typical mode of thought of their time, Tylor and Frazer were both primarily concerned with primitive religion from the evolutionist perspective, which saw cultural difference between societies to be explained by societies' varying degree of cultural development or evolution. Attempting to make sense of ritual from the standpoint of rationality, or in terms of utilitarian logic, such evolutionist thinkers addressed ritual in a rather patronizing manner as "primitive" action which simply reflected a lack of intellectual sophistication.

Tylor's strong belief in an underlying universal "psychic unity" of mankind supposed that humans' minds everywhere thought alike; hence cultural differences could be attributed to differences in evolutionary accidents. Tylor prioritized belief over rite and defined religion, whose earliest form he identified with animism, as the belief in spiritual beings. Frazer and Tylor were not concerned with the meaning of ritual, which was assumed to be simply one facet of religion, interdependent of and inseparable from belief. Ritual was "primitive man's" attempt to control his environment and, since the result could not be assured, it was seen to be an irrational category of human behavior. Hence where means and ends (i.e., the individual's behavior and the concrete goal) appeared to be illogical, ritual behavior was presumed to result from intellectual confusion or inferiority.

Yet ritual is social rather than individual, a social act. Later anthropologists concentrated on the role of ritual in affirming, and therefore maintaining, the solidarity of members of a collectivity. The word "religion" itself, after all, comes from the Latin *religio* meaning a "bond," binding men to obligations and expressing a relationship.

An influential anthropological tradition emerging after evolutionism saw ritual as a product of social life that had to be made sense of in terms of its relation to the patterns of interaction and collective conceptions that unite members of a society or other kind of collective group. It was felt impossible to determine whether religions were erroneous and illusory beliefs, nor in trying to determine the origins of religion. Anthropologists should look instead at the *social functions* of religion and religious practice, including ritual.

William Robertson-Smith's ideas laid out the platform for this more sociological interpretation of religion, propelled further by the work of Emile Durkheim (1858–1917) which followed. Based on his studies of the religions and the cultures of the early Semitic peoples, Robertson-Smith underlined the role of ritual as a practice unifying the members of a given society (Robertson-Smith 1889). He took for granted the validity of the separation of religious and nonreligious domains, prefiguring Durkheim's emphasis on the distinction between the sacred and the profane.

Religious ritual had thus been identified as the primary occasion on which the authority of the social group is asserted. Led by Durkheim (1915), functionalist anthropologists investigated rituals for the contribution they made to the formation and maintenance of a social order. Rituals were commonly understood as key mechanisms in reinforcing the collective sentiment (or, as it was called in French, *conscience collective*) and social integration. In this way, collective rites were the concrete expression of the central role of religion in social life, since they enabled the expression and reaffirmation of the shared values, norms, and cosmologies of the collective group and hence were vital to the perpetuation of the social order itself. Thus ritual in Durkheim's terms was society enacted, formalized, symbolically represented, and constructed; collective rites were the "means by which the social group reaffirms itself periodically."

For Durkheim, religion was "a unified system of beliefs and practices [rites] relative to sacred things, that is, things set apart and forbidden—beliefs and practices which unite into a single moral community called a Church, all those who adhere to them." Durkheim saw religion in its function in establishing and reaffirming group solidarity and as having symbolic significance for a "group" or society. In his study of Australian aboriginal religion, he was concerned with how ritual worked to maintain social solidarity in small, traditional, static and homogenous societies; ritual was about maintaining the status quo. For Durkheim, the rites and ritual events of the Australian aboriginal peoples functioned not only to strengthen the bonds attaching the believer to god, but also fortified the bonds attaching the individual to the social group of which he or she is a member. Through ritual the group became conscious of itself, and therefore whenever the group came together in ritual celebration through symbols or collective representations, the community was reconstituted. Religious rituals were the means by which collective beliefs and ideals—the *conscience collective*—were simultaneously evoked, experienced, and affirmed by the community. Through ritual the sentiments and solidarity of the group were expressed and reinforced by means of the social appropriation and conditioning of individual perception and behavior. Durkheim further suggested that the "public performative aspects of ritual were key to collective effervescence," a heightened emotional state or "delirium," itself the basic notion of the sacred.

In these classic functionalist terms society is seen as a largely homogenous entity, a closed and static system, analogous to an organic entity. British social anthropologists who followed Durkheim continued this line of inquiry by concerning themselves with the social functions of ritual. The most famous of these were Bronislaw Malinowski and Alfred Reginald Radcliffe-Brown.

Bronislaw Malinowski analyzed open-sea fishing magic in the Trobriand Islands and underlined the importance of ritual in alleviating anxiety. Ritual in the form of magic, separate from other kinds of collective ritual, was simply a very practical way for a person to deal with the unknown. People resorted to magic whenever they faced uncertainty or danger, and thus Trobriand Islanders used magic to control such things as wind, the weather, fish supply. While magic was then used to establish control, religion "is born of . . . the real tragedies of human life." He saw that the function of religion and, by extension, ritual activity, was to provide people with emotional comfort, reducing anxiety, above all when they are facing a crisis, especially life crises such as birth, puberty, marriage, and death.

In its more straightforward, practical, and individualistic emphasis, Malinowki's brand of functionalism was distinct from that of *A.R. Radcliffe-Brown,* who focused on the importance of ritual in maintaining social solidarity and the stability of social structures. Following more closely in the theoretical footsteps of Durkheim, Radcliffe-Brown identified totemism as the original form of religion. Totemism, which supposes a mystical relationship between people and nature, was an important aspect of the religions of the tribal Australian aboriginal people. With totemism, people related to nature through their totemic association with natural species, usually animals and plants. Radcliffe-Brown found, however, that the most sacred object in the culture of the Australian aboriginal tribes was not the actual animal or plant but instead the emblem of the natural species; thus totems are sacred emblems symbolizing a common identity. Since rites have the role of affirming and maintaining the solidarity of the collective group, when people came together to honor their totem, they were using ritual to worship the social unity which the totem symbolizes.

Radcliffe-Brown emphasized the notion of society as having a decisive role in shaping individual consciousness. In his famous study of the Andaman Islanders in the South Pacific, he concluded that weeping was not a spontaneous expression of emotion but rather a ritual demanded by custom. Andaman Islanders weep at certain ritual occasions (e.g., peacemaking ceremonies; the meeting of friends, marriages, or at the end of mourning period). Radcliffe-Brown saw this rite to have a specific function: Weeping commemorates occasions "in which social relations that have been interrupted are about to be renewed, the rite serves as a ceremony of aggregation," and as such, weeping in the Andaman Islands affirms social solidarity and cohesion.[4]

Many anthropologists still today, echoing Durkheim and Radcliffe-Brown's Functionalist approach, regard the primary function of collective ritual to be the "expression" or reaffirmation of sentiments of collective loyalty. Rites serve to reaffirm and strengthen those sentiments on which social solidarity depends.

Yet in their preoccupation with ritual's role as a mechanism for group cohesion, functionalist social anthropologists did not concern themselves with explaining the details of the content of ritual. Nor were they interested in ritual's potential role in undergirding relations of power in a given social order. "Society" in functionalist analysis was regarded as a largely homogenous entity with a kind of organic existence. Hence its working could be made sense of in terms of biological reasoning stressing the necessary interpendence of constituent parts directed by the imperative of equilibrium. The framework of analysis was therefore synchronic, emphasizing continuity and the weight of tradition.

But the systemic analogy was still a powerful paradigm within anthropology more generally in the premise that a given cultural phenomenon could be made sense of in terms of its role in maintaining society. While functionalist understandings still inform many analyses of ritual, especially in British social anthropology, another kind of extreme utilitarian functionalist interpretation was focused on the role of ritual cycle in a society's ecological adaptation. The American *cultural ecological* perspective, popular especially in the 60s, is exemplified by *Roy Rappaport's* analysis of the ritual cycle of the Tsembaga (Maring), a tribal agricultural people of New Guinea. Rappaport emphasizes the role of ritual in adaptation to the natural environment.[5] According to Rappaport, religious ritual does "more than symbolize, validate, and intensify relationships"; but rather "ritual, particularly in the context of a ritual cycle, operates as a regulating mechanism in a system, or set of interlocking systems." In other words, ritual is a kind of communication, but the kind of messages it conveys are of practical importance in their relation to prevailing physiological, psychological, and sociological conditions. Rappaport demonstrated that the Tsembaga ritual cycle was central to a complex and self-regulating ecological system across their territory, orchestrating a delicate balance among such variables as person-land ratios, pig farming, patterns of political alliance, and warfare.

Rappaport's argument is that the Tsembaga took part in pig-eating rituals to recover protein deficiencies resulting from periods of warfare-related stress. Thus pig consumption and warfare are related adaptively to the physical resources of the environment. The end of a given period of warfare is marked by the ritual planting of a *rumbin* tree at a traditional site and the sacrificial slaughtering of pigs. This is recognized as a way of thanking the gods for their help during warfare, but Rappaport explains that the extra protein people absorb at these occasions also helps them at a time when they are undergoing severe stress due to illness and injury.

In the same adaptive manner, the slaughter of pigs is also a means for limiting the pig population so that they are not competing with humans for sweet potatoes, an important resource for the Tsembaga. At the festival marking the end of warfare, the number of groups in attendance show to the hosts the kind of support in warfare they can expect should they ever be in need. When the pig herd reaches maximum size for the capacity of the environment, a ritual uprooting of the *rumbin* tree begins a year-long festival ending the ritual cycle; this is a clear signal that a certain state of the ecosystem has been reached, having to do with the balance between the number of pigs, the amount of land under cultivation, and the garden yields.

Thus ritual in Rappaport's analysis is equated to a kind of thermostat—once a certain change in the ideal state of balance occurs, the corrective mechanism will trigger on, much like a furnace. Rituals are then first and foremost a regulatory advice, working to maintain balance in relation to all aspects of the Tsembaga ecosystem. Rappaport saw a systemic relation between aspects—"subsystems"—of the ecosphere, as regulated by ritual cycles which have various effects: The ritual system limits warfare so that it does not threaten the survival of the population, it adjusts the ratio of people to land, encourages trade, and helps the distribution of surplus pig-meat throughout Tsembaga territory. He explains that in addition to communicating this important information regarding the states of the ecosystem, ritual always has some sacred meaning, which lends to the messages communicated a sense of authority, of unquestionable truth.

While Rappaport's analysis of ritual's function within an enclosed system illuminates the relation between various cultural elements and the environment, it presents an oversimplified explanation of ritual which cannot explain many of its aspects, including its change over time.

The classic social anthropological functionalist interpretations of ritual and those of the cultural ecological vein may be seen as similar; they are both concerned to make sense of ritual from the "objective" position of the removed and detached observer, seeing ritual in relation to other domains of given social and cultural contexts. In both perspectives, we see an idea of "society" or culture as possessing a kind of self-regulating mechanism or life of its own apart from its members. In the same way that the human body will regulate itself to maintain equilibrium or homeostasis, shivering when cold to keep blood circulating, fainting when experiencing extreme pain, and so on, society will somehow do the same; it knows what is best for itself, in order to maintain the good of the system.

This kind of functionalist thinking about ritual's role in society and culture tends to overlook not only a large range of data, including the range of significances a ritual may have for a given social group, participants' own interpretations of their ritual acts, similarities between religious and secular ritual, but also the critical questions concerned with *how* rituals convey meaning.

RITUAL SYMBOLISM AND CULTURAL MEANINGS

More contemporary anthropologists adopt approaches to the analysis of ritual far more focused on the relation of ritual to underlying systems of meaning in a given culture or society.

Many anthropologists concerned with ritual symbolism emphasize ritual activity as a fundamental dimension of social life, or in Edmund Leach's words, "the communicative aspect of behavior."[6] Those following this line of enquiry include Edmund Leach and Mary Douglas, who drew from the theories of Claude Lévi-Strauss which shed new light on the relationship between human cognitive processes and the organization discernible in domains of social life, including kinship patterns, myth, and ritual.[7] Levi-Strauss's new anthropological doctrine of Structuralism was based on the idea that realms of culture are structured like a language, and that ritual could therefore be analyzed primarily as a systematically organized mode of communication. Levi-Strauss felt that the interpretation of ritual must go beyond mere symbolic analysis to get at the deeper, implied messages inherent in the form and structure of the event's content.

Later developments in interpretive approaches to cultural analysis dwelt on the dynamics of meaning in culture in a less structured, more holistic manner. A major influence on the study of ritual and religion, Clifford Geertz examines cockfights in Bali—elaborate social events involving a rich complexity of ritualistic (i.e., formulaic) activity and symbolism—for what they reveal regarding the ethos of Balinese society as a whole. From this kind of perspective, a ritual is "read" as a kind of "text" for what it can reveal regarding aspects of social structure and social relations, and related ideologies. The analogy of "text" here is used to refer to any object of interpretation that communicates something about a culture. It corresponds to Geertz's definition of culture—"an ordered system of meaning and of symbols, in terms of which social interaction takes place"—which distinguishes it clearly from the social system.

Cockfighting is a violent sport, a leisuretime activity, a time for gambling, but also a rich drama, which makes it, in Geertz's words, "a Balinese reading of Balinese experience, a story they tell themselves about themselves." Through a "deep" reading of the Balinese cockfight, one can learn about the rules of status in Balinese society and their guiding values. But the outside observer can only penetrate this deep meaning of the rite by looking at it "from the native point of view"— that is, participants in ritual experience the event in a way completely distinct from the perspective of an outside observer. The anthropologist's role is therefore to figure out how the ritual works to reconcile the participants' conceptions of the world, and the fundamental emotions and values associated with such "ultimate" conceptions, or their ethos. Geertz argued that it is in some kind of ritual form that the "moods and motivations which sacred symbols induce in men and the general conceptions of the order of existence which they formulate for men meet and reinforce one another." In other words, ritual integrates strongly charged religious beliefs (the dispositional aspects of religious symbols, or ethos) with people's worldview.[8]

Since it was at such collective events that the shared meanings embodied by public symbols were performed, Geertz's perspective made ritual a window into the heart of social life itself. Geertz's typically American "culturalist" perspective, emphasizing collectively shared meanings and understandings which order social life, signals a divergence from British functionalist priorization of social structures and their maintenance. Yet at the same time, underlying his analysis we can still see a Durkheimian view of society as one of stability and equilibrium.

Beyond views which see ritual as simply concerned with the perpetuation with the world "as is," with a more dynamic approach we can see that ritual is also concerned with some kind of transformation of social reality in the sense of symbolically, spatially, and temporally reorganizing society and lived experience. Communication or interaction between the supernatural world and the earthly world is seen to be possible through certain practical channels: Ritual is one of these. In the words of well-known British social anthropologist Edmund Leach, ". . . the purpose of religious performance [i.e., ritual] is to provide a bridge, or channel of communication, through which the power of the gods may be made available to otherwise impotent men."[9] Religious systems, including conceptions of the supernatural domain, may be seen as reflections or extensions of the social order. Ritual therefore provides a means by which power may be obtained to practically transform or somehow affect the world of the living.

THE RITUAL PROCESS

In understanding the social changes ritual acts are able to bring about, we must keep in mind that any ritual has both instrumental and expressive dimensions. That is, a ritual may actually "do" something in the sense of accomplishing a specific, predetermined goal or having certain pragmatic effects (e.g., moving an individual from one culturally defined social stage to another, appeasing the gods, encouraging rain, uniting the members of the community, etc.), but it also expresses something important about the collective group—the worldview, ideas, values and assumptions basic to a society and shared by its members. Rituals will vary in terms of the relative prominence in each rite of instrumental and expressive dimensions. They thus offer a rich array of cultural information, not only about the ideals and values forming the *conscience collective* in Durkheim's terms, but also about social relationships forming the fabric of collective existence.

Yet how do rituals communicate what they do? Many anthropologists have emphasized ritual as a critical channel of public communication. Whatever ritual does, it does so in part by means of vocal language (utterances, chants, singing, etc.) and in ritual action, or gestures. For these anthropologists, ritual is essentially symbolic and expressive behavior, aimed at communicating certain kinds of social meanings.

Rites of Passage

Rites of passage is a term used to refer to ritual ceremonies associated with birth, puberty, marriage, death, and similar crucial occasions marking critical points of transition in an individual's life. In his classic work *The Rites of Passage* (1909/1960), Belgian sociologist *Arnold Van Gennep* observed that "The life of an individual in any society is a series of passages from one age to another".[10] Van Gennep coined the term *rites de passage* to refer to those "rites which accompany every change of place, state, social position and age." Rites of passage therefore accomplish various kinds of transformations of status of members of any social group, moving them from one position in the social structure to another, and distinguishing them as socially defined beings.

Van Gennep discerned an underlying pattern to all such transition rites which consisted of three stages, each of these elaborated by distinct subsets of ritual activity and symbolism: The first stage was composed of *rites of separation*, a *pre-liminal* stage exemplified by ceremonies such as purification rites, the removal of hair, or scarification, tattoos, and cutting. The next phase was the critical *liminal period* (from the Greek *limen*, meaning threshold), encompassing the rites of transition. During the liminal stage, the individual undergoing the rite is symbolically situated "outside society," and may be subject to certain rules or taboos, or restrictions on his/her behavior or movement. Van Gennep observed that in this period the customary rules of the society may be suspended, "or the rite may be seen as a symbolic death, leading to a new rebirth." In the ensuing *postliminal phase*, the individual is reintegrated or reincorporated into the society in a new status or altered state, symbolized by such changes as the lifting of previous restrictions, the wearing of new clothes, or the sharing of a meal among ritual participants.

Rites of passage are usually associated with tribal societies, where such rituals are more frequently found, often in quite elaborate form, and have a central role in structuring the life of the individual. Yet similar "rites of passage" may be found in so-called "secular" societies such as in North America, even where another kind of social institution (such as school) structures and accomplishes much of the changes of status. Other examples range from more "traditional" rites of passage such as puberty rites and the vision quest of certain North American indigenous peoples, to rites of passage such as confirmations, baptisms, bar and bat mitzvahs, to fraternity, or sports team initiations.

Thus a rite of passage may mark or commemorate any transition in place, condition, social position, or age. While there are some rites of passage a person may undergo alone or in small groups (e.g., a wedding, funeral, or club initiation), these rites have been of anthropological interest especially as collective events wherein several individuals undergo the rite together, at the same time. The important purpose of these rites is to make clear a social transformation, reducing ambiguity, and affirming culturally shaped and shared categories and understandings. Rites of passage, like other rituals, emphasize, affirm, and sacralize as well as ease people through critical changes in social relationships. They perpetuate a sense of continuity and changelessness important to the stability of any social order and may be used to underline and dramatize duty and obligation.

Rites of passage are often linked to critical milestones in a person's physical maturity. Because of this, the staggered social construction of maturation (characterized by abrupt boundaries distinguishing mutually exclusive social categories, e.g., unmarriageable child versus marriageable adult) is made into a smooth continuum by the symbolic assimilation of social maturation to the gradual nature of biological development. As a result, social ideology is naturalized and lent an aura of authority and timelessness.

While Van Gennep's early study highlighted the social importance of rites of passage, it also paved the way for an important later examination of this genre of ritual by Victor W. Turner, an anthropologist working largely in the Durkheimian tradition. Turner's significant contribution to our understanding of rites of passage has been in revealing the properties of the "interstructural" marginal or liminal period of Van Gennep's tripartite structure. Initiation rituals (or "coming-out" rites) are a good example of the effects and significance of rites of passage, especially the liminal stage.

Turner's views on rites of passage are based on his many years of research among the East Afridan Ndembu people of Zambia. The society of the Ndembu is organized according to matriliny, that is, rights and statuses passed through ties between mothers and children. Turner observed how Ndembu initiation rites separated the initiand from the status of child and confer on them the new status of marriageable adult. The two important Ndembu initiation ceremonies he observed are the *mukanda*, or boy's circumcision rite, and the *nkang'a*, or girl's puberty ritual.

The first stage of separation in the rite of passage comprises symbolic behavior indicating the detachment of the individual or group from their former fixed point in the social structure. For neophytes undergoing initiation, the liminal stage is a "betwixt and between" period of limbo when, as liminal entities, they are made structurally invisible, physically removed from their previous status, and symbolically stripped of their identity. During initiation, for example, Ndembu neophytes of either gender are all referred to as *mwadi*, a term describing "initiand." Considered structurally "invisible," they are often secluded, or considered ritually polluting. The Ndembu term for the liminal period as a whole—*kunkunka*—means "seclusion site," further underlining the neophytes' separation from the everyday order.

Turner explained that the symbolism associated with the liminal persona is rich and complex. Much of this "liminal" symbolism is modeled on human biological processes which are likened to structural and cultural processes, and thereby "give an outward and visible form to an inward and conceptual process." Liminality is often likened to invisibility, darkness, bisexuality or to the wilderness. Since neophytes are structurally "dead," symbolism of their liminality is typically concerned with death and decomposition: For example, they may be dressed in black, go naked, or may be covered in earth. In a state of "becoming," the liminality of initiands might also be expressed by symbols of gestation or parturition. In Ndembu boys' initiations, for example, they may be likened to menstruating women, indicating their ritual condition of ambiguity.

Another critical aspect of liminality includes that of complete submission and obedience of initiands to the authority of ritual elders, or persons filling this role. They are expected to obey their elders and accept punishment passively. Neophytes are reduced to a homogenous, uniform state, a complete equality among themselves, stripped of property, status, or clothing indicating their rank or role. Over the duration of their circumcision rite, for example, Ndembu initiands share all food provided to them equally, and sleep together in small groups around the fire. The intensity of this shared experience is conducive to the emergence of an overwhelming and cathartic sense of ritual oneness, a highly charged homogeneity and comradeship Turner referred to as *communitas*.

During the liminal period, sacred knowledge or *sacra*, "the heart of the liminal matter," is shown to initiands in such forms as a secret myth, ritual objects, or special instructions. Like the Ndembu ritual masks with monstrous features which are exhibited to Ndembu initiands, sacra often take a distorted or exagerrated form, with the purpose of promting neophytes to reflect on "their society, their cosmos, and the powers that generate and sustain them." *Sacra* was said by Turner to be especially important in the transformation of persons from one socially determined status to another, inculcating them with the shared norms and expectations associated with their new role. In Turner's words, *sacra* is not about "a mere acquisition of knowledge, but a change in being."

Turner is known best for his unparalleled contribution to understandings of the working of ritual symbolism. In his many influential writings on the religion of the Ndembu, Turner brought to light an incredibly complex symbolic structure. Following Max Gluckman, his teacher at the Marxist-oriented University of Manchester school of social anthropology, Turner shifted interest in the role of ritual in maintaining the structure of society in a condition of stability and equilibrium, to understanding ritual as an active process concerned with the resolution of conflict and contradiction, and perpetuation of the social order.

In his study of Ndembu, Turner focused on *rites of passage* (focusing on death and puberty, and initiation ceremonies), but also *rites of affliction*, associated with various misfortunes believed to result mainly from spirits.

Turner uses the term "ritual" to refer to "prescribed formal behavior for occasions not given over to technological routine; having reference to beliefs in mystical (or non-empirical) beings or power." In Turner's view, rituals provide "decisive keys to the understanding of how people think and feel about . . . relationships, and about the natural and social environments in which they operate."

Turner's work on the properties of ritual symbols did much to illuminate the efficacy of rituals. For him the symbol was in fact "the smallest unit of specific structure in Ndembu ritual". His work is known for the interest it provoked in the pragmatics of symbols. Ritual is the ideal setting in which one can see symbols "in action"; how their "spectrum" or "fan" of meanings ("referents") work together in dynamic ways to bring about certain changes in the social order, such as changing someone from the social status of child to that of adult; or healing tensions or ruptures in the social group. Such ritual transformations, happening on individual or psychological, and social or collective levels, were made possible by the communicative properties of the symbols themselves. These symbols also contributed to ritual's capacity to bring about extraordinary psychological states.

For Turner (following the lead of Lévi-Strauss), ritual symbolism has a "semantic" structure; that is, the relationship between symbols in a given ritual is organized like a language. Among the most important of the attributes of ritual symbolism is the property of "condensation," which has various interrelated aspects: (1) Symbols are *multi-vocal,* in that they can mean many things at once; (2) ritual symbolism allows a *unification* of apparently disparate significata (meanings), but also (3) a *polarization of significata.* Thus a symbol's different meanings are interconnected due to their analogous qualities or by association in people's thought or experience.

In any culture's total complex of rituals, certain symbols may be seen as "*dominant symbols,*" which are recurrent symbols characterized by pronounced multivocality, expressing the shared values on which social life depends. Turner demonstrated how Ndembu ritual symbols refer to the essential needs of social survival (i.e., hunting, reproduction, cultivation). Dominant symbols for the Ndembu are always species of trees, each associated with a particular color. The *mudyi* or "milk tree," for example, is called such because of the milky latex it secrets. For the Ndembu, the milk tree condenses a wide range of associations, including women's breasts, motherhood, the principle of matriliny, and the unity and continuity of Ndembu society.

The milk tree and all other dominant symbols tend to have two opposed poles of meaning. At one end is the ideological (or "normative") pole of meaning, significances that refer to principles of social organization, to kinds of corporate groupings, and to the norms and values inherent in the social structure. At the other, sensory ("orectic") pole cluster the meanings of a natural or physiological character associated with human experiences of an emotional quality, which are hence able to evoke desires or feelings.

In determining the meaning of ritual symbolism, Turner also argued that three levels of interpretation must be distinguished: (1) the level of indigenous interpretation of symbols ("*exegetical meaning*") to be obtained by ritual participants; (2) a symbol's *operational meaning,* or *how* that symbol is *used* during the ritual; and finally, (3) *positional meaning*: What a symbol means as determined by its *relation* with other symbols.

An important mode of symbolic positioning is *binary opposition,* or the relating of two symbolic vehicles whose opposed perceptive qualities suggest, in terms of the associative rules of the culture, a significant contrast. At the heart of the Ndembu's symbolic system, for example, was the color triad white-red-black. Each of these primary colors has a complex span of referents symbolizing both social and organic phenomena. Within a given ritual then, binary opposition may underline one (or more) of a symbol's meanings or referents by contrasting it with one (or more) of another symbol's referents. For example, in the Ndembu classification system, the *mudyi* tree is a white symbol, associated with breast milk. The color white appears to be dominant and unitary, linked to life prosperity, purity, and authority. Another dominant symbol is the "red" *mukula tree* (which exudes a red gum). The *mukula* is considered ambivalent, seen as expressing both danger and fertility. Black, contrasting both white and red, is associated with misfortune, evil, disease, witchcraft, and to what is "hidden."

Much of Ndembu ritual and magical practice can be understood in terms of this color symbolism, wherein different meanings may be conveyed in different ritual contexts. For example, a man who is sterile takes medicine from the *mucheki* plant, which is believed to then make his semen white and therefore fertile. A woman who has problems with lactation will be given the same white sap to "whiten" her "red" breast milk. So colors in Ndembu symbolism have independent significances, but it is only when they are understood in their interaction with other symbols in a ritual context that the full scope of their signification is uncovered. Thus when it appears in a ritual with three or more other symbols, a particular symbol may reveal further facets of its total "meaning." By means of these symbolic operations, whole systems of ritual symbols and actions can be produced through just a small number of oppositions.

Turner underlined the importance of the emotions stimulated by a symbol's association with human physiology—for example, red being associated with blood—in understanding how symbols operate to transfer strong emotions to the social order. His unique contribution in addressing the sensory, material qualities of symbols added a welcome dimension to "semiotic" perspectives of ritual—approaches that focus on the systemic interrelation of symbols within culture. Symbolic communication was enabled by the actual structuring of the ritual event and its confinement to a circumscribed temporal and spatial arena. In addition, the interaction of "normative" (i.e., ideological) and "orectic" (emotional, sensory) poles, produced a heightened, extraordinary experience for all ritual participants. Ritual symbolism was therefore seen by Turner to derive its power to move and channel emotion from the interaction between the two poles.

Anyone who has attended a ceremonial event ranging from a mass, to a funeral, or a wedding—but also to secular collective gathering such as a sports event or a rock concert—knows the powerful feelings which may be brought out of the audience, emotions which are lent extra weight and force due to an overriding sense of the collective spirit (*communitas*) prevailing at the event. Turner argued that this energy becomes transferred to the ideological pole of meanings, the effect of which is "to fuse the obligatory with the desirable." Ritual plays a key part in redirecting the urges and desires of the individual to allegiance to the social order. In this idea Turner is here strongly Durkheimian in assuming a fundamental tension between the innate drives of the individual and society's need for order and control—again imputing to society a kind of independent, almost animate character.

Turner suggested that since the triadic color scheme was based on psychobiological experiences—bodily emissions such as blood, milk and excreta (or bodily dissolution)—it represents a "kind of primordial classification of reality" that provides the basis of other classifications. Blood expresses redness and power, white is linked to the life fluids of milk and semen, and black denotes body dirt and the fluids of putrefaction. Thus, unlike Durkheim (and his nephew Marcel Mauss) who gave logical priority to social categories in religious classification, for Turner it was the human body that was the primary source of all reasoning processes and classifications in cultural symbolism. In his words, "This use of an aspect of human physiology as a model for social cosmic and religious ideas and processes implies that the human body is a microcosm of the universe."

Other anthropologists have illuminated how social classification shapes the decoration, perceptions, and dispositions of the body as these are elaborated particularly in ritual context.

The Social and Ritual Body

Anthropologists have contributed much to our awareness of how symbols and rituals play upon an isomorphism of the personal body and its larger social contexts. The body has been seen as the point of connection between the cosmos, society, and the individual, a mediator of the interaction between the person and society. Victor Turner, as we have seen, showed how in ritual symbolism the social order was literally inscribed on the body, joining biological processes with the process of socialization.

This use of the body as a metaphor in the context of rites of passage can be seen to have two effects: First, it imposes a "natural" significance to categories which are in fact *socially* defined, thereby making them seem timeless and transcendent (and hence unquestionable). As mentioned earlier, the use of "biological" symbols within a puberty ritual, for example, helps make a sudden and arbitrary entry into the social category of "adult" seem natural and inevitable. Secondly, in the way it establishes an identification of personal and social bodies—that is, of the individual, biological being, and the collective group—the metaphor of the body in rites of passage provides a kind of concrete bridge between individual and collective levels of significance, thereby contributing to the formulation of a shared social consciousness.

This connection is demonstrated clearly in the context of Ndembu healing rituals. Turner found that the misfortune befalling an individual could uncover a specific conflict in relations within the community. Ritual is used as a means to settle the conflict by means of curing the patient. Since ordinarily healing rites are public events, with many people from the the local area in attendance, a number of results ensue: Ruptures between village factions were closed as social tensions were defused and more friendly relations was established, the host village gained prestige, and the essential values of Ndembu society were dramatically underlined.[11]

From this same kind of perspective, in an anthropological classic, *Purity and Danger* (1966), anthropologist Mary Douglas observed that the human body is used to symbolize the body politic, or the social structure. Identifying the social body with the "ritual body," Douglas argues that attitudes to the body are central to the system of classification of a given society—the shared categories and attendant meanings by which a given social group makes sense of the world in the course of everyday life. According to Douglas, "the physical experience of the body, always modified by the social categories through which it is known, sustains a particular view of society." Powers and dangers focus on the margins of society, the things seen as threatening since they do not fit the sacred categories by which we perceive the world and order.

Things that are seen not to "fit," or as abnormal (for example, homosexuals in a society ordered according to a dominant doctrine of heterosexuality) become a reference point for standards and perceptions of what is "normal" and therefore
acceptable. In a similar way, bodily orifices and substances—menstrual blood, urine,
feces—are seen as polluting since they reflect these social threats and dangers (in
many cultures such as that of Orthodox Jews, for example, there is a taboo pro-
hibiting men from having intercourse with their wives during their periods). Since
there is continual exchange of meanings between these two bodies, "each reinforces
the categories of the other," thereby ensuring the preservation of the social group.[12]

The fundamental idea of pollution and taboos is to keep principles and categories from contradiction. Van Gennep himself observed that clitoridectomy in the
context of girls' initiation rites in some parts of Africa may be seen as intensifying fe-
maleness by removing from girls those anatomical features which resemble those of
males. (Though this is not formally incorporated into the context of initiation ritual, a parallel could be drawn to the common custom in North America and elsewhere of a pubescent girl shaving her legs to mark her entry into womanhood.) Such
age and gender distinctions are fundamental to the organization of society, transforming individuals into mature ("socially responsible") persons.[13]

In her study on the Tshidi people of South Africa, Jean Comaroff discusses how
social practices structure the body, and so constitute "social beings" through the internalization in people's consciousnesses of critical cultural schemes and values. Comaroff argues that in postcolonial South Africa, the symbols associated with the
Tshidi's Zionist church, as seen especially in Zionist healing rituals and baptism,
focus on the body for objectifying and expressing the image of a reconstructed,
healed individual. At the same time as they help to achieve immediate ritual goals
such as the healing of an individual, the set of Zionist ritual symbols—a significant
blend of Protestant and indigenous African icons—also express a healing or recon-
stitution of the Tshidi people themselves, addressing the ruptures and destruction
of the colonial experience. Harking back to the ritual identification of individual
and collective bodies mentioned earlier, the body is here seen by Comaroff as the mediator of all social action, the medium for the internalization and reproduction of
social values and for the simultaneous constitution of both the individual self and the
world of social relations.[14]

Symbolic anthropological approaches such as Comaroff's are concerned not
with ritual as an autonomous phenomenon or event, but with the role of strategies
of ritual action in the construction of the "social body." They go far beyond earlier
Durkheimian approaches to ritual, which provided us with the basic understandings
of the connection between social structure and religion. Armed with the insight into
ritual given by Turner and others, more recent anthropologists have deepened our
understandings of the connection between ritual and social process. Contemporary
analyses of ritual and history for example, such as Comaroff's, have demonstrated
how ritual can reorient experience or the consciousness of particular groups or social sectors. Such a perspective identifies "ritualization" of human action as a process
involving the production of a transformed social reality.

Work by symbolic anthropologists has paved the way for more inclusive theories of ritual that address many of its basic characteristics, including its complex
communicative aspects and its capacity to alter social reality.

RITUAL AND PERFORMANCE

Anthropological work inspired by symbolic analysis has led to new avenues for analyzing ritual, including its structuring of time and space, its communicative properties, and its "performativeness." This domain of theory emerged in part as a result of a strong dissatisfaction with the traditional categories brought to the study of ritual that were underlain by rigid dichotomies such as sacred/secular, public/private, and society/individual and thereby separated ritual experience from the flow of everyday life.

This "performative" approach to ritual had an early theoretical precedent. Drawing on the work of Milton Singer, Geertz had already discussed religion as being "encapsulated" in specific "cultural performances"—events both secular (such as the Balinese cockfight) and religious—which could be enacted by members of a given society for visitors and for themselves. According to Geertz, such performances represented for the outside observer "the most concrete observable units of the cultural structure" since each performance "has a definitely limited time span, a beginning and an end, an organized program of activity, a set of performances . . ." The events were also regarded as crucial for the transmission of tradition.

In addition, in his own theory of ritual, Victor Turner introduced the concept of the *social drama* to explain the processes through which conflicts within a Ndembu village were resolved. Turner interpreted the social function of ritual in relation to conflict resolution and identified ritual as a mechanism of redress. For both Victor Turner and Max Gluckman, ritual has a politically integrative function. Gluckman for example, saw ritual "not simply as expressing cohesion and impressing the values of society and its social sentiments on people as in Durkheim and Radcliffe-Brown's theories, but as exaggerating real conflicts of social rules and affirming that there was unity despite these conflicts."[15] Rites were the means by which social solidarity was achieved, and the equilibrium and solidarity of the group was restored.

Turner addressed everyday life events which worked to regulate tensions in the social fabric (derived from some kind of breach or violation of "norm-governed social relations"—in other words, the everyday status quo—within a family, work group, village, or nation). Social dramas were embodied by ritual, where because they were concerned with repairing social tensions or conflicts by means of an appeal to fundamental shared norms and understandings, made clear the deepest values of culture. As demonstrated in the example of healing rituals discussed earlier, for Turner ritual was the arena in which purely social conflicts are worked out.

Turner extended the social drama concept to refer to all kinds of different occasions of "plural reflexivity in human social action." Precipitated by crises rooted in contradictions in the social structure, Turner saw such performative events as cultural frames in which aspects of everyday experience could be reflected upon and evaluated, ending in a temporary resolution. Conflicts often arose in Ndembu society, for example, from tensions between the two principles organizing village structure—the rule of matriliny and the importance given to father-son bonds. This contradiction meant that Ndembu village life was constantly in flux, with an unstable village composition and interpersonal relations. For Turner, ritual was an expression of the failure of other "secular" mechanisms to repair conflicts within and between communities.

Drawing attention to the structured, multivocal symbolic character of such occasions and their importance to the social process, Turner also maintained his preoccupation with the reconciliation of individual interests to collective normative codes, showing how these dramatizations were embedded in the natural pattern of daily existence. Such social dramas addressed conflict with the outcome being one of Durkheimian unity. Rituals allowed the structural patterns underlying Ndembu society ro remain intact despite conflict; the nature of this unity was hence *moral*, not political.

Since Turner's work, a subfield of ritual studies has emerged, pushing forth his ideas by focusing on the analysis of ritual in a dynamic and experience-oriented framework. Addressing the complexly layered nature of the communication of meaning in ritual, such analyses of ritual performance have focused closely on less cognitive-oriented modes of signification, addressing the role of the material qualities and dimensions of ritual communication. Thus instead of the "meaning-centred" interpretive approaches which have dominated symbolic anthropology, the focus in many performative analyses of ritual is on nonlinguistic dimensions of the ritual process, particularly on aesthetic aspects.

Some anthropologists have produced insightful work on the signifying power of diverse ritual elements such as song and dance, in an attempt to synthesize the importance of symbolic and performative dimensions of ritual, in relation to their historical contexts. Bruce Kapferer's account of exorcism rituals in Sri Lanka is an example of such contemporary explorations into the dramatic and aesthetic elements of ritual. For Kapferer, ritual possesses a unique logic, its very "performative force" enabling a kind of powerful "metacommunication" of cultural understandings. Performative force here refers to how the form and content of ritual (i.e., dimensions of space, the organization of participants, and certain kinds of stylized behavior) contribute to the ritual's complete effect; to understand the performance as a whole, all aspects of the performance must be taken into account. The goal of exorcism ceremonies is to cure the patient's illness seen to result from demon attack. Through the course of the ceremony, a demonic reality is symbolically created and then destroyed. Kapferer explains that during the ritual, certain rearrangements in the positioning and interaction of participants and audience, and the manipulation of aesthetic expressive media (such as music and dance) are able to actually evoke particular transformations of consciousness. These aesthetic media alter people's perceptions in order to change "the experiential condition of [the] patients and to bring patients back into a normal conception of the world," thus securing a cure.[16]

A performative perspective such as Kapferer's acknowledges the creative power of ritual participants in the transformation of their setting in response to the ritual event as it gradually unfolds.[17] Since the symbolic content of the ritual is tied to people's everyday social environment, the process of ritual communication draws on collectively meaningful symbols and practices which during the performance are drawn upon and reproduced by participants at both unconscious and conscious levels of awareness. The central idea then is that cultural performances do not only depict and express, but these events also have a key role in the construction of cultural meanings, which are (re)constituted during the performance. In this view, ritual does not follow a fixed text as a "scripted" performance in Geertz's terms; instead it is a process of creation where ritual participants negotiate the meanings of given symbols, significances which are to some degree stable, yet also mutable. Again ritual here represents a social space for the enactment of shared cultural understandings or collective aspirations, potentially masking over or resolving conflicts and contradictions in everyday life.

Many such "performative" interpretive frameworks are premised on an interest in the "style" of ritual presentation. "Style" in this sense refers first to the special dramatic mode of symbolic staging that distinguishes ritual as a unique kind of organized communicative action: Many ritual events—from Brazilian Carnaval to a funeral or birthday party—are clearly demarcated, sensuously heightened cultural spectacles distinct from the flow of the everyday. Indeed, this character of "anti-structure"—a clear contrast or opposition to the norm—is key to their efficacy in communication. Yet though we may see a festival, ceremony, or other ritual performance characterized by contingency, disorder, and even chaos, it is underlain at the same time by kind of structure, predictability, and regularity; there is always an implicit established structure of meanings which is being inverted, underlined, or otherwise highlighted.

Second, the notion of the distinct "style" of ritual performance also refers to the dynamic process enclosed in the ritual, the symbolic effect of which operates at both individual and collective levels. Ritual performance is an orchestrated presentation of a particular reality, one that at once reflects and reformulates, in rich material form, the conditions for a special experience of the world.

Contrasting a typical Durkheimian perspective, we may also understand ritual as offering a cultural space for an alternative representation of reality, or of messages which may contrast dominant symbolic codes. In a study of "folk" or "popular" Catholic religion and ritual in the southern Mexican city of Oaxaca, Kristin Norget, for example, discusses the Day of the Dead (the Mexican commemoration of the feasts of All Souls and All Saints at the beginning of November) as such a ritual performance. The colourful and joyful festival, celebrated in its most traditional form by Oaxacans of poor and indigenous origin, commemorates the annual return visit of the dead to the world of the living. In celebration of their visit, people make altars for the dead containing special food and flock to the cemetery to hold vigil beside the graves of their deceased relatives. People also visit among themselves, often exchanging food, as the festival offers the opportunity for the reaffirmation of ties between relatives and friends.

Like other "popular" Catholic ritual performances, the Day of the Dead is a symbolically rich arena of experience involved in the ritual construction of a moral, sacred space clearly distinct from the landscape of the everyday or mundane. This moral domain is constructed by means of unique signifiers of the sacred and the elaboration of "traditional" (i.e., indigenous) forms of sociality and ethical orientations which may contrast the norms and ideals of the upper classes and of the national Mexican *mestizo* society. Ritual practice involved in the Day of the Dead thus symbolically articulates a particular conception of "moral personhood" constituted by various performances of ideals of social interconnectedness and communality, underlain by various metaphors of exchange, commensalism (sharing), and social balance or harmony. Related traditional social values of reciprocity and communality are becoming increasingly eroded in the context of today's Oaxaca, where the present social climate increasingly encourages a more individualistic, "modern" ethos, and elements of indigenous culture are frequently marginalized and devalued.

The Day of the Dead is therefore an arena for the symbolic formulation of a clearly enframed sacred setting and the analogic re-creation of social reality from this construction. To illustrate this notion, since it is defined symbolically as sacred, *processional movement* involved in the festival (such as by the dead to the land of the living, by the living to the graveyard, and by the living among themselves) expresses the meaningful perception of visiting (which entails gift giving or exchange) as sacred activity. In addition to anchoring relations between supernatural and earthly dimensions, gift exchange and reciprocity of varying kinds in the Day of the Dead allow for the affirmation of "sacred" social ties among the living, between both kin and nonkin.

The performative, embodied nature of sacredness in the Day of the Dead means that the concerted significance of the festival is also expressed through the concrete embellishment of certain "sacred" qualities. This can be seen to include the "rich" flavor of much of the most traditional festival foods, which are distinguished by special values of sweetness or spiciness.

Thus both living and dead are seen to enjoy sensual gratification from the cornucopia of foods and special dishes available during the Day of the Dead. The consumption of sensuously rich food is one of several themes prominent in the complex of symbolic processes within the festival, which may be synthesized into the following core message: Visiting, food sharing, and communality are positive, moral, and sacred activities, necessary to the sustenance of personal and social well-being.

As they are not denied a place alongside the living, the dead—*los muertos*—are also crucial mediators between past and present, as representatives of collective memory and morally freighted ideas of "tradition" under threat from today's dislocations of rapid cultural change in Oaxaca and an emerging climate of growing social, political, and economic uncertainty.[18]

Ritual and Theater

Due to the dramatic qualities of ritual, some anthropologists such as Victor Turner have brought attention to the parallels between theater and ritual, emphasizing the similarities in their structuring characteristics and effects. Here rituals and other public collective gatherings are seen as a genre of performance, analogous in terms of the symbolic codes seen to underlie them. On the symbolic level, the dimension of ritual practice is behavior akin to other kinds of stylized cultural practice.

Turner's colleague Richard Schechner explains that the difference between theater and ritual lies only in context and emphasis:

> **Rituals** emphasize efficacy (healing the sick, initiating neophytes, burying the dead, teaching the ignorant, forming and cementing social relations, maintaining (or overthrowing) the status quo, remembering the past, propitiating the gods, exorcising the demonic, maintaining cosmic order. **Theatre** emphasizes entertainment; it is opportunistic, occuring whenever and wherever a crowd can be gathered and money collected, or goods or services bartered . . . [19]

In addition, the two kinds of performance are distinct in that unlike theater, ritual is performed at a regular time and place, and marks days and sites of importance. Yet ritual texts more generally, whether verbal, musical, or theatrical, are fixed and often "sacred" in the sense of having an aura of timelessness and authority. Thus for Schechner the relationship between ritual and theater is an interaction between efficacy and entertainment, which must be seen as poles in a continuum. A performance is called theater or ritual because of where it is performed, by whom, and under what circumstances.

Other anthropologists see ritual as being more a type, rather than a direct analog of drama, in the same way as all religious ceremony. For example, based on his work on the ritual complex of the East African Maasai people, John Galaty (1998) explains that "all rituals entertain, by virtue of rhetoric and aesthetics, but only the Maasai ceremony *transforms*, that is, has social as well as psychological efficacy, this by virtue of being a political event which implicates society as a whole rather than its participants alone." In this view, theatrical performance is distinguished by its entertaining character, separate from the more extensive and profound social transformative effects of ritual.

However, as Schechner himself pointed out, no performance is pure efficacy or pure entertainment: "The relationship between performers, spectators, and performance, like that between entertainment and efficacy, is dynamic, molded by specific social, cultural, and historical developments". Parallels may be seen in ritual and theater as modes of social communication. Certain European Marxist playwrights and dramatic theorists writing in the 30s and 40s (e.g., Bertolt Brecht, Walter Benjamin) formulated a whole philosophy surrounding theater's unique potential for enhancing people's political consciousness. Still today people may be seen to incorporate certain stylized behavior or other dramatic elements into their protest activity (through, for example, the use of masks and special clothing, songs, verses, candles, patterned forms of movement, and so on). This is "aesthetic" ritualistic activity aimed at eliminating the dichotomy between "art" and "life." Thus Schechner states that "performance is more than a mirror of social change . . . it participates in the complex process that *creates* change."

Contemporary theoretical developments in the understanding of ritual have defined it as a dynamic process—symbolically, spatially, and temporally reorganizing society and lived experience. As a result, ritual has become separated in terms of analysis from its associations with religion and approached as a symbolic mechanism integral to the communication and construction of social life, including hierarchies of power.

RITUAL AND POWER

Durkheimian functionalists laid the path for understanding the role of sacred ritual in undergirding the values, norms, and cosmologies which members of a given society subscribe to. In previous sections, we have seen how ritual is an event enclosing a formal, structured ordering of information and experience. But contemporary theorists are also concerned with the way ritual may also operate to determine or mold the construction of categories of the way people think about social life. In other words, such a view focuses on the role of ritual in a religion's construction of what Geertz described as a given "model for" social reality.

Ritual exists in dialectical relationship with the spontaneous, mundane, and indeterminate messiness of everyday life. It is a declaration of form against indeterminacy, a form created and expressed through the ordering of information. As a dialectic of structure and antistructure, ritual works as Turner suggested, a "mechanism that periodically converts the obligatory into the desirable".[20]

How can ritual act as an agent of social control? What role does ritual play in the undergirding of power relations? The prescribed internal structure and content of ritual, its often regular occurence, staged quality, and evocative properties including repetition, impression of a timelessness, and stability, have led many contemporary researchers to pay close attention to the ways that ritual can be used very effectively to reinforce ideological concepts. Rituals often leave little room for dissent, they assert connections, and hence forcefully dramatize certain kinds of explanation and meaning.

According to Catherine Bell, "ritualization" is a strategic arena for the edification of power relations in its participation in the objectification, naturalization, and legitimation of an ordering of power as an assumption of "the way things really are." In his emphasis on the role of ritual in socialization, Durkheim saw ritual as objectifying collective representations and giving them a mystical ethos. Social integration and value consensus were seen as made possible in part by mystical collective effervescences. A focus on *ritualization* sees the Durkheimian assumption of the requirement of solidarity in society as misleading and draws attention to characteristics of ritual to explain how it wields the power it does. Thus, due to its formal properties, including stylized stereotypical language, its performance, and staging, ritual can traditionalize and sacralize anything, allowing the invention of new traditions.

Others contemporary thinkers addressing the relation between ritual and power have examined how predictable social behaviors and attitudes are shaped and "disciplined" by certain patterned social practices to form "docile subjects" of a given social order. This approach is perhaps best exemplified by the social historian Michel Foucault, who examines how "rituals of power" operate to produce what he calls a particular "technology" of the body. Foucault uses the term technology here to refer to the set of socially accepted attitudes and practices which work at the bodily level to shape a shared mindset and, in turn, guarantee the reproduction of a given ordering of power. A clear illustration of Foucault's ideas may be seen in the case of army recruits, who typically must submit themselves to a physically demanding and rigorous training regimen which involves a forceful regulation of their daily physical habits and movements in the course of becoming indoctrinated and transformed into collectively minded, loyal, and obedient soldiers. Here "ritual" refers to any formalized, routinized everyday practices (e.g., regulated especially according to particular arrangements of labor, education, and the legal system) that work on individual bodies or subjects to establish a certain kind of regulated social environment to which people are unwittingly concerned to adapt their behavior. According to this idea, power relations are at work in the very constitution of the "social body," shaping people both in a broad sense as members of a given society, and according to internal sociocultural distinctions such as class and gender. Through their daily participation in this setting, individuals both internalize and reproduce a given social order and the values, expectations, and rules which uphold and perpetuate it.

Other anthropologists are addressing the ways that religious ritual is similar to political ritual, challenging former dichotomies of sacred and profane, or secular.[21] Here the interest is in the connection between power and the sacred in the legitimation of a given social order or ideology. Ritual can assert authority and thus may have a key role in the construction of power and institutionalization of inequality, or hide such patterns under the mask of patriotism and nationalism:

> Ritual helps to define as authoritative certain ways of seeing society: it serves to specify what in society is of special significance, it draws attention to certain forms of relationships and activity—and at the same time, therefore, it deflects their attention from other forms, since every way of seeing is also a way of not seeing."[22]

Following Durkheim, sacralization is not a taken-for-granted aspect of the cultural environment but a socially constructed meaning: Rather, it is how things are treated which makes them sacred. In many societies ritual is used to sacralize a given social order, seen in the still common conception of kinship as an unquestioned divinely given institution, with royal rituals operating to protect and underline the majestic aura of the monarch's authority. In a famous essay on "civil religion", Robert Bellah explains how national rituals and ceremonial in the United States (e.g., the Pledge of Allegiance, Independence Day, presidential inaugurations) draw on idioms and symbols of a generic Christianity in conferring a sacred mystification of power and authority onto the American State and the "American Way of Life".[23]

Ritual and the Invention of Tradition

Attention to the structuring force of ritual dwells on ritualization as a creative practice of selection and innovation. From this perspective, "tradition" is seen not as cultural practice reproduced benignly by members of a community or collectivity. Instead, in Bell's words, it is "a strategic reproduction of the past in such a way as to maximize its domination of the present, usually by particular authorities defined as the sole guardians of the past and experts on ritual."[24]

Ritual is composed of fixed activities as well as acts that mirror changing circumstances. Tradition is underlain by a tension between the ideal order (unchanging structure) on the one hand, and the world of change and compromise (changing history) on the other. Ritual is therefore used to "invent" tradition for the purpose of conveying an impression of legitimized continuity with the past and to make the experience of tradition for people seem fixed. Through the relations that ritual constructs among symbols, values, and social categories, ritual presents a certain configuration of "order." Tradition is thus a set of fixed activities and values inherited from the past and preserved as unchanging, even in oral cultures where the "script" of ritual may appear more amenable to change than in literate cultures.

In his work on the Merina of Madagascar, Maurice Bloch has examined the ritual construction of tradition, analyzing tribal oratory as a form of "social control." Bloch explains that a highly formalized, codified way of speaking distinguishes ritual oratory from everyday speech, thereby creating and maintaining authority. Since this undergirding of "traditional authority" is rooted in an appeal to the past, it is able to deflect challenge and demand acceptance.[25]

Another important aspect of constructed tradition is that of the demarcation of group identity, based on establishing a shared consensus of a group's shared past, but also ways in which that group may be distinguished from other groups. Thus the strategic differences in ritual traditions can integrate particular communities, or it can differentiate them. This may be accomplished by means of the orchestration of rituals in time and space. A good example to illustrate this kind of operation of ritual is given by the phenomenon of pilgrimage. Pilgrimages to sacred shrines around the world have been viewed by those upholding the Durkheimian legacy as having a key role in the formation of group identities, transgressing social and geographic divisions. Other anthropologists, however, argue that pilgrimage is an arena for competing religious and secular discourses as lay and elite participants negotiate conflicting interpretations of the event, reflecting conflicts of power embedded in the society at large.

Ritual as Rebellion

Insights into the logic of ritual have brought to light the way in which a marked contrast to the everyday, normal order of social life is key to their efficacy. Sometimes, rituals dedicated to the perpetuation of the monarchy contain passages in which the accepted order is turned upside down or inverted: The king becomes a beggar, men dress as women, subordinates are raised to a higher social plane—at least temporarily. Max Gluckman observed how such licensed rebellions of this kind formed a part of the Swazi national first-fruits festival, or *incwala*, of the southeastern Bantu kingdom or Swazi. For Gluckman the ceremony is a symbolic representation of the underlying social tensions within the nation as well as its essential unity and cohesion. In these events, the king is publicly mocked and insulted, women assert their dominance over men, and the whole familiar world of established authority is turned head over heels.[26]

Paradoxically, from this ritual rejection of the system come peace, harmony, fertility, and prosperity. The inclusion of these rebellious phases within such establishment rituals Gluckman sees as an institutionalized pressure valve, diffusing social tensions an individual emotions produced by social conflict. The idea is that by periodically ritually rejecting the authority of leaders or by participating in other kinds of "socially rebellious" ritual events, subordinates find their subjection, and prevailing social tensions and inequalities generally, easier to accept. Gluckman extends the concept of ritualized rebellion to include the frequent real rebellions which changed the personnel in power rather than the structure of power itself. One could even see the mischievous ethos characterizing the North American celebration of Halloween as part of a "ritual of rebellion" with a similarly conservative result.

However we should not assume that such "ritual rebellions" are always ultimately about reaffirming the status quo. Indeed, ritual hovers on the delicate line between chaos and order, and therefore is, in Abner Cohen's words, "poised between the affirmation and validation of the established order and its rejection."[27] A powerful capacity of ritual events resides in their very quality as existential "other," or "antistructure" in Turner's terms. Thus although we might see it as a conservative assertion of social ideals, the potential site of the production of and legitimation of unequal social order, because of this ambiguous liminal character, a ritual event has the potential for subversion or the expression of resistance. For Jean and

John Comaroff, for example, ritual's unparalleled creative power derives from its existence in constant tension with more everyday, mundane forms of social action and sources of meanings and values.[28] Ritual's constituent symbols are also inherently ambiguous and permeable, able to soak up new meanings and referents. As with the example of the Oaxacan Day of the Dead described above, a festival or other performative event may serve as a kind of licensed release. But since it represents an unsettling of cherished cultural classifications, ritual inversion can also sometimes be mobilized as a means of remodeling social relations.

Thus public cultural events may enframe a different, positive, and communal ideal "of the people" even while they are acting as a kind of lightning rod for social animosities and tensions. On occasion, ritual expressions of dissent or rebellion may give way to actual social revolt or attacks on the ruling order. For example, popular carnivals, festivals, and fairs in medieval Europe (such as the French celebration of Mardi Gras) were chronically subject to repression by local authorities and the state who were deeply suspicious of the symbolic inversion that saturated such events, as manifest in imagery of the grotesque or in practices of hedonistic revelry which celebrated an inclusive, anti-elite ethos. Historian Natalie Zemon-Davis explains that in Europe in the seventeenth and eighteenth centuries, peasants dressed up as women during popular festivals were known sometimes to attack government officials such as land surveyors and tax collectors. In Europe, such expressions of the distinct aesthetics and cultural consciousness of those "from below" were often in radical opposition to the dominant normative cultural code, and therefore needed to be extinguished or expelled from the pure, unsullied and disciplined social body of "high" culture.[29]

CONCLUSION

Thus, from earlier examinations which limited an understanding of ritual to its role in the religious life of primitive societies, contemporary analyses of ritual are characterized by a relaxation of the connection between ritual and the sacred, while they underscore the connection between ritual, the sacred, and power. Today anthropologists may be found addressing the commonalities between religious ritual and political ritual, and hence between sacred and "secular" power. Ritual and ritual symbols of varying kinds are understood to play a key part in the orchestration and legitimation of power and authority. This has involved a reconfiguration of categories of sacred and profane. Led by an awareness of culturally constructed embodied schemes of perception, enhanced by thinkers such as Foucault, we realize the extent to which the social environment is "ritualized" in the sense of being habitually structured by predictable patterns of human action, and in turn is able to elicit such cultural practices. Thus the new emphasis is on the exploration of the part of ritual not in formulating a timeless, eternal order, but rather one that is historically contingent and socially constructed.

Ritual is primarily a distinct *way* of doing things. It can be seen to distinguish itself from other forms of action, both in terms of obvious differences, and those which can only be seen through a "deep" reading of the event and a plumbing of its symbolic logic. Ritual encodes, actualizes, encourages, and regulates social relationships in a powerful way. Its efficacy can only be completely understood in a semantic framework of interpretation whereby the significance of any symbol or action depends on its relationship within other elements in the immediate context, and in relation to the broader social and historical setting to which the ritual responds. Ritual "works" through a strategic priviliging of certain aspects of a constructed reality whose existence may be underlined, inverted, or denied. But we must also remember that ritual signification also acts—critically—through the body, the culturally given schemes of perception presented in ritual context being internalized in individual consciousness and then reproduced.

Ritual has a crucial role in the construction of our reality, whether that worldview is understood in benign terms as a cosmology or as a "model of" the world which mystifies, and thereby undergirds, a particular ideology of dominance and constellation of power relations. The increased interest by anthropologists in the relationship between ritual and authority has been encouraged in part by the recognition of the political processes at work in the contemporary globalized world, highlighting the role of ritual in the construction of the state, and in formulating new social identities.

Ritual is the creative domain of social life. Its special power to generate, at a profound level, new understandings of the social world is given largely by the emotional pull of ritual symbols. Yet, constituting that liminal space situated between the everyday and the imagined order, ritual action is also characterized by indeterminacy, ambiguity, and flexibility, allowing the shaping of meanings in alignment with particular collective and personal realities. If the imposition of ideas it attempts were direct and explicit, ritual could not have the effect it does. If we recognize the creative power of ritual, we must also accept how it may also be a space for resisting the established order through the assertion of the independent social vision of individuals or subgroups.

NOTES

1. Discussion of anthropological attempts to define ritual may be found in Gilbert Lewis, *Day of Shining Red: An Essay on the Understanding of Ritual*, (Cambridge: Cambridge University Press, 1980); William G. Doty, *The Study of Myth and Rituals*, (Tuscaloosa: University of Alabama Press, 1986); Brian Morris, *Anthropological Studies of Religion*, (Cambridge: Cambridge University Press, 1987). For a critique of the notion of ritual, see Jack Goody's essay, "Against Ritual," in Sally F. Moore and Barbara G. Myerhoff, eds., *Secular Ritual*, (Assen, Netherlands: Van Gorcum, 1977, 25-35).

2. Among theories underlining the distinctiveness of ritual action, see Catherine Bell, *Ritual Theory, Ritual Practice*, (New York: Oxford University Press, 1992). Bell mentions Mary Douglas' *Natural Symbols*, Edmund Leach's *Political Systems of Highland Burma*, John H.M. Beattie's essay "Ritual and Social Change," *Man I* (1966), Stanley Tambiah's "The Magical Power of Words," *Man* n.s. 3, no. 2 (1968), and Ronald L. Grimes, *Beginnings in Ritual Studies* (Lanham, MD: University Press of America, 1982). Theories stressing the relationship between ritual and other kinds of human action include Jack Goody (above), Roy A. Rappaport, *Ecology, Meaning and Religion*, (Richmond, CA: North Atlantic Books, 1979), and Richard Schechner's "The Future of Ritual," *Journal of Ritual Studies* I, no. I:5-33, (1987).

3. See Victor Turner "Liminality and the Performative Genres" in John MacAloon, ed., *Rite, Drama, Festival, Spectacle: Rehearsals Toward a Theory of Cultural Performance*, (Philadelphia: Institute for the Study of Human Issues, 1984), pp. 19-41.

4. For references to Durkheim's 1915 work see endnotes in Chapter Two. For references to Malinowski and Radcliffe-Brown's work see endnotes in Chapter Three. Aside from those theorists discussed, other well-known early functionalist analyses worth mentioning are Henri Hubert and Marcel Mauss' work, *Sacrifice: Its Nature and Function*, (Chicago: University of Chicago Press, 1981 [1898]), and E.E. Evans-Pritchard's masterful *Nuer Religion*, (Oxford: Oxford University Press, 1956).

5. See Roy Rappaport *Pigs for the Ancestors: Ritual in the Ecology of a New Guinea People*, (New Haven: Yale University Press, 1968). Another example of a cultural ecological model applied to ritual may be found in Shirley Lindenbaum's "Sorcerors, Ghosts, and Polluting Women: an Analysis of Religious Beliefs and Population Control," *Ethnology*, vol. II, no. 3 (1972). Marvin Harris adopts a similar, "cultural materialist" perspective toward religious practices in his *Cows, Pigs, Wars and Witches*, (New York: Vintage Books, 1974).

6. See Edmund Leach "Time and False Noses." in Edmund Leach, ed., *Culture and Communication*, (Cambridge: Cambridge University Press, 1976).

7. For staple works in the work of Claude Lévi-Strauss addressing ritual, see *The Savage Mind*, (Chicago: University of Chicago, 1966), and *Tristes Tropiques*, (Paris: Plon, 1955).

8. On Clifford Geertz's analysis of the cockfight see his edited volume *The Interpretation of Cultures: Selected Essays*, (New York: Basic Books, 1973).

9. On Leach's quote see reference in endnote 6, pp. 81-82.

10. See Arnold Van Gennep *The Rites of Passage*, (Chicago: University of Chicago Press, 1960 [1909]).

11. On Victor Turner's work on the Ndembu see Victor Turner, *The Forest of Symbols: Aspects of Ndembu Ritual*, (Ithaca: Cornell University Press, 1967).

12. See Mary Douglas *Purity and Danger*,(New York: Praeger Press, 1960).

13. Another well-known approach to the interpretation of circumcision is that of Bruno Bettleheim's psychoanalytical analysis in *Symbolic Wounds: Puberty Rites and the Envious Male,*(London: Thames and Hudson, 1955). Bettleheim argues that male initiation rites stem from a desire to alleviate fear and envy of women resulting from women's capacity to bear children. Circumcision therefore may be seen, according to Bettleheim, as an attempt to imitate female genital functioning and appropriate women's procreative power.

14. See Jean Comaroff in Jean and Joahn Comaroff, *Modernity and its Malcontents: Ritual and Power in Postcolonial Africa*, (Chicago: University of Chicago Press, 1993). Other works adopting a similar "body-centered" perspective in the analysis of ritual are Janice Boddy's *Wombs and Alien Spirits: Women, Men, and the Zar Cult in Northern Sudan*, (Madison: University of Wisconsin Press, 1989), Dick Hebdige's *Subculture: The Meaning of Style*, (London: Routledge 1979), and Stuart Hall and Tony Jefferson, eds., *Resistance through Rituals:Youth Subcultures in Post-War Britain*, (London: Hutchinson and Company, 1976).

15. See Max Gluckman "Rituals of Rebellion in South East Africa." in Max Gluckman, *Order and Rebellion in Tribal Africa: Collected Essays*, (London: Routledge and Kegan Paul, 1963).

16. See Bruce Kapferer's *A Celebration of Demons*, (Bloomington: Indiana University Press, 1983).

17. Other"performative" approaches to ritual may be found in Stanley Tambiah's essay (above), J.L. Austin *How To Do things With Words*, (Oxford: Oxford University Press, 1962), Erving Goffman's *Interaction Ritual: Essays in Face-to- Face Behavior*, (New York: Doubleday, 1967), Victor Turner's *Dramas', Fields and Metaphors*, (Ithaca: Cornell University Press, 1974), and *From Ritual to Theater: The Human Seriousness of Play*, (New York:Performing Arts Journal Publications, 1982), Dan Ben-Amos and Kenneth S. Goldstein, eds., *Folklore: Performance and Communication*, (The Hague: Mouton, 1975), Sally F. Moore and Barbara Babcock, eds., *Secular Ritual*, (Assen, Netherlands, Van Gorcum, 1977); Richard Schechner and Willa Appel, eds., *By Means of Performance: Intercultural Studies of Theatre and Ritual*, (Cambridge: Cambridge University Press 1989), Johannes Fabian, *Power and Performance: Ethnographic Explorations through Proverbial Wisdom and Theatre in Shaba, Zaire*, (Madison: University of Wisconsin Press, 1989),

Edward Scheiffelin "Performance and the Cult Construction of Reality," *American Ethnologist*, 12:707-24, 1985, Jane Cowan *Dance and the Body Politic in Rural Greece*, (Princeton: Princeton University Press, 1990), and Corinne Kratz *Affecting Performance: Meaning, Movement and Experience in Okiek Women's Ritual* (Washington, DC: Smithsonian, 1994).

18. See Kristin Norget "Beauty and the Feast: Aesthetics and the Performance of Meaning in the Day of the Dead in Oaxaca, Mexico," *Journal of Latin American Lore* 19: 53-64, 1996.

19. See Richard Schechner "Ritual and Performance," in Tim Ingold, ed., *Companion Encyclopedia of Anthropology*, (London: Routledge, 1995).

20. See endnote 11.

21. Works addressing the cultural importance of political ritual include Max Gluckman *Essays on the Ritual of Social Relations*, (Manchester: Manchester University Press, 1962); David Kertzer *Ritual, Politics and Power*, (New Haven: Yale University Press, 1988); Steven Lukes "Political Ritual and Social Integration," in *Sociology: Journal of the Bristish Sociological Association* 9, no. 2 (1975), 289-308; Sally F. Moore and Barbara G. Myerhoff (above); Crystal Lane *The Rites of Rulers*, (Cambridge: Cambridge University Press 1981); David Cannadine and Simon Price *Rituals of Royalty: Power and Communication in Traditional Societies*, (Cambridge: Cambridge University Press, 1987).

22. See Steven Lukes *Power: A Radical View*, (New York: MacMillan, 1974).

23. See Robert Bellah "Civil Religion in America," in *Daedalus*, 96: 1-21, 1967.

24. For Catherine Bell see endnote 2. For more discussion of the role of ritual in the invention of tradition, see Eric Hobsbawm and Terence Ranger's *The Invention of Tradition*, (Cambridge: Cambridge University Press, 1983), and Richard Handler *Nationalism and the Politics of Culture in Quebec*, (Madison: University of Wisconsin, 1988).

25. See Maurice Bloch, ed., *Political Language and Oratory in Traditional Society*. (New York: Academic Press, 1975).

26. See Gluckman reference in endnote 15.

27. See Abner Cohen *Two-Dimensional Man*, (London: Routledge and Kegan Paul, 1974).

28. See endnote 14.

29. See Natalie Zemon-Davis *Society and Culture in Early Modern France*, (Stanford: Stanford University Press, 1965). There is a wealth of literature on popular festivities, social revolts, and symbolic inversion. Other useful resources are Mikhail Bakhtin's classic work *Rabelais and His World*, translated, Helene Iswolski, (Bloomington: Indiana Univeristy Press, 1988); Barbara Babcock, ed., *The Reversible World: Symbolic Inversion in Art and Society*, (Ithaca: Cornell University Press, 1978); Michael D. Bristol's *Carnival and Theater*, (London: Routledge, 1985); James C. Scott, *Weapons of the Weak: Everyday Forms of Peasant Resistance*, (New Haven: Yale University Press, 1985). Important works on millenarian movements include Anthony Wallace's "Revitalization Movements," *American Anthropologist*, LVIII (956), Kenelm Burridge's *New Heaven: New Earth*, (London: Basil Blackwell, 1969), and Vittorio Lanternari's *Religions of the Oppressed*, (New York: Mentor Books, 1965).

Six

Shamanisms:
Past and Present

David Kozak
Fort Lewis College

For centuries, the exotic and romantic image and story line of the shaman as a religious virtuoso who takes magical, hallucinatory flights into the supernatural world, learning from or skirmishing with animal spirits and human ghosts, capturing and returning lost souls, and dwelling in a nether world of trance and ecstacy, has dominated both the scholarly and popular imaginations. The shaman has been perceived and represented as the prototypic, primordial religious practitioner who has direct contact with the supernatural, nonordinary realm of the phantasmic, a perception that has led to the widespread assumption that this is the central defining characteristic of this specialist. Along these lines, the shaman is viewed by some—in the past and in the present—as representative of a person who pursues an "authentic" religious experience and who consider shamanism as an "authentic" religious system when compared to various "inauthentic" institutionalized world religions. This often exotic and romantic image of shamans and shamanisms misrepresents or at least it misunderstands them. And importantly, if not ironically, to understand shamans and shamanisms we must look to ourselves and the stories we have told and continue to tell about them.

The study of shamans and shamanisms has been plagued with a number of conceptual problems. At root is the ethnographic-based difficulty in creating a satisfactory standardized definition. This is because, on the one hand, shamanisms are highly diverse, culturally and historically relative phenomena, encompassing a vast array of social behaviors and beliefs. On the other hand, it is possible to identify shared or perhaps core shamanic phenomena. Yet, to pin a tidy label and definition on what shamanism is, is to risk the social scientific sin of overly particularizing or generalizing a constellation of behaviors and beliefs. Another problem relates to how the shaman's psychological and phenomenological status has taken precedence in the literature. Central to this precedence is the interest in what is today called Altered States of Consciousness (ASC), the affective, inspirational, emotional, and ecstatic states experienced by many shamans. This emphasis is problematic because it largely ignores the very real problems of social history that place each shamanism in context and the individual culture history that drives the transformations that all individual shamanisms experience. While ASC is certainly important, it is debatable that it should be taken as an unproblematic feature of shamanisms. Finally, and related to the emphasis on ASC and shaman phenomenology, is that it has contributed to a line of self-help, self-actualization "New Age," neo-shamanism literature that often bears surprisingly little resemblance to what the ethnographic record tells us of indigenous forms of shamanism.

In this essay I propose to work backwards in that I will begin with a general discussion of the difficulties with the conflation of scholarly and popular writings and perceptions of shamanisms in the present. I then move toward providing a rough working definition and general description of shamanism. How anthropologists and other scholars explain shamanism is outlined prior to my offering three ethnographic (particularistic) case studies. I trust that the case-study approach that focusses on cultural particulars will demonstrate the difficulties inherent in defining the generalities of this subject matter. Moreover, my selection of case studies is intended to juxtapose the so-called "classical" Siberian shamanism with how colonialism, global capitalization, and Christian missionization have differentially affected Tohono O'odham and Putumayo shamanisms. This essay is not intended to be comprehensive—a perhaps impossible task. However, refer to Jane M. Atkinson and Joan B. Townsend for excellent literature reviews and discussions of the relevant issues.[1] Here I offer a more modest goal: to provide the reader a basis for exploring and learning more about this most important religious phenomenon.

THE STORIES WE TELL

Shamans and shamanic traditions continue to captivate both the scholarly and popular consciousness. This captivation has run and continues to run the gamut of admiration to condemnation, acceptance to persecution, emulation to fear. While it may sound strange, shamans and shamanisms as we know them are in part the rhetorical inventions of the Western intellectual and popular cultural imaginations. Oftentimes the stories that outsiders to shamanic traditions tell about them are based less in empirical reality than in the storyteller's own assumptions, stereotypes, desires and expectations about what they themselves want from the exotic "other." The inaccuracies in these stories have less to do with cultural secrecy or of shamans intentionally misleading anthropologists than with the author's failure to appropriately document the phenomena. Perhaps such ill-informed storytelling is innocuous enough, but it is frequently the case that such storytelling serves political, cultural, social, "racial," even personal ends, from the usurping of sacred cultural traditions for personal needs at one end of a continuum to outright state-level political repression, domination, and oppression at the other end. Moreover, shamanism has served as a multivocal symbol for social, political, and religious purposes of the West. For instance, in the past, animistic religions were viewed by late nineteenth-century social evolutionists (e.g., E.B. Tylor, Sir James Frazer) as occupying an inferior or impoverished level of religious evolution and achievement, far behind the assumed superiority of monotheism found in the "civilized" West. Juxtaposed to this unfavorable view, shamanism is today frequently adopted by people who are unhappy with institutionalized and patriarchal Christianity. In the United States, the "New Age," neo-shamanism, and self-actualization movements make much use of shamanic (tribal) symbolism and ideas, taken largely out of context, in order to cobble together a personal religious belief system and ritual practice that satisfies the individual's needs. Whether historically or contemporarily, shamanism is often uncritically evoked as either impoverished as a pagan and archaic religious expression or exalted as the solution to contemporary human ecological, existential, and personal crises.

Anthropologists early recognized the importance of shamanism in human religious history and cultures and have formulated various explanations and interpretations. The explanatory and interpretive stories that anthropologists tell include evolutionary, functional, structural, psychological, Marxist, cultural and political-economic strategies. And while the emphasis of shamanistic research has been on the shaman as healer, as bridge between this and other worlds, as individual, as an evolutionary type, a more recent trend has emerged with an emphasis on the role of the shaman and shamanisms as parts of larger political, historical, and economic contexts in the burgeoning global political economy. Various anthropologists have rightly criticized the emphasis that had been placed on such things as the distinctions made between the so-called "classical" shamans of Siberia and all others, the affective and hallucinatory states that shamans experience, the abnormal personality traits supposedly exhibited by individual shamans, and so on. The emphasis has also been on the universal characteristics shared by shamans and shamanistic systems. In response to the bulk of the literature, some anthropologists have gone so far as to say that "shamanism" is an invented and contentious category of disparate items, ripped out of context, artificially if artfully associated and all of it dreamed up in the West with little basis in reality.[2]

As indicated, anthropologists are not the only ones who find shamanisms of interest. In fact, the scholarly and the popular images merge with shamanism. Today there is a burgeoning popular, nonacademic and practitioner-based interest in shamans, and particularly in their altered states of consciousness, and ultimately in self-help and self-actualization as grounded frequently in Jungian psychology. And while the self-actualization approach is largely denigrated by anthropologists as opportunistic, superficial, and self-serving in its treatment of shamanism, it was originally anthropologists who promoted, if indirectly, the current popularity. It is reasonable to say that the current popular and self-help interest of the neo-shamanism, New Age, and self-actualization movements stem from the publications of anthropologists Carlos Casteñada, Ake Hultkrantz, and Michael Harner, and the religious historian Mircea Eliade.[3] There is a distinct romanticizing and exoticizing of shamanism in their publications which appeals to a consumer group who feels that their lives as members of Western industrial societies are vacuous and that institutional forms of religion are inauthentic. In this literature, whether stated implicitly or not, shamanism offers what is believed to be an authentic method for establishing a relation between the individual and the natural and supernatural worlds.

The overarching rhetorical strategy used by the aforementioned authors is what I call the "shaman-as-hero" archetype, as the striving, seeking, brave, self-assured individual (the image is usually male). With not a little irony, this shaman-as-hero is transformed by such speculations and interpretations into the quintessential laissez-faire "self-made man," the rugged individualist-equivalent of the non-Western, "primitive" world. In other words, the shaman becomes imbued with the idealistic Western characteristics of hyper-individualism in order to better correspond to the lives of people who wish to use shamanism for their own psychic and spiritual needs, rather than for understanding the shaman on his or her own cultural terms. The shaman-as-hero archetype and hero rhetoric, as rugged individualist, thus become acceptable and appropriable. But in this process, the shaman becomes yet another commodity for consumer culture. Herein lies the crux of the storytelling quandary.

The shaman has been used to tell stories distinctly not of the shaman's making. Rather, the stories often tell as much if not more about the tellers of scholarly or popular culture stories. All such characterizations are deeply flawed as they neglect to account for the social context in which all shamans are a part. Shamanism is nothing, after all, if not a community-centered activity. What lacks in much of the literature on shamanisms is an appreciation for the social, political, historical, gendered, and economic contexts that shamans participate in. The struggles of shamans with other shamans, with other villagers, and with outside forces have significantly modified their cultures and religious practices. And the danger of representing the shaman as the rugged individual hero and archetype is that shamanism is trivilized, reduced to a caricature, and is literally eviscerated of its social meaning and context. This trivilization, of course, serves an important storytelling purpose: It affords outsiders easy access to the complex traditions of shamanism without forcing them to understand the intricacies of context or to become part of a community where shamanism is only a fraction of a much larger social and cultural whole. Importantly, it allows the storyteller's imagination to conjure and speculate freely; shamanism as aesthetics rather than science. But this is ideally not what the anthropological study of shamans and shamanisms is about. Rather, anthropologists wish to understand and perhaps partly explain some of the phenomena associated with this compelling and important social role and religious practice. Anthropological understanding is gained up close, through fieldwork observation and participation, through learning the language of the shaman's community, and distinctly not from a "safe" distance where insight derives from one's own imaginative flights of fancy or creative speculation.

DEFINING SHAMANISMS

Defining shamans and shamanisms is not an easy task. In fact, shamanism is truly many things to many people. For myself, I would prefer to avoid making categorical or definitional statements altogether. Yet it is reasonably possible to make a few general statements about shamans and shamanisms. Realize, however, that generalizations on this subject are tentative and any claim must be viewed and evaluated in the context of ethnographic data.

Let us begin by saying that a shaman is a ritualist who is able to divine, predict, and effect future outcomes, provide medical care, who is believed to have direct access to the supernatural, phantasmic realm, and who gains his or her powers and abilities by being tutored by spirits including deceased ancestors. Shamans are frequently skilled orators or singers. The social role of the shaman is often the only or one of only a few distinct social roles available in the culture. This general definition of the shaman shares characteristics with other ritualists known variously as medicine man, medium, spirit or faith healer, priest, oracle, witch doctor, among others.

Origins of Shamanism. For many anthropologists today the origins of shamanism is a moot question because it must remain largely conjectural reconstruction and is ultimately unprovable. Despite this, hypothesizing and research continue. Siberian and Arctic shamanism is considered by some to be the original source and prototypic form of shamanism in the world. The word "shaman" was originally derived from the Tungus (a central Siberian tribe) word *saman,* with the English word shaman being derived from the German noun *der schaman.* Others argue that Tungus shamanism was itself influenced by Buddhism. For this latter suggestion a linguistic affiliation has been explored with the Sanskrit word *sramana,* which translates as "one who practices austerities." Siberian origin also relates to the Bering Straights land bridge hypothesis which explains the peopling of the New World. This hypothesis is widely accepted by archaeologists and argues that the ancestors of today's native Americans migrated from Northern Asia to North America, bringing their religious and shamanic practices with them. This diaspora hypothesis is based on linguistic and physiological data and partly on the similar, cross culturally shared shamanic practices which indicate a common heritage.[4]

Ancient rock art has produced some of the more intriguing sources of data and interpretation regarding the origins question. Several researchers suggest that some rock art styles are actually the renderings of the shaman's altered states of consciousness and of the shamanic cosmos dating to as long ago as 8,000 to 25,000 years. Rock art data suggesting paleolithic origins derive from Lascaux cave paintings in France, southern Africa, and the British Isles and are based on neurologically based entoptic phenomenon. Entoptic phenomena are those visual phenomena that people see while experiencing various altered states of consciousness, visual phenomena that are argued to follow distinctive pan-human patterns and forms. It is claimed that these visual forms and patterns were then chiseled or painted on stone and were used as sacred mnemonic and didactic devices. Moreover, it is argued that shamanistic power came to reside in the shaman's ability to control such altered states and visions and the creation of sacred images.[5]

While it is not possible to know the absolute origins of shamanism, interesting research and hypothesizing continue to be accomplished. The assumption that Siberian shamanism is prototypical and diffused outward, as with all origin theories, must be viewed with a healthy skepticism. The fact that cultures change, adapting and culling beliefs and practices, in myriad patterns, it becomes impossible to pinpoint the genesis of the shamanic science and art.

Where shamanisms are found. Shamans and shamanisms are found throughout North and South America, Siberia, parts of Asia, Polynesia, and Africa, virtually throughout the entire world. The ethnographic record reveals that shamanisms are related to a variety of levels of social structure. Gatherer-hunter, egalitarian populations like the San of southern Africa are the most likely to possess a shamanistic system. Yet, pastoralists like the Tungus of Siberia or the Somali of northeastern Africa and agriculturalists like the Pima of southern Arizona also have shamanic traditions. Recent studies of highly stratified, state-level systems of governing, as in Korea, have also documented the presence of shamanistic systems. Therefore, much of where we find shamanisms depends on how shamans are defined. Gatherer-hunter populations are largely egalitarian with minor status differentiation who subsist on a diet characterized by feast-and-famine food availability which radically fluctuates throughout the yearly cycle. The shaman's role in an often tenuous subsistence setting, for example, is that of mediator between his or her village and the environment where they live and the spirit forces that control food and water availability. The shaman divines to locate game animals and to diagnose and cure spirit sicknesses, soul loss, and sorcery malevolence. Spirit-caused sicknesses are frequently the result of human inattention to or disrespect for the spirit and natural worlds.

Shamanic Cosmos. The cosmos is frequently, though not always, divided into a series of horizontally stacked layers, three or more. Humans occupy a middle earth level that is loosely demarcated by permeable boundaries by upper and lower spirit worlds. The upper and lower worlds are nonphysical in character and accessible only through spiritual means. The various levels are linked and readily accessible to shamans. The spirit worlds are sources of power for human benefit. A version of "balance" between these worlds is the desired state and it is the shaman whose job it is to maintain this balance. Imbalances are manifested in humans as illnesses, or in the lack of game animals, or in natural disasters. As in the human world, so too in the spirit world, there is an emphasis on reciprocity with the spirits who inhabit the supernatural realm. A shaman's job is to keep the spirits happy or at least mollified and fellow villagers healthy. The afterlife locality is conceived of as either an improved version of the human community or an ill-defined place. It is usually not a location of punishment or reward for a person's actions in life. The concept of sin seems to be absent. Spirits, including human ghosts or ancestors, may be malevolent, benevolent, both, or benign. In any case, spirits have a significant impact on the human community.

A Shaman's Training. Direct contact with spirits is a universal feature of the shaman's practice. A shaman's contact with spirits makes the power from the other nonearthly cosmos layers accessible to a larger community of people in the middle earth level. A shaman is taught this power by a spirit(s) and the teaching consists of learning songs, chants, speeches, ritual techniques, and in the construction and use of shaman's tools such as a drum or other musical instruments, clothing, smoke, feathers, rattles, and crystals. A shaman ideally uses this supernatural knowledge and power to aid his or her community members' health and well-being, although shamans are also able to use this power to harm other humans. Frequently, a shaman has the ability for soul flight, or at the very least the shaman is capable of making nocturnal journeys as guided by spirit tutelaries.

A shaman may inherit his or her abilities or be selected by spirits to accept this important social responsibility. A person may be approached by spirits as a child or at any time in one's life for that matter. Often, the selection occurs during an acute or trying period in a person's life such as psychological stress, physical illness, accident, or a "near death" experience. A person often has the choice of accepting or rejecting a spirit's advances, and the shaman role. If a person accepts a spirit's advances, the spirit(s) will tutor their pupil in the shamanic sciences during nocturnal dreams or in hallucinatory or trance-induced states. A shaman's training is a lifelong process and a shaman's abilities and effectiveness may wax and wane over a lifetime.

States of Consciousness. The literature is crowded with discussions of the shaman's altered state of consciousness, Shamanic State of Consciousness (SSC), magic flight, trance, hallucinatory, inspirational, and ecstatic abilities. Made famous by Mircea Eliade, the shaman's ecstasy has come largely to define—as discussed above—much of what we think of as quintessentially shamanic. Altered states of consciousness are either induced with hallucinogenic plants, including fungi, or with nonhallucinogenic alcoholic drinks, tobacco smoke, hyperventilation, meditation, and rhythmic drumming. It is not the altered state per se that is important but rather the communication that the altered state facilitates between spirit-animal and shaman or shaman and the lost soul that he or she searches for. As mentioned above, the altered state is also a time when the shaman is tutored by spirits.

Sacramental Actions. Blowing, sucking, singing, massaging, spitting, smudging, painting, chanting, touching, fanning, seeing, and sprinkling water, ashes, and corn meal are all sacramental actions used by shamans as taught to them by spirit tutelaries. By sacramental I mean how a shaman uses his soul, augmented by the soul(s) of his spirit helpers or tutelaries and tools (i.e., feathers, water, smoke, peyote, or other hallucinogens) to positively affect the soul of a patient and/or of an entire community. The sacramental act of blowing, for instance, may come in the form of singing songs to patients, reciting chants to spirits, or even of blowing cigarette smoke over a patient to illuminate embedded sickness or discover the location of sorcery objects. A sacrament's performative intent is to improve the living condition of a person or of a community through sacredly endowed actions: blessings made physically manifest for all to see. A shaman's sacramental actions are always for good; in comparison, sorcery could be classified as an antisacramental act.

Shamanic Discourses. The verbalizations of shamans provide a rich avenue for understanding shamanism. Songs, chants, narratives, and verbal explanations given by shamans are ways to examine the internal and cultural dimensions and perceptions held by practitioners themselves. This area of research is perhaps the most challenging for an anthropologist as it demands the researcher to possess a firm grasp of the shaman's own language.[6] Text transcription and translation become central in this work and interpretations and explanations of a single or a few key words may be the foundation for an entire study. A rich corpus of song and chant texts has revealed the art of various shamanisms, but also the meaning and centrality of shamanic discourses in the work of healing or divining.

Empirical Observations. Since the social evolutionist E.B. Tylor's time (late 1800s), some anthropologists have argued that religious beliefs and practices are ultimately based in people's systematic observations of the sentient world around them. Empirical observations of the physical world serve as a template for their ultimate conceptions of the soul, human body, the sacred, and the role of religious belief in human affairs. Furthermore, people are also astute observers of human-animal and human-plant interactions. As such, the empirical observations and experiments that people conduct in their natural world serve as the basis for their public and private religious lives.

EXPLAINING SHAMANISMS

Anthropologists use various theoretical orientations to understand and explain the shamanism phenomenon. I will briefly discuss two general orientations: the psychological-physiological and the political-economic. This brief discussion lumps together general tendencies and the two theoretical categories could be divided in other ways.

Psychology and Physiology. The belief that shamans are mentally ill, who suffer from neuroses, psychoses, or schizophrenia, has roots in the eighteenth century. During that time shamanic practices competed, if indirectly, with the ascendancy of rationalist principles being developed with the scientific revolution. At the time, inspirationally or mythically based ways of knowing were being systematically discredited as irrational and as nonsense. The shaman as crazy person penetrated well into the twentieth century with anthropologists such as A.L. Kroeber, Ralph Linton, and A.F.C. Wallace. These anthropologists, using one or another psychoanalytic theory, concluded that the shaman and potential shamans suffer from a number of severe mental or physical complaints. Kroeber (1952) went so far as to say that so-called primitive cultures not only condoned but exalted psychotic behavior, that the shaman's claim to see and deal with spirits was nothing other than a delusional psychopathology. The mental illness theory of the shaman persisted until the 1960s when counter-arguments mounted against this unfortunate interpretation. By the late 1960s shaman's behaviors were considered psychologically normal. And as Jane M. Atkinson has pointed out, the change of attitude that occurred in the 1960s toward shamanic psychology and behavior was affected by changing notions of consciousness in general spurred on by hallucinogenic-modified consciousness in particular and the effectiveness of shamanism as psychotherapy in general.[7]

The continued interest in the psychic states of shamans, anthropologists and other behavioralist researchers, wishing to ground their work on a scientific footing, developed their research around the concept of altered states of consciousness or shamanic states of consciousness. The emphasis of this research is on the phenomenological experience of the practitioner, the crossculturally shared trance-state characteristics, and more recently an interest in the neurophysiological bases of ASC. Of note in this regard are studies related to the role of endorphins and other chemicals released in the brain during rituals. More recently is an interest in what Michael Winkelman calls "neurognostic structures" of the psyche. He argues that shamanism is a biologically based transpersonal mode of consciousness.[8] It is suggested that the capacity for shamanic behavior—that is, trance and vision flights—is a biologically based memory device of sorts, a shamanistic equivalent of a Chomskyan "deep structure" of linguistic ability or a Jungian "archetype" of collective consciousness, whereby shamanic behavior is a hard-wired and universal human characteristic and is evidenced in the similarities shared by shamans in vastly different cultures.

Politics, Economics, and History. Complementing the biological- and psychological-based explanations for shamanism is a recent interest in the political, historical, and economic factors related to shamans, cultures with shamanic systems, and how these relate to state-level and global capitalist structures of power and institutionalized religions. This interest area reflects a general trend in anthropology that emphasizes historical and political economic factors.

Foremost in this approach is an appreciation for how shamanisms have been affected by various state, economic, and institutionalized religious structures. Due to the impacts of colonialism and neo-colonialism, the historical and political economic approach takes for granted that much of what we know of as shamanism today is the result of contact and change initiated by institutions stemming from the West. The implication is that to understand shamanism we must also understand how the structures of power have been manifested at the local level. Thus, much of the published work stemming from this general orientation takes change as inevitable, that shaman-ic-oriented cultures have been victimized, and that the search for pristine and "authentic" versions of shamanisms is fallacious and naíve. In response to the psychological-physiological approaches, to understand shaman psychology, ASC, and ritual actions, the researcher must be rigorous in defining the social, political, and economic context(s) in which individual shamanisms are expressed. Thus, this general approach emphasizes the social rather than the individual, the historical rather than the immediate, the cultural rather than the psychological, and the relations of power rather than altered states.[9]

The primary drawback to this general political economy orientation is that it may sacrifice the richness of local-level interpretations and individualistic articulations for its emphasis on structure, history, and power relations. Real people are often lost in a maze of political and economic and historic factors that seemingly override the agency of individual actors.

In sum, the theories that anthropologists use to explain or interpret shaman-isms are of necessity incomplete. This is because human experience is far more complex and rich than our abstractions of it. Thus, our theories are ways to assist our comprehension of a culturally rich realm of humanness and each theory tends to priv-ilege partial elements of that richness.

THREE CASE STUDIES

Ethnographic description, the product of intensive fieldwork conducted by an an-thropologist who lives for an extended time with the people being studied, is crucial to the work of sociocultural anthropologists. The ethnographic method is perhaps the superior way for understanding shamanisms and it also offers the potential for a critical appraisal and reevaluation of past storytelling inaccuracies and excesses re-garding the study of shamanisms around the world. Because the fieldwork experience demands that the anthropologist live among and participate in the subject's com-munity life and have a familiarity with the host culture's language, the anthropo-logical perspective holds out promise for a nuanced understanding and documentation to be found in this religious-medicinal practice. It is also a valuable source for critiquing the frequently problematic categories, analyses, and assumptions made by outside observers of shamanic phenomena. To illustrate this point and pres-ent a fragment of the diversity of shamanisms found in the world today, and to demonstrate its range of applicability, I here offer three case studies of shamanism in Northern Asia, North America, and South America. The case studies reveal that shamanisms are a complex interweaving of cultural practices, gifted individual prac-titioners, political economic issues, and ASC. They reveal how shamanisms change, how they are influenced by the institutionalized religions like Christianity, and by global capitalism and social change. Each case study demonstrates in its own way how the category of a generalized shamanism is a theoretical oversimplification at best and that shamanisms undergo change and modification to fit the needs of a people.

Siberian Shamanisms

Siberian shamanism is often referred to as the "classical" form that used to exist. Mircea Eliade made Siberian shamanism famous and identified it by their exotic and mystical rituals and costumes, hallucinations, trances, the mastering of spirits, and cosmic travels. Since Eliade's work, many shamanisms have been evaluated and compared with it. As Caroline Humphrey [10] has pointed out, Eliade's characterization is seriously flawed as it lacks social and historical context. Moreover, she criticizes Eliade's representations for effectively crystallizing the current belief in the context-free view of shamanism as a mysterious and purely inspirational phenomenon. In order to offer a context to Siberian shamanism I draw extensively from the research of Roberte Hamayon. [11]

According to Hamayon there are two primary types of Siberian shamanism: hunting and pastoral. Each corresponds to distinct social organizational forms, economic, and political characteristics. Siberian "hunting shamanism" is present in tribal, noncentralized, forest-dwelling societies like the Chugchee. Hunting shamanism is characteristic of the form Eliade spoke of in his writings. "Pastoral shamanism" as found among the Tungus is characterized by people who are patrilineal and patrilocal, who domesticate livestock, and live in regions that border the forest and steppe regions. A potential third type, what Hamayon calls "peripheral shamanism," is only marginally identifiable as shamanism as it is related to state formation and how the traditional shaman's role and power were usurped by Lamaist Buddhist lamas and through the decentralization and feminization of the shaman's role in Siberian shamanic societies. With state formation, institutional religion gains power and pushes traditional inspirational religious practices and beliefs to the margins of society where women may become shamans as men become Buddhist lamas. In many ways state or institutionalized religion delegitimizes shamanism.

The fundamental element of "hunting shamanism" is that spirits of animal species are contacted directly by a shaman who makes compacts with them in order to supply humans with good luck at hunting. The divinely inspired and experienced shaman-spirit compacts assure food availability for human consumption. This compact is not conceived as one-sided in that while animal spirits supply humans with food through hunting successes, the other half of the compact is that humans will eventually supply the spirits with human flesh and blood. Such is the source and cause of much human sickness and death. The task, however, is for the shaman to limit the amount of human sickness and death while maximizing the amount of animal flesh available for human consumption. A shaman's success at this depends on another kind of compact: that of his ritual marriage to the daughter of the game spirit (an elk or reindeer spirit).

The exchanges and compacts established between spirit-animals and humans make them trading partners in an ongoing economic and social relationship. The relationship is a form of generalized reciprocity where the exchanges are never equally balanced and immediate in return. Rather, delayed and nonequivalent exchanges keep the relationship alive and in need of continual tinkering by the shaman and spir-it(s). To balance out their reciprocity would mean an end to their relationship. Thus, a shaman's power resides in his ability to maintain this reciprocity. His authority in the human community, therefore, stems from his usefulness to his peers, in the shaman's ability to secure a plentiful supply of game animals while minimizing sick-ness and death.

The human-animal compacts—of food and marriage—serve as the model of so-cial organization. The dualistic spirit-human relationship is replicated in human-an-imal relations and in the human kinship system of moieties or clan subdivisions. Here, too, in the human world of marriage alliances, society is predicated on com-pacts between moieties just as the shaman makes compacts with the animal-spirit world.

Reliance on the domestication of animals (pastoralism) presents a second type of Siberian shamanism and is related to alterations in inheritance patterns which are linked to changes in social organization which is in turn linked to a transforma-tion in conceptions of the supernatural. With "pastoral shamanism," no longer does food flow directly from compacts made in the supernatural world but it instead de-rives from various locations in the observable environment where grazing and herd-ing occur. For the Tungus, pasturage is associated with patrilineal descent groups (in this case, clan segments), and nearby mountains become the locations where an-cestors reside after death. Patrilocal residence becomes important and land or pas-ture inheritance follows the male line. Sickness is no longer caused by animal spirits but is associated with transgressions of patrilineal kinship rules and by one's ances-tral spirits. Pastoral shamans do not make compacts with spirit animals, nor do they ritually marry the daughter of the game spirit as food comes from other sources. Here the shaman's role changes in that it is entrusted with ensuring the fertility of both the domesticated animals and human villagers. Pastoralist shamans are related to tribal mythology where the shaman is synonymous with the tribal founder.

Here we see that even the classic Siberian shamanism takes several forms. Im-portantly, the forms are related to the mode of subsistence, social organization, res-idence patterns, and whether the shaman has intimate contact with animal spirits or deceased ancestor spirits who participate with the shaman in ongoing reciprocal exchanges.

Tohono O'odham Christian-Shamanism[12]

The Tohono O'odham (formerly known as Papago) of southern Arizona and north-ern Sonora, Mexico, were gatherer-hunters and horticulturalists until the early part of the twentieth century. This form of shamanism is comparable to the hunting shamanism of Siberia. Their subsistence strategy made the best of an existence in the heart of the Sonoran Desert where scarce and unpredictable rainfall made growing corn, beans, and squash very tenuous. Despite this, O'odham subsistence practices emphasized the importance of rain and crop production. In fact, O'odham ritual life—both individual and public—centered around moisture. The public ritual of the annual rain ceremony focused the community's religious sentiments on secur-ing adequate moisture for plant, animal, and human consumption.

Village well-being was symbolized by sufficient rainfall, and the village shaman was in part responsible for securing it. Shamans worked together to sing for, divine, and encourage the rains to fall. They directed the annual rain festivities by overseeing the production of a mildly intoxicating wine brewed from the syrup of saguaro cactus fruits. During the rain dance ceremony, shamans from various villages gave speeches and sang songs to attract the rain clouds from the "rain houses" positioned at the cardinal directions. The proper execution of the ceremony secured the ultimate fertility of the natural and human worlds.

The other central role of O'odham shamans was to diagnose a series of sicknesses unique to the O'odham people. Until the middle of the twentieth century it was thought in O'odham cosmology and medical theory that there were approximately 50 "staying sicknesses" (only O'odham contract them) that were caused by the spirit protectors of various animal-persons (e.g., deer, badger, coyote), insect-persons (e.g., fly, butterfly), natural phenomena-persons (e.g., wind, lightning), humans (e.g., ghosts, prostitutes), plant-persons (e.g., peyote, jimson weed), reptile-persons (e.g., rattle snake, chuckwalla), and bird-persons (e.g., eagle, owl, swallow) species. Being sickened is the result of a human's impropriety or disrespect toward or transgression on the integrity of the spirit species. The person does not know the moment that sickness is contracted, but once symptoms emerge, the person consults a shaman for diagnosis. Once diagnosed, which can take a quick or a protracted form, the person is instructed to have the appropriate curing songs sung for them.

A shaman's ability to diagnose, and to cure, derives from spirit helpers who tutor the shaman during nighttime dreams. Thus spirits both cause sicknesses and provide the means for their cure. This tutoring takes the form of learning songs that are authored and sung by the spirit species to the shaman who memorizes them verbatim. The songs are densely meaningful, haiku-like poems that tell brief stories of experiences that the shaman has had with the spirit, present images of a landscape, or are statements about the quirkiness of the spirit itself.

This version of O'odham shamanism has been modified during the past three hundred years of contact with Spanish, then Mexican, and finally with American colonizers and Catholic missionaries. Catholicism has made significant inroads in O'odham religious culture since their early contact with the Jesuit priest Eusebio Kino in the late 1690s. Catholicism continues to be a strong element of O'odham identity. Another significant source of change came with the introduction of cattle into the U.S. Southwest regional economy. The external influences of Catholicism and cattle capitalism prompted changes in O'odham shamanism in several ways. First, shamans gained power from Christian deities as spirit tutelaries, primarily the saints, but Jesus and God also, just as they did from the traditional spirit-beings. As the O'odham adopted Catholic public rituals and theological beliefs, and as they began to adopt saints for village patrons and for individuals, people began to be sickened by these Christian spirits in a manner similar to that described above. Saint sickness became an illness diagnosed and treated by shamans.

Second, the O'odham also began, by the late 1880s, to be sickened by the instruments of frontier capitalism—cattle and horses (known collectively as devil sickness). O'odham readily adopted a cowboy lifestyle and are still cattle ranchers to this day. Here too O'odham shamans became charged with the responsibility of contending with the new contagions. Today, devil sickness is thought by some O'od-ham to be the most commonly diagnosed staying sickness.

Saint and devil sicknesses in the O'odham theory of sickness and cure represent what I call Christian-shamanism. Not only do shamans continue to use the traditional tools of tobacco smoke, eagle and owl feathers, and crystals to augment their power in diagnostic sessions, but many shamans also use saints' images, a Christian cross, and holy water. Perhaps more telling is the fact that the Christian deities (spirits) also come to shamans in the same manner as the traditional spirits—in dreams, singing and tutoring their human pupils in the diagnostic healing art and science.

Christian-shamanism can be understood as a manifestation of significant political, religious, and economic changes that affected this culture. For the O'odham, shamanism has been effectively used to attend to and ameliorate the changes conceived in the three-hundred-year plus period of colonization and missionization. Some might conclude that the O'odham shamanic system as described has been "corrupted" or "polluted" by the Christian influence. I do not think so, nor do I think that most O'odham think so either. In many ways, the O'odham are merely using all that is available to them to make their lives better and healthier.

Shamanism, Terror, and the Putumayo of Colombia

By the turn of the twentieth century, in the industrializing West, the demand for rubber expanded quickly. Far from the crowded cities of London, Los Angeles, Chicago, and Paris, the Putumayo Indians of the sparsely populated lowland Amazonian jungles of southern Colombia were being forcibly incorporated into the Industrial Revolution as rubber tree tappers. This incorporation was often violent and terrifying. To coerce work out of this recalcitrant labor force, the Putumayo Indians were subjected to systematic torture, murder, and sexual abuses. This troubling period in Putumayo and Colombian social history continues to haunt and permeate the present in the form of *mal aire* (evil wind)[13] and in the shamanistic beliefs and practices that heal it. Current shamanic practice can be partly understood as an attempt to ameliorate the unquiet souls of the violently tortured and murdered Putumayo Indians of the southern Amazon jungle.[14]

Michael Taussig argues in his provocative book *Shamanism, Colonialism, and the Wild Man* that contemporary *yagé* (a hallucinogenic drink) shamanism in southern Colombia is an effort to heal the tortured memories of the violently killed Putumayo Indians. Sorcery and evil air are the two sicknesses that shamans currently treat. It is the latter that stems directly from rubber tapping and Christianization. Currently, both Indians and non-Indians of the region view the ancient ones, called the Huito-to (ancestral Putumayo), as sorcerers, demonic and evil. Huitoto means "the people from below"—below the ground and below in the jungles. They were the people conquered during the Spanish conquest, people who were labeled and viewed by Europeans as evil, devil worshipping idolaters since Spanish times. The ideology of the Spanish was that they were violent, sorcerers, cannibals, and thus fearsome. This ideologically charged characterization persisted until the time of rubber exploration and production. The image of the savage other and of the wild, primordial jungles struck fear in the hearts of the rubber plantation managers. The managers saw Indian conspiracies and treachery everywhere. In their zeal to extract rubber and labor, company managers hired and trained gangs to carry out retribution stemming from their fears of the "savage" Putumayo. Rumors of the atrocities committed by the rubber companies led to an investigation and the eventual publication of Sir Roger Casement's revealing report in 1912 which substantiated the rumors' veracity.

The violent memories created in the colonial, and later the capitalist, contexts revisioned the shamanism of the region. Sickness was now thought to be caused by the evil airs emanating from below in the jungles, from the rotting evil ancestors (savages) buried beneath the ground. This miasmatic theory is perpetuated by locals, native and nonnative alike.

In this context, according to Taussig, Putumayo shamanism is above all else a healing of history, a healing of the excesses of Christian ideology and capitalist extraction. It is as if the former set the stage for the latter. Hence, for the Putumayo, shamanism is the method through which people attend to the horrific memories embedded in the history of the region. It is as if it is history-as-sorcery that today's Putumayo shamans strive to cure.

The three examples come nowhere near exhausting the possible ethnographic variation that continues to exist in the world today. Research into questions of history, global economy, and exploitation add to an already rich anthropological literature on the shaman's ASC, personality, and phenomenological characteristics. It is through a continued documentation of local expressions of shamanism, juxtaposed to macrolevel processes, that our understanding will be improved in this most dynamic arena of human spirituality.

CONCLUSION

The interest and study of shamanism has a long and often checkered history. Shamanism storytellings are varied and continue to be tightly bound to the defining culture's attitude toward indigenous peoples and their cultural practices. In the 1990s shamanisms have not only been tolerated but they have also been exulted as the true, authentic religious expression worthy of emulation. As discussed, this admiration has not always been the preferred story. Yet, this admiration, while meant with the best of intentions, must also be seen as potentially problematic, as it is yet another way people use shamanism in other than their intended contexts. And whether shamanisms are exalted or denigrated, both are equally stereotypic responses. It is my suspicion that shamans and shamanisms will continue to serve the rhetorical needs of members of Western or other dominant societies. It appears that the need for people to tell stories about other people remains strong. It also appears to matter not that the stories are only loosely, at best, based in empirical reality. And as I began this essay, it is important to remember that the stories we tell about others may say more about ourselves than about those of whom we supposedly tell the stories.

NOTES

1. The combined reviews of Jane Monnig Atkinson, "Shamanisms Today," *Annual Review of Anthropology* 21:307-330, 1992 and Joan B. Townsend, "Shamanism," in Stephan Glazier, ed., *Anthropology of Religion: A Hand-* book, (Greenwood Press, 1997), offer a wide ranging and thorough overview of the subjects.

2. Perhaps most strident in this regard is Michael Taussig, who argues in "The Nervous System: Homesickness and

Dada," *Stanford Humanities Review* 1(1):44-81, 1989, that shamanism is a "made-up," "artful reification of disparate practices" that are the creations of academic programs such as religious studies and anthropology. Much earlier, Clifford Geertz in "Religion as a Cultural System," in Michael Banton, ed., *Anthropological Approaches to the Study of Religion*, (London: Tavistock, 1966), came earlier to the same conclusion as Taussig. What Taussig and Geertz criticize are the overly large generalizations and characterizations that anthropologists and others have made of shamanisms, and, particularly for Taussig, how such characterizations reflect Western notions of religiosity.

3. Among the most influential of both anthropology and popular interest in shamanism are Eliade's *Shamanism: Archaic Techniques of Ecstacy*, (Princeton: Princeton University Press, 1964); Castañeda's *The Teachings of Don Juan: A Yaqui Way of Knowledge*, (New York: Ballantine Books, 1968); Harner's *Hallucinogens and Shamanism*, (Oxford: Oxford University Press, 1973); and Hultkrantz's various articles on the subject: "An Ecological Approach to Religion," *Ethos* 31:131-150, 1966; "Spirit Lodge: A North American Shamanistic Seance," in Carl-Martin Edsman, ed., *Studies in Shamanism*, (Stockholm: Almqvist and Wiksell, 1967); and "A Definition of Shamanism," *Temenos* 9:25-37, 1973. Of these works, it is perhaps the first two that have had the longest and most profound impact on shamanic studies in general and popular consciousness in particular.

4. Alice Kehoe in "Primal Gaia," in J. Clifton, ed., *The Invented Indian*, (Transaction Press, 1990); Michael Winkelman in "Shamans and Other 'Magico-Religious' Healers," *Ethos* 18(3):308-352, 1990; Ake Hultkrantz in "Ecological and Phenomenological Aspects of Shamanism, in L. Backman and A. Hultkrantz, eds. *Studies in Lapp Shamanism*, (Stockholm: Almquivst and Wiksell, 1978); J.D. Lewis-Williams and T. Dowson in "The Signs of All Times," *Current Anthropology*, 29(2):201-245, 1988; and Peter Furst in "The Roots and Continuities of Shamanism," in A. Brodzky, R. Daneswich, and N. Johnson, eds., *Stones, Bones, and Skin*, (Toronto: Society for Art Publications, 1977), offer various perspectives of the paleolithic origins question. In general, origins are traced to the Siberian and Arctic shamanisms and are considered the "classic" form. Yet others such as Sergei Shirokogoroff in *Psychomental Complex of the Tungus*, (London:Kegan Paul, Trench, Trubner and Company, 1935) and Mircea Eliade in *Shamanism: Archaic Techniques of Ecstacy*, (Princeton: Princeton University Press, 1964), postulate that Buddhist Lamaism drastically modified Tungus shamanism. Thus, one version of origins suggests that shamanisms have a Tibetan source.

5. J.D. Lewis-Williams' name is synonymous with the work on entoptic phenomena. His works *Believing and Seeing*, (New York: Academic Press, 1981) and "Cognitive and Optical Illusions in San Rock Art," *Current Anthropology* 27:171-178, 1986 are exemplary in this regard. See also his collaboration with T.A. Dowson, "The Signs of All Times," 1988, and "On Vision and Power in the Neolithic," *Current Anthropology* 34:55-65, 1993.

6. *Piman Shamanism and Staying Sickness* by Donald Bahr, Juan Gregorio, David Lopez, and Albert Alvarez, (Tucson: University of Arizona Press, 1974) stands out as one of the first and is still one of finest discussions between a shaman, Gregorio, an anthropologist, Donald Bahr, and two native speaker-translators, Lopez and Alvarez. Bahr has also written on shamanic song texts in "A Grey and Fervent Shamanism," *Journal of the Society of the Americas*, 1991. Other collaborative and innovative work has been completed by Larry Evers and Felipe Molina in *Yaqui Deer Songs*, (Tucson: University of Arizona Press, 1987), Jane Monnig Atkinson's *Wana Shamanship*, (Berkeley: University of California Press, 1989), Anna Siikala's "Two Types of Shamanizing and Categories of Shamanistic Songs," in L. Honko and V. Voigt, eds., *Akademiai Kiado* (Budapest, 1980) and in B. Walraven's *Muga: The Songs of Korean Shamanism*, (Dordredt: ICG Printing, 1985).

7. For arguments against the mentally ill shaman stereotype see Alfred Kroeber, *The Nature of Culture*, (Chicago: University of Chicago Press, 1952); L. B. Boyer, "Shamans: To Set the Record Straight," *American Anthropologist* 71(2):307-309, 1969; D. Handelman, "Shamanizing on an Empty Stomach," *American Anthropologist* 70(2):353-356, 1968; and George Murdock, "Tenino Shamanism," *Ethnology* 4:165-171, 1965, among others.

8. The desire to empirically ground the study of shamanic consciousness has led to this interesting version of sociobiology. For a general discussion of this hypothesis, see C. Laughlin, J. McManus, and E. d'Aquili, *Brain, Symbol and Experience: Toward a Neurophenomenology of Consciousness*, (New York: Columbia University Press, 1992) and Michael Winkelman, "Trance States: A Theoretical Model and Cross-Cultural Analysis," *Ethos* 14(2):174-203, 1986, and "Altered States of Consciousness and Religious Behavior," in S. Glazier, ed., *Anthropology of Religion*, (Westport, CT: Greenwood Press, 1997).

9. A few recent examples of this work include Michael Taussig's *Shamanism, Colonialism, and the Wild Man*, (Chicago: University of Chicago Press, 1987); N. Thomas and C. Humphrey's edited volume *Shamanism, History, and the State*, (Ann Arbor: University of Michigan Press, 1994); and Atkinson's book cited above.

10. Refer to C. Humphrey's "Shamanic Practices and the State in Northern Asia," in Nicholas Thomas and Carolyn Humphrey, eds., *Shamanism, History and the State*, (Ann Arbor: University of Michigan Press, 1994).

11. This section on Siberian shamanism draws heavily from the two works of R. Hamayon: *La Chasse à l'âme: Esquisse d'une Theorie du Chamanisme Siberien*, Société d'ethnologie (Nanterre) and "Shamanism in Siberia," in N. Thomas and C. Humphrey, eds., *Shamanism, History, and the State*, (Ann Arbor: University of Michigan Press, 1994). Her research and writing are exemplary for placing shamanism into a nuanced format rather than reifying much of what is assumed to be true about Siberian shamanism. See also Caroline Humphrey's, "Shamanic Practices and the State in Northern Asia,"

in N. Thomas and C. Humphrey, eds., *Shamanism, History, and the State*, (Ann Arbor: University of Michigan Press, 1994).

12. This section on Tohono O'odham shamanism is based on my own research in various communities on the Sells Reservation and on several published monographs. See Ruth Underhill's classic *Papago Indian Religion*, (New York: Columbia University Press, 1946) and the collaborative work *Piman Shamanism and Staying Sickness* by Donald Bahr, Juan Gregorio, David Lopez, and Albert Alvarez, (Tucson: University of Arizona Press, 1974) . For a detailed treatment of a single

staying sickness see my *Devil Sickness and Devil Songs: Tohono O'odham Poetics*, (Washington, DC: Smithsonian Institution Press, 1999).

13. *Mal aire* is a widespread "folk" illness found throughout parts of North and South America as well as in parts of Europe. Evil air sickness in the New World is thought by most observers to be an import from the Old World.

14. This case study relies on the intriguing and ingenious work of M. Taussig, "History as Sorcery," *Representations* 7:87-109, 1984 and *Shamanism, Colonialism, and the Wild Man*, (Chicago: University of Chicago Press, 1987)

Seven

Sorcery and Witchcraft

Mary Patterson

Melbourne University

There are probably few people in the world today free of preconceived notions about the topic of this chapter. Most children in the Western world have encountered the image of the witch and the sorcerer, even if only through the medium of Walt Disney films. In children's literature this image ranges from the cannibalistic crone of Hansel and Gretel to a much more benign or even humorous figure. Popular culture, particularly in the second half of this century, exhibits a fascination with the occult peculiarly at odds with the secular rationalism seen as characteristic of post-Enlightenment thought in the West. Lately, the familiar image of Satan vies with a more postmodern "enemy within"—the abducting alien. Just as interested in the reproductive capacities and sexual organs of its victims, this creature performs operations on them, usually leaving a contemporary equivalent of the "devil's mark."

At the close of the last century many social theorists thought that increased industrialization in the West and the kind of lifestyle fostered by economic transformation and the spread of more complex technology would inevitably lead to a "disenchantment" of the world. Similarly, as the postcolonial world succumbed to modernization it was assumed that interest in sorcery and witchcraft as explanations of events and as central aspects of cosmology would likewise fade away with literacy and increasing involvement in global economies and Western lifestyles.

But, as we approach the second millenium, the worldviews of ordinary folk in most parts of the planet, including the most technologically advanced, seem stubbornly resistant to "disenchantment." Not only do religions proliferate and revive but in America and the United Kingdom recently, significant groups of people have been convinced of the presence of satanists in their midst, reflecting for them, the reality of the presence of Satan himself. Meanwhile in contemporary Africa, a number of anthropologists have documented the ways in which ideas about mystical evil doing, far from withering away, have become enmeshed in the politics and operation of the postcolonial state. The ability of sorcery and witchcraft ideas and practices to express people's concerns, or as Bruce Kapferer puts it—the "problematics of everyday life," lies in the way in which such practices and ideas are universally conceived. They are subversive of the everyday, yet always very much a part of it—this is the "alchemy of sorcery" that enables it "to metamorphose and maintain a relevance to any situation".[1]

Tradurre e tradire—"to translate is to betray": Italian Proverb

Let me begin my discussion with some very generalized and essentially pragmatic comments about the vexed issue of terminology. Everywhere in the known world humans take stock of their life-world as it impinges on their consciousness via their sense perceptions and the operations of the human mind. Interactions between elements in the posited life-world—living and dead humans, animals, the physical environment, and the products of the imagination—are everywhere thought about and experienced by evolved human beings in their social, cultural, and natural environments in ways that are at once universal and uniquely variable. The categories of the Western social sciences and humanities, so recently devised, that enable us to talk comparatively about human beings inevitably impose a kind of order on our thinking that may not do justice either to the universality or to the variability of modes of being in the world. Anthropologists attempt, with more or less success, to investigate those modes of being in cultures other than their own and are forced, of necessity, to constantly question their own categories and ways of thought in order to render authentically the worldview of others. The study of what we have popularly called the "supernatural" in the West is an excellent example of the difficulties involved in this enterprise. The way in which we take for granted our carving up of the category "the supernatural"—indeed its existence as separate from its equally taken for granted opposite "the natural" is a case in point. Why, for instance, have historians and social theorists been so concerned to explain the persistence of "magic" but not of "religion"? The inherent bias in our way of thinking about these two aspects of the nonempirical realm is also a matter of the history of Western thought, disputation, and tradition, both learned and popular.

In assessing the particular utility of the categories "sorcery" and "witchcraft" with which this chapter is headed, it is useful to remember that not all languages in which social science is written offer us a choice. In French, for example we are provided with only a single category *la sorcellerie* and are thereby forced to pay more attention to the indigenous categories and their attendant meanings. Pocock argues that the terms should be avoided since the way they are used in the literature causes endless confusion. We would do better, he says, to talk of something like " spiritual malpractice."[2] In sections of this chapter I have resorted to variations on such a phrase—"occult practice," "mystical evildoing," and so on—which while cumbersome, help to avoid this problem a little. Because "sorcery" and "witchcraft" are so widely used in the literature, however, with so many different meanings, in this chapter I will refer to all mystical evil doing as sorcery except when referring to other people's work. Clearly it is appropriate to talk about sorcerers and witches in the historical case of English-speaking countries but not necessarily in other parts of Europe.

Pocock makes the excellent observation that within the category of spiritual malpractice recognized around the world, oppositions are frequently made between such things as the manner of operation employed (e.g., controllable/uncontrollable; inherited/acquired; internal/external) and whether the practitioner is motivated by common human feelings like anger, jealousy, and envy or simply malice.

Several of these oppositions have been taken up by anthropologists as justification for the dual labeling system. The being who is thought to operate solely through malice is almost universally credited with extrahuman powers, cannibalistic tastes for human blood and infants, and incestuous and/or perverse sexual desires. The presence of such beings in the world cannot be tolerated. They are most frequently called "witches" in the literature for no other reason than that they resonate with our own deeply entrenched image of the "witch." This image comes, however, from the demonology of the church of the early modern period rather than from the folk views of the mass of the people whose ideas about those with occult powers are never quite so clear-cut. A very important point to bear in mind is that the activities of those who deal with the occult frequently end up being viewed ambivalently no matter how much they wish to identify themselves as only working for the common good.

Traditional Theories

The study of sorcery and witchcraft in the West and the developing world has participated prominently in the debates about the way people think about the world and explain events in their lives and the lives of others. One of the most influential books on the subject, Evans-Pritchard's *Witchcraft, Oracles and Magic among the Azande*, published in 1937, was designed to show how such beliefs and ideas operate in the lives of a non-Western people. Although ethnographers had previously broached the topic of magic, notably Malinowski in his various works on the Trobriand Islanders of Papua New Guinea and in a general statement on the topic in *Magic, Science and Religion*, this was the first full-scale monograph to consider mystical evil doing as a system of thought and to focus an entire work on attempting to explain its operation to a Western audience.

Evans-Pritchard points out that for the Azande, who live in Central Africa on the Nile Congo divide, witchcraft is a constant feature of daily life rather than a topic of abstract speculation or analysis. His major aim was to demonstrate to a European audience that behaviors they might regard as bizarre or beyond comprehension were, given the Zande ideas about why misfortune and death occur, perfectly rational and readily understood. In the Zande worldview there is no simple demarcation between the "natural" and the "supernatural." Witchcraft is a normal occurrence, yet it is at the same time, something that the Azande themselves find somewhat mysterious in the manner of its operation.

When Zande attribute death to witchcraft, as they do in the majority of cases, it is not the "how" that interests them but the "why." In the now famous example Evans-Pritchard gave to illustrate this principle, he describes how the death of a Zande, sitting under a granary to escape the heat of the sun, would not be attributed to the termites that ate through the supports of the granary causing it to collapse and crush him, but rather to witchcraft. Azande know exactly what happens to granary supports when termites eat them; what engages them is the conjunction of events. Why was this particular man sitting under this particular granary at the precise moment of its collapse? Witchcraft is to them the obvious, indeed the only, answer.

The Zande witch is, to all intents and purposes, an ordinary individual who, unbeknown to his or her fellows carries *mangu* or witchcraft substance in their belly. Autopsy and the identification of *mangu* at a suspected witch's death can substantiate an accusation of witchcraft; since this is not a common occurrence, though it may once have been, Azande resort to oracles, the most reliable of which is what Evans-Pritchard calls the "poison oracle." The operation of this oracle involves the consultation of *benge*, a paste made from a plant that is administered to immature chickens, in the past also to humans. Evans-Pritchard identifies this substance as a poison (a variety of strycchnine), but Azande do not regard it simply as a material entity that may or may not kill the fowl, nor however, do they personify it, although they adress it during the consultation as though it were a living being. The poison oracle, and the other less important oracles that the Azande employ, are all categorized as things, yet they are not ordinary things because they can be imbued with a power by the people who use them. Should the various prohibitions and proscriptions that surround their use be broken, they lose their power and resume their mundane character. What the Azande do not do is provide the ethnographer with a neat theory of the operation of witchcraft and oracles.

One of the enduring, and some would argue unfortunate, legacies of Evans-Pritchard's study of Zande witchcraft has been the universalization of the distinction Azande make between sorcery and witchcraft. For the Azande, witchcraft is a physical, inherited substance, intrinsic to the person that might operate even without their conscious intent. Sorcery, on the other hand, is simply bad magic, always extrinsic to the person, aided by the ingestion of "medicines" (plant substances), rites, and spells. Both sorcery and witchcraft may have the same effect and both are always distinct in Zande thought from good magic, even when, used as a protective device, it may cause death or destruction. As we will see in subsequent sections this distinction is not readily maintained in other cultures without doing disservice to the data. However the distinction between intrinsic and extrinsic power is taken as salient by anthropologists using a comparative approach and interested in the meaning of symbolic representations. These will be considered later. Lucy Mair, in her comparative account of witchcraft, while critical of the overuse of the Zande distinction, nevertheless concluded that it was useful to discriminate on empirical grounds between those who are credited with the ability to cause harm simply by their nature and those who must manipulate objects to achieve their ends.[3] Unlike sorcery, she argues, there can never be evidence of witchcraft. However, whether *we* call it sorcery or witchcraft—in this worldview, the evidence is there for all to see—people sicken and die and misfortune occurs.

After Evans-Pritchard's work there was a shift away from looking at ideas and beliefs to a concentration on accusations and their consequences.[4] But accusations are not as simple to study as might appear, since in many societies they are rarely made openly. Often, close kin of someone who has died will allege sorcery while others may accept alternative explanations. Criticisms of these earlier approaches related to the use of static models of society and to their neglect of either indigenous categories of thought or of the complexity of contexts in which accusations may or may not be made.

Regional Perspectives

A question we might well ask at this point is whether it is possible to make more general comparisons both within and between wide geographical areas in relation to sorcery. In the early literature on Africa, several anthropologists commented on the apparent difference between patterns of accusation in that country where accused sorcerer and witch and their victim were almost invariably known to one another and more than likely kinsmen or neighbors, and Melanesia, where accusations appeared more likely to be made against more distant sorcerers of enemy groups. Is it possible to make any generalizations at all about sorcery in Melanesia?

What one can say is that techniques of sorcery, although vastly variable in their details, conform to several common types, many of which are familiar from other regions of the world. The first is the paradigm of sympathetic magic in which the sorcerer manipulates something that has been in close contact with the proposed victim. The items of choice are bodily exuviae such as semen, saliva, sweat, nail or hair clippings, or excreta or some item that has absorbed these substances such as food scraps or clothing or even the soil in which a footprint has been left. The aim may be to cause illness or to cause death. Potent substances are frequently added to the victim's leavings which are then subjected to a ritual treatment in which the sorcerer's power is brought to bear verbally through spells, and through the manipulation of other esoteric objects that often contain ancestral power mediated by the sorcerer. Slow burning, smoking, or burial are common methods. If the sorcerer has a spirit familiar, it may be enjoined to consume the leavings or they may be thrown into a village shrine where the ancestors consume the victim's life-force in retaliation for the desecration. To restore the victim to health, the remains may have to be returned to the victim, neutralized in some way or simply removed from the source of consumption.

Other common methods include the magical introjection of objects like stones or miniature arrows. This is usually accomplished from a distance with the aid of spells and perhaps a spirit familiar. The sorcerer may perform it from a hiding place as the victim passes by or it is accomplished while the sorcerer is in a trance or dreaming. Recovery requires the removal of the objects, something accomplished by a specialist.[5] The use of "poisons," which may or may not be pharmacologically active, is also common. Sorcerers are also said in some areas to be able to induce snakes or crocodiles to attack their victims or to make their victims less wary and therefore more vulnerable to attack.

One of the most dreaded forms of sorcery for which there is frequently said to be no antidote and which is thus often invoked in cases of sudden and unexpected death not preceded by illness involves physical violence as a preliminary. Known as *sangguma, vada,* or *vele* in much of the region, knowledge of this technique is widely distributed in Melanesia. The victim is commonly brought to ambush either by the sorcerer's spells or by the administration of a substance that affects their usual faculties. This variety of sorcery is always carried out by a group of men who, having rendered the victim unconscious, perform an operation on him in which they remove bodily organs and replace them with various items of "poison." They also frequently put slivers of bamboo treated with "poison" under his fingernails, armpits, or in his anus. The victim is magically healed so that the results of the operation are not visible, restored to consciousness, tested to see whether the sorcery has been effective, and if it has, left to wander home, unable to either report on the incident or to name his assailants.

While all these sorts of techniques have prompted some anthropologists to suggest that they are totally imaginary, there is plenty of evidence that this is an unwarranted assumption. It is undoubtedly true that there is lot more talk about sorcery than performance of it. Many of the methods involve the sorcerer in manipulation of objects and recitation of spells. They also involve the specialist in techniques of mental preparation, strict dietary regimes, trance, directed dreaming, and all of the sorts of activities that are more familiar to us in discussions of shamans. Sorcerers, like shamans, need to be in touch with the nonhuman world and frequently conduct their activities in trance and dream. However, in the case of "assault" sorcery, the evidence seems to suggest that, as in the manipulation of objects, such sorcery is practised in some places. The magical operation is performed by the specialist who knows how to do it. It involves the sort of operation commonly performed by shamans except that the items are not only removed from the victim but inserted as well and it presumably involves expert sleight of hand. In one area, it is suggested that the victim's larynx is crushed, in another that a caterpillar that causes swelling of the mucous membranes is pushed into the throat accounting for the inability to speak. There are reports from the New Guinea Highlands of victims who have escaped after the initial assault and the insertion of poison "needles" into the victim. Several similar cases ocurred in North Ambrym, Vanuatu, between the 1940s and 1960s. In one of them the sorcerer was innovative; using wire rather than bamboo slivers, he pushed it into the victim's armpit so far that he died. In another case the novice sorcerer, left to guard the unconscious victim, inadvertently suffocated him when he began to revive before the experts had returned with all of the paraphernalia.

Although sorcerers are frequently specialists, the early literature stresses that the ability to cause disease, as opposed to death, was well known in communities. Just as most people had knowledge of magic that they used in horticulture, hunting, fishing, trading, sexual attraction, and other important areas of everyday life, so too they knew how to cause and cure minor illnesses. Having an antidote meant knowledge of the cause. These techniques, frequently spells and/or various plants, were often the very ones used to protect property. Someone with a recognized minor illness might well assume that they have infringed someone else's property rights and simply ask someone whom they know to possess the curative spell to use it for them. These are precisely the techniques that missionaries everywhere enjoin their converts to give up and it may well be that not only is this sort of knowledge much less widespread than formerly but also that minor ills are more likely to be treated with European medicine where it is available. Persistent illness or misfortune is always another matter. Just as in Western medicine there is a hierarchy of resort in which the increasing persistence or severity of an illness moves the patient along from self-medication to friendly advice to medical practitioners and specialists, so too there is both a hierarchy of resort and a hierarchy of causal agency in Melanesia. At first the sufferer may see his illness or personal failure as minor and "just one of those things"; if it persists it may be because of an infraction of some kind against the ancestors or someone's property. Only when no available cures work and things do not improve will the more serious case of spirit possession or sorcery be invoked.

One thing is clear: In most Melanesian societies in the precontact era warfare and violence were endemic and highly valued pursuits. Extrahuman resources were used against enemies as well as physical aggression. In many regions, given the widespread conviction that humans could harm each other by metaphysical means, every death, particularly of an adult male and always of a leader, occasioned retaliation of some kind. Where analysis frequently seems to get confused is in how the two major kinds of data involved are evaluated. On the one hand, anthropologists have collected statements about indigenous knowledge concerning the causation of illness and misfortune by extrahuman means and on the other they have observed what people do when someone believes themselves to be a victim of some kind of mystical aggression. These two things are not separate in real-life situations and so change over time. Nonetheless it is useful to separate them analytically at a given point. Accusations are very rarely quantified in any way.[6] There are several reasons for this: First, given the average length of fieldwork, an anthropologist would not witness behavior following many deaths so that information concerning accusations will be largely retrospective and structured into a narrative. Second, accusations following deaths are complex processes. Different people may have very different ideas about the cause of death depending on their closeness to the deceased. Open accusation after deaths would appear to be relatively uncommon. Moots or village courts are postcontact institutions and where leaders, particularly hereditary leaders, monopolized access to mystical evil doing they could dispense summary justice. There was no semblance of trial or issues of legitimate defence.[7]

A recent detailed study of sorcery in the largely Buddhist country of Sri Lanka by Bruce Kapferer offers a fascinating view of a region outside Africa and Melanesia. In Sri Lanka's recent history, the demon/god *Huniyam* has become increasingly popular. His name means "black magic" so that even though he has a protective and positive aspect, there is no mistake about his powerful negative side. Shrines to *Huniyam* have proliferated in recent years. Kapferer gives vivid descriptions of the awful ambience of pollution and disgust at these shrines, where sorcery victims and those wishing to protect themselves from its effects gather to curse their enemies and hurl back the force of their distress and anguish at those they suspect of causing their misery.

What makes the Sinhalese and Indian sorcery paradigm unique is its public concentration within the context of organized religion. In Sri Lanka the rites of exorcism, the *kapumas,* and the grand rite of Suniyama, the analysis of which is the center of Kapferer's work, are designed to recenter and reconstitute the victim of sorcery by restoring him or her as a conscious being. The Sinhalese experience of sorcery thus joins together the Buddhist cosmological concerns about the place of humans in the world with the individual's consciousness in its everyday context. Kapferer argues that the anger victims express at the sorcery shrines when they curse their tormentors restores their ability to act in a political and social sense. His phenomenological approach is designed to unify the tendency of analysts to categorize different aspects of experience into sociological, psychological, or anthropological aspects which frequently do violence, he argues, to the embodied and deeply felt power of the experience of sorcery. Clearly this is a valuable perspective, stressing the importance of giving full weight to the indigenous meaning and experience of sorcery, while still taking account of its sociopolitical context. The Sri Lankan situation, in which a rich mythology, cosmology, and ritual practice exist around the phenomenon, contrasts with the situation in many other areas of the world where sorcery and witchcraft practices are so secret and so frequently disowned as appropriate esoteric knowledge that huge difficulties are presented in gaining access to them other than as an "apprentice." This is a position that has difficulties of its own and we will look at some of them in a later section.

The analytic problem of dividing sorcery from other aspects labeled "religion" is seen much more readily in cases like Sri Lanka or India. We encounter this problem as well in the next section where we will look at the great witch hunts of the early modern period in Europe.

Witchcraft and Sorcery in Early Modern Europe: 1450–1750

During the three hundred or so years between the middle of the fifteenth and eighteenth centuries that historians call the "early modern period," the people of Europe and Great Britain experienced plague, wars, vast changes in religion, and the gestation of the modern state. Against this backdrop a massive panic arose at varied times and places about a conspiracy of witches accused of the most horrendous and extraordinary crimes against their fellows. The identification, prosecution, and subsequent executions of these witches have come to be known as "the great witch hunts." Witches, the vast majority, but by no means all of them women, were widely said to be members of a clandestine society in league with the Devil with whom they had made a pact. They attended meetings called sabbats, to which they frequently flew on animals or broomsticks where they performed perverse sexual acts including incest, ate the flesh of murdered infants, and worshipped the Devil. With the Devil's aid they committed frequent offences against persons and property until they were finally apprehended, tried, persuaded to confess, and finally executed. This was the official view of the church and the learned élite that over time infiltrated the world of rural peasants who blamed their neighbors for the ills that befell them. The use of sorcerers or "white witches" or cunning folk to "unwitch," to divine, and to heal and the ubiquity of sorcery or *maleficium* as it was called is the counterpoint to the demonology of the élite.

Over this lengthy period no particular pattern of prosecution emerges. The number of trials increases in some areas, then declines, only to be taken up with some fervor again some years later. Statistics and records are extremely variable in extent and quality though there are now accounts for almost all European regions. There were significant differences even between neighboring countries, such as France and Germany, England and Scotland, Norway and Sweden, and Poland and Russia.[8] The vast majority of prosecutions, maybe 75 percent, occurred within the shifting boundaries of the Holy Roman Empire that included Germany, Austria, Silesia, Bohemia, France, Switzerland, the Netherlands, and parts of Northern Italy. At the start of the period prosecutions gathered momentum in France but by the late sixteenth century at the height of the witch hunts they centred on Germany, where they remained until the seventeenth century.

The extent of the witch hunts has been a subject of some controversy. Estimates of the number of witches executed have varied widely and have suffered, through want of detailed research, and from gross exaggeration. Most numbers accepted as valid by nineteenth-century historians have been drastically scaled down. Based on recent archival research, most scholars agree that for the whole of Europe a figure between 40,000 and 50,000 is probably accurate with some 2,000 in England and Scotland.[9] Historians concentrated on several related issues in interpreting this phenomenon—why did the witch hunts occur when and where they did and what were the factors that influenced their development and their eventual decline? How were popular magic and sorcery related to the image and identification of witches in the period? What was the reality of the witches' sabbat? Did witches exist? Why did the prosecution of witches cease and magical thinking decline?[10]

One of the most important perspectives on the origin of the witch hunts in Europe sees them as the legacy of a long history of persecution of minorities in Europe stretching back to antiquity and predating the Christianisation of the Roman Empire. Norman Cohn in his unsurpassed study *Europe's Inner Demons* traces the antecedents of the witch hunts to the persecution of various groups whose views and activities were able to be labeled unorthodox or heretical by those holding power. The remarkably durable and common features applied to such groups were that they met in secret where they ritually slaughtered and devoured infants and children, held orgies in which sexual intercourse of all kinds was practised including incest, and worshipped some strange divinity in the form of an animal. These activities are always regarded as so antisocial and horrifying that the perpetrators must be exterminated. The elements of this fantasy are first found being used against Jews by Greeks and then in the second century C.E. by Greeks and Romans against Christians who interpreted the Eucharist literally as ritual cannibalism.

The fate of Christians in this period is well known. It is ironic, therefore, that for the remainder of the first millenium it is Christians who, after the conversion of Constantine, apply the myth successively to pagans, Jews, heretics, and all manner of dissenters from a church that was itself riven with dissent as the millenium progressed. Changes in judicial procedure instituted in the thirteenth century had enormous ramifications for prosecution. Prior to this period all criminal cases were dealt with on a personal basis, that is, the accuser was the prosecutor. He brought his case before a judge who would have to be satisfied by incontovertible proof that the accusation was valid. If he was not satisfied, the decision was put in divine hands. God protected the innocent. An accused person would submit to ordeal—grasping a red hot iron or plunging the arm into boiling water. If they were indeed innocent, their injuries would be slight and after exhibiting them before the judge they would be acquitted. Those who could afford it could have champions fight for them. If the accused was declared innocent, the accuser was then liable to prosecution and subject to the penalties that the accused would have received if guilty. The abandonment of this form of procedure known as "accusatorial" for an "inquisitorial" model had obvious consequences. There was an inhibition on prosecuting cases where proof was difficult—as it usually was in accusations of *maleficium.*

When the Church established the Inquisition to aid its prosecution and persecution of heretics and Jews, its methods were gradually taken over by the secular courts. It was this inquisitorial procedure that enabled the witch hunts to gain momentum in the fifteenth century. Prosecution of charges ceased to be a civil matter between accuser and accused but was taken over by the judges and officials of the court. They came to their decision about the guilt or innocence of the accused through interrogation and examination of witnesses, usually carried out in secret. The accused could only be convicted by confession and it was deemed entirely appropriate that a failure to confess should be encouraged by the use of torture. The confession under torture had to be freely confirmed after a short period. If the heretic or witch recanted, they were subjected to renewed efforts, including more torture, to secure the confession necessary for their reconciliation with the church and the safety of their immortal soul. Neither heretics nor witches were always executed in every case. The Inquisition frequently imposed penance after formal reconciliation. At the height of the witch hunts the secular courts were much less merciful. Execution for witchcraft in Europe, as for heresy, was by burning. In England witches were hanged, unless their crime was against the crown and therefore also treason. Executions were public events at which a witch's crimes were read aloud to the assembled crowd. This distribution of knowledge undoubtedly contributed to the content of subsequent confessions. That this procedure of examining suspects was in place was vital to the development of the persecution of witches as we shall see.

While the nocturnal conspiracy, infant murder, cannibalism, and perverted sexual behavior were not new in Europe, the full-blown stereotype did not begin to be applied to peasants accused of harming their neighbors by occult means until the fourteenth century. But confessions did not simply parrot the demonology of the élites and learned judges and inquisitors. They contained a varied amalgam of local folk belief that often included the figure of the Devil, and various other local elements of ancient origin about women flying off with goddesses, and men and women battling witches in their dreams consistent with shamanic and magical ideas.[11] Various kinds of magical practice were endemic; soothsaying, divination, crop protection, and undoubtedly magic to harm people and cause misfortune were all widely practised by a great variety of people. But the increasingly educated élite shared a worldview with the lower and merchant classes that did not separate the "natural" which was the world of the everyday from the unnatural or preternatural which was rare, extraordinary, or magical in which humans were active agents. The "supernatural" realm was divine and characterized by the hand of God. The boundaries between these realms were not uncontested however, and throughout the early modern period there were a variety of views about what was orthodox and appropriate in religion and magic both for the élites and the folk. There were also sceptics, some of them influential but nonetheless in a minority in the early fifteenth century, when they ran the risk of being accused themselves simply by expressing their views. Sceptical positions on the abilities of witches were in earlier centuries promulgated by the church itself. In the ninth century, a guide to bishops that became known as the *Canon Episcopi* denied the possibility of night flight by cannibal women declaring it an illusion inspired by Satan. The Christian church had good reason to attempt to monopolize the metaphysical and they attempted this by denying the validity of popular experience declaring it to be inspired by the Devil. This attitude was to undergo a serious and important transformation. From admonishing silly peasants to give up their untrue but demonically inspired fantasies, the church progressed to accepting the fantasies as a terrifying truth that demanded action, involving the secular authorities in uprooting the evil in their midst.

Several historians have taken up Christina Larner's persuasive argument about the meaning of the witch hunts: She sees Christianity as the first political ideology used effectively by the new regimes of Europe, which in their search for legitimacy needed to expunge all deviants from the body politic.[12] The pursuit of witches, the internal enemy par excellence, had the consequence of emphasising the role of the authorities in protecting the people from this diabolical threat. In areas with strong government, the hunts were frequently lessened by the intervention of authorities. The continuing attempts of centers to gain political control of peripheral areas continued throughout the period and witch hunts can usefully be seen as part of this large-scale, never entirely successful process.[13]

Gender and Witchcraft

The popular stereotype of the witch, as we noted at the start of this chapter, is female. How accurate is it? Some historians have taken a closer look at the evidence for some regions to find some apparently anomalous cases. Robin Briggs, for example, noted that in France gender was not an obvious aspect of prosecutions.[14] Nearly 1,300 cases of witchcraft were put before the *parlement* of Paris on appeal and just over half involved men. Although there was a preponderance of women in the 500 known cases that did not get to appeal, 42 percent were men. In other regions such as Finland and Estonia, a much greater proportion of the accused were male. Against this, however, we have figures of between 70 percent–90 percent women in most other countries. Briggs asks a very pertinent question. Were men better placed to avoid accusation than women? In so many cases the accused women were old, poor, single, and frequently childless. The classic scapegoat figure that we see in other parts of the world is the person of antisocial habits who also has no relatives to defend them.

Anthropologist Ralph Austen suggests that the common attribution of irredeemable evil to women rather than men in Africa occurs because men frequently hold positions of authority and can act as diviners and witch doctors offering protection against witchcraft as well as perhaps being thought to cause it. Their position is always ambivalent but they are in a better negotiating position than the female witch if they are suspected. Women, Austen comments, are usually denied the opportunity to hold such offices.[15] In Europe these roles were open to women but their position as Larner pointed out was ambivalent. Because the majority of prosecutions appear to have been of poor, old women, frequently without support, it is difficult to know whether accused men could deflect accusations and avoid prosecution more readily than women. It does seem likely however. There were of course many women left single and poor by the death of their men in the frequent armed conflicts of this period. We do not know how many of the accused women in Britain or Europe were cunning women but we do know that despite the ideology of witchcraft that closely associated witches with sex, reproduction, and the consumption of children, midwives, though not immune, were not commonly prosecuted. In some regions, there were numerous prosecutions of lying-in-maids, the women, again usually older, who helped out after a woman had given birth. Recent feminist analyses have claimed that historians have virtually ignored the overwhelming number of women who were accused, tried, and executed. In one recent work, for example, Barstow claims that patriarchy and the rise of capitalism were both implicated in the fate of women in the period of the witch hunts, making many more of them marginalized and impoverished and therefore liable to be accused.[16]

Some historians have suggested that it was simply women's association with childbirth and child care that made them more vulnerable to accusation in an era of high infant and child mortality. It was precisely the women most removed from reproduction, however, who were most likely to be prosecuted. In Austen's view the common theme of misappropriation of scarce reproductive resources in witchcraft ideology in Europe and Africa (the blighting of crops, attacks on livestock, murder of children, rendering sterile, etc.) are not unexpected given the need for accumulation in proto-capitalist societies. Representations of the sexuality of witches in both regions express a concern with the "escape of female reproductive power from the enclosed domestic space in which it serves male-dominated communal norms to the open nocturnal realms of self-contained female power."

In cases of possession women also figure prominently. Although theoretically possible without it, possession was commonly also attributed to witchcraft. In one of the world's best known cases, and one of the last, the people of Salem, Massachusetts, found themselves accused by adolescent girls manipulated by one faction of Salem Village. Accusations by the girls who exhibited symptoms of possession began against typical outsiders in the village, all female, who they claimed had bewitched them. The witch hunt ended for two reasons: Accusations were made against the rich and powerful and people began to suggest that the Devil was at work directly, making the girls accuse the innocent.[17] In the early 1950s the investigation that American playwright Arthur Miller was subjected to by the congressional committees presided over by Senator Joe McCarthy into the activities of communists in America inspired him to write a play *The Crucible* based on the Salem events. While sociologists accept the parallels in the structure of all hunts for those labeled deviant, others feel that too much relating to the ideology of witchcraft itself is ignored in this approach. We look at this question again in the section dealing with contemporary allegations of satanic abuse.

The witch hunts ceased in most countries before the legal machinery that enabled them was dismantled. Its end was as varied as its beginning. In most countries of Europe and in England there were no more prosecutions after the late seventeenth century. In Germany where the witch hunt had been most intense, cases were still being brought to trial well into the eighteenth century. While prosecutions ceased, people's ideas about the reality of witchcraft persisted well into the nineteenth century, and some might argue, well beyond. Ian Bostridge sees the fate of the élite discourse of witchcraft as intimately related to transformations of the official point of view which were brought about by a combination of political events and longer term ideological shifts.[18] While judicial resolution of witchcraft ceased to be an option, there were occasional reports of witches receiving summary justice at the hands of their neighbors right through the nineteenth century. Much less research effort has gone into questioning the "decline of magic" than into the details of the witch hunts themselves. Recent findings suggest a continuity of belief in some areas of the countryside in the face of a countervailing trend that associated beliefs in witchcraft with an unsophisticated rural peasantry. When scepticism became fashionable in the eighteenth century among the upper classes, it inevitably drew to it those who might be credulous if it were not more important to appear "modern" and urbane. For the educated and the powerful there was, of course, a range of views as there always had been. Within the established churches faith and reason were reconciled and the devil put back in his box. It appears, however, that the lid was not firmly sealed.

Sorcery, Witchcraft, and Social Change in the Non-Western World

The theme of social change and social upheaval that is prominent in analyses of the European witch hunts became a feature of the second wave of sorcery and witchcraft research in Africa and Melanesia partly as a reaction against what was seen as outmoded structural functionalism, static models of society, and a failure to acknowledge the importance of history. However, there were accounts of the impact of colonialism and conversion and these mostly surfaced in reference to what were called witch finding cults. Anthropologists argued that these cults emerged in Africa to fill the gap left by the colonial governments' banning of mass poison ordeals and the suppression of public confession. These changes in procedure, however, were only part of the answer. Such movements also seem to arise when dominant values are challenged by changing circumstances and/or when social conditions are radically disrupted by famine, warfare, epidemics, invasions, and so on. These are the times when witches are seen to be active in the world and it is likely that these are also precisely the times when more ordinary sorcery gets taken over by the generalist fantasy about the totally evil sorcerer/witch. The identification of this sort of sorcerer does not need previous conflicts or quarrels. The administration of the treatment by the finders compels them to confess. Frequently all who practise divination or any other kind of occult activity hand over medicines and paraphernalia. All protective charms are now obtained from the cult officials. Those declared innocent are thereafter protected from the witchcraft of others. In the 1930s and 1940s in Africa, witch finding cults scoured the countryside for witches but people also traveled great distances to take the witch finding medicine, presumably to prove their innocence and silence their enemies. In some areas such cults had an even longer history. They gathered their own momentum.

Sorcerers and witches are frequently described in contemporary Africa as insatiably hungry. They "eat" others by absorbing their reproductive powers, their children, their sexual fluids, and their flesh. In a zero sum game, one person's advancement can only be at the expense of someone else. When the acquisition of power and wealth is equated with the consumption of human life, it is also frequently tied to ideas about a powerful outside world. How people perceive their access to material resources that come from outside the community has a great deal of influence on their perceptions of security and risk, conflict and danger.

In his study of sorcery and power in Cameroon, Peter Geschiere notes that the association of the upwardly mobile with sorcery is doubly dangerous—it both augments power while serving to undermine it. Sorcery has leveling and accumulative aspects that are particularly tied up with modernization and the postcolonial state.[19] In Cameroon, even in urban areas, the source of witchcraft is always the family. "Kinship still dominates social life" while at the same time kinship ties are placed under increasing pressure. Geschiere describes witchcraft as the dark side of kinship. This nexus will continue to be important, he argues, as long as kinship is forced to accommodate to social conditions yet remains the primary means of security and support for most people.

In a variation of Larner's explanation about the gender bias in witchcraft prosecutions, Andrew Apter argues that Yoruba women's prominence as witches related to conflict between their roles as managers of the domestic sphere in which they competed with co-wives and their prominent economic roles in the local trade markets.[20] He also presents an interesting reanalysis of the Atinga witch finding cult in which hundreds of women were accused of witchcraft. Attributing such movements to social upheaval, Apter argues, diminishes the manner in which Africans were active agents in their own affairs rather than victims swept along by the currents of uncontrollable outside forces. Some of the factors emphasised in earlier anthropological accounts of Yoruba witchcraft were clearly valid. Yoruba co-wives were likely to accuse one another of witchcraft and a common way of referring to witches was "our mothers." But this conflict alone does not explain the structural contradiction and ambivalence in their roles. They also had considerable freedom of movement, sold their husbands' produce, and belonged to trading organizations that pooled resources, rotated credit, fixed minimum prices, and accumulated capital. Apter sees this powerful economic role as subverting the ideology of household labor and reproduction. The witch is seen as draining and consuming reproductive power—she drinks her victim's blood and consumes their vital essence. She can consume a man's sexual energy by "borrowing" his penis to have sex with his wife or another woman. Witchcraft was acquired from one's mother or could be obtained by donating a child as a sort of "entry fee" to the witches' association who would consume it together. The giving up of close kin to demonstrate one's *bona fides* as a sorcerer is not an uncommon idea in sorcery ideology and occurs in many parts of the world.

In addition, Islam, Christianity, colonialism, and the cash economy had wrought immense transformations in social and religious life. Yoruba kings had their powers curtailed while subordinate chiefs were absorbed into the civil service bureaucracy, educating their children to become part of the new local élite. Cocoa became the major cash crop. It is in this context that the Atinga witch finding movement that swept Yorubaland between 1950 and 1951 at the precise moment when the world price for cocoa soared should be considered. Cocoa prices were controlled by the colonial state marketing boards that syphoned off profits in the boom years, while local producers competed for wealth and capital. The power and autonomy of market women flourished alongside anxiety about the work of witches. The arrival of the *Atinga* cult promised a solution. Confirmed witches had to confess and pay a fee of 30 shillings for being cleansed. Many confessed to the mystical killing of children and relatives.[21] The cult was strategic, Apter argues, giving men of the new élite the opportunity to bypass their elders and make new alliances with chiefs who paid them for their witch finding activities. They could also directly intimidate women traders into whose sphere of influence they were intruding. When the cult was banned by the colonial government, the members began attacking the traditional shrines of the female cults, leaving the male ones intact. In this direct attack on women's economic power through a challenge to their mystical powers, Yoruba men entrenched the ideology of witchcraft, ensuring that it would accompany development rather than wither in the face of it.

Some Contemporary Approaches to the Study of the Occult: The Sorcerer's Apprentice

In his comparative study of Melanesian religion, Garry Trompf laments the lack of a style of fieldwork in which the anthropologist seeks training with an adept or expert in esoteric knowledge. Becoming a "sorcerer's apprentice," for example, has not been a common anthropological procedure and there are several practical reasons for that. The dedicated expert practitioner has developed their own knowledge over years of often arduous and perhaps even dangerous contact with the occult. They cannot lightly give up their store of powerful secrets nor are they likely to agree to accept an apprentice who can give at best a couple of years attention to a lifetime's work. Moreover, sorcerers as we have seen rarely admit to the practice of this aspect of their occult dealings. Evans-Pritchard noted all of this when he discussed why he had not himself gone into training with a Zande "witch-doctor" but paid for his cook to be initiated instead. Participation in complex rituals, he felt, interfered with observation but in addition, his position as an honorary noble precluded his involvement since nobles never became witch-doctors.

The most celebrated, yet most controversial and undoubtedly most lucrative, attempt to adopt the "insider" perspective was the account of the late Carlos Casteñada's apprenticeship to the Mexican Yaqui Indian don Juan. The first four books published in the sixties and early seventies began a long debate about the authenticity of the works from which the author remained aloof. Don Juan's existence could not be verified since, according to Casteñada, he refused to be photographed or taped and no one else seemed to have encountered him.[22] The works were published at an opportune moment when the sorts of hallucinogenic experiences recounted by Casteñada as part of his induction were of great interest to young people experimenting with drugs and altered states of consciousness. As well, while there was a considerable literature on shamanism and the occult in other cultures, there were very few detailed expositions on the apprenticeship of a western "rationalist" to an indigenous adept—particularly one like Don Juan who was wonderfully capable of rendering his teaching and philosophy into an accessible form for his pupil. In his turn, the pupil was able to render the whole process of his training and the crumbling away of his "academic" self into a gripping narrative. Whats more, Casteñada was an anthropologist—something that added authenticity to his account.

There have been several assaults on the credibility of Casteñada's work, the most extensive by Robert de Mille who made it quite clear that as far as he could ascertain after extensive research, Don Juan did not exist and the books were works of fiction not fact.[23] In de Mille's view it was scandalous that Casteñada should have been awarded a Ph.D. on the basis that the thesis that became *Journey to Ixtlan* was an ethnography rather than an inspired work of fiction.

A large part of the appeal of Casteñada's work was in the way in which the novice has to be constantly reminded to throw off his "reality" shackles and enter into "a separate reality"—the world of the shaman. Anthropologist Paul Stoller, who decided reluctantly to become apprenticed to a sorcerer while doing fieldwork in the Republic of Niger, was keen to distance himself from Casteñada's efforts. Noting that the Evans-Pritchard option was not open to him because his cook was a woman, he decided to go ahead when a sorcerer interpreted bird droppings on his head as an indication that he had been singled out as an appropriate pupil. Stoller's master, a Songhay *sorko* (sorcerer) admonishes him in a thoroughly Don Juan-like manner. When he fails to see a man's double, Djibo Mounmouni says to Stoller, "You look but you don't see. You touch but you don't feel. You listen but you do not hear."[24] Stoller and his wife Cheryl Olkes present a vivid and exciting version of what a European experiences when he becomes deeply involved in an alternative way of thinking about the world. Some of it he finds extremely disturbing—so much so that he leaves Niger. On returning he is told that some of the procedures he followed at the sorcerer's instruction brought misfortune to the sister of the European at whom they were aimed; the Songhay world challenged the basic premises of his scientific training. What Stoller discovered, he says, is that "sorcery is a metaphor for the chaos that constitutes social relations."

Michelle Stephen was also selected by the Mekeo sorcerer Aisaga who agreed to impart his esoteric knowledge to her if she obtained enough linguistic fluency to dispense with interpreters. The Mekeo live about 110 kilometers from Port Moresby, the capital of Papua, New Guinea. While working with Aisaga, Stephen was taught spells used for various purposes, one of which was to induce particular dream experiences. Dreams are an extremely important aspect of experiential reality in many parts of the world, no less in Melanesia. On reciting certain spells with her teacher she found that her normally ordinary dreams became "disturbing" or simply "persistent." Mekeo see dreams, like the sorcery itself, as another reality in which the dream self operates. Those not adept are vulnerable to the sorcerer's power. For the expert Aisaga, sorcery was part of his definition of self, not simply a means to exert political influence over his kinsmen and neighbors. That it operates to facilitate such an influence is, however, undeniable. Esoteric knowledge, Stephen claims, is only revealed on the death bed to a close relative since its exposure drains part of the self. Stephen found the working relationship with her teacher strained after a time when he began to resent the amount of secret knowledge he had revealed. Sorcery spells and occult dangerous paraphernalia were revealed to the novice who failed to realize the implications of Aisaga's interaction with her. She became implicated in the attribution of illness and misfortune to some of Aisaga's kin and neighbors. Clearly, if sorcery is to be taken seriously as experiential practice, as anthropological apprentices ensure us it should be, its murky ethics have to be taken equally seriously.

All of the anthropologists who have taken on this close and personal approach to the acquisition of esoteric knowledge have claimed to feel their preconceptions and perceptions challenged. Their encounters with seemingly inexplicable and sometimes frightening phenomena cannot be explained within the accepted canons of Western science that divide mind and body, natural and supernatural, real and unreal. If we find this more readily acceptable in reference to exotic cultures distant in space and time, then the material provided by another anthropologist, Jean Favret-Saada, is even more fascinating. Favret-Saada went to the Bocage region of Normandy in France to study sorcery.[25] There she found rural Frenchmen and women attributing their deaths, illnesses, and misfortunes to the occult activities of neighbors and others whom they attempted to combat by employing the services of "unwitchers" who look remarkably like the sorcerers or cunningfolk of the sixteenth and seventeenth centuries—in modern guise of course. Although she encountered difficulties initially because the Bocage people were well aware that they were made fun of in the French press as bizarre survivors of another age, Favret-Saada eventually convinced people that her interest was serious. So serious indeed that she was credited with unwitching abilities herself. In this region, believers say that sorcery "catches' a person to the death and "death is the only thing we know about round here." In a now familiar pattern, individual unfortunate events are accepted as "normal"; only when a series of misfortunes occurs in a family is sorcery suspected and the services of an "unwitcher" sought.

The subject of sorcery, of "being caught," is a hidden subject. It should not be discussed, both for fear of ridicule which is common from local professionals like doctors and clergy but also because it is thought to leave one open to further attack. No one admits to being a sorcerer and public accusations are never made. "Unwitchers" diagnose sorcery and take on mystical battles with the sorcerer who caused the misfortune, rather like the early modern shamans reported by historians. For health to be restored and misfortune to cease, the sorcerer must be killed. The logic of "unwitching" as we have seen so frequently across time and space entails the capacity to harm. While the sorcerer and the "witch-doctor" may be separated linguistically, in practice their position holds within it a central ambivalence. Favret-Saada herself became caught up in the world of sorcery to the extent that, like Stoller, she had to withdraw from the field.

This current trend in a more phenomenological approach to the subject matter has occasioned an edited book in which anthropologists discuss their scientifically inexplicable but experientially vivid field experiences.[26] In the introduction to the volume, anthropologists David Young and Jean-Guy Goulet recommend a method used by Michael Jackson, (the term borrowed, however, from philosopher William James)—"radical empiricism." In this method the anthropologist does not attempt to negotiate the, some would argue impossible, line between participation and observation but to become an "experimental subject" whose experiences are treated as primary data. Some critics argue that too much participation and not enough observation are equivalent to the "intellectualist" fallacy common in the nineteenth century—perhaps we could call it the "experientialist fallacy." The method assumes that we will discover something *more* than the experience encountered by a middle-class, educated, mostly European person when they engage in alien practices. In discussing the experiences reported in their book, Young and Goulet explain most of them as processes of the unconscious. Their approach is essentially rationalist, however, and they disagree with Stoller and Olkes' comment that respect for a culture "means accepting fully beliefs and phenomena which our own systems of knowledge often hold preposterous." They also reject the position, held by some anthropologists, which they rightly regard as extreme, that spirits do exist, and that we should start from this assumption.[27]

But taking our hosts seriously often has unforseen consequences. The novice may become so entangled in their experience that we are only left with their personal journey rather than an empathetic and informed account of sorcery and its context. Sometimes participation in the lifeworld of the sorcerer is not available to the researcher. It may be regarded as inappropriate for reason of social status or gender. Perhaps it is only within the postcolonial political and economic realities of the developing world, for example, that a woman could have become apprenticed to a Melanesian sorcerer and in the context of 1930s colonialism in Africa, a member of the class of the colonizers could not.

Contemporary Witchcraft

Fascination with the occult in the West is not new. In the Renaissance many learned men dabbled in magic and developed philosophies based on what were at the time believed to be texts that originated before the time of Moses. In the late nineteenth century interest peaked again, this time mining Renaissance sources and academic texts for access to secret arcane and esoteric knowledge discarded by the secular scientific world of post-Enlightenment thought. It is out of this latter period that contemporary magic derives most of its history and its largely invented and extremely eclectic tradition. Activities as diverse as tarot card reading, astrology, goddess worship, *wicca,* and ritual magic are popularly seen as New Age hobbies, but to the serious advocates of Neo-Paganism and ritual magic their practices are of a profoundly religious kind, linking them to various ancient traditions of suppressed or neglected esoteric knowledge.

According to Tanya Luhrmann whose study of ritual magic in England is now almost ten years old, there were some several thousand practitioners of "serious magic" in Britain. In the late 80s in the United States she estimated that there were some 80,000 "paganists" or practitioners of *wicca.*[28] Undoubtedly, these figures have by now grown exponentially. While there is amazing diversity in the practice of contemporary witchcraft, contrary to most organized religions, the practitioners themselves do not regard this as problematic. The only dogma is that there is no dogma. Luhrmann notes, however, that some ritual magic adepts are extremely particular about procedure. Most of those involved view their practices as both religious and as "pragmatic, result-producing" activities.[29]

Practitioners of ritual magic, whether they acknowledge it or not, draw from the works of a group founded in the nineteenth century called the Hermetic Order of the Golden Dawn. The founders of the Golden Dawn were freemasons basing their philosophy on a syncretic view of the varied neo-Platonist ideas of Renaissance magicians filtered through the writing of a French cleric who used the pseudonym Eliphas Lévi. Central to this philosophy is the idea that human will power, when trained, can bring about supernormal effects by uniting the microcosm that exists in man with the macrocosm of the universe. Much of the ritual practise was developed by the Golden Dawn's founders from eighteenth-century Rosicrucian practice and recent knowledge of the religion of ancient Egypt uncovered by archaeologists. Among Golden Dawn's better known members were the Irish poet W.B.Yeats and Aleister Crowley, known less for his erudition, magical practice, and poetry than for his "notorious sexual habits."

By 1903 the Golden Dawn had fragmented, ultimately producing several offshoots, the most important of which was founded in 1922 by Violet Firth who called herself Dion Fortune. Her group trained most of the leaders of the major contemporary groups of practitioners of "Western Mysteries" ritual magic who see themselves as a continuation of a "mystery" tradition in the West combining elements of Egyptian, Mithraic, Druidic, Renaissance, Hermetic, and Kabbalistic magic.

While witches also see themselves as part of this tradition, their ethos, as Luhrmann puts it, has more of the shaman than the monk. Some Western mysteries groups have strict requirements for membership such as being a practising Christian, and a solvent parent who is not homosexual or involved in taking drugs. The contemporary practice of *wicca,* while claiming continuity with the ancient religions of Europe and Britain said to have been so viciously supressed by Christianity in the early modern period, owes more to a retired civil servant named Gerald Gardiner than to Margaret Murray. Gardiner claimed that not only did witches survive the persecutions that ended in the eighteenth century but that their knowledge of the "old religion" was hereditary. According to Gardiner and his followers witchcraft was an ancient nature religion featuring the Goddess as well as the horned God. Gardiner's *Book of Shadows,* a twentieth-century compilation of elements from the Golden Dawn, became a handbook for the practice of *wicca.* The irony of this will not be lost on those who know something of the history of folk magic and demonolgy—once more the ideas of the élite take over those of the ordinary cunning men and women.

The major elements of Gardiner's magic are membership in a coven into which novices are initiated bound and blindfolded while undergoing a symbolic scourging; nude "working"; secrecy; use of an altar contained in a circle and of the pentagram and triangle; appeal to the guardians of the four cardinal points; use of water and incense; use of a sword and two knives, one black- and one white- handled and the idea that divine forces are drawn into one or more of the celebrants. Ritual sexual intercourse features in higher initiations in some groups. *Wicca,* as some of its practitioners are happy to acknowledge, is not a unitary ancient tradition but a syncretic amalgam of elements of much more recent origin. Its resemblance to the practices that historians have uncovered in the countryside of Britain and Europe in the early modern period is nonexistent. The sorcery that rural folk knew and practised and the witchcraft attributed to them by both their fellows and those in power existed within a framework of shifting and ambivalent knowledge of how the world was and what sort of creatures inhabited it. Most people believed that it was possible for humans to harm each other by mystical means; most people today do not. Contemporary witchcraft is thus radically different from anything that was known by that name in the past both in its self-conscious largely collective practice and its inherent romanticism.

The appeal of these religions, according to their adherents, is their holism, eclecticism, absence of dogma, and celebration and inclusion of the female principle. They offer the opportunity to include communal and solitary practices that are psychologically appealing. While some groups, particularly the neo-pagans are rarely exclusivist, some ritual magicians are much more closed and hierarchically ordered.

Luhrmann, at the conclusion to her study, takes a rationalist stance to the subject matter. How are we to explain the irrational beliefs of apparently otherwise rational people? It is problematic, she notes, that the majority of the adherents she met were well educated and claimed to "know," rather than to "believe," that their ritual practices worked. However, they also tended to be deeply ambivalent about this knowledge so that they frequently wavered between the claim that magic works and the position that whether it worked or not it was still beneficial, at least psychologically. Modern theologians take a similar position to magicians, Luhrmann argues. Magicians, however, have a harder time reconciling their belief in the efficacy of magical practice since unlike theological beliefs such efficacy is testable. Deep ambivalence to practice accompanies a deep commitment to it.

But if contemporary witches seem not only credulous but quite harmless to secular sceptics, to other sections of the community in parts of the Western world they represent the false face of a much more dangerous, conspiratorial, and clandestine group—the satanists.[30] In the United States during the 1980s and early 1990s, thousands of accusations were made against apparently ordinary citizens, large numbers of whom were convicted of the sexual abuse of children in the context of what has come to be called "satanic ritual abuse." In the United Kingdom in 1988 it was alleged at an international conference that "at least 4,000 children were being sacrificed a year in Great Britain alone" and even that bastion of conservative reporting, the *Times* newspaper, wrote about international conspiracies of satanists.[31] Many of those sentenced in the United States later had their convictions overturned on appeal but according to one source, more than 50 individuals remain in prison.[32] The situation in which these trials and convictions were able to proceed has some disturbing parallels to aspects of the witch hunts of the early modern period examined earlier.

As Norman Cohn pointed out, in relation to the history of European persecutions of heretics and witches, two major things were essential. First is the dissemination and acceptance by those in power of a series of beliefs about the secret activities of the evildoers that defines their evil character and justifies their persecution. The central, indelibly persistent themes in the historical cases were ritualized perverse sex, incest, and the cannibalism of infants. All of these themes appeared in the prosecutions of parents and child-care workers. Second, is the willingness to act on the beliefs by setting in place procedures to apprehend, interrogate, and prosecute suspects. The American trials, though varied in detail, relied on a widespread belief among certain sections of the population, particularly some radical feminist groups, that the sexual abuse of female children had reached epidemic proportions. In addition was another belief, in this case popular with fundamentalist Christians, that clandestine and organized groups of satanists did exist in the community and that they did engage in satanic rituals involving the sexual abuse of children. But as anthropologist Jean la Fontaine discovered in her study of satanic abuse allegations in England, a variety of groups supported the satanic abuse ideas and there was frequently radical differences among them on almost all other matters.[33] The combination of these two beliefs allied to the growing interest in uncovering repressed memories of childhood abuse through therapy, provided a potent mélange of sorcery, sex, and pseudoscience that, with intense media attention, caught the imagination of the public. Undoubtedly modern fascination with the occult, certain genres of Hollywood films and television series featuring witchcraft and satanic themes, a sense of panic about the care of children in a society in which women's roles had undergone rapid change all contributed to a general climate in which, in the most technologically advanced nation on earth, satan could be believed to be alive and well and operating in the suburbs.

For many years it was assumed by experts that children's accusations of incest were false, but the promotion of therapy that was said to unlock memory gave credence to the view that childhood incest was not just common but epidemic, supporting with what was counted as a growing body of evidence, what had been merely a belief. The vigorous promotion of this view to politicians and the relevant authorities enabled various procedures to be put in place to facilitate the detection and prosecution of suspects. Allocation of government funds, the appointment of experts in satanic ritual abuse to influential government instrumentalities in child welfare, medical, and legal areas, production of guidelines for investigation, and the alteration of statutes of limitation all facilitated civil suits and prosecutions. In many cases it was the testimony of children that was used in prosecutions. Children were frequently reluctant witnesses and had to be coerced to "confess" the crimes alleged against them. The article of faith that children could not mention abuse without having experienced it (a reversal of the earlier view) led investigators to adopt a style of interrogation that went against all the existing canons of procedure in dealing with children. Leading questions, bullying, and coercion did not cease with many of these witnesses until they had made increasingly bizarre accusations against their carers. As the marks on the body were used to identify witches, child victims were identified from various signs in their genitalia whether they reported being abused or not. The identification of these signs, developed by medical experts and since totally discredited, escalated the numbers of abused children and prosecutions both in the United States and the United Kingdom.

In response to critics and sceptics, supporters of satanic abuse theories asked how was it possible that so many ordinary people should recount similar experiences if there was no foundation to them? Precisely the same question was posed, as we have seen, about the reality of the witches' sabbat. The answer was complex, and so it is here. What is clear is that human fantasies about evildoing display both a remarkable similarity in certain core areas with an astounding variety that is testament to the powers of the human imagination. The use of particular techniques of interrogation particularly with children and the setting in which therapists uncovered repressed memories provided ample scope for the elaboration of an ancient theme. The idea that among us there are hidden evil enemies, neighbors and kinsmen who could be guilty of the most hideous antisocial crime of all—the crime against reproduction: incest and the cannibalisation of innocent babies—is clearly a recurring cosmic nightmare. When authorities begin to take such things seriously and to act upon them, a dangerous reality of another kind begins to threaten every citizen.

NOTES

1. See Bruce Kapferer, *The Feast of the Sorcery: Practices of Consciousness and Power.* (Chicago: University of Chicago Press, 1997). See pp. 20-21.
2. See D. Pocock in David Parkin(ed.), *The Anthropology of Evil* (Oxford: Blackwell Press, 1985).
3. See Lucy Mair, *Witchcraft* (New York: McGraw Hill, 1969).
4. There were many influential studies of accusations in African societies in this period, for example Mary Douglas' edited volume *Witchcraft Confessions and Accusations* (London: Tavistock, 1970) and Max Marwick's study of the Cewa, *Sorcery in Its Social Setting* (Manchester: Manchester University Press, 1965). Many years before (1944), Clyde Kluckhohn had produced his ethnography, *Navaho Witchcraft*, (Boston: Beacon Press), which combined theories about accusations with a large number of first-hand Navaho accounts of their experiences of witchcraft.
5. See Mary Patterson, 1974–75 "Sorcery and Witchcraft in Melanesia," *Qceania* 45, nos. 2 and 3. Lawrence, in his article on the Garia refers to this kind of sorcery as *sangguma*. It is much more commonly applied to the kind of sorcery involving physical assault described in the following paragraphs. See Lawrence in M. Stephen, *Sorcerer and Witch in Melanesia*, (Melbourne: Melbourne

University Press, 1987). Unfortunately, in this latter work, Melanesia refers only to Papua New Guinea.
6. An exception is Bruce Knauft's ethnography of Gebusi sorcery in which sorcerers are identified instances, though almost never by name. B. Knauft, *Good Company and Violence: Sorcery and Social Action in a Lowland New Guinea Society*, (Berkeley: University of California Press, 1985).
7. See C. W. Watson and R. Ellen's book *Understanding Witchcraft and Sorcery in Southeast Asia*, (Honolulu: University of Hawaii Press 1993) that points out that the predominance of social control theories arising from the analysis of accusations or patterns of social organization characteristic of a lot of the African and Melanesian material did not emerge from the work of Southeast Asian specialists. This is not, of course, to argue that sorcery does not exist in the region but only to say that it may not be as important as elsewhere. More research is needed before we can make a considered judgment on this issue. An important theme in this region is the ambivalent status of the curer-healer who, as almost everywhere else and given the right conditions, can be suspected and accused of sorcery. The recent murders of practitioners called *dukun* in East Java (Indonesia), while probably connected to

other sociopolitical factors as well, are an illustration of the dangerously ambivalent role occupied by occult practitioners in many societies.

8. This point is made in Brian Levack's excellent introductory account, *The Witch-Hunt in Early Modern Europe*, (London: Longman, 1987).

9. See R. Briggs, *Witches and Neighbours: The Social and Cultural Context of European Witchcraft*, (London: HarperCollins, 1996).

10. When historians took up this topic in the seventies, some of them, like Alan Macfarlane who wrote *Witchcraft in Tudor and Stuart England*, (London: Routledge and Kegan Paul, 1970) were influenced by the work of anthropologists on accusations in African villages. Others, like Hugh Trevor-Roper who wrote one of the best-known works of this period *The European Witch Craze of the Sixteenth and Seventeenth Centuries*, (Harmonsworth: Penguin Books, 1969) felt that the unique nature of European history made such comparisons pointless. In the last twenty years a vast amount of research has been carried out in European archives on the witch trials. Recently more attention has been paid to the ideas of the ordinary folk as well as the élite about witchcraft and the practitioners of different kinds of magic and divination and there has been a greater dialogue between anthropologists and historians.

11. Historian Carlo Ginzburg discovered in the archives of the Friuli district of Northern Italy a fascinating case of local beliefs about shamans who battled sorcerers while in trance and the distortion that the Inquisition accomplished by investigating them for witchcraft. Over time *benandanti* as they were called began to confess to "normal" witchcraft activities like going to sabbats. See "Deciphering the Sabbath" in B. Ankerloo and G. Henningsen, eds., *Early Modern European Witchcraft*, (Oxford: Clarendon Press, 1993). Similar beliefs were not confined to Italy. Research in southeastern Europe suggests they may have been quite widespread. In Slovenia and Istria sorcerers called *kresniks* battled with each other in the dreams and trances of those born, like the *benandanti* with a caul (part of the amniotic sack over the head at birth). See G. Klaniczay, *The Uses of Supernatural Power*, (Princeton: Princeton University Press, 1990).

12. C. Larner wrote two important works on witchcraft, one about the Scottish trials called *Enemies of God: The Witch-Hunt in Scotland*, (London: Chatto and Windus, 1981) and *Witchcraft and Religion: The Politics of Popular Belief*, (London: Basil Blackwell, 1984).

13. Students interested in pursuing some interesting recent views on the early modern witch hunts might like to consult the volume of essays edited by J. Barry, M. Hester, and G.Roberts *Witchcraft in Early Modern Europe: Studies in Culture and Belief*, (Cambridge: Cambridge University Press, 1996).

14. See R. Briggs, *Witches and Neighbours: The Social and Cultural Context of European Witchcraft*, (London: HarperCollins, 1996).

15. See R. Austen, *The Moral Economy of Witchcraft: An Essay in Comparative History* in J. Comaroff and J. Comaroff *Modernity and Its Malcontents: Ritual, and Power in Postcolonial Africa*, (Chicago: University of Chicago Press, 1995).

16. See A. Barstow, *Witchcraze: A New History of the European Witch Hunts*, (London: Pandora/HarperCollins, 1994).

17. See J. Demos, *Entertaining Satan: Witchcraft and the Culture of Early New England*, 1982 and R. Godbeer *The Devil ls Dominion:Magic and Religion in Early New England*, (Cambridge: Cambridge University Press, 1992).

18. See I. Bostridge, *Witchcraft and Transformations c. 1650–c. 1750*, (Oxford: Clarendon Press, 1997). The most influential work written on this topic until recently was Keith Thomas' *Religion and the Decline of Magic*, (New York: Charles Scribner's Sons, 1971).

19. See P. Geschiere, *The Modernity of Witchcraft: Politics and the Occult in Postcolonial Africa*, (Charlottesville: University Press of Virginia, 1997).

20 See A. Apter in J. Comaroff and J. Comaroff *Modernity and Its Malcontents: Ritual and Power in Postcolonial Africa*, (Chicago: University of Chicago Press, 1995).

21. The issue of spontaneous confession, that is confession that is not coerced, has always been seen as somewhat problematic. In the case of the witch cleansing cults, it could be argued that there is coercion in being singled out as a witch and since there is no immediate danger, confession is probably psychologically satisfying. It is more problematic of course when the penalty is death, exile, or lengthy incarceration. Such confession occurs across cultures and across time and space. It even occurred recently during the United States satanic ritual abuse panic. By the time the confession had been recanted the defendant had been sentenced to a lengthy jail term. Spontaneous confessions have been attributed to the generally coercive nature of the situation itself, to the desire of mentally unstable persons to be the center of attention, or to the renditions of events that are perceived as real by the defendant who experienced them while in trance or a drug induced altered state. The relative uniformity of some aspects of early modern confessions, both spontaneous and torture induced, has provoked some researchers to claim that cunning folk/sorcerers commonly used ointments containing psychotropic drugs extracted from well-known plants. Historians disagree over the likelihood of the use of such drugs, a common effect of which was the sensation of flight. Some claim that when we examine lists of ingredients for such ointments, we find that they contain materials similar to those used in "poisons" which are not pharmacologically but magically active. For a contrary view see M. Harner, "The Role of Hallucinogenic Plants in European Witchcraft" in M. Harner, ed., *Hallucinogens and Shamanism*, (Oxford: Oxford University Press, 1973).

22. These works were *The Teachings of Don Juan: A Yaqui Way of Knowledge* (Berkeley: University of California Press, 1968); *A Separate Reality: Further Conversations with Don Juan*, (New York: Simon & Schuster,1971); *Journey to lxtlan: The Lessons of Don Juan*, (New York: Simon & Schuster, 1972), and *Tales of Power*, (New York: Simon & Schuster, 1974). Since then another five books have appeared.

23. See Richard de Mille, *Casteñada's Journey: The Power and the Allegory*, (London: Abacus, 1978).

24. See Paul Stoller and C. Olkes *In Sorcery's Shadow: A Memoir of Apprenticeship Among the Songhay of Niger*, (Chicago: University of Chicago Press,1989).

25. See J. Favret-Saada, *Deadly Words: Witchcraft in the Bocage*, (Cambridge: Maison des Sciences de l'Homme and Cambridge University Press, 1980).

26. See D. Young and J. G. Goulet, eds., *Being Changed by Cross-Cuhural Encounters: The Anthropology of Extraordinary Experience*, (Ontario, Broadview Press, 1994).

27. Young and Goulet mention Schweder and Felicitas Goodman as holding this view. (ibid:324).

28. See T.M. Luhrmann, *Persuasions of the Witch's Craft. Ritual Magic in Contemporary England*, (Oxford: Blackwell, 1989).

29. For some more recent accounts of contemporary magic see J. R. Lewis, ed., *Magical Religion and Modern Witchcraft*, (Albany: State University of New York Press, 1996). For an excellent account of what is known of pagan religions in the British Isles, see R. Hutton *The Pagan Religions of the Ancient British Isles*, (Oxford: Blackwell, 1991).

30. Although California hosts the "Church of Satan" whose members call themselves satantists, they have more in common with the neo-pagans just described than with the networks of child abusing monsters alleged to exist by some Americans. Occasional individuals claiming to be "satanists" have been prosecuted for various crimes but there has never been any evidence that these are other than isolated cases.

31. Anthropologist Jean La Fontaine, veteran of African witchcraft research, conducted a government-spon-sored inquiry into the reality of satanic abuse in England, published in 1998. Her work endorses the view taken here that there are enough similarities between the satanic abuse phenomenon of the late twentieth century and the witch hunts of the early modern period despite a gap of some three hundred years to make comparison useful. See Jean La Fontaine, *Speak of the Devil: Tales of Satanic Abuse in Contemporary England*, (Cambridge: Cambridge University Press, 1998.

32. For an excellent account of this phenomenon see D. Nathan and M. Snedeker, *Satan's Silence: Ritual Abuse and the Making of a Modem American Witch Hunt*, (New York: Basic Books/HarperCollins, 1995), and R. Ofshe and E. Watters, *Making Monsters. False Memories, Psychotherapy, and Sexual Hysteria*, (New York: Charles Scribner's Sons, 1994). Journalist Richard Guilliatt published an account of the phenomenon in Australia, *Talk of the Devil: Repressed Memory and the Ritual Abuse Witch-Hunt*, (Melbourne: The Text Publishing Co., 1996). As La Fontaine noted in her work mentioned above, the contemporary phenomenon, while having important local aspects outside of the United States was spread principally in the English-speaking world through the published work of experts and the exchange of information and training in professional conferences, workshops, and so on. In the early modern period demonology was similarly spread through manuals of instruction for interrogators, the training of expert witchfinders, and the travel of influential members of the elite.

33. See endnote 31.

Eight

Aboriginal Religions

Raymond Scupin

Lindenwood University

ABORGINAL RELIGIONS

An enormous variety of aboriginal religious traditions have existed back to prehistoric times. The earliest forms of prehistoric religions are associated with archaeological finds or artifacts that have been interpreted as "religious" or "spiritual." Some of the most ancient artifacts that have been characterized as religious or spiritual include small altars or animal bones that are dated at the time of Neandertal in Europe at around 70,000 B.C.E. Though these artifacts have been subjected to intensive scrutiny and have led to debates within the archaeological community as to whether these artifacts are authentically religious or not, there is no doubt that aboriginal religions were practiced in the distant past. Throughout human prehistory, before the development of writing and religious texts, aboriginal religious traditions flourished in different areas of the world. Some small-scale societies based on food-gathering, hunting, or horticulture have survived in some isolated areas up to the recent past, and into the present. Many of these societies continued to maintain aboriginal religious beliefs and practices based on "nonliterate" or "nontextual" spiritual traditions. These small-scale societies that have managed to sustain themselves over the centuries were affected and are now continually affected by dramatic global changes.

There have been many misleading attempts to characterize all of the aboriginal religions as "primal" or "archaic" traditions that share essential elements.[1] As seen in Chapter 2, many of the nineteenth-century anthropologists and theorists believed that all so-called "primitive religions" were "animistic," involving a belief in a plethora of different spirits. Anthropologists such as Tylor or Frazer (who did not do any field work among these societies) proposed that these early aboriginal traditions represented the original stage in the evolution of religion. In their view, later stages of religious development evolved leading, ultimately to the emergence of full-fledged "civilized" religions such as Christianity. However, contemporary anthropologists, who have done extensive field work among nonliterate small-scale societies find that aboriginal religions are as diversified as many other "literate" religions. As will be seen in this chapter, aboriginal religious traditions range widely from animism to polytheism to monotheism, with sophisticated cosmologies and myths. There is no single stage of development associated with these aboriginal traditions. One other stereotype about the traditional, aboriginal religions is that they were static, unsystematic, rigid, and incoherent. For example, Max Weber held that all traditional religions were static and irrational, whereas the great religious traditions based on religious texts developed rational, systematic formulations. Again, anthropologists in the twentieth century such as Malinowski or Evans-Pritchard and many contemporary ethnographers who did extensive field work among small-scale societies have discovered that aboriginal religious traditions are as flexible, changeable, systematic, and rational as literate religious traditions.

In this chapter for the purposes of illustrating some of the variety of aboriginal religious traditions studied by contemporary anthropologists we will focus on two different areas of the world: native north America and the Pacific Islands. In native North America we will look at the aboriginal religions of the Eskimo or Inuit peoples who are foragers (hunters and gatherers) and the tribal cultures of Iroquois Indians of the Northeast region and the Indians of the Plains region. In the Pacific region we will concentrate on the native peoples of Australia, the Australian aborigines, the peoples of Melanesia, and the native Hawaiians. These different indigenous societies of native America and the Pacific represent a small sample of the wide range and variety of aboriginal religious traditions. In addition to describing the different forms and practices of these aboriginal religious traditions, we will also consider what contemporary anthropologists have learned about how these religions have accommodated to the impact of recent global changes that have affected these societies.

NATIVE AMERICAN RELIGIONS

Traditional Religion Among the Eskimo/Inuit

Groups of native peoples popularly known as the Eskimo have resided in the Arctic area since at least 2500 B.C.E.[2] Some Eskimo live in northwestern Alaska near the Bering Sea, and others live in the arctic regions of northern Canada, extending eastward all the way to Greenland. The majority of the Eskimo refer to themselves as the Inuit, which is also the name of the language spoken by most of these peoples. Traditionally the Inuit peoples were involved in a hunting-gathering or foraging mode of subsistence. A *hunter-gatherer*, or *foraging*, society is a society whose subsistence is based on the hunting of animals and gathering of vegetation. The Inuit were involved in hunting sea mammals such as bowhead whales, seals, and walruses, as well as caribou, musk oxen, an occasional polar bear, and birds. They also fish in nearby waters. Unlike most other foragers, since vegetation was scarce in the arctic regions, most of the subsistence activities of the Inuit were focused on hunting. Although their diet consisted primarily of meat, the Inuit generally satisfied their basic nutritional requirements of carbohydrate, protein, and vitamins (from berries, green roots, and fish and fish oil). They preferred cooked foods, but boiling food over fires fueled by blubber oil was slow and expensive; consequently, the Inuit ate most of their food raw. Most Inuit groups have to move during different seasons to pursue game and other resources. For example, the northwestern Alaska Inuit move from the coastal areas into the interior regions during the summer seasons to hunt herds of caribou. These nomadic behaviors were not arbitrary or spontaneous. Rather, they were carefully planned to minimize labor while providing vital resources. These patterns of mobility represent an admirable appreciation and intimate knowledge of the environment in which these foragers resided.

An extremely complex foraging technology was created by the Inuit to procure animal food resources. The classic Inuit technology has evolved over the past 3,000 years and includes equipment made from bone, stone, skin, wood, and ice. Most of the Inuit resided in snow houses called *iglu*, in the winter, or in homes built of stone, wood, or sod. *Umiaks* (large boats) and *kayaks* (canoes) are used for whaling, sealing, and transportation. Inuit technology also includes dogsleds, lances, fish spears, bows and arrows, harpoons with detachable points, traps, fish hooks, and soapstone lamps used with whale and seal oil for heating and cooking. And, the Inuit have developed sophisticated techniques for curing hides from caribou and seals to make boots, parkas, and other necessary arctic gear. Although most foragers were not able to store food, the Inuit had limited storage capacities. Some Inuit dug holes beneath the permafrost so that they could store meat. The storage of meat, berries, and greens enabled the Inuit to maintain a certain amount of affluence even in winter. They thus had a steady, reliable source of meat and vegetation as a base for subsistence activities.

The social and political organization of the Inuit was based on family and kinship. The two basic elements of social organization for the Inuit are the nuclear family and the band. The nuclear family is the small family unit associated with procreation: parents and offspring. The nuclear family is most adaptive for hunting-gathering societies because of the flexibility needed for the location and easy distribution and exchange of food resources, and the other exigencies of hunting. A band consists of a number of families cooperating and hunting together. Typically, band organization is extremely flexible, with families and individuals leaving and joining bands as circumstances demanded. In addition, personal conflicts and shortages of resources may encourage people to move into or out of bands. An informal political system based on personal characteristics and kinship ties was evident among the Inuit. Political leadership is based on personal characteristics or supernatural powers that the individual is believed to possess. When a particular political leader died, there were no rules of hereditary succession. This lack of rules for succession emphasizes the decentralization of political power and authority in a foraging society such as the Inuit.

One unique tradition described among some Inuit for resolving political conflicts became known as the song duel. The song duel was often used to resolve conflicts between males over various issues. If a conflict involved two males, they would encounter each other in front of a large public meeting. They then insulted each other through improvised songs, and the crowd resolved the conflict by selecting a winner. With the declaration of a winner, the dispute was resolved without the use of any formal court system or coercion.

Inuit religious traditions were based on some traditional mythologies that varied from group to group. One of the creation myths recorded by Franz Boas illustrates some of the basic themes of Inuit life. This narrative myth begins with the tale of a man Inung and his daughter Sedna. Inung had been a widower for some time, and Sedna grew to become a beautiful young woman. Sedna had many suitors who tried to win her heart, but they were not successful in doing so. Eventually, a seabird appeared to Sedna and promised her a life where there was never any hunger and his tent was filled with beautiful warm skins. Sedna flew across the sea with the seabird and reached his home. But upon seeing his home, Sedna realized that she had been deceived. The seabird's home was made up of fish skins and had holes in it. There was no protection from the wind and snow, and her bed was made of tough walrus hides. In her dismay, Sedna cried out for her father. After a year, the father came to visit his daughter in her new home. Hearing about her plight, Inung killed the seabird and took her into his boat. On the way home a heavy storm rose in the water that threatened both of their lives. Inung offered Sedna back to the seabirds and threw her overboard. She clung to the edge of the boat for her life. Inung cut off the first joints of her fingers, and her nails were transformed into whale bones; he cut off the rest of her fingers and they were changed into seals.

The storm subsided and the seabirds believed that Sedna had drowned. Inung allowed her to come back into the boat. However, she had developed a bitter hatred toward her father. After they went ashore, she called her dogs and let them knaw off the feet and hands of her father while he was asleep. When he woke up Inung cursed his daughter and the dogs who had maimed him. The earth then swallowed up the daughter, the father, and the dogs, and they were sent to the land of Adlivan at the bottom of the sea, where Sedna is the goddess. This myth condenses the narratives regarding origins of the game animals and their importance to the Inuit people. The myth attributes the origins of these animals to mistreatment and mutilation of the goddess Sedna. The game animals are under the control of Sedna who releases them to be hunted by the people. Traditional Inuit art products include many items made from ivory, represent these animals controlled by Sedna, and were worn as amulets to enhance supernatural powers and practices.[3] All of the men were carvers and believed that when they took a piece of unworked ivory they were releasing a form of the hidden spirit that was contained in the ivory.

The Inuit maintain a religious belief system that involves shamanistic curers or healers who control and manipulate the supernatural world. In contrast to some of the "literate" religious traditions, Inuit religion does not assume the existence of an omnipotent supreme being. The Inuit believe that every living creature possesses a soul or spirit that is reincarnated after death. Each animal has its own *inua*, or soul or spirit. Thus, game is treated with great respect. They believe that the souls of deceased individuals remain in the vicinity of the living. Most of the Inuit did not maintain a belief in an afterworld, or heaven, in which these souls congregate after death. Rather, they believed that these souls remain close to the natural world. The spirits of animals allow themselves to be hunted and are constantly reincarnated in other animal forms to be hunted again to ensure the Inuit way of life.

Within these general conceptions of spirituality the Inuit believe in *soul loss*, in which a person's soul can be taken from the body as a result of unforeseen circumstances. Soul loss causes mental and physical illness for the individual. It is often believed that the soul has been stolen by another spirit. The Inuit cope with these situations through shamanistic techniques. Two different forms of shamanism are found in Inuit culture. One form is hereditary, passed on through either parent. The more common variety involves people who receive shamanistic powers through direct contact with the supernatural, usually through dreams, visions, or hallucinations. People usually go through an extensive training period before they can begin practicing as a shaman. Inuit shamans learn various relaxation techniques to induce trance states. They also learn methods of healing, curing, and exorcism. These techniques are used to produce group emotional experiences so as to enhance spiritual growth. In many cases, the shamanistic performances work effectively in curing illnesses or resolving emotional problems. Undoubtedly, in certain instances the Inuit beliefs and cultural conceptions surrounding shamanism trigger certain states of mind that produce positive psychological and even physical consequences such as overcoming illness and injuries.

One of the traditional religious ceremonies that illustrates some of the basic themes of Inuit religion is referred to as the "bladder ceremony." This intense religious festival involves the collection of all the bladders of the birds and animals slain during the year. The bladders of seals, walruses, whales, and other animals are inflated and hung in one of the large communal houses in the village. These bladders or balloons are associated with the souls of the game animals. Fires are lit in the house and no noise is made that would disrupt the spirits. The bladders are honored for a period of about four days. The festival includes a number of purification rituals and offerings of food and water. These rituals are aimed at drawing out the souls of the seals and other animals residing in the bladders. After the ceremony the bladders are taken down, deflated, and removed through a hole in the roof of the house. They are then pushed through an ice hole and returned to the underwater home of the goddess Sedna to be reborn as new animals and to return the following year to be hunted. During the ceremony there are dancing, singing, and exchanging gifts of food and other goods throughout the village. The bladder festival symbolizes the renewal, regeneration, and return of the game animals. Part of this renewal involves the creation of new songs by the men, and women give the men new clothing that they have made. The ceremony is an appeal to the spirits for success in the new year.

Colonialism and Religious Change Among the Inuit

Colonial penetration of the arctic region was begun by the Russian expedition of Vitus Bering in 1741. Bering, a Danish explorer, was on a mission to determine where Asia ended and America began. Through this expedition the Russians became aware of valuable fur seal and sea otter skins hunted by the Inuits. At that time the pelts from these animals brought high prices in Europe. Large numbers of Russian fur traders settled in Alaska, leading to colonization of the area. British fur trade companies were also expanding throughout the arctic areas in the region of Canada, and England had colonized vast territories in the Inuit regions. Faced with a decline in fur bearing animals, the Russians sold Alaska to the U.S. government in 1867. Of course, none of the native Inuit peoples were involved in any of these negotiations. The Inuits were simply absorbed into the jurisdiction of U.S. law and government. In addition, the Inuit became dependent on the fur traders as they began to abandon their traditional subsistence to hunt animals for their pelts and obtain goods or cash in return. Another consequence of this colonization of Inuit territory were widespread epidemics. Measles and influenza viruses began to spread quickly among these people, resulting in rapid depopulation.

Christian missionaries began to arrive in the Arctic among the Inuit beginning in the nineteenth century. To reduce their competition for Inuit converts, the major Protestant churches divided their missionary activities into different areas. The Presbyterians and Episcopalians went into areas north of the Brooks Range. The Quaker Church went into the western region, while the Seward Peninsula was assigned to the Congregationalists, Norwegian Lutheran, and the Methodists. Anglican and Catholic missionaries began to move into the Canadian arctic areas in the 1930s. These missionaries tried to develop a whole new way of life for the Inuit. For example, the Presbyterian minister Sheldon Jackson, who became the general agent of education for Alaska in the 1890s, was convinced that the Inuit people had to dramatically change their lifestyle in order to become Christian and "civilized." He directed the attempt to change the subsistence life of the Inuit by introducing reindeer herding. Large quantities of reindeer were imported from Siberia to Alaska in order to facilitate this enterprise. For a number of reasons, including the attempt to take over the reindeer business by nonnative businesses, the reindeer business eventually collapsed by the time of World War II.

The various missionaries wanted to replace the Inuit religion with the Christian tradition, which was viewed as more humane, moral, and "civilized." To make conversion more effective they introduced schools and medical facilities among the Inuit communities. The traditional religions were reinterpreted by the missionaries who taught the Inuit that the spirits described by the shamans were devils in the Christian tradition. The missionaries emphasized that the shamans could not cure measles, influenza, or other diseases that were devastating their communities. They noted that the shamans themselves would often become ill from these diseases. New Christian and Western symbols were introduced to substitute for the older religion and shamanistic rituals. They were taught Christian hymns and prayers to replace the earlier magical practices. Aside from attempting to change their spiritual beliefs, the missionaries began to introduce the norms and practices of Western society into Inuit society.

Beginning in the 1950s and 1960s other missionaries from the Church of the Assembly of God established congregations in several Inuit communities. These missionaries, in contrast to the Presbyterians or Episcopalians, attempted to introduce a more evangelical or fundamentalist form of Christianity. In their church services the Assembly of God members would speak about their salvation and confess their past sins such as drinking, gambling, or smoking. They prohibited all forms of dancing and recreation that were seen to be as immoral. They also emphasized the efficacy of prayer and the immediate intervention of God in daily affairs. They taught that diseases could be healed through the use of prayer and introduced spiritual healing, commonly called "laying on (healing) hands." This faith healing became an important aspect for promoting the Assembly of God churches. The introduction of these new churches produced splits and divisions within the Inuit communities. Converts to the evangelical churches began to view other Protestants as living a less moral life than they were.

Despite the conversion of most of the Inuit peoples to Christianity, many still retain the beliefs and practices of their older tradition. This blend and combination between religious traditions is sometimes referred to as *syncretism* by anthropologists. For example, presently many of the Inuit conceive of the supernatural world as being composed of the Christian God, Satan, and a number of other vague demons. The devils and demons were essentially the same spirits that used to be controlled by the shamans. In fact, shamans who converted to Christianity were believed to be able to retain their spiritual power. They could exorcize demons and devils who possessed individuals and were believed to induce psychotic episodes. Inuit ministers were called in to pray over an individual who had a psychotic experience in the same way shamans might have been called in during the past. Thus, many of the older religious beliefs of the Inuit were flexible enough to become incorporated into the new syncretic blend of tradition and Christianity.

TRADITIONAL RELIGION AMONG THE IROQUOIS

The native American people known as the Iroquois included many different groups who resided in the eastern woodland region of North America. The Iroquois were comprised of peoples such as the Mohawks, Onondaga, Cayuga, Seneca, Oneida, and Huron. Rivers such as the St. Lawrence representing the northern areas of the Iroquois, and lakes such as Lake Champlain and Lake Ontario provided ground for horticultural activities. These horticultural practices probably appeared between 2300 and 1000 B.C.E., although this time frame is not certain. The native people of this region began to raise maize and other crops along with collecting local wild species. The Iroquois constructed their villages with longhouses in the center of the settlement. (Longhouses were large, multifamily housing built with upright posts that supported horizontal poles for rafters. Large slabs of bark, laced together with cords of plant fiber, covered the framework.) Typically, Iroquois males cleared the primary forest around the village and burned the cut litter. In the spring the women planted 15 varieties of maize, beans, squash, and other crops, which females later harvested and processed. The Iroquois left part of the primary forest standing so that deer, squirrels, fox, and bear were available for hunting. The forest also provided nuts, berries, and many species of wild plants. After harvesting the crops in the fall, the men would concentrate their subsistence activities on game such as deer and bear. In the spring, while the women planted crops, the men fished in the many lakes and rivers and also captured birds. Like many other horticulturalists, the Iroquois farmed their fields until the fields were no longer fertile, after which they cleared new fields while the old ones lay fallow. After a generation or so, depending on local conditions, the fertile fields were located far enough away from the village that the entire community moved so it could be closer to the gardens.

Iroquois tribal society was based on matrilineal corporate groupings. A matrilineal group is a descent group in which an individual traces his or her descent through the female line. Matrilineages among the Iroquois resided together in longhouses and had collective rights over tools and garden plots. These matrilineages were also the basic units of production in the slash-and-burn cultivation for maize and other crops. Property was inherited through matrilineal lines from the eldest woman within the corporate group. She had the highest social status within the matrilineage and influenced decision making regarding the allocation of land and other economic rights and resources. The elder matrons within these matrilineages had the power to appoint the *sachem*, a council of leaders within the Iroquois political system. Often they appointed their sons to this position. Women could also influence decisions about peace and warfare and determine whether prisoners of war should live or die. As in many other matrilineal societies, Iroquois women played an important role in organizing subsistence activities and allocating food.

Although it is impossible to sum up the vast array of aboriginal religious traditions among the different groups of the Iroquois, some major features of their indigenous traditions were recorded by a number of missionaries and ethnographers.[4] One of the Seneca origin myths involved a narrative of how twin brothers created the world in primal times. One brother was named *Tarachiawagon* (Good Spirit or Great Spirit) and the other *Tawiskaron* (Evil Spirit). The Good Spirit or Great Spirit created a world that was perfect and utopian. He created human beings, male and female, he created good and useful plants and animals, rivers and lakes that would sustain life for everyone. Simultaneously, the Evil Spirit created the annoying and monstrous animals that were pests for humans. Evil Spirit introduced disease and death. He even tried to steal the sun. The Good Spirit tried to reverse these negative creations but was not able to do it. Eventually, in the narrative, the Good and Evil twins have a cosmic battle with each other. The Good Spirit is victorious but is still unable to eradicate the evils that were created by the bad twin. This native cosmology interweaves both a moral and natural framework for interpreting the world. Evil exists and is manifested by disease, death, pests, which are brought into the world through moral violations against the good. Humans must confront this evil and try to act against it.

The Good Spirit indirectly guided human affairs by countering the energy of the Evil Spirit. According to Iroquois cosmology, both the Good Spirit and Evil Spirit controlled a host of lesser spirits. The Good-Great Spirit managed the spirit of Thunderer who provided rain for the crops. He also governed the "Three Sisters," the spirits of maize, beans, and squash, who were thought to be lovely women. All of the wholesome things in life were associated with the energy forces of the Good Spirit. In contrast, the Evil Spirit supervised lesser spirits who brought pestilence, disease, winter weather, snow, ice, and death. Other spirits associated with Evil Spirit were the False Faces, who could send death and destruction. It was believed that anyone who saw these False Face spirits could become paralyzed. Other spirits controlled by Evil Spirit included witches who could take the form of birds, reptiles, or other animals and do destructive things and create disorder among people.

This native cosmology of the Seneca and many other Iroquois peoples resulted in organizations sometimes translated as the "False-Face Society," consisting of shamans who would prepare masks to impersonate the many forms of the evil twin brother. The masks, which are painted black or red, were usually carved out of a tree and had large eyes made of pieces of metal. The mouth and nose are grotesque, distorted, and exaggerated, and the mask is topped off with a long hank of hair. The masks were considered spiritually powerful and the owners had to treat them with care. The False-Face Society was involved in curing diseases and confronting death and other problems created by the evil twin. The False-Face Society would perform at various religious functions such as the new year's (mid-winter) and green maize ceremonies. Members of the False-Face Society were inducted through a process involving the interpretation of dreams. If individuals had a dream about being a member of the society and had visions of False-face spirits, the dream was interpreted by a shaman, and they were usually chosen as members. The Iroquois believed that dreams expressed inner spiritual energies and forces, and shamans would interpret dreams to help an individual determine a particular life path or choice. There was only one woman member of the False-Face Society at a time. She kept the religious masks and other paraphernalia and was the only one who was supposed to know the real identities of the membership. The False-Face Society shamans would cure a variety of illnesses working against the energy of the Evil Spirit. They would wear the masks imitating and rebuking the False-Face evil spirits. They would perform ritual dances, shake turtle shell rattles, and sprinkle ashes to affect their curing powers. They were also known to be able to eradicate diseases from villages.

Following the impact of colonialism and encounters with Western European industrial societies, many traditional small-scale societies have engaged in resistance movements, known alternatively as *revivalistic, nativistic,* and *millenarian* movements. A *revitalization movement* is an attempt to reinstitute the traditional cultural values and beliefs of a group faced with dramatic changes. Revitalization movements are common in conditions where people experience oppression and deprivation. In some cases, revitalization movements take the form of violent military or political resistance. Generally, however, traditional small-scale societies lacked the technological capabilities to sustain armed resistance against more powerful industrializing societies. In most cases, therefore, these movements are nonviolent or have symbolic forms of violence and have a strong religious element.

The collision of cultures and political economies between the Iroquois and Europeans resulted in a religious revitalization movement. The British and French settlers established fur trade with the Iroquois and nearby peoples during the late 1600s. French traders offered weapons, glass beads, liquor, and ammunition to the Iroquois in exchange for beaver skins. Eventually the Iroquois abandoned their traditional economy of horticulture supplemented by limited hunting to supply the French with fur pelts. The French appointed various *capitans* among the Iroquois to manage the fur trade. This resulted in the decline of the tribe's traditional social and political order. Meanwhile, the intensive hunting of beaver led to a scarcity of fur in the region, which occurred just as the Iroquois were becoming more dependent on European goods . The result was increased competition between European traders and various native Americans who were linked to the fur trade. The Iroquois began to raid other tribal groups, such as the Algonquins, who traded with the French. Increasing numbers of Iroquois males were drawn into more extensive warfare. Thus, the Iroquois became entangled in the economic, political, and military conflicts between the British and French and British and Americans. Wars between the British and the French such as the French and Indian War (1756–1763), and ultimately the American Revolution (1776–1781), which resulted in war between the British and the Americans, had devastating impacts on the Iroquois.

Following the American Revolution the Iroquois were damaged by factionalism, illness, and major land concessions. A number of Christian missionary groups including the Quakers began to become involved in Iroquoian affairs. Under the leadership of the Quakers, the Commonwealth of Pennsylvania granted a Seneca man by the name of Cornplanter and 40 persons land and housing in 1796. One of the houses was called Burnt House. Cornplanter and his half-brother Handsome Lake lived in Burnt House and were visited frequently by Quaker missionaries. According to Iroquois tradition, Handsome Lake had lived a life marked by idleness, drunkenness, and depression. However, in 1799 Handsome Lake appeared to be near death with an illness and had a spiritual vision. In the vision, Handsome Lake had seen three men who told him that the Great Spirit was unhappy about the decline of his people. Handsome Lake continued to have spiritual visions, and was eventually guided into the supernatural world where he met his dead son, and other dead relatives. His spiritual guide said that he would be returned to the land of the living to reveal a new way of life to his people. When Handsome Lake recovered he began to preach the new revealed religion, known as the *Gaiwiio,* "Good Message" or the "Longhouse religion" to the Iroquois. His first gospel to his people contained several themes including a prophecy about the destruction of the world. He was acknowledged as a prophet of this Longhouse religion among his people. He continued his role of a prophet of the Longhouse religion until his death in 1815.

The Longhouse religion had deep roots in the traditional Iroquoian religion; however, it was also influenced by the Quaker and Jesuit missionary teachings. The "Good Message" included various commandments such as prohibitions on using alcohol, which had been devastating the Iroquois, causing high rates of addiction and related social problems. Other commandments included obedience to one's parents, faithfulness in marriage, the care of the elderly, prohibitions against gossiping, boasting, magic, and witchcraft. Other practices were encouraged such as various traditional rituals and dances, but it called for a ban on the traditional medicine societies such as the False-Face society. It also included some Christian concepts such as the existence of a heaven and hell, and how sinners would be condemned to hell, while people who lived good lives would go to heaven. In addition, the Longhouse religion encouraged the Iroquois to accept the Christian missionaries as teachers and to learn as much as possible from them. At the same time Handsome Lake taught his people that they should not be assimilated completely in the mainstream American Christian culture. He encouraged his people to retain their traditional teachings and values. The Christian missionaries, however, were opposed to the traditional elements and values of the Longhouse religion. The Longhouse religion was not recorded until 1845, long after Handsome Lake's death. However, the Longhouse religion with its acceptance of certain Christian beliefs and practices combined with traditional teachings has remained a vital syncretic tradition among many of the Iroquois. This revitalization movement is considered a major factor in the survival of Iroquois traditions and values. And, this Longhouse religion is accepted as a source of moral and religious inspiration for many of the Iroquois up to the present. It combines reforms of traditional values and practices, while preserving Iroquois Indian identity.

RELIGION AMONG THE PLAINS INDIANS

Another region where native American Indians resided is referred to as the Plains area. The Plains region is demarcated by the Rocky Mountains to the west, some of the areas of Canada to the north, the Gulf of Mexico to the south, and the Mississippi river to the east. Within this large expanse of land in North America, there were many different ethnic and linguistic groups. There were seven distinct language families including the Algonquian and Siouan. Within these language families there were numerous ethnic groups. For example, among the Algonquian there were the Blackfoot and Cheyenne, whereas among the Siouan, the largest language family on the Plains, there were the Crow, Omaha, Kansa, Osage, Ponca, Hidatsa, Mandan, Santee, Lakota, Dakota, Yankton, and others. Since there were so many different languages among the Plains Indians, they developed a sign language used to express ideas regarding trade and peacemaking. Archaeologists have traced the native American societies on the Plains back thousands of years. For a long period of their prehistory, these people became proficient at hunting and gathering, and eventually settled in villages, raising a variety of crops in the Plains region. However, following the seventeenth century, after the Spanish introduced horses into North America from their colonies in the Southwest, the life of the native Americans on the Plains was transformed. Horses were traded into the Plains region before the Europeans began to enter this area. With the introduction of the horse into the Plains most of the native American people adopted a new form of subsistence based on buffalo or bison hunting. Peoples such as the Crow and Lakota began to rely on horses to become more nomadic, following the migration trends of herds of bison, using the famed skin tent or "tipi" as temporary shelters, and abandoning their settled horticultural way of life.

The social and political organization of the Plains Indians varied greatly. Some groups such as the Crow and Mandan traced their descent matrilineally, while others such as the Omaha and Kansa had patrilineal descent groupings. The typical nomadic group would follow the bison herd, breaking up into small bands for much of the year, but would come together in larger groups for communal hunts and ceremonies during the summer season when the bison herds would graze on the Plains grasses. Some Plains groups such as the Cheyenne or Crow had councils of elder males who would govern the community and resolve political conflicts. In addition, Plains groups usually had societies for males from different kin groups and bands representing a cross section of the group to serve as police and military associations. These police and military brotherhoods would participate in raids and warfare against other groups on the Plains, but also controlled intragroup conflicts. Elder males were often viewed as individuals who were beyond their aggressive years, and were looked upon as peacemakers. There were also women's societies associated with ritual and craft-making activities.

The Plains Indian religious traditions are as varied and complex as the different groups who live in the region. However, there are some basic resemblances among the religious traditions of the Plains region that have been identified by ethnographers.[5] One common myth that was widespread throughout the Plains had a central character known as Coyote, the trickster. The Coyote trickster could transform himself into any number of appearances. The trickster narratives usually involve the notion that the Coyote can be free of rules, and free of the constraints of time and space in a romantic utopian world. The narratives are often humorous, while at the same time deeply symbolic representing the human desire for freedom. The trickster permits people to experience freedom in a utopian world in a vicarious manner without bringing about chaos and disorder to society. At the same time, the follies that are experienced by the Coyote trickster symbolize the meaning of the boundaries and constraints that are necessary in human life. The trickster is always making mistakes and demonstrates to the people positive values, norms, and practices through negative examples. Among the Crow, Coyote was responsible for creating the earth out of a watery world, forming the mountains, streams, and rivers, animals and plants. He made the first man and the first woman out of earth and breathed life into them. He taught them language and how to live, and how to pray and participate in rituals including the Vision Quest and the Sun Dance.

The Vision Quest ritual and traditions were found widespread throughout many of the Plains Indian societies, and in many other native American societies. The Lakota Sioux referred to the Vision Quest as *Hanbleceya,* "Crying for a Vision." The Vision Quest was associated with male initiation rituals. A young man would attempt to communicate with the supernatural world by going off by himself, fasting for a prolonged period of time, meditating, and sometimes resorting to bodily mutilation (such as chopping off a finger, or cutting away strips of flesh). Through this isolation and self-sacrificing ordeal, each individual male tried to seek a vision and develop a connection with a guardian spirit. Eventually, most males did receive their vision, and the guardian spirit usually appeared in the form of an animal such as a bear or an eagle, or sometimes an inanimate object such as a stone. The guardian spirit would often offer instructions to the young man, teaching special prayers or songs, and most importantly identifying a particular path or life destiny for the young man. Through this spiritual communication the young man typically acquired a new name, and through the vision received guidance about his own personal destiny. The young man might be instructed to become a shaman, a warrior, or to take on another role in life. In some cases the young man's vision would be interpreted by an older shaman to help him choose a particular path. The guardian spirit is frequently manifested in the form of sacred objects or "medicine bundles," which contain skins or bones of animals, seeds, stones, or tobacco and pipes wrapped up in hides representing the sacred power of the guardian spirit. The man carried these sacred relics to continue contact with the spiritual realm whenever facing any type of ordeal in life.

One of the most well known and spectacular religious traditions among many of the Plains Indian societies was the Sun Dance. The Lakota Sioux called the Sun Dance *Wiwanyang wacipi,* "Gazing at the Sun." The Sun Dance was an annual ritual and ceremony that lasted from four to seven days and took place during the summer or early autumn when the various bands of the tribes came together for the bison hunt. The ceremony was performed to engage spiritual power for the tribes and to ensure the continual fertility and survival of the tribes, bison, and other life for future prosperity. Usually one person was responsible for sponsoring the Sun Dance in order to accomplish a particular spiritual goal. However, the ceremony was performed for the whole tribe. Typically, the people would establish their tipis in a circle with a dancing area in the center of the tipis. A tall tree would be selected and cut down to be erected as a sacred pole in the center of the tipis. The participants, young male warriors who had been fasting and practicing purification rites, would dance around the tree for long periods, moving into trancelike states. Many of the male dancers would indulge in self-torture and mutilation. For example, some would have small holes cut into their flesh on each side of their pectorals, and wooden skewers would be inserted through the holes. The skewers were secured to ropes and tied to the central pole. The young man would dance without food or water for a long time, gazing into the sun, and straining to break free of the ropes and having the flesh tear away. The dancers pulled backwards as they danced in time with drum beats, whistles, and singing from the people. Other variations of the Sun Dance included men having their backs pierced and skewered with bison skulls attached.

These men would dance dragging the skulls until the flesh broke. "Breaking free" appeared to symbolize transcending ignorance of the spiritual, and gaining knowledge through fasting and self-sacrifice. In some cases, women also offered flesh from their arms as a personal spiritual sacrifice. The pain and sacrifice of flesh was the ultimate proof of sincerity and devotion to the spiritual world.

Another religious tradition found among the Plains Indian societies was the Sweat Lodge ceremony. The Sweat Lodge ceremony was known as the *Inikaqapi* by the Lakota Sioux. It was a form of purification ritual. In the Sweat Lodge ceremony a number of males would join together with a shaman in a small dome-shaped lodge, or bathhouse, constructed of saplings and blanketed by hides, canvas, and robes to make it airtight and dark. Typically, the men had been fasting and were not drinking water. In the center of the lodge a hole was dug and stones were heated outside and handed into the men by ladles and placed into the center hole. The shaman sprinkled water over the heated stones, creating rushes of steam and hot air filling the lodge. The men would perspire and slap their bodies with switches made from pine boughs or bison tails. Simultaneously they were singing and chanting sacred songs and prayers. During the ceremony from time to time fresh air was allowed to come into the lodge, and the men would smoke a ceremonial pipe filled with tobacco. In most cases, the Sweat Lodge ceremony was a prefatory ritual before going on a Vision Quest, the Sun Dance, or facing an ordeal such as warfare. It was used to purify oneself and renew one's connections to the spiritual world. It also served a social function in instructing the young males in the culture, traditions, and sacred knowledge of the older people.

The Plains Indians and Revitalization Movements

With the expansion of Euramericans westward onto the Plains region, the various groups of Plains Indians were affected dramatically. In 1862 the Homestead Act was passed which sent many Euramerican pioneers westward to settle on land, which was granted to them by the U.S. government. Eventually gold was discovered in the Black Hills that led to the influx of prospectors into the plains. Railways were extended from the East into the Plains Region, bringing more settlers. The rails were also convenient to ship bison meat back to Eastern cities for consumption. This resulted in wholesale slaughter of the bison on the plains. All these factors led to massive resistance and warfare between native American groups and the U.S. Calvary. The U.S. Calvary was sent to enforce peace (through the barrel of a gun). From the 1870s through the 1880s a series of wars and battles between the Plains Indians and the U.S. Calvary changed the way of life on the plains. Native American groups such as the Lakota Sioux were led into battle by leaders such as Crazy Horse and Sitting Bull. Both of these leaders were at the defeat of General George Custer at the Battle of the Little Bighorn in 1876. However, the Plains Indians were outmatched by the forces and technology of the U.S. military and were forced to surrender and were pushed onto reservations. In addition, various epidemics that came into the plains region by the Euramerican population resulted in a massive depopulation of the native American groups.

Ultimately, the native people on the Plains turned to nonviolent resistance, which resulted in two major religious revitalization movements known as the Ghost

Dance and the Peyote Cult. The most well-known revitalization movement was the Ghost Dance movement of the late 1800s.[6] The Ghost Dance originated in Nevada and eventually spread across the Rocky Mountains to the Plains groups such as the Crow, Cheyenne, Arapaho, and Sioux. The movement was associated with the prophet Wovoka, a Paiute Indian in Nevada who was believed to have received spiritual visions of the future during an eclipse of the sun on January 1, 1889. During the 1870s a devastating drought and epidemic of typhoid and measles had wiped out a large number of Paiute Indians in Nevada. Wovoka's father, Tavibo, and another Paiute Indian named Wodziwob, started the first Ghost Dance movement. Tavibo prophesied that a huge earthquake would swallow up both whites and Indians, but after three days the Indians alone would return along with their fish, game, and other sustaining resources. Tavibo created a counterclockwise dance around a fire and taught that this would bring back the dead ancestors of the Indians. This first Ghost Dance movement did not last very long and faded after 1870. Later Tavibo left his family and abandoned his son Wovoka, who was adopted by a white rancher named David Wilson, who renamed him Jack Wilson.

Jack Wilson, or Wovoka, was socialized in this Euroamerican family and was exposed to Christianity and was taught to pray and read from the Bible. Later, when he was 20 he married a Paiute woman, and began to pursue an interest in his father Tavibo's teaching regarding the Ghost Dance. In other words, Wovoka began to teach circular dancing as a means of opening up the Paiute soul to greater spirituality. He also preached a blend of Christianity and native American belief. Wovoka combined teachings about God's love with traditional beliefs in the natural spirituality of the land and nature. By chance on January 1, 1889, Wovoka was ill with a fever when the solar eclipse took place. As the shadow over the sun engulfed him he went into a trancelike hallucination in which he saw himself taken to heaven where he could see and speak with God. He saw God with all of his dead ancestors in a land filled with abundant resources and pleasantness. God told him to go back and tell his people not to quarrel among themselves, and most importantly abandon warfare and live in peace with the whites. God told him that if his people were obedient and faithful they would be reunited with their friends in this other world, where there would be no death, disease, or old age. Wovoka was then given the hypnotic, rhythmic dance and was taught by God that if they performed it at specific intervals they would be able to bring about this event quickly.

After the solar eclipse, Wovoka began to teach the Ghost Dance among his people. He called himself a messiah who was like Jesus, but he never said that he was the Christ. As more people found out about his teaching, delegates from many Indian groups came to listen to him preach. Indians from the Plains began to take home tokens of Wovoka's spiritual power. His Ghost Dance spiritual message began to spread across the Plains area. The Ghost Dance involved a continual and repetitive dancing for hours on end, producing profound emotional experiences for the dancers. Many fell into trances, others collapsed and fell writhing on the ground. It was a dance that induced spiritual transformation. Among the groups influenced by the Ghost Dance were the Lakota Sioux, who had been forced to reside on five reservations in South Dakota. In 1890 the Lakota Sioux leader, Kicking Bear, introduced a special shirt, called a "ghost shirt," that he claimed would protect the Sioux against the bullets of the white soldiers. The wearing of the ghost shirts precipitated conflicts between the U.S. military and the Sioux. The U.S. government became convinced that the Ghost Dance movement was part of a violent apocalyptic war against whites. The secretary of war was ordered to suppress any threatened outbreak of war. On December 28, 1890, 120 men and 230 women and children had set up tipis for the night. They were surrounded by 500 heavily armed white soldiers. Suspecting trouble, the U.S. soldiers began to search the Indian camp for weapons. One young Indian, Black Coyote, refused to give up his weapon. His rifle discharged resulting in a massive shootout between the Sioux and U.S. soldiers. The shootout culminated in a massacre of almost 200 Sioux, including women and children, at Wounded Knee Creek, South Dakota, on December 29, 1890. Following that confrontation, Sioux leaders such as Kicking Bear surrendered themselves to the U.S. military.

Although the massacre at Wounded Knee in 1890 represented the end of the Ghost Dance, this revitalization movement and its relationship to the massacre has remained as a vital sacred metaphor and memory for many of the Plains Indians. The Ghost Dance songs and dances are still heard among the native Americans up to the present. For example, in February 1973, Wounded Knee once again became the site for a violent confrontation between the Plains Indians and the U.S. military forces. Led by leaders such as the Lakota Indians, Russel Means, and spiritual leader Leonard Crow Dog, the organization known as AIM, the American Indian Movement, took over the Pine Ridge Indian reservation at Wounded Knee. AIM accused the tribal government leaders of political and economic corruption, and demanded justice and civil rights for all native Americans. Leonard Crow Dog led a Ghost Dance ritual during the 70-day occupation in order to create solidarity and spiritual renewal among the Sioux at Wounded Knee. (In addition, the Sun Dance ritual was also conducted at Pine Ridge in 1973.) Fire fights between AIM and the FBI and U.S. forces were common throughout the longest siege in American history since the Civil War. The Wounded Knee of 1973 represented the frustration and resentment of many native Americans regarding their conditions after a century of subordination by the U.S. government. The Ghost Dance led by Leonard Crow Dog symbolized the spiritual resurgence and religious renewal of contemporary native Americans on the Plains.

The Peyote Cult

Another form of revitalization movement developed among the Plains Indians on an Oklahoma reservation in the 1880s. Like the Ghost Dance it was also a nonviolent form of resistance, based on a combination of Christian and native American religious beliefs. The movement is referred to as the Peyote Cult. Peyote, the scientific name of which is *Lophophora williamsii*, is a mild hallucinogenic drug contained in the bud of a cactus, which is either chewed or drunk as tea. It is a nonaddictive drug. Traditionally for thousands of years it has been used in some native American rituals for inducing spiritual visions, especially in the Southwest desert areas around the Rio Grande in both Mexico and North America. A number of Navaho Indians in the Southwest became involved in the ritual use of Peyote.[7] During their incarceration on the Oklahoma reservation, some of the Comanche, Kiowa, and other Plains Indians began to combine biblical teachings with the peyote ritual. The ritual took place in a tipi, where the participants surrounded a fire and low altar and took peyote as a form of communal sacrament to partake of the "Holy Spirit." Eventually the

Peyote Cult grew in membership and was legalized on the Oklahoma reservation as the Native American Church (NAC) in 1914. It has spread throughout at least 50 other native American tribes, and approximately 250,000 Indians are associated with the NAC.

NATIVE PEOPLES OF THE PACIFIC

Traditional Religion Among the Australian Aborigines

The archaeological evidence suggests that the people popularly known as the Australian aborigines, or indigenous Australians, inhabited the area between 60,000 and 30,000 years ago. Linguistic, archaeological, and genetic studies indicate that these people came from the area of Southeast Asia. However, after the Ice Ages, and the rise of sea levels in that region, the aboriginal Australians became isolated from the areas of Asia for thousands of years. Approximately 600 distinctive groups of Australian aborigines speaking some 200 different languages resided in various locations of the Australian continent. Because Australia in the driest continent in the world, with the most infertile soil, and unpredictable severe droughts, punctuated by torrential rain storms and floods, and lacking in any domesticable wild plants, the aboriginal Australians took up the hunting-gathering or foraging way of life. However, in different ecological regions of Australia, the indigenous peoples developed different resource strategies. For example, in one area known as the Murray-Darling river system, the aborigines developed unique "fish farms" with elaborate canals up to a mile and a half long to trap migratory fish, especially freshwater eels. Other Australian aborigines were hunter-gatherers, living in deserts that make up at least one-third of the continent. One group, known as the Aranda (Arunta) lived in the interior desert region. They subsisted on the various species of animals and plants found in their habitat. Women and children gathered seeds, roots, snails, insects, reptiles, burrowing rodents, and eggs of birds and reptiles. Aranda males specialized in hunting larger game such as the kangaroo, the wallaby, the large, ostrichlike emu, and smaller birds and animals. Practically every edible plant and animal species has been a part of the aboriginal diet in Australia.

Typically, like other hunting-gathering peoples, the aboriginal Australians lived in bands who foraged and camped together. The size of the bands varied in accordance with ecological resource availability and averaged from 25 to 50 people. Bands were interconnected to one another through marriage and kinship. However, other units of social organization were developed in complex ways among the indigenous Australians. Many of the aborigines had what are referred to as "moieties" that classified the group into two overarching categories. Within these moiety categories there were clans, lineage groups, sections, and subsections that were used to demarcate marriage groupings. Complex marriage rules designated members of different groupings as having to marry only members of other groupings in order to avoid incest. These moieties, clans, lineages, sections, and subsections formed a complex system of marital alliances linking groups with each other to integrate economic, social, and political ties. Political organization among the aborigines was very informal, with leaders selected on the basis of personal characteristics. But these leaders were not capable of coercing other people within the group. The elders within the community had more moral authority over the junior members of society, but political power was widely diffused throughout the group. Like other foraging societies, warfare was not frequent and conflict between groups was highly restrained.

Like other native aboriginal peoples, the religion of the Australian aborigines varied from group to group. However, many of the religious traditions of the indigenous Australians have been described loosely by anthropologists as the "dreaming," which is a complex spiritual concept that acknowledges the interdependence and connections of all parts of the universe.[8] Many of the myths of creation of the various aboriginal peoples refer to the "dreaming" or "dreamtime" as an important element in the beginnings of the universe. For example, among the Aranda of Central Australia the beginnings of the universe were associated with an ancestor known as Karora who was sleeping and dreaming. In a perpetual darkness, Karora was lying at the bottom of the ocean, but there was as yet no ocean, only ground. Through his dreams and wishes he created the flowers; grasses and various animals came out of his navel and armpits. Eventually, the sun began to rise and Karora got up slowly, feeling hungry, groggy, and dazed. He hunted down animals to satisfy his hunger, and cooked them with the fire provided by the sun. At night he fell asleep again and gave birth to a bull-roarer (a carved piece of wood that when twirled in ceremonies produces a roaring music), who was subsequently transformed into a human, Karora's first born son. He awoke and hunted, cooked, and danced with his son. They slept that night, and two more sons were born. This process of sleeping and dreaming went on for many days, giving rise to many sons. Karora remained under the ground in his eternal sleep, but his sons were joined with Tjenterrama, a wallaby, who became their totemic ancestral chief.[9]

In this myth the concept of dreaming results in the creation of the cosmos, the specific environment, and the social order of the Australian aborigines. According to aborigine traditions, the dreamtime exists in the "other world," the world associated with the time of creation, where a person goes in dreams and visions and after death. One common belief is that at the time of creation the "ancestors" deposited souls of all living forms in sacred sites, and eventually these souls or spirits were embedded in all matter such as rocks, water, and all living forms from trees to humans. These sacred sites or places link the mythology and the everyday activity of the aboriginal people. These sacred places are also usually associated with the fertility of the different plants and animals in the region. Various landscape features such as a waterfall or an outcropping of rocks were identified with particular heroic spirits of the myths. Elaborate rock paintings with highly symbolic images of natural phenomena are found near the sacred places for the aborigine societies. It is believed that this art is sacred and can be used to gain access to the spirits of the dreamtime. The rock art is intimately related to nature. Animals, plants, humans, and other components of the natural environment are the major subjects emphasizing the unification of all substance and spirit, which were byproducts of the work of these ancestral beings. All of these spirits come to the world from the dreamtime. The birth of the universe is like a fall from the dreamtime.

As the Aranda creation myth indicates, many of the indigenous Australians believe that the ancestral beings still exist in the dreamtime, where they act as intermediaries between that world and the profane, everyday world of human affairs. The ancestral beings intervene in life, controlling plant, animal, and human life and death. This fundamental belief provides explanations for pain, joy, chaos, and order in human life. The dreamtime is a fundamental and complex conception that embraces the creative past and has particular significance for the present and future. According to aborigine conceptions, life without the dreamtime is highly unsatisfactory. Communication with the supernaturals of the dreaming is a fundamental and necessary aspect of life. The invisible side of life can become visible through rituals, ceremonies, myths, art, and dreams. Many of the aborigines believe that through these activities they can communicate with their ancestral beings. This belief is reflected in aborigine rites of passage. In initiation ceremonies it is believed that the individual moves farther and farther back into the dreamtime. For example, among many aborigines in puberty rituals, which for males include circumcision, subincision (the cutting of the penis lengthwise to the urethra), and other bloodletting actions, the individual is dramatically moved from one status to another through contact with the dreamtime. The rite of passage at death moves the individual into the invisibility of the dreamtime. Rituals had to be used to re-create the ancestors of the dreaming into the present.

The spiritual beings of the dreamtime were linked to the social order, especially the clans of the aborigines through what has been described as totemism. In Chapter 2, we have discussed how Emile Durkheim drew on early depictions of the Australian aboriginal traditions of totemism to develop his theories of religion. The clan, a group in which members traced their common descent, was symbolized by a totemic plant or animal who was believed to be an ancestral spirit of the clan. The ancestral spirits in the dreamtime were usually personified as heroic spirits associated with sacred places. Various rituals were performed by the clan in these sacred places to activate the ancestral spirits to ensure prosperity and the fertility of nature. The dreaming unifies the spiritual world with the social world among the aborigines.

The dreamtime also conveys certain notions of morality. According to most aborigine traditions, the ancestral beings originally lived like other humans and had the capacity for being both moral and immoral, both good and evil. The immoral behavior of the dreamtime beings is highlighted in aboriginal mythology in order to accentuate what is proper and moral in human affairs. Thus, this dreaming religion creates a moral order that functions to sustain social control in the physical world. Although the dreamtime ancestors do not directly punish human wrongdoers, they have provided a blueprint for proper behavior with respect to obligations, reciprocities, and social behavior in general.

Colonialism and Religious Change for Indigenous Australians

Like the indigenous peoples of the United States and most of Canada, the Australian aborigines were colonized and incorporated into the larger nation-state established by the British. The area of Australia was claimed by the British as a colony during the eighteenth century. Captain Cook had explored the coastline and claimed the eastern portion of the continent during his first voyage in 1770. Initially, the British used Australia as a dumping ground for hardened and incorrigible convicted criminals in the hope that they could resolve their social problems at home by exporting them. In time the British policy was broadened to encourage free convicts and other free migrants to settle throughout both the eastern and western areas of Australia. Eventually, more British settlers came to the land "Down Under" to prospect and develop sheep ranches to produce wool. The discovery of gold in the 1850s sent a flood of gold seekers throughout the whole continent. During these colonial years the indigenous Australians lost their land, their autonomy, and often their lives. Epidemics were introduced by the British who brought germs to which the aborigines had had no opportunity to acquire the necessary genetic-based immunities. Smallpox, influenza, measles, typhoid, typhus, chicken pox, whooping cough, tuberculosis, and syphilis began to decimate the aboriginal peoples. In some cases, the aborigines were treated like animals, and were hunted down for alleged preying on settlers' sheep and cattle, which had been considered acceptable by these settlers during the nineteenth century. A large-scale massacre of 31 aborigines occurred at Alice Springs in 1928, the last of a string of violent episodes directed at the annihilation of these people.

The indigenous Australians who managed to survive the period of colonialism had to adapt to new forms of subsistence and lifestyle. They have adopted British-style clothing, work for wages, buy their food, send their children to school, use clinics and hospitals, use automobiles, jeeps, or trucks, and live in settled communities including large-scale cities. Most of them have abandoned their traditional foraging way of life. As a disadvantaged minority, however, with a difference in skin color, they face considerable difficulties in adjusting to the white Australian community surrounding them. Racism and ethnocentrism are still prevalent among some circles of white Australians, which has an effect on employment and educational opportunities. High rates of alcoholism and other social problems are evident within the aboriginal communities presently. Various Land Rights Acts have recently been passed to allow for some legal autonomy and land rights for some of the aborigine population. However, like the United States, or Canada, the Australian government has still not come up with satisfactory solutions in dealing with its indigenous people.

Eventually, various Christian missionary groups began to settle among Australian aboriginal communities in order to convert and "civilize" the natives. However, in contrast to many of the other areas colonized by Europeans, for the most part, the indigenous Australians have not given up their native religious traditions to become Christians. Anthropologist Aram Yengoyan, who did ethnographic work among a group of aborigines known as the Pitjantjatjara in central Australia, illustrates religious developments after Christianity was introduced.[10] A Presbyterian missionary station was established in the 1930s among the Pitjantjatjara. But the missionaries could only count about eight or ten true converts who had given their entire lives and souls to Christianity. Most other indigenous Australian communities showed very few conversions. Though some of the aborigine community attended Christian services, they appeared to be more interested in participating in the choral singing and ritual than accepting the beliefs and doctrines taught by the missionaries. Despite the fact that the missionaries had learned the local language, and the Christian services were in the local language, and the native peoples have respect for the commitment of these missionaries, they did not become true converts.

As Yengoyan notes, the Christian church provided a focus for community gatherings, but it never became an integral part of Pitjantjatjara culture and society. He argues that a number of factors, both social and religious, have accounted for the lack of success of Christianity among the aborigines. In contrast to a focus on future salvation for the individual within the Christian doctrine, the Pitjantjatjara beliefs emphasize how the ancient past and the totemic ancestors affect the future and the present. The future for the individual has no relevance for the aborigine. Also, the individuality expressed in Christian belief is held suspect by the aborigines who stress collective action and strong group affiliation. The key element of conversion to Christianity was to give up the traditional group rituals, especially the initiation rites of passage. But these collective rituals that draw the ancestors of the dreaming into everyday life are the hallmark of community spiritual expression for the aborigines. In addition, the concept of an omnipotent transcendental God is alien to most of the aborigine spiritual experiences. Thus, according to Yengoyan, the traditional religious beliefs, communal values, and practices of the majority of the aborigines are currently not conducive for the process of converting to Christianity.

TRADITIONAL MELANESIAN RELIGION

The Pacific island region known as Melanesia consists of a series of islands north and northeast of Australia such as the Solomons, the Trobriands, New Britain, New Ireland, Vanuatu, New Caledonia, and the second largest island in the world—New Guinea. In Chapter 3 we explored the work of anthropologist Bronislaw Malinowski who studied the culture and people the Trobriand Islands in Melanesia. But many other anthropologists have conducted ethnographic research in Melanesia. Melanesia contained many tribal societies. For example, on the large island of New Guinea hundreds of tribes, speaking some 700 different languages, have been studied by various anthropologists. New Guinea is located just below the equator and the tropical climate that predominates in all areas except the highest mountain regions produces an impressive variety of plant and animal life. Orchids, birds of paradise, large ostrichlike birds known as cassowaries, many parrots, and exotic butterflies are found throughout the island. Dense forests cover 70 percent of the island. In some areas, the forest gets as much as 350 inches of rain per year. Various tribes have been residing in the highland and coastal areas of New Guinea for thousands of years.

Archaeological evidence demonstrates that the island New Guinea has some of the oldest domesticated crops in the world. Agriculture began in the island around 7,000 B.C.E. Early crops include sugar cane, a native species of bananas, nut trees, and the giant swamp taro, and well as other edible grasses and other roots. Another root crop originating in South America, the sweet potato, was introduced from the Philippines where it had been introduced by the Spaniards in the sixteenth century. Sweet potatoes were widely adopted in the highland regions where it grows quickly and gives high yields. Lowland New Guineans on the seacoast and rivers depend heavily on fishing, while those in the highland areas above 4,000 feet developed intensive horticulture, domesticating root crops and raising pigs living in homesteads scattered throughout a clan territory. One group, the Tsembaga Maring, has been studied thoroughly by anthropologist Roy Rappaport.[11] The Tsembaga live in two river valley areas surrounded by mountains. They cultivate the mountain slopes with their subsistence gardens. They plant and harvest the root crops, especially sweet potatoes, taro, manioc, and yams; 99 percent of the Tsembaga diet by weight consists of vegetables, particularly these root crops.

The social organization of the New Guinea tribal peoples consists of various types of clans, lineages, and other descent group organizations and villages that coordinate land ownership and property rights, marital kinship affiliations, and other community relationships. A particular style of political leadership and organization found among some Melanesian groups is referred to by anthropologists as a "big-man" system. Typically, a man who aspires to political leadership has many wives and has formed kinship alliances with other descent groups. In addition, he must accumulate a large number of pigs and grow crops to feed them in large communal feasts. In precontact Melanesia, warfare was also an important strategy for creating alliances among various groups. But political alliances were also created through what are described as pig feasts. When a man had enough pigs, he had a pig feast in which he attracted followers while competing with rival big men. In addition to the material exchanges in the pig feasting activities, usually the "big man" was also very persuasive using ideas, rhetoric, and beliefs to generate political support. If the leader was able to recruit a few hundred men through the "generosity" demonstrated by the feast, these followers demonstrated their political commitment to the big man. These big man systems provided the basis for political and war-making alliances. Warfare was found to be a prevalent feature of many highland New Guinea societies wherein members of one village or clan frequently raided other villages or clans for a variety of reasons including revenge. These wars of revenge were usually related to thefts of pigs or interference with women of the other group.

Since the Melanesian islands have very diverse societies, it is difficult to generalize about religious traditions. However, there are some similarities among the highland groups, as well as among the coastal groups.[12] Generally, Melanesian religions classify the supernatural realm into gods, malevolent ghosts, ancestral spirits, and spirits of the stream and bush. Some groups maintain a belief in multiple spirits that are not transcendent and have an intimate relationship with worldly concerns, whereas other groups have conceptions of one major transcendent spirit. In many tribes the belief in ghosts ties in with general beliefs about human souls. The souls of ancestors may play a role in the community and can promote the welfare of the community. The ghosts of ancestors may be summoned and consulted about developments in future times, and shrines where their bones are kept may come to function like ancestral temples. However, ghosts can influence human activities in negative ways. In some cases the ghosts have to be propitiated or manipulated by bargaining in order to ensure safety for humans.

Various tribes of Melanesia have different myths regarding their origins, and the creation of life. One tribe in the southern highlands of New Guinea known as the Huli explain the creation of the world by various deities known as *dama*.[13] The *dama* include both males and females and often have wives and husbands. The first important deity was Honabe, a female deity who was seduced by a male deity Timbu and gave birth to five other deities, and one female deity. Seven other deities and the first possum and first bird were created through Honabe's menstrual discharge. One of the male deities, Helahuli, married an unknown woman and they had four sons (one of whom was Huli) who became the first human beings and founded each of the different tribes known in the region. Huli had many children with an unknown woman and they were the first humans who began to cultivate taro. Through their activities these first humans flooded the entire area killing every living thing. After the flood the deities re-created the birds, possums, and other animals, and gave birth to the other humans who lived in the region of the Huli. Generally, the various creation myths of Melanesia defined a limited cosmos in the region of the particular tribe. And, typically the myths depicted spiritual beings who had human forms and qualities as well as supernatural powers that gave a group's ancestors the necessary skills of food production, technology, and warfare to be able to survive. After creation these spirits usually departed. However, there were also totemic spirits of the various descent groups who played a role in everyday life for most tribes.

Many of the supernatural creatures can be called into play through various ritual systems. Ritual is at the heart of Melanesian religions. The unseen spiritual world is invoked through various ritual activities to ensure fertility of the crops, animals, and the tribe, and to connect with a powerful spiritual power. Various group rituals were conducted among some tribes that reflected seasonal cycles of nature. One elaborate year-long cycle of rituals known as the *kaiko* is described by Roy Rappaport among the Tsembaga Maring. The *kaiko* began with the planting of sacred trees or bushes that represent men's souls and connects men with specific territories. Every man of the clan touches the bush as it is planted to express his connection and ownership of the land. In the meantime the clan engaged in warfare with other groups in adjacent regions. After the warfare, many pigs were killed, sacrificed to various spirits, and feasted upon. The sacred bushes were uprooted to mark the end of the *kaiko* cycle. According to Rappoport the *kaiko* ritual cycle regulated the relationships between population density, food supplies, and warfare among the Tsembaga. Though Rappoport's interpretation of the *kaiko* cycle has been thoroughly criticized by Melanesian specialists, these types of group rituals were important for many of these tribes. Many other types of collective group rituals such as complex rites of passage in gender-based puberty rituals and funerary ceremonies are highly developed among the Melanesians.

Revitalization Movements Among the Melanesian Islanders

As various Europeans colonized the islands of Melanesia the native people's lives were forever transformed. The Dutch, French, British, and Germans claimed different areas as colonies. The Dutch from their colonial base in Indonesia took over the western half of New Guinea (now known as Irian Jaya, and a province of the country of Indonesia). In the 1880s, German settlers occupied the northeastern part of New Guinea. In the 1890s gold was discovered in New Guinea, and many prospectors from Australia and other places began to explore the region. At the beginning of World War I in 1914, the Australians conquered the German areas. In World War II the Japanese, Australians, and U.S. troops fought bitter battles in New Guinea. After the war Australia resumed administrative control over the eastern half of the island until 1975, when Papua New Guinea was granted political independence. Today, the country of Papua New Guinea (PNG) occupies the eastern half of the island of New Guinea and has about 4 million people.

The colonization of Melanesia was both a dramatic and traumatic experience for native peoples as they faced new systems of economics with the introduction of cash wages, indentured labor, plantations, taxation, new forms of political control, and the unfathomable technologies and the apparently fabulous riches of the whites. Prospectors, traders, and soldiers during the world wars created a highly unstable and unpredictable environment for Melanesian natives. One of the reactions to this rapid change that developed among the Melanesians took a religious and spiritual form. These Melanesian religious responses to Western impact were often loosely labeled as revitalization movements or so-called "cargo cults," a form of millenarian religious movement. Beginning in the nineteenth century and continuing up to the present, these millenarian cult movements have spread throughout many areas of Melanesia. Generally, in New Guinea the coastal or seaboard peoples were contacted first by Europeans and by the end of the nineteenth century were subjected to intensive pressures from the outside world. The highland peoples were contacted much later and were not fully penetrated by the Europeans and Australians until after the 1930s. Many native peoples referred to the European or Australian goods that were loaded off ships or aircraft as *kago*, or as described by anthropologists as "cargo." The native peoples became aware of a dazzling array of goods such as steel axes, matches, medicines, soft drinks, umbrellas, and eventually jet planes and helicopters. Because these native peoples had no exposure to industrial production, they did not see how these Western goods were manufactured. Many, therefore, believed that these goods were generated through spiritual forces, which delivered "cargo" to humans through the spiritual means. Many of the tribal groups of this region attempted to discover the identity of the cargo spirits and the magical-ritual techniques used by Westerners to induce the spirits to deliver the particular commodities.

One New Guinean man who led a millenarian cult movement is known as Yali. Yali had lived in the coastal area of New Guinea, and in the 1950s was recognized as an important future leader of his people by the Australians. He had been a World War II allied war hero fighting against the Japanese. The Australians took Yali to Australia to show him how the industrial goods were produced. Nevertheless, Yali maintained the belief that there must be a supernatural cause or divine intervention for the ability of Westerners to be able to produce cargo. He originated a millenarian cult movement known as *Wok bilong Yali*.[14] Yali began to preach to hundreds of villages throughout New Guinea about how a spiritual techniques needed to be developed to duplicate the white man's delivery of cargo. Over the years of this movement, Yali's teaching ranged from recommending close imitation of the Europeans to opposing white culture and returning to traditional rituals to help deliver the cargo. Although Yali openly rejected the millenarian cult movements beliefs in 1973, after his death many of his followers began to teach that Yali was a messiah equivalent to the white man's Jesus. In their religious literature they propagated these ideas of messiahship by using Yali's sayings to help develop a religious movement that was an alternative to Christianity.

However, some of the millenarian cult movements combined traditional rituals with Christian beliefs in the hope of receiving the material benefits they associated with the white settlers. One movement described by Paul Roscoe developed among the Yangoru Boiken of Papua New Guinea merged some of the millennial teachings of Canadian missionaries from the Switzerland-based New Apostolic Church (NAC).[15] Roscoe describes how on Sunday, February 15, 1981, it was believed that Yaliwan, a leading spiritual and political leader, was going to be crucified, ushering in the millennium. The villagers believed that the earth was going to rumble, hurricanes would arrive, and the mountains would flash with lightning and thunder, and a dense fog would cover the earth. Afterwards, Yaliwan would be resurrected as the native counterpart of Jesus, and the "two" Jesuses would judge the living and the dead. They believed that the whites and native members of the NAC would usher in a new "Kingdom of Rest," described as an earthly utopian paradise with an abundance of material goods and peaceful harmony between native peoples and whites. The millennial teachings of the NAC were interpreted and integrated with traditional Yangoru beliefs of spirits of the dead, and other magical practices. Some of the traditional aboriginal beliefs had millenarian aspects promising the Yangoru economic prosperity and political autonomy. Therefore the NAC missionary teachings based on millenarian views were easily integrated with the traditional beliefs of the Yangoru. Though the crucifixion did not take place, various millenarian movements continue to have some influence on religious and political affairs in Papua New Guinea.

Various anthropologists have attempted to explain the development of the millenarian cult movements of Melanesia. One early explanation by anthropologist Peter Worsley views these millenarian cults as rational attempts at explaining unknown processes that appeared chaotic. The myths and religious beliefs of the cults also helped mobilize political resistance against colonialism. The cults provided an organizational basis for political action for the various Melanesia tribes. Groups who spoke different languages and maintained separate cultures joined the same religious cult. This enabled these people to form political organizations to challenge European and Australian colonial rule.[16] Other explanations rely on more symbolically based phenomena emphasizing how the cargo cults represent the resurgence of aboriginal religious thought, which is more creative and authentic than that of the newer missionary religions that came to Melanesia. Yet, today, most anthropologists recognize that these millenarian cult phenomena are extremely varied. As anthropologists learn more about these movements in different regions of Melanesia they discover that some have millenarian aspects, while others do not. Some of them integrate aboriginal beliefs and practices with the teachings of Christianity, a form of syncretism, while others feature a revival of the aboriginal elements and a rejection of the Christian teachings. A few of the movements have developed into vital political movements, and even violent rebellions, whereas others tend to have a purely spiritual influence. Anthropologists agree that the analysis of these cults is a fruitful area of investigation, and much more needs to be documented through interviews, historical examination, and intensive ethnographic research.

POLYNESIAN CHIEFDOMS: TRADITIONAL HAWAIIAN RELIGION

In the area known as Polynesia in the Pacific, which extends eastward from Hawaii to New Zealand and includes Samoa, Tahiti, and Tonga, various societies referred to as chiefdoms existed. Technically anthropologists define a *chiefdom* as a political economy that organizes regional populations in the thousands or tens of thousands through a centralized hierarchy of leaders, or chiefs. *Chiefs* own, manage, and control the basic productive factors of the economy and have privileged access to strategic and luxury goods. These leaders are set off from the rest of society by various cultural practices and symbols, such as clothing, jewelry, specialized language, and social status. The other aboriginal societies we have discussed above are referred to usually as band and tribal societies. The band and tribal societies are generally "egalitarian" in that there is no concentration of political and economic power or authority within individual families. Though there is considerable variation between different forms of chiefdom societies, they tend to have centralized political economies, and definitive hierarchy and inequality among different groups.

Most chiefdom societies have occupied ecological regions that contain abundant resources, usually more abundant than the resources in the areas inhabited by band and tribal societies. This was certainly the case for the Hawaiian islands. The Hawaiian islands include eight fully inhabited islands, of which Hawaii, with a land area of over 4,000 square miles, is the largest and most heavily populated.[17] Oahu, Maui, Kauai, Molokai, Lanai, Niihau, and Kahoolawe are other islands in the chain. The islands were occupied by humans sometime in the first century C.E. The early settlers were probably from the Society islands or Marquesans and Tahiti and navigated across the Pacific with ingenious sailing techniques. They brought various plants and animals with them to Hawaii as they traversed the vast Pacific. The arable land on the Polynesian islands such as Hawaii is very fertile, and the soil is covered by a dense forest growth. Rainfall is plentiful, and the average temperature is 77 degrees Fahrenheit year-round. The population of the Hawaiian islands before contact with Europeans is estimated at between 400,000 to 600,000.

One important aspect of subsistence for the Hawaiian people was the bountiful harvest from the sea. Fish and shellfish accounted for a substantial portion of their diet. The coconut palm, which grows abundantly even in poor soil, provided nourishment from its meat and milk, as well as oil for cooking. The breadfruit plant was another important foodstuff; if fermented, breadfruit can be stored in pits for long periods of the year, or even years. The Hawaiians practiced an intensive type of horticulture, in which one improves crop production by irrigating, fertilizing, hoeing, and terracing the land. Through intensive horticulture (and near-perfect weather conditions), the Hawaiians were able to make efficient use of small parcels of arable land on the islands. Although this type of agriculture demanded labor, time, and energy, the agricultural yields it produced were tremendous. The Hawaiian's most important crops were taro, yams, and sweet potatoes. Supplementing these crops were bananas, plantains, sugar cane, and gourds. Protein requirements were met by the consumption of seafood and such animals as domesticated pigs, chickens, and, on occasion, dogs. With this environment, foodstuffs, and climate the native people of Hawaii (and other Polynesian islands) had the ecological setting for the development of a highly productive subsistence strategy that provided for the emergence of a complex political economy.

The political economy of the Hawaiian islands was an intricate structure interconnected through extravagant forms of exchange, and norms of etiquette. Economic exchanges, called "redistributional" exchanges, controlled the distribution of food and resources throughout the island areas. In Hawaii, people who were able to redistribute goods and resources among various villages and islands emerged as leaders. After crops were harvested, a certain portion (the "first fruits of the harvest") was directed to local village leaders and then given to higher-level subsidiary chiefs who were more centrally located. These goods were eventually directed toward the paramount chiefs, who redistributed some of them back to the population during different periods of the year. Along with coordinating exchanges, the chiefs could also decree which crops were to be planted and how they were to be used. Within this redistributional system, local leaders and related individuals not only had a higher status and rank but were also able to siphon off some of the economic surplus for their own benefit. This redistributional exchange system among the Hawaiians has been referred to as an early form of taxation.

Whereas the social and political structures of bands and tribes were based on egalitarianism, the sociopolitical structures of the Hawaiian chiefdom were well defined and hierarchal. Hawaiian society was divided into eight different social strata composed of lineage descent groups. The highest ranking noble strata, known as *ali'i*, were district chiefs and their families. Within the highest ranking descent groups, the eldest son inherited the political and social status of the father. Above the *ali'i* were the paramount chiefs, or *ali'i nui*, and the *mo'i* (king) or *ali'i aimoku*, who ruled over an entire island. The paramount chiefs and district chiefs were treated with reverence and extreme deference. They were carried around on litters, and the *maka'ainana*—farmers, fishermen, craftsworkers, and "inferiors"—had to prostrate themselves before the high ranking chiefs. These nobles had a great deal of control over both surplus prestige goods and strategic resources, including food and water. This control enhanced chiefly status, rank, and authority, ensuring both loyalty and deference on the part of those from lower descent groups. In addition, it enabled the chiefs to exercise a certain amount of coercion. They could recruit armies, distribute land and water rights to families, and sentence someone to death for violating certain societal norms. This control of basic resources and judicial authority reinforced the chief's political legitimacy. However, this political legitimacy was buttressed by religious beliefs and rituals, which will be discussed below.

The various families or descent groups—households, lineages, and clans—had a specific ascribed rank within traditional Hawaiian society and were accorded certain rights, privileges, and obligations based on that rank. Social interaction between lower and higher strata was governed by cultural norms and practices used to differentiate the higher status groups from the rest of society. In general, the higher the status and rank, the more ornate the jewelry, costumes, and decorative symbols. Among the Hawaiians, the *ali'i nui* and the *ali'i aimoku*, the highest ranking chiefs, wore feather cloaks consisting of tens of thousands of feathers requiring many generations of commoner labor for their manufacture. The *ali'i aimoku* required a special orator chief to speak to the public. The high chiefs spoke a noble language with an archaic vocabulary containing words that commoners could not use with each other. Other cultural norms involved prohibitions against touching or eating with higher ranking people. Additionally, traditional Hawaiian norms set standards regarding dress, marriage, exchanges, and other cultural practices. Marriages usually took place within one's own descent grouping, and within the *ali'i nui*, marriages were sometimes arranged between brothers and sisters, which ensured the royal legitimacy of the lineage of the chiefs. These cultural norms and practices maintained a high degree of inequality and hierarchy, which was thoroughly ingrained within traditional Hawaiian society.

Aboriginal religious traditions within Hawaii were, in some respects, similar to the religions described for the band and tribal societies. That is, in general they reflected the belief that the spiritual and material aspects of nature could not be separated from each other. Religious world views were oriented to the cyclical pattern of the seasons and all other aspects of nature. The natural order was also the moral and spiritual order. The religious concepts within Hawaiian society were based on oral traditions perpetuated from generation to generation through elaborate cosmological myths. The most elaborate cosmological myth is known as the Kumulipo, which is narrated through religious chanting accompanied by music. The Kumulipo consisted of complex integrated systems of chant, poetry, rhythm, melody, dance (the *hula*), and movement that were used during religious ceremonies. The Hawaiians had a variety of musical instruments, including membranophones made of hollowed wooden cylinders covered with sharkskin, mouth flutes and bows, rhythm sticks, and bamboo tubes. The Kumulipo was chanted by religious specialists, full-time priests, in order to pay homage to their ancestral deities and the *ali'i nui*, who were believed to be descended from these deities. The Kumulipo prayer chant linked the royal chiefly families to the primary gods who were worshiped by the Hawaiians.

The Kumulipo begins with a celebration of the wondrous fertility of the seven stages of the primordial night and darkness. An English translation of the Kumulipo by Martha W. Beckwith[18] provides some sense of the sacred chant:

> At the time when the earth became hot
> At the time when the heavens turned about
> At the time when the sun was darkened
> To cause the moon to shine
> The time of the rise of the Pleiades
> The slime, this was the source of the earth
> The source of the darkness that made darkness
> The source of the night that made night
> The intense darkness, the deep darkness
> Darkness of the sun, darkness of the night
> Northing but night.
> The night gave birth
> Born was Kumulipo in the night, a male
> Born was Po'ele in the night, a female
> Born was the coral polyp, born was the oral, came forth
> Born was the grub that digs and heaps up the earth, came forth
> Born was his [child] an earthworm, came forth

The sacred chant goes on to describe the creation of the many creatures of the sea and land, including a rich pantheon of ancestral spirits of the *ali'i nui*, and the other Hawaiians. One of the most important aspects of the Kumulipo was to develop the traditional genealogies that linked the birth of the *ali'i* to the gods. The chant served to symbolize and legitimize the political and sacred order of aboriginal Hawaiian society.

The Hawaiians believed in four major gods: Kane (the god of life, fresh water, provider of sunshine), Lono (the god of rain, peace, agriculture, and the forest), Ku (the god of war and medicine), and Kanaloa (the god of the ocean and ocean winds). These gods took many different forms. Kane could appear as taro, sugar cane, bamboo, and lightning. Ku appeared as breadfruit or coconut. Lono could be found in rain clouds, sweet potatoes, or gourds. There are also hundreds of lesser gods or goddesses such as Pele (the goddess of volcanoes), Lea (goddess of women and canoe builders), and Laka (the goddess of the hula dance). Another category of spirits included ancestral spirits known as *aumakua* who were familistic deities that could be prayed to for strength, guidance, or inspiration. They could appear as sharks, lizards, birds, fish, owls or the eel. They became personal deities of the *ohana* or families. These family spirits gave spiritual authority to the chiefs or *ali'i nui* of the Hawaiian society.

Since the *ali'i nui* were believed to be manifestations of the gods and sacred intermediaries between human societies and the divine world, Hawaiian chiefdoms have been referred to as *theocracies*, societies in which people rule not only because of their worldly wealth and power, but because of their place in the moral and sacred order. The political and legal authority of Hawaiian chiefs was reinforced by a religious and ideological system known as the "tapu" system, which was based on social inequalities. (The word "taboo" comes from the Polynesian area as reported by Captain Cook on his expeditions there in the eighteenth century.) Social interaction in Hawaii was carefully regulated through a variety of tapus. Elaborate forms of deference and expressions of humility served to distinguish various strata, especially those of commoners and chiefs. The Hawaiians believed that people were imbued with sacred cosmic forces referred to as mana. These sacred forces were powerful and sometimes dangerous. They were inherited and distributed according to a person's status and rank. Thus, *ali'i nui* had a great deal of mana, the subsidiary chiefs, the *ali'i*, had less, and commoners had very little. Violations of certain tapus—for example, touching a member of a chiefly family—could bring the offender into contact with the chief's mana which was believed to cause death. For example, Hawaiian women of the *ali'i nui* had so much mana and sacred power that they were afraid to raise their own children, fearing that they would either cripple the newborn infant or kill it. These women gave their children away to relatives for rearing.

Mana could also be gained and lost through a person's moral actions. Thus, the success or failure of a chief was attributed to the amount of mana he controlled. This was also reflected in the economic and political spheres, in that a chief who was a good redistributor and maintained order was believed to possess a great amount of mana. Conversely, if things went badly, this reflected a loss of spiritual powers. In cases when one chief replaced another, the deposed chief was believed to have lost his powers. There were cases of rebellion among the Hawaiians against *ali'i nui* who were repressive and selfish. But mana could be received by the high chiefs and other people through sacrifices and offerings made to the gods. There were two major sacrificial rituals in Hawaii: the *Makahiki* or so-called New Year's harvest festival devoted to the god Lono, the fertility god, and the annual rededication of the *Luakini* temple. As part of the offerings to the gods during these festivals, human sacrifices were offered. Some of the sacrificial victims had transgressed or violated the sacred tapus. These victims frequently were brothers or cousins who were rivals of the paramount chiefs. It was believed that these human sacrifices would help perpetuate the fertility of the land and the people. Human sacrifice was the prerogative of these chiefs and was a symbolic means of distinguishing these divine rulers from the rest of the human population. Such rituals, sometimes referred to as "rituals of legitimation," effectively sanctioned the sacred authority of the *ali'i nui*.

Colonialism and Religious Change Among Hawaiians

The Hawaiian islands were contacted by the English expedition of Captain Cook in 1778, and the islands were eventually penetrated by traders, whalers, missionaries, and other outsiders. The impact of the Western encounter resulted in a unique religious "revolution" when compared with other aboriginal societies we have discussed in earlier sections. Cook's expedition on the part of the British, which began in the 1760s, set the stage for the colonization of the Pacific. At the time of Captain Cook's discovery of Hawaii, the major chief on the island of Hawaii was engaged in warfare with the chief of the island of Maui, who had already incorporated the islands of Oahu and Molokai under his chieftaincy. The reaction to Cook's arrival during this period was shaped by the aboriginal religious culture. He appeared during the time of *Makahiki,* and he was perceived as someone extremely powerful, perhaps as the god Lono himself, or at the least an important foreign chief. For a variety of different reasons the Hawaiians ended up killing Captain Cook at this time.[19] Later, a man by the name of Kamehameha, who was a nephew of the Hawaiian chief, made a considerable reputation as a fearless warrior in the Maui campaign. When the chief of Hawaii died, Kamehameha became his successor. Because the island of Hawaii offered good anchorage and became a vital strategic point of contact with Europeans, Kamehameha had an advantage over any rivals in trading with European ships. The Hawaiians began to trade their products such as sandalwood with Europeans, and in exchange Kamehameha received guns and light cannon. Eventually he was able to employ European help in conquering most of the other islands of Hawaii and transformed the Hawaiian chiefdoms into a unified, centralized military kingdom or state.

Kamehameha died in 1819 and was succeeded by his son Liholiho, later known as Kamehameha II. Since Western contact, Hawaii continued to be heavily influenced by Western culture. A number of traditional taboos of the Hawaiian culture were being violated on a regular basis. Some of the Hawaiian women were involved in sexual and romantic relationships with Westerners, and openly ate with men, violating traditional taboos. Some of the commoners began to trade openly with Europeans, which also violated traditional norms and taboos, causing tension between the rulers and commoners. Seeing practical advantages for trade with the Europeans and rule over their kingdom, in 1819, Liholiho, the new ruler, and other members of the royal family began to deliberately flout the most sacred traditional taboos of their ancient religion. The royal family began to systematically dismantle the aboriginal religious traditions and practices. This represented a revolutionary transformation in religious thought and culture for Hawaiian society.[20] This transformation of religion was accomplished prior to the coming of Christian missionaries to Hawaii. This religious revolution was resisted by some of the more conservative peoples of Hawaii, and Liholiho had to arm his forces to defeat the more conservative faction within the kingdom. This Hawaiian revolution appeared to be an intentional strategy on the part of the ruling family to enhance their political control over the military kingdom.

The sandalwood trade declined in the 1830s and was transplanted by the whaling industry, which began to dominate commerce in Hawaii. Because Hawaii was located within the vicinity of a major whaling area of the Pacific, New England whalers used Hawaii as a major base for provisioning and relaxation. However, during the 1830s various companies began to develop sugar plantations in Hawaii, which eventually became more successful, resulting in the influx of more Europeans, including various Christian missionaries from the United States. Many of the missionaries were themselves sugar planters, or were connected with the sugar planters. Private property was introduced and land was commodified for sale. As the sugar plantations were developed, substantial native Hawaiian land was lost to the planters. Additionally, the native Hawaiians were subjected to devastating epidemics introduced by the Westerners. Whooping cough, measles, influenza, and other diseases led to rapid depopulation among the native people. As Hawaii became increasingly incorporated into the U.S. political economy during the nineteenth and twentieth centuries, the native population declined to a small minority of about 40,000 people. This depopulation resulted in a labor shortage for the sugar planters, who began to import labor from the Philippines, Japan, and China. In 1893, the United States, backed up by American marines, overthrew the Hawaiian monarchy, and five years later Hawaii was annexed as a colony. Following U.S. colonization, the Hawaiian islands were dominated by U.S. political and economic interests. Eventually, the native Hawaiian population became a marginal group in their own islands.

Through missionary schooling and activities, the native Hawaiian population was forbidden to speak their native language or practice any of their traditional religious or cultural activities, which were deemed to be barbaric, lewd, and uncivilized. These policies led to societal and cultural disintegration for the native population. Combined with the growing Asian population, and new settlers from North America, who were rapidly developing the sugar economy, and the expansion of mass tourism to Hawaii from the mainland United States, the small modern Hawaiian population began to lose not only their native lands but also their cultural and ethnic identity.

Religious Revitalization in Hawaii

As U.S. corporate capitalism and tourism became the dominant forms of economy in Hawaii, every aspect of the traditional Hawaiian culture was affected. Presently the tourist industry generates close to 40 percent of Hawaii's income. Tourists crowd the hotels, restaurants, streets, highways, beaches, golf courses, and parks throughout Hawaii. The advertising industry attempts to promote the image of Hawaii as a romantic and exotic paradise setting where tourists can enjoy the traditional dancing, music, and culture of "primitive" peoples. Ads show skimpily clad women and men dancing before fires on near deserted beaches. The tourist industry is involved in trying to preserve the traditional culture of Hawaii, because it is "good for business." However, native Hawaiians have begun to resist the marketing of their culture. Beginning in the 1970s with a growing awareness of their marginal status in the U.S. political economy, and more familiarity with the civil rights movement in the mainland United States led by various minorities, many Hawaiians have launched a movement known as the Hawaiian Renaissance. The Hawaiian Renaissance has manifested itself as a resurgence of interest in aboriginal Hawaiian culture, including the traditional language and religious beliefs. The movement is fundamentally antitourist. Many contemporary native Hawaiians who are part of the new movement understand that their traditional culture has been mass-marketed and mass-consumed. They feel that their traditional culture has been overly commercialized, and they resent the tourist industry for selling the Hawaiian tradition.[21]

Some of the spiritual elements of the native religious beliefs have been reintroduced and revitalized in the context of the Hawaiian Renaissance movement. For example, a number of native Hawaiians have become involved in environmental activism. In doing so, they draw on traditional religious beliefs. They are attempting to prohibit the destruction of the rain forests and other natural settings by developers. The native people emphasize a spiritual renewal and refer to traditional Hawaiian gods and goddesses that are associated with the natural areas in order to protect these areas from destructive tourist and commercial forces. In some areas, the native Hawaiians are restoring some of the ancient temples or *heiaus*. Native Hawaiians can be seen making offerings to the god Pele at the rim of Halemaumau Crater in the Hawaii Volcanoes National Park. Some aboriginal young people complain about their parent's conversion to Christianity and the negative views expressed by Westerners about their traditional culture and religion. However, most importantly, the revitalization of their religious culture is part of an overall attempt to preserve their heritage and reclaim their cultural identity and selfhood. As these native peoples of Hawaii were subjected to overwhelming and traumatic cultural change, they found that they were marginalized in their own land. After losing their land, their autonomy, and their culture, these native Hawaiians have been involved in reconstructing and reinvigorating some of their aboriginal spiritual beliefs as a means of repossessing their cultural identity.

CONCLUSION

In contrast to the early simplistic misconceptions about aboriginal religious traditions proposed by early anthropologists and theorists such as Marx, Weber, or Freud (see Chapter 2), twentieth-century ethnographers, through their research, have demonstrated the immense variety and complexity of religions found among these nonliterate native peoples. There is no single distinguishing feature of these aboriginal religions, other than that they are based on oral traditions that are transmitted from generation to generation. These traditions do not differ in kind from the other various religions of humankind. Contemporary ethnographers have shown that these religions are comparable in many ways to the other literate religious traditions that will be discussed in following chapters. As seen above in these native societies of North America and the Pacific, these aboriginal religions exhibit tremendous complexity and sophistication in their religious symbols, cosmologies, myths, and rituals. We can no longer think of these aboriginal religions as any more irrational, mystic, simple-minded, prelogical, or otherworldly than any other religious traditions of humans. Through their sustained research, contemporary ethnographers have provided new insights about the beliefs and practices among indigenous peoples, which definitively refute older misunderstandings of these aboriginal religions.

Presently, contemporary anthropologists are facing great opportunities and challenges in the research among native people. These small-scale societies have been affected by the enormous changes produced by colonialism in every corner of the globe. These global changes have endangered these societies, resulting in depopulation, loss of land and political autonomy, and deprivation. Despite these global changes, we have seen how some of the native people have transformed and reconstructed, and occasionally combined the aboriginal religious beliefs and practices with other religious traditions. Ethnographers today are attempting to document how these native people are remolding and refashioning their religious traditions. In addition, many of these native people have become educated in the Western tradition. Some have chosen the field of anthropology in order to join the contemporary ethnographers as colleagues in the endeavor to better comprehend the aboriginal religions and the continuing process of religious change. This new challenge and opportunity to work along with native people trained in anthropology will open up new perspectives and insights into the study of these aboriginal religions. More collaboration along these lines will produce further appreciation and awareness of the vitality and significance of these important nonliterate religious traditions.

NOTES

1. One of the foremost religious scholars who attempted to characterize all aboriginal religions as essentially similar was the Romanian scholar Mircea Eliade. Eliade suggested in books such as *The Patterns of Comparative Religion*, trans. Rosemary Sheed (New York: Meridian Press, 1963) and *The Sacred and the Profane: The Nature of Religion* (New York: Harcourt, Brace and World, 1957) that all aboriginal religious traditions or "archaic religions" had the same elements. According to Eliade the same symbols, myths, and rituals were found in these "archaic religions" throughout the world. For example, he proposed that all of the "archaic religions" had symbols and myths about sky deities, moon and sun gods and goddesses, and other fertility spirits. Eliade's work has had a tremendous influence on the field of religious studies.

2. There is an enormous ethnographic literature on the Eskimo or Inuit societies. One of the classic studies is Asen Balikci, *The Netsilik Eskimo* (Prospect Heights, IL: Waveland Press, 1970). Nelson Graburn's *Eskimos without Igloos* (Boston: Little, Brown, 1969) is also an informative ethnography. Another good ethnography focusing on the Alaskan Inuit is Norman Chance's *The Inupiat and Arctic Alaska: An Ethnography of Development* (Fort Worth, TX: Holt, Rinehart, and Winston, 1990). An excellent survey of Inuit culture from prehistoric to modern times is given in the *Handbook of North American Indians*, vol. 5, ed. David Damas (Washington, DC: Smithsonian Institution, 1984). A sensitive account of Inuit shamanism is H.G. Gallagher's *Etok, A Story of Eskimo Power* (New York: Putnam's Sons, 1974). A good reconstructive account of Inuit religion in its traditional form is found in William W. Fitzhugh and Susan A. Kaplan's *Inua: Spirit World of the Bering Sea Eskimo* (Washington, DC: Smithsonian Institution, 1982). A comprehensive bibliography for Inuit religion is given by John Fisher in his essay "Bibliography for the Study of Eskimo Religion," *Anthropologica*, n.s. 15 (1973): 231–271.

3. Franz Boas collected this myth from the Central Eskimo and it was published in his book *The Central Eskimo*. [Lincoln: University of Nebraska, 1964 (1888)].

4. A major early source on the Iroquois was written by anthropologist Lewis H. Morgan in 1851. His work entitled *League of the Ho-De-No-Sau-Nee or Iroquois*, 2 vols. (Rochester, NY: Sage) is a detailed description of one group of Seneca living between 1841 and 1850.

5. An early study of the Plains Indians is Robert H. Lowie, *The Crow Indians*, 1935 (reprinted 1956, New York), and Lowie's *Indians of the Plains*, 1954, a survey of the Plains Indians after they acquired horses. Peter Nabokov, 1967, *Two Leggings: The Making of a Crow Warrior* is a good biographical and ethnographic account of one man's quest for leadership during the period 1840–1920. John G. Niehardt, *Black Elk Speaks*, 1961, is a description of a Lakota Sioux shaman's dreams and the influence it had on his life.

6. The classic account of the Ghost Dance is by the Smithsonian anthropologist James Mooney, who documented this revitalization movement in the 1890s in a book called *The Ghost-Dance Religion and the Sioux Outbreak of 1890*, ed. A.F.C. Wallace [Chicago: University of Chicago Press, 1896 (1965)]. A recent in-depth account of the Ghost Dance is by Alice Kehoe titled *The Ghost Dance: Ethnohistory and Revitalization* (New York: Holt, Rinehart, and Winston). Other books include a speculative evolutionary approach by Weston LaBarre called *The Ghost Dance: Origins of Religion* (Garden City, NY: Doubleday, 1970) and D.H. Miller *Ghost Dance* (Lincoln: University of Nebraska, 1959).

7. David Aberle wrote an ethnographic study of the Peyote cult among the Navajo called *The Peyote Religion Among the Navajo*, Viking Fund Publications in Anthropology, no. 42 (New York: Wenner-Gren Foundation for Anthropological Research, Inc, 1966). Paul Steinmetz did an ethnography of Peyote use among the Lakota titled *Pipe, Bible and Peyote among the Oglala Lakota* (Stockholm: Almqvist & Wiksell International, 1980).

8. The literature on Australian aborigine religion is enormous. For a good general account of the dreaming religion, see Robert Tonkinson's *The Mardudjara Aborigines: Living the Dream in Australia's Desert*, 2nd ed. (New York: Holt, Rinehart, and Winston, 1991). A classic overview of the dreaming religion is W.E.H. Stanner, "The Dreaming," in W.A. Lessa and E. Vogt, eds., *Reader in Comparative Religion: An Anthropological Approach*, 4th ed. (New York: Harper and Row, 1979).

9. This Aranda myth comes from T.G.H. Strehlow, *Aranda Traditions* (Melbourne: University of Melbourne Press, 1947).

10. This example of the reluctance to convert to Christianity for the aborigines is drawn from Aram Yengoyan, "Religion, Morality, and Prophetic Traditions:

Conversion among the Pitjantjatjara of Central Australia," in Robert W. Hefner, *Conversion to Christianity: Historical and Anthropological Perspectives on a Great Transformation* (Berkeley: University of California Press, 1993). Despite the lack of converts among the aborigines, Yengoyan does note that the mission effort has had widespread effects on the aboriginal communities. The missionaries were at the forefront of serving aboriginal reforms for better health care, employment, and self-determination.

11. Roy Rappaport's *Pigs for the Ancestors: Ritual in the Ecology of a New Guinea People* [New Haven, CT: Yale University Press, 1984 (1968)] is a classic ethnography of a highland Melanesian community.

12. One early anthology that contains a number of essays on Melanesian religions written by anthropologists is edited by Peter Lawrence and Mervyn Meggitt and called *Gods Ghosts and Men in Melanesia: Some Religions of Australian New Guinea and the New Hebrides* (London: Oxford University Press, 1965). An attempt to characterize Melanesian religions is done by G.W. Trompf in *Melanesian Religion* (Cambridge: Cambridge University Press, 1991).

13. This Huli myth is described by anthropologist R.M. Glasse in "The Huli of the Southern Highlands" in Peter Lawrence and Mervyn Meggitt, *Gods Ghosts and Men in Melanesia: Some Religions of Australian New Guinea and the New Hebrides* (London: Oxford University Press, 1965).

14. The classic description of Yali's movement is in Peter Lawrence's book *Road belong Cargo: A Study of the Cargo Movement in the Southern Madang District, New Guinea* (Manchester: Manchester University Press, 1964). Two other works dealing with the cargo cults are Kenelm Burridge's *New Heaven, New Earth* (Oxford: Basil Blackwell, 1969) and Glynne Cochrane's *Big Men and Cargo Cults* (Oxford: Clarendon Press, 1970).

15. Roscoe describes this millenarian movement in "The Brokers of the Lord: The Ministration of a Christian Faith in the Sepik Basin of Papua New Guinea," in Victoria Lockwood, Thomas G. Harding, and Ben J. Wallace, eds., *Contemporary Pacific Societies: Studies in Development and Change* (Upper Saddle River, NJ: Prentice Hall Press, 1993).

16. Worsley's analysis of cargo cults is found in his *The Trumpet Shall Sound: A Study of 'Cargo Cults' in Melanesia* (London: Paladin, 1970).

17. For anthropological accounts of traditional Hawaiian society see Irving Goldman *Ancient Polynesian Society* (Chicago: University of Chicago Press, 1970); Marshall Sahlins, *Historical Metaphors and Mythical Realities: Structure in the Early History of the Sandwich Islands Kingdom* (Ann Arbor: University of Michigan Press, 1981); and *Islands of History* (Chicago: University of Chicago Press, 1985); and Valerio Valeri, *Kingship and Sacrifice: Ritual and Society in Ancient Hawaii*, Paula Wissing, trans. (Chicago: University of Chicago Press, 1985).

18. The Kumilopo chant was carefully translated by Martha Warren Beckwith and can be found in her *The Kumulipo: A Hawaiian Creation Chant* (Honolulu: University of Hawaii Press, 1972). Beckwith has an older standard work collecting much of the mythology of traditional Hawaiian society entitled *Hawaiian Mythology* (New Haven, CT: Yale University Press, 1940).

19. A fascinating debate within anthropology has developed regarding the death of Captain Cook and the way in which he was perceived by the Hawaiians. Marshall Sahlins in his books *Historical Metaphors and Mythical Realities: Structure in the Early History of the Sandwich Islands Kingdom and Islands of History* (see note 17) argues that Cook was believed by the Hawaiians to be the god Lono, who appeared at the time of sacrifice, and for a variety of reasons was killed. Gananath Obeysekere in *Apotheosis of Captain Cook: European Mythmaking in the Pacific* (Princeton, NJ: Princeton University Press, 1992) argues that Sahlins misinterprets the evidence and advocates the view that Cook was not perceived as a god, but as an important chief who was sought as a powerful ally who had military and economic resources, and that he commanded a lot of mana. Sahlins in a later book *How "Natives" Think, About Captain Cook, for Example* (Chicago: University of Chicago, 1995) attacked Obeysekere's thesis. In this book, Sahlins interprets the ship's logs and later Hawaiian writings to establish that the Hawaiians did understand Cook as connected with the god Lono. For an interesting assessment of this debate see Robert Borofsky's "Cook, Lono, Obeyesekere, and Sahlins," *Current Anthropology* 38 (2): 255–282. 1997.

20. The Hawaiian cultural revolution as it became known among anthropologists has been explained by Malcolm Webb in "The Abolition of the Taboo System in Hawaii," *Journal of the Polynesian Society* 74 (1):21–39, 1965, and William Davenport in "The Hawaiian Cultural Revolution: Some Political and Economic Considerations," *American Anthropologist* 71 (1): 1–20, 1969. The Hawaiian revolution is also taken up by Marshall Sahlins in his two major books on Hawaii (see note 17).

21. For an overall analysis of the Hawaiian political economy and culture and recent change, see Elizabeth Buck's *Paradise Remade: The Politics of Culture and History in Hawai'i* (Philadelphia: Temple University Press, 1993). For commentary on the contemporary native Hawaiian movement, see Jonathan Friedman's "Narcissism, Roots and Postmodernity: The Constitution of Selfhood in the Global Crisis," in S. Lash and J. Friedman, *Modernity and Identity* (Oxford: Basil Blackwell, 1992), and Friedman's *Culture Identity and Global Process* (London: Sage Publications, 1995).

Nine

African Religions

Jeffrey Carter
University of South Carolina

Any study of African religions faces a dilemma from the start. It encounters the immense diversity of religious phenomena on the continent. With a geographical area more than three times the United States and over 500 million people organized into more than 50 countries and several hundred ethnic groups, Africa is one of the most culturally and religiously complex regions in the world. Adding to this complexity are the lasting consequences of European colonialism. As Britain, France, Germany, Portugal, and Belgium maintained colonies in Africa during the late nineteenth and early twentieth centuries, the indigenous peoples on the continent, to varying degrees, adopted new cultural, religious, linguistic, political, and economic patterns. The Africa of today is a place of diversity sprouting amid diversity, of Western values and materials blending with traditional ways of life. Equally so for religion. Most contemporary communities include elements both traditional and modern, both African and Western, both international and local. The richness of African religions reflects this cultural diversity and historical complexity.

At the same time, anthropologists have commonly simplified their studies in Africa by making distinctions and bracketing various domains of interest. For example, many researchers distinguish between the northern, predominantly Islamic region of the continent along the Mediterranean Sea, and the larger, more diverse, southern area south of the Sahara desert. They refer to the former as "North Africa" and the latter as "Tropical," "Black," or "Sub-Saharan" Africa. Similarly, the history of Africa has allowed anthropologists to differentiate between indigenous forms of religion (usually called "African Traditional Religions"), Islam (which gained a Sub-Saharan foothold in approximately the eleventh century), and Christianity (which arrived in West Africa in the fifteenth century). Using these various distinctions, early anthropological investigations of religion in Africa concentrated on various examples of traditional religions as they were present among individual ethnic groups in Sub-Saharan Africa. During the early twentieth century, trained anthropologists sought to study examples of religious life in Africa that were, as much as possible, immune to the influences of Christianity and Islam. These studies produced a great number of outstanding ethnographies, which when read together, comprise what can be understood as "African religions." More recently, however, anthropologists studying religion in Africa have focused their attention on how historical processes have led Christianity and Islam both to affect, and be affected by, traditional religious beliefs and practices.

This chapter will identify and discuss the major themes, issues, and areas of interest that constitute the classical ethnographic study of traditional religions in Africa. It will present a general framework for understanding African religions while attempting to characterize the diversity of religious forms on the continent. This chapter will also briefly examine Christianity in Africa, paying particular attention to how both Christianity and traditional religions inform indigenous new religious movements.[1]

THE AGENTS OF AFRICAN RELIGIONS

At the heart of traditional African religions is a belief in the reality of superhuman agency. Across the African continent, people experience reality as greater than the empirical aspects of nature and society. Along with tangible realities, there exist for African religions a variety of gods, goddesses, impersonal spirits, and forces. Furthermore, most traditional African religions assert these three domains—the social world (human beings), the natural world, and the supernatural world—are mutually dependent. Instead of autonomous realities, these domains exist in an ordered system of relationships. Far from being chaotic, these domains of reality and the mutually defining relationships between them constitute a "religious cosmos." While the detailed content of a community's conception of the religious cosmos (for example, the number and type of gods it recognizes) varies among ethnic groups, it essentially serves as an ordered system of meanings around which people in Africa traditionally orient their lives. In other words, the religious dimension of traditional life in Africa—what it means to be a religious person—revolves around knowing the nature of, and relationships between, the religious realities constituting the cosmos, and then molding one's behavior, defining one's identity, even structuring one's community accordingly. This section begins the task of characterizing the different ways various ethnic groups across Africa define and organize their religious cosmos.

The most prominent superhuman agent in traditional African religions, generally speaking, is the "Supreme Being" or "High God." Devotees maintain these beings possess abstract superhuman qualities such as unsurpassed greatness, transcendence, ultimacy, and superiority. Much like other monotheistic conceptions of divinity, many African High Gods are all-knowing, or omniscient. For example, the Yoruba-speaking peoples of southwest Nigeria refer to their High God (*Olódùmarè*) as "the discerner of hearts." High Gods are also omnipresent. This is the case for the Nuer of southern Sudan, for they claim their High God (*Kwoth*) is everywhere "like the wind." Equally common, ethnic groups believe their High God is omnipotent, that is, all-powerful, capable of anything, almighty. Hence the Dinka, another ethnic group in Sudan, refer to their High God (*Nhialic*) as the "One with power and strength."

These transcendent qualities lead many African ethnic groups to associate their High God with the sky. In fact, many groups believe the High God now dwells in the sky, separated from the earth, because a mythic human being committed some transgression such as acting greedy, disobeying a divine command, or being jealous. With few exceptions, High Gods are so transcendent, they have no temples, special priests, annual festivals, or images devoted to them. At the same time, however, most African High Gods also possess traits that give them a certain immanence. They are in some ways close to the human world, involved in human affairs, personal and concrete in character. For example, most African ethnic groups understand their High God to be male, some even describing Him as their "father" or "friend." High Gods are frequently master creators, essentially good, merciful, and kind beings. They are ultimately responsible for creating life, and for insuring human health and prosperity. High Gods also can demonstrate anger, however, and some groups, such as the Nuer, associate them with misfortune, even death.[2]

Despite this conception of the High God, the traditional religious experience of superhuman agency in Africa is not singular. For most ethnic groups, in fact, the religious cosmos also includes a pantheon of lesser deities, the size and character of which vary from group to group. For example, the Yoruba recognize more than four hundred gods (*òrìsà*), while the Dinka identify less than five deities (*yeeth*). The character of these many gods likewise varies tremendously from group to group, and from deity to deity within a single pantheon. Some are associated with distinctive activities or abilities of the High God, for example the power to create, to bestow wisdom, or grant fertility. Other deities are associated with powerful or significant aspects of nature like the sun, rain, certain rivers, or animals. Some were once historical human beings, who because of their strength, bravery, or other heroic trait, become deities after their deaths. Still others are associated with particular human activities or experiences like agriculture, blacksmithing, or medicinal healing. Most religious traditions know and remember these gods through myths, proverbs, songs, or other forms of religious literature, and through prayer, sacrifice, possession states, divination, or other ritual activities (see below).

These gods have diverse, though specific, identities as well—usually a particular gender, demeanor, and a set of preferences and aversions regarding food, colors, and numbers. Understood to be powerful and authoritative within certain domains of influence, these lesser gods provide blessings but can also cause misfortune for human beings. Most significantly, these many gods, when compared to a group's High God, are more dynamic and immediate, more manifest and specific, as forms of divine power. Consequently, worshippers do devote temples to these gods, often represent them with altars and images, employ priests and prophets to communicate with them, and conduct regular rituals in their honor. For most ethnic groups in Africa, people live their daily religious lives, quite literally, in relation to these many gods.[3]

E.E. Evans-Pritchard's ethnographic study of the Nuer provides a fine example of an ethnic group's belief in multiple superhuman agents. They distinguish between two categories of lesser divinities (*kuth*): "spirits of the above" (*kuth nhial*) and "spirits of the below" (*kuth piny*). The Nuer further divide the "spirits of the above" into two main types. The first type, known as the "spirits of the air" (*kuth dwanga*), includes a spirit associated with human sickness named *deng*, another named *teny* who is responsible for fashioning human beings, and a female spirit associated with rivers and streams named *buk*. The second type of "spirits of the above" is the *colwic* spirits, and is composed of the spirits of people killed by lightning or found dead in the wilderness. The Nuer believe their "spirits of the below" embody creatures or things on earth. They claim "totemic" and "totemistic" spirits link specific lineages or individuals with various species of plants or animals like lions, reptiles, or cattle with certain markings. Similarly, material substances such as fire, ashes, or pieces of wood may contain spirits the Nuer call "nature sprites" (*bieli*) and "medicine spirits" (*kulangni*). Overall, a variety of gods, goddesses, and spirits, each of different importance and recognition, populate the Nuer religious cosmos.[4]

Along with High Gods and lesser deities, most African religions recognize another class of superhuman agency: ancestors. While not every African group actively worships ancestors, most assume recently dead family members can continue to influence their descendants. These beings are the "living dead." Ordinarily, they are individuals whose socially admirable qualities like moral integrity, longevity, and wealth allow them to retain a degree of prominence after death. In this way, surviving family members, by remembering the name, character, and exploits of their ancestors, likewise keep alive certain social relationships, rights, and responsibilities. Since ancestors are senior members of the community and therefore are invested with the authority and status of age, they deserve respect, and in some cases gifts of appreciation, or acknowledgment of their power and abilities. A great many African ethnic groups claim ancestors are most concerned with maintaining the moral and social order of their surviving communities. For this reason, many African traditional religions believe ancestors can punish wrongdoers by causing misfortune but can also assist (grant favors to) those family members who act morally. In his ethnography of the Tallensi of Northern Ghana, the British anthropologist Meyer Fortes describes people making frequent offerings of food, beer, and grain to ancestors. Noting the importance of parenthood for the social structure of this group, Fortes concludes that ancestor worship is an extension of ordinary filial piety, a continuation of expected social relations between parents and children. Just as children respond to the punishment and protection of their parents, adults likewise treat their ancestors. Not quite gods, but certainly no longer mere human beings, ancestors are family-specific superhuman agents who, when remembered and treated appropriately, can provide substantial benefits in the material world.[5]

Many African religions include in their religious cosmos an understanding of what constitutes a human being. Along with the physical body, human beings are composed of an immaterial essence, an ethereal or spiritual component with religious significance. Unlike most Western conceptions of the "soul," however, many African groups such as the Fang of Gabon, the Lugbara of Uganda, and the Bambara of Mali posit the existence of multiple souls for every individual. While their number and character vary widely among African religions, souls are associated in general with different body parts like the heart, breath, and head; they have distinctive functions and ordinarily survive the body after death. Most ethnic groups, for example, tie one or more of these surviving souls to the idea of ancestors. Similarly, many African religious traditions hold that one or more of a person's souls becomes temporarily replaced, driven out of the body, or superseded when that person experiences spirit possession (see below). Some ethnic groups also claim that when dreaming, a person's soul travels out of the body so it can, for example, communicate with distant relatives, or engage in other extraordinary activities common to dreams.

The Yoruba religious conception of the human being, to cite one example, includes a physical body and two (though some say five) different immaterial parts.

Before an individual's birth, one of the Yoruba lesser deities (*Òrìsànlá*) first forms his or her body (*ara*). Then the High God (*Olódùmarè*) adds a portion of divine breath to the body, thereby providing it a "life," "spirit," or "soul" (*èmí*). Finally, the enlivened body receives another spiritual component called the "inner head" (*orí*). The Yoruba understand this soul to determine (though not absolutely) the quality of an individual's life. For this reason it is sometimes referred to as the person's "destiny," or "ancestral guardian spirit." The Yoruba, much like other African ethnic groups, understand human beings to be more than simply biological beings. Rather, religious components derived from the High God, from various lesser deities, and ancestors, together constitute the full nature of human beings. Human beings have religious significance and hence should be understood as integral parts of the religious cosmos.[6]

Many African ethnic groups, particularly those in West Africa, arrange the superhuman agents consituting the religious cosmos hierarchically. Beginning at the top with the High God and moving down through the lesser deities, ancestors, human beings (including their souls), animals, and objects, the cosmos takes on a certain order. Higher beings have more power, more transcendent qualities, and more general significance for the community at large. Proceeding down the hierarchy, beings are more socially differentiated, closer to the world of human activity, and more frequently implicated in ritual behavior. The practical significance of this hierarchical arrangement for religious life varies throughout the continent, but it further illustrates the systematic nature of African traditional religions. As they relate to each other, these superhuman agents are known and named and can be placated, befriended, and offended. They are powerful beings that ultimately constitute the core of religious life in traditional Africa.

RITUAL IN AFRICAN RELIGIONS

Defining ritual has been, and remains, a controversy for the anthropological study of religion. Most simply however, ritual is religious action or behavior; it refers to people doing something religiously. Of course, this definition requires a distinction between religious and nonreligious action. While this too is a controversy, for African religions at least, ritual can be understood as action conforming to religious beliefs. It is any behavior structured, defined, modified, or limited by the nature of the religious realities a community holds true. Said differently, ritual is activity a group organizes in accord with its conception of the religious cosmos—the system of relationships between human beings, superhuman beings, and the natural world that constitute the ultimate source of meaning for the community. Whether public or private, ritual refers to the variety of things individuals and communities do to create and maintain their relationships to the religious cosmos.

As a structured form of activity, ritual tends to exhibit three basic traits. First, rituals ordinarily display some degree of repetition. People may repeat them periodically, for example annually at harvest time, or monthly with the cycles of the moon. Also within a single ritual performance, participants may repeat certain individual actions, acts like chanting a phrase or assuming a particular posture. While it is true ritual performances also include various improvised elements, as a whole they are historically and/or internally continuous. After repetition, most rituals furthermore have a specific context for their performance. They occur at established times such as sunrise or midnight, at special places like shrines or mountain tops, and for distinctive purposes, for example to ensure safe passage of the deceased into the realm of the ancestors. Third, rituals tend to be formal concerning content. Any given ritual will include specific objects, symbols, words, activities, even individuals, just as it will exclude others. In this way, ritual is, among other things, an enacting of the participants' (ritual performers') conception of propriety. Together these three traits (repetition, a customary context, and formal content) make participating in ritual not only structured (as is the religious cosmos) process, but also structuring activity. It literally creates for participants a sense of pattern and order in their lives, organizing the chaotic and generating meaning out of uncertainty.[7]

An important class of ritual activity in African traditional religions is "rites of passage." First discussed by Arnold Van Gennep early in the twentieth century, rites of passage mark the major transitions human beings undergo over the course of their lives. Gennep noticed that around the world societies understand bodily changes (for example at puberty) to parallel changes in social and religious status. People perform rites of passage to recognize and make real these changes from one mode of being to another. Rites of passage define anew a participant's social, religious, and physical identity. The most important of these transitions are the movement from womb to childhood (birth), from childhood to adulthood (puberty), from adulthood to procreative adulthood (marriage), and from life on earth to the afterlife (death). Gennep also noticed that rites of passage ordinarily have three phases or stages. The first, the "pre-liminal phase," is marked by separation from a participant's present mode of existence. It suggests the removal of an old identity, a breaking of the ties and relations associated with that identity. This phase may include forms of cutting (of hair for example), fasting, purification, or physical ordeals—all acts symbolic of separation. The second stage, the "liminal phase," is a transitional phase, a neutral zone between identities. With the old status now nullified and the new status not yet created, only nonstatus, nonstructure, nondistinction, and equality remain. The liminal phase, being a period of nonidentity, is a time of radical potential, an opportunity for rebirth, re-creation, and transformation. It can include symbols that suggest isolation, silence, or asceticism. The final phase, or "post-liminal phase," is distinguished by features of incorporation. This phase establishes the new mode of existence. It takes the potential of the liminal phase and creates new relationships, a new order, identity and status. This final phase often involves community wide celebrations such as meals, the exchange of gifts, and the giving of new names. All together, the three phases that constitute rites of passage may be aligned with natural cycles, represented with images of death and rebirth, or depicted by movement through space, for example through doors, or from inside to outside. By organizing and orienting the basic periods of human life with the overall religious cosmos, rites of passage place and replace individuals within a meaningful world.[8]

The attitudes and actions surrounding pregnancy and birth demonstrate that these physical events are religiously significant as well. Traditionally in Africa, people believe pregnancies can fail for religious reasons, and therefore to insure their success ritual precautions must be observed. For example, when a woman determines she is pregnant she may begin to carry protective charms designed to ward off evil spirits such as witches (see below). She will most likely begin to observe special taboos whereby she avoids certain activities like sexual intercourse, or particular objects like oily foods for example. Disregarding these restrictions may harm the mother or the developing child. Similarly an expectant mother may pray to any number of superhuman agents (gods, ancestors, etc.) and ask for success in her pregnancy. Depending on an ethnic group's particular customs, the actual birth may take place in the mother's house, in her parent's dwelling, or in a special birthing house outside the main village. Sometimes professional midwives, usually older women, will assist with the birth. Most ethnic groups do not ignore the placenta or treat it haphazardly. As a symbol of the baby's old identity and attachment to its mother, some ethnic groups, such as the Wolof of Senegal and the Yansi of the Democratic Republic of Congo, deliberately separate the placenta from the child (suggesting a pre-liminal intention) by burying it or casting it into a river. Recalling the liminal phase, many ethnic groups seclude the mother and child for a number of days immediately following birth. Following this seclusion, a family will celebrate the successful incorporation (the post-liminal stage) of the new baby into the community. The parents may hold a feast for invited guests, receive gifts, and conduct a special naming ceremony that acknowledges the baby's new identity within the group. As it is lived within traditional African religious communities, birth is only the beginning of a life punctuated by rites of passage.[9]

Puberty signals the next occasion when ritual redefines the social and religious status of an individual. Here, ritual marks the passage from childhood into adulthood. This is the event when young boys and girls become men and women, when they become full members of society qualified for marriage. Across Africa, communities hold separate puberty ceremonies for boys and girls. Ordinarily, though this is less true for female puberty rites, young people over a range of ages undergo this rite of passage as a group. These co-participants form what anthropologists call an "age-grade" or "age-set." Over the course of their lives, members of an age-set enjoy mutual support, perhaps offering each other financial or other forms of assistance when needed. Effectively being born into adulthood together, they treat each other, even refer to each other, as siblings. Some ethnic groups like the Limba of Sierra Leone combine their puberty rituals with initiation into gendered secret societies as well. For such groups, all eligible boys periodically join one secret society and all girls join another. Here too, an individual's social and religious identity depends upon being initiated into one of these societies. Other ethnic groups such as the Yoruba of Nigeria have no formal puberty rites but do initiate young people into different cultic groups.

Even as their details vary, puberty and initiation rituals ordinarily display the three phases common to rites of passage. Most of the activity for these rituals occurs during a period of seclusion when all those being initiated live together separated from the rest of the community. Leading up to this seclusion the initiates may be assigned a mentor, someone who will care for them during the seclusion. This person may also be responsible for teaching the initiate the cultural knowledge required to be an adult, for example the specifics of the society's religious and social virtues, information about sex and gender roles, and perhaps secret doctrines or esoteric rituals. Also during this period, the initiate may be forced to memorize certain songs or myths, to follow strict taboos, and to endure a range of physical discomforts such as sleeplessness, unusual foods, or scarification. Significantly, this is also the time when many ethnic groups in Africa circumcise boys and girls. Here, cutting in the bodily area of fertility can symbolize a young person's separation from childhood and readiness for reproductive adulthood. Following the period of seclusion, the initiates return to the community to celebrate and proclaim publicly their new status as adults. They may acquire a new name and begin to dress differently, each indicating their new status, and in the end, claiming the new rights and obligations it entails.[10]

The next important rite of passage in an individual's life is marriage. The rituals of marriage accomplish the proper transition from adulthood into *procreative* adulthood. For postpubescent individuals, the ritual practices of marriage identify and sanction a new reproductive status. They allow a man and a woman to create one of the most widespread values in Africa—children. Children are important to society because they serve as new members and thus perpetuate it. Being named after an ancestor, or being recognized as a devotee of a certain god or goddess make children religiously valuable because they thereby help maintain a family's relationship with the superhuman realm. They have an economic value as well because they can assist with a family's agricultural or market chores, and on a personal level, people value children because they are responsible for properly burying their parents. Indeed, for many ethnic groups, being married means having children, so much so, that couples failing to reproduce are at best incompletely married, if married at all.

Beyond the importance of children, marriage gains significance because of the social relationships it creates. As individuals marry outside their lineage, as they practice exogamy, marriage is essentially a bonding of families, more than that of the couple. Marriage is a corporate matter where frequently parents, in some cases through an intermediary, arrange for their children's mate. Most marriage customs in Africa involve the groom's family giving various gifts such as cattle, money, food, or household goods to the bride's family, paying the so-called "bride-wealth" or "bride-price." Along with the children produced, which in these societies usually stay with the groom's lineage, this payment realizes the contractual agreement made between families. It thereby creates, through the act of exchange, recognizable social relations, rights, and obligations.

A majority of African societies recognize polygyny, the practice of a man marrying more than one wife. Men often prefer additional wives for the added social and financial prestige they bring, and many women prefer polygyny for the additional help with household chores co-wives provide. At the same time, relatively few African men marry additional wives because doing so requires more resources like a larger house and greater quantities of food. In addition, jealousy and competition between co-wives tend to trouble polygynous households, and many ethnic groups think this kind of resentfulness contributes to witchcraft. Wedding ceremonies vary widely in Africa, but they tend to include features of the pattern described above for rites of passage. Weddings commonly involve crossing a threshold of some sort, a period of seclusion for the couple, dancing, gift exchange, thanksgiving prayers and sacrifices, and communal meals.[11]

Death, for traditional African religions, is not the end of human existence, not truly the elimination of a person. Instead, it simply indicates a departure or a passing away, for only the physical portion of what constitutes a human being actually dies. A person's immaterial portions (or souls) move on and survive in another world, in an "after-life," or in what some call the realm of the ancestors. Much like birth, puberty, and marriage, death is another passage, another religious transition human beings undergo. It transforms a person's physical, social, and religious status from that of the living into that of the "living dead" (the ancestors). Most ethnic groups in Africa traditionally trace the origin of death to a mythic event where the immortality associated with the superhuman realm ends following human disobedience of divine commands, a sexual offense, murder, or some other fault.

Methods for disposing of the corpse vary tremendously across Africa, but burial is certainly the most common. Some groups bury their dead inside the family house or courtyard, while others rely on organized cemeteries. Even within single groups, there is a degree of variation here, with the two most important factors determining the character of a particular burial being a person's social status while alive, and the manner in which he or she died. For example, most ethnic groups do not perform customary burials for infants, apparent suicides, or other examples of "bad death." The bodies of such people may be simply abandoned in a remote or uninhabited area. It is common to orient graves toward the East and to bury with the body various material goods that may be useful in the afterlife such as personal belongings, food, money, or weapons. Other ethnic groups shave the deceased's head, undress the body, or place it in the fetal position within the grave. Funerals in Africa vary greatly as well, but generally they last several days, weeks, even months, and include a formal period of mourning, prayers, and sacrifices, and a postburial celebration recognizing the successful passage of the deceased into the afterlife. With few exceptions, traditional African conceptions of the afterlife suggest it differs little from life on earth. Only in rare cases does it include the notion of a judgment that leads to punishment or reward. Instead, death is the final step in the life cycle of being human, a simple move, realized through ritual, from this world to the next.[12]

Following rites of passage, there is another extremely widespread and frequently performed ritual act in Africa: prayer. Ethnic groups across the continent acknowledge their relationship to superhuman agents by communicating with them through prayer. Believing in the reality of the religious cosmos, human beings use speech, among other things, to connect with the various powerful beings enlivening the world around them. Prayer allows people to deliver messages, express concerns, and ask questions they believe are relevant to their place in the religious cosmos. At formal occasions like rites of passage, and at informal times such as when a person feels threatened for some reason, prayer permits both individuals and groups to tap the power superhuman agents possess to affect things on earth. For example, many prayers in African religions focus on petition and ask to receive health, wealth, children, or another form of material welfare. Others are statements of thanksgiving that recognize and declare gratitude for good fortune. Some prayers simply announce praise for, or assert the powers and abilities of, one superhuman agent or another, and still others are explicit confessions, statements of wrongdoing conceded to propitiate a disapproving superhuman being such as an ancestor. Whether performed kneeling, standing, or bowing, whether facing the East, the altar of a shrine, or some other particular direction, prayer employs the power of speech to invoke a named superhuman being, to honor and praise him or her, to communicate troubles or concerns, and in the end, to solve them. In Africa, prayer represents one of the fundamental ritual techniques to solve life's problems.[13]

Second to prayer, though in some ways of equal importance, sacrifice is another common ritual practice in traditional African religions. Most simply, religious sacrifice involves the forfeiture or destruction of something valuable for a religious purpose, that is, to influence the current state of the religious cosmos. It ordinarily means enduring a voluntary deprivation whereby the sacrificing party transfers what is lost to the superhuman realm in the hopes of some favorable response. Some sacrifices benefit individuals, for example when a parent might immolate a chicken as part of a prescribed healing ritual for a child, and others benefit groups, such as when a village offers food-crops following a successful growing season. The materials sacrificed, that which is given up, vary widely from example to example, but they tend to be either animals like cows, goats, chickens, and birds, or edible items such as grains, fruits, root-crops, and prepared foods. They can also, however, be liquids like water, oil, and beer, or other symbols of wealth like money and cloth. The mode of sacrifice, how the materials are forfeited or destroyed, likewise varies widely. In Africa, blood immolation, which can include decapitation and/or dismemberment, is the most common mode of sacrifice if an animal is the offering. The animal's blood may be collected and poured as a libation or perhaps employed in a further ritual act such as a bath. Other sacrificial items may be abandoned in the wilderness, cast into a river, buried at a crossroads, or simply presented at a shrine. Generally, the recipient of a sacrificial offering will be one of the superhuman agents discussed above—the High God, one of the lesser deities, an ancestor, or another spirit.

The reasons for sacrificing, the purposes behind sacrificial ritual, vary from context to context. One common reason people in Africa sacrifice is propitiation, that is, to remove the anger of, and resulting punishment by, a superhuman agent. Much like a payment for wrongs done, a person can appease an offended deity or ancestor, for example, by offering a particular sacrifice. Second, prevention of harm or misfortune is another reason why a person might offer a sacrifice. Here the sacrificing party assumes the recipient of the sacrifice has the power to prevent some potential danger or accident. Some sacrifices in Africa, thirdly, are made to express thanks to a superhuman being thought responsible for an occurrence of good fortune. When things go well, a person may sacrifice something in the hopes that such good fortune will continue. Finally, people in Africa sometimes sacrifice to fulfill a vow or promise to a superhuman agent. For example, a barren woman might promise to sacrifice a goat to a god if he helps her deliver a healthy child. She may even make a sacrifice before becoming pregnant, hoping to persuade the god to help her be successful. All together these reasons for sacrifice—propitiation, prevention, thanksgiving, and the contractual—represent different avenues of relationship between human beings and superhuman agents. Consequently, sacrifice, much like prayer, can be understood as a ritual means by which human beings establish and sustain the network of meaningful relationships they value between themselves, superhuman beings, and the natural world.[14]

In his ethnography *Nuer Religion*, Evans-Pritchard devotes considerable attention to sacrifice. He describes the Nuer sacrificing on many occasions—when faced with impending danger, when suffering with sickness, at funerals, marriages, and births—but he claims most Nuer sacrifice is piacular, that is, performed to assist individuals suffering from barrenness, sickness, or some other affliction. Since the Nuer understand the High God or one of the lesser deities to be the cause of these personal crises, Evans-Pritchard uses the term "desacralization" to describe this form of sacrifice. In this case, he suggests, sacrifice "removes" the interference of a superhuman agent by accomplishing an expiation for wrongdoing. The Nuer consider oxen the ideal victims, but they sacrifice goats and particular species of plants as well. Evans-Pritchard also claims Nuer sacrificial rituals can be divided into four acts. The first, "presentation" (*pwot*), involves tethering a victim to the ground and on occasion pouring a libation of milk, beer, or water over the tethering peg. During the next step, "consecration" (*buk*), the person hoping to benefit from the sacrifice rubs ashes on the animal victim, thereby establishing a symbolic link with it. Third, the officiating male will offer an "invocation" (*lam*), which is basically a prayer, to the superhuman recipient of the sacrifice stating the intention behind the ritual. Finally, the "immolation" (*nak*) or killing of the victim occurs so that its blood can drain out onto the ground. Not all Nuer sacrifices strictly follow this pattern, but generally, Evans-Pritchard tells us, the Nuer believe a superhuman agent "takes the life" of the animal victim, which is symbolized by its blood and breath, while the sacrificing party keeps, and in most cases, eats the victim's flesh. Partly a ransom or bargain, partly an expression of honor or homage, and partly an atonement or purification, sacrifice for the Nuer, and many other African ethnic groups, is a regular dimension of their religious life.

Anthropologists and other scholars of religion have offered a number of theories to explain the cultural phenomena associated with religious sacrifice. Discussing all of them is beyond the scope of this chapter, but among the earliest, Edward Tylor argues that human beings sacrifice because they think giving gifts to gods will win their favor and avoid their wrath. The French sociologists Henri Hubert and Marcel Mauss claim that sacrificial victims serve as intermediaries or mediums of communication between the sacred and profane realms. For them, sacrifice establishes moments of relationship between the sacred and the profane, while allowing them to remain separate. Noting how many sacrificial rites include a communal feast where participants eat the sacrificial victim, W. Robertson Smith suggests that this meal is an occasion for human beings to commune with the recipient of the sacrifice, for example the deity or ancestor of the clan. Here, sacrifice brings together and unifies the human and superhuman realms. Finally, Evans-Pritchard favors a theory of substitution. He points to the fact that expiation is the most common purpose behind Nuer sacrificial rites, notes that the Nuer believe the victim's blood carries away the defilement needing expiation, and argues that the victim serves as a substitute for the person benefiting from the sacrifice.[15]

RELIGIOUS SPECIALISTS

Within any religious community, certain individuals may distinguish themselves by virtue of their possessing special religious abilities, skills, or knowledge. These religious specialists have some form of privileged access to one or more dimensions of the religious cosmos. For a number of reasons, some people simply excel at contacting, and in some cases manipulating, various supernatural beings and forces. As a result, such individuals ordinarily gain a degree of religious authority within their communities, and in many cases, social and political prestige as well. This section examines three important traditional religious specialists in Africa.

A widely reported religious phenomenon in Africa is spirit possession. Indicated by a dramatic altering of their consciousness, possessed people often report disturbances in perception such as a loss of memory, or sense of time or space. Such people frequently gain the ability to perform superhuman feats such as licking hot iron, piercing body parts, or demonstrating extreme physical endurance or strength. They may exhibit drastic changes in physiognomy like assuming unusual postures, or speaking in peculiar voices. Most commonly, ethnic groups attribute these changes to a lesser deity or ancestral spirit, but rarely, if ever, the High God, taking control of a person. A superhuman being temporarily "possesses," "haunts," "enters," "rides," "mounts," or "marries" a human being. A possessed person, in other words, essentially serves as a medium for a superhuman being to express itself physically, make demands upon devotees, or perhaps provide information.

Possession states exhibit different levels of dissociation and lucidity, persist for various lengths of time, but tend to reoccur once a person is initially possessed. Over time, certain individuals within a community may gain the ability to control their possession states, and given the proper ritual context, which may include rhythmic music, dancing, and role playing, such individuals may become possessed at will, thus allowing them to serve the wider community. Variously referred to as "spirit mediums" or "prophets," such individuals effectively become religious specialists known to be spokespersons for possessing superhuman agents. Instead of learning or inheriting their position, typically a superhuman agent will call, inspire, or even force an individual to accept the religious duties of prophecy. Prophets are usually charismatic men and women who serve individuals or small groups seeking occasional contact with a particular superhuman agent. Evans-Pritchard describes prophets among the Nuer (*gwan kwoth*) as those people who "have" some form of "Spirit" and hence gain "spiritual powers" ordinary people lack, for example the ability to foretell events, to divine advice during war, and to heal certain diseases. Generally, prophets play a role in maintaining traditional social and religious values, but in some instances, particularly during historical moments of rapid social change, prophets can galvanize resistance against (or, paradoxically, support for) the perceived forces of change. An example here is the prophet-led Maji Maji revolt of 1905–1907 in Tanzania. Overall, prophets serve as yet another conduit for the relations structuring the religious cosmos in many African religions.[16]

Beyond prophets, there is a second common type of religious specialist in Africa: priests. These are respected individuals in a community who function as ritual experts. Priests know the details, in some cases esoteric details, of a community's ritual practices, and thus act as officials or leaders in ritual contexts, for example during rites of passage and regularly scheduled communitywide festivals. Being a priest is a matter of occupying an institutional office defined by a body of knowledge and skills. Consequently, a priesthood is a learned profession, sometimes inherited from generation to generation. Priestly authority stems from knowing well the skills to perform the recognized duties of the priestly office, and unlike prophets, does not follow from a charismatic personality. Also different from prophets, priests ordinarily do not experience spirit possession. Rather than acting as the corporal medium for a superhuman agent to address human beings, priests act as representatives for human beings wishing to communicate with the superhuman realm. Priests speak for the people, while prophets speak for the gods.

Again turning to the Nuer for an example, there are so-called "leopard skin priests" (*kuaar twac*), individuals who serve their communities by settling feuds, taking and verifying oaths, and conducting sacrifices on the behalf of others who have committed especially serious misdeeds like murder, incest, or adultery. This Nuer example, combined with the one above, makes it clear that some societies have both priests and prophets. In some cases, a community's priest may be called upon to interpret the behavior or speech of a prophet. In other cases, the same person can function as both types of religious specialist, for example when a prophet has occasional priestly roles like officiating at a community ritual. Together, priests and prophets represent specialized religious figures, people who make possible avenues of meaningful connection between the human and superhuman realms.[17]

A few ethnic groups in Africa organize themselves socially, politically, and religiously around the notion of a divine or sacred king. More than simply a political leader, a sacred king is yet another type of religious specialist, for he is thought to possess "divine power" and thereby to personify one or more aspects of the superhuman realm. Sacred kings are similar to prophets since they are incarnations of the divine, but different from prophets since kings ordinarily are not possessed. Furthermore, sacred kings are similar to priests because their authority derives from their office rather than their personality, but different from priests since kings are only rarely responsible for the ritual activity of individual cult groups. Often, a community's myths will include an explanation for the origin of kingship, a description of the rules and process of royal succession, and an account of the king's responsibilities. Given his exalted position ("second to the gods" as the Yoruba describe their kings), however, a king's major responsibility is to ensure the well-being of his kingdom. He accomplishes this duty, generally speaking, by providing a form of divine sanction or validation through his presence at major communitywide religious events like harvest or new year festivals. Yet he also insures the health of his kingdom by living in accord with a variety of prohibitions thought essential to maintaining his own health.

If a sacred king should become seriously ill, too old, or weak, or if the general well-being of a community begins to suffer, for example from a famine, flood, or epidemic, the community may decide to inaugurate a new king. For some ethnic groups, these rituals of royal succession traditionally include killing the out-going king. Made famous by James Frazer, this phenomenon of regicide has been reported among the Banyoro of Uganda, the Shona of Zimbabwe, the Shilluk of Sudan, and others. Underscoring reports that a successor king would eat certain body parts of his predecessor, Frazer understood regicide to be a community's attempt to preserve their king's religious power by magically transferring it to his successor. The entire community of people dependent on the king may participate in such a royal succession ritual. Other ethnic groups such as the Swazi of Swaziland enact annually a public festival where the king, without relinquishing his office, undergoes a symbolic death and rebirth. Coinciding with certain natural cycles, this ritual renews the political and social dimensions of sacred kingship as an institution. It is thought to replenish the fertility of nature, and ultimately to ensure the religious prosperity of the community at large.[18]

All together prophets, priests, and sacred kings are the three most important religious specialists in Africa. Some ethnic groups recognize other specialists such as "rain-makers," "medicine-men," and "diviners," but ordinarily these can be classified as one of the three types discussed above. In all cases, however, these are individuals who assist their communities with their uncommon religious abilities, skills, or knowledge.

HEALING IN AFRICAN RELIGIONS

When people encounter problems in their lives, failures, perhaps poverty, or infertility, they naturally desire to know the reasons for such experiences. African religions, much like other religious traditions around the world, offer people explanations for suffering, and in most cases, provide concrete techniques by which it can be counteracted or prevented. Healing, broadly construed, refers to the various responses human beings have toward disease, misfortune, and suffering when it occurs in their lives. It is a cultural process built upon three important components. First, an ethnic group's approach to healing will include a number of possible etiologies. There will be a system of beliefs that posit the possible causes of disease both for individuals and groups such as families, and whole communities. Second, African systems of healing always include some process of diagnosis where the precise cause of any particular instance of disease or suffering can be determined. Finally, every system of healing will also be able to prescribe a means of treatment aimed at removing the diagnosed cause of an illness. This section examines how the notion of healing, understood in terms of etiology, diagnosis, and treatment, provides a general rubric that can tie together much of what constitutes traditional religious life in Africa.

The etiology of disease for traditional African religions is firmly rooted in the general understanding of the religious cosmos described above. Essentially, all three dimensions of the religious cosmos—superhuman agents, human beings (society), and the natural world—can potentially cause disease. Beginning with the supernatural (superhuman) world, most African ethnic groups recognize that their High God, lesser deities, and/or ancestors can create problems for human beings on earth. If these powerful beings are neglected, offended, or disobeyed, they may choose to punish those people guilty of such acts. The various superhuman agents populating the traditional religious cosmos, in other words, expect human beings to act in certain ways, not only religiously, but socially and politically as well. Therefore, if someone breaks a rule—acts cruelly, commits murder, adultery, or incest for example—he or she can expect to receive any number of negative consequences from one or more religious beings. This being true, following the rules, doing what is expected, and respecting given human-divine relations are ways to avoid this particular source of suffering in African religions. Likewise, ignoring or in some way fouling recognized ideal human-divine relations is one possible cause of disease. The only protection from this cause is acting ethically.

While most African ethnic groups recognize this cause, it is not of equal importance for every group. It does, however, predominate among nomadic, hunter and gatherer groups like the !Kung of Botswana, the Mbuti Pygmies of the Democratic Republic of Congo (Zaire), and the Dinka of southern Sudan. Evans-Pritchard observes the preponderance of this attitude toward suffering and disease among the Nuer as well. He describes the Nuer notion of *thek* ("respect" or "avoidances") and claims it constitutes a system of restrictions, of things that should remain separated, and of actions that should be avoided. Ignoring *thek* relationships, showing some disrespect, leads to the High God (*Kwoth*) or some other deity such as *deng* punishing the transgressor. Consequently, when afflicted with an illness or misfortune of some sort, the Nuer look to uncover the fault committed so that it might be excused and the punishment lifted. For this model, knowing the nature of the fault and the identity of the castigating superhuman being becomes crucial in alleviating the suffering, in curing the disease.[19]

The second common etiology of illness for most African traditional religions, besides superhuman agents, is other human beings. Members of a person's community, even immediate family, can ultimately be responsible for any kind of misfortune, disease, or trouble. Sedentary or agricultural groups tend to emphasize this etiology of suffering. Most ethnic groups distinguish between two different supernatural techniques by which human beings can harm each other: sorcery and witchcraft.

Beginning with sorcery, many people in Africa traditionally recognize the existence of unseen, impersonal forces and powers that can be concentrated in material objects or substances. Human beings can manipulate these powers and thereby bring about changes in the material world. Anthropologists have called this manipulation "magic." According to James Frazer, two principles organize such manipulation so that there are effectively two basic types of magic, each employing one of the principles. There is "imitative magic" where "like produces like," where eating snails slows you down, for instance, and there is "contagious magic" where "part affects part," where destroying an enemy's discarded hair harms that enemy, for example. In the African context, anthropologists have observed how certain people combine various substances and speech ("spells") and expect magical results. After making these composite materials, these charms, amulets, powders, or figurines, people may bury them at critical locations such as along a footpath, or perhaps apply them to the body by wearing them as a bracelet or dissolving them in a bath. They may eat them, or simply destroy them in a more elaborate ritual. When driven by anger, envy, malice, or profit and designed intentionally to harm, this behavior constitutes sorcery, and those people who practice sorcery, for example, the *nde beshèn-gu* of the Kapsiki ethnic group in Cameroon, are "sorcerers." They are malicious human beings who employ magic to harm their enemies, and hence for African religions, are a potential source of suffering.[20]

The belief in witchcraft, in the activity of witches, is an extraordinarily widespread, though not universal, phenomenon in Africa. Many ethnic groups describe witchcraft as evil because, like sorcery, it is a cause of affliction that resides within the human community even as it employs supernatural powers. Unlike sorcery, however, most traditional African religious systems believe witches cause harm psychically, that is without manipulating any physical substances (charms) or speech (spells). Also different from sorcery, which is a learned technique effectively open to all, witchcraft is something inherited or acquired unwittingly. A witch may cause harm to others unconsciously or involuntarily, not knowing his or her thoughts are responsible for someone's accident, illness, or unhappiness. Some groups, such as the Azande in the Democratic Republic of Congo, understand these powers to emanate from a "witchcraft-substance" (an actual physical mass that can be discovered by autopsy) present in the body of a witch. Some ethnic groups such as the Yoruba believe witches (*àjé*) are usually women (especially old women), while more rarely, other groups such as the Lugbara say witches (*oleu*) are predominantly men. Most African ethnic groups believe witches, or at least their spirits, can change into animals, particularly nocturnal or predatory animals like birds, snakes, bats, or leopards. Witches, according to many African accounts, can fly great distances at night, and meet in groups at the tops of trees. People claim witches "consume" their victims in a psychic sense—eating the soul, drinking the blood, or breaking the backbone of victims so that they "waste away." Witches tend to attack people they know, for example co-wives, competitors, or others who inspire feelings of jealousy. They tend to engage in bizarre and antisocial behavior as well. They may walk on their hands, dance naked in the forest, or perhaps secretly defecate in public places.

These attitudes toward witches and witchcraft, while different for various ethnic groups, offer yet another explanation for human misfortune and disease. With respect to witchcraft, a person's failure or illness is neither a god's punishment for some misdeed, nor the work of a sorcerer's magic. It is instead the supernatural consequences of someone thinking malicious thoughts. Here, it is not the victim's fault when things go wrong. Rather, someone he or she knows is secretly a witch and is causing the harm. Discovering the identity of witches within a community thus becomes a priority for most African religions. Some groups, for example the Azande, rely on accusation. Normally with the help of divination (see below), a person may be accused of being a witch, and be proven guilty or innocent after a series of ordeals like handling hot metal or ingesting special poisons. If found guilty, such individuals may be banished from the community or even killed. Other African groups, for example the Ashanti of Ghana, identify witches only after individuals confess to practicing witchcraft, that is, to having wished harm upon someone and obtaining results. Reproducing such results can, over time, drive men and women to reveal publicly their belief in their powers of witchcraft. These witchcraft confessions are more common in West African ethnic groups.[21]

The third commonly recognized etiology of disease, after superhuman and human causes, is natural causes. Most ethnic groups in Africa admit that some illnesses have physical explanations. For example, a person may be suffering from an insect or snake bite, or perhaps from the effects of a poor diet. Clearly, diseases can simply be the result of some material interference with a person's body. Even so, this explanation does not exclude the possibility of a secondary immaterial or supernatural cause. While a snake bite may explain certain physical symptoms, it does not explain why the snake chose to bite one person and not another, or in fact, why it chose to bite at all. Thus, even though there may be obvious natural reasons behind a disease, the ultimate question "Why me?" may often require a religious answer in the end.

All together, the three basic etiologies of disease for traditional African religions stem directly from the three dimensions of the religious cosmos—superhuman agents, human beings (society), and the natural world. Put differently, an ethnic group's understanding of the religious realities structuring the cosmos will also determine its conception of what can cause disease and other forms of suffering. In general, however, the basic source of misfortune in traditional African religions is a failure to live in accord with the nature of the religious cosmos and the principles of communal value that inform it. Ultimately, every form of suffering is caused by being misrelated to one or another social, metaphysical, or material reality. It is caused, in other words, by fouled human-human, human-divine, or human-natural relations. For African traditional religions, being properly placed within the religious cosmos guards against suffering, just as acting contrary to the order of things inevitably brings trouble.

Knowing the possible etiologies of disease, the next important component of healing is diagnosis. Here the goal is to determine which of the many possible causes is responsible for a given illness or misfortune. Since the procedures for treatment of disease vary according to different causes, healing depends on proper diagnosis, but since many of these causes originate in the supernatural realm (gods, ancestors, witches, etc.), most patients are unable to diagnose their illnesses. Fortunately, there is a culturally recognized technique effective at diagnosing all forms of human suffering. Widely observed throughout Africa, this technique is called divination.

Divination is a ritual process by which human beings can obtain or reveal otherwise inaccessible, obscure, or extraordinary information about their place in the religious cosmos. It is a ritual means to answer troubling questions, to diagnose problems, and in some cases, to provide solutions. For example, divination can furnish insight into the future, perhaps determining if it will be safe to build a house on a particular plot of land. It can provide an interpretation of past events such as why a father's child recently died, and it can offer explanations for present problems such as a woman's infertility. Diviners are individuals who possess the special skills required for divination and therefore can be consulted whenever someone might need their services. The diviners of some ethnic groups, such as the poison oracle diviners of the Azande, gain their abilities after learning a set of skills during a period of apprenticeship, and thus should be classified as priests (see above)—though of course not all priests practice divination. The diviners of other ethnic groups, like the rattle diviners of the Nyole in Uganda, become possessed by a deity when divining. These so-called "mediumistic diviners" should be classified as prophets. As either priests or prophets, therefore, diviners are also, generally speaking, religious specialists.

The details of divination techniques vary widely, but divination systems generally include two main aspects. First, most African systems of divination (though not all—the main exception being some that employ mediumistic diviners) involve the handling of certain objects so that random results appear. Whether it be shells, pebbles, bones, seeds, or lengths of twig, diviners will deliberately manipulate these objects, perhaps toss them on the ground, select them from a pile, or transfer them from hand to hand. No matter what form of divination, however, it is necessary for diviners to present themselves as neutral mediums through which this apparent randomness can arise. This neutrality is important because clients believe these results ultimately represent the will of a deity, and thus any interference from the diviner would distort the message, answers, or diagnosis they contain. Second, diviners are skilled at interpreting the meaning of these random looking results. Though this task may be the responsibility of the client or even another religious specialist, divination systems ordinarily include a formal process whereby they convert what appears to be random, for example the pattern of shells on a tray or the words of a prophecy, into concrete knowledge or information. Through this act of interpretation, the client finally receives what he or she is seeking from the divination session—meaningful information about his or her problem.[22]

A widely known example of divination in Africa is the Ifá system practiced by the Yoruba people of Nigeria. In this divination system, individuals become diviners (*babaláwo*) after a long apprenticeship of learning complex rituals and memorizing a vast corpus of oral texts. Ifá diviners use this knowledge to communicate with the Yoruba "god of wisdom" (*Òrúnmìlà*), a being who knows the destiny of every human being on earth, and hence knows the solution to every personal problem someone might face. In the Ifá divination system, the diviner holds 16 palm nuts in his or her left hand, and with the right, attempts to scoop up the nuts. The size of the nuts, however, makes this is a difficult task, and usually one or two remain in the left hand. If two nuts remain, the diviner makes a single finger mark in a thin layer of sawdust that is spread on a small, decorated wooden tray. If one nut remains, the diviner makes a double mark on the tray. Repeating this hand-to-hand transfer of nuts eight times produces an identifiable pattern of single and double marks, one of 256 possible combinations, each of which corresponds to a distinct chapter (*Odù*) in the Ifá corpus of oral texts. These chapters are composed of a collection of narratives, each describing a mythical divination session where a client with a certain problem consults a diviner, receives instructions to perform a certain ritual that usually includes sacrifice, and after performing it, solves the problem. With a particular chapter identified, the diviner next recites all the stories he or she knows for that chapter, and if the divining has been done correctly, the client's problem will be mentioned in one of the stories. In this way, the client receives, in narrative form, a precise diagnosis of his or her immediate concerns. The Yoruba Ifá system of divination, much like others in Africa, demonstrates that what appears random (both the client's suffering and results of the palm nut manipulation) is in fact ordered.[23]

With a particular cause of an affliction identified, traditional African religions offer distinct modes of therapy as well. Here too, as with diagnosis, most ethnic groups recognize special individuals who have the skills and knowledge to treat diseases. While some observers have used terms like "witch-doctor," "medicine-man," and "herbalist" to refer to these individuals, they are better understood as religious specialists (see above). In other words, these "healers" are people who have an unusual capacity to access the superhuman realm, either because of inspiration (prophets), of learning (priests), or of succession to an office (kings). Much like those who diagnose disease, individuals who excel at administering traditional medical treatments must be specially equipped to deal with the supernatural beings and forces that cause most human misfortunes. In some cases, like the Ifá diviners of the Yoruba, African ethnic groups rely upon the same person to diagnose disease and to prescribe treatment. Other groups consult different religious specialists, perhaps a prophet for diagnosis and a priest for treatment. The details of traditional therapies vary, but African religions typically recognize three main, and occasionally overlapping, types of medical treatment—magical preparations, sacrificial rites, and cultic initiations.

Just as sorcerers can manipulate impersonal forces or powers to cause harm, other individuals can employ these techniques to heal. Healers can combine various substances like parts of animals or plants, recite particular incantations like the names of deities, and instruct patients to perform certain rituals. A patient might ingest compounds, apply them to the body as an ointment, dissolve them in a bath, burn them as incense, or perhaps embed them in a small wound. Most ethnic groups understand this beneficial magic ("white magic") as a particularly suitable prevention and cure for the evil ("black") magic of sorcerers, and in some cases, for the machinations of witches as well. In other words, these "medicines" work when other human beings, the second category of etiology described above, are the cause of a person's suffering. They are also seen as effective treatment for natural causes of illness, the third category of etiology described above. The individuals who prepare these medicines tend to be priests, in some cases priests of deities known to excel at such activities. For example, many of the Yoruba-speaking peoples of Nigeria recognize a "god of medicine" (*Òsanyìn*) whose priests have learned a vast amount of information about herbal medicines. These individuals, having access to the capacities of a superhuman agent, offer healing by making magical preparations.

A second common healing technique in Africa is sacrifice. Since superhuman beings are sometimes the direct cause of human affliction, the first category of etiology described above, and since sacrifice is an effective means for human beings to influence these beings, many ethnic groups understand it as therapeutic as well. Indeed, propitiation, one of the central purposes for sacrificing (see above), is meaningful in the context of healing. For example, divination might reveal that a patient's suffering is due to an ethical infraction of some kind, thus making sacrifice to the offended superhuman agent an appropriate expiation. In this way, an individual may forfeit or destroy a valuable animal to appease the anger of a deity or ancestor causing an affliction. The Yoruba Ifá system of divination serves as a good example here because most of the diagnostic narratives it uses also include concrete therapies that ordinarily center on sacrifices. Therefore, when patients select an Ifá story applicable to their particular disease, they can use that story as a model, and perform the ritual sacrifice it describes to achieve the same therapeutic results. Religious specialists who treat patients with sacrifices tend to be priests. They are individuals who know the detailed protocols these ritual therapies often require.

Some African ethnic groups view being initiated into a secret society or cultic group another effective form of religious healing. Sometimes called "cults of affliction," "rituals of affliction," or "drums of affliction," this phenomenon is well known in central and southern Africa. Many societies such as the Ndembu of Zambia have cults of affliction capable of healing all misfortunes whether they be caused by natural events, superhuman intervention, or the malicious intentions of other human beings. In most cases, experienced members of a particular cult group can divine if a patient's affliction is being caused by the deity that the group worships. If so, it means the patient's illness indicates a divine calling, and thereby his or her therapy must include becoming a member of the cult. While the details of the initiation rituals vary from cult to cult, they may include sacrifice, ritual purifications such as baths, or stylistic modes of dress. Ordinarily however, this initiation process revolves around extended periods of singing, dancing, and drumming (the sound of the drum suggesting the voice of the attending superhuman agent), where the cultic deity ultimately possesses the afflicted individual. This initial spirit possession denotes successful initiation, and qualifies the new member for the community support of the entire cult group. After prolonged membership in the cult, some new initiates go beyond simply being healed and become ranking priests or prophets capable of diagnosing the afflictions of potential new members. They become religious specialists whose knowledge of this form of healing qualifies them to serve the broader community.[24]

Finally, the general significance of healing for African traditional religions follows from the fact that all the main topics discussed earlier in this chapter inform or affect it in some way. For example, the superhuman agents populating the cosmos are important to healing because, depending on the particular context, they can cause human suffering, for example when ancestors punish moral infractions, but also offer therapy such as when they accept sacrificial offerings. The same is true for the social realm, the second dimension of the religious cosmos; it can harm, for example through the activity of witches, yet also heal, for instance by offering membership in a cult group. Likewise for the natural world—it too can create problems for people, such as with snake bites, or serve as a source of healing materials when it provides plants for medicines. All of this is to say, for African traditional religions, life is a matter of creating, maintaining, or modifying the quality of one's relationships with the three dimensions that constitute the religious cosmos. Indeed, as any of these relationships become flawed, the result is sickness, suffering, or misfortune. Thus, therapy is simply a matter of repairing those flawed relations. It may require the assistance of a religious specialist, but no matter the precise context, healing in traditional African religions is a matter of *ritual*. All the basic therapeutic techniques described above—magical preparations, sacrificial rites, and cultic initiations—can be understood as different ritual attempts by religious people to modify their relationships with the world around them, to replace themselves differently in the religious cosmos. Overall, healing is not only a customary religious concern in Africa; it is also an organizing metaphor for the essential beliefs and practices of traditional African religions.

CHRISTIANITY AND NEW RELIGIOUS MOVEMENTS IN AFRICA

Thus far, this chapter has discussed the "classical period" of anthropological research into the different religious traditions of Africa. It has ventured to describe, using the results of this research, the key concepts and themes that constitute traditional religious life in Africa. We should remember, however, that as early as the fourth century, Christianity found converts on the African continent. Consequently, most contemporary African societies consist of several different religious communities, some adhering to traditional forms of religion, and others accepting different forms of Christianity and Islam. This final section will briefly summarize the history of Christianity in Africa and introduce the notion of syncretism as it applies to new religious movements.

The first Christian communities in Africa began in the fourth century with the Roman Empire's conversion. It remained in the north of the continent, spreading into Nubia and Ethiopia during the fifth and sixth centuries, but died out everywhere, except in Ethiopia, with the rise of Islam in the seventh century. Later in the fifteenth century, Portuguese Catholic missionaries following trade routes along the west coast of Africa established a few churches, but they eventually collapsed due to a shortage of clergy and declining financial support. These two initial failures, however, contrast with the broad success of Christian missions beginning in the late eighteenth century. As European governments established colonies throughout the African continent, various denominational missionary societies sponsored mission churches and schools with the general objective of converting as many native Africans as possible. These European mission churches were largely successful because they tied together religion, education, and the economic advantages of Western modernization so that access to one required acceptance of the others. In the late nineteenth century, second-generation Christians began to voice dissatisfaction with missionary practices that limited African leadership roles and that forced segregation based on race. This opposition gave rise to a number of splinter groups that became independent African church denominations, for example the "Ethiopian churches" in southern Africa and the "African churches" in West Africa. Finally, in the early twentieth century, during the peak of colonial activity, a number of indigenous Christian religious movements arose. Variously referred to as "zionist," "spiritual," or "prophet" churches, these religious movements are widespread in Africa and in some cases broadly popular even today. Prominent examples include the Aladura churches in Nigeria, the churches of Simon Kimbangu in central Africa, and the churches of Isaiah Shembe in southern Africa.[25]

The founders and leaders of these indigenous African Christian movements are often charismatic prophets. Much like the pattern of initiation into cults of affliction described above, many of these founders report falling ill, and after recovering, receiving via possession messages from a divine being. Some of these messages include directions to establish a new religious community. As evidence of this divine calling, these prophet figures typically demonstrate extraordinary powers of healing, and thereby are able to attract followers. Many observers have labeled the beliefs and practices of these movements "syncretistic" or "syncretisms." Anything composed of a blend of two or more otherwise distinct sociocultural or religious elements can be described by the academic term "syncretism." In this case, these religious movements are syncretistic because they apparently combine prophecy, prayer, possession states, an emphasis on healing, and other aspects of traditional African religions with aspects of Christianity like the Bible, the doctrine of the trinity, and belief in paradise after death. Some scholars have suggested that the negative effects of colonialism like oppression, powerlessness, racism, disease, and the cultural collapse due to Western education played a role in the rise of these new religious movements. When faced with a crisis, these religions promise a better alternative. Consequently, some prophet leaders claim their mission is to reform a present religious system, while others advocate succession from the dominant social order. Still others seek to restore a lost utopian past, or simply to offer relief from current personal or social problems. In each case, however, these new religious movements furnish alternatives by recombining old and new cultural or religious forms in ways that respond meaningfully to changing historical conditions. Even today, they continue to be one of the most popular avenues of religious life in Africa.[26]

CONCLUSION

This chapter has argued that traditional religious life in Africa recognizes and responds to an organized system of realities, a religious cosmos. While acknowledging variation in how ethnic groups characterize the nature of their religious cosmos, this chapter has also suggested this variety has limits. It forms significant general patterns. Hence, along with nature and society, people throughout Africa believe their world includes superhuman beings who can affect the quality of human life on earth. Experiencing the effects of these beings, these gods and ancestors for example, religious people in Africa act in certain structured ways. In other words, they perform religious rituals. With the help of a priest or a prophet, a community may celebrate a rite of passage at the death of an elder, pray for a divine favor, or offer a sacrifice to prevent a potential danger. When suffering or afflicted by some disease, individuals may consult a diviner to discover whether a witch is tormenting them. Finally, encountering foreign religious traditions may inspire some individuals to integrate traditional religious forms and novel religious ideas. The anthropological study of religion in Africa has focused, and will continue to focus, on the cultural and historical particularities that fall within but also challenge these general patterns.

NOTES

1. Space limitations, unfortunately, make it impossible for this chapter to cover the nature and importance of Islam in Africa. Indeed, even the examination of Christianity presented here is spare so that the chapter can do justice to "African traditional religions." For more developed discussions of Christianity and Islam, see other chapters in this volume.

2. For further information on African conceptions of High Gods see (among others): J. B. Danquah, *The Akan Doctrine of God,* 2nd ed. (London: Frank Cass & Co., Ltd., 1968); E. E. Evans-Pritchard, *Nuer Religion,* (Oxford: Oxford University Press, 1956); Edwin W. Smith, ed. *African Ideas of God: A Symposium,* 3rd ed. (London: Edinburgh House Press, 1966).

3. See the following selected sources for more on these "many gods." Andrew Apter, *Black Critics and Kings: The Hermeneutics of Power in Yoruba Society* (Chicago: The University of Chicago Press, 1992); Karin Barber, "How Man Makes God in West Africa: Yoruba Attitudes Towards the Orisa," *Africa* 51, no. 3 (1981): 724–745; Marcel Griaule, *Conversations with Ogotemmeli: An Introduction to Dogon Religious Ideas* (Oxford: Oxford University Press, 1965); Melville J. Herskovits, *Dahomey,* 2 vols. (New York: J.J. Augustin, 1938); R. S. Rattray, *Ashanti,* (Oxford: Clarendon Press, 1923).

4. E. E. Evans-Pritchard wrote three major books on the Nuer: *The Nuer: A Description of the Modes of Livelihood and Political Institutions of a Nilotic People* (Oxford: Clarendon Press, 1940); *Kinship and Marriage Among the Nuer* (Oxford: Clarendon Press, 1951); *Nuer Religion* (Oxford: Oxford University Press, 1956). For a more contemporary ethnography, see Sharon Elaine Hutchinson, *Nuer Dilemmas: Coping with Money, War and the State* (Berkeley: University of California Press, 1996).

5. For more material on ancestors, see Meyer Fortes, *Oedipus and Job in West African Religion* (Cambridge: Cambridge University Press, 1959); Jack R Goody, *Death, Property and the Ancestors: A Study of the Mortuary Customs of the Lodagaa of West Africa* (Stanford, CA: Stanford University Press, 1962); Igor Kopytoff, "Ancestors as Elders in Africa," *Africa* 41 (1973): 129–142.

6. Other anthropological studies of concepts of the soul in Africa include Wande Abimbola, "The Yoruba Concept of Human Personality," in *La Notion de Personne en Afrique Noire* (Paris: C.N.R.S., 1973), 73–89; John Beattie, "Representations of the Self in Traditional

Africa," *Africa* 50, no. 3 (1980): 313–320; Meyer Fortes, "On the Concept of the Person Among the Tallensi," in *La Notion de Personne en Afrique Noire* (Paris: C.N.R.S., 1973), 238–319.

7. See the discussion of ritual in this volume, but for ethnographies especially concerned with African ritual, see Margaret Thompson Drewal *Yoruba Ritual: Performers, Play, Agency* (Bloomington: Indiana University Press, 1992); John Middleton, *Lugbara Religion: Ritual and Authority Among East African People* (London: Oxford University Press, 1960); S. F. Nadel, *Nupe Religion* (Glencoe, IL: The Free Press, 1954); Victor Turner, *The Forest of Symbols: Aspects of Ndembu Ritual* (Ithaca, NY: Cornell University Press, 1970).

8. On rites of passage, see Arnold Van Gennep, *The Rites of Passage,* trans. Monika Vizedom and Gabrielle L. Caffee (Chicago: The University of Chicago Press, 1960); Max Gluckman, "Les Rites de Passage," in *Essays on the Ritual of Social Relations,* ed. Max Gluckman (Manchester: Manchester University Press, 1962); Victor Turner, *The Ritual Process: Structure and Anti-Structure* (London: Routledge & Kegan Paul, 1969).

9. For further reading see Ronald Cohen, *The Kanuri of Bornu* (New York: Holt, Rinehart and Winston, 1967); James W. Fernandez, *Bwiti: An Ethnography of the Religious Imagination in Africa* (Princeton, NJ: Princeton University Press, 1982); T. M. Ilesanmi, "Naming Ceremony Among the Yoruba," *Orita* 14, no. 2 (1982): 108–119.

10. For more on puberty and initiation rituals, see J. T. Brown, "Circumcision Rites of the Becwana Tribes," *Journal of the Royal Anthropological Institute* 51 (1921): 419–27; J. Lorand Matory,. *Sex and the Empire That Is No More: Gender and the Politics of Metaphor in Oyo Yoruba Religion* (Minneapolis: University of Minnesota Press, 1994); Audrey I. Richards, *Chisungu: A Girl's Initiation Ceremony among the Bemba of Zambia* (London: Travistock Publications, 1956); Gunter Wagner, *The Bantu of Western Kenya: With Special Reference to the Vugusu and Logoli* (London: Oxford University Press, 1949).

11. See the following sources for further discussions of marriage in Africa: Laura and Paul Bohannan, *The Tiv of Central Nigeria* (London: International Africa Institute, 1953); Daryll Forde, ed., *Ethnographic Survey of Africa* (London: International African Institute, 1953; N. A. Fadipe, *The Sociology of the Yoruba* (Ibadan: Ibadan University Press, 1970); A. R. Radcliff–Brown, and D.

Forde, eds., *African Systems of Kinship and Marriage* (London: Oxford University Press, 1950); I. Schapera, *Married Life in an African Tribe* (Evanston, IL: Northwestern University Press, 1966).

12. Sources on death and conceptions of the afterlife in Africa include Hans Abrahamsson, *The Origin of Death: Studies in African Mythology* (Uppsala: Studia Ethnographica Upsaliensia, 1951); Maurice Bloch, *Placing the Dead: Tombs, Ancestral Villages, and Kinship Organization in Madagascar* (London: Seminar, 1971); Max Gluckman, "Mortuary Customs and the Belief in Survival after Death among the South-Eastern Bantu," *Bantu Studies* 11 (1937): 117–136; Jack R. Goody, *Death, Property and the Ancestors: A Study of the Mortuary Customs of the Lodagaa of West Africa* (Stanford, CA: Stanford University Press, 1962).

13. See also Meyer Fortes, "Prayer," In *Religion, Morality, and the Person: Essays on Tallensi Religion*, ed. by Jack Goody (Cambridge: Cambridge University Press, 1987), 22–36; John S. Mbiti, *The Prayers of African Religion* (Maryknoll, NY: Orbis Books, 1975); Aylward Shorter, *Prayer in the Religious Traditions of Africa* (New York: Oxford University Press, 1975).

14. Sacrifice is a topic of discussion in many ethnographies of African peoples, but see particularly J. Omosade Awolalu, *Yoruba Beliefs and Sacrificial Rites* (Essex: Longman, 1979); E. E. Evans-Pritchard, "The Sacrificial Role of Cattle among the Nuer," *Africa* 23, no. 3 (1953): 181–197; Luc de Heusch, *Sacrifice in Africa: A Structuralist Approach,* trans. Linda O'Brien and Alice Morton (Bloomington: Indiana University Press, 1985); Henri A. Junod, *The Life of a South African Tribe,* 2nd ed. (London: Macmillan & Co., Ltd., 1927).

15. See also Henri Hubert, and Marcel Mauss, *Sacrifice: Its Nature and Function,* trans. W.D. Halls (Chicago: The University of Chicago Press, 1964); Nancy Jay, *Throughout Your Generations Forever: Sacrifice, Religion, and Paternity* (Chicago: University of Chicago Press, 1992); W. Robertson Smith, *The Religion of the Semites: The Fundamental Institutions* (New York: Schocken Books, 1972); Sir Edward B. Tylor, *Primitive Culture: Researches in the Development of Mythology, Philosophy, Religion, Language, Arts and Custom* (New York: Brentano's Books, 1924).

16. See John Beattie, and John Middleton, eds. *Spirit Mediumship and Society in Africa* (New York: Africana Publishing Corporation, 1969); Fremont E. Besmer, *Horses, Musicians, and Gods: The Hausa Cult of Possession-Trance* (Zaria: Ahmadu Bello University Press, 1983); Erika Bourguignon, ed., *Religion, Altered States of Consciousness, and Social Change* (Columbus: Ohio State University Press, 1973); Sheila S. Walker, *Ceremonial Spirit Possession in Africa and Afro-America: Forms, Meanings, and Functional Significance for Individuals and Social Groups* (Leiden: E.J. Brill, 1972).

17. See also Daryll Forde, ed. *African Worlds: Studies in the Cosmological Ideas and Social Values of African Peoples* (London: Oxford University Press for the International African Institute, 1954); E. Bolaji Idowu *Olodumare: God in Yoruba Belief* (London: Longman's Press, 1962); Godfrey Lienhardt, *Divinity and Experience: The Religion of the Dinka* (Oxford: Clarendon Press, 1961).

18. For more information on kingship in Africa, see E. E. Evans-Pritchard, *The Divine Kingship of the Shilluk of the Nilotic Sudan* (Cambridge: Cambridge University Press, 1948); S. F. Nadel, *A Black Byzantium: The Kingdom of Nupe in Nigeria* (London: Oxford University Press, 1942); Jacob K. Olupona, *Kingship, Religion, and Rituals in a Nigerian Community: A Phenomenological Study of Ondo Yoruba Festivals* (Stockholm: Almqvist & Wiksell International, 1991); Benjamin C. Ray, *Myth, Ritual, and Kingship in Buganda* (Oxford: Oxford University Press, 1991); Michael W. Young, "The Divine Kingship of the Jukun: A Re-evaluation of Some Theories." *Africa* 36 (1966): 135–152.

19. Here are three ethnographies salient to this discussion: Richard Katz, *Boiling Energy: Community Healing Among the Kalahari Kung* (Cambridge, MA: Harvard University Press, 1982); Godfrey Lienhardt, *Divinity and Experience: The Religion of the Dinka* (Oxford: Clarendon Press, 1961); Colin M. Turnbull, *The Forest People: A Study of Pygmies of the Congo* (New York: Simon & Schuster, 1961).

20. Most discussions of sorcery are combined with witchcraft, but for more information, see M. G. Marwick, "The Sociology of Sorcery in a Central African Tribe," *African Studies* 22, no. 1 (1963): 1–21; John Middleton, and E. H. Winter, eds., *Witchcraft and Sorcery in East Africa* (London: Routledge & Kegan Paul, 1963); Godfrey Wilson, "An African Morality," *Africa* 9 (1936): 75–98.

21. See the chapter on witchcraft in this volume, but for works dealing explicitly with Africa see Jean Comaroff, and John Comaroff, eds., *Modernity and Its Malcontents: Ritual and Power in Postcolonial Africa* (Chicago: University of Chicago Press, 1993); E. E. Evans-Pritchard, *Witchcraft, Oracles, and Magic Among the Azande* (Oxford: Clarendon Press, 1976); Lucy Mair, *Witchcraft* (New York: McGraw-Hill, 1969); S. F. Nadel, "Witchcraft in Four African Societies," *American Anthropologist* 54 (1952): 18–29; Victor W. Turner, *Schism and Continuity in an African Society* (Manchester: Manchester University Press, 1957).

22. For further information on African systems of divination, see E. E. Evans-Pritchard, *Witchcraft, Oracles and, Magic Among the Azande* (Oxford: Clarendon Press, 1976); Philip M. Peek, ed., *African Divination Systems: Ways of Knowing* (Bloomington: Indiana University Press, 1991); Victor Turner, *Revelation and Divination in Ndembu Ritual* (Ithaca, NY: Cornell University Press, 1975).

23. Sources on Ifá divination include Wande Abimbola, *Ifa Divination Poetry* (New York: Nok Publishers Ltd., 1977); Wande Abimbola, *Ifa: An Exposition of the Literary Corpus* (Ibadan: Oxford University Press, 1976); William Bascom, *Ifa Divination: Communication between Gods and Men in West Africa* (Bloomington: Indiana University Press, 1969); Judith Gleason, *A Recitation of Ifa, Oracle of the Yoruba* (New York: Grossman Publishers, 1973).

24. Other ethnographic sources dealing with healing beliefs and practices include A. Buckley, *Yoruba Medicine* (Oxford: Clarendon Press, 1985); John Janzen, *The*

Quest for Healing in Lower Zaire (Berkeley: University of California Press, 1978); Una Maclean, *Magical Medicine: A Nigerian Case-Study* (Middlesex, England: Penguin Books, 1971); Victor Turner, *Drums of Affliction: A Study of Religious Processes among the Ndembu of Zambia* (Oxford: Clarendon Press, 1968); Monica Wilson, *Communal Rituals of the Nyakyusa* (London: Oxford University Press, 1959).

25. For more information on Christianity in Africa, see G. Bond, W. Johnson, and S. Walker, eds., *African Christianity: Patterns of Religious Continuity* (New York: Academic Press, Inc., 1979); Jean Comaroff, and John L. Comaroff, *Of Revelation and Revolution: Christianity, Colonialism, and Consciousness in South Africa*, Vol. 1 (Chicago: The University of Chicago Press, 1991); Jean Comaroff, and John L. Comaroff, *Of Revelation and Revolution: The Dialectics of Modernity on a South African Frontier,* Vol. 2 (Chicago: The University of Chicago Press, 1997); Rosalind I. J. Hackett, ed., *New Religious Movements in Nigeria* (Lewiston, NY: The Edwin Mellon Press, 1987); Elizabeth Isichei, *A History of Christianity in Africa: From Antiquity to the Present* (Grand Rapids, MI: Eerdmans, 1995); J. D. Y. Peel, *Aladura: A Religious Movement Among the Yoruba* (London: Oxford University Press, 1968); Lamin Sanneh, *West African Christianity: The Religious Impact* (Maryknoll, NY: Orbis Books, 1983).

26. See also Jean Comaroff, *Body of Power, Spirit of Resistance* (Chicago: The University of Chicago, 1985); James W. Fernandez, "African Religious Movements," *Annual Review of Anthropology* 7 (1978): 195–234; James W. Fernandez, "Politics and Prophecy: African Religious Movements," *Practical Anthropology* 12, no. 2 (1965): 71–75; Charles Stewart and Rosalind Shaw, eds., *Syncretism/Anti-Syncretism: The Politics of Religious Synthesis* (London: Routledge, 1994); Harold W. Turner, *Religious Innovation in Africa: Collected Essays on New Religious Movements* (Boston: G.K. Hall, 1979).

Ten

Classical Religions
of the Old World

Michael Fuller and Neathery Fuller
St. Louis Community College

Archaeological evidence from the Old World has identified several locations where human populations expanded in size from very small groups (often termed bands and tribes) into larger populations called complex chiefdoms. One of the most significant traits of the latter is the appearance of a permanent position of political leadership. In certain circumstances, such as in the Nile River and Euphrates River valleys, the next phase of growth involved a process called urbanization where up to 80 percent of the population lived permanently in towns and cities. The first cities had sharply defined social positions, long-distance trade, and struggles among the elite of different city-states. Writing was born out of the necessity of the first cities to manage the economic resources being concentrated in these early states. We equate the early city-states in Egypt and Syro-Mesopotamia with the term "civilization."

EGYPTIAN RELIGION

The shift from complex chiefdoms to early states began in Egypt during the preliterate period of Egyptian history that dates from 5500 to 3150 B.C.E. Archaeological excavations at the ancient cities of Naqada, Ballas, and Hierakonpolis have uncovered complex burial rituals and subtle clues to religious beliefs before the use of hieroglyphic writing. Sir Flinders Petrie recognized that some graves at Naqada were divided into halves, with the north half of the grave reserved for offerings of food and drink. The south end of the graves at Naqada contained the human skeletal remains, personal objects such as jewelry, and wavy-handled jars that contained scented vegetable fat. The offerings of food and ointment were clearly for use in the afterlife. The burial custom at Naqada dictated body placement in a flexed position with the face turned toward the west. The orientation toward the west is very significant because later Egyptian religion would identify the west with the location of the Land of the Dead. Mummification was not practiced during this period of Egyptian prehistory, but the impetus for it was clearly present.[1]

A small number of clay figurines of female forms were placed as grave offerings in burials dated 4000 to 3500 B.C.E. Some of the figurines, such as the one from burial 2 at El-Mamariya, show arms arched overhead in a gesture more typical of a dancer than a mourner. The beaklike faces of the female figurines contrast sharply with the graceful lines of the breasts and hips. The figurines may represent a specific goddess associated with fertility and afterlife, or signify a dancing ritual with priestesses in specific costumes. Painted pottery of the same period represents the dancer female forms as larger than the accompanying male forms.

Egypt during the first centuries of urbanization consisted of dozens of nomes (small chiefdoms), each under the control of its own ruler who recognized a local god. The nomes were be unified by military conquest into a single preindustrial state between 3150 and 3050 B.C.E. A leading Egyptologist, Fekri Hassan, has argued that Egyptian religion during the period of state formation held an all-powerful female deity at the center of Egyptian belief and that the goddess was associated with birth, death, and resurrection. The attributes and rituals of this principal Egyptian goddess changed as the political system in Egypt evolved from dozens of independent chiefdoms into a unified state. The gods Osiris, Horus, and Re would rise to displace the goddess from the central position in Egyptian religious belief, but they did not cause the extinction of the goddess cults. The cults of Isis, Hathor, and Neit would remain central to Egyptian religion for over 3,000 years.

The most powerful religious idea that emerged with kingship was the concept that the king was the incarnation of the god Horus and the son of the god Re. This meant that the living king was the ultimate link between the Egyptian people and the Egyptian deities. Many of the first hieroglyphic inscriptions demonstrate the use of theophoric names which refer to Egyptian gods and goddesses. A carved piece of ivory from the tomb of Queen Neit-hotep at Naqada bears her name and the name of King Hor-Aha. The queen's name can be translated as "Neit is pleased." Hor-Aha translates as "Fighting Hawk" and is an allusion to the god Horus who is associated both with kingship and the first capital city of Upper Egypt, Nebkan/Hierakonpolis. An ivory panel from the tomb of Neit-hotep dates from circa 3050–2890 B.C.E. and shows the royal couple celebrating a ceremony called "Receiving the South and North" which had both political and religious ramifications.

The well-being of the Egyptian king was essential to the prosperity of his kingdom and this well-being was ensured by the *Sed* religious festival. The ritual was celebrated at a point 30 years after the king's coronation. The purpose of the ceremony was to reassert the king's sovereignty and included rituals of robing, enthronement, and receiving homage from the leaders of each nome. The origins of the *Sed* festival began at the unification of Egypt into one state and these rites continued for over two thousand years. The famous Narmer macehead shows the first king of a unified Egypt participating in the *Sed* festival.

Evidence from recent archaeological discoveries at the site of Nihal Tillah in southern Israel shows that the political and religious reach of Egypt during the period of state formation was not limited to the Nile River Valley. The specific discoveries include an elaborate Egyptian style tomb, imported Egyptian pottery (including examples bearing the name of King Narmer), an amulet associated with the goddess Neith, and fragments of clay impressed with seals inscribed with Egyptian hieroglyphics. The Egyptian colony at Nihal Tillah carefully segregated their living quarters and food preparation vessels from their Canaanite neighbors at the nearby settlement of Tell Halif. It is too early to speculate on how this Egyptian colony may have affected the development of religious traditions among the native Canaanite groups or how the Canaanite religious beliefs could have influenced the Egyptian colonists, but the site demonstrates a significant level of contact at a date of approximately 3150 B.C.E.

Egyptian religion experienced a lengthy continuum of certain rituals and beliefs, but it is also essential to note that many changes were introduced during the span of the Old Kingdom (2686–2181 B.C.E.), Middle Kingdom (2040–1782 B.C.E.), and New Kingdom (1570–1070 B.C.E.). These included changes in the religious practices related to principal deities, mortuary customs, and household worship.

The Old Kingdom (ca. 2686–2181 B.C.E.) began with a shift of political power from the cities of Hierakonpolis and Abydos to the city of Memphis situated near the location where the Nile River Valley broadens out to form the Nile delta. Paralleling the geographic shift was an elevation in status for the gods of Memphis and Heliopolis. The local god of Memphis, Ptah, is described in a creation epic as having a primary role in creating the other gods and goddesses. Likewise, the temples at Heliopolis of the Sun god named Re and the local god named Atum achieved positions of authority that would last for over a thousand years.

The third Dynasty of Egypt is remarkable because of the construction of the multiterraced step pyramid that was meant to commemorate and protect the remains of King Zoser. The pyramid of Zoser at Saqqarah was constructed in approximately 2670 B.C.E. It would be overshadowed quickly by the great pyramids constructed to honor and protect the three famous fourth Dynasty kings, Khufu, Khafre, and Menkaure.

An important source of information concerning Egyptian religion during the Old Kingdom (2686–2181 B.C.E.) comes from the Pyramid Texts which were inscribed on the interior walls of the pyramid of Unas and the kings of the sixth Dynasty. The Pyramid Texts consist of spells designed to assist the soul of a king in his goal of reaching a pleasant afterlife. The total number of spells, gathered from several sources, appears to be 400. By the time of the Middle Kingdom, some of these same spells were written inside the interior of mummy coffins. Later, during the New Kingdom, an elaboration of the Coffin Text spells would evolve into the important "Book of the Dead" which contained 192 spells. It is important to note that the "Book of the Dead" described beliefs tied to the Old Kingdom and Middle Kingdom as well as spells based upon writings that were created during the New Kingdom.

The end of the Old Kingdom is marked by a brief collapse in the political system of kingship in Egypt. The First Intermediate Period (2181–2133 B.C.E.) was marked by internal conflicts and, according to some reports, social anarchy. This period saw changes in both religious beliefs and practices. The city of Abydos grew as a center of worship for the god Osiris because a new religious concept proposed that the soul of a deceased person would become one with Osiris in the afterlife. Other religious ideas that developed during this period include the doctrine of the *ba* (soul) and the concept of judgment after death. At this time, the heart of a deceased person was weighed against the symbol and spirit of truth, law, and justice.

The return of a strong, centralized kingship marks the beginning of Egypt's Middle Kingdom Period (2133–1786 B.C.E.). This was a time of great literary and artistic development in Egyptian history. The Middle Kingdom saw the rise of the cult of Amun in Thebes which, in turn, would give rise to one of the greatest temple complexes in the ancient world.

Egypt was not closed to outside contact during the Middle Kingdom. Contact with Syro-Mesopotamia and Crete continued as indicated by a handful of finds in Egypt, Greece, and Lebanon. One such discovery was a foundation deposit made by King Amenemhet II at the temple of Montu at Tod (just south of Luxor). The offering consisted of silver cups (from Crete or Lebanon), cylinder seals in the Babylonian style, and amulets made from the blue gemstone, lapis lazuli. The amulets were of Syro-Mesopotamia design and made from raw material obtainable only in Afghanistan.

The political structure of Egypt was shaken during the Second Intermediate Period (1786–1567 B.C.E.) when political and economic control of the Egyptian Delta was lost to a mixed population of Asiatic peoples called the Hyksos in contemporary Egyptian texts. The Hyksos would equate their Syro-Mesopotamian god with the Egyptian god Seth. The Hyksos capital city was Avaris in the northeastern quarter of the Delta at the modern site of Tell Daba. The Hyksos maintained a complex social and economic relationship with the kingdoms in Syro-Mesopotamia as demonstrated by elite Hyksos artifacts found in a royal tomb at Ebla in Syria.

Avaris, the Hyksos capital in Egypt, included temples built in a typically Canaanite pattern. The native Egyptian princes in Upper Egypt organized an army, defeated the Hyksos, and pursued the retreating Hyksos population into Syro-Mesopotamia. Successful military campaigns by several Egyptian kings of the New Kingdom, some reaching as far north as the Euphrates River in Syria, laid the foundations for an almost 300-year period during which Egypt controlled vast areas as colonies.

The New Kingdom (1567–1085 B.C.E.) marks the period of Egypt's greatest geographic control. One Egyptian outpost was at the ancient (and modern) city of Gaza which the Egyptians referred to as "Plunder-of-the Ruler." An Egyptian outpost in the Jordan River Valley was situated at the site of Beth Shean (called in Egyptian, Beth-sa'l or Beth-sa'el). Ruins of at least two Egyptian temples have been uncovered at Beth Shean, but it is unclear if they were meant for use by Egyptian troops garrisoned at the city or by the Canaanite citizens of the city.

Significant changes in Egyptian religious tradition occurred during the New Kingdom. The god Amun became the national god of Egypt and his temple at Luxor was expanded and lavishly decorated. The concepts of afterlife and judgment of the soul are elaborately described in "The Book of the Dead."

A religious, political, and artistic revolution took place briefly during the New Kingdom under the guidance of King Amenhotep IV ("Amen is pleased"). He shifted political and religious power from Thebes to a newly designed city named Akhetaten ("the Horizon of the Sun Disk") and changed his name to Akenaten which translates as "Servant of Aten." His actions were guided by his strong personal, religious convictions. Implementation of his new belief increased the power of the king at the expense of the cult of Amun in Thebes. The exact religious vision of Akenaton has been characterized as "monotheistic" in sharp contrast to the proceeding "polytheistic" belief pattern of Egyptian religion where many gods and goddesses were recognized. A few scholars have tried to link the monotheism of the ancient Hebrew with the Aton cult in Egypt. The evidence for such a connection is very circumstantial and hard to prove. What is clear is the polytheistic nature of Egyptian religion quickly reasserted itself after the death of Akenaton. Subsequent foreign domination of Egypt by the Persian, Greek, and Roman empires did not extinguish the long-held beliefs in traditional Egyptian deities, but added to them. The last vestiges of ancient Egyptian religion came to an end with the conversion of the temple of Isis at Philae into the Church of Saint Stephen Egyptian during the reign of Justinian (527–565 C.E.). The grip of monotheism in Egypt would be tightened with the arrival of Islam into Egypt during the seventh century C.E.

SYRO-MESOPOTAMIAN RELIGION

Hunting and gathering bands scattered across wide sections of Syro-Mesopotamia (modern Syria, Iraq, Israel, Palestine, and Jordan) where they established settled villages as early as 8200 to 8000 B.C.E. Sheep, goats, and cattle replaced the protein that hunters once obtained from wild gazelles. Domesticated wheat and barley replaced gathered wild seeds that for millennia had been the principle source of dietary carbohydrates. Domestication of plants and animals did not occur within a single generation, but once groups adapted to this new food production process, they locked themselves into a cycle of population growth, intensification of work, innovations in domestic architecture, and creation of new religious rituals.[2]

Archaeological discoveries at the site of Mureybet along the Euphrates River in Syria document the changing religious rituals during the period when plant and animal domestication was shifting the economic and architectural patterns of life. The shift from hunting-gathering to food production at Mureybet occurred between 8000 to 7600 B.C.E.; the change was mirrored by a shift from circular outline houses to rectangular houses. A new religious ritual began in approximately 7600 B.C.E. and continued until the abandonment of the site in 6800 B.C.E.. This ritual included reverential treatment of human skulls which were placed on red supports inside domestic houses. Postcranial (skeleton minus the skull) remains were buried beneath the floor of the house.

Skull consecration rituals have been practiced by many diverse cultures and the most common anthropological interpretation for such rituals is that they are designed to keep the soul and wisdom of a family's elders within the household. Children were buried intact beneath the floor of each domestic structure. Perhaps deceased children had not achieved wisdom that needed to be conserved. More likely, the religious belief was that a child's spirit would be reborn within the same household.

Between 4500 and 3500 B.C.E. the food production system intensified with the introduction of irrigation agriculture along the Euphrates River and human settlements grew in size to become towns. In this period, burial ritual changed also. Communities began to use cemeteries that were separated from the residential sector of a site. In one case, at the archaeological site of Eridu in Iraq, 200 graves were discovered by archaeologists. Many contained paired burials of a male and female and are interpreted as a husband and wife burial. Personal jewelry and pottery vessels for food offerings were found in the graves. Smoked fish and cooked meat offerings were included to nourish the dead on their journey to the afterlife.

Temples at early towns dating from 4500 to 3500 B.C.E. sites were not focused on mortuary rituals, but upon rituals to ensure the success of their agricultural system.

Many early towns contain only one temple, but at the site of Tepe Gawra in Iraq, three temples stood side by side. A few centuries later, when written inscriptions provide names for deities such as An (god of sky and heavens), Enlil (god of rulership), Enki (god of the sweet waters of the earth), Shamash (sun god and is concerned also with justice), and Inanna/Ishtar (goddess of love and war).

Rich oral traditions concerning the principal gods and goddesses of Syro-Mesopotamia eventually would find their way into the written cuneiform texts of the Sumerians and Babylonians. Among these religious traditions is an account of creation that depicts two deities named Apsu (primordial waters under the earth) and Tiamat (personification of the sea). Their union creates four generations of gods who are so annoying that Apsu plans to achieve quiet by eliminating his offspring. The god Ea slays Apsu, occupies his house, and creates the god Marduk and his spouse, Damkina. Tiamat opposes Ea and the other lesser gods with an army of monsters and, at the outset, appears predestined to overpower and eliminate her rebellious children. Marduk defeats her and creates the world by splitting her body and using half to form the heavens and half to form the earth. The wounded sockets of her eyes become the sources of the two great rivers of Syro-Mesopotamia: the Tigris and the Euphrates. Marduk's significance is underlined further by his creation of humans as lesser beings suitable to work for and serve the gods.

Several ancient cities in Syro-Palestine have produced libraries containing thousands of tablets. Such discoveries usually come after years, sometimes decades, of careful excavation. The most remarkable archive from ancient Syria was discovered by Italian archaeologists investigating the ruins of an ancient city-state called Ebla. Extensive excavation at Ebla has demonstrated that the city thrived for 800 years and that the urban center included extensive palaces, temples, workshops, and royal tombs. Ebla's economy was fueled by its agricultural surpluses and textile industries while trade brought special objects to the kingdom. These included lapis lazuli from Afghanistan and carved stone vessels from Egypt. Cuneiform texts from Ebla provide clues to its pantheon of approximately 40 principal deities. The gods included Kura (principal god of the city), Haddad (storm god), Dagan (lord of the region), Rashap (god of underworld), Adamma (underworld goddess and spouse of Rashap), Ishara (principal goddess of the city), Ishtar (goddess of love and war), and Idabal (god associated with the Orontes Valley). Two sanctuaries at Ebla are associated with the goddess Ishtar. The larger sanctuary (monument P3) probably surrounded a sacred tree associated with the goddess, while Temple D on the acropolis of the city included an elaborately carved stele representing the winged goddess, human worshippers, and a variety of supernatural creatures such as bullmen and winged sphinxes. Other temples discovered at Ebla include Temple N, dedicated to Shamash (sun god) and Temple B, sacred to Reshap.

Complex patterns of urban growth and abandonment at the end of the third millennium coincide with the expansion and political ascension of the West-Semitic tribes called Amorites. An Amorite king named Yaggid-Lim established a powerful lineage at the ancient city of Mari which would eventually be displaced by Shamshi-Adad, founder of the subsequent Assyrian Empire. The story of Mari began in the third millennium and comes to an end when the palace of King Zimri-Lim is destroyed (in approximately 1759 B.C.E.) by King Hammurabi of Babylon. Mari is of particular importance to scholars of ancient history because approximately 15,000 cuneiform documents were discovered during decades of careful excavation by French archaeologists. Physical remains of three temples have been identified near the palace. The temples were dedicated to the goddesses Ishtar, Ninizaza, and Ishtarat. Cuneiform texts attest to the importance of several deities including Itur-Mer (lord of the land of Mari), Shamash (the sun god), Dagan, and a principal pantheon totaling approximately 40 gods and goddesses. The duplication of deities between Ebla and Mari suggests that changes in ethnic and political groups did not require the abandonment of gods and goddesses who were linked integrally with the land.

During the time period 3000 to 2000, ancient cities were established in both the interior of Syria and along its Mediterranean coastline. Ugarit is the best documented Bronze Age city on the Mediterranean coast. Artifacts found in the ruins of Ugarit point to trade routes reaching south to Egypt and west to the Mycenaean culture in Greece. The kingdom of Ugarit fell victim to an invading group called the Sea Peoples between 1180 and 1175 B.C.E.. The ruins of Ugarit include two main temples which were dedicated to Dagan (god of the fertile plains of Syria) and Baal (god of strength and fertility). Cuneiform texts mention El (father of the gods), Athirath (goddess of the sea and spouse of El), Anath, Mot (death), Rashap, Dagan, Nikkal, and Kotarot.

Aramaean and Neo-Hittite principalities rose in power after 1200 B.C.E., but their autonomy would be curtailed as the Assyrians annexed the cities of Syria to their empire. An exceptional temple from this period is found at Ain Dara in the Afrin valley near Aleppo. The iconography of the Ain Dara temple links it with Ishtar, the goddess of fertility. The exterior of the temple is decorated with carved designs of mountain gods, sphinxes, and lions. The continuity of Ishtar in the religion of Ebla, Mari, Ugarit, and Ain Dara is not coincidental but reflects a religious tradition that began in the Neolithic period. The incorporation of Syro-Mesopotamia into the empires of Persia, Greece, and Rome would not extinguish the religious tradition. The end of the ancient beliefs would come with the expansion of Christianity and Islam into the region.

GREEK AND ROMAN RELIGION

The earliest expressions of prehistoric religion in Greece are reflected in male and female figurines manufactured from clay, bone, and soft stone. Interpretation of these figurines is problematic and will always be open to debate. One approach equates the female figurines with three goddesses who symbolized the "Great Mystery" of nature, life, and death. The male figurines are interpreted as the brothers, partners and consorts of the goddesses. They include a Strong and Dying God of vegetation, a phallic god (the prototype of Hermes—god of fertility), centaurs, and male gods that served as the guardians of forest and wild animals.

The religious tradition of prehistoric Greece changed with the migration of Indo-European speaking people during 2200 to 2100 B.C.E.. Their arrival coincides with destruction deposits at several archaeological sites such as Lerna, Tiryns, Asine, Zygouries, and Corinth. The most common name given by ancient writers for this new population is "Achaeans" and it is clear that they introduced several new gods and goddesses into Greek religion while retaining reverence for the older traditions of fertility, death, and rebirth.[3]

A second model of change in Greek religion has been proposed by writers who envision diffusion and colonization from Egypt as influencing social and religious changes in Greece during the period 3000 to 2000 B.C.E.. For example, it has been proposed that the city of Athens is derived from the Egyptian term Ht Nt which translates as Temple or House of Neit. Most classical scholars and archaeologists are unconvinced by the "Black Athena" arguments. Trade contacts between the various Old World civilizations is evident, but the evidence religious borrowing or colonization is still very circumstantial.

The Achaean conquest of Greece did not include the island of Crete where a non-Greek speaking population, called the Minoans, would continue to flourish. The Achaean population in mainland Greece evolved into the powerful Mycenaean civilization which extended its control onto the island of Crete during the fifteenth century B.C.E.. Unfortunately, the written inscriptions of the Minoans, preserved in a script designated as Linear A, are still undeciphered. The first written record of Greek religion is found in the Linear B tablets associated with the Mycenaean civilization.

The term "Mycenaean" is derived from the ruined city of Mycenae where extensive archaeological excavations have uncovered an elaborate palace, a cult center, and two royal cemeteries. The palaces of this period were richly decorated with wall paintings that included a variety of motifs including religious themes. The Mycenaean civilization arises in approximately 1700 B.C.E., extends to the Greek islands around 1200 B.C.E., and declines significantly by 1100 B.C.E..

The gods and goddesses listed in the Linear B tablets include several names and titles familiar to students of Greek mythology. Five principal goddesses were addressed with the honorific term *Potnia* which can be translated as "Mistress." These include Hera (*Dapu ritojo potinija*), Athena (*Atanaotinija*), Artemis (*Potinija asiwija*), Demeter or Leto (*Sitopotinija* which means "Grain Mistress") and Aphrodite (*Potnia*). The term *Potnia* is an Indo-European word and it may have replaced an older, indigenous Greek word which was *Ariadne* (the proper name for the daughter of King Minos in the mythic tale of Theseus and the killing of the Minotaur). Among the Linear B inscriptions are the terms "mystery" and "initiate." These terms are linked during the rise of the Greek city-states (480–320 B.C.E.) with the worship of Demeter and Persephone at the sacred site of Eleusis. Archaeological excavations have confirmed ritual activity at Eleusis during the Mycenaean Period. Like Eleusis, the sacred site of Delphi was a religious site that would continue from the Mycenaean period throughout Greek history until it was closed by pressure from Christians. Delphi was famous for its oracle that was consulted as well as the Sanctuary of Athena Pronaia and the Sanctuary of Pythian Apollo.

Male deities recognized in the Linear B inscriptions include Apollo (*Paiawon*), Ares (*Enualios*), Zeus, Poseidon, and Hermes. The familiar gods and goddesses existed with less familiar deities that included Eleuthia (goddess of childbirth), Enyalios, Smintheus, Zagreus, Ephimedeia, Erinys, and Sito. One clue to the ritual practices during the Mycenaean civilization comes from the Linear B tablets which list offerings provided for the various gods and goddesses. For example, one tablet lists the offerings for either a sacrifice or banquet in honor of Poseidon. The offerings included one bull, four rams, wheat, wine, honey, fifteen cheeses, perfumed olive oil, and two sheepskins. A linear B tablet from the Mycenaean palace at Pylos lists offerings of perfumed oil for the king, the goddess Athena, and the god Poseidon. The oil was offered to the gods during ritual meals and, in one case, for the "anointing of robes." Also from the palace at Pylos comes a fascinating tablet that lists 13 deities who are to receive offerings. Included in the list are Zeus, Hera, Hermes, and several obscure deities. Each deity received an offering of a golden cup while 9 of the deities received human offerings. Women are listed as offerings to the goddesses while men are the offerings for the gods. It would be appealing to think that the designation of human offerings was a metaphor to describe an individual who would serve as a priest or priestess, but the tablet seems to clearly designate these individuals as human offerings, literally "victims." Greek legends address the practice of human sacrifice and the Pylos tablet may record this practice in a particularly expensive ritual meant to appease a group of gods and goddesses.

Painted images of gods and goddesses appear in the frescoes that decorated the walls of Mycenaean and Minoan palaces in ancient Greece. Among the representations of goddesses is a female figure identified by her flounced skirt and interpreted as a Great Mother Goddess or Mistress of Animals. An image of her appears in the Ayia Triadha Minoan Villa where she is associated with wild creatures in a rocky landscape. She is sometimes associated with griffins, mythic creatures which may have served as her guardians. One of the many frescoes from the palace of Knossos is known as the "Sacred Grove and Dance." It shows a large group of men and women who watch 14 priestesses dancing in a sacred grove of olive trees. It has been suggested that the figure-of-eight shield motif found in many frescoes was associated with a female war goddess who would evolve into Athena. Also, two fresco fragments from Mycenae have been linked with Hera in her role as protector of children, marriage, and family.

Many scholars use the term "Dark Age" to refer to the centuries between the collapse of the Mycenaean civilization in approximately 1100 B.C.E. and the rise of Archaic Greece in approximately 700 B.C.E.. This period corresponds to the introduction of iron technology throughout the Mediterranean region. Two contrasting models have been proposed for the collapse of the Mycenaean civilization. Some scholars support a Dorian invasion from the north while other scholars prefer an explanation involving a social uprising within the Mycenaean cities in which the Dorians played a role. The Linear B script disappeared during the Dark Age, but cultural traditions and memory thrived. Composed at the end of the Dark Age or beginning of the Archaic Period is the famous cycle of Homeric poems that recount the exploits of Mycenaean princes and warriors during the Trojan War. The poems provide detailed information concerning many aspects of life including relationships between specific deities and warriors on each side of the conflict. It is unclear how much of the religious information had been "modernized" at the time that Homer lived. Some of the religious information contained in the *Iliad* and *Odyssey* must reflect practices and beliefs during the Mycenaean period which had continued into the Archaic period. Many goddesses are mentioned in Homer's epic including Athena (daughter of Zeus), Aphrodite (daughter of Zeus), Artemis (daughter of Zeus and sister to Apollo), Demeter (sister of Zeus and Great Mother Goddess), Eileithi'a (goddess of childbirth), Erinys (a fury and goddess of curses), Hera (wife of Zeus and queen of the gods), and Persephone (wife of Hades and daughter of Demeter). Gods mentioned by Homer include Apollo (son of Zeus and Leto), Ares (son of Zeus and god of war), Dionysos (god of wine), Hades (god of the underworld), Helios (sun god), Herakles (son of Zeus and Alkmene), Hermes (son of Zeus and messenger of the gods), Kronos (father of Zeus), Poseidon (brother of Zeus and god of the sea), and Zeus (son of Kronos and king of the gods). Homer makes it clear that the home of the gods was Mount Olympus. The gods and goddesses mentioned by Homer would remain the principle deities of Greek religion until their eventual replacement by the spread of Christianity.

The gods portrayed in Homer's writing are vibrant and passionate deities. Hera and Athena are clearly enemies of the Trojans while Apollo and Aphrodite are their supporters. The power of the gods and goddesses is an interesting puzzle, because no single deity could dictate the outcome of the war. In fact, the gods and goddesses sometimes seemed powerless to prevent events which disfavored them. For example, Homer records the death of Sarpedon who was the son of Zeus and Laodamia. The king of the gods wanted to postpone the death of his son but was rebuked by Hera who knew that even Zeus could not cheat the Fates.

Greek deities would bestow blessings upon humans only when the worshippers honored them in their temples, sanctuaries, and household shrines. Failure to perform specified rituals could result in a deity's decision to punish an individual by disease, early death, accident, or by dissolving their security through war. If properly worshipped, the Greek gods and goddesses would provide prosperity and happiness.

One special form of divine blessing was provided by oracles at a handful of sacred temples. The most famous of these oracles was called the Pythia and she resided at the Temple of Apollo in Delphi. Other Apollo temple complexes with oracles were located at Delos, Didyma, Claros, and Daphne. Different procedures were used to determine Apollo's answer to an inquiry. The least expensive and most commonly used procedure involved dropping or drawing small counters (such as beans) and interpreting their number and distribution. More complex answers were obtained when the prophetess uttered Apollo's answers. Direct prophecies were given on the seventh day of each month. Before she could prophesy, the Pythia had to be purified ritually by bathing first in special water and then in the smoke of burning laurel leaves. Individuals bringing questions to the oracle were ritually purified in the water issuing from a spring located downslope from the Temple of Apollo. Each individual petitioning the oracle would leave an offering of a small cake on the main altar and a sacrificed sheep or goat on the inner hearth. The sacrificial cakes were purchased in the temple complex at a significant expense.

Large animals designated for sacrifice, such as a sheep or bull, had to be unblemished. Ritual purity required that the animal approach the altar of its own will; often, fresh grass or grain were used as encouragements. Water was sprinkled on the animal's head to induce a shaking response that implied its willingness to submit to the sacrifice. The animal was killed by having its throat cut and a small portion of the meat was thrown onto the altar fire. Most of the meat would be divided among the individuals who had paid for the sacrifice. Meat was not a significant component of Greek diet, so the roasted meat obtained from a sacrifice was always a welcome treat. Those participating in the sacrifice might partake in the ritual meal in a banquet hall within the sacred precinct. The ancient writer Plutarch wrote, "It is not the abundance of wine or the roasting of meat that makes the joy of the festival, but the good hope and belief that the god is present in his kindness and graciously accepts what is offered."

Temples dedicated to various gods and goddesses were found in every major Greek city and in the areas controlled by the Greeks. As the Greek world expanded by colonization and conquest (specifically those of Alexander the Great), the sphere of Greek religious beliefs and practices also expanded. Many aspects of Greek religion would spread further as the Romans absorbed the colonies and kingdoms that had once been under Greek control and added new provinces by the conquests of the Roman legions. Every medium-sized Greek (and later Roman-controlled) city would have a principal temple and several smaller temples or shrines. Each temple was equipped with an open-air altar where public sacrifices were offered by priests and priestesses. Individuals wishing to honor a deity could offer a bloodless sacrifice of incense, wine, fruits, vegetables, or a small cake. Animals were more potent sacrifices, but also much more expensive. Large cities had an elaborate calendar of festival and sacrifice days for the different temples within the city walls. Athens boasted the largest number of scheduled religious festivals with more than half the days of each year earmarked for one or more festivals. In Athens the third day of each month was celebrated as Athena's birthday while the sixth day of each month was sacred to the goddess Artemis. The Athenians honored Apollo, the brother of Artemis, on the seventh day of each month.

Special attention was always shown to a city's patron god or goddess. Merchants were wise to curry the favor of Hermes (Roman Mercury) because he could speed and safeguard their commerce. Offerings to the goddesses Tyche were of value because she ensured the strength of a city's walls against military attack.

Greek religious beliefs concerning the afterlife evolved through time. Homer offers a moderately pessimistic picture of an afterlife in Hades where there is neither pleasure nor pain. For example, the *Iliad* contains a passage in which a ghost describes life on earth for a slave as better than the afterlife of a mortal king in Hades. Such a pessimistic view may not have been held by everyone even during the time that Homer was writing. Individuals hoping for a pleasant afterlife, a paradise, were drawn to religious beliefs that are often called "Mystery Cults." The most famous of these were the Eleusian Mysteries involving Demeter and Persephone. Other mystery cults involved Hercules, Dionysios, and Orpheus.

The mystery cult of Demeter and Persephone was celebrated each year at the major sanctuary of Eleusis near Athens. Those who qualified and participated in the ritual at Eleusis expected to be blessed during their lifetime and in the afterlife. The hymn to Demeter promised "Richly blessed is the mortal who has seen these rites, but whoever is not an initiate and has no share in them, never has an equal portion after death, down in the gloomy darkness." The final ceremony of the Eleusinian Mysteries took place in a large initiation hall called the Telesterion where the ritual involved "something done, something said, and something shown," The roots of the Eleusinian Mysteries probably extend into the culture of Bronze Age Greece as evidenced by the presence of Mycenaean artifacts buried beneath the later buildings at Eleusis.

The popularity of mystery religions among the Romans demonstrated that they held no prejudice against non-Roman gods or goddesses who offered special or extraordinary blessings. The Romans saw no reason to exclude sanctuaries of potent foreign deities from their cities. Thus, underground sanctuaries to the god Mithras (a god borrowed from the Parthian Empire in modern Iraq and Iran) would spread across the Roman Empire from Syria to England. Temples to Isis and Serapis were constructed in Italy at cities such as Rome and Pompeii.

In one sense, it is unfair to portray the mystery cults as only providing an insurance policy for a pleasant afterlife. A mystery cult transformed its members by providing a catharsis, a mind cleansing experience, by bringing a member to a state of emotional collapse, and then implanting a new idea. One ancient writer of the fourth century C.E. insisted that his life would not be worth living if he "could not celebrate the most sacred mysteries which unite the human race." Romans drawn to the mystery cults were prone to see the traditional Greek deities (such as Zeus, Hera, Athena, Apollo, etc.) as religious fossils and their priests without a genuine sense of enthusiasm and excitement.

Greeks and Romans felt that worship of one deity did not exclude acknowledgment of other gods or goddesses. Sacrilegious behavior to a deity was obviously dangerous and the act of a foolish or deranged person. When Christianity began to spread inside the Roman Empire it was first viewed as another mystery cult offering blessings such as those given by the Eleusian or Dionysian Mysteries. Christians refused to have Jesus viewed as equal to the Greek and Roman gods whom they rejected and denounced. The hostility of some Christians to the mystery cults and to the traditional religious rituals caused the Romans to treat Christians as dangerous individuals practicing a religion barely removed from atheism.

Christianity differed from the mystery cults and traditional Greco-Roman religions on several levels. For example, Christians were critical that membership in a mystery cult often began with a free initiation but required fees paid to the priest or riestesses to learn the "secrets" needed to move to the highest stages of a cult. This prevented individuals without moderate incomes from moving beyond initiate. The early Christians argued that such a practice was a moneymaking scheme, not a real faith. Non-Christians could not fathom what was especially good about Christianity since it cost nothing to join and even welcomed poor individuals within its membership. The unresolvable differences between Christianity and the Greco-Roman religions created a tension which resulted in the persecution of Christians. Centuries after Jesus, the Christians finally found themselves with powerful influence in the family of various Roman emperors. This gave them the authority, in the later years of the Roman Empire, to close the temples and shrines of all deities except Jesus.

NOTES

1. There are many books and television programs dealing with ancient Egyptian culture and religion; some are more credible than others. Three of the best summary volumes concerning Ancient Egypt include *The Chronicles of the Pharaoh* (London: Thames and Hudson, 1994) by Peter Clayton, *A History of Ancient Egypt* (Oxford: Blackwell Press, 1993) by Nicolas Grimal, and the *Cultural Atlas of the World: Ancient Egypt* (Alexandria, VA: Stonehenge Press, 1990) by John Baines and Jaromír Málek. Discussions of the origins of Egyptian religion are contained in *Egypt before the Pharaohs* by Michael Hoffman (Austin: University of Texas, 1991) and an article by Fekri Hassan entitled "Primeval Goddess to Divine King" in *The Followers of Horus*, edited by Renée Friedman and Barbara Adams (Oxford: Oxbow Books, 1992).

A very clear summary of Egyptian religion is contained in *Egyptian Myths* by George Hart (Austin: University of Texas, 1990) and an older and more exhaustive discussion can be found in *Ancient Egyptian Religion* by Henri Frankfort (New York: Columbia University Press, 1948). A comprehensive discussion of many aspects of Egyptian religion can be found in *The Gods and Symbols of Ancient Egypt* by Manfred Lurker (London: Thames and Hudson, 1980).

2. A number of resources are available concerning the religions of ancient Syro-Mesopotamia. A good summary is contained in *Mesopotamian Myths* by Henrietta McCall (Austin: University of Texas, 1990). The context of Syro-Mesopotamian myths and ancient societies is addressed in the *Cultural Atlas of Mesopotamia and the Ancient Near East* by Michael Roaf (Oxford: Facts on File, 1990), *Ebla to Damascus: Art and Archaeology in Ancient Syria,* edited by Harvey Weiss (Washington DC: Smithsonian Institution Press, 1985), *Syrie Mémoire et Civilisation,* produced by L'Institut du Monde Arabe (Paris: Flammarion, 1993).

3. We encourage students interested in the religion of ancient Greece to consult the rich collection of material contained in *Perseus 2.0* CD-ROM database, edited by Gregory Crane (New Haven, CT: Yale University Press, 1996) which is also available as a Web site. Related to the Perseus 2.0 project is an excellent summary volume, *Ancient Greece from Prehistoric to Hellenistic Times* by Thomas Martin (New Haven, CT: Yale University Press, 1996).

Perspectives on the origins of Greek religion can be found in *The Civilization of the Goddess: The World of Old Europe* by Maria Gimbutas (San Francisco: Harper, 1991), and *The Birth of Greece* by Pierre Leveque (New York: Harry N. Abrams, 1994). Additional information is contained in *Reading the Past: Linear B and Related Scripts* by John Chadwick (Berkeley: University of California Press, 1987). Insights into Minoan religion is found in *Aegean Frescoes of Religious Character* by Litsa Kontorli-Papadopoulou (Goteborg: Paul Astroms, 1996). There are many resources concerning Greek religion during the Classical period. One resource that describes the classical tradition and the following Christian tradition is *Backgrounds of Early Christianity* (Grand Rapids, MI: Eerdmans Publishing, 1987).

The controversial evidence of Egyptian influence in ancient Greece is outlined in the mutlivolume series entitled *Black Athena* by Martin Bernal (New Brunswick, NJ: Rutgers University Press, 1987 and 1991). Books critical of the Black Athena perspective include *Not Out of Africa* by Mary Lefkowitz (New York: Basic Books, 1996).

Eleven

New World Religions of MesoAmerica and North America

Michael Fuller and Neathery Fuller

St. Louis Community College

Scattered from Canada to Chile are earth and stone mounds that are silent witnesses to complex religious traditions that began thousands of years before Columbus arrived in the New World. Most of these low mounds were constructed as memorials for the dead and reflect a commonly held belief in an afterlife. At some prehistoric towns and cities (such as La Venta, Tikal, Copan, Tenochtitlan, Cahokia) we find massive mounds that rise hundreds of feet above the surrounding land surface and represent man-made mountains. The summit of the largest mounds were capped with temple structures where a variety of gods and goddesses were offered sacrifices. In many cases, the archaeological investigation of the temple pyramids and temple mounds have shown them to be multilayered structures constructed over several centuries. One explanation of the cycles of temple construction lies in the nature of the political power system where rulers or kings added new edifices to existing pyramids to demonstrate their right to power. A second explanation involves a deeply held belief among many of the New World civilizations that "measured units of time" needed to be celebrated with sacrifices and new temple facades.

The term MesoAmerica is used by scholars to describe parts of modern Mexico, Guatemala, Hondorus, and Belize where several cultures evolved into city-states. What traits define a city-state? The basic three features of a city-state include

1. A population of over 5,000 individuals supported by an agricultural economy,
2. Living in a discrete territory governed by elite within the state, and
3. A central government that has the power to make rules and laws.

One school of scholarship equates the word "civilization" with the concept of city-state, while other scholars would add extra requirements such as a system of writing, mathematics, and literature.[1]

OLMEC RELIGION

If you accept the more liberal definition of civilization, then the Olmecs are the oldest civilization to develop in MesoAmerica. The name for this civilization derives from the historic period when the Aztecs identified the people living along the southern Gulf Coast of Mexico as *Olmeca*, literally, "people of the rubber country." Michael Coe has proposed that the ancient name of the Olmec was preserved in an Aztec legend as *Tamoachan*, "nation on the eastern sea."[2]

The writing system of the Olmec is a hieroglyphic script, one of four or five hieroglyphic writing systems that developed during the Preclassic period in Mexico. Some scholars have argued that the Olmec civilization was the mother culture of all later Mexican cultures. Recently, several scholars have acknowledged evidence of borrowing and interaction between the Olmec and other groups but argue that it is inaccurate to assume that any one culture, such as Olmec, was the "mother culture" of the region. Interaction between the Olmec and other MesoAmerican cultures occurred on several levels, ranging from trade in raw materials to selective borrowing of religious iconography.

The oldest Olmec city is San Lorenzo Tenochitlán which thrived between 1200 and 900 B.C.E. This city was located along the floodplain of a tributary of the Río Coatzacoalcos in the modern Mexican State of Veracruz. The people of San Lorenzo Tenochitlán maintained raw material trade ties that stretched from Guatemala to the Mexican highlands. The artistic accomplishments at San Lorenzo included the carving of 70 stone monuments which conveyed both religious and political themes. The most famous of these monuments are the nine colossal stone heads that portrayed their kings wearing headgear related to the sacred ballgame or warfare. The stone heads weigh up to 3 tons and measure up to 3 meters (9 feet) high. The raw stone for the heads was brought from the Tuxtla Mountains more than 70 kilometers from the city. The heads were buried ceremonially just before the city's abandonment.

One school of scholars has attempted to link the flat nose features of these colossal heads with African faces and identified San Lorenzo as a point of contact between Old and New Worlds. This argument seems most unlikely to almost all archaeologists and anthropologists who conduct fieldwork in either the New World or the Old World. There is an absence of artifacts, linguistic evidence, and genetic evidence to identify the Olmec as a hybrid of Old World and New World peoples. The creation of colossal stone heads took place not only at San Lorenzo Tenochitlán, but also at the Olmec cities of La Venta and Tres Zapotes.

The stone quarried in the Tuxtla Mountains had special significance to the Olmec. Archaeologists and art historians hypothesize that one particular volcanic peak, San Martín Pajapan, was a sacred location in their creation story. They commemorated this association by placing a life-size statue of a kneeling figure in the saddle of San Martín's crater. It is likely that the Olmec saw the figure as the creator god who performed the supernatural act of separating the sky from the earth. The creator god holds the trunk of the "World Tree" which he used to separate the earth and sky. His headdress is decorated with an image of the cleft-headed god and a maize plant.

Further commemoration of the San Martín Pajapan volcano appears in the Olmec city of La Venta. This city was founded on an island in the marshland formed by the Tonala River in Mexico. Radiocarbon dates place its beginnings around 900 B.C.E. and its destruction at approximately 400 B.C.E.. The heart of the site is dominated by a 32-meter high artificial mound that the excavator recognized as a replica of San Martin Pajapan. Adjacent to this artificial mound are platforms, elite burials, and three massive mosaic pavements formed from green serpentine. The artisans of La Venta carefully arranged the mosaic blocks to represent a stylized face of a jaguar. Artisans also crafted stelae (carved stone pillars) decorated with images of the Olmec king communing with supernatural spirits and joining with the supernatural World Tree. These stelae were installed at the base of the replica volcano to emphasize the separation of the city's ruling elite from ordinary citizens. This intentional placement underscored the special relationship between human life and the spirits of creation. The rich iconography of the Olmec monuments looks convincingly like a royal claim to divinity, if not during the king's lifetime, at least after death.

The major platforms, tombs, and replica volcano at La Venta are aligned on an axis 8 degrees west of north. This same alignment occurs at the site of San Jose Mogote and one interpretation suggests that the alignment was chosen intentionally to match the point on the horizon where the Big Dipper rests at summer solstice. It is possible that the Olmec envisioned the Big Dipper as a skyform of the Jaguar god. Its disappearance below the horizon may have been the stimulus for a myth cycle in which the god departs from the sky to enter the Underworld.

The Olmec religion included rituals that required elaborate offerings of jade celts, jade figurines, and serpentine figurines. Six celts and sixteen figurines were found in Offering Number 4 at La Venta. One interpretation proposes that the crescent outline formed by the celts are a row of teeth in the mouth of the Olmec creator deity. This god may have been associated with an earth serpent or a jaguar deity.

La Venta was destroyed and its monuments were defaced in approximately 400 B.C.E.. One anthropologist has argued that each successive generation of Olmec rulers tried to outspend their predecessors with expensive and elaborate religious rituals and building programs. The ruling elite may have been motivated by a wish to please their principal gods and demonstrate to the populace that they could ensure blessing for all Olmecs. The escalating budget for "ritual sanctification" rose until it overwhelmed the meager economic surpluses and triggered an economic crisis. The religious and political power of the elite dissolved once their ritual behavior proved ineffective.

MAYA RELIGION

Excavations at the site of Nabke in Guatemala have uncovered a Maya city with major structures as early as 600 B.C.E. Many major Maya cities (Calakmul, Dzibilchaltún, El Mirador, Uaxactun, Tikal, Tintal, Cerros, Cuello, Lamanai, Nohmul, and Chalchuapa) boasted pyramids, ballcourts, and palaces from 400 B.C.E.to 250 C.E. Thus, as the Olmec civilization disappeared, the Maya civilization appeared and covered a larger territory in MesoAmerica.[3]

Analysis of the Maya religion is greatly aided by the hieroglyphic inscriptions found carved on stelae and painted on pottery vessels. Historical records from the Spanish Conquest of Mexico indicate that thousands of books written in Maya hieroglyphics were kept in scattered Maya communities. Regrettably, almost all of these were destroyed by the religious zeal of the Spaniards. The destruction of the Maya books and persecution of the literate elites ended one phase of the Maya's literary heritage. It would not be until late in the twentieth century that major breakthroughs would be made in translation of the Maya hieroglyphic language.

One way to understand Maya religion is to realize that the major cities were equipped with breathtaking pyramids, ballcourts, and palaces. The pyramids were called *Witz*, meaning "mountain," and were crowned with temples at their summits. To pass through the temple doorway was, literally, to step into the mouth of the supernatural world and the abode of the ancestors. It is likely that only a handful of elite religious and political leaders entered the temples. The majority of a city's population watched ceremonial activities from the plaza area in front of the temple. The largest temple at the site of Chichen Itza was revered as the "Creation Mountain" and the plaza in front of the temple was the symbolic primordial sea of creation. Near the "Creation Mountain" temple at Chichen Itza is the massive ballcourt and the impressive *cenote* (the surface entrance to an underground pool of water). Both were seen as physical features that connected the Middleworld (earth's surface) with the nine planes (and nine Lords) of *Xibalbá* (the Underworld). The elevated sacred mountain (the Temple) reached toward the 13 planes of the Upperworld.

Pictorial and inscriptional evidence indicates that blood sacrifices were required for many, if not the majority, of rituals involving the elite. Often, this was accomplished with the blood of captives. However, the blood of the elite themselves was required for some specific rituals. The location for these elite sacrifices was in the temples atop the major pyramids and in the royal palaces. An example of such a ritual, performed by the elite of a minor Maya city, is portrayed on the painted walls of a temple at the site of Bonampak.

Maya artists painted a series of murals at Bonampak to document the steps taken by the city's ruler, Chaan Muan, to prepare his son for the throne. The first step in series of ceremonies begins with the visit of 14 rulers of other Maya cities on December 14, 790. This episode was triggered by an event of ominous portent: a solar eclipse. The second ritual occurred on November 15, 791 when the temple was "ensouled" with a sacred spirit. Additional rituals required blood from human sacrifices. The artists portray a series of battles in which the victorious Chaan Muaan watches his opponents retreat from battle. Then the mural panels shift the action back to Bonampak where a group of the captured warriors are stripped and prepared for ritual. The faces of the captives show a range of emotions including horror and glances that beg for pity. The blood offering from the captives was not the only blood offering made during the final ceremonies. Blood offerings were made also by members of Chaan Muaan's household who used stingray spines and stone blade knives to obtain the necessary blood. The royal family's blood would have been sprinkled upon sheets of paper that were burned. This allowed the blood to become smoke and rise toward the heavens. The Bonampak mural portrays the serious religion ceremonies associated with ensuring the succession of power from father to son. The scenes include elite processions, musicians, dancers, captives awaiting sacrifice, and the members of the royal family.

Human blood was a powerful offering to the Maya gods. Other strong offerings included the sacrifice of powerful animals like the jaguar. For example, King Yax Pac of Copan inaugurated a special monument designated as Altar Q with the sacrifice of 15 jaguars. The monument is a commemoration to 15 generations of his ancestors who served as kings of Copan. Each jaguar must have been seen as an offering to one ancestor.

The religious rituals of kings like Yax Pac and Chaan Muaan were probably not the same as the rituals practiced in small Maya villages or observed by individual farmers along the edge of their cornfields. We can gain insight into the beliefs and rituals of the nonelite by examining the religion of the Lacandon Maya who live in the jungle near the ruins of Palenque. Most modern Maya, descendants of the ancient Maya, have become Roman Catholics but still retain some vestiges of their pre-Christian religious tradition. The Lacandon Maya have not adopted Christianity. They still burn the sacred incense, called *copal*, to appease and nourish a small number of ancient Maya deities. The Lacandon call themselves the *Hach Winik* ("real people") and wear a very distinctive, loose fitting white tunic called a *xicul*. They still make offerings to *Kanank'ash* ("Lord of the Forest"), *K'ak'* ("Lord of Fire"), *Mensabak* ("Bringer of Rain"), and *Hachakyum* ("Great Lord- Creator"). One ceremony, supposedly held on an eight-year cycle, requires separation of the men from their families and corn fields for one month. The men seclude themselves in a "god house" for a month of chanting. A drink called *balche*, made from fermented tree bark, is part of the ritual as well as the burning of sacred *copal* (dried tree sap). The ceremony ends with the ritualistic painting of jaguar-patterned dots on each man's skin before he emerges from the "god's house."

TEOTIHUACÁN RELIGION

Between 200 C.E. and 700 C.E., the city of Teotihuacán developed in the Basin of Mexico. The name of the city is an Aztec word which means "Place of the Gods." Its maximum population was estimated at between 125,000 and 200,000 individuals living in a 20-square-kilometer area. The city's urban landscape was dominated by two huge pyramids. The largest, the Pyramid of the Sun, was built above an ancient lava tube cave that was probably viewed as their cave of creation. Rituals involving fire, water, shells, fish spines, and distinctive pottery vessels were conducted in the cave beneath the Pyramid of the Sun. The smaller pyramid is designated as the Pyramid of the Moon. These were not the only religious features of the city, just the most massive.[4]

A twofold religious system has been proposed for Teotihuacán. One level comprises household religion and ritual while the other consists of "state" religion. One remarkable difference between the art of Teotihuacán and Maya art is the near absence of specific portraits of ruling elites in Teotihuacán. They are not depicted as dominating weaker men nor are they shown communing with supernatural spirits. Humans are definitely less powerful than the deities at Teotihuacán and it is doubtful that the city's ruler was considered divine during his lifetime or after his death. One suggestion has been put forward that the political structure at Teotihuacán may have been an oligarchic republic.

The pantheon of Teotihuacán deities can be studied by examining the painted wall murals, moldmade figurines, and stone sculptures found at the site. The gods and goddesses worshipped at Teotihuacán included a Sun deity, Moon deity, Venus deity, Old Fire God (similar to the later Aztec God called *Huehueteotl*), Storm God, and Great Goddess. The Storm God shared some characteristics with the later Aztec God named *Tlaloc* and the contemporary Maya rain God named *Chac*. Rain was a critical factor in the social and economic viability of all ancient cultures in MesoAmerica. The important deity identified as the Great Goddess was portrayed wearing a nose pendant and a bird in her headdress. The importance of her cult may be related to her ability to transcend with impartiality the factions associated with various male, militaristic cults.

In approximately 750 C.E. the city was partially destroyed by a fire. Temples and elite residences were burned and images of the deities were smashed. The city was resettled but never rebuilt to its previous scale. The selective nature of the destruction could be attributed to a social revolution carried out from within the society, but outside conquest cannot be totally discounted.

AZTEC RELIGION

The Aztecs recorded the year 1 Flint (1324) as the date when the Mexica arrived and founded their great capital city Tenochtitlan. One of their first building projects was a shrine to honor *Huitzilopochtli* (Hummingbird on the Left), a deified hero, patron of war, and associated with the sun. Eventually this shrine would be replaced by the grand Templo Mayor with its twin shrines to *Tlaloc* and *Huitzilopochtli*.[5]

A sixteenth-century Spanish writer was impressed by the many Aztec deities, including gods who had been appropriated from neighboring, captive populations. The most powerful, supreme deity of the Aztecs was *Tezcatlipoca* ("Smoking Mirror") who was associated with destiny or fate. This deity played a crucial role in the rite of kingship prayers. Also of great importance in Aztec religion was *Tonatiuh*, the sun. He also played an important role in the coronation of a new king and human sacrifices were particularly pleasing to him.

Tlaloc, the rain deity, was portrayed with a goggle-eyed mask, heron-feather headdress, and often carrying a cornstalk or a symbolic lightning-bolt wand. Related to *Tlaloc* was a female deity of ground water, *Chalchiuhtlicue* ("she of the jade skirt"). Considered a sister of *Tlaloc*, her shrines were built near springs, streams, irrigation ditches, and aqueducts.

Aztec religion, like the Maya religion, involved offerings of human blood. This practice has to be understood in the context of the Aztec creation story. The world begins with two primordial deities named *Ometecutli* ("Lord of Duality") and *Omexihuatl* ("Lady of Duality"). They produced four sons, each of whom is associated with a specific color and direction: *Xipe Totec* (a vegetation deity associated with red), *Tezcatlipoca* (an omnipotent deity associated with the jaguar and the color black), *Quetzalcoatl* (windstorms that bring rain associated with white), and *Huitzilopochtli* (patron of war associated with blue). *Quetzalcoatl* and *Huitzilopochtli* are charged with continuing creation and they create the lessor gods, fire, human beings, the calendar, the underworld, the heavens, water, and the earth. A series of five discrete episodes of time, defined by the Aztecs as "suns," transpire after creation is finished. Each age is brought to a close as a result of battles fought between the four sons of *Ometecutli* and *Omexihuatl*. The Aztecs believed that they were created during the time of the fifth sun when the god *Quetzalcoatl* journeyed to the underworld and received from *Mictlantecuhtli* (god of death, darkness, and underworld) the bones and ashes of the humans who died during the time of the fourth sun. The god *Quetzalcoatl* grinds the bones and ashes of the fourth sun humans, then he adds his own blood to the mixture by performing an autosacrifice (spilling his own blood as Maya kings were required to do in certain rituals). *Quetzalcoatl* mixes the blood from his penis into the ground ash and bone. The first male child and first female child emerge from the mixture; they are the ancestors to all Aztecs. *Quetzalcoatl* gave his own blood to make humans. Thus humans must repay a "blood debt" to the gods. Human sacrifice is the means of this repayment.

There were many other components in the explanation of human sacrifice by the Aztecs. In one sense, Aztec deities were mortal to the extent that they had to be fed. Offerings of human blood provided their nourishment, and they reciprocated by providing regular rains, fertile soil, and keeping the sun on its daily cycle. The Aztecs believed that the gods would go hungry and the world would come to an end without human sacrifice.

CHACO CANYON AND MISSISSIPPIAN CULTURES

Two discrete locations in North American became centers of complex cultures that functioned as early states before declining and collapsing. Unlike the Maya, we have no preserved writing systems in North America to assist in reconstructing their political and religious institutions. The extent to which civilizations in MesoAmerica interacted with the populations in Chaco Canyon and the Mississippi Valley is still an area of intense archaeological interest. A minimal level of trade between Chaco Canyon and MesoAmerica have been demonstrated, while no direct evidence of MesoAmerican trade materials have been identified at any of the major sites of the Mississippian culture. Evidence for limited ideological interaction between MesoAmerica and the Mississippian culture has been inferred based upon the similarity of some public monuments (flat-topped temple mounds, astronomical observatories, plazas) and artistic motifs (long-nosed god, death god, jaguar god).[6]

Chaco Canyon flourished between 850 and 1130 C.E. with 13 large towns and hundreds of smaller villages situated in modern day Arizona. An extensive network of more than 250 miles of roads radiated out of the Chaco Canyon area. There is good evidence that the artisans at Chaco Canyon processed turquoise from mines near Sante Fé and traded with MesoAmerican merchants for copper bells, parrot feathers, and other exotic items of beauty.

The largest of the Chacoan towns is called Pueblo Bonito and it contained over 500 rooms surrounding a central plaza that is neatly divided into two halves by a masonry wall. Most of the rooms within the pueblo were square or rectangular in shape with the exception of the kivas—circular, semisubterranean rooms used by specific religious orders. One kiva at Pueblo Bonito measures 55 feet (approximately 16 meters) in diameter and must have served for religious rituals of great significance to the whole community. Each large town in Chaco Canyon contained a number of small kivas in proportion to the total number of rooms and at least one great kiva. The assumption, based upon the practices of modern Hopi and Zuni people, is that each kiva would be sacred to a specific *kachina* (spirit force–god/goddess) responsible for various aspects of nature such as rain, corn germination, sun, and so on. Most small kivas, like the modern kivas of the Hopi and Zuni, were constructed with a small indentation in the center of the floor. This feature in a modern kiva is termed the *sipapu*, the symbolic representation of the point where humans emerged from the third world onto the surface of the fourth world where the Hopi and Zuni still live. Both of these people, who are linguistically and culturally distinct, have emergence stories that are associated with specific locations in the Southwest United States.

Several large, fortified urban sites developed in the Mississippi Valley and its tributary valleys during the period 1000–1450 C.E.. Of these cities the largest was Cahokia Mounds situated near the modern city of St. Louis (itself built on top of a daughter city of Cahokia). The Mississippian people depended upon corn for a major component of their diet and they cultivated a corn race that was more reliable and productive than the varieties available to the preceding Woodland cultures. The presence of wooden stockades around many Mississippian sites reflects the pervasive problem of raiding and warfare between coalitions of different towns and cities. Cahokia, the largest of these cities, covered over 5 square miles (14 square kilometers) and probably supported a population as large as 50,000.

The center of Cahokia was dominated by a large, multiterraced earthen mound that looks down upon a large plaza area. The large mound is locally known as Monks Mound to commemorate the small Catholic church that was built on its lower terrace by Catholic missionaries in the late 1700s or early 1800s. Archaeological exploration on the summit of the mound has exposed the outline of a large temple constructed out of wood. Various assumptions link the temple with the worship of a sun god, but it is likely that the mound was also seen as a point of creation/emergence. Construction on the mound began in the nineth century C.E. and subsequent building phases added additional mass to the mound over 300 years. Recent conservation efforts to stabilize Monks Mound have detected the presence of a stone pavement buried deep within the interior of the mound; its exact purpose has yet to be determined.

An astronomical observatory, designated as the "woodhenge" by archaeologists, was constructed at approximately the same time that construction began on Monk's Mound. The first phase of the observatory involved 24 wooden posts designed to mark the rising and setting points of the sun during evenly spaced periods of time. Special care was given to ensure that posts coincided with the specific days termed equinoxes and solstices. The woodhenge observatory was rebuilt almost every hundred years, and the number of posts increased by 12 during each rebuilding. Observations of the sun were used to control both the agricultural cycles of planting and harvest as well as ceremonial cycles. There is evidence of two or three contemporaneous woodhenges at Cahokia during its period of maximum population; approximately two dozen astronomical observatories have been documented at various Mississippian sites and it is certain that more will be identified with continued excavations.

The collapse of Cahokia did not mean extinction of its population or its belief system. The Natchez, a historic chiefdom living in the lower portion of the Mississippi Valley, are seen by some scholars as the bearers of the religious ideology that found its greatest expression at Cahokia. The combination of ethnographic and archaeological data suggests that the religion of Cahokia focused on the issues of fertility, purification, revitalization, and ancestor worship. At least two annual rituals can be hypothesized based on the archaeological and ethnographic data. The first is the ritual called "Great Busk" which took place in July when the Great Sun was honored. The ceremony was probably associated with the color red (on some ceremonial vessels), sacred fire, blood, and life. The second ceremony was associated with the capture and rescue of the Great Sun and its associated concepts of revitalization and rebirth.

The social hierarchy of the Natchez, thought to be related to the earlier hierarchy of Cahokia, involved a supreme leader known as "Great Sun" and a leader of warriors called "Tattooed Serpent." There is definite artistic imagery for the "Great Sun" at Cahokia, but no imagery that can be associated with "Tattooed Serpent." The artistic tradition at Cahokia does include falcon imagery (on a stone tablet, shell embroidered blanket, and copper plates) which must have been the symbol of the warrior leader and those serving under him.

The Natchez did not allow the feet of their supreme leader to touch the earth. His wives, guards, and retainers were sacrificed to accompany him into the afterlife, and this seems to be the exact situation represented in a mass grave found under mound 72 at Cahokia. In this situation, human sacrifice functioned in a different mode than the examples among the Maya and Aztec.

CONCLUSIONS

Our discussion of religious traditions in the New World has not included the evidence of the rich heritage that developed in Peru (Inca, Moche, Tiahuanaco, Huari, Chavin) because that would double or triple the amount of information presented in this chapter. Their religious traditions continued many of the themes discussed for the state religions in MesoAmerica and North America but also added new distinctive features. Common to all of the religious traditions of the New World is a concern with the question of human origins and rituals designed to ensure the reliability of food supplies based upon agriculture.

Emergence stories are a common feature among the most advanced cultures in MesoAmerica and North America. Often, the elite within a given civilization linked themselves with the creator, which gave the elite remarkable social position and power. The exceptions to this rule appear to be the religious traditions at Teotihuacán and in Chaco Canyon. In many cases, a gradual ideological creep must have allowed the elite to shift their position from "friends of the divine" to that of living gods.

The concept of cycles of sacred time and ritual can be seen in several city states in MesoAmerica and North America. Groups such as the Maya and Aztec created complex recording technologies involving hieroglyphic writing and observations of the sun, moon, and planet Venus. Linked with the measuring of time was the concept of offerings (often human sacrifices) needed to ensure the continuity or time, life, and fertility.

NOTES

1. The criteria for defining civilization have been discussed by the French historian Fernand Braudel in his book entitled *On History* which was translated into English by Sarah Matthews (Chicago: University of Chicago Press, 1980). The archaeological perspective on the same question is addressed by Ruth Whitehouse and John Wilkins in *The Making of Civilization* (New York: Al-

fred A. Knopf, 1986). Difficulties with terms such as tribe, chiefdom, and early states have arisen among scholars. Colin Renfrew, the author of *Archaeology: Theories, Methods and Practice* (New York: Thames and Hudson, 1991), classifies the Mississippian cultures as a chiefdom. Henri J. M. Claessen provides further discussion of the issue of "state" in the *Encyclopedia of*

Cultural Anthropology (New York: Henry Holt and Co., 1990) and Gary M. Feinman discussed the issue of "chiefdoms and nonindustrial states" in the same encyclopedia.

2. Karl Luckert analyzed the artifacts and architecture of the Olmec civilization in *Olmec Religion: A Key to Middle America and Beyond* (Norman: University of Oklahoma, Norman, 1976). His perspective on the role of the jaguar in Olmec art departs from the mainstream of Olmec scholarship, but his other insights are very compelling. The most current background on specific sites and New World civilizations (including the Olmec) is contained in *The Oxford Companion to Archaeology* (New York: Oxford University Press, 1996) which was edited by Brian M. Fagan.

3. A concise summary of the Maya civilization is contained in *Maya Civilization* written by T. Patrick Culbert (Washington DC: Smithsonian Books, 1993). Advances in deciphering the Maya inscriptions have led to new perspectives on the Maya as reflected in recent books such as *Maya Cosmos: Three Thousand Years on the Shaman's Path* (New York: William Morrow and Co., 1993) by David Freidel, Linda Schele, and Joy Parker. Scholarship on Maya civilization has produced many new historical insights such as those contained in *A Forest of Kings: The Untold Story of the Ancient Maya* by Linda Schele and David Freidel (New York: William Morrow and Co., 1990).

4. See George L. Cowgill, "State and Society at Teotihuacán, Mexico," *Annual Review of Anthropology* 26:129–161, 1997, for current theories concerning Teotihuacán. An excellent source of information for this ancient civilization is the volume titled *Teotihuacan: Art from the City of the Gods* (New York: Thames and Hudson, 1993) which was edited by Kathleen Berrin and Esther Pasztory.

5. Elizabeth Hill Boone produced a wonderful summary of the Aztec Civilization in *The Aztec World* (Washington DC: Smithsonian Books, 1994). Other useful sources concerning Aztec religion include *The Aztecs* by Richard F. Townsend (London: Thames and Hudson, 1992) and *Aztecs* by Inga Clendinnen (Cambridge: Cambridge University Press, 1991), .

6. An insightful discussion of Cahokia and its religious beliefs can be found in *Prehistory of the Americas* prepared by Stuart J. Fiedel (Cambridge: Cambridge University Press, 1992). Detailed information concerning the site of Cahokia is presented by Melvin Fowler in *The Cahokia Atlas: A Historical Atlas of Cahokia Archaeology* (Springfield, IL: Illinois Historic Preservation Agency, 1989). Discussion of Cahokia and Chaco Canyon are provided by Brian M. Fagan in *Ancient North America: The Archaeology of a Continent* (New York: Thames and Hudson, 1991). An insightful analysis of politics and religion at ancient Cahokia is found in an article by Patricia J. O'Brien titled "Cahokia: The Political Capital of the 'Ramey' State?" *North American Archaeologist* 10(4), 1989, and in an article by Patricia O'Brien and William P McHugh titled "Mississippian Solstice Shrines and a Cahokian Calendar: An Hypothesis Based on Ethnohistory and Archaeology," *North American Archaeologist* 8(3), 1987.

Twelve

Vedic and Hindu Traditions

Maxine K. Weisgrau

Barnard College

As practiced by hundreds of millions throughout the world, Hinduism raises some important issues for the discussion of religion as a universal human undertaking. In some ways it is unique among the world's religions. There is no one founding figure associated with its origins as in Christianity, Buddhism, or Islam. There is no single text or scripture that unites its followers. Its dogma is not based on one omnipotent deity, nor does it encompass a single moral code. It has no internal structure or centralized institutional authority. Even thinking about Hinduism as a single, unified religious system is foreign to most of its history.

The history of Hinduism encompasses the evolution of South Asian cultures, languages, and the region's multiple religious traditions. This essay will trace some major historical events and philosophical themes in the formation of Hinduism and will discuss the present day context of its practice in India and abroad. It therefore combines many forms of knowledge about the region's culture and history; the research of archaeologists and linguists will be discussed along with that of anthropologists and religious scholars.

Multiple and intersecting strands of knowledge—both South Asian sources and Western translations and interpretations—contribute to the contemporary understanding of Hinduism. The documentation of all these sources is beyond the scope of this essay, but it is important to consider at the outset that the languages and words used to talk about Hinduism have social and political histories themselves.

REPRESENTING HINDUISM: SCHOLARSHIP AND STEREOTYPES

Observers, scholars, and rulers from abroad have profoundly influenced the representation of South Asian religion and culture. Many of the terms now routinely used for aspects of Hinduism derive from nonindigenous languages. For example, the word "caste," which denotes the social divisions associated with South Asian Hinduism, comes from a Portuguese word, *casta*, for animal breed or lineage.

The very term "Hindu" is a borrowed one with no exact equivalent in South Asian languages. The word is believed to originate from *sindhu*, an Indo-European word for sea, used by Middle Easterners three to four thousand years ago for the extensive Indus River region in what is now Pakistan. Some scholars claim that Persians subsequently modified the word to "hind" and used the term for the geographic area that now comprises Pakistan and the Indian states of Rajasthan and parts of Gujarat.

Greek and Roman historians commented on South Asian cultures over two thousand years ago and left their mark on historiography and terminology. Megasthenes, who left accounts of social and political life in what is now the Indian state of Bihar ca. 300 B.C.E. applies the term "Indika" to refer to the entire South Asian region. Middle Eastern historians of 1000–1300 C.E. use the term Hindu to denote both the religion and the region within which its followers reside.

The term "Hinduism" doesn't come into use until the 1820s, when British colonial rulers added the suffix "ism" to conform to European nomenclature for religious systems. ". . . [I]t was only in the nineteenth century that the many indigenous Indian religious formations were collectively named 'Hinduism.' Before this, not only did these groups not have a name for themselves as a religious unity, but for the most part they did not consider that they were members of a single religious collectivity."[1] Single-term designations for religious affiliation were thus imported and propagated throughout India during the British colonial period.

As the result of centuries of migration, colonialism, and globalization, some aspects of South Asian culture and Hinduism are familiar to non-Hindus around the world; however, misconceptions and stereotypes abound. The dominant image of Hinduism in the contemporary global imagination is of an "ancient" and "timeless" culture, phrases that invariably appear when foreign journalists report on India. Despite technological advances and participation in the global economy as well as the profound influences of Middle Eastern and European cultures on its history and culture, India is still described as ancient and unchanging.

This is due in great part to what foreign historians have written about India, and the assumptions brought to their scholarly discourse. This historiography discusses India's history with different terms and concepts than those used to discuss the histories of European states. Ronald Inden suggests that Indology, the European study of Indian civilization, is dominated by an intellectual framework that essentializes the caste system, reducing all of Indian civilization to this single phenomenon. The ultimate effect of this Orientalist Indology has been to consider caste "as though it were the unchanging (substantialized) agent of the civilization, from the rise of the Indus Valley culture and the arrival of the Aryans down to the present day of regionalism and caste in electoral politics . . ."[2] Inden offers an alternative interpretation of caste-based institutions throughout Indian history as having important political and economic functions within which individuals and groups influenced governance and decision making. This approach to Indian history draws parallels with, rather than differentiating it from, European political history.

Some journalists writing about contemporary India comment on what they perceive as inherent contradictions between the practice of Hinduism and contemporary modernization and industrialization. For example, a recent newspaper article in the *New York Times* on participation in pilgrimage and bathing rituals in holy rivers of India remarks that the "passion for ancient rituals among the country's 700 million Hindus shows no sign of flagging" despite the nation's advanced technology.[3] In this and many other newspaper and magazine articles, the practice of Hinduism in modern India is represented as anachronistic, and passion for its rituals as newsworthy by foreign journalists. As anthropologists familiar with contemporary Indian religion have documented, improved communications and transportation in India, as well as computer technologies, are actually facilitating knowledge about and practice of Hinduism.

Aspects of Hinduism, as well as other Asian religious philosophies, have historically attracted European and American followers, and are most recently integrated into some "New Age" religious movements. Many of these Western reinterpretations of Hinduism stress its spirituality in contrast to the materialism of the West. While the complex philosophical traditions of Hinduism have much to offer students of religious thought, this simplistic duality obscures the compatibility of India's religious systems with its technologically advanced, consumer-oriented economy.

Throughout its long history, Hinduism, like all the other world religions, created, adapted, and reinterpreted its core set of beliefs and practices on new landscapes. Although not associated with missionary activity and conversion, Hinduism has spread globally since its inception as its followers pursued trade and migration. This process is documented as long ago as the third century B.C.E. during the reign of the Emperor Ashoka, when followers of the early Brahmanical religions of India traveled to and traded throughout Southeast Asia.

Nineteenth-century migration of followers of Hinduism is linked to colonization and indentured servitude; in the Caribbean and parts of the South Pacific descendants of South Asian bonded laborers now thrive in trade, industry, and government. With the post-1960s wave of South Asian immigration to the United States and Canada, Hinduism is truly a global religion; its followers are located throughout Asia, the Caribbean, North America, the Pacific, and Africa.

Its beliefs and practices have both absorbed from as well as contributed to other religious systems. Hinduism is therefore best envisioned as a continuously evolving tradition that blends a set of core beliefs based on a textual tradition with localized and modernized interpretations and practices. In both South Asia and abroad Hinduism is continuously and historically embedded within political process and is intrinsically linked with civil society, identity politics, and state building.

SOUTH ASIAN CIVILIZATION: BEGINNING POINTS

Recent scholarship on the archaeology and linguistics of the South Asian region is shedding new light on the complex history of population movements and the evolution of political and religious traditions. This information provides a useful lens through which to view proto-Hindu history and philosophy.

Archaeological excavations in what is now northwestern India and Pakistan have uncovered cities, towns, and agricultural settlements that flourished for four thousand years along the alluvial plain of the Indus river and its now-dry tributaries. At its height (ca. 2600–1900 B.C.E.) this Indus Valley civilization encompassed more than 250,000 square miles of land, twice the area inhabited by contemporaneous Sumerian and Egyptian cultures.[4]

The Indus Valley civilization was diversified and complex; over 1,500 settlements, towns, and urban centers had trading and political links to each other, as well as to Mesopotamia and parts of Africa. There is also evidence of a unified system of weights and measures that facilitated and unified this geographically far-flung trade. Distinctive patterns of abstract fish scale designs and fig leaves begin to appear on pottery and small ceramic seals throughout the Indus valley by 2800 B.C.E. Although these symbols have yet to be deciphered, some scholars believe they are evidence of an early Indus Valley writing system.

The economic success of these communities is evidenced by a rapid growth in population around 2600 B.C.E., and the emergence of two major urban centers, Mohenjo-Daro and Harappa. Both these cities had a well-planned urban design of multistoried housing complexes, uniform roadways, and water and sewage systems. The Great Bath at Mohenjo-daro may have served as a public bath or ritual center.

The uniform architecture and layout of the city suggest some form of central government, but the sociopolitical structure of this period has yet to be identified. Objects have been unearthed that suggest some form of religious ideology but there is as yet no conclusive evidence of a permanent class of religious specialists. Bovine animal and plant motifs, what may be phallic images, and females with exaggerated breasts and hips are repeated in many different forms in the material record. These images may represent evidence of pre-Hindu deities and icons, but as the Indus script is not yet decipherable the meaning and uses of these suggestive images are unclear.

By about 1900 B.C.E. these once-thriving urban centers began to enter a period of decline and were eventually abandoned. By 1300 B.C.E. the archaeological record reveals an emerging pattern of complex settlements in the Ganga and Yamuna river regions to the west in what is now northern India.

The explanation for the decline and eventual abandonment of the Indus Valley cities has been debated by historians, archaeologists, and linguists for over a century, as have the language and culture of its inhabitants. The first archaeologists to excavate the Indus Valley cities in the early 1920s formulated the now-contested scenario of the "conquest" of the Indus Valley region and the sacking of its cities by peoples originating in Central Asia. This scenario suggests that these so-called "Aryan" invaders descended on the cities of the Indus Valley in armed, horse-drawn chariots, destroying cities and decimating the local population, replacing them with a new language and culture group. Early proponents of this theory based some of their historical scenarios on translations into English of the *Rig Veda*, a collection of sacred hymns and stories that mentions the victories of Aryan peoples, described as fair and light-skinned, over dark-skinned inhabitants, or *dasas*.

In translating and studying Sanskrit texts, nineteenth-century European linguistic scholars discovered the shared origins of Sanskrit and some other South Asian languages with other languages of the Indo-European language family, including French, English, and Greek. These linguistic discoveries shaped historical scenarios that suggested that civilizations of the Indus Valley were associated with the Dravidian group of languages spoken in the southern parts of India. Dravidians were therefore believed to have been conquered by and replaced with the more technologically advanced invaders originating in Central Asia. These "Aryan invaders," some scholars believe, introduced a hierarchically based social system for separating themselves from indigenous conquered people while utilizing them as a forced labor pool of servants and bonded laborers.[5]

More recent archaeological and linguistic scholarship has refined the discussion of Indo-Aryan population movements into South Asia and suggests a series of gradual migrations spanning two thousand years. This population movement may have originated in the middle of the third millennium B.C.E. in what is now the south-central Russian steppes and radiated outward in several directions. These Indo-European migrants used the spoke wheel and fabricated weapons of copper and bronze. Some settled in Europe; others migrated further southward into the Middle East and then westward into South Asia.

The population groups who eventually migrated south into the Iranian plateau and Indian subcontinent are referred to as Indo-Aryans. Evidence of small groups of Indo-Aryan population groups appears in the archaeological record in the Indus River Valley as early as 2000 B.C.E.; by 1200 B.C.E. they controlled the Punjab region and by 600 B.C.E. they had gained political and social control over the Gangetic plain and most of northern India.

Linguistic scholars now suggest that the Indo-Aryan migrants and indigenous Dravidian language-speaking groups interacted with and absorbed language and culture from each other. One linguist calls this contact between these two groups "biculturalism and bilingualism."[6] Material evidence also suggests that over a period in excess of one thousand years successive groups of Indo-Aryans migrated into various regions of the Indus Valley. They interacted with Dravidian language speakers in variety of ways in a bilingual and culturally complex environment. The indigenous population and language groups were eventually absorbed into a political and cultural system dominated by the Indo-Europeans.

Explanations for the abandonment of the Indus Valley cities now focus on processes of environmental shifts and natural disasters, including dramatic changes in the course of the Indus river during the period of urban decline. Flooding and other ecological disruption may have prompted mass migration of settlers westward into the Gangetic plains. Disease, epidemics, and agricultural failure may have also prompted out-migration. There is scant material evidence of military conquest or invasion to totally account for the decline of the Indus Valley civilization, but this scenario about the early history of the subcontinent persists and resonates in the contemporary politics of the region.[7]

INDO-ARYANS AND THE VEDAS

The most enduring contribution of the Indo-Aryans is a massive collection of texts and sacred scriptures composed and orally transmitted in an early form of Sanskrit known collectively as the Vedas, composed and formulated over hundreds of years beginning approximately 1800 B.C.E.. The religious system associated with the Vedic literature is referred to as Brahmanism.

The precise dating of composition of these texts is virtually impossible; their composition evolved over several centuries, and they were not recorded in written form until hundreds, or in some cases, thousands of years after their composition. The *Rig Veda*, for example, was not written down until about 600 B.C.E.; the earliest surviving texts date from about 1200 C.E. Some scholars believe that during the periods of oral transmission the sacred texts were transmitted intact from one generation to another; others suggest that oral traditions will invariably result in regional changes and modifications in the texts over time.

This enormous body of sacred literature is believed to have been "revealed" to sages who transmit these revelations to their followers orally and thus "hear" this sacred wisdom. Later Sanskrit texts distinguish between *sruti*, divine revelations of the Vedas, and *smriti*, human knowledge and traditions contained in the auxiliary texts to the Vedas.[8]

The four Vedas or *Samhitas* in approximate chronological order are *Rig Veda*, *Sama Veda*, *Yajur Veda*, and *Athara Veda*. Later expository prose texts, attached to and commenting on each of these Vedas, are collectively called *Brahmanas*. The *Upanishads*, the latest of the Vedas, includes philosophical commentary and observation compiled between 800 B.C.E. and the fifteenth century C.E. Additional texts, *Vedangas* (literally "the limbs of the Veda"), are a compendium of commentary that do not share the revelatory status of the Vedas, but they have come, over time, to be categorized within the Vedic corpus.

The Vedas are concerned with prayer, ritual, and sacrifice; the Sanskrit term *brahman* has many meanings, including the prayers themselves and the power inherent in their recitation. The same term denotes the ritual specialists (alternatively Anglicized as "Brahmin") who had exclusive access to the language and content of the Vedas. Because of their control over the performance of sacrifices and ritual necessary for both personal and political order, Brahmans emerge as a significant status group in early Indian history.

RIG VEDA

The *Rig Veda* is the oldest of the Vedic compilations. Among the world's oldest intact religious texts, it consists of over 1,000 hymns containing a total of 10,000 verses. Composed over several hundred years, it was compiled into a single collection in approximately 1200–1000 B.C.E. The work as a whole was transmitted orally by religious specialists who had exclusive access to these texts.

The creation of the universe is discussed in the *Rig Veda*, with many different scenarios proposed. In some hymns the gods Indra and Varuna are described as the creators of the universe; in the *Atharva Veda* in a hymn to *Kala*, or Time, an intellectual abstraction is described as its source. In the following Creation Hymn the poets of the *Rig Veda* are vague and provocative concerning the question of creation of universe. An explanation is presented, immediately followed by the suggestion that perhaps even this explanation is unsound.

> There is neither non-existence nor existence then; there was neither the realm of space nor the sky which is beyond. What stirred? Where? In whose protection? Was there water, bottomlessly deep?
>
> There was neither death nor immortality then. There was no distinguishing sign of night nor of day. That one breathed, windless, by its own impulse. Other than that there was nothing beyond.
>
> Darkness was hidden by darkness in the beginning; with no distinguishing sign, all this was water. The life force that was covered with emptiness, that one arose through the power of heat.

Desire came upon that one in the beginning; that was the first seed of mind. Poets seeking in their heart with wisdom found the bond of existence in non-existence.

Their cord was extended across. Was there below? Was there above? There were seed-placers; there were powers. There was impulse beneath; there was giving-forth above.

Who really knows? Who will proclaim it? Whence was it produced? Whence is this creation? The gods came afterwards, with the creation of this universe. Who then knows whence it has arisen?

Whence this creation has arisen—perhaps it formed itself, or perhaps it did not—the one who looks down on it, in the highest heaven, only he knows—or perhaps he does not know.[9]

The *Purusha-Sukta*, Hymn of Man, is one of the most famous of the Vedic hymns. It makes the first known reference to the division of human society into four social orders or *varna*: *Brahman*, priests or ritual specialists; *Kshatriya*, warrior princes and chieftains; *Vaishya*, a group including agriculturalists, merchants, and traders; *Shudra*, laborers and servants to the three other varna. There is little evidence to suggest that the varnas of the *Purusha-Sukta* correspond directly with the fully articulated ranked and hierarchical system of caste and *jati* (localized caste groupings) of later periods of Indian social history. They were more likely a philosophical expression of the components of an idealized, religiously informed society in which the four described groups contribute to an interdependent social and political order.

This hymn describes the creation of the earth and heavens, animate life, human society, and the poetics of *dharma*, or ritual law. They all originate from the sacrifice and dismemberment of the cosmic giant *Purusha*, the primeval Man whose origin is unclear.

The Man has a thousand heads, a thousand eyes, a thousand feet. He pervaded the earth on all sides and extended beyond it as far as ten fingers.

It is the Man who is all this, whatever has been and whatever is to be. He is the ruler of immortality, when he grows beyond everything through food.

Such is his greatness, and the Man is yet more than this. All creatures are a quarter of him; three quarters are what is immortal in heaven.

With three quarters the Man rose upwards, and one quarter of him still remains here. From this he spread out in all directions, into that which eats and that which does not eat.

From him Viraj was born, and from Viraj came the Man. When he was born, he ranged beyond the earth behind and before.

When the gods spread the sacrifice with the Man as the offering, spring was the clarified butter, summer the fuel, autumn the oblation.

They anointed the Man, the sacrifice born at the beginning, upon the sacred grass. With him the gods, Sadhyas, and sages sacrificed.

From that sacrifice in which everything was offered, the melted fat was collected, he made it into those beasts who live in the air, in the forest, and in villages.

From that sacrifice in which everything was offered, the verses and chants were born, the metres were born from it, and from it the formulas were born.

Horses were born from it, and those other animals that have two rows of teeth; cows were born from it, and from it goats and sheep were born.

When they divided the Man, into how many parts did they apportion him? What do they call his mouth, his two arms and thighs and feet?

His mouth became the Brahmin; his arms were made into the Warrior, his thighs the People, and from his feet the Servants were born.

The moon was born from his mind; from his eye the sun was born. Indra and Agni came from his mouth, and from his vital breath the Wind was born.

From his navel the middle realm of space arose; from his head the sky evolved. From his two feet came the earth, and the quarters of the sky was form his ear. Thus they set the worlds in order.

There were seven enclosing sticks from him, and thrice seven fuel-sticks, when the gods, spreading the sacrifice, bound the Man as the sacrificial beast.

With the sacrifice the gods sacrificed to the sacrifice. These were the first ritual laws. These very poets reached the dome of the sky where dwell the Sadhyas, the ancient gods.[10]

As these excerpts illustrate, the *Rig Veda* embodies diffuse and often paradoxical philosophies impossible to reduce to a single systematic description or statement. But some general characteristics and themes can be identified. The Vedic hymns resonate with images of the natural environment: Climate, seasons, and natural events are personified as living and animate essences of the universe, which is pervaded with a cosmic sense of order. This cosmic order, *rita*, is overseen by the gods but supersedes even their power; it links humans and the natural word to the deities who are sometimes guardians, sometimes creators, of the natural realm. The gods or *devas* and female *devis* are both anthropomorphic and closely identified with essential forces of nature. They are not ranked or hierarchical, although they are associated metaphorically with different realms of the universe.

Vedic philosophy generally divides the universe into three realms: the celestial, the atmospheric, and the terrestrial. Varuna, among the most powerful of all Vedic deities, is associated with the celestial realm; Indra, Usha, goddess of dawn, and Surya, the sun deity, are all associated with the atmosphere. Soma, the deity invoked in sacrifice rituals, and Agni, the god of fire and warfare, have a relationship to the terrestrial realm.

The god Indra is often identified with the power of thunder, lightning, and rainfall—critical elements for the survival of agro-pastoral peoples. Indra's celestial powers are also linked to warfare; his cosmic battles with demons (*dasas*) were interpreted by some scholars as evidence of actual battles between indigenous Indus Valley inhabitants and the invading Indo-Aryans. There are also references to divine and semidivine creatures that do not fit into this tripartite division: forest dwelling spirits, demons, female consorts of the gods, and abstractions of human qualities, including Faith and Anger.

The performance of sacrificial ritual is a dominant theme in many of these texts. These rituals are described in the Vedas as being performed in two different contexts: the domestic and the political. Sacrifice as ritual to maintain domestic order is associated with the gods Agni and Varuna, the deities of fire and maintainer of social order. Public performance of sacrifice rituals had a different goal: challenging death and achieving the immortality of the deities. These rituals are associated with the warrior deity Indra and the god Soma, and were significant mechanisms by which competing chieftains established political authority and legitimacy.

Soma is a multifaceted element of ritual: It is the name of both the hallucinogenic liquid ingested during the ritual (made from an as yet unidentified plant) as well as the deity invoked during the ceremony. After having completed the Soma rituals, the sacrificer is believed to have attained immorality. The following hymn to the god Soma from the *Rig Veda* describes his awesome and elusive power.

> This restless Soma—you try to grab him but he breaks away and overpowers everything. He is a sage and a seer inspired by poetry.
>
> He covers the naked and heals all who are sick. The blind man sees; the lame steps forth. Soma, you are a broad defense against those who hate us, both enemies we have made ourselves and those made by others.
>
> Through your knowledge and skills, rushing forward you drive out of the sky and the earth the evil deed of the enemy . . .
>
> . . . Be kind and merciful to us, Soma; be good to our heart, without confusing our powers in your whirlwind.
>
> King Soma, do not enrage us; do not terrify us; do not wound our heart with dazzling light. Give help. When you see the evil plans of the gods in your own house. Generous king, keep away hatreds, keep away failures.[11]

Some of the dialogs in the *Rig Veda* portray mortal women and female deities boldly challenging the authority of their husbands and consorts. Others describe females pursuing their sexual partners with candor and lustfulness equal to their male counterparts. Alongside this sexual bantering, however, are references to the dangers of female sexuality and the primacy of the spiritual and ritual power associated with male celibacy. Some observers find in these intriguing and somewhat paradoxical references evidence of gender equality in the Vedic period which subsequently disappears in texts and Hindu social norms of later periods of history.

In the Vedic philosophical system there is no distinction between religion and the attainment of material or worldly pleasures, and no dichotomy between the "sacred" and "profane" realms of existence. The literature addresses divine and abstract issues as well as problems of daily life. Some of its prayers and incantations are designed to attain success in secular activities, like warfare, gambling, or travel. Other Vedic dialogs and commentaries reflect domestic concerns, including sexuality, adultery, incest prohibitions, and marital harmony. The poets seem to be suggesting that all activities, whether abstract contemplation about the nature of the universe or the details of family life, are infused with cosmic meaning. In the Vedas, ". . . religion extends out into every aspect of life, not merely the official religious moments."[12]

BRAHMANAS AND RITUAL SACRIFICE

Prose texts collectively called Brahmanas, associated with the period of approximately 1200 B.C.E. to 600 B.C.E., are appended to each of the four Vedic Samhitas. These commentaries elaborate on ritual sacrifice and the nature and use of prayer, or brahman. During this historical period, pastoral nomadic Indo-Aryan society transformed into settled agrarian lifestyle, a transition facilitated by iron-producing technology which allowed these agriculturalists to develop the plow and to clear the heavily forested Gangetic plain.

As in many other parts of the world, settled agriculture in South Asia corresponded with significant social and political developments. Agriculture provides many of the material conditions necessary for supporting large densely populated and economically diverse communities. Economic and political specialization creates status and class distinctions associated with different occupational groups and their differential access to valued resources.

Throughout the Gangetic plains emerging political leaders drew on the Vedic rituals to legitimize and extend their authority by public and conspicuous displays of ritual and ceremony. The rulers and the Brahmans who controlled the performance of ritual formed the interdependent classes that divided political and religious leadership.

The Brahmanas expand on the concepts of ritual and sacrifice articulated in earlier texts of the *Rig Veda*, as well as redefine the nature of cosmology and the pantheon. In the Brahmanas the gods are no longer the omnipotent creators of the universe but are rendered powerless before the magic of ritual. This "demotion" of the deities from omnipotent to servant may be a symbolic representation of the structure of a society in which the king's political power is tempered by the ritual power of Brahmans. As the king's authority was linked with his ability to compel the gods to grant his wishes, the role of sacrifice, and of the ritual specialists in the king's court, grew. Elaborate state sacrifices, such as the *Asvamedha* (horse sacrifice) and the ceremonies surrounding royal coronations, developed during the period of the Brahmanas and suggest increasing reliance of the political rulers on the Brahmanical class of ritual specialists.

The Brahmanas expand on the themes of domesticated social order and individual immortality, and the concurrent role of ritual specialists as critical to attaining these goals. These two themes, the domination of religious process by the Brahmans and the tension between individual salvation and the goals of political order, are creative forces that underlie much of the subsequent history of South Asian religious and philosophical traditions.

The Upanishads and Challenges to Brahmanical Authority

The Upanishads, the latest works of the Vedas, are speculative and philosophical discussions appended to the four Vedic Samhitas. The oldest of these texts were composed between 800 and 400 B.C.E; the latest were composed as late as the fifteenth century C.E. As a body of work the 112 Upanishads are designated Vedanta, the end of the Veda. They expand on concepts and ideas already articulated in the Vedas and generally attempt to reconcile the role of the individual behavior and action within the larger philosophical framework of cosmic order.

The Upanishads explore the nature of knowledge, the role of the *guru* or teacher, and the position of the Brahman in this increasingly personal exploration for ultimate meaning and reconciliation. Some of these texts critique the exclusive control of Brahmans over ritual language, knowledge, and practice. In this verse fragment, exclusive reliance on ritual, and presumably the specialists who perform them, is analogous to blindness to the true meaning of religious devotion that dooms the ignorant to interminable cycles of death and rebirth:

> . . . when the flame flickers as the oblation fire has been kindled, then, between the offerings of the two portions of clarified butter one should proffer his principal oblations—an offering made with faith . . .
>
> Unsteady, indeed, are those boats in the form of sacrifices, eighteen in number, in which is prescribed only the inferior work. The fools who delight in this sacrificial ritual as the highest spiritual good go again and again through the cycle of old age and death.
>
> Abiding in the midst of ignorance, wise only according to their own estimate, thinking themselves to be learned, but really hard-struck, these fools go round in a circle like blind men led by one who is himself blind . . . [13]

The Upanishads contain debates and dialogs between teachers and disciples which articulate the processes of transmigration of the soul (*atman*) and rebirth (*samsara*), the perpetual wandering of the soul through a cycle of birth and rebirth, associated with pain and suffering of mortal cycles of life and death. The principal of *karma* suggests that the conditions of each rebirth are directly dependent upon an individual's actions in previous lives. In these discussions *moksha*, or release from mortal pain, is not obtained through ritual practices, which may at best provide some temporary relief to this cycle, but ultimately through an individual's withdrawal from preoccupation with the material world.

The Upanishads, while containing elaboration of philosophical issues of tremendous subsequent importance, still maintain their Vedic affiliations. They do not reject the Brahmanical order, but they expand on ideas articulated throughout the Vedas which were given less importance during earlier periods of ritual and political development. And while they articulate the root metaphors of karma, samsara, and moksha, the Upanishads do not dictate any single formula by which to achieve spiritual liberation; rather they articulate multiple philosophical and intellectual perspectives. Many of the philosophical concepts in the Upanishads are similar to those associated with early Buddhism and with Jainism, demonstrating the religious syncretism and interactions of this period in South Asian history.

The Emergence of Classical Hinduism

The philosophical and religious environment throughout South Asia by the sixth century B.C.E. is one of enormous dynamism. Several concurrent threads in philosophical and religious thought are apparent from the texts and proliferation of non-Vedic movements associated with this period. The political power of the Brahmans may have been partially eclipsed by more individualistic cults and ascetic movements associated with the worship of a single deity, but they maintain their social and philosophical influence through their continuing exclusive access to Sanskrit religious texts and ritual.

Many other religious movements emerge as challenges to Brahmanical hegemony. Buddhism and Jainism, which continue to flourish in contemporary forms, were founded by historically documented warrior-princes, each of whom lived in Northern India during the sixth century B.C.E. Mahavira, the first Jain prophet, and

Siddartha Gautama, later called the Buddha or Enlightened One, inspired followers by their own life examples. They abandoned their political power and high station in the material world and adopted ascetic lifestyles, seeking self awareness as a path to liberation through meditation and nonviolence.

The more orthodox Vedic traditions continue to evolve and flourish and articulate multiple philosophical and performative norms. The literature of this period includes the first description of *yoga*, a system of psychophysical practices that draws from ascetic traditions.

Another major contribution of this period is the Dharmashastra literature, religious law, and treatises stressing the social order of society according to adherence to the principles of *dharma* and *varna*. The term dharma refers to an evolving concept, first introduced in the Vedas, of order and duty. It has both a generalized meaning of what constitutes the order of the universe and any individual's duties within the world; in the Dharmashastras the concept is more clearly articulated as a system of differential duties according to social position, gender, and life stage.

Dharma is also articulated within the framework of the oppositional characteristics of purity and pollution. The Dharmashastras all recognize and presuppose the concept of pollution, which can be either permanent, attached to a person throughout his or her lifetime by virtue of birth group, or impermanent and subject to reversal by ritual. The major sources of pollution are substances related to death or to bodily fluids. Pollution is transmittable and "contagious" both directly and indirectly; food and water can be polluting by virtue of the form of its preparation and/or the ritual status of the person who prepares it.[14]

One of the most often-quoted of all the Dharmashastras is the Manava Dharmashastra, or the Code of Manu (ca. third century C.E.). This work rearticulates varna theory and contains a description of the various rights, duties, and obligations of each of the four varna. The Code of Manu also describes the punishments meted out to members of these groups for violations of social and ritual order; the most serious of those punishments are reserved for the lowest groupings who presume to either criticize or emulate the behaviors of the "twice-born" or Brahman, Kshatriya, and Vaishya varna.

The distinction between the Shudra category and the other three varna eventually leads to the emergence of the concept of Untouchability. The exact process by which Untouchability emerges in Hindu traditions is difficult to document historically; some scholars believe it has its earliest expression in the Dharmashastras. Sprinkled throughout these and Buddhist texts of this period are references to "excluded" groups—social groupings whose members, by virtue of occupation, are excluded from interaction with the twice-born varnas, and who are distinguished from Shudras. Some texts mention the division of the fourth varna into "included" and "excluded" Shudras. While it is tempting to seek direct parallels between textual and historical references to social groupings outside the pale of varna categorization and Untouchability, no sources directly link these textual references to the hierarchical and ranked caste-based practices, based on rules of marriage and concepts of purity and pollution, that emerge later in Indian social history.

Just as society as a whole was divided into four categories in the Codes of Manu, so too is the life of a twice-born man; each of these stages was associated with particular rights, duties and obligations of behavior and ritual. The first stage requires a boy to study with a guru or teacher, maintenance of a celibate lifestyle, and become learned in the Vedas. The second stage, or householder, is devoted to marriage, family, and accumulation of wealth. The third stage is one in which a man turns over to his sons his material possessions and retreats into the forest to live an ascetic lifestyle of contemplation and poverty. The final stage of renunciation (*sannyasin*) requires severing connections with worldly goods and sensual attachments. Ideally the sannyasin wanders without possessions, naked and alone, relying entirely on others for food and shelter. Through this progression of ideal life stages a man approaches the goal of moksha, or release from eternal rebirth. The articulation of the third and fourth stages resonates with principles articulated in the Buddhist and Jain texts and reflects the assimilative and syncretic characteristics of the religious environment of this period.

The period of the emergence of Classical Hinduism (ca. 300–700 C.E.) is associated with the efflorescence of worship of Brahma, Vishnu, and Shiva. This three-part pantheon, mentioned in the Vedas, integrates the three interdependent principles of creation, protection, and destruction. Brahma worship declined early in the history of Hinduism; Vishnu and Shiva remain in the iconography and worship cults of classical Hinduism as preeminent figures of divine power in the Hindu pantheon.

Vishnu, in his various forms and incarnations (*avatars*) is a prominent figure in the great epics *Mahabharata* and *Ramayana*. Both these works originate in the Sanskrit oral poetic traditions; they were, and continue to be, told and retold by bards to public audiences. Their narrative forms have been adapted to integrate local language, preferences, and images. This tradition continues; both epics were recently adopted into widely popular serial dramas, with weekly episodes appearing on the state-owned Indian national television system, *Doordarshan*, for over two years.

Both epics describe great battles, wars, and rivalries for power between Kshatriya clans. Human conflict is mirrored through the participation of gods, demons, animals, and the cosmic forces themselves. The *Mahabharata* contains one of the most famous sections of all Sanskrit poetry, the *Bhagavad Gita*. In it Vishnu appears as Krishna, a prince with superhuman characteristics who both participates in and manipulates events. Toward the end of this great epic about a cosmic war of succession between rival clans, Krishna engages in a dialogue with the prince Arjuna, who is suddenly seized with doubt and fear over fighting his kinsmen, teachers, and allies. Krishna argues that dharma, or duty, is not incompatible with mortal warfare and encourages Arjuna to both military prowess and spiritual devotion.

In the *Ramayana*, Vishnu appears in the form of Rama, a prince of Ayodhya who throughout this epic engages in life and death struggles with Ravana and other demons. A major narrative thread of the *Ramayana* concerns the abduction of Rama's loyal and devoted wife Sita by Ravana; this narrative provides the backdrop by which Sita's selfless devotion and loyalty to her husband and his family are continually demonstrated. Sita's example of constancy and selflessness to her duties as wife and daughter-in-law, to the point of her own voluntary self-destruction, continues to provide a model of the ideal wife, mother, and daughter-in-law in contemporary Hindu society.

The multiple aspects of Shiva evolve fully in the *Puranas* (literally Ancient Stories), a compendium of popular and public religious instructional texts and legends compiled over almost one thousand years. The Puranas are regarded by some as "the Bible of modern Hinduism" in that they contain, in popular and accessible form, many of the enduring myths and stories of the Hindu deities.

Shiva is an extremely complex character who is both creator and destroyer, benevolent and fearsome, ascetic and erotic. These various aspects of Shiva are not generally represented as separate avatars, as in the case of Vishnu, but as various aspects of his character. He has a more remote domain, both literally and figuratively, than does Vishnu. Shiva resides as a great ascetic on the Himalayan Mount Kailash; he intervenes in earthly events but always retreats back to his mountain abode. In material expressions of temple art and religious sculpture he appears in many different forms, one of the most famous being Nataraj. With one raised foot, encircled by a ring of flame, his dance inspires both the creation and destruction of the universe.

While women figure prominently as wives and mothers in the *Mahabharata* and *Ramayana*, the concept of the female deity evolves in the Puranas and other literary and artistic forms of the fifth, sixth, and seventh centuries C.E.. The major male deities have wives or consorts: Lakshmi is the consort to Vishnu; Parvati to Shiva, and Sarasvati to Brahma. These female deities symbolize earthly powers beyond their wifely status; Lakshmi is the goddess of prosperity and domestic good fortune, and Sarasvati the goddess of knowledge. More significantly the goddesses embody *shakti*, the divine, energizing power of all deities, whose source is distinctively female. The male deities require shakti, in the form of their consorts, to transform their passive powers into action; Shiva and Vishnu are therefore often represented in temple art and iconography accompanied by their consorts. The power of the goddesses emanates from within themselves; they are therefore often unaccompanied by their male consorts.

Some Puranic texts make reference to a great unmarried goddess with supreme and violent powers; she appears in one form as Durga, the warrior goddess born from the collective anger of all the gods. She is portrayed carrying weapons, riding on a lion, and draped in a necklace of skulls. Durga is interpreted in many local idioms and throughout the classical and modern periods of Hinduism, and appears, for example, as Kali, the black goddess, in Bengal, where she is honored annually in the Durga *puja* (worship and celebration) as the champion of tribals and other downtrodden peoples.

Temple Worship

From the period of approximately 700 C.E. onward Hindu temples emerge as sites for both worship and secular affirmation of the princely political functions. The efflorescence of temple building throughout India from the first millennium onward bespeaks not only a flourishing and somewhat unified religious system (although always decentralized and nonhierarchical in structure) as well as a vibrant economic system by which temple patronage and fundraising supports the arts and crafts of temple complex construction. These monumental structures, some rising 300 feet, dominated the landscape with their carvings and massive images honoring the deities. Equally important to their religious significance, temple complexes were also an expression of local and regional political unity and the power and influence of rulers.

Various cults of deities and multiple interpretations of the earlier practices of Brahmanism and Hinduism prompted the alternative modes of worship associated with this chronological period. Among them are *Bhakti,* or devotional movements, which stress personal devotion to the deities through songs and prayers in local languages, usually expressed through group following of a particular saintly prophet or poet.

India's religious tapestry was further enriched by the migration of ethnic and religious traditions from the Middle East. Muslim, Christian, and Jewish merchants inhabited India's trading centers. Parsis, adherents of the ancient Iranian religion of Zoroastrianism, sought religious refuge in India beginning in the tenth century C.E. and continue to maintain a distinct religious identity in urban centers throughout India. India's religious environment throughout the first millennium was characterized by the followers of multiple, co-existing ideological systems.

Foreign Rulers in India

Throughout the second millennium C.E. foreign rulers controlled much of the subcontinent. Their political and social influence was profound; equally significant and enduring is the impact of Islamic and Christian ideologies and philosophies.

The western frontier of India was periodically invaded and successfully defended by Indian princes and local rulers for two hundred years before the successful incursions of Mahmud, the ruler of Ghazna (now Afghanistan) in the eleventh century C.E.. These military incursions didn't result in permanent settlements until 1206, when the Ghurids, a successor dynasty in Afghanistan, established the Sultanate of Delhi, which lasted over 300 years under several different dynasties.

The Mughal empire was founded in India by the central Asian warrior-prince Babur. Descended from Ghengiz Khan and the Turkish conqueror Timor, Babur led the defeat of the Delhi Sultanate in 1526 and established the empire named for his Mongol forebears. At its height the Mughal Empire controlled vast regions of what is now northern India and Pakistan. Although lasting only three centuries, this dynasty is associated with some of the most dramatic accomplishments in painting and architecture, including the magnificent Taj Mahal in Agra. These Islamic rulers of India were for the most part tolerant of their subjects' multiple religious traditions. During the 50-year reign of Babur's grandson Akbar (1556–1605) the Delhi court was a cosmopolitan center of religious, artistic, and literary production, meticulously documented in miniature paintings and illustrated manuscripts.

Some forms of Hinduism integrated elements of Sufism or Islamic devotional prayer and dance. The Muslim weaver-poet Kabir (1440–1518) attracted a large following among both Muslims and Hindus with his poetry devotional songs. His followers pursued a spiritual path that rejected the orthodox sectarianism of both Islam and Hinduism, encouraging instead a syncretic spiritual path of personal devotion to and identification with a single deity.

The Sikh religion emerges in the Punjab region of northern India among the followers of Guru Nanak (1469–1538), whose own life symbolizes some of the syncretism between Hindu and Muslim traditions of the period. He was born into an upper-caste family in a village inhabited by both Hindus and Muslims, and was well versed in both religious ideologies. His writings and teachings articulate a system of personal devotional worship of an omnipotent single creator. The followers of Guru Nanak gradually identified themselves as a separate religious community and mobilized political opposition to both Mughal and British rule. Some Sikh followers aspired for Khalistan, a separate state; this proposal was rejected at the time of independence and partition but some Sikhs continued to press their demands for political autonomy through the early 1980s.

The first Europeans to reach India were Portuguese; when Vasco da Gama sailed into the Malabar (southwestern) coast city of Calicut in 1498, it was a thriving port city inhabited by traders and merchants of all religions from Asia and Eastern Africa. The Portuguese dominated Indian Ocean trade for the following century using the coastal island of Goa as their economic and political base in India. Goa also became a Christian religious settlement, attracting the first European missionaries to India. In the late sixteenth century the Mughul Emperor Akbar invited Jesuit missionaries from Goa to join religious and philosophical discussions in his court.

French and British trading settlements followed in India's coastal port communities in the seventeenth century; by the early nineteenth century the British ousted their European trading rivals and consolidated their power over the Indian princely states. British and Canadian Protestant missionaries came to India after the mid-nineteenth century. While not converting large numbers of followers they made their most significant inroads among the poor and low caste, and among tribal groups. They were also important in influencing British social policy and provided extensive input in articulating the colonial agenda of social and educational reforms.

Indian intellectuals like Rammohan Roy of Bengal (1772–1833), who was a scholar of both European and South Asian religions, critiqued some of the gender and class-based inequalities of Hinduism. He sought in both Sanskrit texts and European religious and political histories the basis for a socially relevant Hinduism.

The intellectual descendants of Rammohan Roy, poets and writers throughout the nineteenth and early twentieth centuries, reinterpreted Hinduism as a philosophical as well as political force in British India. The life and writings of the great Mohandas K. Gandhi (1869–1948) illustrate how this towering historical figure integrated some of the theories of South Asian religious traditions, particularly those of nonviolence (*ahimsa*) into the nationalist movement's political strategy. *Satyagraha*, the strategy of nonviolent noncooperation with British rule (a term Gandhi coined and defined as the force born of truth and love or nonviolence) mobilized his followers in a national movement that led to the independence from British rule in 1947.

The religious pluralism that had marked centuries of India's history was not maintained during the colonial and postcolonial periods. Most scholars attribute the onset of violent Hindu-Muslim conflict in South Asia in the twentieth century to colonial period manipulation of the economic and political interests of different religious groups. Immediately following independence, Gandhi was assassinated by a Hindu extremist, who felt he had made too many concessions to the Muslim minority during preindependence negotiations that resulted in partition of India, Pakistan, and East Pakistan (later the independent state of Bangladesh).[15]

The legacies of Hindu-Muslim conflict still resonate in contemporary politics of India. In the late 1980s "Hindutva," or Hindu nationalism, emerged as a major political agenda. Subsequent erosion of voter support for the Congress party, associated with Gandhi, Nehru, and other great political architects of the independence movement, ushered in a period of increasingly communalized and religiously identified coalition building in Indian national and local politics.

Being a Hindu in Modern India

This brief survey of the major textual and historical forces shaping Hinduism only hints at the breadth and scope of religious diversity in modern India. Differences among its 30-plus states and union territories are as profound as the differences among European nations; language, population density, religious traditions and majority religious affiliation, climate, literacy rates, levels of urbanization and industrialization are just some of the important factors that distinguish different states and regions of the country. The snow-covered mountains of Kashmir, with its majority Islamic population, is a world away from the Hindu-dominated regions of the tropical south. In between are the fertile agricultural regions of India, Christian-dominated regions of Goa and Kerala, the Tribal or Adivasi regions of Assam, Bihar, Rajasthan, and Madhya Pradesh, as well as cosmopolitan cities. Although the majority of India's population of almost 900 million still resides in small towns and villages and is engaged in some form of agricultural production as a primary income activity, India's industrial centers rival in technology and marketing sophistication those of Europe and the United States.

Anthropologists have documented the wide variety of social, ritual, and religious practices, particularly in Indian villages.[16] The multiplicity and variety of ritual and ideological systems throughout India, and the proliferation of local deities and mythologies, present analytic challenges to scholars of Hinduism and religion in general. How can these local interpretations be reconciled with the great body of Sanskritic literature and philosophy contained in the oral and written texts of Hinduism?

One theory employs the opposing concepts of "great tradition" and "little traditions"—the former referring to a scriptural, pan-Indian ideological civilization guided by the texts and liturgy of Sanskrit literature and the latter localized co-existing systems of actual practice. This dichotomy contains within it inherent forms of hierarchy and authenticity, the "great tradition" representing a pan-Indian tradition drawing on the Sanskrit texts and their interpretation. Anthropologist C. J. Fuller suggests that understanding the practice of Hinduism lies in ordinary people's practices and beliefs. He distinguishes popular Hinduism, locally articulated religious practices found in the contemporary practice of Hinduism, from textual Hinduism, the philosophical ideas and sacred texts that are primarily the domain of scholars. While the themes of major texts are often present in popular Hinduism, they do not dominate the religious concerns in people's daily lives.[17]

Equally diverse are the manifestations and practices of Hinduism between the northern "Hindi belt" and the southern regions of India. Tribal religious and social practices also vary from mainstream Hindu norms. Despite these variations, however, some generalizations about Hinduism in contemporary India can be made.

The practice of Hinduism suffuses daily life—food, living arrangements, family composition, gender relationships, even where people actually live and with whom—all contain within them norms and ideals expressed by religious traditions. The main expressions of Hinduism are personal and domestically situated. This personal relationship with the deities is compellingly expressed by the care lavished on images in household altars which are often clothed in hand-knit and hand-stitched garments that are changed with the seasons. Many Hindus begin their day with prayer and devotional songs to the images of deities housed in prayer niches or special rooms of their houses. Offerings of money, *ghee* (clarified butter), and special foods to the household images are made daily and throughout the cycle of holidays and feast days of the Hindu religious calendar.

Formal life-stage rituals, like weddings and funerals, are generally supervised and executed by Brahman priests in domestic settings. People regularly visit local temples, both as part of prayer services and for personally motivated exhortations or appeals to favorite deities. The temple itself is conceptualized as a deity's residence or abode. Through its physical layout the temple guides the orderly performance of worship, which culminates in *darshan* or viewing of an image of the temple's major deity in a small enclosed central chamber. *Puja*, a combination of prayer and offerings, is guided by a ritual specialist who is an employee of the temple community. Circumambulation of the temple structure, stopping for prayers and offerings at the images of secondary gods and goddesses, completes the worship experience.

Pilgrimage, journey to sacred sites and temples, is an integral part of the practice of Hinduism. Some of these sacred sites are associated with holy rivers; the Ganges itself is a pilgrimage site as are the cities of Benares and Hardwar on its banks. Temple pilgrimage sites may have specific references to a deity or mythological event; for example, the cities of Mathura and Brindavan are associated with different periods and events in Krishna's life and are regularly visited by his devotees. Whatever the location, the modern pilgrim temporarily enacts some of the traditions of the sannyasin, leaving the comforts of home for a spiritual journey. With the conveniences of modern travel and hotels and restaurants catering to all classes of travelers, and increasingly to nonresident Indians returning on visits, the pilgrimage tends to combine religious experience and tourism, in a seamless and noncontradictory way.

Caste Identity and Modern Hinduism

Probably no subject about India has generated more written commentary than the institution of caste. The division of society into ritually and economically significant groupings continues to inform the Indian social and political landscape. As has been mentioned, the actual history of the evolution of the caste system is difficult, if not impossible, to document.[18] Caste is based on some social principles that, in combination, characterize this South Asian-derived system: endogamy; commensality; hierarchy; purity-pollution distinctions; and traditional occupational specializations.

Castes are endogamous groups based on patrilineal descent; one marries within one's caste group (endogamy) and one's caste affiliation is determined through one's father's caste grouping. There are restrictions on commensality; under caste principles the people from whom one accepts cooked food and water is one of an equal or higher caste ranking. Caste groups are ranked hierarchically, based on the principles of purity and pollution; the higher the ranking, the higher the level of purity. Some of this purity and pollution derives from the traditional occupational specialization of the group; the status that derives from polluting traditional activities is shared throughout the group and is not based on an individual's actions.

In common practice most people refer to their *jati*, rather than "caste" or "varna." There are thousands of jatis throughout India; most of these terms reflect local linguistic and historical derivation and have regional meaning and ranking.

For example, the jati associated with animal tanning and the hauling of carcasses in parts of Rajasthan is Meghwal; in the state of Uttar Pradesh the same occupational and social status is known as Chamar. And more importantly, in terms of local identity a Meghwal of Rajasthan does not have kin or jati affiliation with a Chamar of Uttar Pradesh.

In contemporary Indian politics these affiliations are being forged through political parties and voting blocks attempting to unite diverse low-status poor and oppressed peoples throughout India. The term *dalit* is gaining national acceptance as a pan-Indian social category mobilizing political alliances among groups of people previously divided by jati category and local hierachical divisions.[19]

While the caste system in India is generally believed to be an unchanging and rigid social hierarchy, in actual practice the system contains mechanisms for social change. The traditional system of caste and jati identity is based on residential patterns and intergenerational familiarity with one's rural neighbors and their descent groups. Economic status, apart from birth grouping, emerges as an important mechanism of identity in modern India, often superseding kin-based caste identity. For example, migration from agricultural villages to urban centers allows individuals to redefine their identities according to modern occupations of factory workers, teachers, computer specialists, medical practitioners, and so forth. The anonymity of urban centers somewhat eases this, and one's economic and professional status may counterbalance more traditional identity categories.

Since independence the government of India has had an extensive and controversial affirmative action plan in effect. The Reservation System is so-named because it guarantees or reserves a certain number of seats in state and national legislatures, state-owned colleges and universities, and in government employment, to qualifying castes and tribes. The benefits are extended to all members of the Scheduled Castes and Scheduled Tribes (so-designated by virtue of inclusion on the government's list, or schedule, of qualifying jati). These benefits are intended to help eliminate some of the social and economic discriminations that derive from low-caste status and lack of access to institutions of mobility. They have their roots in the nationalist movement of the early twentieth century, and the efforts of Mahatma Gandhi and other social reformers of the independence period to eliminate some of the stigmas and disadvantages associated with birth into low-status groups. These programs have become increasingly politicized, as various governments have attempted to either increase or decrease the number of qualifying groups. While increasing the range of benefits appeals to dalit voters, upper-caste groups are likewise expressing their resentment of extending these benefits through the ballot box.

In rural communities traditional occupations are being replaced with more "ritually neutral" forms of employment and access to economic resources. Although large land owners continue to be mostly upper-caste members, low-caste and tribal group members now have access to land ownership and are exercising that right all over India. But abandoning traditional occupations does not eliminate the stigma of "untouchability."

Illiteracy, particularly in rural areas, continues to be a major problem throughout India. The illiteracy rates are highest in rural communities; however, villagers are increasingly realizing the value of education for their male children, and are (more slowly) coming to realize the value of literacy for girls as well. Access to many of the educational and employment benefits under the Reservation System is based on the equivalency of a high-school education, so tapping into these benefits is dependent upon schooling for children.

Village and town residential patterns continue to reflect to some degree jati neighborhoods; this is not surprising as sons inherit the homes and lands of their fathers, and bring their new wives to live in their extended households with their parents and male siblings. Their sisters marry generally within their jati and go to reside in similar households in other villages. This inheritance and virilocal postmarital residence pattern tends to perpetuate the jati composition of local neighborhoods. As villages expand and agriculturalists build new houses, they establish new residential patterns based on access to land and home-building sites rather than traditional jati neighborhoods.

Many anthropologists have described and recorded examples of Sanskritization movements, whereby a local jati group will orchestrate group mobility by adopting the ritual and occupational patterns of an upper-caste group.[20] One such movement among the Meghwal jati in southeastern Rajasthan in the late 1980s was initiated by a small group of wealthy jati members whose families have made comparatively large fortunes in the traditional occupation of scavenging and animal hide processing. These *panchayat* or jati council leaders are now urging all Meghwals to cease any activities involving the handling of animal skins or the hauling of carcasses.

The ban on handling leather or animal skins has not yet been entirely accepted throughout the region and in all villages. Resistance is based on the constraints of household and village economies. Some village-based leather workers and shoemakers, who supplement their meager agricultural income with their traditional jati occupation, resent the intrusion of town and city elites into their fragile household and village economies. Some fear that if they refuse to remove carcasses, this would create conflict with the upper-caste groups, particularly with the Rajputs.

As many Meghwals are already small-scale agriculturalists the question of practicing traditional polluting occupations is becoming moot. The goals of the movement are slowly being integrated into the jati panchayat discourse as issues of social and educational reform. In addition, the use of the courts and other state institutions are increasingly being used as vehicles for addressing caste-based discrimination.[21]

While caste matters in modern Indian life, the factors that contribute to both individual and group identify are far more complex than the one designation of jati affiliation. Economic status, employment, education, political party affiliation, and personal skills and abilities also contribute to the multiple status that shape the trajectory of one's life and family.

Women and the Practice of Hinduism

As has been discussed previously, the practice of Hinduism includes daily rituals and practices associated with the domestic realm; many of the ideological norms define appropriate and acceptable behavior for women. Many of the norms and restrictions on women's public activities are articulated through the concept of *parda* (a word which translates literally as curtain, referring to the partition that traditionally divided the male-dominated from female-dominated spaces of large houses). The practices relating to parda are believed by some scholars to be borrowed from the Islamic traditions, as it is not mentioned in the Vedas or other Hindu texts.

Even when parda is observed, it does not equate with female isolation. Although the senior women of traditional households that observe this practice rarely leave their homes and property, they are completely up-to-date on the news of the day; newspapers, television, radios, as well as a steady stream of relatives, servants and tradespeople keep these women apprised of both local and global events. Within these households women, particularly as they mature and become *Dadi*, or the senior woman in a multigenerational household, are active participants in household and family business decision making.

Most marriages are arranged and follow the virilocal postmarital residence pattern whereby women after marriage reside in the extended households of their husbands' family. Arranged marriages generally evolve into warm, loving, and supportive relationships that include the financial and emotional support of a wide range of family members.

Marriage and family norms throughout India assume that a woman will be under the financial and emotional control of male family members throughout her lifetime. Divorce, even in cases of physical or emotional abuse, is generally discouraged.

Women must fight aggressively for access to inheritances from their fathers, despite civil law stipulations that are intended to ensure equal distribution of inheritance among sons and daughters. And if they do manage to inherit what is rightfully theirs under the law from their fathers' estates, women must then at times struggle, legally and personally, to protect that inheritance from their husbands' control.

The dowry system, despite legislative efforts to eliminate it, is still a significant issue in arranging marriages and often places daughters at a distinct disadvantage to their brothers in negotiating marriages and protecting their rights after marriage. Dowry-related disputes after marriage are often the cause of dissension and conflict between the families of a married couple; dissatisfaction with dowry settlements often haunts a marriage for decades. The physical abuse of women by their husbands, when it occurs, is often traced to long-simmering resentments over disputed dowry or perceived failures of the wife's family to deliver promised dowry. The preferred strategy of resolving these marriage disputes is often for a third party—in the case of urban families this could be an attorney or employer—to negotiate a settlement by which it is agreed that physical violence stops and the marriage continues—but often without resolution of the underlying emotional or financial issues.

Many families express the belief that once a woman marries she is the concern of her husband's family, and no longer the responsibility of her parents or brother. After marriage brothers may refuse their sisters long-term or permanent residence in her natal home, out of fear of her claims on the paternal estate. The dowry she carries to her husband and his family at marriage is often seen as her "premortem" inheritance settlement from her father, and as such is sometimes interpreted as the end of her natal family's financial, and sometimes social, responsibility for her.

Dowry death (abuse of women in their in-laws' homes in an effort to increase dowry-related payments from the women's families, abuse that occasionally escalates to a level resulting in the death of the daughter-in-law) has recently become the focus of international media attention. This issue has galvanized women's organizations throughout India to effectively lead a multipronged attack on some of the more socially conservative aspects of police and law enforcement, raising the awareness level of legal institutions to the criminality of domestic abuse generally in Indian society.

Obviously the range of actual behaviors is wide and varied; some families actively intervene in cases of their daughters' or sisters' abuse; parents and brothers may welcome them back to their natal households in times of crisis. But generally emotional, residential, and financial independence of women is discouraged; even in urbanized, cosmopolitan cities like Bombay and New Delhi, an unmarried or divorced woman living independently experiences many forms of social discrimination.[22]

Hinduism and National Political Identity

This brief historical sketch of Hinduism demonstrates its ability to adjust, adapt, and respond to cultural and other forms of change around it. Hinduism in India entering the twenty-first century continues this process. Contemporary Indian politics is characterized by a resurgence of religious-based coalition building and the emergence of ruling coalitions with a specifically religious appeal to voters. Voter discontent with the corruption and economic stagnation associated with the secular Congress party, which held political domination throughout India since independence, has been articulated in elections in the early 1990s through support of various political parties with a specifically "Hindutva" or Hindu nationalist agenda.

The explosion of nuclear devices in India in mid-1998 was celebrated by some as a symbol of the political power of the Hindutva agenda. The Bharatiya Janata Party, or BJP, which leads the coalition government that replaced the congress-dominated government, faces voter challenges over their inability to solve domestic economic problems, eliminate corruption, and halt inflation that has dramatically affected the price of basic food commodities throughout India.

Due to the economic success of many South Asian immigrants, Hinduism abroad is flourishing. Major centers of Indian immigration throughout Europe, the United States, and Canada boast newly constructed Hindu temples which employ traditional forms of art and architecture; the demand for these skills abroad has stimulated demand for traditional artisans in India. In diaspora communities the temple complex is a site of worship and religious training, as well as for educating a new generation of overseas-born youngsters in the culture of the region from which their parents hail. Language classes, cooking demonstrations, and Indian dance instruction co-exist comfortably in these religious complexes with ritual, prayer, and meditation.[23]

Melas or fairs, corresponding with the Hindu cycle of holidays are an opportunity for displaying the food, dance, clothing, and artistic traditions to a diverse public audience. Local politicians also utilize these gatherings to publicly express their support for causes and positions sympathetic to the political leanings of the South Asian community hosting the event.

Newly constructed Hindu temple complexes in North America draw on computer technologies to serve multiple interests of their members; many of them have Web sites, special-interest "chat rooms," and other forms of computerized technology and communications systems. They offer services of secular concerns to the community, including college preparatory courses, academic tutoring, and classes to help prepare students to take standardized college entrance exams.

Web sites and SAT preparation courses may seem at first glance to run counter to Western ideas about temples as a sites of worship; on closer consideration, however, these activities are the continuation of religious traditions from South Asia. Hinduism is a dynamic religious tradition that has continuously adapted to many forms of change, as well as reforming itself from within. The history of Hinduism resonates with this seamless blending of the ideological, political, economic, and domestic concerns of the community enacted within its spiritual spaces.

NOTES

1. "Introduction," by Richard H. Davis in *Religions of India in Practice,* ed. Donald S. Lopez, Jr. (Princeton: Princeton University Press, 1995), p. 5.

2. *Imagining India* by Ronald Inden (London: Blackwell Publishers. 1990), p. 83. The critique of the historiography of South Asia is expanded in a series of publications collectively referred to as Subaltern Studies, scholarship that documents the often-ignored role of nonelites throughout history. See *A Subaltern Studies Reader 1986–1995,* ed. Ranajit Guha (Minneapolis: University of Minnesota Press, 1997).

3. "Ancient Hindu Festival Thrives in Computer-Age India" by John F. Burns, *New York Times,* April 16, 1998, A10.

4. See "Birth of a Civilization" by Jonathan Mark Kenoyer, *Archaeology* 51 (Jan./Feb. 1998): 54-61 and *The Archaeology of Early Historic South Asia: The Emergence of Cities and States* by F. R. Allchin (Cambridge: Cambridge University Press, 1997).

5. Indian historian Romila Thapar suggests that this construction of early Indian history resonates with the social and racial constructions of nineteenth-century European culture. For a discussion of European racial theory and the interpretation of Indian history, see "Ideology and the Interpretation of Early Indian History" in Romila Thapar's *Interpreting Early India* (Oxford: Oxford University Press, 1992), and *Aryans and British India* by Thomas R. Trautmann (Berkeley: University of California Press, 1997).

6. See Franklin C. Southworth "Reconstructing Social Context from Language: Indo-Aryans and Dravidian Prehistory," in *The Indo-Aryans of Ancient South Asia: Language, Material Culture and Ethnicity,* ed. George Erdosy (Berlin De Gruyter, 1995).

7. See Romila Thapar's "Imagined Religious Communities? Ancient History and the Modern Search for a Hindu Identity" in *Interpreting Early India* (Oxford: Oxford University Press, 1992).

8. Throughout the balance of this essay, Sanskrit terms will be transliterated by omitting diacritical marks indicating Sanskrit phonemic forms not found in English.

9. *The Rig Veda: An Anthology,* translated and annotated by Wendy Doniger O'Flaherty (London: Penguin Books, 1981), p. 25.

10. Ibid., pp. 30–31.

11. Ibid., p. 121.

12. Ibid., p. 229.

13. *Sources of Indian Tradition,* Wm. de Bary et al. eds (New York: Columbia University Press, 1958), p. 28.

14. Some scholars believe that the oppositional forces of pollution and purity, combined with the social hierarchy, endogamy, and rules of commensality, form the essence of the South Asian caste system. Louis Dumont in *Homo Hierarchicus* (Chicago: University of Chicago Press, 1980) says that the caste system is reducible to the basic principles of the opposition between pollution and purity and the hierarchical model of society inherent in it. He particularly focuses on the relationship between Brahmans and Kshatriyas, priests and kings. For a critique of Dumont see Inden 1990 and Nicholas B. Dirks, *The Hollow Crown,* 2nd ed. (Ann Arbor: University of Michigan Press, 1993).

15. The nationalist period of Indian history is detailed in Stanley Wolpert's *A New History of India,* 4th ed. (Oxford: Oxford University Press, 1992), a comprehensive and concise history of the South Asian region. For a recent biography of Gandhi, see Judith M. Brown's *Gandhi Prisoner of Hope* (Oxford: Oxford University Press New Delhi, 1992).

16. William and Charlotte Wiser's *Behind Mud Walls* was originally published in 1930 and updated in several subsequent editions, including the 1989 edition with an appended essay by anthropologist Susan Wadley, "The Village in 1984" (Berkeley: University of California Press, 1989). *Village India,* edited by McKim Marriott (Chicago: University of Chicago Press, 1955), is a collection of ethnographic essays on religion, caste, and social life in rural communities. *The Remembered Village* by M. N. Srinivas (Berkeley: University of California, 1976) is a widely read ethnography by the Indian-born and British-educated anthropologist M. N. Srinivas, who conducted fieldwork in a village in Mysore in South India from which his family originated. *Society in India* by David G. Mandelbaum (Berkeley: University of California Press, 1970) is a comprehensive, two-volume reference on social, cultural, and religious life in rural India based on field studies. Ronald Inden critiques the anthropology of village studies in Chapter Four of *Imagining India.*

17. C. J. Fuller's *The Camphor Flame: Popular Hinduism and Society in India* (Princeton: Princeton University Press, 1992) contains a discussion of the "great tradition/

little tradition" debate in anthropology, and differences in ritual and religious practices in the north and south of India.

18. For a description of multiple theories on the origin of the caste system in India see Morton Klass, *Caste: The Emergence of the South Asian Social System* [Prospect Heights, IL: Waveland Press, 1997 (1980)].

19. See *The Untouchables: Subordination, Poverty and the State in Modern India* by Oliver Mendelsohn and Marika Vicziany (Cambridge: Cambridge University Press, 1998).

20. The anthropologist M. N. Srinivas first describes this process in *Religion and Society Among the Coorgs of South India* (Oxford, 1952).

21. For a discussion of this Sanskritization movement among the Meghwals of Rajasthan, see Maxine Weisgrau *Interpretation of Development: Local Histories, Local Strategies* (Lanhorn, MD: University Press of America, 1997), pp. 30–31.

22. For an introduction to the large and varied literature on women in India, see *Women in India: Two Perspectives* by Doranne Jacobson and Susan S. Wadley (Manohar, 1995); *Don't Marry Me To A Plowman: Women's Everyday Lives in Rural North India* by Patricia Jeffery and Roger Jeffery (Boulder: Westview, 1996); and *Siva and Her Sisters: Gender, Caste and Class in Rural South India* by Karin Kapadia (Boulder: Westview, 1995). For a historical perspective on women in India, see *Recasting Women: Essays in Indian Colonial History*, Kumkum Sangari and Sudesh Vaid eds. (New Brunswick: Rutgers University Press. 1990).

23. See *From the Ganges to the Hudson: Indian Immigrants in New York City*, by Johanna Lessinger (Boston: Allyn and Bacon, 1995).

Thirteen

Buddhism

Marcia Calkowski
Regina University

Buddhism has been described by religious scholars and popularizers as being "an atheistic religion," a psychological religion, and a religion of renunciation. Anthropologists, however, look at Buddhism within specific cultural and social contexts and ask not what Buddhist doctrine says, but rather such questions as how do Buddhist practitioners interpret this doctrine, and how do these interpretations, Buddhist ritual practices, and forms of monastic organization relate to sociocultural concepts and practices? Before we turn to the specific approaches anthropologists have taken to these general questions, we must look at the origin, initial development, and spread of Buddhism.

THE ORIGINS OF BUDDHISM

The Buddhist tradition emerged from the teachings of Siddharta Gautama, later known as Buddha ("the enlightened one") or Lord Buddha. Siddharta Gautama was born about 560 B.C.E. in Lumbini, which presently lies just north of Nepal's southern border with India and about 100 miles from the Indian city of Benares. As the son of Shuddhodanna, a rajah or hereditary ruler of a local principality, Siddharta Gautama was born to a life of privilege and luxury. His mother, Maya, was known as a woman of exceptional virtue who dreamed auspiciously that a white elephant had entered her womb. Ten months later she gave birth to Siddharta beneath a grove of trees on the night of the full moon in May amid supernatural portents. Maya died seven days after giving birth, which was later interpreted by Buddhist sages as signifying that as she had fulfilled her great purpose in life, to give birth to a Buddha; she could fulfill no other.

    The prince's name Siddharta was bestowed on him by his parents and means "he who has attained his goal." Siddharta was raised by his mother's sister and tutored, as would befit a noble's son, in the arts, sciences, and athletics. But since his father, the rajah, had been given a prophecy that his son was destined either to be a great ruler or a homeless wanderer, Siddharta's education fell short of exposing him to the harsher realities of life. To prevent his son from turning to religion and adopting the life of an ascetic holy man, the rajah took substantial precautions to shelter Siddharta from any knowledge of suffering. He built three palaces suited to the different seasons for his son to occupy and staffed them with only youthful attendants. Whenever Siddharta ventured outside these palaces, his father made certain that the sick and elderly were out of sight. In his adolescence, Siddharta married a princess called Yashodara, who gave birth to a son Siddharta named Rahula. Since Rahula means "chain," Buddhist sages suggested that the name reflected Siddharta's dissatisfaction with the life he led.

In his twenties, Siddharta undertook four journeys which were to transform his perception of the world. During the first journey, Siddharta noticed a feeble old man and learned that aging was the future of every being. On his second journey, he encountered a man wasting away from a repelling illness and thus became aware that illness was an ever-present possibility of existence. The third journey exposed Siddharta to the cremation of a corpse, acquainting him with the fate of all mortals. These discoveries destroyed his peace of mind and put his father's efforts to cheer him to naught. On his fourth journey, Siddharta encountered a wandering holy man who traveled with his begging bowl and radiated contentment.

Concluding that he could restore his peace of mind if he followed this holy man's example, Siddharta stole away from his wife and child while they slept and embarked on what at first appeared to be a traditional Hindu search for knowledge. Siddharta shaved his head and shed his princely garments for a simple yellow robe. He took instruction from Brahminic gurus and applied himself to yoga exercises in an attempt to unite his self with the origin and meaning of the universe. But Siddharta, unconvinced that his gurus could reveal the path to enlightenment, chose to take up the path of extreme asceticism, which was currently popular among Jains and followers of other sects. He reached a grove by a flowing river and resolved to sit under the trees and subject his body to the strictest ascetic practices such as sitting on thorns and consuming only one grain of rice per day. As a result, Siddharta grew extremely gaunt, but reasoned that to discipline the body would clarify the mind. However, after maintaining this asceticism for five years, Siddharta concluded that he was no nearer to enlightenment than he had been before beginning these practices, and that rather than clarifying his mind through the severe discipline of his body, his body was failing to sustain his intellect. Thus, Siddharta resolved to restore his bodily health and again took up the path of a homeless wanderer with his begging bowl. As he sat under a banyan tree (a fig tree), a young village woman presented him with a bowl of rice she had prepared as an offering. Siddharta's acceptance of this bowl drew sharp criticism from five fellow ascetics and marked his determination to seek another path to enlightenment.

To that end, Siddharta broke his journey at what is now called Bodhgaya, seated himself beneath a fig tree which came to be known as the Bodhi tree or the "tree of knowledge," and began to meditate on the nature of his failure to achieve salvation. It is under this tree that he finally attained enlightenment and became the Buddha in a three-stage process. During his first night of meditation, he witnessed his previous lives. During the second night of meditation, he envisioned the continuous cycle of birth, death, and rebirth, and the law that perpetuated it. On the third night of meditation, he realized the four noble truths, which account for suffering in the world, the cause of this suffering, the possibility of release from suffering, and how to attain that release. Upon completing these meditations, Siddharta was the Buddha, which meant that as an enlightened one, he could escape at once from the cycle of existence, *samsara*, and attain *nirvana*. The legends that sprang up recounting the life of the Buddha state that the demon Mara, who had tried unsuccessfully to tempt the Buddha away from his goal, now encouraged him to seize his own salvation rather than to remain in the earthly domain to help others attain enlightenment. But the Buddha once more frustrated the demon Mara and determined to set in motion the turning of the "wheel of teaching" or the "wheel of Buddhist dharma."

THE EMERGENCE OF THE SANGHA

At the Deer Park in Benares, the Buddha discovered the five ascetics who had left him when he accepted rice from the village woman. Though prepared to jeer at him for abandoning the ascetic path, the five men were overwhelmed by the serenity radiating from the Buddha and sprang forward to serve him. In his famous first sermon delivered at the Deer Park, the Buddha advised that neither the path of indulgence nor of extreme self-mortification led to enlightenment, and that the one who would find truth must follow the Middle Path, a path mediating these extremes. The five former ascetics became the Buddha's first disciples. Other disciples soon gathered around the Buddha to be ordained by him as monks. As his teachings spread, the number of disciples, many of whom came from afar to hear the Buddha's teachings, rapidly expanded. To accommodate so many new disciples, the Buddha authorized monks he himself had ordained to ordain others, but this expansion of the order also called for implementing a program to coordinate monastic education with the functional necessities of maintaining a monastic institute, and establishing rules of conduct for the monks.

Accordingly, the Buddha aligned certain monastic activities with particular seasons, deeming the dry season as the opportune time for himself and his disciples to go forth and deliver sermons to the laity, and the three months of the wet season as a time of monastic aggregation and retreat from the world. During the wet season, the monks were to focus on their education and self-discipline. The *Sangha*, as the monastic brotherhood is called, required its members to shave their heads, wear simple yellow robes, carry begging bowls, engage in daily meditation, and subscribe to what Buddhists commonly refer to as "taking refuge in the three jewels." The three jewels are the Buddha, the Dharma (the law of Buddhist doctrine), and the Sangha (the monastic order). To take refuge is accomplished by stating "I take refuge in the Buddha. I take refuge in the Dharma. I take refuge in the Sangha." The Buddha's disciples also obeyed Ten Precepts:

1. Do not destroy life.
2. Do not steal.
3. Do not be unchaste.
4. Do not lie.
5. Do not take intoxicants.
6. Eat in moderation and not after noon.
7. Do not witness dancing, singing, or theatrical performances.
8. Do not wear garlands, perfumes, or jewelry.
9. Do not sleep on a high bed.
10. Do not accept gold or silver.

Of these precepts, the first five were prescribed for those who could not abandon the householder's life, but who, nonetheless, wished to attach themselves to the order as lay associates. Lay membership proved very significant in the development of Buddhism since it is lay members who often donated their properties to the order, thereby providing land for the construction of many monasteries. Women also sought admission to the order. Although the Buddha was initially averse to ordaining women since he apparently believed that women perpetuated the cycle of rebirth, according to tradition, his stepmother and his wife eventually persuaded the Buddha to accept them as disciples and to found an order of Buddhist nuns.

About 483 B.C.E., when the Buddha was about 80 years of age, he took ill after a meal in a small town northeast of Benares and passed into what Buddhists call *parinirvana*, the death of his physical self and his entry into *nirvana*. Tradition describes this passage as ecstatic, and the cremation of the Buddha's body as accompanied by a great earthquake. To the disciples he had attracted over his 45 years of teaching, the Buddha left the Doctrine and the Rules of Monastic Discipline.

THE DOCTRINE

The Buddha's method for attaining salvation rejected philosophical speculation, religious devotion, and, of course, extremely ascetic practices. He did subscribe to two major tenets of Hinduism, the Law of Karma and the cycle of rebirth, but envisioned a far greater flexibility for karma than Hindu doctrine permitted. The Law of Karma postulates that one's particular situation in life, which constitutes the status of one's rebirth, is the product of the accumulation of one's positive and negative actions in previous existences. The Buddha held that if one attained proper mindfulness in one's present lifetime, one could transcend the negative consequences of one's previous lives; in other words, one could escape what was considered one's fate according to the law of karma.

With respect to rebirth, the Buddha broke with the Hindu tradition that an immortal soul passed from one lifetime to the next and proposed that what was considered the immortal soul was rather an aggregate of ever-changing states of being, which included the body, perception, feelings, dispositions, and reasoning. But the Buddha's interpreters observed that the Buddha never proclaimed that some sort of entity did not pass through the cycle of rebirth according to the dictates of karma. Although the entity, "soul," or personality of one's previous existence would not be identical to that of one's present existence, the two are connected causally. In the same way, one's present "aggregate of being" will shape one's future existence. It is important to note that in societies where Buddhism took root, great emphasis is always placed on directing the "entity" of the dead person toward a good rebirth, which implies that Buddhists believe not only that the "entity" of one lifetime is indeed connected to that of the next lifetime, but also that action can be taken, independent of the "entity's" karmic destiny, to improve the future formation of that entity.

The Nature and Cause of Suffering

No matter how improved the nature of an entity's rebirth might be, the resulting individual would, nonetheless, be subject to great suffering. The Buddha conceived of suffering as the product of a twelve-part sequence of cause and effect. The first two parts result from the previous life, the second eight parts arise from the present, and the remaining two parts relate to future existence. Known as Dependent Origination or the Chain of Causation, this sequence stipulates that ignorance is the ultimate basis of all suffering. Ignorance of the impermanence of the self and the world, which continues from previous lives, shapes one's "aggregate of being" at birth. As a result, one recognizes the reality of the world and of one's self, a recognition that leads, in turn, to the emergence of one's individuality. Individuality constitutes the expression of the five senses and the mind. The senses and the mind encounter other individuals and things, producing sensations in the process. Sensations excite desire, and desire causes one to cling to existence. This clinging to existence brings about the process of becoming, which, in turn, precipitates a new state of existence, a new birth. But this new existence will also entail the experience of aging, death, grief, suffering, and despair.

Buddhist texts give considerable attention to the specific conditions that bind individuals to an endless cycle of rebirth, and, thus, to conditions that must be eliminated. These conditions include "the Three Intoxications"—greed, hatred, and lust; "the Five Hindrances"—the desire for sensual pleasures, sloth, ill-will, inattention, and doubt; and "the Ten Fetters"—belief in the reality of the self, doubt, belief that performing rituals can attain salvation, lust, anger, desire to be reborn in the worlds of form, desire to be reborn in the worlds of formlessness, pride, self-righteousness, and ignorance.

The Transcendence of Suffering

The Buddha achieved his ultimate understanding of the nature of suffering during his third night of meditation under the bodhi tree. This understanding was reflected in his realization of the Four Noble Truths and the Eightfold Path, which form the basis of Buddhist teachings. The Four Noble Truths state

1. All existence is suffering: birth, aging, illness, anxiety, misery, pain, despair, and the inability to satisfy one's desires.
2. The source of suffering is desire and ignorance.
3. Suffering must be eliminated. One must escape the cycle of rebirth and enter *nirvana*, the blessed state of nonexistence.
4. The way to eliminate suffering is to follow the Eightfold Path.

The Eightfold Path, the Buddha's prescription for a proper orientation toward life, constitutes a middle path to the attainment of enlightenment. It requires the acceptance and practice of the following:

1. Right knowledge—referring to the understanding of the Four Noble Truths.
2. Right attitude—cultivating an attitude of peacefulness and goodwill as opposed to that of sensual desire and malice.
3. Right speech—not lying or gossiping but directing one's speech toward harmonious interaction with others.
4. Right action—adhering to moral actions.
5. Right occupation—not injuring others through one's occupation.

6. Right effort—eliminating evil impulses and nurturing good ones.
7. Right mindfulness—avoiding the dictates of desire in one's speech, deeds, and emotional state.
8. Right composure—attaining the intense level of concentration that enables the practitioner to resist what would distract him or her from the goal of attaining salvation.

The Canonization of the Doctrine

After the Buddha's death, his disciples were concerned with preserving the Buddha's teachings and presenting them in a systematic form. To that end, the disciples held a council in Rajagha. The conclusions reached by this council were reviewed about 100 years later by what came to be called the Second Buddhist Council in Vesali. A third council was held in 253 B.C.E., nearly 200 years after the death of the Buddha, under the patronage of the great Indian King Ashoka in Pataliputta. During this third council, a thousand monks worked for about nine months to classify and corroborate the Buddhist traditions which had been transmitted orally for hundreds of years. But the Buddha's teachings were not to become codified in written texts until about the first century C.E., when they emerged as the Pali Canon, the comprehensive teachings of the Buddha written in the Pali language. The selection of the Pali language may have served to emphasize that Buddhism was a tradition markedly distinct from Hindu traditions, which were codified in Sanskrit. The original Pali Canon was written on palm leaves and entitled the *Tripitaka*, meaning "the three baskets," since the Buddha's teachings were divided into Monastic Rules (*Vinaya pittaka*), Discourses (*Sutta*), and seven supplemental works (*Abhidhamma Pitaka*). The Discourses were mainly the teachings of the Buddha himself but also incorporated several texts composed after the Buddha's lifetime, including, among other works, accounts of the life of Siddharta Gautama and his predecessors and the *Jataka* tales, stories the Buddha himself purportedly recalled about his previous lives.

SCHISMS WITHIN THE ORDER
AND THE SPREAD OF BUDDHISM

Tradition holds that the Second Buddhist Council occasioned fierce debates over issues of doctrine and Buddhist discipline. Those who supported a more moderate approach to the strict discipline of early Buddhism and a more liberal interpretation of doctrine resolved to form a new order of Buddhism, which they called Mahasanghika, meaning "members of the Great Sangha." Although the second council may not actually have been the venue for these debates, the schism would have at least followed the second council closely in time. The monks who continued to support the orthodox path were called, in Pali, Theravadins, "Followers of the Teachings of the Elders." The term "Theravadin" came to refer to older Buddhism in general. Those who formed the Mahasanghika order came to call themselves "Mahayana," which means "great vehicle," and referred derisively to the rival Theravadin Buddhism as "Hinayana." This reference to great and small vehicles derives from the Mahayana comparison of samsaric existence to a burning house. The only means of escape from the burning house is an animal cart, but since the Hinayana cart is so small, it only allocates room to the few faithful practitioners, leaving the rest of humanity to perish. The schism following the second council, however, did not merely divide the Buddhist order into two branches. Over the next 300 years, an additional 16 sects emerged.

Because of these sectarian divisions, Buddhism might never have achieved its missionary success. Buddhism was to be embraced, however, by none other than Ashoka, one of the greatest warrior kings in Indian history. Ashoka was the grandson of Chandragupta, the founder of India's first empire, the Mauryan Empire. Chandragupta had forced the garrisons left by Alexander the Great out of India and had then set himself to create his own empire. Ashoka, who ascended the throne in 273 B.C.E., added more lands to this empire but eventually found himself regretting the violent means and suffering that his conquests entailed. The Buddhist teachings to which Ashoka had been exposed affected his conscience and led him not only to adopt Buddhism, but also to take great interest in its propagation. Ashoka expressed his remorse for causing so much suffering by having his declaration of regret engraved on a rock as an enduring public edict. By 256 B.C.E., Ashoka issued 35 additional rock edicts, urging his subjects to live peaceably and observe Buddhist precepts, and had them placed in different regions of his empire.

Ashoka, however, was a world conqueror, not a monk or meditator, and very likely recognized a political utility in urging his subjects to live peaceably, to obey a common law, and to contribute to the unity of his empire. Ashoka, thus, was interested in promoting Buddhism as a state religion. He sent his officials to the far reaches of his empire to deliver sermons on the Dharma, thus allocating the role of Buddhist missionary to government officials. Ashoka stressed tolerance of Jains and Brahmins but took official measures to discourage splits within the Buddhist order. Tradition cites this concern as the basis of Ashoka's sponsorship of the Third Buddhist Council to reform the Sangha. Ashoka envisioned Buddhism as a world religion and sent missionaries to Gandhara, Kashmir, Syria, Egypt, Greece, and the Greek North African colony of Cyrenaica. From Gandhara and Kashmir, Buddhism spread to Central Asia and reached China by the first century C.E. In 372 C.E. the first Buddhist missionary from China arrived in Korea, and Japan was introduced to Buddhism in 552 C.E. through a gift from a Korean King.

Ashoka also sent his son Mahinda and daughter Sanghamitta to convert the royal court of Sri Lanka. Ashoka's children fulfilled their father's wish and Buddhism became the state religion of Sri Lanka by the second century B.C.E. The success of Ashoka's Buddhist mission was enhanced by popular enthusiasm for the relics the missionaries brought from India. These relics included what are purported to be the begging bowl, a tooth, and the collarbone of the Buddha, and were enshrined in magnificent reliquaries. According to tradition, Mahinda and his fellow missionaries had committed the entirety of Buddhist teachings to memory but had no written texts themselves. The task of inscribing these teachings was left to Sri Lankan monks, who wrote these texts down in their language, Sinhalese.

In the fifth century C.E., the Indian Buddhist scholar Buddhaghosa traveled to Sri Lanka to compare the Sinhalese with the Pali texts and compiled authoritative commentaries on Theravada doctrine. Theravada Buddhism emerged as the dominant order in Sri Lanka in the first century C.E. and flourished there until the fifth century C.E., when political upheaval and Tamil invasions from India, followed in the sixteenth century by European colonization, led to a decline of Buddhism in Sri

Lanka. Buddhism enjoyed a resurgence in Sri Lanka in the latter half of the nineteenth century and today is the dominant religion.

Following Ashoka's death in 232 B.C.E., the Mauryan empire declined. Buddhist legend cast Ashoka as the exemplary Buddhist monarch, a fierce conqueror who was transformed into a champion of Buddhism and who ruled his empire under the guidance of Buddhist principles. But the centralized bureaucracy of Ashoka's Mauryan empire was based upon the government officials' loyalty to Ashoka. Ashoka's less charismatic successors were unable to command such allegiance and the great Mauryan empire disintegrated. Several polities emerged in place of the Mauryan empire. While some of these polities were hostile to Buddhism, one polity, that of the Kushana kingdom of northwestern India, would nurture the development of the Mahayana Tradition. The Kushana kingdom's most celebrated ruler, King Kanishka, converted to Buddhism and sponsored the Fourth Buddhist Council in Kashmir. A significant outcome of this council was the codification and promotion of doctrines which were later to be embodied as Mahayana doctrine. Unlike the Theravadins, Mahayanists held that Gautama Buddha was a divine being to be both worshipped and adored for choosing to be born in the world out of compassion for the suffering of sentient beings. The Mahayanist emphasis on the Buddha's choice to be born in the realm of *samsara* led Mahayanists to redefine a *bodhisattva*, which early texts defined as a person who would become enlightened, as a Buddhist savior who would guide humans toward enlightenment. This new definition of *bodhisattva* added a social dimension to the attainment of salvation. Mahayanists also stressed, more strongly than Theravadins, that the Buddha must have existed in some heaven prior to his taking birth in the world and that there were Buddhas who preceded Siddharta Gautama just as there were Buddhas who would appear in the future. Under King Kanishka's patronage, the Mahayana Tradition expanded into Central Asia.

Another kingdom emerging after the fall of the Mauryan Empire, that of the Satavahanas of southwestern India, was brahminical but patronized Buddhism in order to promote trade, which provided an important source of state revenue. In the south of India, Buddhism continued to prosper in coastal towns which harbored merchant sailors who were to spread Buddhism to Southeast Asia. From around 200 B.C.E. to 300 C.E., the mercantile community in India enjoyed a rapid expansion and important trade routes were established from the subcontinent to other lands. Merchants from Gujarat on India's west coast and from the coastal towns of southern India set sail for Burma, Cambodia, Malaya, Sumatra, Java, and Bali by at least the first century C.E. With them, the merchants brought Indian concepts of government and culture, which resulted in the establishment of the Indianized kingdom of Funan in Cambodia around 100 C.E., and of Champa in southern Vietnam in 192 C.E. These kingdoms were Hindu or Hinduized in the sense that they were modeled on the Hindu polities extant in India in the post-Mauryan period. The ruling class appear to have been Hindu, since the Funan king Jayavarman worshipped the Hindu god Shiva; however, the local population embraced Buddhism and the worship of Vishnu. In the ninth century C.E., Jayavarman II established Angkor as the capital of the Khmer kingdom of Cambodia and built the mile-square Angkor Wat.

Jayavarman II broke with the Hindu royal court tradition in having himself declared a devaraja or god-king. In Hindu polities, the king possessed secular power but was subordinate morally to the authority of the brahmin priest, who wielded spiritual power. By identifying himself with Shiva, Jayavarman II became divinized, and the brahmin priest reduced in status to a mere vehicle for ceremonially uniting Shiva with the king. With the reign of Jayavarman VII (1181–1215), Angkor became Theravadin and the ruler was identified as a Buddharaja or living Buddha. The influence of these Cambodian kingdoms was extensive. Funan, which endured until about 600 C.E., exercised control over Champa and the Malay state. In the twelfth century C.E., the Khmer kingdom conquered the northern state of Vietnam, Champa, and the Mon state of Burma. The Mons had spread Buddhism in southern Burma and central Thailand but were supplanted politically by the kingdom of Pagan. Influenced by the Sinhalese tradition of the tenth to twelfth centuries which held that the king was a bodhisattva who was empowered by the sangha to gain the throne and to defend Buddhism, Pagan introduced another variation to the relationship between religion and the royal court in Southeast Asia in its cult of the dharmaraja. As a dharmaraja, the king saw himself as a bodhisattva whose task it was to restore Buddhism. What is more, the Pagan royal court dispensed with the role of the brahmin priest altogether, since a dharmaraja crowned himself in fulfillment of the sangha's request.

The first Thai kingdom, the Sukhodaya (1100–1350), was influenced by both the Pagan and Sinhalese royal courts. The Sukhodaya king was enjoined to rule righteously but to relinquish his throne on religious holidays to monks, who would sit on the throne and explain Buddhist doctrine. The Sukhodaya kingdom succumbed to the important Thai kingdom of Ayutthaya which enjoyed strong religious ties to Sinhalese Buddhism. Ayutthaya borrowed many cultural institutions from the Khmer kingdom which it had defeated, including the cult of the Khmer royal court, and combined the dharmaraja with the devaraja cults to establish the king as the absolute moral authority.[1]

Vajrayana Buddhism

By the seventh century C.E., a major school of Buddhism branched off from the Mahayana Tradition. This school, the Vajrayana or "thunderbolt vehicle," is also known as Tantric Buddhism, and co-evolved with Hindu Tantrism in northern India. Vajrayana Buddhism held that enlightenment was not best achieved through studying texts, but rather through the practice of mystical exercises under the tutelage of a guru. The object of these exercises was to experience fundamental reality, the state of voidness or emptiness, which is the realization that there is no difference between *samsara* and *nirvana*. These mystical exercises included the meditational practice of visualizing deities, yogic exercise, the utterance of sacred syllables and prayers (*mantra*), and elaborate rites which incorporated mystical diagrams (*yantra*), gestures (*mudra*), the playing of ritual instruments, sacred dances, and circular diagrams composed of grains of colored sand and representing the realms of deities.

Vajrayana Buddhism is frequently referred to as Tibetan Buddhism, since it was in Tibet that Vajrayana Buddhism developed its most sophisticated philosophical doctrine, elaborate ritual form, and political as well as theological authority. According to tradition, Buddhism arrived in Tibet through the auspices of two princesses, one Chinese, the other, Nepali, who were given, as tribute, in marriage to the Tibetan empire's great King Songsten Gampo, who ruled from 643–650 C.E. Tibetans also encountered Buddhism in the seventh century in the oases of Central

Asia, in northwestern India and Bengal, in China, and in Nepal. Songsten Gampo and his immediate successors were known as Tibet's "religious kings" for their promotion of the translation of Buddhist texts into Tibetan, the importation of Buddhist scholars, and the building of monasteries. Tradition also places a particular emphasis on the eighth-century missionary efforts of an Indian tantric practitioner known as Padmasambhava, "the lotus-born one," as critical to the spread of Buddhism in Tibet and Bhutan.

In Tibet, four major sects of Vajrayana Buddhism emerged: the Nyingmapa, Sakyapa, Kargyupa, and Gelugpa, whose most famous practitioner is the Dalai Lama. The Gelugpa sect gained ascendance in Tibet under the auspices of Mongolian princes, who were instrumental in the development in the seventeenth century of a theocratic Tibetan state headed by the Dalai Lama. The Mongolians, in turn, who had embraced Tibetan Buddhism from the thirteenth century contributed to its emergence in Siberia. Tibetan Buddhism also became the state religion of both Sikkim and Bhutan in the seventeenth century, and continued as the state religion of Ladakh after Ladakh seceded from the Tibetan empire in 1533. Vajrayana Buddhism, in a form distinct from that of Tibetan Buddhism, was introduced to Nepal in the fourth century C.E. and continues to be practiced by the Newaris of the Kathmandu Valley.

The spread of Buddhism to Tibet was to play a pivotal role in its preservation since Buddhism almost disappeared in India by the end of the twelfth century. Tibetan scholars who had come to study with Indian Buddhist masters were responsible for translating Buddhist texts into Tibetan, which proved to preserve texts whose Sanskrit versions were lost.

The Decline of Buddhism in India

Several factors contributed to Buddhism's decline in India. The devotional cults developing in Mahayana Buddhism and the emergence of Tantric Buddhism may not have distinguished themselves significantly from parallel developments in Hinduism. Theravadin Buddhism, which in India did not constitute a state religion as it did in Sri Lanka, may have had greater difficulty attracting lay patronage, and Muslim invasions led to the destruction of monasteries and the slaughter of Buddhist monks.

THE ANTHROPOLOGY OF BUDDHISM

One of the major focuses of anthropological research in Buddhist societies has been the relationship between a "world-renouncing" religion that posits the denial of the ego as the path to salvation and the individual and social interests of the lay community that supports the Buddhist Sangha. Traditional Buddhist societies, whether Theravadin, directed to individual enlightenment, Mahayana, with its emphasis on the Buddhist savior, or Vajrayana, which guides practitioners toward directly experiencing enlightenment, have impressed many religious scholars as being doctrinally inconsistent with the principle tenets of Buddhism. One basis for this perception of inconsistency emerges in light of the fact that the laity and even the monastic communities in these societies propitiate a host of supernatural beings or engage in ritual practices that either have no connection to, or even seemingly contradict, Buddhist prescriptions for salvation. Some anthropological responses to this problem have suggested that several parallel "Buddhisms" exist in a society[2] or that "dual causalities" may be found in Buddhist interpretations of karma.[3] Let us examine more thoroughly the issue of Buddhism and animism.[4]

BUDDHISM AND ANIMISM

Melford Spiro[5] considers this problem in relation to the elaborate cult of *nat* worship in Burma, a cult whose practitioners are Theravadin Buddhists. A *nat* is a supernatural being whose power is superior to that of humans and who can affect the lives of humans for better or for worse. A *nat*, then, can cause suffering, but this attribute appears to contradict Buddhist concepts of suffering. Buddhism defines the origin of suffering as desire, but the law of karma accounts for the existential circumstances of individual human beings, or the cause of personal suffering. One's karma is the cumulative effect of one's good and bad deeds and thus locates one's existential position, one's relative happiness or suffering, in the present life. But Spiro notes that the Buddhist assignment of personal responsibility for suffering is emotionally unsatisfying, since (in the Theravadin tradition) there is no escape from one's karma. He draws upon anthropological theories of functionalism and of culture and personality to argue that the Burmese worship of *nats* supplies a more emotionally satisfying causality of suffering since it deflects the responsibility for personal suffering from those who suffer. Spiro is intrigued by the question of how the existence of *nats* and their attributed powers may be rationalized in view of a belief in the doctrine of karma.

Initially, Spiro found the Burmese to be inconsistent and even contradictory in their expressed beliefs concerning the existence of *nats*. Women consistently professed their belief in *nats* and were said to be their most fervent propitiators, while men often voiced skepticism as to the existence of *nats*. The basis for this gender discrepancy is in the relative cosmological status assigned men, women, and *nats*. The Burmese accord men a higher mode of existence in the 31 realms of existence than *nats*, but women rank beneath men in this ordering. Thus, women would not subvert the hierarchy by showing their respect for *nats*. Spiro concludes that men propitiated *nats* in their homes despite the fact they disbelieved in them for social reasons such as keeping up appearances, placating wives, or escaping any assignment of blame should a household member fall ill. Many of Spiro's informants claimed to uphold doctrinal orthodoxy by denying the possibility that *nats* could harm either pious Buddhists or those with good karma. Burmese intellectuals and the army opposed *nat* worship, but for different reasons. Burmese intellectuals tended to find *nat* worship in direct conflict with Buddhism. The army, on the other hand, embracing modernization and economic development, felt that "magical thinking" had no utility and that *nat* cults simply drained capital.

Spiro is less interested in the question of what the Burmese believe about *nats*, however, than that of why the Burmese hold these beliefs in the first place. To answer the latter question, he begins by tracing the historical basis of *nat* worship to both indigenous Burmese animistic beliefs and to the cosmological schema that accompanied Buddhist teachings to Burma. He then applies a psychological analysis, arguing that the persistence of *nat* belief could be traced to factors influencing the development of a Burmese child's personal orientation or perceptual set, a development which generates mutual suspicion in interpersonal relationships and both reinforces and is reinforced by a belief in harmful supernaturals. Spiro's third mode of analysis is to consider the relationship of *nat* cults to Burmese social structure. It is on this level, Spiro argues, that *nat* cults join Buddhism as a vehicle for integrating Burmese society, since the structure of *nat* cults appears to be modeled after the traditional Burmese political system.

However, although *nat* cults are patterned after the Burmese political system, they differ from it since *nats* emerge as symbols opposing both political and religious authority. Important *nat* festivals present carnivalesque atmospheres where Buddhist values, such as sobriety, are flaunted. Furthermore, a patient who has been possessed by a *nat* will commonly vent his or her frustration with Buddhism during an exorcistic seance. Spiro casts such an occasion in terms of the Freudian theory of the personality, whereby the entranced patient has an unconscious ego, a dissolved superego, and, therefore, an unrestrained id that can vent the patient's primary impulses.

Spiro concludes his analysis of *nat* cults by identifying several strategies used to resolve the tension between Buddhism and *nat* cults that both confer Buddhist legitimacy on *nats* and assert the subordination of *nat* cults to Buddhism. One strategy, for example, is to follow a *nat* propitiation conducted chiefly by women with a Buddhist ritual led by men. But despite these strategies, and the fact, Spiro asserts, that animistic beliefs and rituals are indeed compatible with orthodox Buddhism (which recognizes evil spirits as the manifestation and delusion of ignorance), Spiro observes that the Burmese continue to find *nat* worship incompatible with Buddhism.

Beyond the issue of doctrinal conflict, Spiro locates a second basis for the inner conflict Burmese experience with respect to *nat* cults in the opposing orientations to the world, or ethos, expressed in Buddhism and *nat* propitiation. Whereas Buddhism stresses morality and a life of reason, *nat* worship indulges the senses, the emotions, and the pursuit of worldly goals. In practice, however, Burmese Buddhists pursue the goal of a good rebirth, and not that of salvation. This suggests that Burmese Buddhist practice is instrumentally parallel to *nat* worship in that the Burmese apply Buddhist means to achieve what amounts to a worldly end. If, as others have suggested, Burmese Buddhism and animism exist as a religious continuum, Spiro argues that the poles of this continuum constitute two distinct religions. Buddhism retains its precedence in Burma because its teachings are accepted as normative, its values are sacred, it draws the investment of considerable psychic energy, and its superior religious power is unquestioned. *Nat* cults, which the Burmese themselves do not consider a religion, serve to enforce and strengthen the integrity of the Buddhist religion in Burma, because they serve needs prohibited by Buddhism. In this way, *nat* cults protect Buddhism from either opposition or the corruption that would ensue should Buddhism be manipulated to address too worldly ends.

In *Buddhism and the Spirit Cults in North-east Thailand*, Stanley J. Tambiah[6] shares Spiro's interest in the persistence of spirit cults alongside Buddhism but disagrees with Spiro's argument that *nat* cults and Buddhism constitute two distinct religions. Tambiah, in contrast, suggests that Buddhism and spirit cults exist in a "field of religion" where various practices and beliefs are complementary, hierarchically ranked, and/or linked. Tambiah found Buddhism and spirit cults to be separate collective representations that reflect both different ethical notions and different approaches to the supernatural. For these reasons, Tambiah categorizes their relationship as complementary. Issues of hierarchy emerge, for example, in the fact that both Buddhist and spirit cult practitioners ethicize the use of spiritual power and rank those in possession of such power according to moral superiority. Linkages between Buddhism and spirit cults are evident in myths and rites which identify the conversion of *nagas*, a type of serpent spirit, into agents of Buddhism. Importantly, Tambiah views the idiom of gift giving and making offerings as a critical distinction between human communication and reciprocity with the Buddha and divine angels, as opposed to human communication and reciprocity with the spirit world. The latter, Tambiah argues, is characterized by coercive bargaining. Thus, Tambiah offers considerable insight into the logic of different sets of practices and separate collective representations within a single religious field. In arguing that the analyst's task is to seek out the logic of these differences, a logic expressed according to what is considered to be distinct and what is considered to be related, Tambiah supports a structural analysis of the religious field.

Incorporated into Tambiah's notion of a field of religion is the relationship of Buddhism to Thai village society. He observes that an anthropological study of Buddhism as a popular religion will likely differ dramatically from the approach of a philosopher or religious scholar because the anthropologist will focus on how the monastic institution is integrated with village social structure and concerns. The collective monastic life, based on the association of members of the same sex, is structurally opposite to the collective life of domestic households, which is based on the distinction and complementarity of the sexes. The monastic community may also be distinguished from the lay community in that it is entirely dependent on gifts from the lay community for its existence. However, the monastic and lay communities are enmeshed in ties of mutual reciprocity that are grounded in the concept of merit. Villagers conceive of and evaluate behavior in terms of merit and demerit, concepts that derive from doctrinal Buddhism. Merit, however, is popularly understood as merit that can be made by the giving of gifts to monks and to the wat or temple, or as merit that is acquired by the monks' acceptance of the gifts. The notion that merit can be acquired through the monks' willingness to receive gifts implies that in this instance, the receiver of the gift is superior to the giver, and is consistent with the doctrinal view that monks are spiritually superior to the laity.

Thai villagers center on merit-making activities as their primary religious activity in order to work toward a good rebirth as well as to achieve a peaceful mind. Unlike the attainment of salvation, which in Theravadin Buddhism is a highly individualistic pursuit, merit making may be a social endeavor conducted by households, kin groups, or even by the entire village. Moreover, one individual or group can make merit on behalf of another, which is, in itself, a meritorious activity. Merit is thus transferable, and such transference is institutionalized in Thai society. According to a lay evaluation, financing the building of a wat (temple) significantly outranks other modes of merit making and is followed, in descending order of merit accrual, by becoming a monk, having a son become a monk, contributing to the repair of a wat, contributing to certain religious ceremonies, giving food daily to monks, observing certain religious ceremonies, and observing the five basic Buddhist precepts. Tambiah notes that certain of these activities are clearly restricted to the wealthy, but that ordinary villagers can achieve substantial merit by either becoming monks themselves or having their sons ordained. The fact that almost every household can afford to feed monks and does so on a daily basis contributes to the low ranking given this merit-making activity. The high ranking assigned to wat building as well as to becoming a monk or having a son become a monk reveals that merit making integrates two lay prestige systems, the religious and economic.

Wat financing, however, is a rare event, while ordination to monkhood has become for many young men a rite of passage. Tambiah bases this assessment on the fact that young men frequently opt to be ordained as monks without having undergone the preparatory stages of temple boy and novice as prescribed by doctrinal Buddhism, and on the very short time these young men remain monks. Tambiah assesses these departures from doctrinal Buddhism in terms of two systems of relations, one obtaining between the agricultural cycle and collective wat rites, and the other between parental and filial generations. The Buddhist Lenten season, which marks the birth, enlightenment, and death of the Buddha, coincides in Thailand with the rainy season when agricultural labor in the rice fields is at a minimum. The monks' retreat during the Lenten season is interpreted by villagers as directly linked to the success of the crop. Furthermore, the ordination of a few novices just prior to the beginning of the Lenten season is viewed as conferring merit on local village guardian deities, which also contributes to the rain required for agricultural fertility. Young men seeking ordination as monks typically arrange their ordinations to coincide with the onset of the rainy season only to resume lay life at the end of the Lenten period. To become a monk for the short span of the Lenten season serves a twofold purpose: On the one hand, the families of the monks are not deprived of laborers during critical periods of agricultural activity; on the other, the young men accomplish their goal of attaining merit for themselves and for their parents. The relationship between the monks and their parents is one of institutionalized reciprocity. A young man cannot become a monk without the sponsorship of his parents but equally enables his parents to obtain merit by their very act of sponsorship. Upon his ordination, the new monk immediately transfers merit to his parents, thus binding together the monastic and lay communities through the idiom of merit.

Rejecting the religious historian view that lay Buddhism is necessarily antithetical to doctrinal Buddhism, Tambiah concludes that merit making asserts a preoccupation with death that also implies rebirth and is thus an orientation that is consistent with the doctrinal emphasis on death and its aftermath, which underscores the transitional nature of existence.

In *World Conqueror and World Renouncer,* Tambiah explores the Buddhist theory of society, specifically the relationship between the monk and the king (who categorically encompasses householders) or between the Buddha and the Chakravartin, the ruler who wields the wheel of dharma and develops a historical analysis of the Buddhist polity in Thailand. He introduces the term "galactic polity" to refer to the model of rule patterned after Ashoka's Mauryan empire. Tambiah invokes the metaphor of a galaxy to describe a political structure consisting of an imperial central entity around which revolve lesser political replicas which are constantly in motion, either splitting off from the center or becoming incorporated in it. This model posits a *chakravartin* who encompasses lesser kings, who in turn encompass lesser rulers. The *chakravartin,* then, does not stand as a totalitarian authority, but rather as a ruler who influences people through the example he sets and through his various agencies.

A *chakravartin*, for example, may influence people through what we might call his "virtual physical presence." This means that while the ruler himself is not physically present, his authority is represented by statues made in his image, or, after his death, by his relics. King Ashoka set the precedent for this strategy by declaring that Buddhist relics and statues were equivalent to the regalia of king and state. In the distant reaches of his empire, where he may not have exerted much direct political control, Ashoka endeavored to assert his authority by enshrining relics. He thus invoked Buddhism to legitimate his sovereignty. The royal cult that emerged around Thai monarchs incorporated Ashoka's strategy to secure political authority by stockpiling bone fragments from the cremated remains of royal rulers in the palace. The relics themselves were regarded as such potent symbols of the ruler's sovereignty that the legitimacy of any given or would-be ruler was determined by his physical proximity to these relics. Thus, those who usurped the throne and banished the heirs of the former rulers far from the palace were the credible rulers by virtue of their physical association with the royal relics.

Succession to the Thai throne was frequently accomplished through rebellion, calling the legitimacy of many rulers into question. To redress this problem, rulers sought legitimacy from the Buddhist Sangha and the divine status conferred through a court ceremony. The modern Thai polity utilizes kingship to legitimate the concept of the nation, to which the king is subservient, and is ruled by a military dictatorship empowered by a military-civilian bureaucracy. But this modern polity continues certain galactic polity patterns. The concept of nation is strongly associated with Buddhism. Political offices, each with its coterie of followers, are elaborately ranked, and the Sangha, so important to the legitimation of rulers in Thai history, sustains certain dialectical tensions with the polity. At the same time, the modern Sangha has evolved a hierarchical structure that parallels that of the modern Thai state.

In *The Buddhist Saints of the Forest and the Cult of Amulets*,[7] Tambiah presents another important dimension to the understanding of Buddhism in Thailand with his study of the cult of the saints, the forest-dwelling monks who follow the path of the "homeless wanderer" and, therefore, occupy the "periphery" of the galactic polity. He investigates the dynamics of center-periphery relations by examining the distinction between the "establishment Sangha" of the village and cities and the ascetic, forest-dwelling monks, and the relationships that obtain between each of these two branches of the Sangha, the ruler, and the laity. During times of political unrest, natural disasters, or the intensive engagement in politics on the part of the establishment Sangha, the Thai monarchy sought to regain its legitimacy through the charismatic authority of the forest-dwelling monks, who were invoked to purify the Sangha. Although the royal family and the military establishment continue this tradition in contemporary Thai society, elites in Thai banking and commerce and other members of high society echo this tradition by seeking to enhance their reputations and stockpile of grace through their identification with the charisma of forest monks. This is accomplished through the burgeoning cult of sacred amulets, which embed and objectify the merit of the saints of the forest. Since the forest saints who bless and even manufacture these amulets are decidedly "unworldly" in their orientation, the amulets imbued with their power are believed to amplify the worldly benefits of protection and success that accrue to those who possess them.

Despite their origin as objects fashioned through the devotion of saints and, therefore, as objects charged with mystical power, the amulets typically become highly salable in the marketplace. The lay view holds that amulets lose their mystical power through successive economic exchanges, which, in turn, causes such amulets to be eventually forgotten while new ones become fashionable. Thus, unlike the sacred relics and statues of the Buddha whose movement from one principality or kingdom to another carried with it the legitimacy conveyed by their undiminished spiritual power, the cult of amulets may appear to respond to crises in political legitimacy in a fundamentally different manner. The entry of sacred amulets into the marketplace subjects them to a comparative evaluation that is based upon the quantification of mystical power in terms of money. But the most valued of amulets remain out of circulation and in the hands of the elite who sponsored their manufacture. Tambiah thus concludes that the cult of amulets is driven by the same ideology that applied historically to the legitimation of Southeast Asian kings, an ideology that recognizes differentials of power and social control in the lay social hierarchy. By this logic, the ruling elite and the wealthy possess the most sacred amulets and consequently more merit than their social inferiors.

HIMALAYAN BUDDHISM

Buddhism in the Himalayan region follows the Vajrayana tradition, which reflects complexities with respect to such issues as the fate of the transmigrating consciousness or that which takes rebirth, avenues through which karmic destiny can be altered, and practitioner specializations. Vajrayana Buddhism accommodates much of what anthropologists working elsewhere have labeled "magical animism" or spirit cults. Christoph von Fürer-Haimendorf,[8] in his pioneering ethnography of the Sherpas of Nepal, stressed that Sherpa religion, which had its roots in Tibetan traditions, did not divide Buddhist doctrine from the worship of local deities.

Anthropologists whose work centers on issues of Buddhism in Himalayan cultures have investigated such topics as the relationship between Buddhism and householding, Buddhism and the social hierarchy, Buddhism and problems of succession, Tibetan Buddhism and shamanism, the Tibetan Buddhist polity, Buddhist nuns,[9] the relationship of Buddhist to non-Buddhist practices,[10] divine madmen,[11] Tibetan Buddhist law,[12] and Western assumptions about Sherpas as Buddhists. [13]

My own research[14] investigates the ways in which Tibetans in the exile community in India, Nepal, and the West are currently recognizing young children, often about two years of age, as the reincarnations of Tibetan spiritual masters or *tulkus*. A *tulku* is believed to be the incarnation or embodiment of the consciousness of a deceased spiritual master or lama. If that spiritual master has reached a high enough level of spiritual attainment, Tibetans believe that he, and, occasionally, she, can determine the precise circumstances of his or her rebirth—that is, select his or her parents and the time of the birth itself. What complicates the matter is the Tibetan view that a given *tulku* might reincarnate in as many as five distinct aspects. This means that one *tulku* might be identified as the "body" incarnation of his or her predecessor, and another, as the "speech" incarnation, "mind" incarnation, "wisdom" incarnation, or "activity" incarnation. The parents of *tulkus* often experience auspicious dreams prior to the child's birth and the birth itself may be accompanied by meteorological phenomena such as rainbows. What I have found particularly intriguing in my research is the variety of divinatory strategies resorted to by Tibetan monastic officials, lamas, and by the Dalai Lama in determining the legitimacy of a *tulku* candidate, and the narratives recounting evidence that a young tulku has demonstrated his recollection of a past life.

BUDDHISM, HOUSEHOLDING, AND HIERARCHY

Sherry Ortner, in *Sherpas Through Their Rituals*,[15] examines conflicts and parallel orientations between Buddhist ideology and domestic life among Sherpas of the Solu valley of Nepal. In the context of status, social exchange, and the life cycle, she analyzes a key ritual, *Nyungne*, in terms of the ways it transforms these conflicts into an appropriate religious orientation. Sherpa society is composed of clans organized around the principle of patrilineal descent and Sherpas follow a pattern of land inheritance that gives equal shares to all sons, including sons who elect to become monks. Marriage is the occasion when fathers transfer land to and build houses for their sons and endow their daughters. Since a Sherpa man's primary claim to social status is his headship and management of a productive estate, each time his child marries, his status is reduced.

In addition to the economic threat to the head of a Sherpa household posed by the marriage of his children, marriage is also seen as the disruption of the *nying-je* bond between mother and son. The mother-child relationship, and, in particular, the mother-son relationship, is conceived as the greatest expression of mutual love. This relationship serves as a metaphor for *nyingje*, the compassion expressed by the bodhisattva who takes rebirth in the realm of samsaric existence to guide others toward enlightenment. Sherpa weddings stress relationships of exchange and mutual assistance that are contracted between members of different households but do not emphasize the bonds between parents and children. Sherpa tradition also decrees that the youngest son inherits the house of his parents and is expected to take control of the parental property and care for his parents in their old age. Elderly parents thus find themselves in a role reversal, no longer self-sufficient but dependent upon their children for survival.

Nyungne is a four-day ritual held during the Buddhist holy month marking the birth, enlightenment, and death of Lord Buddha. It is a time when the laity can acquire merit by remaining celibate and practicing acts of renunciation. Normally, only older adults participate in this ritual. They spend the ritual period in the temple, fasting, not speaking, praying, and prostrating in atonement for their sins to an image of Chenrezi, known in Sanskrit as Avalokitesvara, the Bodhisattva of Compassion. This asceticism emphasizes the participants' nonengagement in social transactions.

Ortner describes the Sherpas' view of Chenrezi, who embodies both male and female attributes, as a perfect parent, a compassionate or "motherly" male. This characterization of Chenrezi enables the *Nyungne* ritual, in Ortner's assessment, to be what Clifford Geertz,[16] in his discussion of cultural symbolism, would call a "model of" and a "model for" old age. The Nyungne ritual constitutes a "model of" old age in that its participants are conceived of as asexual, not working, no longer property owners, and socially isolated. But Nyungne reorients these realities into a positive "model for" old age by directing participants toward an identification with Chenrezi. In the Mahayana and Vajrayana Traditions, one identifies with the deity in the process of meditating on that deity. With respect to the *Nyungne* ritual, Ortner interprets the identification claimed by participants as an expression of the primal experience of mutual love. Since parties involved in a love relationship are interchangeable, humans become Chenrezi in the process of identifying with Chenrezi. In this sense, then, the ritual participant who initially assumes his or her dependency on the universal Chenrezi-mother, becomes the universal Chenrezi-mother, the universal parent.

Ortner sees the *Nyungne* ritual as utilizing the classic symbolism of rites of passage to achieve a powerful transformation of the participant's social orientation as a dependent, low-status elder into a religious orientation that not only earns great merit but also casts the participant as a universal parent. Furthermore, Ortner suggests that the *Nyungne* ritual, with its asocial emphasis and cultivation of ties between participants and Chenrezi as a universal parent, may be seen as antimarriage and, more generally, as antisocial. This, Ortner argues, would reflect the Sherpa conception of the household as autonomous and as a refuge from the outside world.

In her analyses of other Sherpa rituals, Ortner continues to incorporate psychological and social levels of interpretation. She views the Sherpa treatment of the corpse in funerary rituals as expressing the belief that pollution emanates from the corpse and from the demons who are attracted to it. Essentially, Ortner argues that the Sherpas fear pollution because it upsets the proper integration of the psychic self. Ideally, the self is composed of an ascendent spiritual aspect which presides over the physical and demonic aspects. Physical pollution, the result, for example, of excessive drinking, renders the individual lazy and stupid. Demonic pollution, on the other hand, causes anger and violence. A corpse, which no longer possesses a spiritual aspect, is highly polluting because it constitutes an excess of the internal physical component of the self, while also vulnerable to the violence of demons, who symbolize others. According to Ortner, the pollution of death is caused by the disintegration of the hierarchy of the aspects of the self. Sherpa funeral rituals emphasize this disintegration by manipulating the hierarchy of the corpse's "self." The physical aspect, which is the sole aspect of the self remaining in the corpse, is first elevated to a godlike status, but just prior to its cremation, the corpse is offered as food to demons. Thus, the physical aspect is assigned a status that is either too high or too low to be appropriately integrated into the self. The cremation is followed by a feast at which the normal Sherpa social hierarchy, so dramatically enacted at other feasting occasions, is suspended. This feast, in turn, is followed by an exorcism which subdues demons through the lay enactment of violence toward demonic effigies. Ortner interprets this ritual as an expression of mock violence directed toward the rich by the poor, and, thus, as a status inversion of the living.

Ortner locates another instance of status elevation in the ritual reading of texts to guide the soul to a better rebirth during the 49-day period between death and rebirth, a standard ritual practice in both Theravadin and Mahayana Buddhism. She argues that this transfer of merit to the soul sends it on to a better rebirth than what the soul morally deserves—that is, the destiny determined by the "soul's" karma. The completion of the 49-day period is also followed by a feast during which the social hierarchy is suspended. But the exorcism following this second feast illustrates a peaceful, and, therefore, more spiritual, method of subduing demons. The restoration of a proper integration of the self, symbolically expressed through the second exorcism, is reflected by the restoration of the normative social hierarchy. In this way, Ortner again combines a psychological with a sociological analysis by finding a link between the integration of the self and the integration of society.

Ortner also examines the Sherpa (and Vajrayana) practice of temporarily embodying Buddhist deities in dough offering cakes placed on Buddhist altars. Sherpas observe numerous ritual events in which they make offerings to Buddhist deities in order to gain their general protection or, as is the case with exorcisms, to secure their active assistance in subduing demons. The problem Sherpas face in making such requests of the Buddhist deities is that the deities abide in blissful states beyond the cycle of suffering and rebirth. Ortner argues that the deities must be drawn out of their state of self-absorption in order to combat demons. The rituals accomplish this end by calling upon the deities and inviting them to "sit" in dough offering cakes for the duration of the ritual. The deities are thereby embodied, and embodiment carries certain important implications in Sherpa culture. Embodied deities are subject to the same sorts of social manipulations that hosts ply on their guests. Guests, like embodied deities, can be put in a good mood through food and drink offerings and then persuaded to fulfill the hosts' requests. Moreover, embodying the deities is akin to polluting them, which, Ortner finds, makes the deities angry. But arousing passion in the deities and then directing that passion to combat forces of evil is a ritual goal. Ortner suggests that a basic pattern of Sherpa Buddhist ritual is to provide a "model of" and a "model for" a complex emotional state—positive anger, the morally appropriate attitude for subduing demons. The compassion of the deities is thus invoked through the mechanisms of hospitality, which are the mechanisms of social alliance, while the strategies of hospitality, which are normally perceived as self-serving and egotistical, are incorporated into the religious context of serving universal needs.

MONASTIC SOLUTIONS TO PROBLEMS OF SUCCESSION AND STATUS

Robert Paul[17] examines Sherpa and Tibetan concepts of descent, Sherpa religion, Tibetan saintly biographies, epics, dramas, and royal traditions in light of psychoanalytic theory. He endeavors to show that each of these contexts, which concern political and sacred authority, addresses the problem of succession to a position of authority and reveals Oedipal symbolism. Freud identified in what he termed the "Oedipal complex" a paradoxical model of the relationship between senior and junior males where both groups are consumed by the competing passions of mutual hatred and love. Junior males kill senior males in order to succeed them; senior males kill junior males to remove the threat they pose; but both senior and junior males are morally enjoined not to kill each other. Freud noted, however, that in reality, senior males must die and junior males live to succeed them. To Freud's paradoxical relationship, Paul adds three corollaries: (1) Anyone benefiting from someone's death is guilty of that death; (2) anyone so guilty must be punished by death; and (3) a person dies only because someone has killed him or her.

Paul locates a resolution to the paradox of intergenerational male relationships and his three corollaries in certain principles underlying institutionalized monasticism. Firstly, he argues that Sherpa culture exhibits two parallel lineage systems. One of these systems is based on biological reproduction; the other, on the reproduction of symbolic information through Buddhist initiations and teaching. The latter system is driven by karma and enables disciples to reproduce their master through strictly cultural, as opposed to biological, means. In Vajrayana Buddhism, disciples receive mystical initiations from their masters and, thereby, entitlement to spiritual power from their masters. The transmission of the teachings and spiritual power from master to disciple ultimately creates a spiritual lineage of disciples who can trace their specific doctrinal orientation and spiritual power to one ancestral guru. As the guru's teachings and spiritual power are transmitted from one generation of disciples to the next, the guru's spiritual lineage reproduces itself asexually.

Secondly, Paul observes that the parallel lineages were intertwined in Tibet where monasticism was highly institutionalized. While older sons would succeed their fathers in the worldly realm, younger sons typically joined monasteries where their paternal uncles resided. In this way, religious power passed from paternal uncle to nephew, and the transmission of both worldly and spiritual power could take place in one family. Thus, Tibetan patterns of succession equated the relationships of father to son, master to disciple, and paternal uncle to nephew. In turn, these patterns enable a different sorting out of the Oedipal paradox. Paul argues that the Tibetan pattern of inheritance in the biological lineage created a succession rivalry between a male property owner's younger brother (who did not inherit) and that male's son, as opposed to a rivalry between a father and son. Within one family, then, parallel lineages could be represented by two sets of brothers, one in the senior and the other in the junior generation. The monk brother in each generation would observe celibacy and certain ascetic practices, which, from a psychoanalytic perspective, would be the symbolic equivalent of castration (again equated with being killed) and atonement. Following this line of psychoanalytic logic, the four males would fulfill the requirement of the paradox that a senior male be alive, a senior male be "killed," a junior male be alive, and a junior male be "killed." Moreover, in the monastic context, Paul argues, the negative relationship between paternal uncle and nephew and the positive relationship of guru and disciple are unified in the intergenerational biological relationship of two monks.

In the premonastic Sherpa religious system, where spiritual masters, known as lamas, married, sons received spiritual power from their fathers. But the lamas required their sons to undertake a period of ascetic hermitage when those sons came of age. By the same token, the fathers entered ascetic retreat when their sons gained full maturity. In this case, taking up ascetic hermitage symbolizes the castration/killing and atonement served by entering the monastery, and the four roles outlined above are played by two people.

A further dimension to Paul's discussion of Sherpa and Tibetan Buddhist institutionalized resolutions to Oedipal rivalries is the role of the reincarnate lama. Tibetans and Sherpas generally understand a reincarnate lama to be the rebirth of a spiritual master. In other words, unlike ordinary humans, the successive reincarnations of this spiritual master are viewed as the continuation of a distinct personality. This implies that it is the same person taking rebirth in different bodies. Paul finds the reincarnate lama to be the ultimate solution to problems of succession. The reincarnation is not related biologically to his predecessor, and if he is the same person as his predecessor, he need not kill and succeed his predecessor. On the other hand, if the predecessor and the reincarnation are separate persons, the predecessor or senior dies only to live again, and the current reincarnation, the junior person, atones for his succession by accepting the role of the celibate, world-renouncing monk. In the reincarnate lama, then, Paul finds the four roles of the Oedipal scenario enacted by one person.

The question of why celibate monasticism was introduced only recently in Sherpa areas is taken up by Sherry Ortner in *High Religion*.[18] Sherpa social order reveals a contradiction between hierarchy and egalitarianism. Both principles are visible, for example, in Sherpa descent and inheritance patterns. The investment of authority in the eldest son acknowledges hierarchy, but the practice of apportioning the sons' inheritance equally reflects egalitarianism. However, Ortner notes that the equal inheritance rule actually contributed to the largely economic division between what the Sherpas call "big" and "small" people, since the inheritance rule would favor economically not simply the sons of large property owners, but also men with the fewest brothers. Another factor contributing to the division between big and small people was tax collection, which effectively prohibited small people from having the capital to engage in trade, and, thus, like the big people, to increase their wealth. The tax collector appears to have been a traditional role carried out by an important man in Sherpa society. Tax collectors typically enhanced their own wealth substantively and, therefore, "big" men competed for the position.

Sherpa temple founding stories have four parts. They begin with an intense rivalry either between brothers or between two men who both seek the position of tax collector, move on to the departure of the hero and his acquisition of a protector (a person of great power and authority), follow this with the hero's defeat of his rival with the assistance of the protector and the hero's collection of followers who support his legitimacy, and conclude with the defeated rival's departure from the scene. Ortner observes that this pattern is reflected in Sherpa offering rituals, where demons may be substituted for the hero's rival. Ortner finds that this pattern, or cultural schema, suggests that big people can acquire great merit and legitimacy, a "big" name, by submitting themselves to the power of a protector. Thus, the temple founder's potency coupled with his humility may be seen as mediating the Sherpa contradiction between hierarchy and egalitarianism. The hero's submission to a higher authority, which supports hierarchy, enables him to defeat his rival on the plane of egalitarian competition.

Ortner's theoretical interest with respect to the founding of Sherpa celibate monasteries, is not only in locating recurring cultural schema, as revealed in the stories of the founding of temples and the twentieth-century histories of important sponsors of monasteries, but also in the actors' motivations for contributing to their construction. The establishment of Sherpa celibate monasteries, which began in the early 1900s at a time when the social division between big and small people became more marked, followed the temple-founding pattern insofar as big people were concerned. The small people, however, were also enthusiastic participants in the construction of these monasteries. Acquiring merit is, of course, a major motivation for both big and small people. However, apart from the acquisition of merit, Ortner argues that big and small people were enthusiastic about the monasteries for inverse reasons. The legitimacy of big people at this time was being undermined due to political and economic factors. From the big people's perspective, then, sponsoring monasteries was a quest for legitimacy through the expression of humility, lack of ego, and a concern for others. On the other hand, the small people, who by this time were enjoying unprecedented access to material resources, were expressing their bigness, their ability to acquire protectors (such as British mountaineering patrons), and their ability potentially to challenge the big people.

Another dimension to the question of the actors' motivation may be found in Ortner's investigation of who populated the celibate Sherpa monasteries and the Sherpa nunnery. Sherpa monks and nuns tended to the children of big people, because a son or daughter could not enter a monastic institution or nunnery without the parental financial support that was simply not a possibility for small people. But what often distinguished Sherpa monks and nuns is the fact that were they to remain in the secular world, they would experience downward mobility. Monks were typically middle sons who stood to inherit neither their fathers' status nor their fathers' houses. Daughters, even daughters of big people, could receive meager dowries from their fathers, which would prevent the possibility of making a good ("big") marriage. But joining a monastery or nunnery provided the big person's child with the opportunity to achieve high status in terms of religious merit and avoid sinking social status. What is more, Ortner finds evidence that many Sherpa monks and nuns joined celibate institutions in the twentieth century to escape the marriage manipulations imposed on them by their parents. Ortner highlights this fact to show that the intentions of actors, in this case, the popular enthusiasm for the founding of celibate monasteries, had unexpected consequences for the marriage system.

BUDDHISM AND SHAMANISM

Geoffrey Samuel, in *Civilized Shamans*,[19] centers his anthropological study of the development of Tibetan (Vajrayana) Buddhism and the patterns of Tibetan polity on the practitioner's orientation and argues that Tibetan Buddhism synthesizes very distinct religious practices and orientations, which accounts for the establishment in Tibet of both a clerical and shamanic Buddhism. The Vajrayana Buddhism that was introduced to Tibet shared two important features with indigenous shamanism: (1) The bodhisattva ideal, which links social responsibility to enlightenment, resonated with the shaman's sociocentric focus; and (2) tantric ritual techniques, which promise a quick but difficult path to enlightenment, parallel a visionary shamanic experience. Tibetan secular rulers utilized celibate academic monasticism, with its hierarchical structure of power, as a source of political legitimacy. However, unlike Theravadin Buddhism, Vajrayana Buddhism offered a way to immediately redirect the consciousness. If "instant" enlightenment is possible, then it is possible to escape karmic consequences. Since, as Samuel notes, Theravadin Buddhist monastic rituals are preoccupied with karmic consequences, Vajrayana Buddhism subtly altered the ideal of the monastic career. This alteration was possible because Vajrayana Buddhism is oriented towards the lama, a spiritual master who is not necessarily celibate, male, or even affiliated with a monastery, but who has the capacity to initiate practitioners into various levels of tantric practice. The lama, then, makes it possible for practitioners to transcend karma.

A lama's status was mainly determined by his (or her) reputation, and disciples were steadfastly loyal to their lamas. Although the development of lama-centered social groups[20] would seem to have threatened political centralization in Tibet, lamas became instead an integral part of Tibetan monastic structure, uniting shamanic with established monastic techniques. Samuel identifies the emergence of the reincarnate lama as a product of the synthesis of clerical (monastic) and shamanic elements in Tibetan Buddhism. However, the synthesis of clerical and shamanic elements emerged in two distinctive forms by the end of the nineteenth century. The politically dominant Gelugpa sect, which included the Dalai Lama, was concerned with centralizing—that is, orienting Tibetans, politically and spiritually, toward Lhasa. Thus, what Samuel calls the clerical, institutional emphasis of the Gelugpa sect would serve this purpose. The opposite trend of nonsectarianism, decentralization, and a more shamanic emphasis emerged in eastern Tibet.

Stan Mumford[21] approaches the relationship of Tibetan Buddhism to shamanism as a dialogical process that generated Tibetan Lamaism. To study this phenomenon, Mumford located an area in Nepal where recently resettled Tibetan refugees, including lamas, encountered strong shamanic traditions of the local Gurung community, who are believed to have migrated from Tibet long ago. A key distinction Mumford found between the shamanic and lamaic orientations was that the former promotes an ideal of harmonious cosmic balance to be achieved through practices of reciprocal exchange, while the latter emphasize the doctrine of karma that calls for the individual accumulation of merit. For example, shamanic rituals stress the notion of reciprocal exchange between humans and supernatural beings, whereas lamaic rituals call for the propitiation of guardian deities because the latter serve the dharma. The blood sacrifices so essential to maintaining good relations with the shamanic deities are condemned by Tibetan lamas as guaranteeing ritual sponsors and practitioners a long sojourn in hell. The Tibetan lamas, however, practice rituals where they "sacrifice" dough effigies. Thus, by focusing on the interpretations given by Tibetan lamas and Gurung shamans of their own as well as each other's rituals, Mumford concluded that shamanic and lamaic ritual practices represented historical layers of tradition.

BUDDHISM AND NATIONALISM

The relationship between Buddhism and nationalism, which Tambiah[22] and Keyes[23] have investigated in Thailand, has been a particular anthropological research focus in Sri Lanka, where violence between Sinhalese Buddhists and Hindu Tamils has raged since the late 1970s. The transformation of Sinhalese Buddhism in the nineteenth century contributed to the emergence of this violent Buddhist nationalism.

On this topic, Bruce Kapferer[24] argues that the revitalization of Buddhism in nineteenth-century Sri Lanka can be related to the development of a capitalist economy and the emergence of a middle-class ideology. Sinhalese exorcisms, rituals designed to treat patients suffering from ghostly or demonic attack, emerged under colonial rule as a tradition of the weak, and continue in postcolonial times to constitute ritual cults that the Sri Lankan middle-class views as unorthodox and, therefore, as the practices of inferior classes. Richard Gombrich and Gananath Obeyesekere[25] refer to the Buddhism that emerged in Sri Lanka as a result of the impact of British colonial power on Sinhalese society in the nineteenth century as "Protestant Buddhism." Protestant Buddhism became the religion of the Sinhalese middle class, who were educated in English-medium schools run by Protestant missionaries. The diffusion of Protestantism in this educational context supported the "rationality" of the Buddhist religion but not the ecstatic ritual practices associated with the spirit cults. Gombrich and Obeyesekere view the development of Protestant Buddhism as a historically significant transformation of Buddhism and imply that it is connected to the emergence of nationalist movements in Sri Lanka.[26]

Kapferer[27] argues that Sinhalese nationalist ideology views the nation or people as a hierarchical social order which is encompassed by the Buddhist state. Since Buddhism encompasses the state, and the state encompasses the nation, what unifies the nation as a hierarchical social order is submission to the ideology that this hierarchy is cosmically determined according to Buddhist dharma. In Sinhalese society, the integrity of individuals depends upon their encompassment by (or ability to fit into) the hierarchy and the unity of the whole. According to this ideology, Hindu Tamils should also be encompassed by the state, although they rank below Sinhalese Buddhists in the hierarchical order. Since Tamil nationalists reject such submission to the state, Kapferer concludes that the principle of hierarchical encompassment is attacked. This would, in turn, situate Tamil nationalists, from the perspective of Sinhalese nationalists, as powerful independent beings metaphorically akin to demons.

Tambiah, in *Buddhism Betrayed?*,[28] shows that the participation of Sinhalese monks in the fierce nationalism and violence that has emerged in Sri Lanka since 1977 is not simply a continuation of Sangha becoming periodically engaged in politics, which was a pattern in precolonial Sri Lanka as well as in Burma and Thailand, but rather the product of the modern state. What distinguishes current monastic involvement in politics from previous historical periods is that the current monastic organizational structure patterns itself after political parties, and the traditional monastic orientation to the ethical doctrinal aspects of Buddhism is no longer emphasized.

Ronald D. Schwartz,[29] a sociologist who employs anthropological modes of analysis, discusses a protest by monks in Tibet on the last day of the Lhasa Monlam festival in March 1988, when hundreds of monks were killed by Chinese soldiers, in terms of the relationship of the festival to the traditional Tibetan theocratic state. Monlam is a ten-day prayer festival which follows the celebration of the Tibetan New Year and commemorates the victory of Buddhism over other doctrines and reenacts the submission of the Tibetan state to Buddhism. Although the traditional Tibetan state from the mid-seventeenth century to 1951 was a theocracy headed by the Dalai Lama, who wielded both spiritual and temporal power, the Monlam festival marked the distinction of spiritual and secular rule within Tibet's capital, Lhasa. The Monlam festival continued the rituals of reversal characteristic of New Year celebrations by taking political control of Lhasa away from secular authorities and turning it over to Drepung Monastery. The attendance of secular state officials at Monlam ceremonies signified the submission of these officials to Buddhism, and, at the same time, renewed the spiritual legitimacy of the secular aspects of the Tibetan state. Prior to the Monlam riot of 1988, the Chinese Government thought that by symbolically presenting its officials as the patrons of religion, it could replace the political legitimacy, in the view of the Tibetan people, of the Dalai Lama's government. However, Schwartz points out that from the perspective of the traditional Tibetan polity, the monks predictably seized this dramatic opportunity to deny the legitimacy of the Chinese Government in Tibet, with fatal results.

CONCLUSION

Ethnographic studies of Buddhism reflect a variety of analytical approaches and a broad range of specific foci. Anthropologists have shared a particular interest in how a world-renouncing religion is socially accommodated, how it serves the needs of the self as well as of society, how it encompasses apparent doctrinal and practical paradoxes, and how it integrates monastic institutionalism with the careers of wandering seekers of enlightenment. Anthropologists have also investigated the relationship of Buddhism to colonialism and Buddhism both as an expression of resistance and that which is resisted, all brought to the fore by dramatic ethnic tensions in Sri Lanka. Anthropological research has shown that strategies developed by the great King Ashoka continue to be deployed in Sri Lanka, Southeast Asia, and even in present-day Tibet.

NOTES

1. Stanley J. Tambiah, in *World Conqueror and World Renouncer* (Cambridge: Cambridge University Press, 1976), gives a detailed comparison of early Buddhist kingdoms in Southeast Asia.
2. Melford E. Spiro, in *Buddhism and Society* (Berkeley: University of California Press, 1970), identified three separate Buddhist systems: one concerned with release from samsaric existence or attaining nirvana (Nibbanic Buddhism); one concerned with karma and obtaining a good rebirth (kammatic Buddhism); and one concerned with magical protection (apotropaic Buddhism).
3. Articles addressing apparent contradictions between doctrine and practice include Gananath Obeyesekere, "The Great Tradition and the Little in the Perspective of Sinhalese Buddhism, *Journal of Asian Studies* 22(2): 139–153, 1963; Gananath Obeyesekere, "Theodicy, Sin and Salvation in a Sociology of Buddhism," in *Dialectic in Practical Religion* E.R. Leach, ed. (Cambridge: Cambridge University Press, 1968), pp. 7–40; David Lichter and Lawrence Epstein, "Irony in Tibetan Notions of the Good Life," in *Karma*, Charles F. Keyes and E. Valentine Daniel, eds. (Berkeley: University of California Press, 1983), pp. 223–260; and Charles F. Keyes, "Merit-Transference in the Kammic Theory of Popular Theravada Buddhism," in *Karma*, Charles F. Keyes and E. Valentine Daniel, eds. (Berkeley: University of California Press, 1983), pp. 261–286.
4. Articles specifically addressing the relation of Buddhism to animism include Michael M. Ames, "Magical-animism and Buddhism," in *Religion in South Asia*, Edward B. Harper, ed. (Seattle: University of Washington Press, 1964), pp. 21–52; and Michael M. Ames, "Buddha and the Dancing Goblins: A Theory of Magic and Religion," *American Anthropologist* 66(1):75–82, 1964.
5. Melford E. Spiro, *Burmese Supernaturalism* (Upper Saddle River, NJ: Prentice Hall, Inc., 1967).
6. Stanley J. Tambiah, *Buddhism and the Spirit Cults in North-east Thailand* (Cambridge: Cambridge University Press, 1970).
7. Stanley J. Tambiah, *The Buddhist Saints of the Forest and the Cult of Amulets* (Cambridge: Cambridge University Press, 1984).
8. Christoph von Fürer-Haimendorf, *The Sherpas of Nepal* (London: John Murray, 1964). In *Morals and Merit* (Chicago: University of Chicago Press, 1967), a survey of concepts of social morality across South Asia, von Fürer-Haimendorf examined notions of merit in the context of social morality among Sherpas and Tibetans.
9. See Hanna Havnevik, *Tibetan Buddhist Nuns* (Oslo: Norwegian University Press, 1992), and Anna Grimshaw, *Servants of the Buddha: Winter in a Himalayan Convent* (Cleveland, OH: The Pilgrim Press, 1994).
10. David Holmberg, *Order in Paradox* (Ithaca: Cornell University Press, 1989).
11. John Ardussi and Lawrence Epstein, "The Saintly Madman in Tibet," in *Himalayan Anthropology*, James F. Fisher, ed. (The Hague: Mouton, 1978), pp. 327–338.
12. Rebecca Redwood French, *The Golden Yoke* (Ithaca: Cornell University Press, 1995).
13. Vinceanne Adams, *Tigers of the Snow and Other Virtual Sherpas* (Princeton: Princeton University Press, 1996).
14. Marcia S. Calkowski, "Returning and Exile: The Recognition of Contemporary Tibetan Reincarnations," n.d.
15. Sherry B. Ortner, *Sherpas Through Their Rituals* (Cambridge: Cambridge University Press, 1978).
16. Clifford Geertz, "Religion as a Cultural System," in *The Interpretation of Cultures* (New York: Basic Books, 1973).
17. Robert Paul, *The Tibetan Symbolic World* (Chicago: University of Chicago Press, 1983).
18. Sherry B. Ortner, *High Religion* (Princeton: Princeton University Press, 1989).
19. Geoffrey Samuel, *Civilized Shamans* (Washington, DC: Smithsonian Institution Press, 1993).

20. Barbara Aziz, in *Tibetan Frontier Families* (Chapel Hill, NC: University of North Carolina Press, 1978), describes the leadership roles of several Tibetan lamas in an ethnography of Tibetan refugees from D'ing-ri.

21. Stan R. Mumford, *Himalayan Dialogue: Tibetan Lamas and Gurung Shamans* (Madison, WI: University of Wisconsin Press, 1989).

22. Stanley J. Tambiah, in *World Conqueror and World Renouncer* (Cambridge: Cambridge University Press, 1976).

23. Charles F. Keyes, *Thailand: Buddhist Kingdom as Modern Nation-State* (Boulder, CO.: Westview Press, 1987).

24. Bruce Kapferer, *A Celebration of Demons* (Bloomington: Indiana University Press, 1983).

25. Richard Gombrich and Gananath Obeyesekere, eds., *Buddhism Transformed; Religious Change in Sri Lanka* (Princeton: Princeton University Press, 1988).

26. Gananath Obeyesekere, in *The Cult of the Goddess Pattini* (Chicago: University of Chicago Press, 1984), shows how the Sinhalese employed the Ashokan model of the just Buddhist king in a ritual to criticize the excessive demands placed on them by Sinhalese kings.

27. Bruce Kapferer, *Legends of People, Myths of State: Violence, Intolerance, and Political Culture in Sri Lanka and Australia* (Washington, DC: Smithsonian Institution Press, 1988).

28. Stanley J. Tambiah, *Buddhism Betrayed? Religion, Politics, and Violence in Sri Lanka* (Chicago: The University of Chicago Press, 1992).

29. Ronald D. Schwartz, *Circle of Protest* (New York: Columbia University Press, 1994).

Fourteen

Traditional Religions of China

John L. McCreery
Sophia University

INTRODUCTION

Turn back the clock a century. You have graduated from university and accepted a post with one of the great British trading companies that operate out of Hong Kong. To reach China from England, you must travel by ship. En route, your ship will stop in Italy, Egypt, India. Wherever it stops, you have a few days to explore the country-side and pursue your interest in comparative religion.

Italy is strange but also familiar. With its crucifixes, candles, incense, priestly vestments, carnivals and saints days, Italian Catholicism may seem a bit exotic. Still, it is Christianity, the most common form of religion in Europe. Its churches, priests, and doctrines are not all that different from what you imagine when you think of religion in the West.

In Egypt you encounter Islam. Mosques replace churches. Friday not Sunday is the holy day, and religious images are forbidden. But Islam also has its saints and festivals. Islam is, like Christianity and Judaism, a religion of the Book. All three are monotheistic religions rooted in belief in one, transcendent God, who exists apart from his creation and reveals His will through prophets whose words are recorded in canonical, sacred texts: the Torah for the Jews, the Bible for Christians, the Koran for Muslims. For believers in all three religions, their faith is the mark of membership in an exclusive religious community.

In India you encounter Hinduism. Here, too, there are temples, rites, and festivals. The division between Brahmin and warrior castes recalls a familiar division between priestly and secular authorities. But instead of one God there are many—goddesses as well as gods, and a seemingly endless variety of both. Stranger still, devotion to one does not preclude the worship of others. Instead of one sacred Book, you find a seemingly endless list of scriptures, commentaries, folktales, and myths. There are, to be sure, similarities between their content and what you find in the sacred Books of the monotheistic religions of Europe and the Middle East. There are, however, no rabbis, priests, or judges with the power to determine which are canonical and which are not.

You may note, too, that Hindu creation myths do not describe a singular event. Instead of a one, definitive pronouncement, "Let there be light," creation in Hindu thought is an endlessly repeated dream. Mystics of all schools seek to free themselves from the dream by losing their mortal selves in the great Self that is God. In this archetypically mystical religion, the mystic's search for that true Self has replaced submission to God's revealed Word.[1]

Then, at last, you arrive in China. Here, again, there are temples, rites and festivals; images like those of Catholic saints or Hindu gods and goddesses; fire, incense and offerings. When, however, you ask, "What is the religion of China?" you hear two surprising answers. Some say that China has three religions: Confucianism and Daoism, both indigenous to China, and Buddhism, imported from India. The other says that China has no religion. The three religions aren't religions at all, but schools of moral philosophy. The religious customs of the masses are only superstitious magic.

If you live long enough—to the middle of the twentieth century—you will also hear some scholars say that there is, after all, one Chinese religion.[2] It is not, however, a monotheistic religion; there is no single high God. Like Hinduism, Chinese religion is polytheistic and only in one of its many dimensions—the worship of ancestors—exclusive. But in contrast to Hinduism, there is no Creator who exists apart from His creation. The world does have an invisible dimension, the realm of spirits; all spirits—whether gods, ghosts, or ancestors—exist, like the human beings they resemble, inside the one, self-sustaining, natural order of things.

In Chinese religion, mysticism aims, not to escape from a world seen as a dream, that is, as a snare and illusion, but instead to become one with the constantly changing cycles of Nature. Ritual is seen in functional terms, either as essential for maintaining social or cosmic order or, more pragmatically, as a means of achieving the long life, wealth, and numerous descendants that define worldly success.

Like a Chinese banquet, the religious life of the Chinese combines many elements: Some can be identified as Daoist, Buddhist, or Confucian; others are labeled folk or popular religion and described as shamanistic.

At the core of this complexity is ancestor worship, to which everything else is related. Before the revolutions of the twentieth century, the worship of the ancestors was encompassed and elaborated by rites performed by emperors and mandarins: The cult of the imperial Chinese state. In traditional Chinese communities in Taiwan and Southeast Asia, communal and sectarian worship of gods and the exorcism of ghosts continue to surround and complement the domestic cult of the dead. In the People's Republic of China, all three were officially regarded as "feudal superstition" and targeted for suppression. In recent years, however, they have once again become widespread.

WORDS TO THE WISE

As we look more closely at all these aspects of Chinese religion there are several key points to keep in mind. There are temples; there are sects. There are private belief and public practice. But there is no Church separate from the state, no sharp boundary line that separates religion from other institutions. Chinese religious cosmology reflects this social reality; there is no transcendent God, only spirits who are part of the social and natural order, just like the human beings whom they outwardly resemble and whose fundamental nature they share.

We should also bear in mind that while we speak of "Chinese religion," China is a very large country with a population that is now around 1.2 billion people, a quarter of the world's population. Chinese religious attitudes exhibit every conceivable shade from fervent belief to indifference and active atheism, and a wide range of variation can be found in rural villages as well as towns and cities. In a study of religious belief in a village in Taiwan, anthropologist Steven Harrell interviewed fourteen villagers. Three, he found, were religious enthusiasts, village theologians who had each developed his own idiosyncratic version of Chinese religious cosmology. One, an old woman, was the village atheist; she stated bluntly that traditional religion is nonsense. The other ten participated in ancestor worship and festivals because, "it's the custom."

The communist revolutionaries who founded the People's Republic of China were heirs not only to Karl Marx's conviction that religion is "the opiate of the people" but also to a long indigenous tradition of scholarly skepticism. It was, after all, Confucius himself who said that while a gentleman acts as if the spirits are present in ritual, he devotes himself to worldly affairs and keeps the spirits at a distance. Many educated Chinese continue to follow his advice.

In attempting to understand Chinese religion we cannot, therefore, be satisfied with statements that say, "the Chinese believe this" or "the Chinese do that." Our goal must be instead to discover the range of possibilities for religious belief and practice that the world of Chinese religion provides and to understand the motives that incline individuals who occupy different positions in Chinese society to act on some of these possibilities while, perhaps, rejecting others.

We must recognize, too, that attitudes may change depending on circumstances. Even in premodern China, a mandarin who seemed a sober Confucian while holding imperial office could still be a Buddhist or Daoist mystic in private life and hire Buddhist monks or Daoist priests to perform their rituals at his parents' funerals. A despiser of "superstition" might still turn to a Daoist magician or medium when faced with disease or misfortune. Even a modern intellectual can feel the pull of "superstitious" beliefs if her child is sick or when death draws near at the end of life.

HOW DO WE STUDY CHINESE RELIGION?

Here we will use two approaches to explore the possibilities that Chinese religion provides. Our first approach is historical and based on the observations of historians and archaeologists. Here we must always keep in mind the sources on which their conclusions are based.

Three points are critical: First, China is the world's oldest continuously literate society, and the sheer volume of historical texts is enormous. One source suggests that the 25 imperial histories alone would require 45 million words in English translation. In Chinese the Buddhist Canon is 74 times the length of the Christian Bible, while the Daoist Canon is a library that runs to several thousand pages in its latest edition. In contrast the number of scholars who study these materials is small. In history as well as in archaeology, new discoveries continue to appear. Suppressed texts, hidden away sometimes for centuries, surface periodically.

Second, while the overall volume is enormous, what is available varies widely from one point in Chinese history to another. Relatively few texts survive from before the invention of woodblock printing on paper during the late Tang (581–907). Starting in the Song (907–1276), the trickle of materials suddenly becomes a mighty river.[3]

Third, almost everything we have in writing represents the views of an educated, literate minority, the scholar-gentry from whom the mandarins who governed imperial China were recruited. As a consequence, we may know a great deal about what went on at the imperial court and almost nothing at all about religious beliefs and practices in towns and rural villages away from the imperial court. This bias is especially strong in descriptions of pre-Song religion.

Our second approach will be through the work of anthropologists who have studied Chinese religion firsthand. For historical and political reasons, most of this research has been concentrated in Taiwan and Hong Kong, overseas Chinese communities in Southeast Asia, and, more recently, in parts of Southeast China. In addition, much of this work has been done in rural towns and villages. The primary focus of this research has been on the relationship between Chinese religion and forms of social organization in rural society. What Chinese religious life is like in North China or in modern Chinese cities is something we know far too little about. There is a certain irony here, for, to begin our historical survey, we must start on the North China plain.

PREHISTORIC AND ANCIENT RELIGION

The civilization we now call "Chinese" appeared on the North China plain around 2000 B.C.E. It is then, archaeologists tell us, that a complex, Bronze Age civilization began to emerge in an area long inhabited by Neolithic farmers. It is during this period that we first find evidence for metal working, horse-drawn chariots, states with political hierarchies governing large territories, walled cities, and writing. Traditional Chinese histories written centuries later associate this transition with a legendary dynasty called the Xia, replaced around 1600 B.C.E. by the Shang, the dynasty for whom we have the first reliable historical records.[4]

Diviners employed by the Shang kings wrote messages on oracle bones, either turtle shells or the shoulder blades of cattle. Hot pokers touched to the bones produced cracks from which the kings determined the spirits' response. While some of the messages were prayers to the kings' ancestors, others were addressed to a high god Di who may have been (scholars are still arguing) the kings' highest ancestor. Di's name was later incorporated into *Huangdi*, the word we now translate as "emperor," and into *Shangdi*, "Lord on High," a term now used by Protestant Christians to translate the word "God."

Besides the oracle bones, excavations of Shang sites have also revealed the rammed earth foundations of palaces, temples, and altars, bronze vessels used to make offerings of wine and food, and physical evidence that human beings as well as animals were sacrificed to the royal ancestors. Tomb 1001 at Anyang, constructed for a king who reigned around 1200 B.C.E., contained the remains of 90 followers who accompanied the king to his death, 74 human sacrifices, 12 horses, and 11 dogs.

It is clear that the Shang king was the chief priest of the state as well as its secular ruler. This combined role, which contrasts sharply with the separation of priest and king in Indian civilization and the separation of church and state in the Christian West, has remained characteristic of Chinese religion ever since. What is less clear is whether the Shang priest-king was also a shaman or medium.

Precise definitions of "shaman" and "medium" are terms hotly debated by experts in the history of religion.[5] Here "shaman" refers to someone who goes into trance and interacts with spirits through visions. In contrast to the shaman, who remains conscious while in trance, the medium is possessed by a spirit and unconscious of what the spirit does. Both are distinguished from the priest or magician who does not go into trance and acts consciously on the basis of expert knowledge of ritual instead of revelations received through visions.

What is clear is that mediums and shamans, magicians and priests have all been present throughout the history of Chinese religion and that members of educated elites have tended to despise mediums and shamans and the magicians who work with them. In other words, those who see themselves as masters of conscious knowledge acquired through education tend to reject those whose powers depend on inspiration, or worse yet, possession by spirits. We have noted, for example, Confucius's advice that a gentleman keeps spirits at a distance. In contrast, in the novel *Fengshen Yan-i* (*The Tale of the Infeudation of the Gods*), we read that the last Shang king, a cruel and despotic tyrant, was bewitched by fox spirits.

THE RISE AND FALL OF THE ZHOU

Around 1050 B.C.E. the Shang were overthrown by the Zhou. The Confucian classic, the *Book of Documents*, describes the overthrow of the Shang as the victory of just and noble warriors over a decadent and despotic king who no longer deserved his throne. Here we see for the first time the idea Heaven had transferred its mandate from a dynasty that had lost its virtue to a new imperial family whose virtue was fresh and unblemished. The dynastic cycle, the idea that dynasties begin with sages and end with despots whose misrule angers Heaven, has remained central to Chinese political and religious thinking ever since.

Zhou religion resembled that of the Shang but with certain important changes. Under the Zhou, the custom of voluntarily "following one's lord" into death would continue, but human sacrifices were on a smaller scale. Increasingly, images were substituted for human victims. Divination with oracle bones declined, giving way to a new system using the whole and broken lines that would later be codified in the hexagrams of *The Book of Changes*.

The first Zhou kings were, it seems, capable rulers. Confucius identified them as sages and argued that later rulers should emulate their example. But like the Shang before them, the Zhou would see their power fade. By the period called Eastern Zhou (770–256 B.C.E.), the North China plain was once again filled with warring states.

CONFUCIANISM AND DAOISM

Kungzi, who came to be known in the West as Confucius, lived at a time when the Zhou kingdom had already collapsed (551–479 B.C.E..). Appalled by the chaos of the world in which he found himself, Confucius traveled from one to another of the states that were struggling to replace the Zhou, attempting to persuade their rulers to model themselves on the ancient sages. If, he argued, rulers would display the human-heartedness called *ren*, Heaven would recognize their virtue, people would flock to support them, and unity and order would be restored.

In the *Analects*, a book which records discussions between Confucius and his disciples, we find that human-heartedness can be displayed in many ways, avoiding war and excessive taxation among them. But the most important by far is sincerity in behaving according to *li*, the proprieties exemplified by sacrificial ritual. Human-heartedness governed by *li* means conforming to social distinctions. Subjects should be loyal, children filial, wives obedient, friends faithful; subordinates should always defer to superiors.

Daoists were also disturbed by the chaos around them. But Laozi, the author of the *Dao De Jing* (*Classic of the Way and Its Virtue*), saw the rituals prescribed by Confucius as obstacles to living naturally. For Confucius, the *dao*, the way of Heaven, lay in performance of ritual that maintains social distinctions. To Laozi, social distinctions were the origin of strife and conflict. To live in accordance with the *dao* was, he taught, to follow the model of nature, which is wholly indifferent to human desires and treats everyone alike.

While Confucius and his disciples attempted to reform society, Daoists preferred to drop out. Thus, for example, the Daoist sage Zhuangzi was sitting one day by a river fishing when two emissaries from the king of Chu approached him with the king's offer to entrust to him the management of all his domains. Zhuangzi replied,

> I have been told that in Chu there is a holy tortoise that died three thousand years ago. The king keeps it in the great hall of his ancestral shrine, in a casket covered with a cloth. Suppose that when this tortoise was caught, it had been allowed to choose between dying and having its bones venerated for centuries to come or going on living with its tail draggling in the mud, which would it have preferred?

When the officers agreed that that tortoise would prefer to go on living in the mud, Zhuangzi told them to go away and, "leave me to drag my tail in the mud" (adapted from Waley).[6]

INDIGENOUS ALTERNATIVES

Confucianism and Daoism were only two of several schools of philosophy that flourished as the Zhou collapsed. One of the most influential was a school called the Legalists. While Confucianists argued that moral behavior exemplified in ritual is the key to an orderly society, the Legalists argued that the only activities of value to the state are agriculture and war. As they saw it, the only way to ensure social order and enable the state to defeat its enemies is a rigid system of clearly stated laws enforced by strict rewards and punishments.

While both Confucianists and Legalists were primarily concerned with social order and Daoists with living in harmony with nature, the Cosmologists were interested in how nature works. It was they who conceived a cosmos created through the interaction of *yang* (bright, male, active) and *yin* (dark, female, passive) forces and developed the theory of the Five Elements (wood, fire, earth, metal, and water).

THE IMPERIAL SYNTHESIS

It was, in the end, the state of Qin, organized on legalist principles, that extinguished the Zhou, conquered all the other states, and made its king, Qin Shihuangdi, the first emperor of China. But while legalist principles won the war, they lost the peace. The collapse of the first emperor's dynasty shortly after his death discredited a strictly legalist approach and led to renewed interest in the moral authority preached by Confucianists.

Thus it was that during the long-lived Han Dynasty (202 B.C.E. to 220 C.E.), a modified Confucianism became the empire's official ideology. Han Confucianism was a wide-ranging synthesis that combined Confucian political ideals with rituals rationalized in terms of Yin-Yang cosmology and legalist laws and punishments. While the emperor would help to ensure social and cosmic order through correct performance of ritual, his ministers could use force to suppress invaders and rebels. This all-encompassing system would form the overall framework for Chinese religious thinking.

DAOIST RELIGION AND BUDDHISM

As the Han collapsed during the second century C.E., Daoism was reborn. Now, however, it had ceased to be a quietist philosophy. Adherents of Daoist sects saw Laozi as a god and regarded his writings as sacred texts. In sharp contrast to the original Daoist philosophers described above, who rejected the state and its rituals, these new religious Daoists created an alternative state with rites modeled both on those of the dynasty it challenged and those of Buddhism, a new competitor from India. By rebelling against the Han, the Daoist sect known as the Way of Great Peace (also known as the "Yellow Turbans") became the first in what would become a long history of sectarian rebellions against the Chinese state.

Buddhism had arrived in China during the late Han. The dynasty's collapse then provided fertile ground for the spread of the Buddha's message that the world's suffering is caused by desire and the only path to salvation is to eliminate desire. Like the Daoist hermitage the Buddhist monastery offered an escape from the wars that wracked the dynasty's end. By the time Buddhism reached China, however, the Buddha's original philosophy was only one of its elements. Great temples, statues, and esoteric magical rites all added to its appeal.

The founders of China's next great dynasty, the Tang (581–907 C.E.), saw both Daoists and Buddhists as sources of magical power and legitimacy. While Confucianism continued to provide the core of official ideology, during this period Daoists and Buddhists also became powerful competitors for imperial patronage. Sometimes one or the other would gain the upper hand and see its rival proscribed, but overall both enjoyed a golden age. That golden age would come to an end during the Song (960–1276 C.E.).[7]

THE BIRTH OF MODERN "TRADITIONAL CHINA"

Shang oracle bones and excavations give us our first glimpses of divination, ancestor worship, sacrifice, and funerals. Confucian and Daoist classics date back to the Zhou.

With the Han imperial synthesis providing an overall framework, Buddhist and Daoist rituals elaborated at the Tang court are the models for rites that are still being performed as the twentieth century draws to a close. It is during the Song, however, that all these elements seem to come together in forms still visible today.

During the Song, China was repeatedly invaded by nomadic warriors from central Asia, Mongolia, and Manchuria. As refugees fled these nomadic invaders, the bulk of China's population shifted to what is now southern China, where the climate is warm and wet, the important grain is rice, and numerous waterways made moving goods from one place to another much simpler than in the north. Woodblock printing vastly increased the supply of books and also made it possible to print paper money. With a larger money supply, a denser and more literate population, and increased trade, commerce flourished.

Political institutions were also changing. The idea of an empire governed by bureaucrats recruited through examinations that test their knowledge of Confucian texts goes back to the Han. But during the Han and Tang and even the Northern Song (the period before the Jurchen expelled the Song from the north), imperial politics had been the preserve of large aristocratic families. The collapse of the north destroyed many of these families and seriously weakened others, creating new opportunities for ambitious men from the south. The number of candidates who trained for the imperial examinations far exceeded, however, the number of available posts. Those who failed to achieve the goal of official appointment became the literate gentry who dominated throughout the remainder of China's imperial history. Members of this class, who had, after all, devoted much of their formative years to the study of Confucian classics, became strong supporters of the great Song revival of Confucian thought called Neo-Confucianism.

In its Neo-Confucian form, Confucianism absorbed ideas from Daoism and Buddhism but eliminated both as political rivals. During the Song, Neo-Confucian thinkers not only established the canon, the Five Classics and the Four Books, that would serve as the basis for educating imperial bureaucrats into the twentieth century. They also created the basic institutions—genealogies, ancestor halls, and lineage estates—that would structure society in southern China down to the present day.

In contrast to Confucianism, both Buddhism and Daoism would see their fortunes decline. Buddhism has retained an institutional base in its temples and monasteries, and its celibate monks hold a near-monopoly on performance of funeral rites intended to ensure that the dead pass safely through the courts of Hell. In contrast, Daoists, who typically marry and raise families and are indistinguishable from other Chinese when not performing their ritual duties, have in the main become purveyors of ritual expertise. They operate, in effect, as religious entrepreneurs who compete not only with Buddhists and each other but also the spirit-writing cults, spirit mediums, geomancers, and fortunetellers with whom they overlap.

AN IMPERIAL INTERLUDE

In historians' accounts of the Song, an anthropologist enters a familiar world. There is, however, one major difference. In the Song and subsequent dynasties, the Yuan, Ming, and Qing, China was still an empire and the emperor still a priest-king whose character and correct performance of ritual were seen as essential for cosmic as well as social order.

The Qing, the last imperial dynasty, reached its peak in the eighteenth century, during the 60-year long reign of the Emperor Qianlong. His reign was, writes Angela Zito, "as famous for its imperial displays and ceremonial performances as for its literati scholarship and vast text-editing projects."[8] So concerned was Qianlong with correct performance of ritual that never once, despite the pressures of ruling a vast empire, directing wars on its boundaries, and making six imperial tours from Beijing to the Yangtze valley, did he miss a single Sacrifice to Heaven.

The Sacrifice to Heaven was one of four Grand Sacrifices in an annual ritual calendar that also included court audiences, reception of foreign guests, rites of mourning, and ceremonies associated with war. It began, like the other Grand Sacrifices, with a period of intense preparation. While the emperor and other participants went into seclusion to prepare themselves by meditation that emptied and centered their minds, other officials were busy assembling and inspecting materials and setting the scene for the ritual's performance. Official guides spell out the following steps:

1. Viewing victims
2. Achieving seclusion
3. Inspecting victims
4. Writing prayerboards
5. Viewing killing of victims
6. Placing spirit thrones, pitching tents, displaying vessels for offerings
7. Reviewing prayerboards
8. Departure of phoenix carriage (carrying the emperor) from palace
9. Viewing spirit thrones, altars, vessels, hall of seclusion
10. Arranging and standing
11. Inspection of filled vessels
12. Differentiating places
13. Inviting spirits to take places
14. Approaching the altar, ritual washing taking place
15. Welcoming the spirits
16. Presenting jade and silk
17. Bringing forward the flesh of the victims
18. Initial oblation
19. Middle oblation
20. Final oblation
21. Receiving felicitous liquor and flesh
22. Sending off the spirits
23. Watching the burning/interring of offerings
24. Returning spirit thrones
25. Returning to palace in phoenix carriage

Painstaking care ensured correct performance of the ritual. But, in contrast to Southeast Asian or Himalayan kings who reincarnate Hindu gods, the emperor was not divine. He was, says Zito, "a privileged exemplar of correct embodiment and perfect practice." He was, in other words, a model for his officials and, through them, a model of correct behavior for every Chinese.

What, then, had become of this model when, two centuries later, anthropologists began to study Chinese religion in Taiwan, Hong Kong, and Southeast China? What is Chinese religion today?

SPIRITS AND THE RITUAL PROCESS

If you spend a year in a traditional Chinese community, you will see an annual round of rituals addressed to the spirits who inhabit a Chinese cosmos fundamentally unchanged since the Han imperial synthesis. In the world of the spirits, the empire lives on. Besides the ancestors, there are gods who resemble imperial officials and ghosts who upset the social and cosmic order with sickness, misfortune, and death.

As you watch the rituals addressed to these spirits you will see them differentiated in numerous, clearly visible, ways. Depending on the part of China you live in, the details may vary a bit. But wherever you live they are likely to resemble those described by Stephen Feuchtwang in a study of a small mountain town in Taiwan.[9]

The town is composed of neighborhoods and the neighborhoods of households, the smallest territorial units of local society. The town has a temple where it houses and worships the heavenly gods who watch over it. Each neighborhood has a shrine to Tu Di Kong, the local god of the soil. Each household has its own altar. On one side, stage left, sit the images of the gods to whom the household's members feel a special relationship; on the other, stage right, sit the wooden tablets on which are written the names of the ancestors of the men of the family whose members form the core of the household, a group of people who eat together, sharing food cooked on a single stove. An incense burner that hangs from the eves of the room in the center of the house where the household altar is located is a place for offerings to Tian Kong, the Lord of Heaven, also known as the Jade Emperor. In front of the altar is a table where offerings of food and spirit money are placed during worship and food is arranged for banquets.

The rituals addressed to the household gods and ancestors follow the same basic pattern as worship in temples. Offerings of food and spirit money are placed before the spirits. Incense is lit and the spirits are invited to partake of the food. Prayers spell out what their worshipers hope to obtain from the spirits. Divining blocks, a pair of wooden crescents, flat on one side, round on the other, are tossed to determine the spirits' response. One round and one flat side up means "yes." Two round sides up means "no." Two flat sides up, with the blocks rocking on their round sides, means that the spirits are laughing. The rite ends when the food is withdrawn, the spirit money is burned, and the spirits are sent on their way.

The pattern is similar, whatever the type of spirit involved. Details differ, however, depending on whether the spirits are ancestors, gods, or ghosts. We have, for example, been using the word "worship" to describe the ritual process. Chinese distinguish two types of rites: propitiating ghosts and honoring gods and ancestors. Silver is offered to ancestors and ghosts (the commoners in the world of the spirits). Gods require gold. Offerings of food may be raw or cooked, served whole, or cut up and ready to eat. In rituals performed by individual households, ghosts are propitiated at rites performed outside in the street. Gods are first addressed by worshipers facing outward into the street but may be invited inside. Ancestors are worshiped indoors, facing the altar and away from the street.

These details may seem confusing, but what they do is dramatize distinctions that require different types of spirits to be treated in a manner appropriate to their status. The ancestors are family who live inside the house. The ghosts are potentially dangerous strangers. The gods are more powerful than either. Some gods are moral paragons who uphold the social and natural order. Some may resemble the ancestors and provide useful blessings, but power is inherently dangerous. Neither clearly "us" or "them," the gods are betwixt and between.

We should note, moreover, how the ritual drama ends. Whatever the type of spirit addressed, the final act is sending the spirits away and burning spirit money to clear the debts owed to them. Here we see a sharp contrast with the monotheistic religions which originated in the Middle East, where maintaining an enduring relationship with the one God is the core of both religious belief and ritual. In China relationships between worshipers and their gods depend on reciprocity in exchanges of offerings and blessings. Even ancestors who fail to provide the children and material wealth required to provide for their worship are likely to be forgotten.[10]

In contrast to the mystic religions of India, whose ultimate aim is the dissolution of the worshiper's worldly self in the larger, eternal Self that is God, here both gods and ancestors are worshiped then sent away. The basic pattern of ritual seems to conform to Confucius's advice to act with sincerity in ritual, as if the spirits are truly present, but otherwise to keep a wary distance from them.

ANNUAL FESTIVALS

As in other religious traditions, the Chinese year is punctuated by festivals. The high point of the annual cycle is the Chinese New Year, which typically falls in February or March. The season begins on the sixteenth day of the last month of the old year, the last day on which the God of the Soil is worshiped. It ends on the sixteenth day of the first month of the new year, when the worship of the God of the Soil resumes. The twenty-fourth day of the last month is when the household gods are sent off to Heaven, the fourth day of the new year, the day on which they return. On New Year's Eve, the whole family should gather to worship its ancestors. This night is the point in the year when the family is most turned in on itself. On New Year's Day, neighbors go out to greet and congratulate each other, renewing their relationships with society outside the family.

The fifteenth day of the New Year is the Lantern Festival. A day on which the Lord of Heaven is worshipped, it is balanced by the Ghost Festival held in the seventh month, when ghosts are released from Hell and must be propitiated. We must note, too, the annual festival on the birthday of the god to whom the town's temple is dedicated. Classical explanations relate these three pivotal events in the annual calendar of festivals to the spiritual rulers of Heaven, Earth, and Man or Heaven, Earth, and Water, respectively.

The New Year is not the only time that the ancestors are worshiped. At the Bright and Pure festival in the spring, the family gathers again, to clean its ancestors' graves. Offerings are also made on the first and fifteenth of each lunar month, when the moon is new and the moon is full. The God of the Soil is worshiped on the following days, the second and sixteenth. Here again we see the pattern described above, first a day on which the family turns inward to worship its ancestors, followed by a day on which it turns outward to renew ties outside the family.

ANCESTOR WORSHIP

The Shang Dynasty (c. 1600–c. 1050 B.C.E.) oracle bones that are China's earliest historical records tell us that the Shang kings sacrificed to their ancestors. In the *Analects* we find that when Confucius was asked to define filial piety, he answered, "That parents, when alive should be served according to *li*; that when dead, they should be buried according to *li*; and that offerings should be made according to *li*." Narrowly speaking, the *li* mentioned here means "ritual" or "ceremonial"; more broadly it means "propriety," following proper forms of behavior, like those elaborated in the rituals described above.

According to Mencius, the most revered Confucian philosopher after Confucius himself, the greatest of all sins is to have no sons to carry on the ancestral line and continue the ancestors' worship. "Sons" is the operative word. Traditional Chinese society is a patrilineal society in which the family surname and the right to a share of the family property descends from father to son. When daughters marry, they leave the family in which they were born to join another. The duty of a daughter-in-law is to serve her parents-in-law, to worship her husband's ancestors, and, above all, to provide the sons to continue his family line.

These principles are strongly rooted in an agricultural society where a family's primary asset is land passed down from one generation to another. The virtue prized above all others is *xiao*, filial piety. The younger generation serves the elder, providing their elders with food and other material goods. In exchange they receive their lives, care, and education in childhood, a dowry if a daughter, and, if a son, the right to inherit and become an ancestor. Chinese ancestor worship extends this pattern of exchange to include the dead as well as the living. For the dead, in traditional Chinese belief, depend on their living descendants for the means to survive and prosper in the realm of the spirits after they die.

The most powerful expression of *xiao* is the funeral by which the dead, who if left unburied, will become angry, hungry ghosts, are transformed into honored ancestors. There are, says James Watson,[11] nine critical steps:

1. The survivors of the deceased sob and wail. The wailing is loud and dramatic. It is both a public announcement that a death has occurred and demonstration of sincere grief.
2. The mourners dress themselves in hoods, robes, and shoes made of white cloth, sackcloth, and hemp. There are many variations, each of which clearly indicates a mourner's precise relationship to the deceased.
3. The corpse is bathed, ideally by the children or spouse.
4. Spirit money and paper models of items to be used in the afterlife (e.g., houses, furniture, servants, vehicles) are burned to transmit them to the world of the spirits. Offerings of food are also provided.
5. A soul tablet is prepared to house the soul of the dead. A tablet is prepared for all except those who die as infants or as wandering strangers. It becomes the object of ancestor worship in the home.

6. Specialists are hired to assist at the funeral. More is at stake here than a simple economic transaction. Someone from the community must accept money before the corpse can leave it.
7. Music is provided to settle the corpse and sooth the soul.
8. The corpse is sealed in the coffin, and then
9. expelled from the community.

These steps are universal throughout China. What happens next is more variable. In a manner reminiscent of many of the peoples who inhabit Southeast Asia, southern Chinese bury the coffin for seven to ten years. Then they exhume and clean the bones which are placed in a large ceramic pot and eventually reburied in a permanent tomb. Northern Chinese are revolted when they hear of this custom, but their own customs—for example storing coffins above ground for several years until other deaths allow spouses or parents and children to be buried together—are equally shocking to those who live in the south.

However the corpse is disposed of, the result is the same. The ancestor's soul is divided. The *hun*, its heavenly component, is brought home to be worshiped in the form of an ancestor tablet placed on the family's domestic altar. The *po*, its earthly component, is left at the grave. Once each year in the spring, at the Bright and Pure festival, the family will gather to clean the grave. As we shall see later, how the grave is sited may also affect the family's fortunes.

ANCESTORS, GODS, AND GHOSTS

The rites of burial and sacrifice are, says Laurence Thompson, sanctioned both by fear of the dead becoming vengeful demons and by hope that the dead will become benevolent gods. Who, then, are these demons, these ghosts, and these gods? If ancestors are members of the family, ghosts are hostile, hungry strangers. The gods are often described as heavenly bureaucrats, the spiritual counterparts of officials whose task is to represent the Heavenly state that governs the natural order. As often with things Chinese, the reality is more complex.[12]

"Family" in a narrow sense means *jia*, the household composed of people who form an economic unit and share food cooked at a common stove. The ideal is a *jia* composed of three or more generations, for grandparents, parents, and children all living together are visible proof that the members of the parents' generation have succeeded in their filial obligations to care for their own parents and continue the family line.

"Family" in a larger sense is *zu*, the lineage composed of *jia* who share common ancestors. The ideal lineage is a long and distinguished line of eminent men whose names are carefully recorded in the lineage genealogy. An ancestral hall provides a place to worship the ancestors shared by the families that make up the lineage, and land set aside as lineage property provides the income that pays for their worship.

The simplest definition of "ghost" is those who have neither family or lineage to see to their worship. Lacking descendants to feed them, ghosts are always hungry. With no one to burn spirit money for them, they are stuck in Hell, unable to pay for their sins. Hungry, needy, and angry, ghosts are hostile to the living and will seize any opportunity to harm them. It is hardly surprising, then, to find that much of Chinese religious activity consists of charms and exorcisms, the beating of gongs, the setting off of firecrackers, the building of spirit walls, and the like—all aimed at warding off ghosts, the vengeful demons the unworshipped dead become.

Some gods are, indeed, heavenly bureaucrats, and those who judge the dead as they pass through the Courts of Hell are one especially good example. Among Buddhism's contributions to Chinese religious ideas is the concept that karma determines rebirth in successive lives. Perhaps as early as the Tang (581–907 C.E.), but certainly by the Song (907–1276 C.E.), the Chinese had begun to conceive of karma in highly bureaucratic and monetary terms. In the Chinese view of karma, each rebirth adds to a burden of karmic debt recorded in divine ledgers. When the dead pass through the courts of Hell, their debts are adjusted by the gods who judge them to reflect the good and bad deeds they performed while alive. Those with descendants who burn plenty of spirit money can pay off their debts, thus securing a better rebirth or even eternal life in Amida Buddha's Western Paradise.

This view of Hell suggests that the gods are, in essence, heavenly bureaucrats, spiritual counterparts of the mandarins who governed late imperial China on behalf of the emperor. The mandarins were scholar-officials who qualified for official positions by passing the imperial examinations. The gods are divine officials appointed to their posts as rewards for virtuous behavior during their mortal lifetimes. Besides the judges in the Courts of Hell, other good examples include the Directors of Fate who inhabit the stars we call the Big Dipper, the God of Moats and Walls whose domain is a town and the region around it, and the local God of the Soil who watches over a neighborhood. All hold positions in a hierarchy that roughly mirrors the organization of the Chinese imperial state before the revolutions that unseated the last emperor in 1911. All are conceived as male and are known by the titles attached to their offices.

But some of China's most popular gods are goddesses, and others, while male, have demonic origins. The most widely worshiped divinity in Chinese religion is the Boddhisatva Guanyin, who is generally represented as a kindly, motherly woman. Southeast China's most popular cult is the worship of the Heavenly Consort Mazu, a favorite of merchants, fishermen, and seamen. Among the more demonic gods is Na-cha, the Third Prince, who began his supernatural career with violent, unfilial exploits that cause no end of trouble for his parents. Marshal Wen, a god worshiped to avert plagues, started out as a demon spreading plagues.

It appears, then, that far from being confined to idealized bureaucrats, the gods and goddesses worshipped in Chinese popular religion are a highly varied lot. They are, in effect, a cross section of powerful and potentially useful spirits who are neither ancestors (spirits who are kin) nor ghosts (spirits who are poor, thus hungry and hostile). Some have local roots; some are well connected in many different localities. They are powerful but also dangerous. Sometimes they will grant their worshipers favors. Then, again, they may not. What their worshipers look for is *ling*, the power to grant their wishes. An anecdote collected by Valerie Hansen nicely captures the pragmatism characteristic of Chinese belief.

> One day Li Mama told me she had gone to pray to a new god. I asked her why she had decided to pray to that particular deity, and she replied that the deity was *ling*. As I had

never heard the word before, Li Mama explained that a god was *ling* when he or she responded to requests. People in Taipei usually prayed when sick, or before taking the competitive college entrance examinations, or when hoping for a child. And if the deity cured them, or enabled them to get into a good university, or brought them a son, then that particular deity was *ling*. Li Mama had visited this new temple hoping that the god was *ling*, but if he was not, then she would go to another god. Her point was clear: people pray to gods to get things done, and they judge gods on the basis of their ability to perform miracles.[13]

THE WORLD OF YIN AND YANG

Like their human counterparts, the power holders, kin, and dangerous strangers who make up Chinese society, gods, ghosts, and ancestors do not exist in a realm which is separate from the natural order. They are part of the natural order and subject to its regularities. The basic concepts are ancient, going back at least to the period of the Warring States (403–221 B.C.E.) before the first emperor unified China.

An ancient Daoist text says: "The Dao gave birth to the one, the one gave birth to the two." The two are *yang* and *yin*. *Yang* is bright, active, male, the sun, dryness, the positive pole. *Yin* is dark, passive, female, the moon, wetness, the negative pole. Through their interactions *yang* and *yin* give birth to all the myriad things that constitute the world. They are often presented as complementary, but their relation is hierarchical. *Yang* is always the greater, encompassing the lesser *yin*, a model of as well as a model for male dominance in a patrilineal society.

An alternative model, now always combined with the *yang* and *yin*, is based on the *wu xing*, a term variously translated as the Five Elements, Five Agents, Five Phases, or Five Operational Qualities. Wood, fire, earth, metal, and water: The *wu xing* correspond to the five senses, the five internal organs, the five sounds, the five colors, the five flavors, and the five relationships.

- They control the five directions (east, south, center, west, and north)and the five seasons (spring, summer, mid-summer, autumn, and winter).
- They produce each other: wood giving rise to fire, fire to earth, earth to metal, and metal to water.
- They also check each other: Water checks fire, fire metal, metal earth, earth water.

More elaborate schemes include the eight trigrams and sixty-four hexagrams of the *Classic of Changes* and the ten heavenly branches and twelve earthly stems used for calendrical and astrological calculations.

The shared assumptions in all these systems are that nature moves through repetitive cycles whose permutations and combinations affect the fates of humans and spirits alike. Prior to the twentieth century, Chinese historians would use these basic concepts to interpret the rise and fall of imperial dynasties. These same concepts provide the basic framework of Chinese medicine, acupuncture, martial arts, and fortunetelling.

To see these concepts at work, let's look more closely at *feng-shui*, "winds and waters," the art of geomancy, aligning graves and buildings to improve the luck of those associated with them. Our example is a grave, somewhere in southern China, but the same principles apply to homes, temples, and imperial palaces. Nowadays, they may also be used in planning office and apartment blocks.

In the case we examine here,[14] a southern Chinese family has saved enough to build a proper tomb for its ancestor and has hired a geomancer to recommend a lucky site. A well-chosen site will not only make the ancestor's earthly soul more comfortable; it will also channel good fortune to his descendants. Ideally the grave should be on a slope, facing south to receive the *yang* rays of the sun. The mountain behind it should be gently rounded. Sharp peaks are not only inherently threatening; they also leave gaps through which cold *yin* winds from the north can blow. The site should form a U, like the courtyard of a traditional house, with ridges from the mountain gently cradling the place where the grave is located. The ridge to the east, the Azure Dragon, another *yang* symbol, should be slightly higher than the ridge to the West, the *yin* White Tiger. A stream should flow across the slope below the grave. Its water symbolizes wealth; ideally it should collect in a pool. Things to be avoided include roads, power lines, or streams that run perpendicular to the grave. They will drain away luck and provide a path for *yin* forces that bring misfortune to the family.

Care must be taken in choosing and planning a grave, for not all descendants share the same fate. A site and alignment within it that are lucky for one branch of the family could mean disaster for another. To ensure that nobody takes unfair advantage and, more directly, because geomancy involves calculations that only an expert knows how to do, the usual pattern in choosing a grave is to seek expert help.

WHO, THEN, ARE THE EXPERTS?

If you've read this far, you may be feeling that the world of Chinese religion is a very complicated place. Your feelings are shared by most Chinese. Funerals are complicated, but Buddhist monks and other specialists know what to do. A chronic sickness or run of bad luck may be a sign that an ancestor is angry, you are being attacked by a ghost, or perhaps you've offended a god. Which is it and what to do about it? A Daoist priest or a spirit medium may have the answers you need. Will a marriage or business venture be successful? You may want to see a fortuneteller.

Broadly speaking, the experts you consult range from those like the geomancer or fortuneteller who draws on expert knowledge recorded in written texts to the spirit medium possessed by a god. The medium is unconscious; it is the god who knows what to do. Buddhist monks and Daoist priests may fall in the middle of the spectrum, appealing either to texts or to personal revelations to justify their advice.

At one end of the range are those who, when dressed to perform ritual, present themselves in the style of traditional literati. They wear long gowns and slippers. Their movements and gestures are carefully controlled. Their rites are accompanied by courtly music. At the other end are mediums who appear barefoot and half-naked. While in trance they may beat themselves bloody with swords or spiked balls. That they seem to feel no pain is seen as a demonstration that they are truly possessed by their gods.

While Buddhist monks and Daoist priests identify themselves with particular religious traditions, geomancers and fortunetellers avoid religious identification, presenting themselves instead as practitioners of traditional sciences. Spirit mediums may only say that they *bai shen*, that is, honor the gods.

Daoist priests present themselves as the heirs to ancestors who passed down to them the esoteric knowledge required to perform the communal rites of renewal called *jiao*. Imitating the emperors and mandarins of old and representing a tradition traceable back to the Han, they look down on mere *fashi* (masters of magic), who may seem more like shamans, attributing the powers they wield to their own encounters with the gods they serve.

A critical point to remember, however, is that all of these various specialists are, in effect, consultants who compete in a market for ritual knowledge and services. None have the authority to impose their own particular view of the Chinese religious cosmos on others. For diplomatic reasons, both the Peoples Republic of China and the Republic of China on Taiwan legally acknowledge the principle of freedom of religion.[15] Prior to the twentieth century, the imperial state might enforce its claim to exemplify the natural order of things and suppress challenges to it. In practice, however, little attention was paid to competing religious and ritual perspectives until they became mass movements.

SEERS AND REVOLUTIONARIES

As described above, much of Chinese religion is keyed to recurring ritual cycles and easily interpreted in functional terms as contributing to a self-contained cosmic and social order. Some rituals, like the annual cycle of festivals or the rites of cosmic renewal performed by Daoist priests, are tied directly to the passage of time. Others, like funerals or weddings or the rituals that surround childbirth, reflect moments in individual lives. The image that all of these rites dramatize is that of a self-contained world in constant but regular change.

There are times, of course, when sickness or misfortune disrupt this smoothly running cosmos. Daoist priests, magicians, and mediums like those described above may then be called upon to perform healing rituals designed to exorcise the ghosts on whom problems are blamed and restore the cosmic and social order.

When times are good and change fits comfortably within conventional cycles, these recurring and occasional rituals may suffice to make life meaningful, to make misfortune endurable, and to promise that better times will come. What happens, however, when change is too fast or disasters and calamities too widespread?

Chinese history is filled with examples of sectarian movements whose response to widespread misfortune has been to challenge the power of the state and the cosmic assumptions on which it is based. We have already mentioned the late Han Daoist sect called the Way of Great Peace. This sect, however, was only the first of numerous similar sectarian movements that appear over and over again throughout China's history.[16]

Taizu, the founder of the Ming dynasty, was a commoner who started his career as a White Lotus rebel against the Yuan. During the Qing, White Lotus rebels whose aim was the restoration of the Ming became the focus of a widespread rebellion that lasted eight years, cost the empire the equivalent of five years' revenue, and devastated large parts of the empire. White Lotus beliefs included a view of cosmic cycles that owes as much to Indian concepts of destruction and rebirth as indigenous Chinese thinking. They appealed to the hopes of poverty-stricken peasants that the Maitreya Buddha would descend into the world, utterly destroy the current system, and begin a new era of peace and prosperity.

Another famous example is the Great Taiping Rebellion of 1851–1864 whose millennial hopes were rooted in its founder Hong Xiuquan's visions—an eclectic mixture of Christianity (Hong presented himself as Jesus' younger brother) and indigenous Chinese ideas (the rebels' political-military system was based on the *Rituals of Zhou*). Like the Yellow Turbans of the Way of Great Peace, the Taiping rebels were defeated and suppressed. But again the cost was high. Years of civil war had devastated the countryside, weakened the central government, and left large areas of China in the hands of generals turned warlords who began to fight among themselves.

The Communist revolutionaries lead by Mao Zedong can perhaps be seen as the latest of these movements. Like the White Lotus rebels who overthrew the Yuan, they too rebelled against a corrupt and decadent state, justified their actions in terms of imported—this time Marxist-Leninist—ideas, and succeeded in seizing the Mandate of Heaven.

Scholarly works on Chinese religion and mysticism often portray a world in which the elements resonate with each other like the notes in a well-tuned harmony. The imperial Great Sacrifices, the Daoists' rites of cosmic renewal, and the annual round of festivals all lend strong support to this view. The Yin-Yang cosmos, with its endlessly repeating cycles and rhythms, provides the conceptual framework for all these rituals. As we end this survey of Chinese religion, we should, however, also remember all those times when harmony collapsed, when sects proclaimed new revelations, and the music of the Dao became a battle hymn.

NOTES

1. For more on the difference between the prophetic religions of the Middle East, Indian mysticism, and China's "religion of harmony," see Julia Ching, *Chinese Religions* (Maryknoll: Orbis Books, 1993).

2. See, for example, the argument in Laurence G. Thompson, *Chinese Religion: An Introduction*, 5th ed. (Belmont, CA: Wadsworth Publishing Company, 1996). The volume cited here is the latest edition of the classic starting point for all serious modern thinking about Chinese religion. It is definitely the place to start when exploring the subject further.

3. This and the following point are taken from Valerie Hansen, *Changing Gods in Medieval China, 1127–1276* (Princeton, NJ: Princeton University Press, 1990), a book on which this essay draws heavily. There is no better introduction to the critical Song period in which Chinese religion began to assume its modern shape.

4. The account presented here is taken largely from Patricia Buckley Ebrey, *The Cambridge Illustrated History of China* (Cambridge: Cambridge University Press, 1996) and John King Fairbank, *China: A New History* (Cambridge, MA: Harvard University Press, 1992).

5. See, for example, the discussion in Jordan Paper, *The Spirits Are Drunk: Comparative Approaches to Chinese Religion* (Albany: State University of New York Press, 1995).

6. Arthur Waley, *Three Ways of Thought in Ancient China* (Garden City, NY: Doubleday Anchor Books, 1939), pp. 57–58. Waley is not only a classic in the field but also delightful to read.

7. The account of the Han synthesis and the subsequent history of Buddhism and Daoism presented here is based largely on Arthur F. Wright, *Buddhism in Chinese History* (Stanford, CA: Stanford University Press, 1959).

8. Angela Zito, *Of Body and Brush: Grand Sacrifice as Text/Performance in Eighteenth-Century China* (Chicago: University of Chicago Press, 1997). This book is one of the finest analyses of imperial ritual currently available. See also, Howard J. Wechsler, *Offerings of Jade and Silk: Ritual and Symbol in the Legitimation of the T'ang Dynasty* (New Haven, CT: Yale University Press, 1985).

9. Stephan Feuchtwang, "Domestic and Communal Worship in Taiwan," in Arthur P. Wolf, ed., *Religion and Ritual in Chinese Society* (Stanford, CA: Stanford University Press, 1974), pp. 105–130. This volume is to the

modern anthropology of Chinese religion what Thompson is to its history, an indispensable starting point for anyone with a serious interest in the subject.

10. These ideas are developed at greater length in John L. McCreery, "Why Don't We See Some Real Money Here?" *Journal of Chinese Religions*, No. 18, 1990 pp. 1–24 and John L. McCreery, "Negotiating with Demons: The Uses of Magical Language," *American Ethnologist*, 22 no.1, 1995.

11. From Watson's "Introduction" to James L. Watson, and Evelyn S. Rawski, *Death Ritual in Late Imperial and Modern China* (Berkeley: University of California Press, 1988); *Eighteenth-Century China* (Chicago: University of Chicago Press). Watson's and Rawski's parallel introductions to the volume are a striking demonstration of the difference in perspective that historians and anthropologists bring to the study of Chinese religion.

12. For several accounts of Chinese deities with ghostly origins and nonbureaucratic characteristics, see Meir Shahir, and Robert P. Weller, eds., *Unruly Gods: Divinity and Society in China* (Honolulu: University of Hawaii Press, 1996).

13. See Valerie Hansen. *Changing Gods in Medieval China, 1127–1276* (Princeton, NJ: Princeton University Press, 1990).

14. Taken directly from Daniel L. Overmeyer, *Religions of China* (San Francisco: HarperCollins, 1986).

15. For an interesting account of the status of Chinese religion both in Taiwan and in mainland China by a serious scholar with firsthand experience in both places, see Kenneth Dean, *Taoist Ritual and Popular Cults of Southeast China* (Princeton, NJ: Princeton University Press., 1993).

16. Susan Naquin, 1976, *Millenarian Rebellion in China: The Eight Trigrams Uprising of 1813*; David K. Jordan, and Daniel L. Overmeyer, 1986, *The Flying Phoenix: Aspects of Chinese Sectarianism in Taiwan*; and Robert P. Weller, 1994 *Resistance, Chaos and Control in China: Taiping Rebels, Taiwanese Ghosts and Tiananmen* (Seattle: University of Washington Press) are all rich sources of information on this subject.

Fifteen

Japanese Religions

C. Scott Littleton

Occidental College

INTRODUCTION

This chapter surveys the origins, history, sacred texts, deities, rituals, paths toward salvation, ethical principles, and other aspects of the magico-religious belief systems—Shintō, Buddhism, Confucianism, Daoism, Christianity, and the so-called "new religions"—that have shaped Japan's religious consciousness in the course of the last millennium and a half. Of these several belief systems, the most influential have been Shintō and Buddhism, and it upon these two fundamental traditions, the one indigenous and the other imported, that we shall focus in what follows.

Shintō, or the "Way of the Gods," the indigenous Japanese belief system, is primarily concerned with matters of this world, such as marriage, physical well-being, plant, animal, and human fertility, and the land itself. In contrast, the Mahayana Buddhist sects that have impacted Japan since the middle of the sixth century C.E. have from the outset been more concerned with moral, philosophical, and spiritual matters, and with death and the hereafter.

Like most other fundamental features of Japanese civilization—as opposed to culture in the fundamental anthropological sense—Buddhism came to Japan from China, the great mother civilization of East Asia. To be sure, Buddhism's ultimate origins were in North India some 2,500 years ago (see Chapter Thirteen), and the monks who, in 552 C.E., introduced Buddhism to the Yamato court were Koreans. But the sacred Buddhist texts, or sutras, had long since been translated into Chinese, and in order to read them the newly converted Japanese aristocrats (it would be several centuries before the new faith spread widely throughout the population) were forced to learn to read Chinese characters. Thus did literacy arrived in Japan, and along with it far more than the sutras. Confucianism and Daoism also made their appearance in Japan at this time, and, although with a few exceptions, such as the role played by Neo-Confucianism at the Tokugawa court (see below), they never attained the status of full-fledged religious sects, both belief systems have exerted considerable influence on both Shintō and Japanese Buddhism.

However, despite the tremendous impact of Chinese religious beliefs, philosophy, literature, art, architecture, music, dance, political theory, and so forth, Japan remained culturally distinct from its neighbor across the Yellow Sea. Then, as in more recent times, the Japanese penchant for borrowing and readapting soon manifested itself, and the Buddhist sects that diffused to Japan, all of which belong to the Mahayana branch of the religion (see Chapter 13), soon became—and have remained—uniquely Japanese.

Another important element in the Japanese religious mix is Christianity, which, as we shall see, was first introduced by Jesuit missionaries in 1549, only to be ruthlessly suppressed at the end of what some historians have called Japan's "Christian century."[1]

More recently, Japan has witnessed the emergence of a multitude of what are called in Japanese *shinko shūkyo*, that is, "new religions." The earliest of these new creeds were stimulated by the social chaos that accompanied the last three decades of the Tokugawa Shogunate (1837–1867) and the rapid economic development that followed World War II. But again, the end result has been quintessentially Japanese, a relatively seamless blend of foreign and indigenous ideas, customs, rites, and beliefs.

This "blending" process is what anthropologists call *syncretism*, that is, the fusion of otherwise disparate religious beliefs and practices into a single system, and it is a prime feature of Japanese religion–together with what can best be described as a high degree of "ambiguity tolerance." Both of these processes have had a profound impact on Japanese religious consciousness, almost from its inception. With some important exceptions, most Japanese consider themselves to be both Shintōists *and* Buddhists and see no inherent contradiction in practicing two faiths with such radically different roots. For example, the overwhelming majority of Japanese are married according to Shintō rites.[2] At the same time, an equally overwhelming majority are buried according to Buddhist rites and interred in cemeteries attached to Buddhist temples.

Moreover, the two major Japanese belief systems, together with Daoism, Confucianism, and, at various times, Christianity, have by no means remained wholly separate.[3] Shintō deities, or *kami* have become Buddhist *bodhisattvas* (or *bosatsu*, as they are called in Japanese), and vice versa; and Daoist deities and Confucian ethical principles have been integrated into both the Shintō and Buddhist traditions. In this chapter we shall look at both the specifics of these several faiths *and* the ways in which they have commingled, especially at the popular level.

THE HISTORICAL DIMENSION

The Roots of Shintō

Shintō's origins are shrouded by the mists of prehistory.[4] Whether the earliest known Japanese prehistoric tradition, the Jōmon culture (ca. 11,000 to 300 B.C.E.), knew the *kami* faith, at least in anything like the form we know it today, is an open question. We do know that these preliterate, seminomadic foragers, and fisher folk made stylized ceramic female figurines, or *dogu*, that emphasized the hips and breasts.[5] Like analogous figurines in other prehistoric cultures, such as Upper Paleolithic Europe, the Jomon *dogu* probably reflect the presence of a fertility cult. However, the precise nature of the religious beliefs that surrounded these figurines is unknown. We do know that they were often placed in or near graves after being deliberately broken, or "killed," thus releasing the spiritual essence of the *dogu*. But whether that "essence" was a prototypical Shintō kami is anybody's guess.

After the arrival of the more complex Yayoi culture, ca. 300 B.C.E., we begin to see iconographic materials that do indeed seem Shintō-like. Among the grave goods associated with these simple rice cultivators, whose homeland probably lay somewhere in Southeast Asia or South China, are small images of raised storehouses that are strikingly similar to the architecture of the most sacred of all Shintō shrines: the Grand Shrine of the Sun Goddess at Ise. We also find female fertility images as well as stone clubs that appear to have a phallic symbolism. Indeed, the introduction of paddy rice agriculture seems to have engendered rituals associated with sowing and harvesting that were probably fundamentally similar to rice-related Shintō ceremonies that persist to this day in many parts of rural Japan.

Closely associated with this Yayoi fertility cult were comma-shaped jewels called *magatama*, ceremonial mirrors, and sacred swords, all of which play an important part in Shintō mythology and in the rituals surrounding the enthronement of an emperor. Most scholars suspect that many of the tutelary *kami* associated with the attested ancient clans, or *uji*, that is, the *ujigami*, date from this period. The most important of these *ujigami* was, of course, Amaterasu, the Sun Goddess, the mythological progenitor of the Yamato *uji*, that is, the Imperial Family.

In the late fourth century, Japan was conquered by horse-riding nomads from Central Asia, who seem to have constituted a ruling elite rather than an invading population, and a new form of burial appeared: the *kofun*, or tumulus, hence the designation Kofun Period.[6] Around the periphery of these massive, keyhole-shaped tombs were often arranged small, votive figurines of horses and armed warriors known as *hanniwa*, which were believed to accompany the deceased chief on his journey to the afterworld.

All the while, the power of the Yamato, or Imperial *uji*, was growing. By the beginning of the sixth century the Yamato Emperor, based in the region that still bears this name, exercised at least a nominal authority over most of the country south and west the Kanto plain. It was into this embryonic state, in either 538 or, more traditionally, in 552, that the first major contingent of Buddhist missionaries arrived in Japan as a good-will gesture from the king of Paekche in southwestern Korea to his Japanese "brother." (A few Buddhist missionaries may have reached Japan from China over a century earlier, but their influence seems to have been slight.)

Early Japanese Buddhism

At first, there was a fair amount of conflict between those members of the Imperial court who enthusiastically embraced the new religion and those who resented its intrusion. However, in 587, the Soga *uji*, which championed Buddhism, managed to defeat a conservative coalition headed by the Mononobe family, and the future of Buddhism in Japan was assured. As a result, when young Shōtoku Taishi, or "Prince Shōtoku" (574–622), second son of the first Buddhist emperor and an ardent Buddhist himself, was appointed regent on behalf of his aunt, the Empress Suiko, he was able, in 592, to declare Buddhism the official religion of the Yamato court.[7] Shortly thereafter he founded (and perhaps designed) a major Buddhist temple complex at Horyuji, near Nara, and throughout his career worked tirelessly to advance the Buddhist cause. It is for these reasons that he is often described as the "founder" of Japanese Buddhism.

It should be emphasized that Shōtoku Taishi's contributions to the development of Japanese religion were not limited to his activities on behalf of Buddhism. He was also steeped in the Chinese classics and did as much as anyone to introduce Confucianism and Daoism to Japan. In 604 he promulgated his famous "Seventeen Article Constitution," which draw heavily on both Buddhist and Confucian ethical principles. In short, by the time of Shōtoku Taishi's death in 622, Japan had moved from a peripheral, barely literate proto-state to a civilized and highly sophisticated empire closely modeled on that of China.

The "Nara Schools" and Heian Buddhism

In the two centuries that followed, Buddhism rapidly expanded its influence among the Imperial aristocracy.[8] Between 625 and 738, the six so-called "Nara Schools" (from the fact that most were–and still are–headquartered at Nara, the first permanent imperial capital, 710–794) were founded: Jojitsu (625), Sanron (625), Hosso (654), Kusha (658), Kegon (736), and Ritsu (738). Each had a link to a parent temple in China. A good example of such a connection can be seen in the case of Sanron, which derived from the Chinese San-lun sect. The best known of these early Buddhist "schools" is probably Kegon, whose massive wooden headquarters, the Todai-ji Temple in Nara, which houses a huge bronze statue of the Buddha, is one of the most famous buildings in Japan.

With a few exceptions, however, the mass of the population remained essentially outside the Buddhist orbit until the early Heian Period (794–1185), when two famous monks, Kōbō- daishi (774–835) and Dengyō-daishi (762–822) returned from China in 806 and founded, respectively, the Shingon (from Chinese Chen-yen) and Tendai (from Chinese T'ien-t'ai) sects. Both were headquartered on mountain tops near Heian (modern Kyōto), which became the imperial capital in 794: Shingon on Mt. Koya and Tendai on Mt. Hiei, which rises up directly behind the city. From these bastions, priests journeyed far and wide throughout the countryside, founding temples and monasteries, and, as a result, the number of converts to the new faith rose rapidly.[9]

Nevertheless, Shintō remained firmly intact. Unlike the missionaries who, at approximately the same time (the ninth and tenth centuries), brought Christianity to Northern Europe and were in the habit of tearing down "pagan" shrines and erecting churches in their place, the Buddhist missionaries founded their temples next door to the Shintō shrines and proclaimed that there was no conflict between the two faiths, and that the Buddhist *bosatsu* and the indigenous *kami* were but different aspects of the *same* fundamental religious concepts.

By the end of the Heian Period (1185) this sense of inclusiveness led to the development of Ryōbu Shintō, or "Double Shintō," in which *kami* and *bosatsu* were formally combined into single divine entities. This theological fusion was often visually represented by images of human figures (*kami*) "dreaming" of their Buddhist counterparts (*bosatsu*), ethereal images floating above them in cloudlike "balloons."

Kamakura Buddhism: Hōnen, Shinran, Nichiren, Eisai, and Dōgen

The last years of the Heian Period were characterized by a bloody civil war between two clans, the Minamoto and the Taira, for control of the Imperial court. The end result of this conflict was the establishment of the office of *shōgun*, or "generalissimo," and the onset of a 400-year period of almost constant internal strife, which, in turn, caused many Buddhist priests to suspect that the chaotic "third age," or *mappō*, in the Mahayana eschatology, had dawned. Given the increasing social instability, it was difficult, if not impossible for the average person to devote the time and effort needed to achieve salvation in the traditional fashion, that is, by intense meditation on the meaning of the sutras (see below).

Thus, an "easier" path to salvation was needed, and it is not fortuitous that the early years of the Kamakura Period (1185–1333), so-named because the new shogunal capital was located in Kamakura, near modern Tokyo, were a time of great religious ferment in Japan. Indeed, no period in Japanese history has produced more major religious reformers.

The earliest of these was Genku, better known as Hōnen (1145–1215).[10] Hōnen eventually became dissatisfied with the orthodox Tendai dogma, and, in 1175, he began to preach the extreme importance of reciting *nembutsu*, that is, recitation of the phrase *Namu Amidu Butsu*, or "I put my faith in Amida Buddha," which was central to the Tendai creed. Shortly thereafter, drawing upon the teachings of Tao-cho, Shan-tao, and Chih-I, he inaugurated the Jōdō-shū, the earliest Japanese version of "Pure Land" Buddhism, which had taken shape in China several centuries earlier.

Drawing on the *Lotus Sutra* (see below), Hōnen preached that if one did *nembutsu* repeatedly, and especially just before dying, Amida Buddha would take pity on the supplicant's soul and cause it to be reborn in the "Pure Land" (also called the "Western Paradise"). Reflecting the chaotic spirit of the era, Honen asserted that all human beings were inherently too wicked to achieve salvation on their own, even if they lived apparently perfect lives. The only hope, he asserted, was to throw oneself on the mercy of Amida.

Another version of the "Pure Land" idea, one that was to loom even more importantly in subsequent Japanese religious history, was preached by Hōnen's chief disciple, Shinran (1173–1263).[11] What sets Shinran's theology apart from Hōnen's is his emphasis upon what he came to call the "Primal Vow," that is, an absolute commitment to Amida as one's "personal savior," to use a familiar Christian expression. It is this aspect of Shinran's thought that admits of a comparison to what Martin Luther preached some three centuries later. Like Luther, Shinran held that an all-embracing, intensely personal faith in the power of the divine—in this case Amida Butsu rather than Jesus Christ—was the key to salvation. It did not matter how often one recited *nembutsu*, or whether one said it just prior to death. A single, intensely fervent *namu Amida Butsu*, in which the supplicant opened his or her heart to the bosatsu, was all was really needed to gain eventual rebirth in the "pure Land." Although it is framed in the context of a vastly different religious tradition, this idea is strikingly similar to Luther's concept of "justification by faith."[12] Ultimately, what counts is the compact between the supplicant and Amida Butsu. Indeed, the power of *nembutsu* permits a true believer to become one with the Maitreya Buddha, the "Buddha-Yet-to-Come," just as Protestant Christians who achieve a state of grace are assured life everlasting in the company of Jesus.

Initially, Jōdō Shin-shū was extremely exclusivistic, rejecting other Buddhist concepts as well as the Shintō *kami*. However, in the fifteenth century, the "second founder" of the sect, a monk named Rennyo (1414–1499), subtly reshaped Shinran's ideas in such a way as to make them more palatable to the ordinary Japanese, for whom religious exclusivity was inherently foreign.

A third, albeit far more controversial Kamakura Period religious reformer, who did indeed preach exclusivity and who, like Hōnen and Shinran, spent time in his youth at the Mt. Hiei, was a curious figure called Nichiren (1222–1282).[13] Almost from the beginning of his studies, Nichiren had come to entertain a great many doubts about the efficacy of the Pure Land beliefs, especially as regards the power of *nembutsu*, as well as those espoused by the Zen sects (see below). He had come to regard the *Lotus Sutra* (see below) as the supreme authority. Indeed, the text itself, with its doctrine of universal salvation (see above), seemed to possess an awesome power, and he encouraged his followers to chant what came to be called *daimoku*: a *nembutsu*-like phrase, *Nammyohō renge kyō*, "I take my refuge in the *Lotus Sutra*." All other Buddhist beliefs, including the belief that Amida had the power to save souls, were rejected.

In 1253, after leaving Mt. Hiei, Nichiren began to preach against the Jōdō and Zen sects and promptly earned the enmity of local officials, who exiled him to Izu. This was the first of a series of banishments and incarcerations he was to endure in the course of the next decades. For example, in 1268 he asserted that only by adopting his sect as the sole religion of Japan could the Mongols be prevented from invading. His denunciations of the shōgunal authorities in Kamakura became so virulent that he was arrested for treason and sent to Sado Island under a sentence of death—which was later revoked.

Quarrelsome, charismatic, fanatical, a super-patriot, and absolutely convinced that his was the only truth, Nichiren and his ideas cut against the Japanese grain; no other Buddhist reformer preached exclusivity, and this aspect of his teaching was widely resented from the beginning. As a result, the two sects based on his teachings, Nichiren-shū and Nichiren Shō-shū, remained relatively unimportant until this century, when the later sect, supported by an organization called the Soka Gakkai, the "Value-Creating Society," launched a campaign to revive the teachings of its founder.[14]

Before leaving this most important era in Japanese religious history, we need to consider two additional major contributors, Eisai (1145–1215) and Dōgen (1200–1253), who were instrumental in introducing the most famous of all Japanese Buddhist traditions: Zen.[15]

At age 13, Eisai joined the monastic community at Enryakuji and diligently studied the *Lotus Sutra* and other Tendai teachings. However, he eventually became disillusioned with the laxity of monastic discipline, and, in 1168, set out on a five-month pilgrimage to China, visiting the major T'ien-t'ai (Tendai) temples and collecting sacred texts that had not yet been translated into Japanese.

It was in the course of a second pilgrimage to China, from 1187 to 1191, that he became acquainted with Hsu-an Huai-ch'ang, master of the Lin-chi sect of Ch'an Buddhism. After he became enlightened, he returned to Japan to preach what came to be called, in Japanese, the Rinzai sect of Zen, the Japanese articulations of the Chinese words Lin-chi and Ch'an. Forced to leave Enryakuji, he made his way to Kamakura, where he gained the patronage of Hōjō Masako, Yoritomo's widow. As a result, the Rinzai sect rapidly attracted members of the new samurai warrior aristocracy. Among Eisai's more important works were *Shukke Taikō*, "Essentials of the Monastic Life" (1192), *Kōzen Gokku ron*, "Promulgation of Zen as a Defense of the Nation" (1198), and *Nihon Buppō Chukō gammon*, "A Plea for the Revival of Japanese Buddhism" (1204).

Dōgen, founder of the Sōtō Zen sect and, by birth, an aristocrat, also studied at Enryakuji, and, like Eisai, became disenchanted with what he believed to be its spiritual laxity. He also came to see a contradiction between the Tendai doctrine that all men intrinsically possessed the "Buddha-nature" and, at the same time, the admonition to engage in a continual search for enlightenment. As a result of these doubts, he left Mt. Hiei and entered Kenninji, a Rinzai monestary.

Six years later, he, too, made a pilgrimage to China, where he ended up studying under a T'sao-T'ung (in Japanese, Sōtō) master, Chang-weng Ju-ching. When he returned to Japan he set about introducing this sect, that is, Sōtō, with its emphasis on sitting *zazen*, that is, cross-legged in the lotus position, as a prerequisite for *satori*, or enlightenment. Unlike Eisai, who advocated the study of the *koans*, mantralike statements (or enigmatic questions, the most famous of which is "What is the sound of one hand clapping?"), as the path toward *satori*, Dōgen felt that individual discipline, focusing on an intense understanding of one's Buddha nature, was the key to spiritual enlightenment. This idea was elaborated in *Fukan Zazengi*, "A Universal Promotion of *Zazen* Principles" (1227).

Dōgen went on to achieve great fame, and, like Eisai, enjoyed the patronage of the shōgunate. He was also a prolific writer, and many of his treatises, including *Gakudō yōjinshu*, "Instructions on Learning the Way" (ca. 1234), are considered classics.

Although Japan has produced a great many subsequent religious thinkers and scholars, none have rivaled the galaxy of reformers that appeared between the birth of Hōnen 1133 and the death of Nichiren in 1282. Between them, they established the religious framework that still governs Japanese Buddhism, a framework which has also had a profound impact on the subsequent evolution of Shintō as the two faiths have sought to find common ground.

The "Christian Century"

As indicated earlier, Christianity was introduced to Japan by a band of Jesuits in 1549.[16] Their leader was St. Francis Xavier, a companion of St. Ignatius de Loyola and one of the founders of the order (the Portuguese had begun trading with Japan in 1545). The new religion was supported, implicitly, by Oda Nobunaga (1534–1582), a daimyō (feudal warlord) who began the process of reunification by making effective use of European military technology, especially cannon and muskets. The new faith spread rapidly. Indeed, by the early 1580s, three of the most powerful daimyō of Kyūshū, the southernmost of the four main Japanese islands, together with their subjects, had converted to the new religion, and there were large pockets of Christians in other regions, including Kyōto, the capital. The total number of converts is hard to estimate, although it may have been as high as 150,000 at the time of Nobunaga's death (see below).[17]

In 1571, using cannon he had obtained from the Portuguese, and perhaps encouraged by his Jesuit advisors, Nobunaga reduced the vast Tendai establishment atop Mt. Hiei to rubble, thereby eliminating a powerful adversary. Tendai and several other Buddhist sects, notably the Ikkō sect, which controlled large areas in the vicinity of Kyōto and Nara, had made common cause with several daimyō families that were threatened by Nobunaga's rise to power. The Buddhist clergy also resented the growing influence of Nobunaga's Jesuit advisors; indeed, although there is no tangible evidence that he converted to Catholicism, one of the last portraits of Nobunaga before his untimely death in 1582 (he was captured by a rival and forced to commit suicide) depicts him wearing a crucifix. The considerable wealth accumulated by the Tendai and Buddhist clergy was confiscated and distributed among his followers.[18]

Nobunaga was succeed by his chief general Toyotomi Hideyoshi (1536–1598), who made an accommodation with the Buddhists and, in 1597, began to persecute the Christians. A number of Jesuit novices were crucified—the so-called "Japanese Martyrs"—and missionaries were asked to leave the country immediately.[19]

Under Hideyoshi's successor, Tokugawa Ieyasu (1542–1616), founder of the Tokugawa shōgunate and the leader who completed the reunification of Japan under a single authority, the persecution became less intense. However, the third Tokugawa shōgun, Ieyasu's grandson Tokugawa Iemitsu, who was a fanatical Buddhist, zealously enforced the ban on Christianity. For example, persons suspected of harboring Catholic ideas would be asked to urinate on an image of the Virgin; if they refused, they would summarily be executed. Faced with this level of repression, most of the Christian daimyō and their subjects—even in Kyūshū—renounced the new religion, and by the 1640s, Japan's "Christian century" had come to an end. However, a handful of Japanese Christians, mostly in and around the Kyūshū city of Nagasaki (still the seat of the Roman Catholic primate of Japan), went underground, as it were, and practiced their faith in secret. By the time the edicts against openly practicing Christianity were repealed in 1872, and Catholic missionaries were allowed to return to Japan, the Secret Christians had been devoid of any ties with Rome for over two centuries. They were so far removed from the faith of their ancestors that the majority refused to rejoin the Church and continue to form a tiny but unique piece in the modern Japanese religious mosaic. (In the early 1870s, after the ban was lifted, a variety of Christian denominations, Protestant as well as Catholic, once again took root in Japan. However, they have only been marginally successful in attracting converts. Today, there are approximately 600,000 Christians in Japan, out of a total population of almost 130,000.000.)[20]

The Shintō Revival

During the Tokugawa era, Buddhism, especially the Pure Land sects, was in the ascendancy, along with with Neo-Confucianism (see Chapter Fourteen), which formed the basis of the Tokugawa approach to statecraft and ethics.[21] However, in the later part of the eighteenth century, thanks to the efforts of Mootori Norinaga (1730–1801) and other Shintō scholars, interest in the ancient religious and mythological texts (see below) was revived. A century later, in 1868, the "Shintō revival," as it has come to be called, was a major factor in restoring the Imperial institution to the center of the Japanese political arena, and, by extension, the subsequent modernization of Japan. (Other primary factors here were, of course, the "opening up" of Japan by Commodore Matthew Galbraith Perry's "Black Ships" in 1853 and the collapse of the Tokugawa economic system, which was based on an increasingly unworkable feudalism.) In the years immediately following the Meiji Restoration, Shintō became the state cult (i.e., "State Shintō"; it was not officially designated as a "religion") and Buddhism went into a brief eclipse.[22] However, by the 1880s the historic balance between the two faiths had been restored and continues to the present. Since the end of the Second World War in 1945 neither Shintō nor Buddhism nor any other religious faith has been officially recognized by the state.

SACRED TEXTS

As far as Shintō is concerned, the most ancient and important sources of religious ideas are the *Kojiki* and *Nihonshoki*, which date, respectively, from 712 and 720 C.E.[23] However, neither of these texts is equivalent to the Western (and, to a lesser extent, Buddhist) concept of "scripture," that is, a divine revelation. Rather, they are genealogically focused chronicles that extend, in both cases, well into the early historic period.

The *Kojiki*

The *Kojiki*, or "Record of Ancient Matters," the oldest surviving text in the Japanese language, was compiled—"creatively edited" is perhaps a better way to describe it— by a single scholar/courtier, Ōnō Yasumarō, from a number of earlier texts, some of them apparently written but unfortunately long since lost, and others oral. These were for the most part genealogies of the several powerful *uji*, or clans, that dominated Japanese political life during the Nara Period (710–794), the most important, of course being the Imperial, or Yamato clan. Each traced the descent of the *uji* in question back to a particular *kami* (that is, god or goddess).

As Japan was then actively engaged in borrowing almost every conceivable culture trait from China, it was only natural that she would borrow the Chinese concept of an imperial chronicle, which served to legitimate the ruling dynasty. With this in mind, Ōnō was commissioned to pull together a coherent Imperial genealogy, one that would establish for all time the supremacy of the Yamato clan. It is in the early sections of this text, which ends approximately a hundred years before Ōnō's time, that we find the primary account of Shintō cosmology and theogony (see below).

The Nihonshoki

The second primary Shintō text, the *Nihonshoki*, that is, the "Chronicle of Japan," was complied eight years after the *Kojiki* by a panel of editors as a "corrective" to Ōnō's text. The leading *uji* were dissatisfied with Ōnō's work even before it was complete. The court therefore acquiesced in their demands and commissioned the *Nihonshoki* from a committee of courtiers. Unlike Ōnō, who produced a remarkably straight-forward narrative, the authors of the *Nihonshoki* felt compelled to retell each major mythological event from a variety of perspectives, reflecting the versions sacred to each of the major clans. The result was a jumble of compromises, redundancies, and, on more than one occasion, contradictions.

Unlike the *Kojiki*, the *Nihonshoki* was written in classical Chinese, and the text contains a great many Chinese mythological themes. A good example is the Pan-Gu story, which appears at several points in the text almost unchanged. However, the *Nihonshoki* does contain a treasure trove of tales that shed a great deal of light on the range and diversity of ancient Shintō mythology and upon the *kami* that animate that mythology.

The Core Shintō Mythology

As expressed in the *Kojiki, Nihonshoki,* and other ancient texts, such as the *Fudoki,* or provincial chronicles (713), the *Manyoshu* (ca. 760), which includes poems based on religious as well as secular themes, and the *Engishi* (tenth century), which includes a large body of *norito,* or ritual prayers for public ceremonies, the core of the mythology upon which Shintō is based can be summarized as follows.

In the beginning, there were seven successive generations of invisible heavenly gods. However, the eighth generation included the Japanese "Adam and Eve," Izanagi and Izanami, who were commanded by their divine forebears to "solidify" what, to this point, had been a chaotic, roiling, jellylike mass. Standing on the "Floating Bridge of Heaven," they dipped a jeweled spear into this roiling mass and managed to create an island, called Onogoro. Then, at the behest of the gods, they descended to this island, in the center of which was a tall pillar.

The primal pair then noticed their gender difference and mated with each other. However, because Izanami, the female member of the pair, spoke first as they circled around the pillar, their first offspring was a "leech-child," that is, a monster. The entity was floated away in a small boat.

After consulting the heavenly *kami*, they realized that Izanagi should speak first, as a man should, and from then on Izanami began to give birth to a variety of islands and gods, culminating with the birth of the Fire God. The latter deity's birth so burned Izanami that she died and went to Yomi, the primordial land of the dead.

However, Izanagi was disconsolate. In a vain attempt to get his beloved wife back, he made a visit to Yomi, but in his eagerness disregarded his dead wife's plea not to look upon her. What he saw horrified him, and, pursued by a now demonic Izanami (who had eaten the food of the dead) and the so-called "Hags of Yomi," he barely escaped after blocking off the entrance to the land of the dead with a great boulder.

In order to rid himself of Yomi's pollution, he decided to bathe in the Hi river. When he wiped his left eye, there was born the Sun Goddess Amaterasu; from his left eye issued the Moon God Tsuku-yomi; and from his nose emerged the recalcitrant thunder god Susanō. Having fathered these and a set of other, lesser divinities, Izanagi, like a great many early Japanese emperors, decided to retire. He gave overall sovereignty to his daughter Amaterasu, the night to Tsuku-yomi, and the sea to Susanō.

But the latter *kami* was unhappy with this arrangement, and, after refusing to accept the outcome of a contest in which the sovereignty would go to the sibling who could produce the greatest number of offspring (Susanō produced the most children, but Amaterasu's brood included more males, and she was declared the winner), he defied his sister's authority.[24] Susanō raged through Heaven, tramping down the dikes between the divine rice paddies, defecating in the fields, and finally heaving a flayed horse through the roof of the Divine Weaving Hut, killing one of Amaterasu's handmaidens.

The assembled gods demanded that Amaterasu do something about her recalcitrant brother, who was creating chaos. But rather than face the problem, she shut herself up in Ama no Iwato, the "Heavenly Cave of Darkness," and had to be tricked into reappearing so that the crops could grow and the creative process continue. (That this episode contains the image of a solar eclipse has often been suggested.)

Shortly after the Sun Goddess's return, which is an extremely important event in Shintō theology, Susanō was banished to the "Reed Plain," where he fathered a lineage of earthly deities. Eventually, Amaterasu ordered her grandson Honinigi to extend her sovereignty over the earth in general and, in particular, over the most powerful of Susanō's descendants: a divinity called Ōkuninushi, the "Great Lord of the Country" (see below). A modus vivendi was achieved, and Honinigi's great-grandson Jimmu, became the first emperor of Japan, from whom all subsequent emperors, including the current one, are traditionally believed to descend. Thus ended the Age of the Gods.

The *Lotus Sutra*

Although a variety of sutras were introduced to Japan as early as the late sixth century C.E., by far the most important sacred text in Japanese Buddhism is the *Lotus Sutra*, or *Hokkekyō* in Japanese.[25] Purportedly based on sermons preached by the historical Buddha himself (that is, the Shakyamuni) the *Lotus Sutra* is one of the most important religious texts in the Mahayana Buddhist tradition per se (see Chapter Thirteen).

The central thesis of the *Lotus Sutra* is that all life has the potential for becoming enlightened and has within it, at least to some degree, the so-called Buddha-nature"—which can be glossed as a capacity for an all-encompassing compassion, together with the serenity that comes with having renounced all desire. This idea leads, in turn, to the notion that salvation was possible, if only one's "Buddha-nature" could be fully realized. To realize it, the worshiped must devote him- or herself to a life of prayer and meditation, and must seek the help of a variety of *bodhisattvas* (see Chapter Thirteen). Every devotional act brings one closer to realizing one's "Buddha-nature," and each time a *bodhisattva* is supplicated, the soul of the supplicator inches closer to the ultimate goal: permanent release from the endless cycle of death and rebirth—or, in other words, the achievement of *nirvana*. As we shall shortly see, all of the major Japanese Buddhist sects that sprang from the Tendai tradition are predicated on the *Lotus Sutra*, including the Pure Land sects preached by Hōnen and Shinran, and especially the sect founded by Nichiren (see below).

The *Sun Sutra*

Another important Japanese Buddhist text is the *Sun Sutra*, or *Dainichi-kyo* in Japanese, the principal text of the Shingon sect (see above). It emphasizes the so-called Vairocana, or Sun Buddha and is characterized by an elaborate set of Tantric, that is, esoteric beliefs and practices. According to the *Sun Sutra*, the entire cosmos emanated from the Sun Buddha, and the goal of the worshiped is to understand the inner meaning of this process.[26] Like the *Lotus Sutra*, the *Sun Sutra* holds that Buddha-nature is inherent in every person and that one can become enlightened in a single lifetime. However, the path to such enlightenment is via the esoteric knowledge and "higher truths" contained in a highly complex *mandala*, or symbolic representation of the cosmos, rather than via professions of faith in the soteriological capabilities of the *bodhisattvas*.

There are, of course, a great many other sacred texts in Japanese Buddhism, not the least of which are the writings of Kōbō-daishi and Dengyō-daishi, as well as those of Hōnen, Shinran, Nichiren, Eisai, and Dōgen (see above). There are also the Zen *koans*, or sacred riddles, attributed to the Bodhi Dharma, who brought the Indian concept of *dhyana* (meditation) to China in the fifth century C.E., but when it comes to the primary sources of Japanese Buddhism, tradition, the Lotus and *Sun Sutras* have had by far the greatest impact, all things considered.

RITUALS AND SACRED CEREMONIES

Like all religions, Japan's faiths have their fair share of rituals and sacred ceremonies. Indeed, one of the distinguishing features of religion in Japan is the abundance of local religious festivals, both Shintō and Buddhist. In addition to such widespread observances as *Obon*, the Buddhist celebration of the return of the dead to their ancestral homes (mid-August), which is accompanied by dancing and the cleaning of gravestones, and *Shogatsu Matsuri*, the three-day New Year festival, at which time people visit local Buddhist temples and Shintō shrines and pray for good luck and prosperity during the year ahead, almost every temple and shrine has its own, unique ritual calendar. Moreover, each Buddhist sect and Shintō shrine is characterized by special rituals and ceremonies, and the same holds for the "new religions" (see below). A good example of such a sect-specific Buddhist ritual is the famous *goma*, or fire-purification ceremony, which occupies a central place in Shingon worship.

The Goma Ceremony

Thought by some scholars to be related to the ancient Hindu soma sacrifice, the Shingon fire-ritual focuses on the purification of the worshiper and provides an avenue for all concerned priests and congregation alike, to be transported symbolically by the flames to a higher realm of consciousness.[27] The priests pile up small strips of wood, each inscribed with a prayer or passage from a sutra. The pile, which usually takes the form of a square of interlaced layers, is then ignited, and *goma*, or sesame seed oil, a sacred substance, is poured on the fire, making the flames leap and dance. As the sacred smoke rises, the priests fumigate various objects given to them by members of the congregation—women's purses, drivers licenses, wallets, photographs of loved ones, and so forth—thereby rendering them pure and, by implication, safe from harm. At the close of the ceremony, each member of the congregation receives a dab of sesame seed oil on the forehead as a sign both of purification *and* exposure to the esoteric realm symbolized by the flames and the smoke. (Having participated in several *Goma* ceremonies, the author can attest that the atmosphere created by the fire and the accompanying chants by the Shingon priests is indeed conducive to other-worldly thoughts and meditations.)

Household Rites

Other Buddhist rituals include funeral ceremonies—as we have indicated, almost all Japanese funerals are conducted according to Buddhist rites, the one major exception being Imperial funerals, which are totally Shintō in form—and a variety of rites performed at *butsudan,* or household Buddhist altars. Most of the latter rites are related to the family ancestors. Generally, such rites—burning incense and offering small dishes of rice to the ancestor spirits—are performed in the early morning, as both Buddhism and Shintō agree that sacrality is intimately associated with the dawn of the new day, with the emergence of the sun from the abyss of night. Indeed, the *Sun Sutra,* the primary Shingon text (see above), emphasizes this aspect of the Buddha-nature in its account of Vairocana's enlightenment.

Household rites also play an important role in Shintō, and the syncretic character of Japanese religions, one of the principal themes of this chapter, is clearly demonstrated by the fact that in a great many Japanese homes the *kamidana,* or Shintō "god-shelf," is located directly above the *butsudan.* The head of the household (or his wife) is generally responsible for "feeding" the family *kami,* that is, the Shintō incarnations of the ancestral spirits venerated at the *butsudan.* The food consists of a small dish of rice, a tiny cup of *sake,* that is, rice wine, and perhaps a piece of daikon, the Japanese radish.

Among the most important of all Buddhist household rites is the veneration of wooden ancestral tablets, called *ihai,* a practice that complements the worship of ancestral *kami* enshrined in a family's Shintō *kamidana.* Indeed, this is yet another area where the two faiths overlap in the popular tradition, as the names memorialized on the *ihai* and in the *kamidana* are, of course, one and the same.

A Neighborhood Matsuri

By far the most important Shintō ritual, at least as far as the local community is concerned, is its annual (or, in some case, semiannual) *matsuri.*[28] Virtually every Japanese urban community, neighborhood, village, or *buraku* (village quarter) plays host to such a festival, which centers on the local shrine. There are two basic types of *matsuri*: an ordinary festival, or "shadow *matsuri,*" which does not directly involve the local *kami,* but is still centered on the shrine and culminates in the carrying of a portable shrine, called a *mikoshi,* around the neighborhood, and a *taisai,* or "major festival," which does indeed involve the local Shintō deity. *Taisai* typically occur every three years, although they may occur more frequently, and at certain major shrines on an annual basis. In both varieties, however, the three basic constituencies of the community served by the shrine, the merchants' association (*shōtenkai*), the neighborhood residents' association (*chōkai*), and the shrine elders' association (*sōdaikai*), cooperate to "present" a positive image of the neighborhood, village, and so forth, to the larger community, and, at the same time, reinforce their own sense of social solidarity and local pride.

The *taisai* celebrated in a Tokyo neighborhood I shall call "Daigaku-chō" (University Neighborhood) is a triennial event focusing on Amaterasu, the *kami* enshrined in a small shrine called the Tenso-*jinja* (or shrine), one of thousands of shrines throughout Japan that venerate the Sun Goddess (see above), the most important of which being the Ise-*jingu* (see below).[29] In Daigaku-chō, the *matsuri* traditionally takes place over a two-day period in early September. In the morning of the first day, young children, girls as well as boys, carry a children's *mikoshi*, about a quarter the size of the adult version, around the neighborhood and thereby learn the local traditions. In the afternoon a Shintō priest from a nearby shrine (the Tenso-*jinja* is too small to have its own *guji*, or full-time priest), assisted by the local *sōdai*, performs a ceremony at the shrine, in which he chants *norito* and purifies the shrine and its contents. That evening, there is entertainment on the shrine grounds, in some years by a Shintō theater troop, who perform *kagura*, or sacred theater, and in others by a traditional dance group. Itinerant *matsuri* concessionaires, called *rōten*, set up their stalls and sell souvenirs and traditional festival foods, such as *okonomiyakai*, an egg dish prepared on a grill, and various varieties of fried noodles.

Early the next morning the acting *guji* removes the sacred (and rarely seen) image of Amaterasu from the inner precincts of the shrine and places it in the waiting *mikoshi*. Then, rotating teams of 30 or 40 young men and women, chanting *Wa shoi! Wa shoi!* (untranslatable), carry the portable shrine up one narrow street and down another. The procession, which halts frequently for liquid refreshments, is led by the priest and the elders and includes singers, a young man impersonating the guardian demon Tengu, a *taiko* drum, and the *sodai*.

After six or seven hours, the procession returns to the shrine grounds, and the priest removes the image from the mikoshi and returns it to the inner shrine, where it will remain until the next *taisai*, two years hence. The fundamental purpose of this ritual is to sacralize the neighborhood served by the *jinja* by periodically exposing it to the sacred aura emitted by the image in the *mikoshi*, which also, of course, sacralizes the carriers. A *matsuri* is therefore a joyous, indeed ecstatic occasion, one in which the participants partake of the essence of the local *kami* and, in the process, experience godlike feelings.

Over and above participating in neighborhood festivals and household rites, a great many Japanese go to temples and shrines individually to ask the blessings of the local *bosatsu* or *kami*, especially when faced with some personal crisis. In a temple, this usually involves burning a stick of incense as an offering to the deity and wafting the smoke over the body. At a shrine, the worshiped first rinses his or her mouth and hands, then approaches the outer portion of the shrine and drops an offering, usually monetary, into the collection box. Then, after clapping twice and/or pulling a bell rope to alert the deity that a worshiped is present, with head bowed and hands clasped, the request is articulated. For example, a mother might ask the *kami* to help her son or daughter pass an entrance examination. When the request has been made, the worshiper claps again and leaves the shrine. (If the request is granted, good manners dictate that the petitioner return to the shrine to thank the *kami* for its beneficence.)

TEMPLES, SHRINES, AND SACRED MOUNTAINS

There are two major types of religious institutions in Japan: Buddhist temples (*otera*) and Shintō shrines (*jinja*). Although their architecture and accouterments differ significantly, temples and shrines, together with the relative handful of Christian churches (*kyokai*) found mainly in the larger Japanese towns and cities, form welcome islands of sacred space in what has recently become one of the most intensely developed and secular societies on the planet. The same thing can be said for the mountains that have become sacred to one or the other (and sometimes both) of the two faiths.

Temples

The prototypes of Japanese Buddhist temples originated in China. Initially the Japanese followed the Chinese custom of building temples atop mountains, which is why so many Japanese Buddhist temples include the word *san*, or mountain, in their names. The Japanese monks considered their temples to be daughter institutions of the ones they had visited in China. Good examples of this fascination with mountain tops can be seen in the great Tendai temple complex on Mt. Hiei (see above), as well as the Shingon temples that adorn Mt. Koya. Unlike churches, cathedrals, synagogues, and other Western religious institutions, Japanese (and Chinese) Buddhist temples typically consist of a complex of buildings: the *kondo*, or main hall, which contains sacred images of the Shakyamuni and other buddhas and bosatsu; the *daikodo*, or lecture hall; and various treasuries, storehouses, priestly residences, and, more often than not, a five-story pagoda (*goju no to*), which often houses a religious relic. Wherever feasible, the complex is surrounded by a garden, some parts of which, like the famous Zen garden at Ryōangi Temple in Kyōto, are themselves sacred places and foci of devotion.

A famous example of such a temple complex can be seen at Horyuji, near Nara, which was built in 607 C.E. by Shōtoku Taishi (see above) and is held to be the oldest surviving set of wooden buildings in the world. In addition to the architectural elements just mentioned, the complex includes ten major structures, several of which are officially designated "national treasures" by the Japanese government.

Shrines

Like their Buddhist counterparts, Shintō *jinja* typically include a complex of several structures, and, save for the tiny shrines one finds on the roofs of department stores and other high-rise buildings, are almost always located in natural settings—even if this setting consists of but a few trees shading an open space used by neighborhood children as a playground.[30] If the pagoda is a distinguishing (but not universal) feature of Japanese (and Chinese) Buddhist temples, the *torii* gate, which, in its simplest form, consists of a pair of posts topped by two crossbars, one of which extends beyond the uprights and the other is usually tucked between them. The *torii* serves to mark the boundary between the outer (and impure) secular world and the sacred space of the shrine. When one passes under it, one symbolically sheds the pollution accumulated in that outer world.

Like Buddhist temples, most shrines are in fact complexes, including, in addition to the *torii*, the *honden*, within which the sacred image of the *kami* is kept, one or more storehouses, an outer building, in front of which the faithful pray and make offerings, and a stone water tank for the ablutions—rinsing the hands and mouth—that are required before one approaches the *kami*. The oldest Shintō shrines were simple, open-air, stone altars. However, by the early years of the Common Era, shrines began to be built on the model of thatched-roof rice storehouses. The most famous example of such a shrine is the Ise-*jingu*, the most sacred of all Shintō complexes.

The Ise Jingu

Located southeast of Nara in Mie Prefecture, near the coast, Ise is actually a grand complex of shrines. The most important of these, the Naiku, or "Inner Shrine" and the Geku, or "Outer Shrine," are dedicated, respectively, to the Sun Goddess, Amaterasu, and the Rice Goddess, Toyouke-omikami. The Inner Shrine is the most sacred of all Shintō shrines and for more than a millennium has been the object of pilgrimages from all over Japan. But what makes Ise truly unique is the fact that, since the seventh century, every building in the complex has been totally rebuilt every 20 years. Thus Ise is at once extremely old and always new. The symbolism here is extremely important: With each rebuilding (the most recent was in 1993), both the Sun Goddess—the divine ancestor of the Imperial family—and the Rice Goddess are themselves renewed. And, by extension, the vitality of both the Imperial line and the rice crop, without which the nation could not survive, are ensured.

The ground on which the previous cycle of Ise buildings stood, which lies next to the current "generation" of shrines, is carefully preserved and will, when the cycle comes around again, become the loci for the next "generation" of buildings. The previous buildings are torn down only after the new ones are completed and the sacred images have been ritually transferred by the distinctively clad Ise priests. Indeed, for a brief period, one might think one was seeing double, as the architecture of the two sets of side-by-side shrines is absolutely identical. Pieces of the disassembled buildings are subsequently distributed to shrines throughout Japan. Thus, every 20 years, as these pieces are incorporated into the walls of these shrines, the essence of the Ise *kami* pervades the Shintō universe.

Beginning in the Nara Period, many shrines began to reflect Chinese design elements, such as upturned roofs and bright, vermillion paint instead of natural, unpainted wood. It is perhaps not fortuitous that, as Shintō shrines came to resemble Buddhist temples, the process of syncretism between the two faiths proceeded accordingly. Indeed, almost every major Buddhist temple complex includes at least one Shintō *jinja*. Another curious result of this process was the movement known as Shugendō, which took shape in the Heian Period and involved a fusion of Buddhist *bosatsu* and Shintō *kami*, especially the *kami* that were believed to live atop mountains. Spread by mystics known as *yamabushi* (literally "mountain warriors"),[31] the movement survives to this day in parts of Northern Japan and is practiced in buildings that are at once *otera* and *jinja*.

Sacred Mountains

This fascination with the sacredness of mountains pervades both Buddhism and Shintō. As we have seen, two of the most important Buddhist temple complexes, the headquarters temples of the Tendai and Shingon sects, were established, respectively, on Mounts Hiei and Koya. The most famous of all Japanese sacred mountains is, of course, Mount Fuji, or Fuji-san, which is traditionally conceived as a major *kami*. It has long been a place of mass pilgrimage, and each year thousands of Japanese climb Fuji-san to worship at the small Shintō shrine at the summit. (In the nineteenth century, when travel was far more difficult, a Fuji cult developed wherein small replicas of the famous mountain were erected at local Shintō shrines in many parts of Japan and "climbed" by those who were unable to get to the real thing.) Fuji-san is also sacred to several Buddhist sects, and the main Nichiren Shō-shū (see below) temple is nestled in its foothills so as to absorb the mountain's spiritual essence.

In addition to mountains, a host of other major features of the landscape are held to be sacred, both by Buddhists and by Shintōists. One example is the magnificent Tachi waterfall in Wakayama Prefecture, which, like Fuji-san, is widely conceived to be a powerful *kami*. Indeed, almost every distinctive Japanese rock outcrop, river, hill, and waterfall, as well as mountain, has some association with either a local Buddhist temple, a Shintō shrine, or both.

DIVINE BEINGS

We have already mentioned several of the divinities, Buddhist as well as Shintō, that are worshiped in the temples and shrines just discussed. Indeed, some of them are important to *both* faiths. An early example of such a figure was the semilegendary, warlike Emperor ōjin (ca. 300 C.E.), whose spirit later became an integral element of the Shintō war god Hachiman (also sometimes referred to as a *bosatsu*; see above). Hachiman is widely enshrined throughout Japan, and his shrines are favorite venues for the christeninglike ritual called *omiyamairi*, literally, "honorable going to a shrine," in which infants—in the case of Hachiman *jinja* (*miya* is a synonym for *jinja*), primarily male infants—are taken to shrines for the first time and purified by the priests. At the same time, Hachiman's image is to be found in a great many Buddhist temples, where the figure is venerated as a *bosatsu*.

Buddhist Deities

In addition to Hachiman, three Buddhist deities loom especially large in Japanese Buddhism: Amida, Kannon, and Jizo. Amida *butsu*, who, as we have seen, plays such an important role in the Tendai sect and its Pure Land offshoots, derives from the ancient Sanskrit figure Amitabha, a *bodhisattva* who is believed to have voluntarily postponed his own salvation (that is, his entry into Nirvana) until all human beings had been saved (see below).

After Amida, the most popular Buddhist *bosatsu* is Kannon, who derives immediately from the Chinese figure Guanyin and ultimately from the Indian deity Avalokiteshvara, and to whom worshipers turn for mercy and forgiveness. Indeed, almost every Japanese community of any size has at least one Kannon temple.

Variously depicted as male and female, Kannon is the protector of women in childbirth, of children, and of dead souls. The deity is often described as Senju Kannon, or "Kannon of the Thousand Arms," each of which is stretched compassionately toward the believer. He/she is often accompanied by a miniature Amida, who rests on his/her head. The *bosatsu* Jizo is also concerned with children, but particularly with the souls of those who have died (or, in modern time, those who have been aborted). Tiny *Jizo-yas*, or temples to Jizo, are ubiquitous, and are readily identifiable by a cluster of small images of the *bosatsu* wearing red scarves around their necks and often clothing worn by deceased children in the neighborhood. He is also the protector of all those who are suffering pain, and is believed to have the capability to redeem souls from Jigoku (hell) and to lead them to the Western Paradise. Indeed, in the popular tradition, both Kannon and Jizo, although clearly Buddhist figures, have effectively become *kami* and are worshiped as such by vast numbers of Japanese.

Some Shintō Deities

When it comes to the indigenous Shintō deities, it is traditionally held that there are eight million *kami*, which is another way of saying that the number is well-nigh infinite. It is therefore impossible in this chapter to mention more than a tiny fraction of this vast pantheon. We have already considered the primary deities—Izanagi and Izanami, Susanō, Amaterasu,—who populate the core mythology, and who emerged during the so-called "Age of the Gods." Another important group of *kami* include the rice god Inari and the so-called *Shichifukujin*, or the "Seven Lucky Gods," who personify a variety of desirable characteristics or conditions.

Inari is widely venerated as the deity who ensures an abundant rice harvest and, by extension, general prosperity. As a result, his cult is especially important to merchants. Inari's messenger and guardian is the fox, and images of these animals are prominently displayed at every Inari *jinja*. In ancient times, Inari was also considered to be the patron of swordsmiths as well as rice farmers and merchants.

The most popular of the "Seven Lucky Gods" are Daikokuten and his son Ebisu, both of whom personify material abundance. Often enshrined together, Daikokuten is typically depicted with a large sack slung over his left shoulder, while Ebisu carries a sea-bream under his right hand and a fishing rod in his left. Other members of the group include Benten, the personification of skill in music and other arts; Fukurokuju, who ensures popularity; Hotei, who presides over contentment and magnanimity; and Jurojin and Bishamonten, the embodiments, respectively, of longevity and benevolent authority.

Yet another figure who looms large in the Shintō pantheon is the previously mentioned *kami* Ōkuninushi (or Daikokusama,), "the Great Lord of the Country" (see above), who is frequently identified with Daikokuten. Widely worshiped for his power to enrich those who venerate him, Ōkuninushi is enshrined at the Izumō-taisha shrine in Shimane Prefecture, near the Sea of Japan. After the Ise-*jingu* (see above), it is the most sacred Shintō shrine in Japan.[32]

In addition to the figures who populate the major Shintō myths and legends, almost any person or object can be enshrined as a *kami*. We have already considered the semihistorical roots of the Shintō-Buddhist figure Hachiman (see above).

Another widely worshiped *kami* who is based on an undoubted historical figure is called Tenjin, or "Heaven Person."

A brilliant administrator-scholar, Tenjin (845–903), whose real name was Sugawava no Michizane, was at the peak of his career as a member of the Heian court when several jealous colleagues conspired against him. Falsely accused of malfeasance in office, Tenjin was banished from his beloved native city and spent the rest of his life as a restless political exile. After his death, his accusers suffered divine retribution, as did Heian. Fires and pestilence were everywhere. The authorities finally decided to appease Tenpin's angry spirit by building a major shrine to his *kami*—the Kitano Temmangu, which remains one of the most important Shintō shrines in modern Kyōto. Things soon returned to normal, or so the legends goes. Indeed, Tenjin has long since become a major member of the Shintō pantheon and is enshrined throughout Japan. Considered especially helpful when it comes to matters relating to education, he is still regularly invoked by students (and/or their mothers) who are about to take major examinations and by scholars seeking divine help in their research.

More recently, the founder of the Tokugawa dynasty, Tokugawa Ieyasu (see above), was enshrined by his grandson at Nikko in 1645, and, in modern times, figures like the Emperor Meiji, under whose reign (1867–1912) Japan began its pell mell rush toward modernization, and Admiral Tōgo Heihachiro (1847–1934), who defeated the Russian fleet at the Battle of Tsushima Straits in 1905, have become important *kami* and are worshiped extensively. Indeed, the principal shrine to the spirit of the Emperor Meiji, the Meiji-*jingu*, has become the most important Shintō shrine in Tokyo.

DEATH, SALVATION, AND THE AFTERLIFE

There is, as we said at the outset, a significant difference—perhaps "division of labor" would be a better way to put it—between Shintō and Japanese Buddhism when it comes to the matters relating to death and the afterlife. Shintō is the "life-religion." It is primarily concerned with the here and now, with reproduction, the abundance of nature, including agriculture, and human and animal fertility. The only real concern the *kami* faith has with anything that might possibly be considered "salvation" is the concept of *oharai*: the purification of the natural world and all those creatures, including human beings, that dwell in it. Indeed, much of Shintō ritual involves spiritual cleansing. A *kannushi*, or priest (a *guji* is the chief priest of a shrine), is expected to perform *oharai* on almost every ritual occasion. Waving a sacred *sakaki* (pine) branch, and chanting appropriate *norito*, he (or sometimes she) attempts to remove whatever pollution may have contaminated the person, place, or thing. This can include possession by evil spirits or demons.

Exorcizing Evil Spirits

The Japanese word for "demon" is *oni*. Most *oni* are invisible, but some are thought to be animal spirits who have the capability of possessing someone. Among the most feared of animal spirits is the fox spirit. To be possessed by a fox spirit is to invite all sorts of calamities, including illness and death. In parts of rural Japan, especially in the north, where old customs and beliefs tend to linger, the aforementioned *yam-abushi*, the practitioners of Shugendō (see above), are considered particularly adept at removing such spirits and thereby restoring the victim to good health. Another variety of evil spirit is the *obake*, or ghost. These entities, too, are believed capable of causing much harm, and they can be driven off with appropriate rituals.

Paths to Nirvana and the "Western Paradise"

If the exorcizing of evil spirits and other supernatural pollutants is as close as Shintō gets to salvation, in the Western theological sense, the latter notion is the central focus of most Japanese Buddhist sects. (Zen is an exception, but even here the achievement of *satori*, or sudden enlightenment, on the part of someone sitting *zazen* is, in the last analysis, a form of "this world" salvation; see above.) Indeed, Buddhism is the quintessential Japanese "death religion." The Buddhist's ultimate goal is to achieve *nirvana*, or "release" (see Chapter Thirteen). To this end, a variety of ritual procedures are prescribed, most of which involve extensive—and intensive—meditation.

However, as we have seen, the Pure Land sects, in which the *bosatsu* Amida plays a central role, are concerned not with ultimate salvation, but rather rebirth in a land—sometimes also called the "Western Paradise," where the deceased will have the time to perfect his or her spirituality and eventually achieve *nirvana*. It was thus a "halfway house," as it were, between the pain and suffering of the mortal world and final and perpetual release.

Amida was central to achieving this partial salvation, because he was believed to have a vast amount of compassion for human beings and has postponed his own achievement of *nirvana* so as to help others reach the safe harbor provided by the Pure Land. The key was absolute faith in Amida's ability to ensure such a rebirth, a faith expressed in the recitation of the *nembutsu* (see above).

It was, of course, still theoretically possible for one to achieve *nirvana* directly, that is, via the "hard path" of intense meditation and attention to spiritual cleansing. But Hōnen (see above) was convinced that most human beings were inherently so wicked that even a well-nigh perfect spiritual life in this world was probably not enough to achieve ultimate salvation.

Compounding this dilemma was the widespread assumption on the part of the Buddhist clergy that the universe had reached the "third age," the age of increasing disorder, evil, and chaos known in Japanese as *mappō* (see above). Therefore, what amounted to a shortcut to salvation was vital if more than a tiny handful of souls were to avoid the eternal fires of the Buddhist hell, or Jigoku. Thus, professing faith in Amida became a vital part of the Japanese "way of death," and it is not accidental that, as was mentioned earlier, almost all Japanese cemeteries are attached to Buddhist temples, especially Pure Land temples (that is, temples belonging to the Jōdō-shū and Jōdō Shin-shū sects).

To be sure, it is possible to be buried according to Shintō rites, and there are at least two Shintō cemeteries in Tokyo. One of them is reserved for the Imperial family, whose funerals are traditionally Shintō in form. Indeed, the funeral of the late Showa Emperor (Hirohito) in 1989, which was presided over by *kannushi* from the Ise-*jingu* and other major shrines, was a prime example of such a Shintō funeral. But as we have said, the overwhelming majority of Japanese choose to be buried according to Buddhist rites and to have their ashes interred in a Buddhist cemetery.

ETHICAL PRINCIPLES AND PATHS TOWARD ENLIGHTENMENT

All religions are concerned with ethics, with the ways in which human beings ought to relate both to one another and to the world around them, and Shintō and the Japanese Buddhist sects are no exception. At the same time, most, if not all religions share a concept that can best be described, borrowing a phrase from Buddhism, as "paths toward enlightenment" (in Christianity, this might be referred to as achieving a "state of grace"). However, the two Japanese faiths approach these matters from vastly different—albeit complementary—perspectives.

It has sometimes been said that there is no clear-cut Shintō ethic, and that the Japanese rely in all cases on their Buddhist heritage for guidance in human relationships. This can be disputed.[33] At the core of Shintō theology is the idea that harmony, or *wa*, between the human community and the natural world is inherently good, and that anything that fosters this harmony is, ipso facto, good, while that which disrupts it is bad. This idea, of course, extends to human relationships, and the notion of harmony in the natural sphere extends to social harmony.

Although the idea that Japanese culture is wholly predicated on a "shame" ethic rather than a guilt-based ethic has rightly been criticized,[34] the idea that the individual is far less important than the group (or groups) to which he or she belongs (see below) is extremely widespread and is thoroughly consonant with the Shintō harmony ethic just mentioned. Thus, the "face," or *tatemae*, that an individual presents to the outside world is intimately bound up with his or her membership in an *ie*, or household. The household *kami* form an integral part of this relationship, and conformity to the rules is in large (but by no means total) measure constrained by the shame, or loss of face, not only among his or her peers but among the *kami* enshrined in the *kamidana*, that an individual experiences when he or she violates a rule. Indeed, the assumption underlying the presence of the rules themselves it that they are necessary for the maintenance of *wa*, without which both society and the natural world would disintegrate and chaos would reign.

To be sure, much of this way of thinking was stimulated by Confucian and Daoist ideas, which have been part of the Japanese cultural mix for over 1,500 years. But these Chinese ideas have been strongly underscored by the indigenous Shintō ideology just discussed, which grew out of the clan-centered social organization of prehistoric and ancient Japan.

Again, it should be emphasized that the Shintō ethic, which reached its apogee during the "State Shintō" era (1872–1945), when obedience to the Emperor became the noblest form of behavior—up to and including sacrificing one's life for his benefit (e.g., the *kamikaze* pilots in World War II)—is, like Shintō itself, very much a "this-world" phenomenon, with little or no emphasis placed on reward or punishment in the afterlife.

The Buddhist ethic is, of course, very different, at least when it comes to constraining factors—as we shall see, the two faiths converge and support one another in providing guidelines for human conduct. As we have seen, the central focus of most of the Buddhist sects is "otherworldly." It centers on the afterlife and the ultimate fate of the soul.

From the outset, Mahayana Buddhism per se has had a well-defined concept of evil, of the wickedness inherent in human nature. Thus, the goal of all who follow the Way of the Buddha is to achieve salvation (see above) and thereby avoid eternal punishment for their sins. As we have seen, this can be accomplished in a variety of ways, from deep meditation leading to enlightenment to good works and/or the recitation of *nembutsu.*

But when it comes to daily life, the two ethical traditions reinforce one another. Thus, to subordinate oneself to the group and behave in such a way that the group—family, workplace, school, and so forth—does not lose face is consonant with both the Shintō emphasis on harmonious relationships and the Buddhist goal of avoiding desire and selfishness and thereby cleansing the soul of its inherent wickedness.

As we have seen, the Zen sects—Rinzai and Sōtō—are an exception to this rule in that they are less concerned with enlightenment (and/or salvation through the recitation of *nembutsu*) as a passport to a better life in the hereafter than with achieving a sudden enlightenment that will help the believer cope with the demands of *this* world. The Zen sects have had a profound influence on a wide range of Japanese arts, including the martial arts. From the outset, the sect appealed to the military aristocracy that came to power at Kamakura after 1185, and it was there that Eisai found the greatest support for his ideas when he returned from China (see above). Young samurai found that the discipline involved in sitting *zazen* and, if possible, achieving *satori* made them better fighters. At the same time, the simplicity, the intense focusing of the mind that is so intimately related to Zen meditation, eventually inspired a uniquely Japanese aesthetic. In the visual arts it is known as *shibui*, or elegant simplicity, and in literature as *wabi-sabi*. This same aesthetic is also present in the *chanoyou*, or tea ceremony, which also focuses the mind, involves intense discipline, and takes place in harmonious and simple surroundings. Indeed, it is no accident that the greatest of all tea masters, Senrikyu, was a sixteenth-century Zen monk.

SOCIETY, RELIGION, AND POLITICS

Almost a century ago, the eminent French sociologist Émile Durkheim pointed out that religion and society everywhere are inextricably bound together, and that the former is necessarily a "collective representation"—a projection, if you will—of the latter.[35] Durkheim's thesis is amply demonstrated by the two faiths that dominate Japanese religious life. The beliefs and practices of both Shintō and Japanese Buddhism have been profoundly shaped by the norms and values of Japanese society. Indeed, there are certain fundamental aspects of Japanese culture that must be taken in to consideration when assessing the role played by religion in Japan, ancient or modern. The most important of these is the subordination of the individual to the group, which many scholars think has it roots in the necessity for close cooperation and collective decision making in paddy rice cultivation—which, until very recently, has been the prime source of Japanese sustenance. The irrigated rice paddy, which was introduced to Japan in the latter part of the first millennium B.C.E., is extremely labor intensive; until recently, each rice plant must be individually inserted into the soggy ground. Even in modern times, with sophisticated farm machinery, rice cultivation is, at bottom, a family affair, one in which all members of the household must subordinate their own personal proclivities and work together as a close-knit team for good of the crop—and, by extension, for mutual survival. At a broader level, it is a village affair, one in which a cluster of linked households assist one another in planting, weeding, and harvesting. Farm equipment has traditionally been shared; indeed, the Japanese word for village, *mura*, comes from a root which means "gathering, coming together."

This necessity for close cooperation and consultation, and a concomitant absence of marked individualism, has marked both Shintō and Buddhism from the outset. Both religions, as we shall see, place great emphasis on the community and its well-being, whether it be a household, a rice-growing village, a feudal domain dominated by a close-knit body of samurai who placed loyalty to their lord above life itself, or the "salarymen" employed by modern corporations who are attempting to carve out an international market share. The Japanese ethos, epitomized by the expression "the nail that sticks up will be hammered down," has always made subordinating oneself to the larger social unit a prime virtue.[36]

Moreover, in ancient Japan, society was organized into *uji*, or clans, and, as we have seen, the roots of the *kami* faith are intimately intertwined with the collective values fostered by these all-encompassing social institutions. Indeed, the tutelary *kami* enshrined in a local *jinja* is still called the *ujigami*, or "ancestral clan deity," despite that fact that the *uji* system, as a major force in Japanese life, has been defunct for almost a millennium. More recently, the *ie*, or extended household, which supplanted the *uji* as the feudal system took hold after 1185, has given rise to a deep-seated emphasis on the family in both Shintō and the more popular Buddhist sects (again, Zen is something of an exception). Households, urban or rural, and *not* individuals are still the principal units when it comes to membership in a shrine or temple.

Another fundamental feature of Japanese social organization that, until recently, was mirrored in the country's religious institutions is the disparity between the sexes. Traditionally, women have played a relatively minor role in the country's religious life. To be sure, in prehistoric times there were reigning empresses, as well as high priestesses of Ise—after all, the *kami* enshrined there, Amaterasu, is the queen of Heaven and the head of the divine family. But 1,500 years of exposure to Confucian ideas about the relative importance of men and women have taken their toll.

In recent years, however, the worldwide women's movement has begun to affect Japanese thinking about gender relationships, including those that affect religious beliefs and practices. Nowhere is this better exemplified than in the increasing numbers of Shintō shrines that permit young women to carry *mikoshi*.

Women and Matsuri

Traditionally, carrying a *mikoshi* was a young man's privilege. To be sure, most larger shrines had a complement of *miko*, that is, unmarried teenage girls, typically daughters of local worthies, who assist the *kannushi* in performing various rituals and who sell charms and fortunes to persons visiting the shrine.[37] However, these shrine virgins were not permitted to carry *mikoshi*. Indeed, women were expected to play a supportive role in the processions that are the heart of any *matsuri*, providing refreshments for the carriers at rest stops and cooking the dinner after the portable shrine has been returned to the *jinja*. But since the late '70s, in neighborhood after neighborhood, young women are gaining the right to join their brothers and husbands in carrying the *kami* through the streets. In a Tokyo neighborhood the author has studied extensively over the last 20 years, this change occurred in 1987. In March of that year, six months before the festival, a member of the Women's Committee (*Fujinbu*) of the Neighborhood Association (*Chōkai*) informally pointed out that young women were carrying *mikoshi* in nearby *matsuri*, and that perhaps the time had come for their own neighborhood to follow suit.

What happened next is a classical example of Japanese decision making, religious or secular.[38] After every major component of the neighborhood had discussed the proposal informally—and had come to a consensus that it was a good idea—it was formally approved by the *Chōkai-chō*, the head of the Neighborhood Association, who has overall responsibility for the festival. Thus, when a group of young women approached the organizers a week or so before the *matsuri* and asked to be included in the roster of carriers, they were immediately assigned to *mikoshi*-carrying teams, just as if they had always been part of the scene. This episode—and others like it in recent years throughout Japan—proves that even the most overtly conservative elements of the Shintō religious tradition can be affected by such political movements as feminism and the push for social and economic equality between the sexes.

The Yasukuni Shrine

In many respects, the most politically controversial Japanese religious institution, Shintō or Buddhist, is the Yasukuni Shrine in Tokyo, where the enshrined *kami* are the souls of Japan's war dead, from the creation of the Imperial Army in 1871 to the end of World War II. Exacerbating the inherently controversial nature of such a shrine, thanks to Japan's postwar commitment to pacifism, is the fact that, from time to time, prominent members of the government—sometimes including the Prime Minister—stop by to pay their respects. When this happens, the Japanese media have a field day. The political left, raising the specter of prewar State Shintō and its intensely nationalist ideology, accuses the government officials in question of violating the 1947 Constitution's clear separation of the state from involvement in any religion; the right claims that the Yasukuni Shrine is a private religious institution, and that those who pray there do so as private individuals. Making matters more complicated is the fact that in recent years there have been repeated attempts to make the Yasukuni-*jinja* into the equivalent of the Tomb of the Unknown Solider in Arlington National Cemetery, that is, a place where visiting foreign dignitaries could lay wreaths. But so far, the bill has failed to receive a majority in the Diet, and the controversy continues.

On the whole, the several major Buddhist sects have been at once far less controversial politically *and* less responsive to the kinds of pressures for change that have led to women carrying *mikoshi*, to say nothing of a significant increase in the number of women Shintō priests in recent years (a development that the more conservative shrines have adamantly opposed). There are few if any women Buddhist priests, and, although Japanese women do probably spend more time praying in temples than their menfolk, their role in the religious hierarchies remains minimal.

The one mainstream Buddhist sect that has become controversial in modern times, thanks largely to Soka Gakkai (see below), the lay organization, that supports it, is Nichiren Sho-shū. In the 1960s, Soka Gakkai formed a political party called Komeito, the "Clean Government Party," which was widely seen to be an attempt to politicize this Buddhist sect. This sentiment lingers, despite the fact that Komeito early on formally renounced its ties to Soka Gakkai.

THE NEW RELIGIONS

As we indicated at the outset, mainstream Buddhism, Shintō, Confucianism, Daoism, and Christianity are by no means the only religions to be found in contemporary Japan. Since the early nineteenth century, the country has given birth to a host of *shinko shūkyo*, or "new religions."[39] The great majority of these are spinoffs, as it were, from Shintō, although most are heavily infused with ideas drawn from a variety of sources, including Buddhism, the Chinese traditions just mentioned, Christianity, and, in modern times, even Western occultism. Indeed, the Japanese genius for syncretism seems to know no bounds!

The impetus for the first *shinko shūkyo* was the growing chaos and disorder that accompanied the decline of the Tokugawa system in the early nineteenth century.[40] By the 1830s, organized Shintō and Buddhism had grown stagnant and unresponsive to the changing social conditions, especially in the countryside, and the time was ripe for charismatic individuals to proclaim new faiths. Among the first of such individuals to appear on the scene was a farmer's wife named Nakayama Miki (1798–1887), who founded a "new religion" that eventually came to be called Tenrikyo.[41]

Tenrikyo

In 1838, while nursing her sick son, Nakayama-san was possessed by a *kami* who identified himself as Ten-taishōgun, the "Great Heavenly Generalissimo." In a series of possessions in the course of the next several years, Ten-taishōgun told Nakayama-san that he and his nine subordinate entities were the only true *kami*, and that they had chosen her to spread what came to be called the "Heavenly Truth," or *tenri*. Thus was born the Tenrikyo sect. The *kami*'s message was eventually written down in a 1711-verse poem, completed in 1883, called the *Ofudesaki*, "The tip of the Divine Writing Brush." In it can be found the collected revelations the founder received about the nature of heaven and especially of the *kami* who dwell there. Their relationship to human beings was analogous to that of a parent to his or her children. Thus, the prime manifestation of the godhead in the Tenri faith is what is called the Oyakami, or "Parent God."

Tenrikyo eventually became a recognized Shintō sect, and it remains today one of the most successful of the "new religions." Although it is primarily rooted in the Shintō concept of a hierarchy of *kami*, the religion founded by Nakayama Miki incorporates a number of concepts borrowed from Pure Land Buddhism, including salvation through intense professions of faith, in this instance in the power of Oyakami, and a well-defined afterworld. From its headquarters in Tenri City, near Nara, Tenrikyo has long since spread throughout Japan and has been carried to Hawaii, North America, Brazil, and wherever else Japanese have migrated.

By the end of the Meiji era in 1912, 13 Shintō-based sects, including Tenrikyo, had been recognized by the Japanese government, and most of them were *shinko shūkyo*. However, Shintō is far from the only source of these new faiths. Several movements have sprung directly from the Buddhist tradition. By far the most influential of these is Soka Gakkai, which as we have seen, is closely related to the Nichiren Shō-shū sect.[42]

Soka Gakkai

While Nichiren Shō-shū itself is by no means a true "new religion," the aforementioned Soka Gakkai, or "Value Creating Society," which was founded by Makiguchi Tsuesaburo (1871–1944) in the late 1920s, is generally considered to be one. By the outbreak of World War II in 1941, Makiguchi and his principal disciple, Toda Josei (1900–1958), had attracted only a few thousand disciples. But their intense devotion to the *Lotus Sutra* and the teachings of Nichiren were deemed subversive, and the organization was suppressed by the military regime.

This fact alone gave the movement an impetus with the American Occupation. In any case, under Toda's leadership, and spurred by the social upheavals that accompanied Japan's rapid postwar economic growth, Soka Gakkai grew rapidly. Its appeal was primarily to the massive numbers of people who were migrating to the cities from rural areas and who, as a result, had lost the social networks that are so important to Japanese life everywhere. By the late-1960s, led by Toda's successor, Ikeda Daisaku (1928–), the Soka Gakkai had attracted over 11 million members—all of whom were devout believers in the quasi-magical power of the *Lotus Sutra*, and the chant "*Nammyoho renge kyo*." A great many non-Japanese members were recruited, including the famous African-American singer Tina Turner and television actor Patrick Duffy.

At the same time, the cult's quasi-military organization, penchant for mass rallies, and demand for an almost total commitment on the part of its members raised suspicions among a great many Japanese that Soka Gakkai was but the tip of an iceberg that included a plot to take over the government. This suspicion, which subsequently turned out to be totally incorrect, was fueled when the Komeito political party was founded (see above). At present, under Ikeda-sensei's continuing leadership, Soka Gakkai remains an important force in Japanese religious life, although its membership has declined somewhat in recent years.

As we said, there are a vast number of "new religions"—one estimate runs as high as 200,000!—some of which have but a tiny handful of members.[43] A good example of such a small movement is Shokyo Mahikari, or the "Divine Light" movement, which was founded in the early 1960s.[44] It emphasizes healing and is based an extraordinarily broad-based theology that includes both Shintō and a variety of Buddhist elements, as well as the legend of the lost city of Atlantis! Another example is Agonshū, which became prominent in the 1980s. Founded by Kiriyama Seiyū in 1978, it combines traditional Shintō beliefs with those of the Shingon sect (see above) and the prophecies of the sixteenth-century French seer Nostradamus.[45]

The most notorious "new religion" in recent years is, of course, Aum Shinrikyo, a Buddhist offshoot that was implicated in the February 1995 attempt to poison the Tokyo subway system with Sarin gas. Like almost every other *shinko shukyo*, from

Tenrikyo on, it is (or was) centered around the person of a charismatic leader, in this case a young man named Shoku Asahara, who, as this is written, is currently on trial in Tokyo for the crime just mentioned.

In sum, despite some deplorable excesses and garbled theological underpinnings, the "new religions" provide vivid evidence that the impetus to religious innovation is very much alive and well in modern Japan. That the belief systems upon which this chapter has focused—Shintō and the mainstream Buddhist sects—will ultimately benefit from this impetus is likely, given the Japanese penchant for seamlessly blending tradition and innovation, not only when it comes to religion, but also in the culture as a whole.

NOTES

Note: All Japanese names appear in the traditional East Asian fashion, that is, surname first.

1. For example, H. Byron Earhart, *Japanese Religion: Unity and Diversity,* 3rd ed., (Belmont, CA: Wadsworth Publishing Company, 1982), pp. 121–123.

2. In recent years it has become fashionable to have a second ceremony performed by a Protestant minister. This necessarily involves a quick change of clothes on the part of the bridal couple, from the traditional Japanese wedding *kimono* to a Western-style wedding dress and a tuxedo.

3. For a comprehensive overview of Japanese religion as a whole, see Earhart.

4. For an overview of Shintō, see Ono Sokyo, *Shintō: The Kami Way* (New York: Tuttle, 1962). See also Joseph J. Spae, *Shintō Man* (Tokyo: Oriens Institute for Religious Research, 1972); Stuart D. B. Pickens, *Shintō: Japan's Spiritual Roots* (Tokyo: Kodansha International, Ltd., 1980); and C. Scott Littleton, "Shintō," in *Eastern Wisdom,* ed., C. Scott Littleton, (New York: Henry Holt, 1996).

5. The classic modern work on the earliest phase of Japanese prehistory is J. E. Kidder, *Japan before Buddhism* (London: Thames and Hudson, 1959). See also L. Melvin Akins and Takayasu Higuchi, *Prehistory of Japan* (San Diego, CA: Academic Press, 1982); and Gina Lee Barr, Karl L. Hutterer, and Richard J. Pearson, *Windows on the Japanese Past: Studies in Archaeology and Prehistory* (Ann Arbor: Center for Japanese Studies, University of Michigan, 1986).

6. For an overview of the "horse rider" theory, see Gari Ledyard, "Galloping along with the Horse Riders: Looking for the Founders of Japan," *Journal of Japanese Studies* 1:217–254, 1975; see also Egami Namio, "The Formation of the People and the Origin of the State of Japan," *Memoirs of the Toyo Bunko* 23:35–70.

7. See John Whitney Hall, *Japan: From Prehistory to Modern Times* (New York: Dell Publishing Company, 1979), pp. 41–42.

8. See Matsunaga Daigan and Alice Matsunaga, *Foundation of Japanese Buddhism,* Vol. 1 (Los Angeles: Buddhist Books International, 1974).

9. See Michael R. Saso, *Tantric Art and Meditation: The Tendai Tradition* (Honolulu: University of Hawaii Press, 1970); Yamasaki Taiko, *Shingon: Japanese Esoteric Buddhism* (Westminster, MD: Shambala Publications, Ltd., 1988), especially.

10. The classic work in English on Hōnen is Havelock Coates and Ryugaku Ishuzaka, *Hōnen, the Buddhist Saint: His Life and Thought* (Kyōto: Society for the Publication of Sacred Books of the World, 1925). See also Matsunaga and Matsunaga in note 8.

11. For an overview of Shinran's life and thought, see Alfred Bloom, *Shinran's Gospel of Pure Grace* (Tucson, AZ: University of Arizona Press, 1965). See also Takamichi Takahatake, *Young Man Shinran: A Reappraisal of Shinran's Life* (Blasdell, NY: Wilfrid Laurier University Press, 1987).

12. For a discussion of this parallel and its implications, realized and otherwise, see James H. Foard, "In Search of a Lost Reformation: A Reconsideration of Kamakura Buddhism," *Japanese Journal of Religious Studies* 7:261–291.

13. For a sympathetic assessment of Nichiren and his ideas, see Anesaki Masaharu, *Nichiren the Buddhist Prophet* (Cambridge, MA: Harvard University Press, 1966). A more balanced view of the Nichiren tradition can be found in Noah S. Brenner, *Soka Gakkai: Japan's Militant Buddhists* (Louisville, KY: John Knox Press, 1968).

14. As we shall see, in the post-World War II period, the Soka Gakkai and Nichiren Shō-shū gained millions of supporters—although the controversial nature of Nichiren's doctrine of exclusivity, coupled with his insistence that the *Lotus Sutra* is the only valid Buddhist text, remains a sore point among a great many contemporary Japanese Buddhists and Shintōists. See Brenner.

15. The literature on Zen is vast. For an overview of the history of Zen, see Heinrich Dumoulin, *A History of Zen Buddhism* (New York: Pantheon Books, 1963). See also D. T. Suzuki, *Zen and Japanese Culture* (New York: Pantheon Books, 1959); and Alan Watts, *The Way of Zen* (New York: Pantheon Books, 1957).

16. See C. E. Boxer, *The Christian Century in Japan: 1549–1650* (Berkeley: University of California Press, 1951).

17. This figure comes from a report to the Vatican by the Jesuit Visitor Valignano (1539–1606); see Hall, p. 140.

18. Although far more violent, this curious episode in Japanese history recalls Henry VIII's dissolution of the

English monasteries in 1535–36 after divorcing Catherine and breaking with Rome. In both cases, the wealth obtained from formerly powerful monasteries aided the confiscator in consolidating his power. For Henry VIII's attack on the English monasteries, see Christopher Hibbert, *The Story of England* (Harrisburg, PA: Phaidon Press Limited, 1992), pp. 109–112.

19. See Hall, pp. 142–159 in note 7.
20. See Edward O. Reischauer, *The Japanese Today: Change and Continuity* (Cambridge, MA: Harvard University Press, 1988), p. 212, who states that Christians number less than 2 percent of the modern population.
21. In 1704 the Tokugawa family founded the only Confucian temple in Japan, which still stands in the Hongo district of what is now Tokyo and is still a center for Japanese Confucian studies.
22. On the history of State Shintō, see Helen Hardacre, *Shintō and the State, 1880–1980* (Princeton, NJ: Princeton University Press, 1989).
23. The standard English edition of the *Kojiki* is Donald Philippi, *Kojiki* (Honolulu: University of Hawaii Press, 1968). The best translation of the *Nihonshoki* is still W. G. Aston, *Nihongi [=Nihonshoki]: Chronicles of Japan from the Earliest Times to A.D. 697* (Rutland, VT: Charles E. Tuttle, 1978 [first published in 1896]).
24. This motif is curiously similar to the legendary events that decided the sovereignty of Rome in 753 B.C.E. Like Susano, Remus disputed the outcome of a divinatory contest and defied the power of his twin brother Romulus. Unlike Remus, the Japanese figure was banished rather than killed, but the similarities are too close to be the result of chance; see Derek Hoffman, "Parallels in Myths Exemplified by Disputes among Twin Sibling Divinities," Occidental College (unpublished research paper), 1998. Indeed, a number of motifs here have counterparts in Western mythology: Izanagi's vain attempt to rescue Izanami from Yomi reflects the ancient Greek myth of Orpheus and Eurydice, while the idea that the goddess ate food in the land of the dead and was thereby tied to it reflects the Persephone myth. Also, in later sections of both the *Kojiki* and *Nihonshoki* the exploits of the greatest of all Japanese legendary heroes, Yamato-takeru, include a great many "Arthurian" traits, including the hero's magical, Excalibur-like sword, Kusanagi. How these tales managed to get to Japan is still an open question, although many scholars now believe that the steppe-spawned "horse riders" who invaded Japan in the fourth century (see above) were the principal agents of diffusion. For a discussion of the Yamato-takeru legend from this perspective, see C. Scott Littleton, "Yamato-takeru: An 'Arthurian' Hero in Japanese Tradition," *Asian Folklore Studies* 54:259–274, 1994.
25. A recent English translation of the *Lotus Sutra* can be found in Burton Watson, *The Lotus Sutra* (New York: Columbia University Press, 1993). For an assessment of it on Japanese Buddhism, see George Tanabe and Willa J. Tanabe, eds., *The Lotus Sutra in Japanese Culture* (Honolulu: University of Hawaii Press, 1989).
26. For a succinct discussion of the *Sun Sutra* and the Vairocana Buddha, see Earhart, pp. 80–83 in note 1.
27. See Yamasaki, pp. 172–175 in note 7.
28. The literature on *matsuri* is extensive. See, for example, Michael Ashkenazi, *Matsuri: Festivals of a Japanese Town* (Honolulu: University of Hawaii Press, 1993). See also A. V. Sadler, "Carrying the Mikoshi: Further Notes on the Shrine Festival in Modern Tokyo," *Asian Folklore Studies* 31:89–114 (1976); and C. Scott Littleton, "The Organization and Management of a Tokyo Shintō Shrine Festival," *Ethnology* 25:195–202.
29. See Littleton, "The Organization and Management of a Tokyo Shintō Shrine Festival" in note 28.
30. For a comprehensive account of account of a Shintō *jinja*, see John K. Nelson, *A Year in the Life of a Shintō Shrine* (Seattle: University of Washington Press, 1996).
31. For a discussion of Shugendō and the *yamabushi*, see Carmen Blacker, *The Catalpa Bow* (London: Allen and Unwin, 1975), pp. 165–168.
32. Like the Ise-*jingu*, the Izumo-*taisha* shrine is built of wood and thatch and has been rebuilt frequently, although not at any regular intervals.
33. For a discussion of Shintō ethics, see Spae, pp. 51–59 in note 4..
34. The chief proponent of this idea was the well-known American anthropologist Ruth Benedict, who elaborated on it in *The Chrysanthemum and the Sword* (Boston: Houghton Mifflin, 1946).
35. See Émile Durkheim, *The Elementary Forms of the Religious Life* (New York: Collier Books, 1961 [1912]).
36. For discussions of these matters, see Nakane and Reischauer in notes 20 and 38.
37. The ancient *miko* were shamans who were possessed by *kami* while in a trance state and served as healers, etc.; see Blacker, pp. 104–126 in note 31. However, most modern *miko* play a role in Shintō analogous to that played by altar boys in Roman Catholicism.
38. See, for example, Nakane Chia, *Japanese Society* (Berkeley: University of California Press, 1970).
39. For an overview of the "new religions," see H. Neil McFarland, *The Rush Hour of the Gods: A Study of the New Religious Movements of Japan* (New York: Macmillan, 1967). See also Ian Reader, *Religion in Modern Japan* (Honolulu: University of Hawaii Press, 1991), especially pp. 194–233.
40. See Hall, pp. 233–253 in note 7.
41. For a concise, albeit doctrinal history of this sect, see *A Short History of Tenrikyo*, published by the Tenrikyo Kyokai Honbu (the Main Tenrikyo Church, Tenri), 1956. See also Dendobu Kaigai, *Tenrikyo: Japan's New Shintō Movement; Its Faith and Doctrines, History, Institutions and Mission Work Described* (Tenrikyo Board of Overseas Missions, Tenri, 1935).
42. See Brenner in note 13, A less objective account can be found in *The Nichiren Shosho Sokagakkai* (Tokyo: Seikyo Press, 1966).
43. See McFarland in note 39.
44. See Winston B. Davis, *Dojo: Exorcism and Miracles in Modern Japan* (Stanford, CA: Stanford University Press, 1980).
45. See Reader, pp. 208–233 in note 39.

Sixteen

Judaism

Jack Glazier
Oberlin College

INTRODUCTION

Judaism, the religious observances and beliefs of the Jewish people, comprises an ancient, ordered set of rituals, symbols, tenets, and practices. Studies of the great world religions frequently entail a systematic examination of abstract principles regarded as the encapsulation of the creed or doctrine of the faith. This approach is characteristic of studies in the field of comparative religion. To understand Judaism from an anthropological point of view, a different mode of analysis is necessary for two complementary reasons.

First, while anthropologists share with scholars of comparative religion an interest in the interrelated principles and beliefs defining a particular faith, the anthropologist goes further. He or she also aims to understand religion within the framework of community life. The anthropologist wants to grasp how religion shapes social experience and is in turn affected by it. In other words, an anthropological approach to religion closely examines how beliefs, practices, and even written texts considered sacred are connected to other aspects of human culture and how their meanings change over time. In this view, religion is regarded as a dynamic phenomenon, inextricably connected to the broad stream of social life. It is an organic part of human communities.

Second, Judaism does not conceive of divinity as an abstract, distant force but rather emphasizes the relationship of the community to God in personal terms. That relationship is to be realized in daily life and human interaction, where each person should guide his or her behavior according to the ethical and moral obligations of Judaism. The grounding of the religion in the shared reality of a community is thus particularly congenial to an anthropological understanding, because the latter also emphasizes the ways in which people organize and think about their own experience. Certainly, Judaism is generally regarded by its adherents as a religion focused on community life rather than on otherworldly preoccupations far removed from the practical concerns of living. While belief is of course important in Judaism, the moral and ethical behavior of people in consonance with their religious teachings is preeminent. Judaism is thus tightly woven into the reality of daily living.[1]

The anthropologist also regards religion as a part of human culture, rooted in particular times and places and, of course, subject to change. Practices detailed in the Hebrew Bible, for example, bear only a partial resemblance to the religious actions of later centuries as a result of rabbinical commentary and interpretation of the ancient text. The religion has steadily evolved and changed in step with the shifting historical circumstances of diverse Jewish communities worldwide.

Two brief examples should make the point. One might consider current controversies in Israel between highly religious, or orthodox Jews, and their less observant neighbors over such matters as maintaining the Sabbath. The former group calls for a strict adherence to the Biblical rules about the day of rest. They protest the flow of traffic through their neighborhoods on the Sabbath since driving violates the injunction to refrain from labor. They criticize their more secular Jewish neighbors, who choose to drive on the day of rest without concern about the Biblical commandment. Clearly, there is a considerable difference between these two segments of Judaism over belief and its relationship to behavior, and that relationship plays itself out in the way people organize their lives. The orthodox feel so aggrieved at what they see as the profanation of the Sabbath that they sometimes hurl verbal abuse and even rocks at those driving through their neighborhoods.

Closer to home, American Jewish groups no less than their neighbors of other faiths have over the past three decades responded to the feminist movement, which has of course affected many domains of life beyond religion. Within traditional Judaism, only men could serve as rabbis or otherwise perform various functions within the religious service. Although the traditional community of Jews remains resistant to the ordination of women as rabbis and to their elevation to a more egalitarian religious position, other segments of Judaism now accept female ordination and grant to women the same prerogatives traditionally enjoyed only by men. Women rabbis, at least beyond the precincts of orthodoxy, are no longer a novelty.[2]

These two cases illustrate the conflict between long-standing convictions and challenges to tradition by people seeking a more comfortable fit between Judaism and the modern world. Indeed, such tensions occur in other faiths as well, where conservative practices and beliefs face severe challenges from adherents eager to reconcile traditional religion with science and modernity. This issue will be taken up again at the conclusion of this chapter. The examples also establish an important general point, namely that Judaism is responsive to change and can only be understood in the broad context of culture and history. Even "traditional" Judaism is evolving, and the reformulations of Judaism continue. As a religion, it is not monolithic but instead exhibits a considerable diversity amid its core beliefs and values. This chapter aims to lay out those common elements within Judaism that link diverse communities—Ethiopian Jews, American Jews, Russian Jews, North African Jews, and others—while noting some of the cultural and historical differences and innovations across Jewish communities.

ORIGINS

Judaism begins with the Biblical patriarch Abraham when, according to Jewish belief, God established a covenant with him. Abraham is also revered by Islam as the lineal forebear of its founder and prophet, Muhammad. Jewish tradition regards the covenant as a divine promise to Abraham and his descendants that they would enjoy the special blessing of God. They in turn were obligated to obey the divine word. Emphasizing monotheism and ethical behavior, Judaism was embraced by the ancient Hebrews, yet their practices also differed in important ways from the subsequent Jewish tradition of ancient Israel and, of course, from what constitutes modern Judaism. For example, the sacrifice of livestock to God, so ubiquitous in the Old Testament, ceased to be a part of Jewish observance more than two thousand years ago. The religion of Abraham also evolved with the first five books of the Hebrew Bible, or *Torah*, received by Moses. It constitutes the core sacred text of Judaism from that time (approximately 3,500 years ago) to the present and makes clear the way the covenant changed from the era of Abraham to that of Moses.

With the Roman conquest of the Middle East and the destruction in the year 70 of the Christian era of the Temple in Jerusalem, the ancient Jewish state of Israel ceased to exist. It became a province of the Roman Empire. Many people were then dispersed well beyond their ancient homeland to other parts of the Roman world. This dispersion, or Diaspora, eventually resulted in the formation of Jewish communities throughout western and eastern Europe, North Africa, and the eastern Mediterranean. The continuing diffusion and cultural diversification of Jewish settlements over the subsequent centuries also included the founding of Jewish communities in India, China, and the Western Hemisphere

CENTRAL BELIEFS

The theme of historical change and community diversity among Jews is balanced by the common elements that cut across the differences. It is thus possible to identify the central tenets and religious values of Judaism. These center on God, the Land of Israel, and the *Torah*, yet these ideas do not yield to dogmatic formulations. Judaism is characterized by flexibility in belief, partly because no hierarchical religious authority, as in Catholicism, codifies and enforces religious precepts. While rabbis throughout the centuries offered interpretations of the sacred texts, their variant understandings stood side by side in the Jewish tradition. Doctrinal assertions about belief are also distinctly out of place in Judaism, since the religion tends to value ethical practice and moral action above letter-perfect conformity to abstract theological or ritual rules.

Believing that people are created in the image of God, Judaism emphasizes that human beings are uniquely capable of performing good deeds over the course of their lives. The Hebrew term for such righteous acts (*mitzvot*, sing; *mitzvah*) provides insight into a person's connection to God, for the term also means a divine command. Thus one who acts with kindness and compassion to help a fellow human being is literally carrying out God's will, thus realizing the divine presence, even in the most familiar routines and interactions of daily activity. Every good deed performed is, in effect, a religious act. This, rather than ecstatic experience or sudden revelation, marks the Jewish encounter with God. While in many respects God remains unknowable, the observance of commandments makes God manifest in the world, sometimes in the most simple ways of helping others. In a sense, God's creation is an unending process, continuing to unfold in the virtuous actions of people.

Put somewhat differently, the Jewish tradition believes that God is revealed in history, that is, through the action of people within a community.

By the same token, the *Torah*, first revealed by God to Moses as a divine guide to moral and ethical human conduct, is believed to be more than an ancient document. It is often described as "living," thus suggesting that the teachings of the *Torah* are as relevant to the modern world as they have been to all other historical periods.

Judaism is also inseparably bound to the land of Israel. Beginning with Abraham, commanded by God to settle in Israel, the land has remained an intimate part of Jewish consciousness. Even through the 20 centuries of exile between the Roman conquest and the establishment of the modern state of Israel in 1948, the land promised to the Biblical patriarchs and their descendants beckoned in Jewish prayers and liturgy for a return of its people. The prayers refer variously to the land of Israel or places within that are equally charged with religious significance—Jerusalem, Zion, and other holy sites, for example. Returning to the Promised Land depended, however, on the coming of the messiah. When the Jewish people had shown themselves worthy, they believed they would achieve the messianic deliverance that would restore them to their ancient and sacred homeland, ending once and for all two thousand years of exile. Thus for this vast expanse of time, a religious longing expressed in prayers for the land characterized the Jewish communities of the Diaspora.

The covenant between the Jewish people and God raises the question of "the chosen people"—an idea easily misunderstood. While Jewish scholars certainly discuss the special relationship implied by the covenant, they have interpreted "chosenness" in several ways, none of which includes unique privilege or an arrogant, ethnocentric sense of superiority or entitlement. Thus, the idea of a chosen people is not exclusionary, for all people are believed to be entitled to the rewards of the divine plan. Instead, the Jews were chosen to serve God in particular ways that would guide others in living morally and ethically. "Chosenness" effectively means that the covenant placed particular responsibilities on the Jewish people to demonstrate by their own actions the universal truth of God's commandments. There is thus in the concept of the "chosen" a tension between the very particular and specific relationship of one nation to God and more general meanings that encompass all of humankind.

Jews also ask many of the same kinds of religious questions raised by their Christian neighbors, yet Jewish belief points to different answers. While both traditions confront the enduring problem of human sinfulness, for example, Judaism rejects ideas about original sin or an inherently depraved human nature. Rather, people are regarded as self-determining in that they can choose to act in esteemed and righteous ways or in a sinful manner. With their inevitable human shortcomings and imperfections, people in the course of their lives will act reprehensibly as well as admirably. Judaism recognizes this dual human capacity and urges both the expiation of sin in prayer and continuing efforts to follow one's higher inclinations in order to fulfill divine expectations.

It should be clear at this point that Judaism is a religion focused on this world. Accordingly, the concept of heaven is little developed, and hell hardly at all. While the Bible refers to a place where the soul goes after death, it is at best a vague conception. In ancient Judaism, some concern about heaven and hell entered the tradition under Persian influence. But for the most part, heaven remains an indistinct notion lacking any physical description in Jewish writings. In the Jewish tradition, heaven and hell are experienced in this life as the rewards and punishments for human actions. Upright and honest living provides its own satisfactions. Heaven and hell representing physical locales where divinity dispenses rewards and punishments for behavior on earth are decidedly absent from the Jewish tradition.

Connected to the Christian concept of hell is of course the character of Satan. Here, too, Judaism differs from Christianity, for Satan as a personification of evil is of negligible importance, despite various references to Satan in the Hebrew Bible. The contact between ancient Judaism and external influences, such as those from Persia, introduced the personified evil of Satan into the Jewish tradition. Yet in some ways the idea of a force of evil competing with God is at odds with the Jewish notion of divine omnipotence. Moreover, the Jewish value on free will and the human power to make decisive choices for good or ill leaves no room for a concept of Satanic temptation or the related idea that a power of pure evil is at work in the world. Judaism takes a critical view of beliefs that absolve people of responsibility and so the tradition also rejects notions of a preordained fate directing people's lives.

TEXTS

The preeminent text of Judaism is the *Torah*, the first five books of the Hebrew Bible. In the form of a sacred scroll of parchment that is handwritten in Hebrew, the *Torah* has a central place in each synagogue, where it is stored within a cabinet known as the ark. During each Sabbath morning service, the *Torah* is ritually removed from the ark amid great ceremony and then read in successive portions throughout the year.

In Jewish belief, the *Torah*, however, is more than a holy object. The term also represents the essence of a way of life that extols devotion to God, life-long learning, reason, wisdom, and ethical conduct. Sometimes spoken of as the "living *Torah*," it is not frozen in time but rather has continued to impart its meanings to the Jewish people throughout history. *Torah* also refers to other writings, particularly the rabbinical commentaries contained in the *Talmud*. Consisting of more than 60 books written between the fourth and the sixth centuries, the *Talmud* records the thinking and decisions of rabbis during that period. It is a massive collection of lore, parables, aphorisms, and other wisdom as rendered by learned rabbis in the course of their textual interpretations. It represents the authoritative statement of Jewish law. In light of its extraordinary difficulty and complexity, the study of the *Talmud* is taken up by relatively few people, mainly rabbis and religious scholars. That the *Talmud* was transmitted over many generations as part of the oral tradition is remarkable. Written down approximately at the beginning of the third century, this codified oral tradition is known as the *Mishnah* and consists of a number of parts examining such topics as marriage and divorce, civil affairs, and ritual purity. A much larger part of the *Talmud* is the *Gemara*, completed in the sixth century, and consisting of commentary on the *Mishnah*.

Another principal text of Judaism is the *Midrash*, which dates from the same period as the *Talmud*. It consists of additional rabbinical reflection, commentary, and questions on the Bible. A creative tradition resembling the *Midrash* has been revived in recent times as people interpret Biblical text in line with contemporary questions inspired by feminism and other current social concerns. Once again, this reflects the fact that Judaism is a steadily evolving tradition.

When considering the texts of any religion, an important question arises about how they are to be interpreted. Some individuals read the Bible as history, that is, as an actual record of events and people. Everything from the most routine descriptions to miraculous accounts about Joshua at Jericho or Moses parting the Red Sea ring with literal truth. While some orthodox Jews maintain this fundamentalist understanding of the sacred texts, most people regard the events of the Bible as symbolic. In other words, they do not read the Bible as history but rather as a narrative containing lessons of great value. Even in ancient times, *Talmudic* scholars might read the text literally while also pointing out the larger truths contained in the narrative.

For example, in Genesis 18:10–14, God informs Sarah and Abraham that they will have a son. Remarking about Abraham's advanced age as well as her own, Sarah laughs at the prospect of bearing a child. But God tells Abraham only of Sarah's comment about herself. He does not report that the idea of fatherhood for a man of Abraham's advanced age provoked her amusement. While few people would take this story as a literal representation of actual events—the personal encounter of very aged prospective parents with supernatural agency—they can nonetheless gain insight of considerable importance from this simple story. Against expectation, the reader discovers that even God can lie at times. But God does so not out of perversity or deceit, but rather to maintain the harmonious relationship between Abraham and Sarah. Otherwise, Abraham might have taken offense had he known of Sarah's doubts about his capacity to father a child. The moral of God's own misrepresentation is simple but compelling. A lie that serves the interests of peace is justified. It should be emphasized that this is an ancient interpretation that stood alongside a reading of the text in literal terms. While few continue to adhere to the belief that the narrative represents history, traditional Jewish texts remain rich with symbolic meanings that scholars continue to discern as guides to appropriate moral action within the community.

ORTHODOX, REFORM, AND CONSERVATIVE JUDAISM

Jewish religious behavior ranges from strict, highly observant practice to liberal forms of the religion that readily adjust tradition to the imperatives of social change. Orthodoxy refers to the strictest forms of Jewish ritual practice as dictated by Jewish law, or *halacha*. The latter Hebrew term refers to the body of rules recorded in the *Talmud* and in subsequent documents, especially the sixteenth-century compilation, entitled the *Shulhan Arukh.*

Illustrative of Jewish law are the dietary, or kosher rules (*kashrut*) prescribing what can and cannot be eaten. These rules derive from the books of Leviticus and Deuteronomy as well as from rabbinical interpretations in the *Talmud*, the exclusions apply only to certain meats, fowl, and marine and aquatic life; all vegetables and fruits are acceptable.

For example, the book of Leviticus specifies that animals such as cattle, goats, and sheep which have cloven hooves and chew their cud are permissible for the table. Pigs, on the other hand, are prohibited, for although they have cloven hooves they do not chew cud. They are, in effect, outside the acceptable category and must not be eaten. Moreover, of those animals that can be eaten, consumption of their blood is strictly prohibited. Blood as the symbol of life belongs only to God. Additionally, strict rules forbid the mixing of milk and meat products during meals and require separate cooking utensils and dishes for preparing and serving meat and dairy foods. As to the rules governing the consumption of fresh water or sea creatures, one may only consume fish that have fins and scales. Shellfish, such as lobsters, shrimp, oysters, mussels, and the like are prohibited. Fowl that may be eaten include only those birds that can fly and do not kill prey, and indeed no carnivorous animal is acceptable under the kosher laws.

Just as the concept of the Chosen People sets Jews apart from others, so too do the strict rules of classification in the dietary laws separate foods into acceptable and unacceptable categories. The rules are complex, but observing them as well as all other codes pertaining to the entire gamut of human activity reiterates the Jewish commitment to live according to divine will. The anthropologist Mary Douglas argues persuasively that the dietary rules are metaphors about holiness in the sense of wholeness and perfection. Each meal thus enables people to express their belongingness to a distinct community defined by its adherence to rules that reiterate divine models of holiness.[3] Following the dietary laws is an important symbol differentiating orthodox Jews from all other people, including Jews who do not feel bound by the code.

Despite some internal variations within orthodoxy, this wing of Judaism on the whole is notable for its resistance to change. Many Orthodox Jews believe that the *Torah* was literally bestowed by God on Moses and the Jewish people and is therefore sacred and beyond challenge. It embodies divinely inspired precepts for proper behavior in every phase of life. Consequently, the laws of Jewish living that are rooted in the teaching of the *Torah* must be followed. While orthodox Judaism has made important accommodations to modernity, its position is, on the whole, highly conservative, always leaning more to a preservation of tradition rather than its modification.

A particularly noteworthy segment of orthodox Judaism is the Hasidic movement. It originated in Poland in the eighteenth century. Hasidic Jews, while highly orthodox, practice a mystical Judaism that finds the divine presence in all places. A particularly joyful religious observance is the rule. Hasidic Jews find sacred value in music, dance, and the like, and the most basic activities can take on spiritual significance. Thus exultation in worship—the expression of pure feeling and emotion—provides the same route to God as the dedicated study of sacred texts carried on by religious scholars. Consequently, Hasidism found many eager followers among common people. Additionally, unlike other orthodox communities, the Hasidim look to their rabbis as charismatic leaders with special powers enabling them to perform miracles. The Hasidic communities are noteworthy for their high birthrates. Additionally, the Hasidim actively recruit non-Hasidic Jews, seeking to persuade them to take up a highly observant orthodox way of life. Their population is 200,000 in the United States, with at least half that number living in New York state. Hasidim also reside in Europe and Israel. Hasidic men are immediately recognizable by their distinctive black dress, beards, and earlocks, worn in accord with the Biblical command. Hasidic women dress in extremely modest fashion, including head coverings, long sleeves to cover the arms, and dresses that are similarly undisclosing.[4]

Until the eighteenth century, most Jews lived in Europe in segregated semi-autonomous communities dominated by the authority of rabbis and elders, who in turn were guided by the sacred texts of Jewish law. There was little alternative to orthodox practice within the ghetto communities. By the end of the eighteenth century, however, a political and social movement of profound significance ushered in radical changes in Jewish life, including a weakening of the authority of traditional rabbis. Orthodox belief and practice, in effect, were losing their grip. Specifically, in several areas of Western Europe, Jews were granted citizenship and civil rights. Jews were no longer obligated to live only in certain designated areas. With the move toward political and social equality, the enforced exclusion of Jews from schools, political office, the military, and from particular occupations came to an end in Western Europe.

As traditional rabbinical authority was diminishing, Jews were experiencing greater tolerance from the wider society. Some left the fold through intermarriage and conversion to Christianity. Many others, however, sought to modify the traditional religion, bringing it into harmony with modernity. They wanted to extend the process of social and political liberalization to religion, emphasizing only those aspects of Judaism that were consistent with the rationality and modern thought. Beginning in Germany, this movement toward religious liberalization became known as Reform Judaism. It rejected many of the ancient rules and beliefs, such as the dietary laws, that seemed irrational or incompatible with scientific understanding. Whereas the rules may once have existed to promote good health, in the reasoning of religious reformers, modern scientific understanding about hygiene and food preservation rendered the dietary laws obsolete. Among other reform measures was the use of vernacular language in prayers to replace Hebrew.

Additionally, Reform Judaism eliminated seating segregation by sex in religious services, and since the 1970s the ordination of female rabbis has become routine. Of utmost importance in considering the many liberalizing changes of Reform Judaism is the questioning of traditional authority—orthodox rabbis and the sacred texts. In the name of modernity and enlightenment, Reform Judaism was inclined to modify those practices and beliefs that seemed out of step with scientific progress and the greater social acceptance that Jews had managed to gain, particularly in Western Europe and in the United States.

At the end of the nineteenth century, a number of American Jews found the efforts of the German Jewish reformers too extreme. As a result, Conservative Judaism emerged as a distinctly American branch of the religion. It has spread elsewhere but enjoys its greatest strength in the United States. Conservative Jews believe some adaptations of Jewish law to contemporary life should proceed, but they are unwilling to go as far as Reform Jews in ignoring or updating ancient tradition. Changes should occur only with moderation. Some Conservative synagogues welcome the full participation of women on a par with men, and the ordination of Conservative women rabbis is a recent but still controversial phenomenon.

Reconstructionism, a small offshoot of Conservative Judaism, emphasizes Jewish peoplehood and how it has evolved as a civilization. Apart from purely religious matters, issues of common culture, however secular they may be, figure importantly in Reconstructionism. Its conceptions of divinity are diffuse but do not include the idea of a personal God, and Reconstructionism is more willing than Conservative Judaism to question the most fundamental tenets of the faith, such as the nature of

God and the role of sacred texts in modern life. Reconstructionism, like Reformism, promotes the ordination of female rabbis and women's full participation in Jewish ritual.

RELIGION OR ETHNICITY

Anthropologists conventionally regard ethnicity as the complex of factors that define distinctive cultural groups in pluralistic nation-states. Among the features that characterize the ethnic group are a shared language and religion, a sense of common history, and a wide range of cultural practices, including styles of dress, folklore, and narratives, foodways, naming practices, language, and music. In the United States, many hyphenated ethnic identities such as Irish-American, Japanese-American, Mexican-American, and so forth, reflect the cultural diversity of the nation and its history. As these identities suggest, one becomes a member of an ethnic group by birth, not by choice. One cannot decide to become Irish. To what extent do Jews in America or in other nation-states constitute an ethnic group?

The Jewish religion has always accepted converts into its ranks, although Judaism, unlike Christianity, does not actively engage in efforts to proselytize. In this respect, Judaism as faith is set apart from ethnic groupings determined solely by parentage. Just as one can become Catholic (but not become Irish) so too can an individual choose to become Jewish, if he or she is willing to undergo the process of conversion under the supervision of a rabbi. Yet the matter is not quite so simple because Jewish communities around the world are marked by distinctive cultural features that extend beyond the purely religious. These cultural emblems represent the ethnic dimension of Jewish life—the distinctive practices and beliefs that define any community and shape the identity of people born into it.

The anthropologist Robert Redfield distinguished between the Great Tradition and the Little Tradition—two concepts that should help clarify the religious and ethnic dimensions of the Jewish experience across cultures.[5]

The Great Tradition refers to the sectors of culture controlled by a literate, learned elite that attempts to codify or systematize belief and practice. The elite or intelligentsia present, in effect, an official version of the religion. In Judaism, features of the Great Tradition include Hebrew, long considered a sacred language reserved for worship and religious study, rabbinical authority, the sacred texts referred to earlier, ritual observances marking the Hebrew calendar, prayer, and liturgy. These Great Tradition characteristics transcend place and time. That is, they define Jewish religious life throughout the world in various, culturally diverse communities of Jews. For example, Sabbath observance in Jewish houses of worship in different parts of the world—Cleveland, Buenos Aires, Rome, Tunis, Jerusalem— will, with some variation, comprise a corpus of Hebrew prayers, *Torah* readings, and synagogue rituals.

Complementing the Great Tradition is the Little Tradition, or the ethnic features of community life. The Little Tradition is deeply rooted in the experience of daily living, delimiting as it does an entire cultural complex of activities and outlooks within a community. The ethnic dimension of Jewish life is also implicated in an interesting paradox. Jewish people may identify closely with the distinctive cultural characteristics of their communities yet not attend religious services or even participate in Jewish rituals or observances. They might even claim to be atheists while expressing a determined pride in their Jewishness! Nonetheless, the Little Tradition also includes "domestic religion," or the religious rituals centered in the home.[6] It is the province of ordinary people, a matter of customary behavior that is sanctioned by the experience of parents and grandparents rather than the pronouncements of rabbis and other religious authorities. It is the domain of folk religion and, indeed, rabbis representing the Great Tradition were not friendly to many of its features. While rabbinical scholars are the arbiters of the Great Tradition, the people of a community represent the final authority on matters pertaining to the Little Tradition.

A brief comparison of Ashkenazic and Sephardic Jews will illustrate the distinction between the religious, Great Tradition features of Judaism, on the one hand, and its ethnic and Little Tradition characteristics, on the other. Ashkenazic Jews derive from central and eastern Europe, where they lived for centuries. Most inhabited small towns in Russia or Russian-controlled territory under a succession of czars. Ethnically, their way of life centered on the Yiddish language and the culture embedded within it. Yiddish is a Germanic language that not only shares many common lexical and grammatical roots with modern German but also reflects in its vocabulary word borrowing from Hebrew and from the languages of neighboring Slavic communities of central and eastern Europe. Along with the language, distinctive foods, patterns of courtship, folklore and belief, and religious observance within the home, other customs large and small made up the content of the Little Tradition of Ashkenazic Jewish communities over the course of six hundred years.

In contrast to the Ashkenazic Jews, Sephardic Jews derive from Spain, where they flourished for centuries in generally amicable co-existence with their Muslim and Christian neighbors. With the onset of the Inquisition in 1492, however, they were expelled from Spain. Finding safe haven in the eastern Mediterranean under the control of the Ottoman Empire, Sephardic Jews broadly shared the Great Tradition of Judaism with the Ashkenazic communities of central and eastern Europe. They held in common liturgical and religious practices, ritual observances, and Hebrew texts, and the use of Hebrew in worship, although there were certainly differences of tone and coloration amid the common features. But on the smaller canvas of the Little Tradition, the Jewish exiles from Spain sketched an ethnic tradition that was quite different from the portrait of local Ashkenazic culture. They were, in other words, culturally and linguistically distinct. The Sephardim were not Yiddish speakers but rather used Ladino as their first language. Ladino was based on fifteenth-century Spanish and also steadily incorporated lexical elements from Turkish and other languages spoken in their new home.

Differences in naming practices exemplify Little Tradition, or ethnic differences between Jewish communities that still share commitments to the orthodox practices defining a single Great Tradition. Among Ashkenazic Jews, parents name their children after the dead, usually kinsmen. In the folklore of Ashkenazic communities, it is said that a Jewish soul does not rest until a child has taken the name of the dead person. To name a child after a living person is almost unthinkable, for it portends the imminent death of that person. It is feared, in anthropological terms, as an act of sympathetic magic. This naming pattern derives from the folk beliefs of Yiddish-speaking communities periodically devastated by antisemitic violence. Carrying on the names of those who perished thus became a time-honored, commemorative tradition. It is not, however, sanctioned by the authority of sacred texts.

Otherwise, one might expect the same pattern to occur among equally religious Sephardic Jews, but it does not. Instead, the latter honor living kinsmen by naming children after them. This practice is an equally venerable Little Tradition custom that nevertheless distinguished Sephardic from Ashkenazic Jews. When Ashkenazic and Sephardic Jews have inhabited the same communities—a development occurring in the wake of immigration to Israel beginning in the 1950s and to America in the early twentieth century— friction between the two groups occurred. In America, for example, some Ashkenazic Jews mistakenly questioned the Jewish authenticity of their Sephardic neighbors on the basis of Little Tradition differences, such as naming practices.

THE HEBREW CALENDAR AND THE RITUAL CYCLE

The Hebrew calendar, unlike the standard, or Gregorian, calendar is based on the lunar cycle. The moon requires 29.5 days to orbit the earth, and each cycle marks a separate Hebrew month. By this reckoning, only 354 days elapse in each year, thus falling 11 days short of the solar year. To avoid a widening gap between the Hebrew calendar and the earth's actual movement around the sun, an entire month is periodically added to the calendar. Otherwise, various holidays and festivals geared to particular times of the year would soon occur out of season. While the Gregorian calendar marks 365 days in a solar year, the actual number is a fraction more, thus requiring a much less drastic adjustment of an added day every fourth year, or leap year. Various symbolic expressions, in this instance the differing representations of time in Judaism and Christianity, provide important attributes of distinctiveness and identity for the two historically connected religions.

Jewish tradition includes both major and minor holidays. The former are sanctioned in the Bible and require "time out of time"—that is, they usually mandate cessation of work and a suspension of familiar activities. These include the Sabbath, New Year (Rosh Hashonah), the Day of Atonement (Yom Kippur), and Passover. Minor holidays, on the other hand, such as Hanukah originated after the Bible was written and do not entail major breaks with normal activities and customary labor.

The ritual cycle is marked weekly by the Sabbath observance. Jewish holy days always start at dusk immediately before the first full day of the observance. The Jewish Sabbath, accordingly, begins at sundown on Friday evening and concludes at dusk on Saturday. This characteristic pattern derives from the Book of Genesis, where the first day begins with evening followed by morning. The Sabbath is redolent with meaning, for it evokes the very act of creation. God made the world in six days, reserving the seventh for rest. The day of rest is thus consecrated as a time outside the workday pattern of labor. At the end of the creation, God invests humanity with the task of stewardship over the world and the responsibility for using nature wisely and benevolently. God's sovereignty is recognized both by the day of rest and by work itself that not only nurtures the human body but also the soul.

Friday evenings are traditionally joyous times in Jewish homes. The profane routine of the work week gives way to a family observance of the Sabbath, including candle lighting, a traditional activity for women. The candle lighting ushers in the Sabbath, providing a kind of timeless unity across the generations that have performed precisely the same act. Blessings, including the *kiddush,* or prayer of sanctification, are intoned to proclaim the holiness of the day of rest. Additionally, a specially prepared meal served on the best dishes is set out. Because many kinds of work, including cooking, are prohibited on the Sabbath, the foods are prepared during the day. Religious services are held in synagogues on Friday night and additionally on the Sabbath morning, Saturday, at which time the *Torah* is read. As Friday night and Saturday morning formally honor God the creator, the afternoon of the Sabbath may be devoted to reading religious texts, to resting and eating, and to enjoying the leisure of a special day. The actual extent of Jewish observance of the Sabbath is very wide, ranging from the most scrupulous performance of all the rituals among the orthodox to synagogue attendance without adherence to the rules preventing work.

Besides the weekly Sabbath celebration, the Hebrew calendar marks a series of recurrent, ancient seasonal observances with deep religious significance. Only a few can be considered here. They vary in importance. Many are joyous festival days while others resonate with the most profound themes of existential meaning and self-examination. Of the latter observances, none is more serious than the two holidays marking the Jewish New Year (Rosh Hashonah) and the Day of Atonement (Yom Kippur). Known collectively as the High Holidays, the New Year and the Day of Atonement occur over a ten-day period of penitence. Mercy and forgiveness are the themes of the New Year synagogue service that is periodically signaled by the sounding of the *shofar*, or ram's horn. The piercing sound of the *shofar* is a kind of awakening of the faithful to the need for reflection and self-examination. At the same time, an intense awareness of God's power pervades the community.

The Day of Atonement, the holiest day in the Jewish calendar, is the culmination of a process of penitence and renewal—a new beginning at the onset of a new year. People seek expiation of their sins and reconciliation with others by asking forgiveness from those they have wronged over the year, thus attempting to reestablish within the community a harmony that has given way to discord over the previous months. Only then is it possible to gain divine forgiveness. The 24-hour observance includes private and collective confession of sins as well prayers that seek release from promises made but not fulfilled. The solemnity of the Day of Atonement is also inscribed by fasting in order to divert attention away from mundane concerns and bodily comforts as one stands before God to ask for absolution. It is a time above all for spiritual self-examination and the most personal efforts to take stock of one's life. Although many Jews do not embrace orthodox practice and fail to observe the strictures of Jewish ritual, it is significant that the New Year and the Day of Atonement remain important for many of these individuals. Even for those who remain aloof from Jewish practices throughout the year, the High Holidays represent core symbols of Jewish selfhood and perhaps the only calendrical occasions drawing them to the synagogue. Such annual synagogue appearances effectively represent a public performance of one's identity.

In the spring, Jewish communities worldwide celebrate Pesach, or Passover, a holiday infused with themes of new life, renewal, and freedom. Probably originating in a festival for the harvest of early grains, Passover accrued the additional meanings of freedom and liberation contained in the story of the exodus from Egypt more than three thousand years ago. Delivered by God from bondage and led to their own land by Moses, Jews at Passover recall their enslavement and commit themselves to the extension of freedom to all people.

The memory of affliction as well as the joy of freedom find expression in the ritual practices of Passover, especially in the *seder*, or ceremonial meal, prepared on the first two nights of the eight-day celebration. An elaborate food symbolism, blessings and prayer, readings, and songs evoke the servitude in Egypt as well as the exultation of freedom. The order of ceremonies derives from the *haggadah*, a booklet placed before each seder participant and containing the Passover story as well as the prayers, songs, and symbolic interpretations of the seder meal.[7] No food is more closely associated with Passover than *matzah*, or unleavened bread. A mixture of flour and water that is rapidly baked, the *matzah* recalls the ordeal of slavery in severely limiting what foods people could prepare. Indeed, any food containing yeast is strictly prohibited during Passover. At the same time, *matzah* conveys the hope of freedom for it was the food of the escaped slaves, hastily leaving Egypt and thus lacking the opportunity to bake yeast bread. The dynamic qualities of Jewish ritual are evident in innovations within the *haggadah* and *seder* to accord women a place equal to that of men. Creative Passover celebrations and indeed innovations in other Jewish rituals are now common. Even orthodox practice has not been unyielding to such creative modifications.

A well-known but minor holiday in the Jewish tradition is Hanukah, meaning "dedication" in Hebrew. Celebrated in December, it commemorates the struggle of Jews in the second century B.C.E. against their Syrian overlords led by King Antiochus. He banned Jewish religious practice and profaned the Temple. Led by the Maccabees, a priestly lineage, a company of Jewish fighters bent on maintaining Jewish worship defeated the Syrian enemy against staggering odds and reconsecrated the Temple. As the story goes, only sufficient oil was present to kindle the Temple lights for a single night, yet miraculously the oil burned for eight days. For this reason, Hanukah, also known as the "Feast of Lights," lasts eight days, counted each night by the lighting of one additional candle in the *menorah*, or ceremonial candelabrum. Significantly, Jewish tradition has focused almost exclusively on the miracle of a one-day supply of oil lasting eight days rather than on the extraordinary feat of arms by a small military contingent defeating an overwhelming force.[8] Hanukah is thus a holiday of hope and recommitment, calling on Jews to recognize the divine presence within the Jewish community.

Although historically a minor holiday, it is noteworthy that Hanukah has become perhaps the most widely observed festival in the Jewish ritual cycle. Its popular practice is an apt index of the dynamics of Jewish community life, particularly in America, where cultural accommodation and assimilation have reshaped the Jewish experience. Hanukah represents one among many instances of expressing Jewish identity without sacrificing participation in the economic and social routines of day-to-day living. During the eight days of the festival, parents need not miss work nor Jewish children school to attend religious services as is the case during the High Holy Days. The home, instead, is the primary locale for observing Hanukah. Moreover, the December date of the holiday, its child-centeredness, and its tradition of gift-giving inevitably associate it with Christmas, thus boosting its popularity. Also, like Christmas, Hanukah has undergone a commercialization replete with greeting cards and an exaggeration of the gift exchange aspect of the holiday. Over the past 25 years, the holiday has further entered into the consciousness of the non-Jewish world, particularly through strenuous efforts in some American Jewish communities to erect oversized *menorahs* in public spaces alongside Christmas trees and other familiar emblems of the season.

THE LIFE CYCLE AND RITES OF PASSAGE

Since the pioneering efforts of the early twentieth-century scholar Arnold Van Gennep, anthropologists have been particularly attentive to ritual performances that mark the socially defined transitions in the life cycle of individuals.[9] The Great and Little Traditions of Judaism provide a particularly rich ground for the study of these venerable anthropological phenomena. These are social events centered on the family but extending outward to other kin and friends within the community. While the individual transition motivates the ritual event, its full meaning, as in so many other aspects of Judaism, depends on community acknowledgment, support, and participation.

One of the oldest rites in Judaism—a ritual practice that even predates the *Torah*—is *brit milah*, or the convenant of circumcision performed on the eighth day following the birth of a baby boy. Unless the newborn is at some health risk, the ritual must take place on schedule. While some rites cannot occur on such holy days as the Sabbath or on the Day of Atonement—marriage and funerals, for example, cannot be performed on those days—circumcision must proceed.

Anthropologists have documented the extensive distribution of circumcision rites worldwide and have observed that traditional societies in the ethnographic record by and large do not perform the ritual on newborns. Rather, it frequently occurs, for example in African societies, as an initiation of youth on the cusp of manhood. The newly circumcised, who often undergo the rite collectively, may begin a period of warrior service before taking their place as responsible adult males in the community. In effect, the ritual enables society to reproduce itself. Additionally, circumcision serves as a symbol that socially differentiates the community from those that do not perform the rite. Initiates may also undergo other bodily modifications, such as ear piercing, the filing of teeth, or scarification that likewise serve to distinguish the community from others. These anthropological insights dovetail with Jewish religious rationalizations of circumcision that designate it as "the seal of God," or, sometimes as "the seal of Abraham."[10] Circumcision is thus a social inscription on the flesh, a symbolic representation of incorporation into the religious community that perpetuates both itself and the divine will through the individual.

The actual rite of circumcision customarily occurs in the presence of ten adult men, who constitute a religious quorum. The operation is performed by a specialist known as a *mohel*, or circumciser. Nowadays a Jewish physician with religious training may perform the operation or may simply be in attendance as the *mohel* proceeds.

Traditionally, women were not present, and even the mother was excluded from the circumcision of her son. Such prohibitions have loosened considerably in most communities. Although no comparable ancient ritual incorporated a baby girl into the religious fold, religious innovations along these lines have occurred. It is now common for a family to conduct a naming ceremony in the synagogue for the infant girl and to emphasize the covenantal relationship that she too, as part of the Jewish community, will have with God.

The circumcision of males remains a vital feature of Jewish communal identification and self-definition. It has proven remarkably resistant to reformist critiques of Judaism dating from the nineteenth century. These critiques repudiated as unenlightened primitive survivals of ancient and medieval practice a wide range of orthodox observance, including the dietary laws, Jewish nationality, and the physical separation of men and women in religious services. Circumcision, too, fell under close scrutiny and recent questioning of its religious value has again surfaced, although the current critique within Judaism is confined to the social margins of Jewish life. It retains its core significance for Jewish communities throughout the world.

When a boy is 13, he becomes a "son of the commandment," or *Bar Mitzvah,* which makes him a full-fledged member of the Jewish community. He accepts all of its responsibilities as a result of a synagogue ceremony on the morning of the Sabbath, when he reads some portion of sacred text—the *Torah* and a selection from the Prophets. By so doing, he exercises for the first time the right to participate fully in the religious life of his community centered as it is on the reading and study of the *Torah.* He may now be counted for the religious quorum, or *minyan,* made up of a minimum of ten men (and women in many communities) required for a religious service. The celebrant is feted within the community, receiving as he does many gifts, often at a celebration hosted by his parents. As in so many other dimensions of Jewish life, the communal focus of the ceremony is critical, affirming as it does not only the requisite knowledge and religious understanding of the young person but also the public celebration and social recognition of the event.

An increasing consciousness of the exclusionary features of much of traditional Judaism has resulted in the development of the Bat Mitzvah, "the daughter of the commandment," for girls at the age of 13. Originating in Reform congregations and later taken up in Conservative Judaism, the *Bat Miztvah* has also gained some limited recognition among the orthodox. It provides yet another illustration of the adaptive, flexible quality of Jewish belief and practice in relationship to broader cultural currents, in this case concerns about women's role in Judaism. Beyond the *Bat Mitzvah* innovation, the religious coming of age has undergone other, adaptive shifts, particularly in the United States. These changes are related to the dynamic nature of Jewish communities and altered meanings of the life cycle in the modern world.

Amid the blandishments of secular living, the *Bar Mitzvah* in many places indicates only that one has undergone sufficient Jewish education to read the holy text. It is often the point at which Jewish learning under the guidance of rabbis ceases. As synagogue members get caught up in many organizations, both Jewish and non-Jewish, effectively reducing the pervasive significance the synagogue once had, recognition of adult status by the synagogue lacks its older import. That is, when the synagogue did not have to compete with other affiliations and other modes of prestige and achievement, it enjoyed a greater role in the lives of its congregants. Paradoxically, as its larger significance has attenuated, the coming of age ceremony of *Bar Mitzvah* and, now *Bat Mitzvah,* provides the occasion for parties and celebrations out of all proportion to the prayers, modest toasting, and repasts that traditionally celebrated the event.

Following the religious coming of age marked by the *Bar Mitzvah* or *Bat Mitzvah,* marriage is the next major life cycle event that is celebrated. Commanded in the Book of Genesis—"Be fruitful and multiply"—people enter marriage as a holy act.

Another sacred text, the *Talmud*, states that a married couple should have one son and one daughter, at least. Celibacy and childlessness are abnormal and pitiable states in traditional Judaism. The marriage ceremony itself takes place beneath a ceremonial canopy (*chupah*), evocative of the home the couple will have together. Their unity is also expressed by sharing a cup of wine.

The marriage ceremony consists of two parts. The first, *kiddushin* (sanctification), culminates in the bride and groom presenting rings to each other. This follows their pledge to join together their individual religious commitments and to maintain collectively the terms of the covenant, including raising children in the Jewish faith and leading an ethical life. The second part of the marriage ceremony consists of the recitation of seven blessings resonating with the hopeful expectation of marital happiness, explicitly likened to the paradise of Adam and Eve as well as to the messianic order to come. The ceremony concludes when the groom steps on a wine goblet, smashing it to pieces. While this act represents a joyous conclusion to the marriage ceremony amid expressions of congratulations from those in attendance, it also evokes the memory of the Roman destruction of the Temple in Jerusalem. Thus began the Diaspora and the many Jewish travails in various lands of exile. The marriage ceremony, consistent with the recurrent Jewish religious emphasis on communities, thus widens the circle outward from married pair, to family, to immediate community, to the Jewish people as a religious collectivity with all its joys and sorrows.

Over the past three decades, rates of intermarriage between Jews and Christians have increased dramatically. According to some surveys, between 40 and 50 percent of Jews marry non-Jewish spouses. Rabbis and Jewish community leaders, especially, express concern about Jewish continuity and survival, owing not only to intermarriage but also to a low overall Jewish birth rate.

Traditional conceptions of the family and male-female relationships have undergone various challenges from liberal and reform-minded segments of the Jewish community. Feminism, as already noted, has caused many Jewish women to reconsider their roles within the family and the traditional male-centered dimensions of the religion. Within this new framework of questioning, some highly orthodox Hasidic women even betray a gender consciousness that oddly shares some common ground with feminism.[11] Fundamental critiques of customary family arrangements have issued from observant Jews who are also homosexual. Whereas traditional Judaism defines homosexuality as an abomination (re: Book of Leviticus), some people are attempting to reconcile it with Jewish practice. Jewish homosexuals and a gay synagogue are recent topics of anthropological research.[12]

Anthropologists have long noted that across cultures death and its attendant funerary observances are no less a part of a ritualized passage than birth, puberty, and marriage. So, too, in Judaism, mortuary practices are observed with great care in order to ensure the passage of the soul to the world beyond and to assist the survivors in reconciling themselves to the loss of a loved one. The mourners are also in a kind of social transit, moving through their condition of bereavement in order to reenter a normal social state. Thus observations of the treatment of death within Jewish communities provide additional evidence for the anthropological claim that funerary rites perform social functions as much for the living as for the dead.

Burial should occur within 24 hours of death, unless a Sabbath or other designated holy day intervenes. Then, the burial must be delayed until the holiday ends.

In traditional Judaism, cremation did not occur since it physically destroyed a body created in the image of divinity. Among some Reform Jews and others, cremation is no longer rejected. The deceased should be buried in a linen shroud in a modest wooden coffin, although orthodox Judaism traditionally laid the deceased to rest directly in the earth. Judaism spurns display and ostentation in funerary rites, and wealth differences expressed by more elaborate funeral ceremonies are considered unseemly. Moreover, traditional Judaism rejects flowers and musical performance as out of keeping with the sadness and mourning of death. While the notion of life after death is, on the whole, not a central issue in Jewish religious thought, some orthodox Jews believe in a resurrection of the body. More liberal interpretations of the question focus instead on the immortality of the soul and even the role of memory in preserving the essence of the dead person.

Mourners consisting of the closest kin of the deceased traditionally rend a small portion of their clothing but nowadays wear a black ribbon that has been cut. At the home of the deceased, commencing on the day of the funeral, close kin begin a week long observance, known as *shiva*, the Hebrew term for seven, referring to seven days of "sitting." During that time, friends and more distant family visit the bereaved, providing fellowship, comfort, and community support. Mourners, particularly the children of the deceased, typically attend synagogue services or sometimes hold the religious service at home in order to recite the prayer for the dead (*kaddish*) that should be intoned three times a day. Following the week-long *shiva*, the survivors continue the mourning period, although less rigorously for another three weeks. During this time, they should refrain from normal social enjoyments and public entertainment. At the end of this period, life may then resume its familiar rhythms, but the children of the deceased should continue for approximately one year to attend the synagogue in order to recite the prayer for the dead. Thereafter, on the yearly anniversary of the parent's death, it is customary to light a candle to the parent's memory and to say the mourner's prayer.

THE HOLOCAUST AND ISRAEL

Jews throughout the world have for centuries defined their Jewishness in accord with traditional prayer and rabbinic teaching that link the Jewish people to the Biblical Land of Israel. The modern state of Israel has also shaped to an extraordinary degree Jewish consciousness and self-definition over the past half century. Fifty years ago, the reemergence after two millennia of a modern Jewish state—a restored homeland for an in-gathered Diaspora and a revitalization of Hebrew as the national language—seemed to fulfill many centuries of prayer following the Roman Conquest of the Holy Land. Israel's meaning in Jewish self-conception is all the more significant in light of the nation's rebirth in the aftermath of the systematic destruction of most of Europe's Jews during World War II. Prior to the war, the Jewish population of Europe was approximately 9 million. By 1945, it had been reduced by about two-thirds. Many of those who perished had attempted to flee Europe but found few places willing to issue visas. Of those countries that did accept Jewish refugees, their immigration quotas were small. These severe restrictions thus consigned many people to their doom. At the end of the war, some of the remnants of once flourishing Jewish settlements throughout Europe reconstituted themselves in the new state. Throughout contemporary Jewish communities, Israel is thus seen as a permanent refuge where beleaguered Jews from anywhere can find a secure home that was nonexistent for the victims of Nazism. No longer in contemporary Jewish consciousness will Jewish communities anywhere have to endure threats to their physical safety. Consequently, the modern Jewish state and the Holocaust are interwoven in contemporary thinking and represent the two most pivotal events in modern Jewish history.

Over the past half century, Jewish immigrants from many places—Morocco, Tunisia, Ethiopia, Russia, Iran, Turkey, Iraq—have sought a new start in Israel. The Middle Eastern and North African origin of many of the immigrants has significantly changed the initial, European Jewish character of the country. Numerous anthropological studies have documented and analyzed not only Jewish communities in the Middle East but also the complex process of Jewish immigration to Israel from various places. Included in these studies is the way the country itself has had to respond to its stream of newcomers and the linguistic and cultural diversity they bring.[13] Multiple Jewish ethnicities, in other words, characterize modern Israel.

At various periods in modern history, momentous secular social and political movements have swept through Jewish communities, particularly in Europe. It is paradoxical that the restoration of a Jewish nation, prayed for over the course of 20 centuries, did not come about through divine or messianic intervention but through an activist political movement known as Zionism.[14] Like other political movements for national liberation and other social movements studied in various parts of the world by anthropologists, Zionism represented the strategy of a self-conscious minority group, at times subject to physical threat and attack and politically and economically disenfranchised. Toward the end of the nineteenth century, the Zionist movement had persuaded large numbers of people that the answer to the problem of Jewish vulnerability throughout European history lay in the founding of a Jewish state. The activism of the Zionist movement from the end of the nineteenth century until the founding of Israel in 1948 achieved its political ends, in the words of an Israeli writer, by "closing the prayer book and boldly engaging reality."[15] In this context, Judaism refers not only to religion but also to nationality, politics, and culture.

Currently, Israeli society is caught up in a domestic conflict between the highly orthodox who argue that state policy should represent an extension of Jewish religious law and the more secular segments of the population who reject the effort to give the orthodox a determining role in how society is ordered. Most Jews value a pluralist conception of Judaism within modern Israel that would not confer on orthodox rabbis any special privilege as arbiters in religious and cultural matters. To return to the example set forth early in this chapter, the orthodox not only continue to limit their own activities within their neighborhoods but also aim to control the behavior of others. Whether it concerns driving on the Sabbath, or patronizing restaurants, or seeking entertainment on the day of rest, secular-minded Jews and others of a liberal religious bent must contend with the efforts of the most religious segments of the population to influence public policy.

The division between the ultra-orthodox, on the one hand, and the secular and liberal interpreters of Judaism, on the other, encapsulates a central issue in the modern world. The past quarter century has witnessed a resurgent religious orthodoxy that cuts across the world's great religions. The political force of the ultra-orthodox in Israel has as its counterparts Islamic fundamentalism in much of the

Middle East, militant Hinduism in India, and the Christian right in the United States. Certainly, devoted religious practice and belief can foster a strong sense of community, spirituality, and meaning and can do so in an atmosphere of mutual respect. This occurs, for example, among the substantial numbers of American Jews who have questioned their secular way of life and returned, often selectively, to the orthodox practices of their forebears without seeking to impose their views on others.

Rigorously observed, text-based faiths now vehemently contend with secularism or other religions in various parts of the world and question the value of religious or intellectual pluralism. That is, they challenge the legitimacy of multiple religions and modes of thought within the nation-state as well as the intrusion of modern values into their own creeds and practices. Such conflicts occur not only in authoritarian states but also in democratic countries. To the extent that fundamental adherence to a religion also motivates people to seek limits on the expression of alternative social or religious practice and thought, the prospects for cultural tolerance can only be dim.

NOTES

1. For a very good discussion of the relationship between anthropology and the study of Judaism, see Harvey Goldberg's "Introduction: Reflections on the Mutual Relevance of Anthropology and Judaic Studies" in *Judaism Viewed from Within and Without*, ed., Harvey Goldberg (Albany: State University of New York Press, 1987). The volume comprises nine anthropological essays, including contributions on Judaism in America and in Israel.

2. In recent years, anthropological and social scientific interest in gender issues and women in Judaism has proliferated. See, for example, Barbara Myerhoff, *Number Our Days* (New York: E.P. Dutton, 1979); Lisa Gilad, *Ginger and Salt: Yemeni Jewish Women in an Israeli Town* (Boulder: Westview Press, 1989); Riv-Ellen Prell, *Prayer and Community: The Havurah in American Judaism* (Detroit: Wayne State University Press, 1989); Debra Kaufman, *Rachel's Daughters: Newly Orthodox Jewish Women* (New Brunswick: Rutgers University Press, 1991); Lynn Davidman, *Tradition in a Rootless World: Women Turn to Orthodox Judaism* (Berkeley: University of California Press, 1991); Susan Starr Sered, *Women As Ritual Experts: The Religious Lives of Elderly Jewish Women in Jerusalem* (New York and Oxford: Oxford University Press, 1992).

3. Mary Douglas, *Purity and Danger* (London: Routledge, 1966).

4. A very good collection of articles on Hasidic Jews in the United States appears in Janet S. Beclove-Shalin's *New World Hasidim: Ethnographic Studies of Hasidic Jews in America* (Albany: State University of New York Press, 1995).

5. Redfield's concepts are discussed in his *Peasant Society and Culture* (Chicaco: University of Chicago Press, 1956).

6. Barbara Myerhoff, *Number Our Days* (New York: E. P, Dutton, 1979), pp. 256–257.

7. For a noteworthy study of Passover by an anthropologist, see Ruth Gruber Fredman's *The Passover Seder* (Philadelphia: University of Pennsylvania Press, 1981).

8. Emil L. Fackehnehim, *What is Judaism?* (New York: Macmillan, 1987), pp. 222–223.

9. Arnold Van Gennep, *The Rites of Passage* (Chicago: University of Chicago Press, 1960). By the 1960s, the study of rituals of initiation, particularly by Victor Turner, renewed interest in Van Gennep's seminal work.

10. Theodore H. Gaster, *The Holy and the Profane* (New York: William Sloane Associates, 1955), p. 52.

11. Debra Kaufman, *Rachel's Daughters: Newly Orthodox Jewish Women* (New Brunswick: Rutgers University Press, 1991).

12. Moshe Shokeid, *A Gay Synagogue in New York* (New York: Columbia University Press, 1995).

13. See, for example, Shlomo A. Deshen and Walter P. Zenner, eds., *Jewish Societies in the Middle East: Community, Culture, and Authority* (Lanham, MD: University Press of America, 1982); Gilad, *Ginger and Salt* (Boulder: Westview Press, 1989); Harvey Goldberg, ed. *Sephardi and Middle Eastern Jewries* (Bloomington: Indiana University Press, 1996); Guy Haskell, *From Sofia to Jaffa: The Jews of Bulgaria and Israel* (Detroit: Wayne State University Press, 1994); Herbert Lewis, *After the Eagles Landed: The Yemenites of Israel* (Boulder: Westview Press, 1989); Walter F. Weiker, *The Unseen Israelis: The Jews from Turkey in Israel* (Lanham, MD: University Press of America, 1988); Alex Weingrad, ed., *Studies in Israeli Ethnicity* (New York: Gordon and Breach Science Publishers, 1985).

14. Zionism was one of several important secular political movements springing from the Jewish communities of Europe. It represented a movement for national liberation that culminated in the founding of the modern state of Israel. Shlomo Avineri, *The Making of Modern Zionism* (New York: Basic Books, 1981).

15. Akiva Turk, "Tisha B'Av in the Age of the Third Temple," *Midstream* (August/September 1991):11.

Seventeen

Catholicism

Michael Dean Murphy

The University of Alabama

CATHOLICISM[1]

Go out into the whole world and proclaim the Good News to all creation."[2]

All variation is abhorrent to Catholic thought.[3]

What the Christian believes today about God, life after death, the universe, is not what he believed a millennium ago . . .[4]

INTRODUCTION

Quite apart from its significance as one of history's greatest religions, the Roman Catholic Church is also arguably the most influential corporate group in human history. The great missionary task set out in Mark 16:16 has been accomplished to a remarkable degree by Christianity's biggest denomination. Indeed, the largest single religious group of any kind, the Catholic Church[5] claims about one billion members, or roughly one out of every six living human beings. With a presence in virtually every part of the planet, the Church controls vast, literally uncountable, resources and—by its own, if not others', reckoning—it has been in existence for nearly 2,000 years. In addition to its enormous role in human religious history, then, the Catholic Church could well be taken as the very model of a highly successful multinational corporation, managing to extend and sustain its influence in the widest variety of political, cultural, and social environments.

The Catholic Church has not enjoyed this spectacular success, however, by actually living up to its widespread reputation for the sort of inflexibility and conservatism implied in Durkheim's remark. Indeed, what appears to many outsiders (and some believers, as well) to be rock-ribbed social and theological conservatism in the short run, looks quite different when the institution is regarded from the temporal perspective that its own leaders adopt, one that is much longer than the human life span. As Asad suggests, the Catholicism of today is not the Catholicism of a thousand years ago, or even one hundred years ago for that matter. Similarly, the extent of its selective tolerance of local variation in belief and practice comes into sharp focus when one examines the religion, as anthropologists have done, not only in its European heartland, but in the many distant places where it has made its presence felt.

The paradox of the Catholic Church is precisely that while it is characterized by a relatively efficient, hierarchical, and centralized authority structure organized around the papacy based in Rome, the actual expression of Roman Catholic beliefs and practices varies in interesting ways in the many different sociocultural settings in which the religion has taken root. It is, perhaps, the effort to understand the play between these opposed unifying and diversifying tendencies that has been the emphasis of much of the anthropological research on Roman Catholicism.

This chapter will begin with a discussion of the basic demographics and social organizational features of contemporary Roman Catholicism. Then, the history of its development up to the present will be briefly sketched before turning to a consideration of its central beliefs and rituals. The greatest strength of the anthropology of Catholicism is its proclivity for studying this religion as it is actually conceptualized and practiced by ordinary believers and for linking the vernacular forms of this religious tradition to other features of local social and cultural life. Accordingly, the local expression of Catholicism will be examined in two quite different communities, one in Spain and the other in Papua, New Guinea. Although it would be quite impossible in a chapter of this size to describe fully the range of local articulations of Catholicism, it is hoped that these two examples will serve to indicate how this religion has shaped and been shaped by the very different societies in which it has flourished. Many interesting topics relevant to the study of this important religion cannot even be mentioned here, much less pursued, but perhaps this brief introduction to Catholicism will pique the interest of the reader and motivate him or her to explore it further.[6]

THE CATHOLIC PRESENCE IN THE WORLD

The doctrine, the ritual practices, and the organization of the Catholic Church emerged in the Middle East with the teachings of Jesus Christ, came to maturity in Europe, especially in Rome, and spread to the rest of the world principally in the context of European colonialist expansion. The English word *catholic* is derived from the Greek adjective *katholikos*, which means "general," "total," or "universal." Although it was used earlier to refer to the entirety of the Christian Church (rather than its many individual Christian communities), by the third century C.E. the term was employed principally to distinguish the "true," that is, mainstream, church from a variety of heretical movements that had splintered off from it. Another meaning of *catholic*, one quite germane to this chapter, is the notion that the Church views itself as open to all humans—whatever their social, cultural, or racial characteristics may be and wherever they are found on earth. In the fourth century C.E., Cyril of Jerusalem argued that the Church was catholic, both universal and total, precisely because it teaches all the peoples of the earth everything that is necessary for salvation.

One of the principal outcomes of the reforms of the Church's Second Vatican Council (1962–1965) was the Decree of Religious Freedom (*Dignitatis Humanae*), which stipulates that all people enjoy the freedom to allow their own conscience to determine their religious beliefs and affiliations. Nonetheless, the leadership of the

Church will probably not be satisfied with anything less than the conversion of all people everywhere. Although the complete fulfillment of the central mission of the Church is unlikely to occur any time soon, especially since Roman Catholicism is currently losing ground in its traditional bastions of Europe and Latin America, the progress made so far is unrivaled by any other global, proselytizing religion.

How many Catholics are there? How are they distributed throughout the world? Where is Catholicism dominant in the world and where is it of scant significance? Following United Nations criteria, Table 17–1 presents the numbers of adherents to Roman Catholicism in six continental areas as of mid-1996. Clearly, Europe and the Americas are the strongholds of Roman Catholicism, accounting for fully three-quarters of all of the Catholics in the world. Of the 18 countries with the most Catholics (listed in Table 17–2), 14 of them are American or European. Asia, the world's most populous region, remains the least Catholic in the world by quite a large margin, but Africa is the continent in which contemporary efforts at missionization seem to be bearing the most fruit.

One important caveat to keep in mind, however, is that the figures cited here refer both to self-reports on census forms and to the numbers of people whom the officials of the Church regard as members by virtue of *baptism,* or initiation into the religion. Inevitably included as "Catholics," then, are people who do not fulfill the minimal ritual obligations to be Catholics in good standing or who no longer profess belief in the central dogmas of the Church. Moreover, regarding oneself as a Catholic (or being so counted by either secular or ecclesiastical officials) does not preclude simultaneous participation in other religious traditions. For example, Brazil is the country with the most number of Catholics (135 million), yet many self-proclaimed and/or officially recognized Catholics there are also involved in other religious traditions quite exotic to it, such as Umbanda. Indeed, fully 60 percent of the people surveyed in one study regarded Catholicism and Umbanda as complementary and only 11 percent saw them as in conflict with one another.[7] In short, exactly who counts as a member of the Catholic Church is a matter of some dispute and inherent ambiguity.

TABLE 17–1 The Worldwide Distribution of Roman Catholics, 1996

	Total Population	*Number of Christians*	*Number of Roman Catholics*	*Catholics as Percent of All Christians*	*Catholics as Percent of Total Population*
World	5,804,120,000	1,955,229,000	981,145,000	50.2	16.9
Africa	748,130,000	360,874,000	125,376,000	34.7	16.8
Asia	3,210,091,000	303,127,000	94,250,000	31.1	2.9
Europe	727,678,000	555,614,000	269,021,000	48.4	37.0
Latin America	490,444,000	455,819,000	408,968,000	89.7	83.4
North America	295,973,000	255,542,000	75,398,000	29.5	25.5
Oceania	28,973,000	24,253,000	8,452,000	34.8	29.2

SOURCE: This table is based on information presented in "Worldwide Adherents of All Religions by Six Continental Areas, Mid-1996," *1997 Britannica Book of the Year* (Chicago: Encyclopedia Britannica, Inc., 1997), p. 311.

TABLE 17–2 Countries with Greatest Number of Catholics, 1993

Brazil	135,160,000	Argentina	29,965,000
Mexico	83,815,000	Germany	28,599,000
United States	56,399,000	Peru	20,380,000
Italy	55,728,000	Venezuela	18,638,000
Philippines	52,325,000	Zaire	18,583,000
France	47,625,000	India	14,585,000
Spain	37,039,000	Canada	11,972,000
Poland	36,616,000	Chile	10,761,000
Columbia	31,298,000	Nigeria	10,587,000

SOURCE: The information in this table is taken from *1994 Catholic Almanac* (Huntington, IN: Our Sunday Visitor Publishing Division, 1993).

THE ORGANIZATION OF THE ROMAN CATHOLIC CHURCH

Coordinating the religious activities of a billion devotees is, of course, a most daunting organizational task. Over its long history Roman Catholicism has evolved what is arguably the most complex social organization and bureaucracy of any religious body. Indeed, the formal structure of the Church is so complicated that very few ordinary believers are aware of more than its broadest outlines. Yet fewer still are aware of the pressure, sometimes subtle and sometimes implacable, that the elaborate and very hierarchical ecclesiastical authority structure of the Church brings to bear on local Catholic communities to conform to minimal universal standards of belief and practice. The fundamental tension in this religion is between sometimes remote, authoritative forms of Catholicism and those local practices and religious preoccupations of what is often called "popular" Catholicism. Frequently, this central dynamic of the religion is localized. Often a local elite supports clergy-promoted universal standards against those devotions and beliefs of the common people that they regard as heterodox, "superstitious," or even pagan.[8]

Fundamental to the organization of the Catholic religion is the distinction between the *laity* and the *clergy*. Christianity was nearly two hundred years old before some came to be called "priests" and nearly another two centuries would pass before the emergence of the monastic and religious orders. The laity (derived from the Greek *laos*, or "people") originally consisted of all believers, but now the term has come to refer to that still vast number of Roman Catholics who are not members of the clergy. The clergy consists of those Catholics who have been initiated into the ecclesiastical state by the conferral of *Holy Orders*, which empowers them in the ministry of the sacred. There are only three clerical ranks: deacons, priests, and bishops. Clerics of all three types are required to meet disciplinary observances not required of members of the laity: They must pray the Liturgy of the Hours every day, for example. The clergy must obey and show respect for their own bishops and for the pope. They are excluded (although this has not always been so) from holding public political offices. Except for permanent deacons who were married prior to their ordination, the clergy must observe the rule of celibacy, a rule which has been consistently observed only since the eleventh century.

The role of the *deacon* in the early church is not entirely clear, but that ecclesiastical status eventually became a transitional condition before entering the priesthood. With the Vatican Council II (1962–65) reforms, however, the deaconate was restored as a separate ministry within the Catholic Church. The deacon can preach, give counsel to the laity, and serve as a teacher of Church doctrine. This restored office was clearly intended to provide a visible link between the laity and the priests. A permanent deacon (as opposed to one in a transitional state prior to becoming a priest) is a man who is ordained for life and is subject to all laws associated with being a member of the clergy. No unmarried man who becomes a permanent deacon may subsequently marry, yet deacons are typically obliged to earn a living from secular employment. There are approximately 18,000 deacons in the world, with over 10,000 of them in North America alone.[9]

A *priest* (or *presbyter*) is an ordained cleric who performs the basic ministry of the Church. Numbering nearly 400,000 in the world, priests celebrate the Mass, hear confessions, baptize babies, anoint the sick, counsel parishioners, and preside over funerals and most of the other religious services provided for the laity.[10] Priests are of two principal types: regular and secular. The approximately 150,000 *regular* priests belong to one of a large number of religious orders or congregations. They are "regular" (from *regula*, or rule) because they live apart from secular society in groups that follow a religious rule of varying degrees of strictness but which usually dictates vows of chastity, obedience, and poverty among other observances specific to each order. Among the most important orders are the Benedictines, Dominicans, Franciscans, and Jesuits, but there are many others. Women cannot be priests, but as *nuns* they may enter into a wide variety of religious orders open exclusively to women. These monastic, canonical, and mendicant institutions are all characterized by some sort of centralized authority structure that exists apart from, and in some sense parallel to, the diocesan structure that governs secular priests. At the risk of oversimplification, it may be said that throughout the history of the Church, the regular clergy and religious orders have been used by the papacy to keep in check local bishops and the priests under their administration. Functioning as extraterritorial institutions, the religious orders often have been deployed by distant Church authorities in their efforts to damper religious localism and nationalism.[11]

Secular, or *diocesan*, priests are clergy who serve and minister to the laity in *parishes*, the most numerous and the smallest territorial units of the Church. They are "secular" because they do not separate themselves by special religious rule from the secular world of the laity. Many secular priests are *pastors*, that is, clerics entrusted with the care of a parish by the local bishop. Pastors are not only charged with officiating over the sacraments and instructing parishioners in matters of doctrine and rite, they also administer the financial, property management, and other mundane affairs of the parish. Secular priests are ordained by and serve at the pleasure of the local bishop.

Bishops have received the highest level of ordination, usually after serving for some time as priests. Most of the approximately 4,000 bishops of the Catholic Church are *diocesan bishops*, or *ordinaries*, who preside over a *diocese*, the most important administrative-territorial unit of the Church. The diocese is subdivided into parishes and bishops closely oversee and coordinate the work of the parish priests. Although the process by which bishops are selected can be complicated, ultimately it is the pope, the Bishop of Rome, who chooses, appoints, and reassigns them to particular dioceses. *The College of Bishops* consists of all bishops (including auxiliary and retired ones) and works under the leadership of the pope. Functioning as the successors to the apostles, the authority of the College is generally expressed when it meets in *Ecumenical Councils.* Whatever action this body proposes becomes authoritative once the pope accepts it.

Over the centuries the balance of power between the pope (and his bureaucratic apparatus) and the bishops has shifted back and forth. Since the Second Vatican Council, bishops of a nation or region have convened conferences or synods to address problems of both local and global significance. A more venerable feature of Church organization is the grouping together of a number of dioceses to form *provinces* under the direction of the bishop (called in this instance a *metropolitan*) of its most important diocese. The metropolitan usually receives the title of *archbishop* and sometimes the greater honorific of *cardinal.* Typically the bishop of a country's most important diocese is a cardinal and is also referred to as a *primate.* Cardinals constitute a key advisory group for the pope. Upon his death they convene to elect his successor.

The *pope* is the Bishop of Rome and the supreme authority of the Roman Catholic Church. Indeed, in matters of faith and morals the pope's judgment is regarded as infallible, as incapable of error. A quite extensive and complex bureaucracy, the *Roman Curia* (or, "court"), has evolved to serve the papacy through a variety of offices, councils, tribunals, and other organizational entities. Chief among them are the *Secretariat of State* and the nine *Congregations*, which collectively serve as the central administration of the Church. The papacy and the Curia are based in a palace known as the *Vatican*, which also gives its name to the *Vatican City State.* Vatican City is the official residence of the pope, but it is also the world's smallest sovereign and independent state, consisting of only 100 acres situated in the middle of the city of Rome. The term "Vatican" is often used to label the entire papal bureaucracy which serves as the chief instrument for centralizing and unifying the far-flung expressions of Catholicism.

In addition to the clerical offices and institutions just described, the Catholic Church is characterized by a large array of lay religious groups such as charitable, educational, medical, and service organizations, including confraternities and sodalities. Notable among them in the twentieth century are the Legion of Mary, the Knights of Columbus, and Opus Dei.

Mart Bax, a Dutch anthropologist, has used the concept of "religious regimes" to address the social (as opposed to cultural) complexities of Catholicism in a region of the Netherlands and in the great contemporary pilgrimage site of Medjugorge in Bosnia-Herzegovina.[12] Bax's insightful work illustrates quite clearly that the different officially recognized groups and institutions within the Church (such as the secular clergy and their colleagues within the religious orders) often work at cross-purposes as they pursue different social and theological agendas and seek to shape to their own advantage the relationship between the clergy and the laity. Thus, to the great cultural variation characteristic of the Catholic Church must be added the considerable social complexity that has arisen within its own institutions as they have developed over nearly two thousand years of history.

AN HISTORICAL OVERVIEW OF ROMAN CATHOLICISM

Origins

The Roman Catholic Church identifies its origins with the very beginnings of Christianity in Palestine, that is to say, with the life and teachings of the Jewish religious innovator Jesus Christ (circa 3 B.C.E. to 30 C.E.) and with the evangelical work of his original apostles and other early followers. Setting aside the issue of the emergence of sects which were either branded as heretical or which hived off on their own accord, during the first millenium after Christ's death Christianity and Catholicism were one and the same. Central to Catholicism's claim to Christian authority is that it is the original church founded by Christ and that it enjoys an unbroken chain of priestly ordination, known as *apostolic succession*, from the first communities of early Christianity established by Christ's apostles up to the contemporary church. Indeed, the key to the primacy of the current pope, John Paul II, is that he is the two hundred sixty-second direct successor to St. Peter, the first Bishop of Rome.

If the sympathetic observer cannot help but be impressed by the historical ability of the Catholic religion to adjust to nearly every sociocultural niche into which it is introduced, it should be remembered that the specific context in which early Christianity emerged was itself decidedly multicultural, drawing upon a heady mixture of Jewish, Hellenistic, and Roman cultural traditions and social forms. Although at first Christ's apostles limited their missionary work to Jews, members of that ethnic group were scattered throughout the Roman Empire and Christianity was rather quickly taken to them from Jerusalem. St. Paul, himself a Jew in diaspora in Asia Minor, successfully argued that the teachings of Jesus Christ should be brought to non-Jews or *gentiles*, as well, and he not only established the first church for gentiles in Antioch (Syria), he also traveled throughout the Roman Empire seeking to introduce Christianity wherever possible to whomever was receptive to its message.

Although Christianity quickly adopted not only the languages (Greek and Latin) of the Roman world, but also much of its philosophical modes of expression, at first it spread mostly (although certainly not exclusively) among the lower social strata of the Empire. The infrastructure of the Roman Empire was instrumental in all of this early missionary work and is reflected still, nearly two thousand years later, in the organizational forms of the Church described above. Although five great sites, or *patriarchal sees*, of Christianity emerged in the Mediterranean world at Jerusalem, Antioch, Alexandria, Constantinople, and Rome, it was the latter which quickly became the center of gravity for what would evolve into the *Roman* Catholic Church. Rome was not only the hub of the civilized world, it was also intimately identified with the lives of the greatest of the apostles, Paul and Peter. While early Christian communities enjoyed a degree of institutional and doctrinal autonomy, during the early centuries of the development of Christianity, the Roman church came to occupy an increasingly important role in the overall structure of the religion.

Christianity and the Roman Empire

The gradual process of ecclesiastical centralization and cultural standardization was greatly advanced by the conversion to Christianity in 312 C.E. of the emperor

Constantine and his subsequent Edict of Milan (314 C.E.) which legalized Christianity throughout the empire. If during its first three centuries Christianity had suffered varying degrees of official persecution, by the close of its fourth the religion had been elevated to the status of the state religion of the entire Empire. It is perhaps ironic that the removal of the seat of the Roman Empire to Constantinople in 330 C.E. strengthened rather than weakened the position of the emerging Roman Church. This transfer of secular authority to the east left the pope, in his capacity as the Bishop of Rome, in a better position to contend with the now distant Emperor for spiritual authority. When, in the fifth century, the western regions of the Empire crumbled under the assault of the so-called "barbarians," the Roman Church under the pope vigorously pursued the religious conversion of the invading (principally Germanic) peoples. The process of culturally absorbing the conquerors of the western Empire began with the conversion of Clovis, King of the Franks, in 496 C.E. and culminated in 800 C.E. when Pope Leo III elevated Charlemagne, another Frankish king, to the position of Roman Emperor in the West.

During the Middle Ages the Church not only succeeded in converting most Europeans to Christianity, it also served as a formidable force for the integration of cultural and social forms in the continent. Yet, if Catholicism "civilized" (or perhaps more accurately, "romanized") the northern peoples, it is equally true that they in turn "europeanized" what was before an essentially Mediterranean Church. By the end of the first millenium C.E., Roman Catholicism was the official religion of every European state. The emergence during the seventh century of Islam, a competing proselytizing religion, also served to consolidate the importance of the Church based in Rome. The rapid expansion of Islam throughout the Near East, Eastern Europe, North Africa, and even Western Europe's own Iberian Peninsula, not only swallowed up three of the five patriarchal sees (Jerusalem, Antioch, and Alexandria), but also unified Western European resistance against a powerful, missionizing competitor. The most famous manifestations of this resistance were the protracted Christian Reconquest of Iberia and the various Crusades to liberate the Holy Lands. The Crusades often had a decidedly international character as the battle against Islam served to unite, albeit only transiently and partially, diverse European peoples in the conduct of what they regarded as a holy war.

The Eastern Schism

Another great challenge to Christianity came from within rather than from without. The mutual antagonism of Rome and Constantinople, the two patriarchal sees remaining outside the Islamic sphere of influence, culminated in a complete break in mid-eleventh century. The Eastern Schism split Christianity into separate western (essentially Roman and Latin) and eastern (Byzantine and Greek) communions. The eastern churches had not only suffered disproportionately from the incursions of Islam, they also resented western theological and liturgical innovations and bridled under Roman claims of supremacy and primacy. Although these problems had been brewing for centuries, the definitive split occurred in 1054 C.E. when the pope in Rome excommunicated the Eastern Ecumenical Patriarch. Since that time the Eastern Orthodox Churches have spread by missionary activity from the original four, non-Roman, patriarchies to Greece and the Slavic peoples of eastern Europe and to other places in the world where these people migrated. Each of the Orthodox Churches, unlike those eastern churches still in communion with Rome, is relatively autonomous and self-governing.

The Role of Catholicism in the Formation of "Western Europe"

Throughout the Middle Ages and for sometime afterward the Catholic Church and the secular social orders of Western Europe continued to develop an intimate relationship with each other. During this period of Church history many of its institutions came to take on definitive and distinctive forms. For example, the intellectual life of Western civilization was immeasurably advanced by the growth of monasticism which not only called for its monks to withdraw from the concerns of the secular world but also provided an institutional basis for the preservation of the classical heritage of Greek and Roman scholarship. Indeed, the Roman Church sponsored the first European universities which were originally organized as seats for religious education, but which ultimately have come to be centers for the advancement of all branches of human knowledge and learning.

The broad outlines of a continental European civilization began to take shape precisely during a period in which the Church provided a heterogeneous region with transsocietal models of social organization and a transcultural set of beliefs and practices. The Catholic Church had a central role in the emergence of many of the features of social organization and culture that we now take to be essentially European: the modern nation-state, the principles and forms of judiciary processes, varied musical forms and traditions, the aesthetic and engineering principles of monumental architecture, and the elaboration of norms and motifs for narrative, poetry, painting, and sculpture, to name but a few. The creative, if only partial and often-contested, convergence of ecclesiastical and secular interests throughout the premodern period fixed important features of a common European experience, an experience that transcends the many linguistic, social, and cultural factors that distinguish the societies of the continent and tend, to this day, to pull them apart on occasion.

Colonialist Expansion and Protestant Contraction

Two pivotal events in the history of Catholicism occurred within a quarter century of one another around the turn of the sixteenth century. As every school child in the United States knows, in 1492 Christopher Columbus discovered the Western hemisphere for the Europeans, thereby inaugurating the most spectacular opportunity for the expansion of Catholicism since the conversion of the European "barbarians." Although since the Eastern Schism Catholic missionaries had been active in parts of central Europe, in the Moorish occupied Iberian peninsula, and in Asia, it was the "discovery" of the New World that heralded the most concentrated and highly organized efforts at religious conversion in Church history. As European nations vied with one another for colonial possessions, the Catholic Church (and shortly afterward the various Protestant denominations) mounted vigorous campaigns to convert the newly subjugated peoples of the Americas, Asia, Africa, and Oceania.[13] One measure of the success of these efforts to extend the influence of the Church beyond Europe is that Latin America now has many more Catholics than Europe and Brazil is the most populous Catholic nation in the world.

In 1517 Martin Luther presented his 95 theses against the custom of indulgences (i.e., the purchase of the remission of sins through good works, prayers, or money), thus initiating another schism within the religion, this time splitting Western Christianity into Catholic and Protestant confessions. During the preceding centuries the papacy had evolved into an enormous bureaucracy in which corruption was rampant. In the fourteenth and early fifteenth centuries the removal of the papacy to Avignon and the resulting furor over multiple claimants to papal succession brought the ecclesiastical institutions of the Church into great disrepute. A number of other unfortunate practices such as the purchase of Church offices, the multiple occupancy of these offices, and clerical arrogance of every sort produced widespread disillusionment with the clergy. After first decrying indulgences, which he regarded as both theologically suspect and a source of corruption, Luther set out a thoroughgoing critique of the theology of the Catholic Church. Luther's criticism extended to very central issues of belief and practice including the doctrine of sacramentalism, the authority of the pope, the role of human action in salvation, the institution of monasticism, and the exclusive privilege of the clergy to interpret sacred Scriptures.

What began as an effort at reform within the Catholic Church quickly developed into a schismatic movement that spread throughout Northern Europe, diversifying into Lutheran, Calvinist, Anabaptist, and Anglican forms, among others. By the beginning of the seventeenth century these "Protestant" movements, as they came to be called, had taken hold in Germany, Switzerland, Holland, Scandinavia, and Great Britain. Then, as now, the principal position shared by the various Protestant churches is a thoroughgoing rejection of the authority of the pope and the elaborate, hierarchical organization that had evolved around the papacy.

If the singular historical achievement of the Catholic Church had been to accommodate sociocultural diversity within a single, clearly defined organizational structure, once Protestantism slipped free of the grip of that ecclesiastical authority, little stood in the way of a creative process of social fission and cultural fragmentation as new beliefs, practices, and forms of religious organization proliferated among Western Christians. Some secular leaders promoted the rise of nationalistic Protestant churches, motivated less by theological concerns than by a desire to weaken the sway held in their lands by what they regarded as a foreign power (i.e., the Vatican and the papacy).

In the face of this formidable threat to its influence in Europe, the hierarchy of the Catholic Church mounted a vigorous campaign, known as the *Counter-Reformation,* to contain and reverse its losses. The single most important form that this offensive against Protestantism took was the *Council of Trent* which convened in 25 sessions from 1545 to 1563. What emerged from Trent was a resounding reentrenchment of virtually all of the doctrines Luther opposed. The Council vindicated tradition, not just scripture, as a source of divine revelation, thus facilitating variation in liturgy (i.e., public prayers and rituals) based on the distinct traditions and customs of the various Catholic communities of the world. This position provided a measure of flexibility for Catholic missionaries just as they endeavored to spread the religion to colonized places and peoples quite exotic to the European cultural matrix in which the religion had matured.

The Struggle with Modernity and Socialism

While the Council of Trent also sought to address positively the clerical corruption at the heart of the Reformation movement (e.g., by establishing seminaries for the instruction of priests), on balance it proved to be a reactionary solution to a changing secular world. Tridentine doctrines set the Church on a collision course with the profound intellectual, political, and economic challenges that lay ahead: the European Enlightenment, the end of monarchy, the rise of science, the gathering dominance of industrial capitalism and the socialist reaction to it.

Vatican Council I (1869–1870), only the twentieth general council in Church history, was conceived of by Pope Pius IX as a response to the perceived tidal wave of secularism sweeping across the world. A plethora of "isms"—atheism, rationalism, materialism, liberalism, socialism, and nationalism—were condemned as "modern error." Indeed, Vatican I entertained nothing less than the complete repudiation of the economics, politics, and aesthetics of a nascent modernism. This rigid stance, only truly relaxed a century later, has continued to stigmatize the religion as anachronistic and inflexible in the eyes of many outside observers.

The First Vatican Council's dogmatic rejection of modernism was accompanied by an equally dramatic blow to any possible rapprochement with the Protestant branches of Western Christianity: The Pope was declared to be infallible in matters of faith and morals. This doctrine continues to be the single greatest point of disagreement between Catholics and other Christians, both Protestant and Orthodox alike. Yet, Church officials came to view socialism and atheism, not alternative Christianities, as their greatest enemies in the modern era.

Long identified with the traditional secular authorities of Western Europe, the Catholic Church lost many nominally Catholic members of the working classes to the various radical workers movements that had emerged as the continent industrialized. By the turn of the twentieth century anticlericalism flourished in places like southern Spain, where both urban and rural workers saw the Church as aligned with the landowners and capitalists that they regarded as class enemies.[14] Prior to and during the Spanish Civil War (1936–1939) the hostility felt by many workers for the Church was clearly expressed in attacks on its institutions (e.g., the burning of churches, monasteries, and convents) and by the murder of thousands of priests and nuns.

Indeed, the Spanish Civil War was portrayed by both sides as essentially a religious war, or more accurately, a clash between a traditional, conservative brand of Catholicism and atheistic socialism. This fratricidal conflict was merely one of the most palpable manifestations in the twentieth century of the mutual enmity between the officials of the Catholic Church and the proponents of a variety of leftist social movements. William Christian has documented how the republican repression of the Church in Spain stimulated various popular religious manifestations, often in the form of apparitions of Mary and Christ.[15] When beleaguered by the state, its historical ally, the Spanish clergy turned to popular religious forms to shore up its support with the laity.

Of course, some Catholics, even some Catholic clerics, embraced the politics of the left, most notably in a movement known as *Liberation Theology*.[16] This movement is most closely associated with Latin America and draws inspiration from Marxist thought in its fight against the oppression of the poor and the powerless by international capitalism. Nonetheless, the Catholic hierarchy, on the whole, engaged in a bitter struggle against socialism in its many guises, both in the capitalist West and in those countries of the former Soviet bloc which had been Catholic prior to the imposition of communism following World War II. The wary co-existence between Catholicism and communism there has attracted the attention of such excellent ethnographers as George Saunders and David Kertzer for Italy, a country which is simultaneously the very seat of Catholicism and since World War II a nation frequently governed by leftists.[17]

Yet it must also be pointed out that twentieth-century Church authorities (notably Popes Pius XI and Pius XII) also promoted the disengagement of the missionary movement outside Western Europe from its colonialist heritage. For example, both popes advocated the ordination of indigenous priests and bishops in mission societies, rather than continuing to import them from Europe. In a fascinating article, Michael Angrosino describes how, in fact, the Church has incorporated (and modified) the anthropological concept of culture to advance its efforts at missionizing non-Western peoples in this century.[18] The growing concern with accommodating cultural variation within the globalizing Church culminated in the Second Vatican Council.

Vatican II and Its Aftermath

Clearly, the single most transformative event of the twentieth-century Church is the Second Vatican Council (1962–65) which, four centuries after the Council of Trent, essentially reversed the course set by Tridentine principles and reiterated by Vatican I. Among its many pronouncements, too numerous to even mention here, were the renewed emphasis on the role of the laity in the Church, the assertion of the importance of the pursuit of world peace and social justice, and the call for ecumenicalism, or greater cooperation and unity among all the branches of Christianity. Vatican II emphasized that all humans enjoy the right to pursue religious freedom of expression and that the Catholic Church is not the only avenue toward salvation. Importantly for the average Catholic, Vatican II produced significant changes in the liturgy of the Church, including abandoning Latin as the universal language of the mass. The adoption of the vernacular in the celebration of most masses is just one example of a new emphasis on incorporating cultural differences into what essentially was a rather Eurocentric religion.

Since Vatican II, and possibly stimulated by the concerns of some traditionalist Catholics who regarded some of its provisions as unwarranted concessions to modern, secular society, the Church has been divided between competing liberal and conservative wings who not only disagree on theological issues but on social ones as well. The number of Catholics willing to enter the ranks of both the secular and the regular priesthood has declined significantly. The role of the laity and, especially of women, in the governance of the Church has also been a source of sometimes bitter contestation. Nevertheless, the contemporary Church has not suffered any serious schismatic movements of the sort that were experienced in the sixteenth century and this is despite a lively discourse about basic elements of Roman Catholic belief and practice.

BASIC BELIEFS AND RITUALS

> It is preeminently the Christian church that has occupied itself with identifying, culti-
> vating and testing belief as a verbalizable inner condition of true religion. (Talal Asad
> *Genealogies of Religion*, p. 48, 1993)

If, as Asad implies, belief is at the heart of Roman Catholicism, then its complex religious doctrine begins with the simple conviction that Jesus of Nazareth is
both fully human and fully divine. Jesus is the incarnation on earth of God (the
Supreme Being) for the purpose of securing the redemption of humankind. Suc-
cinctly stated, Catholics believe that the sins of the first humans, Adam and Eve, caused
them to be cast from an earthly paradise, the Garden of Eden, and removed them from
full communion with God, who created them and everything else in the universe.
This *original sin* is the inheritance of all human beings, a condition that alienates them
from God. The texts of the Old Testament of the Bible are accounts of God's direct
intervention in the efforts of the Jews, the Chosen People, to reestablish their communion with God. The New Testament records the life and teachings of Jesus, who
while miraculously born of a human mother, the Virgin Mary, is the Son of God. As
God's embodiment on earth, Jesus opened the gates of heaven through his life, suffering, death, and resurrection, thus providing all human beings with the means for
their salvation. Catholics affirm that redemption is attainable through Jesus and the
Church that he established on earth to assist people in the salvation process after his
Ascension (or translation) into heaven, shortly after his resurrection from the dead.
    Catholics believe that at the end of this earthly life, the souls of all human be-
ings will enter into one of three realms or states of being. Those who have been absolved of their sins will go to *heaven* which is paradisiacal principally because the souls
admitted there, or *saints*, enjoy the beatific presence of God. The souls of those people who must still pay for sins that are not of such a magnitude as to condemn them
definitively go to *purgatory* until such time as they are prepared to enter heaven. Finally, those who die without repenting and being absolved of mortal (very serious)
sins are condemned to an eternity of punishment in *hell*. It is worth noting that while
most believers regard these three realms as real places in which one enjoys or suffers
the consequences of God's judgment of their mortal lives, some contemporary
Catholic theologians emphasize that heaven, purgatory, and hell are not cosmological locations but states of being in direct communion with God or not, either temporarily or permanently. While, as we shall discuss shortly, many souls are certified
by the Church as having attained heaven, Church doctrine does not require Catholics
to believe that anyone has ever been condemned to hell. Ultimately, the point of all
of the Church's teachings, ritual practices, missionary activities, and organizational
efforts is to ensure that as many souls arrive in heaven as possible.
    Roman Catholicism is monotheistic, but complexly so. One of its most dis-
tinctive doctrines is that of the *Holy Trinity*. According to this belief, God is unitary,
but expressed in three distinct persons: the Father, the Son (Jesus Christ), and the
Holy Spirit. The basis of belief in the Trinity, as in other Catholic doctrines, is faith
rather than human reason. That is to say that while the Catholic Church does not es-
chew the use of the logical faculties of human beings to accept elements of obligatory belief, ultimately it is God who provides people with the grace necessary to have

faith in that which is beyond human, rational comprehension. Grace, or the love of God, and the effects of that love in humankind, is the source of the key Christian virtues of faith, hope, and charity.

The Virgin Mary, while herself entirely human, is the only saint entitled to special veneration, known as *hyperdulia*. Catholicism is unique among the three major branches of Christianity (the other two, of course, are Protestantism and Orthodox Christianity) in according to her progressively greater honors and increasingly superhuman qualities over time. Mary was declared the Mother of God in the fifth century at the Council of Ephesus (451 C.E.). Fundamental to the Catholic understanding

---

The Nicene Creed

An historically important statement of Roman Catholic belief, this creed was first formulated in the fourth century after Christ.

We believe in one God,
The Father, the Almighty,
Maker of heaven and earth,
Of all that is seen and unseen.
We believe in one Lord, Jesus Christ,
The only Son of God, eternally begotten of the Father,
God from God, Light from Light,
True God from true God,
Begotten, not made, one in Being with the Father.
Through him all things were made.
For us men and for our salvation
He came down from heaven:
By the power of the Holy Spirit
He was born of the Virgin Mary, and became man.
For our sake he was crucified under Pontius Pilate;
He suffered, died, and was buried.
On the third day he rose again
In fulfillment of the Scriptures;
He ascended into heaven
And is seated at the right hand of the Father.
He will come again in glory to judge the living and the dead,
And his kingdom will have no end.
We believe in the Holy Spirit, the Lord, the giver of life,
Who proceeds from the Father and the Son.
With the Father and the Son he is worshipped and glorified.
He has spoken through the prophets.
We believe in one holy catholic and apostolic Church.
We acknowledge one baptism for the forgiveness of sins.
We look for the resurrection of the dead,
And the life of the world to come. Amen.

of Mary is her perpetual virginity (hence her principal epithet). That is to say, Mary miraculously retained her virginity before, during, and after the conception and birth of Jesus. The doctrine of the Immaculate Conception was established by Pope Pius IX in 1854, stipulating not that Mary was a virgin, but that she was conceived without original sin, just like her son Jesus. In 1950, Pope Pius XII asserted in the doctrine of the Assumption that all Catholics must believe that at her death Mary was taken up, body as well as soul, into heaven. At present there is within Catholicism a powerful movement calling upon the current pope, John Paul II, to accord to Mary the triple status of Mediatrix, Co-Redemptrix, and Advocate. The first stipulates that all of the graces that come to humankind through the suffering and death of Jesus are channeled through her. The second states that Mary participates in the redemption of humanity accomplished by her son. The third indicates that the petitions and prayers of the believers on earth are transmitted to Jesus through the intercession of Mary.

Non-Catholic Christians have long criticized the emphasis on the cult of the Virgin Mary and it is a particularly important point of distinction between Catholics and most Protestants. Should John Paul II (or one of his eventual successors) grant the quality of Co-Redemptrix to the Virgin Mary, it would not only strain the relations between Catholicism and the rest of Christianity, but it would also stir considerable controversy within the Church itself. This contentious issue highlights a more general and distinctive position of the Catholic Church: Its authority is based not just on sacred scriptures but on tradition as well. There are only 12 relatively brief mentions of the Virgin Mary in the New Testament, yet the Church not only accepts many nonscripturally based beliefs about Mary, it also continues over time to add to the list of her extraordinary, superhuman qualities and accomplishments. Perhaps, the most salient of Mary's characteristics, and one of the reasons for her enduring popularity among Catholics, is her role as a mediator between humans and God. In that role Mary has appeared in visions to more Catholics in the twentieth century (at least 400 well-documented cases) than in the previous three centuries combined. The growing anthropological literature on marianism has explored both the psychodynamic import and the politics and social organization of this most distinguishing feature of contemporary international Catholicism.[19]

The Catholic Church is also characterized by an elaborately developed *cult of the saints*. Saints are exemplary Catholics who are certified as having attained salvation, who are considered to be worthy of veneration, and who can be called upon to intercede with God on behalf of the faithful. Believing that the saints enjoy the Beatific Vision (the face-to-face personal experience) of God in heaven is a fundamental feature of Catholic doctrine as is the belief that death does not sever the communion that links all Catholics together. Saints often serve as patrons for communities, nations, ethnicities, occupations, or other social categories of people. For example, St. Joseph, the husband of Mary, is the patron of carpenters because that was his profession. St. Patrick is the patron saint of Ireland because he is credited with converting the people of the island to Christianity. St. Francis of Assisi safeguards animals because of his love for them during his lifetime. Indeed, there is a vast panoply of patron saints for virtually every imaginable social or personal condition: from poets (St. Cecilia) to pawnbrokers (St. Nicolas), from philosophers (St. Justin) to postal workers (St. Gabriel), from athletes (St. Francis de Sales) to invalids (St. Roch). The

---

The Hail Mary

One of Catholicism's most popular prayers, the Hail Mary, is derived from the angel Gabriel's salutation to Mary when announcing that she was about to become the Mother of God. It is the principal prayer of the Rosary and its second part clearly establishes the mediating role of the Virgin.

Hail Mary, full of grace:
The Lord is with thee.
Blessed art thou among women,
And blessed is the fruit of thy womb, Jesus.

Holy Mary, Mother of God
Pray for us sinners,
Now and at the hour of our death.
Amen.

Church officially recognizes as saints only a small subset of the entire body of those Catholics who are believed to have attained salvation. It does so through an elaborate, and usually very lengthy, quasi-legal process known as *canonization*. Anthropologists have shown most interest in documenting and understanding the local, as opposed to official, sociocultural processes involved in the sanctification of exemplary Catholics. Most noteworthy in this literature is the splendid work of Candace Slater who describes how local people in Brazil and Spain have fashioned devotions to holy people they regard as saints and for whom they have developed commemorative pilgrimages.[20] Christopher McKevitt, writing about the cults centered around the Italian holy man Padre Pio draws our attention to the very different perspectives taken on Catholic religious virtuosi by local people and more distant admirers.[21]

Catholics also believe in *angels*, both good and evil, who are spiritual beings, neither human nor divine. Derived from the Greek word *angelos*, which means "messenger," angels are generally depicted not only as delivering messages from God to humans, but also as interceding with God for the benefit of people and otherwise taking an active role in human affairs. Although it is not part of official dogma, many Catholics believe that each person is assigned a special *guardian angel* whose task it is to protect and advance their spiritual and physical well-being. In the sixth century C.E., Denys the Areopagite described nine distinct kinds of angels organized into three hierarchies, each containing three choirs.

Satan (from a Hebrew word meaning "adversary"), sometimes referred to as *Lucifer* ("light bearer"), is a member of the lowest choir of the lowest hierarchy of angels. Satan's historical career began as a member of the heavenly court of God whose function it was to accuse humanity of its wrong doings. Over time he became transformed by tradition into the opponent of God and the leader of all evil angels and demons. Catholic dogma emphasizes that all such devils were created good by God but turned from him through their intentional disobedience. While official doctrine indicates that Satan and other devils have very limited power over humans, they may loom very large in the minds of some Catholics as Michael Taussig has demonstrated for South Americans and John Ingham for Mexican Catholics.[22]

If a *sacrament* is the external sign, or indication, of something sacred, then Roman Catholicism is a deeply sacramental religion in which the invisible presence of the divine is experienced in a mediated fashion through symbols and ritual acts. The principal rituals of Catholicism are the seven sacraments whose enactment produces, renders visible, and delivers God's grace to their celebrants. *Baptism* is that ritual through which a person is initiated into the Catholic Church and incorporates him or her into the Body of Christ, pardoning all sins, including original sin. *Penance* (or the *sacrament of reconciliation*) traditionally involved the oral confession of sins to a consecrated priest, thus reconciling the sinner with God and Church. Since Vatican II, general forms of the absolution of sins have been recognized that do not require private confession of sins to a priest. *Confirmation* is the ritual recognition of Catholic maturity. Prior to the Vatican II reforms, baptism ideally was celebrated shortly after birth, followed by First Confession (penance) and First Communion at about seven years (the age of reason). Confirmation followed at about the age of ten as a sacrament of mature commitment to the faith. Although infant baptism is still the norm, since the Vatican II reforms, the sacraments of baptism and confirmation have been revised for adults in the *Rite of Christian Initiation of Adults.*

Marriage has been designated as a sacrament by the Church since the sixteenth century. Unlike the other sacraments, marriage is not technically administered by an ordained priest or bishop, but rather by the couple consenting to the bonds of matrimony. The priest who presides over the ceremony merely serves as the Church's official witness to the spiritual and social contract freely entered into by the bride and the groom. That the Church takes the state of marriage seriously, then, is indicated not only in its well-known prohibition of divorce, but also in the careful preparatory measures taken to ensure that all proper conditions for valid consent are met. If it should be determined after the fact that any of these conditions did not apply at the time of the marriage, then it may be annulled.

Holy Orders is the sacrament by which men (and only men) are initiated into the priestly offices (including those of deacon, priest, and bishop), thus bestowing upon them the authority to preach and to administer other sacraments. Ordination is presided over by a bishop who confers on the candidate power over the sacred. As already noted, Catholic priests are enjoined to be celibate (hence they may not marry), a requirement that has become increasingly controversial as the number of Catholics willing to enter the priesthood has declined precipitously in this century.

The *Anointing of the Sick* (formerly known as *extreme unction*, or the "last anointing") is rendered to those who are seriously ill and in danger of death. It may be administered only once per serious illness and cannot be offered to those awaiting execution. Technically the anointing is not a sacrament of the dying, yet many Catholics regard it as such and it is often called upon when all hope of recovery is lost and death is regarded as imminent.

Clearly, the principal ritual of Roman Catholicism is the sacrament of the *Eucharist,* or as it is commonly referred to, the *Mass.* The mass commemorates the death and resurrection of Jesus Christ by symbolically reproducing the Last Supper and by offering thanks for all that God has done for humanity. Catholics believe that during the Eucharist the Holy Spirit descends upon the assembled. Moreover, Catholics believe that transubstantiation takes place, that is, the transformation of the bread and wine offered during the Eucharist into the substance of the body and blood of Christ. The actual reception of the Eucharist is known as *Holy Communion*, which typically, but not exclusively, takes place in the context of the celebration of the mass.

Catholics are required to attend mass each Sunday (or Saturday evenings) and on other designated days of holy obligation (which may vary from episcopal conference to conference). Catholics must also partake of Holy Communion at least once a year during the Easter season in the spring. Masses are often celebrated in conjunction with other sacraments, particularly baptism, confirmation, marriage, and holy orders. It is noteworthy that the liturgy of the mass has evolved over time and continues to do so. For example, one of the most important innovations of the Vatican II reforms of the 1960s was the abandonment of Latin as the universal language of the mass. The mass is now usually performed in the vernacular language of the assembled.

The centrality of the sacraments in the practice of Catholicism cannot be overestimated, with the Eucharist taking pride of place. Nevertheless, there are many other rituals and devotions, some fully recognized by ecclesiastical authorities and others not, that enliven the sacred calendars of diverse national and regional Catholic traditions. In a beautifully written and evocative account of Irish Catholicism as it is practiced in southwest Donegal, Lawrence Taylor has documented the many different "occasions of faith" in which believers there express Catholicism in their own culturally and historically unique manner.[23] Among these are included pilgrimages to Holy Wells, Charismatic Renewal prayer meetings, and pilgrimages to both Irish and international holy places.[24] There are many such popular devotions (characterized by prayer forms, sacred objects, and ceremonies) which, while nonliturgical, are regarded as worthy expressions of Catholic faith by Church officials. Among them are also included the recitation of the Rosary, the performance of the Stations of the Cross, devotion to the Sacred Heart of Jesus, the Miraculous Medal novena, and many others.[25] In some parishes and dioceses these popular devotions are encouraged by clerics and in others they are not. In many Catholic settings throughout the world there are rich traditions of devotions to particular advocations of the Virgin Mary and to patron saints. Vernacular Catholicism may also be expressed in elaborate processional rituals, in activities associated with confraternities and other lay religious organizations, and in other highly particularized, place-specific religious ceremonies and festivities. Some of these observances clearly bear the influence of other, non-Christian, religious traditions. With few exceptions anthropologists have elected not to study the sacraments, preferring instead to document the vast panoply of local ritual expressions of Catholic faith. Just one notable example, among many, is the fascinating comparative study of vernacular rituals in Spain and Latin America undertaken by George Foster.[26]

Although admitting the authenticity of some visions and other sorts of private mystical experiences, Catholicism emphasizes the social aspects of a faith sustained by social tradition and articulated through symbols, institutional structures, and the sacraments. In contrast to the iconoclasm of many Protestant denominations of Christianity, Catholicism embraces the use of sacred images and representations of Christ, the Virgin Mary, and the saints. Catholic ritual deploys incense, candles, sacred music, and often is set in a church or cathedral ornately decorated with paintings, stained glass windows, statues of Christ, Mary and the saints, and elaborate crucifixes. Catholic clerics array themselves in distinctive vestments laden with symbolism of ancient vintage. The great Catholic cathedrals of Western Europe, which continue each year to attract believers and secular tourists in the millions, may best be understood as medieval multimedia instructional devices that were designed to engage the senses, inspire awe, and instruct the mostly illiterate Catholics who worshiped within. They also served to physically represent the power and authority of the ecclesiastical hierarchy and the Church itself.

Despite elaborate provisions for the instruction and inspiration of the illiterate among the faithful, the sacred texts (notably the Old and New Testaments of the Bible), catechisms, instruction manuals, missals, encyclopedias, dictionaries, and theological works of this most literate and literary religion have played an important role in universalizing the Church. Moreover, a vast educational system—surely unique among the world's religions for its scale—has developed in the Catholic world. Roman Catholic institutions of religious and secular instruction range from preschools and kindergarten through research institutions. Currently, according to one estimate, there are 450 Catholic colleges and universities in the world with an equal number of seminaries, finishing schools, and vocational schools. As of 1990 there were 8,500 Catholic elementary and secondary schools in the United States alone and over 100,000 such institutions worldwide.

Even with all of the resources available to the Catholic Church's universalizing efforts—its elaborate and centralized bureaucracy; its complex literary, theological, and canonical apparatus; and its huge, uniquely global, educational system—there remains a great deal of local variability in the expression of beliefs and practices in world Catholicism. In some cases variation is due to selective attention to, or studied disregard of, certain Catholic beliefs and practices. For example, Catholic Pentecostals in the United States have focused on the events of the original Pentecost and have elaborated new rituals around their understanding of the contemporary presence of the Holy Spirit in their midst.[27] On the other hand, a substantial amount of polling data and other evidence indicates that many other American Catholics choose to disagree with or ignore the position of the ecclesiastical hierarchy about such specific issues as divorce, contraception, priestly celibacy, and the proper role of women in the Church. They continue to view themselves as Catholics in good standing, choosing to ignore the features of the "official" religion with which they disagree. Examples such as these from the United States can be found throughout the Catholic world, but let us now consider in a bit more detail two examples of the dialectical relationship between the universal Church and local expressions of Catholic religiosity.

CATHOLICISM IN A SPANISH VALLEY

The nation of Spain is intimately associated with Roman Catholicism, and not only because the Spanish people were converted to Christianity very early in the religion's history (in the first century, according to some). Long before there was a "Spain," that is, a single nation of people with a national culture, the Iberians were Christians. Indeed, one cannot separate the gradual process by which the various people of Spain united politically from the prosecution of an enormously protracted holy war, the *Reconquest*. Only after more than seven centuries of struggle did Spanish Catholics succeed in wresting the peninsula back from the Islamic Moors and it is not farfetched to claim that this experience has marked their national commitment to Catholicism ever since.

Forged in religious militancy, the history of "official" Spanish Catholicism is characterized by a vigorously exclusionary and sternly orthodox tone. One need only mention its banishment of the Jews and Muslims from the nation, its famously lengthy Inquisition, its extraordinarily successful rejection of Protestantism, and its rigid authoritarianism during the long Franco dictatorship of this century. During much of its history, then, Spain has been a bastion of orthodox Catholicism in which religion and the state have frequently been tightly interwoven, with the latter very often enforcing the dictates of the clergy on the religious lives of the laity.

Of course, despite the best efforts of inquisitors, stern cardinals, and military dictators, Spanish Catholicism is hardly a homogeneous phenomenon: There is interesting variation in the practice of this religion over time, from region to region, and from city to village. As already indicated, views about Catholicism in southern Spain are highly polarized. Some working-class people harshly reject the Church, its clergy, and its institutions, while many others selectively elect which doctrines to believe and which observances to keep. However, in choosing a site in which to study Spanish Catholicism in 1968–1969, anthropologist William Christian selected a fairly isolated setting well known for the religious devotion of its people: the Nansa Valley of the Province of Santander in northern Spain.[28]

The Nansa Valley is geographically divided into a number of vales, or naturally circumscribed regions. The upper three vales, where Christian focused most of his attention, are furthered divided into from four to nine villages, each of which makes use of four kinds of lands: gardens, cornfields, meadows, and uncultivated *monte*, usually mountainside covered with ferns and gorse. Given the high level of rainfall in the valley, the people there are principally dedicated to the herding of beef and milk cattle, supplemented by their gardens and maize fields. At most only 15 percent of the population of any of the villages earns a living from nonagricultural pursuits.

Although some men in the valley express a mild skepticism about the priests, most of them attend mass every Sunday, contribute to the support of the Church, and fulfill the other religious obligations imposed by the clergy and by local convention. Most women recite the rosary every day and the valley produces many priests and nuns for the Church. Christian notes that women assume the role of the family's representative to priest and Church and are responsible to ensure that all the members of the family fulfill their personal and collective religious obligations.

Christian describes interesting patterns in the personal and public devotions of the people of the valley. There is a good deal of local variety as different villages pursue slightly different devotions and earn reputations for greater or lesser religious fervor. Yet, in a setting in which Catholicism has no competition from other religions and in which religious observance is intimately linked with the fulfillment of collective obligations, much of that variation can also be accounted for by differences in the level of emotional commitment to optional religious observances. Some families, and every village in the valley has at least one, are identified as *core* parish families. They are closely associated with the priests and their exemplary performance of both oblig-atory and optional religious practices is extolled by them. They generally are among the first to adopt the newest devotions that the priests periodically seek to introduce into the valley. These families may have kinship ties with the priests and often they are wealthier and better educated than most of their fellow villagers. On the other hand, other families are *peripheral* to the religious life of the community for a variety of reasons. Some are simply so poor that they have ceased to even try to keep up appearances and others do not bother to do so because of ideological or intellectual reasons. Still others attend mass every Sunday and perform other public observances that are expected of them, but, as Christian puts it, "their heart is not in it." For them religious participation is a matter of minimally complying with social expectations and, on occasion, seeking the intervention of divine figures for the resolution of practical problems.

Apart from the celebration of the sacraments there are two additional devotional systems at work in the valley. The first, and apparently the oldest, involves activities (pilgrimages, processions, vows, and other religious rituals) associated with *shrines* and the images of divine personalities that reside within them. These highly individualized images are generally statues of Mary, Christ, and various saints that have come to be fixed in the landscape of the valley. Shrines are *localized* sites of devotion in both the social and the geographical senses of that term. They invest particular places in the landscape with sacredness and the landscape, in turn, imparts special local meaning to them whatever the circumstances of their introduction into the valley. It seems likely that practices similar to these shrine devotions existed in the valley before it was Christianized and that, as has happened in many places in the world, these preexisting observances were gradually, but ultimately quite thoroughly, Catholicized over time.

The second system of optional religious activities consists of *generalized devotions* that are neither territorial nor local in their orientation. Devotions such as those organized for the *souls in purgatory* or for the recital of the *rosary* had no particular social or geographical reference when they enter the valley. If they involve images at all, any version of the standardized representation of the image will do. For example, any particular depiction of the *Sacred Heart of Jesus* is just as suitable as any other. Put differently, one representation of the Virgin Mary may be part of the shrine system, attracting devotion from a quite specific social category or group (e.g., *Our Lady of the Lowlands* is the patroness of a village), whereas another statue of Mary (e.g., *Our Lady of Fatima*) may be part of a generalized devotion that has great significance for the universal Church but lacks any connection to local groups or social identities. These generalized devotions invariably have been brought to the valley by priests, many of them members of monastic or mendicant religious orders, who seek to promote greater interest in the repentance of sin, the pursuit of personal redemption, and salvation. These devotions tend to be personalistic and familial rather than communal. That is, they are pursued by individuals and families, not social groups based on a sense of common, territorially based, identity. Generalized devotions focus on the life to come after death, not on the regulation of social order in this life.

Christian explains that the system of shrine devotions, on the other hand, is organized precisely around the problem of imposing order in the here-and-now and attaining well-being in the social world of the valley. The changing popularity of particular shrine images tracks important shifts in the local social structure of the Nansa Valley. The shrines, distributed through the valley and beyond, are intimately linked to some of the most important social identities recognized by the people: The nation, the region, the province, the vale, the village, and the barriada (a village segment) all have their shrines. Many shrines attract devotees from one, and only one, of the several moral communities important to each person. Drawing upon shrine and death records (which record bequests and death masses called for by the deceased), Christian convincingly demonstrates how the rise and fall over time in the attendance at particular shrines mirrors the shifting social importance of the different identities linked to them. Currently, an increased interest in regional and national shrines reflects the waning importance of the village as the people are drawn more deeply—socially, culturally and economically—into the world beyond the valley. As the nature of social life in the valley changes, the shrine system adjusts accordingly.

Shrines are mechanisms through which people seek the intercession of particular representations of Mary, Christ, and the saints. Christian notes that the Nansa people regard these supernaturals as intermediaries between themselves and God, a relationship of mediation that is replicated in other social and familial arenas, as well. People also seek the intervention of powerful patrons to serve as buffers between themselves and a distant government, just as they expect the mother of the family to intervene with the father on behalf of their children. Thus, exchanges among humans and exchanges between humans and divinities are both conceptualized in terms of mediation. People pursue shrine devotions both to resolve all manner of specific practical problems (e.g., sickness, poverty, poor weather, unemployment, anxiety, etc.) and to ensure that the balance of social and divine relations is maintained.

Generalized devotions address the problem of sin and the ultimate consequences for the individual of either overcoming temptation or not. There has been a constant flow of new, generalized devotions into the valley for at least the past 400 years, as agents of the universal Church, principally members of the religious orders, periodically attempted to redirect the spiritual practices of the people away from their local and practical concerns towards the Tridentine preoccupation with sin, with purgatory and hell, and with personal redemption. That these persistent efforts to replace the shrine observances have failed to displace the local devotions is due in no small measure to the penchant of Nansa people for taking new generalized devotions and converting them to local ones.

One example must suffice. Perhaps as long ago as the early seventeenth century, the Franciscans introduced a general devotion to the *souls in purgatory* as a means by which villagers could pray to God to hasten the promotion to heaven of those suffering souls. Presumably this activity would also cause devotees to reflect on their own sins and attend to their own redemption and salvation. This devotion eventually was reinterpreted in local terms and now devotees pray not *for* the souls to reduce their punishment in purgatory, but rather they pray *to* the souls, asking that they intervene with God to alleviate human physical illness.[29] Thus, the souls in purgatory have been drawn into the local system of divine intermediaries. Indeed, despite the fact that this devotion enjoys no concrete representation in the form of a stylized statue, three of the villages in which it is inordinately strong both lack other patron statues and maintain special side altars dedicated to the souls. In an important sense the generalized notion of a collectivity of suffering souls has become a patron saint for some communities. As a result of this dialectic between universal and local expressions of Catholic faith, the religious history of the valley has been marked by a continuous flow of novel general devotions into the area as each externally introduced religious innovation in due course is co-opted and transformed by local religious culture.

If there is a discernible increase in general devotions, as Christian notes, this is probably due mostly to the progressive integration of this formerly isolated valley into the wider world. But there is a new threat to the shifting balance maintained between these two kinds of Catholic practice. Post-Vatican II priests, typically quite young ones from outside the valley, now preside over many of the parishes of the valley. Most of them express little enthusiasm for either kind of traditional practice. Instead, they exhort their parishioners to study sacred scriptures and involve themselves with issues of charity and social justice. If this represents a religious transformation in the making, as Christian suggests it might, then it is one whose ultimate course will be difficult to predict. While clearly constituting a monumental change of course in official Catholicism, it seems very likely that the provisions of Vatican II, like those set forth four centuries earlier by the Council of Trent, will ultimately be *locally* interpreted and adapted to suit the great economic, social, and cultural changes in store for the people of the valley.

CATHOLICISM IN A PAPUA-NEW GUINEA VILLAGE

Unlike Spain, the nation of Papua-New Guinea (or PNG) does not immediately summon up a strong association with Roman Catholicism. While Melanesia has long attracted the notice of anthropologists interested in religion, until recently they have tended to give short shrift to the variety of Christianities which in this century have come to dominate the religious landscape of this part of Oceania. Although Christianity came to Melanesia only very lately, there are, as John Barker has observed, "few places where Christianity has spread so quickly or permeated so thoroughly."[30] Indeed, by 1980 over 85 percent of the people of Papua New Guinea described themselves as Christian. Although Roman Catholicism is but one of a number of Christian denominations at work there, it has dominated some regions, among them the East Sepik Province in which over 70 percent of the people claim membership in the Church.[31] The spectacular success of Catholicism there, of course, means neither that indigenous beliefs and practices have been entirely supplanted, nor that all elements of universal Catholicism have been addressed with equal enthusiasm and depth of understanding. Once again, as has occurred throughout the long history of the religion, local versions of Catholicism are taking shape.

In the mid-1970s anthropologist Michael French Smith undertook ethnographic research in Kragur village which is located on the island of Kairiru.[32] Whereas William Christian searched for a setting in Spain in which to study best the observance of Catholicism there, Smith had a different initial agenda. He was interested in understanding how Papua New Guinean villagers were reacting to their exposure to Western cultural and social forms. Kragur village is somewhat removed from the mainstream of regional politics and economics despite being located only 12 miles by air from the mainland village of Wewak, the principal community of the East Sepik Province of Papua-New Guinea. Once there, Smith discovered that Catholicism figured importantly in the evolving relationship between the villagers and the wider world into which they were being implicated. Indeed, one of his first observations was that the widespread reputation that Kragur had for its devotion to Catholicism was well founded and he resolved to study the religion in this most exotic of locales.

The 200 residents of Kragur are organized into patrilineal residential units called *koyeng*. Each *koyeng* is presided over by male heads of household who are related to one another through common male ancestors. Some *koyeng* are regarded as relatively more prestigious than others because of their possession of important traditional magic used to control the weather and to enhance the fruitfulness of their subsistence activities. The authority of "big men," as traditional leaders are called, is vested in their control over this magic. Some leaders also gain authority by virtue of their official positions in the administrative system that has developed in PNG. As part of their incorporation into the national and provincial administrative apparatus, the people of Kragur participate in the system of village councils.

Although Kragur villagers do own some European clothing, kerosene lanterns, metal tools, and Western cooking utensils, to a large extent they live a subsistence lifestyle based on what they produce for themselves. Their principal staple is taro, but they also grow and consume yams, sweet potatoes, and sago palms. They also fish and hunt wild game (mainly wild pigs). While these people do earn a modest amount of money from the sale of copra, garden produce, and other very small scale commercial activities, most of the money that flows into Kragur comes from the earnings of village men who work for wages off-island. The remittances they send back to Kragur are used to purchase the few necessities that the villagers do not grow or produce themselves, to pay taxes, and to provide fees for the education of their children. Although, Smith notes, the scarcity of money is a constant preoccupation with many villagers, their local economy is basically a subsistence one characterized by the delayed reciprocal exchange of goods and services. Thus, Kragur village has long been very much isolated from (and marginal to) regional, national, and global economic and social systems.

The attenuation of that isolation began at the end of the nineteenth century when German Catholic missionaries of the Society of the Divine Word began the process of bringing Catholicism to the mainland of Papua New Guinea. Smith estimates that sometime between 1900 and 1910 one of their mission ships visited Kairiru island. Thus, their initial direct encounter with European civilization was mediated through an effort to convert them to Catholicism. Soon after that first contact, some island men were taken in by the missionaries who introduced them to wage labor off-island and undertook to instruct them in the beliefs and practices of their religion. One of these trained, lay catechists[33] came to live and work in Kragur village in the 1920s and by 1930 had succeeded in drawing the local people into Catholicism to such an extent that they abandoned the central institution of their indigenous religion: the men's cult. A few years later European priests came to the island and formally baptized the Kragur converts. A school to train additional lay catechists was established on the island which eventually became a Catholic high school.

Although Catholicism had only been introduced 50 years before Smith first came to the village, the depth of its influence in the religious lives of the people is reflected in the great difficulty that the anthropologist had in reconstructing the indigenous religion that it had so recently displaced. Indeed, Smith concluded that a complete account could not be compiled of the Melanesian religion being practiced in Kragur prior to its conversion to Catholicism. This is not to say, of course, that all elements of traditional religious belief and practice had been erased from village life, but rather that the original integrity of the religious system was lost, even in memory.

Nonetheless, the Catholicism of Kragur is both selective and, in some sense, sketchy, partly because the villagers have never enjoyed a resident priest. Each evening a prayer meeting is conducted in the village plaza in front of a wooden altar bearing a small statue of the Virgin Mary. The meeting begins with children praying and singing hymns. Typically, adults later join them. Eventually, a lay religious leader calls upon all assembled to pray in front of Mary's altar. A separate church building has been erected to house Sunday religious services. Since they have no priest, they do not conduct a mass, but each Sunday nearly the whole village assembles there to be led in prayer by Ibor, the acknowledged lay leader of Catholicism in the community. These Sunday services are characterized by the enthusiastic recitation from memory of prayers and the energetic singing of hymns in Pidgin, a lingua franca used in PNG. Many Kragur Catholics celebrate Christmas Eve by trekking overland to the Mission school to hear midnight mass, an event which takes two days to accomplish and represents something of a hardship to its participants. Other Catholic holidays are celebrated as well, including Easter and All Souls Day during which they decorate their European style cemeteries and participate in processionals that would be easily recognizable to Catholics in Nansa Valley.

Kragur Catholics enthusiastically participate in these daily, weekly, and annual religious activities and they also express their religion in other ways. For example, Kragur Catholics enjoy displaying their pictures of Jesus and Mary and they invariably cross themselves before beginning a meal. There is an active, but small, chapter of the Legion of Mary in the village. Its members promote attendance at the evening prayer meetings and Sunday services and they were instrumental in the placement of a life-sized statue of the Virgin on a nearby mountain top. Because native Melanesian clerics are still relatively rare, Kragur people are quite proud that one of their own has become a priest who serves elsewhere in PNG. In general, the villagers have earned their regional reputation for being devout Catholics and they enjoy this distinction.

Despite their commitment to their recently adopted religion, many villagers clearly struggle to understand certain key tenets of universal Catholicism. Such notions as "heaven," "hell," and "sin" are quite vague to them, if not downright implausible. Smith quickly discovered that few could explain what these concepts mean and those who did have firm convictions about them did not often agree on details of belief. For example, one villager told Smith that sin is just "a word for making people afraid." This conceptual confusion is perhaps understandable given that prior to the arrival of Catholicism, Kragur people entertained no notion of an afterlife in which humans endure punishment or enjoy rewards based on how they conducted their lives while alive.

Many Kragur people simply do not know what to make of the Catholic "God." It must be disconcerting to the representatives of the universal Church that Kragur people have great difficulty comprehending a remote and powerful deity who is interested in taking account of their daily activities and keeping a tally, as it were, of their good deeds and bad. Like the Catholics of Nansa Valley, Kragur people model family relations onto their relationships with the supernaturals. However, some villagers go well beyond most Spanish Catholics when they explicitly identify their deceased mothers and fathers with the Virgin Mary and God. For villagers to say "My God is my father," testifies to the resilience of the traditional Melanesian concern with the spirits of deceased ancestors, a central feature of their indigenous religion. Some Kragur people believe that all prayers directed to "God" are actually received by their ancestors. Others entertain the view that "God" might be a species of *masalai*, or potentially dangerous "nature spirit" who is part man and part serpent. Still others seek to identify "God" with a traditional deity named *Wankau*, a supernatural figure who created the earth and provided humans with important foundational knowledge. But *Wankau* is always depicted in very human terms whereas the Catholic God strikes Kragur people as very abstractly good and judgmental. Perhaps most tellingly, a number of Smith's informants claim to have no clear comprehension of what or who God might be.

On the other hand a number of Catholic beliefs resonate quite well with indigenous religious views and these have been relatively well received. For example, if the people have had some problems in conceptualizing a Catholic "God," they have much less difficulty relating to the "Virgin Mary," even if there might be some tendency to identify her with one's deceased mother. Indeed, Smith states that for Kragur villagers the Virgin Mary is more important as a supernatural than is God the Father or Jesus Christ. Proof of this includes the fact that most intercessionary prayers are directed to her, not to God. In part their appreciation of Mary is due to the fact that she is a much more anthropomorphic figure than is the relatively abstract notion of God. Smith argues also that Mary's quality of perpetual virginity is particularly attractive to a people who believe that sexual intercourse not only weakens the efficacy of magic but also constitutes a threat to physical well-being and material prosperity. That priests and nuns are required to be celibate makes perfect sense to the villagers because they believe that the practitioners of magic must curtail sexual behavior if they are to be effective. Similarly, the Catholic concept of prayer was easily understood by Kragur people because of its similarity to other beliefs about traditional magic. They are particularly keen to learn formulaic prayers like the rosary because in times of dire necessity they believe that its precise recitation will produce an intervention on their behalf by the Virgin Mary. As in their traditional magical spells, it is not necessary to understand the meaning of the Catholic prayers, but they must be performed correctly if they are to produce the desired results. Indeed, Smith suggests that when the missionaries first presented themselves to Kragur community, the villagers probably regarded Catholicism as the rather potent "magical basis of the European way of life."

Whether explicating those features of universal Catholic beliefs that challenge the comprehension of Kragur people or detailing those elements of Catholic doctrine which have been more easily assimilated to preexisting traditional beliefs and practices, Smith makes clear that this very small Melanesian village harbors a great deal of variation in opinion on virtually all of the momentous issues of religion. Going beyond issues of religious consensus, however, Smith examines the subtle manner in which even the highly localized and variably interpreted form of Catholicism that has emerged in Kragur has prepared villagers for increased participation in the

Western capitalist system that they are gradually, but as yet far from completely, being drawn into. Even though the version of Catholicism entertained by Kragur people is highly adapted to their own culture and their own cultural concerns, it nonetheless has greatly facilitated the implantation in the village of key Western capitalist notions and social forms (e.g., "punctuality," "money," "work for wages," "schooling," "elected councils"). Apart from its great impact on the religious lives of the people of Kragur, Catholicism has clearly created the kind of "discipline" upon which involvement in the world economy is predicated. In fact, Smith argues that one possible explanation for why Kragur village has thoroughly embraced a religion so exotic to its own cultural assumptions is that the villagers view it as an excellent vehicle for their successful involvement in the world beyond their Melanesian village.

Exactly how Kragur Catholicism will develop may be influenced, in part at least, by two circumstances, one external and the other internal in origin. Although at first the Catholic missionaries sought to eliminate pre-Christian religious customs and beliefs, a new attitude of tolerance for at least some of the old forms has developed as one response to the very same Vatican II reforms whose implementation is altering the profile of popular devotions in Nansa Valley. Although Catholicism has been so persuasive that much knowledge of the old religious ways is lost, others in similar circumstances elsewhere have easily reinvented ancient traditions. But more intriguing is another potential source of innovation. Some Kragur villagers, reflecting on their continuing poverty and powerlessness relative to Europeans despite their acceptance of Catholicism, suspect that they have not been given the full and most powerful version of the religion by those who introduced it to them. Thus, they have begun to construct their own understanding of those "true" beliefs and devotions that might lift them out of their social and economic plight, but which have been hidden from them, they believe, by the representatives of the official Church. This perception, and the religious imagination that it stimulates, constitutes a potentially creative source for the future elaboration of a local version of Catholicism that goes well beyond the simple accommodation of a preexisting religion with a recently introduced official Catholicism. If many villagers adopt this view, they may well begin to elaborate their Catholicism along lines that diverge significantly from the interests of the missionaries who originally delivered the religion to them.

Other examples, could be cited which explicate the complex interplay between local social conditions and cultural constructions (both sacred and mundane) and the universalizing forces of Catholic organization, belief, and practice. Many ethnographic accounts attest to the remarkable ability of Roman Catholicism both to modify the religious views of people quite exotic to the cultural heritage in which it matured and, simultaneously, to accommodate local versions of itself almost anywhere. Although often depicted by its detractors as a rigid and authoritarian religion whose social and theological conservatism makes it unwieldy in the modern (or postmodern) world, a careful examination of Roman Catholicism's historical expansion and its fundamental strategy of cultural accommodation suggests that the secret to the phenomenal success of the world's largest, most multi-ethnic, religion is precisely the long-term organizational and cultural flexibility that some believe it lacks.

NOTES

1. I am indebted to Kathryn Oths, Milady Murphy, George Saunders, Ray Scupin, Richard Krause, David Jordan, and Elizabeth Throop for their most helpful comments on earlier drafts of this chapter. I wish, also, to acknowledge my teachers, Marc Swartz and the late Cèsar Graña, for introducing me to the anthropology of Catholicism. Special thanks go to my compadre, Juan Carlos Gonzalez Faraco, for an enlightening 15-year dialogue on Catholicism as it is expressed in his native southern Spain.

2. Mark 16:16

3. Emile Durkheim *Suicide*. (New York: The Free Press, 1951) p. 158, [orig. 1897].

4. Talai Asad *Genealogies of Religion*. (Baltimore: The Johns Hopkins Press, 1993) p. 46

5. For the sake of convenience I have adopted the convention of referring to the Roman Catholic Church as the "Catholic Church" or the "Church," but the reader should be advised that there are other Christian denominations, not considered here, that also regard themselves as "Catholic," notably some Anglican and Orthodox Christians. Moreover, a number of other churches are in communion with the Roman Church and accept the authority of the pope; examples include Maronite, Antiochene, Chaldean, Armenian, and Alexandrian rites. This chapter treats only the Roman Church.

6. The anthropological literature on Roman Catholicism is as far-flung as the religion itself. Many ethnographic monographs about Catholic peoples, while not focusing on religion, do include enlightening chapters or sections on local expressions of Catholicism. Some book-length ethnographic treatments of Catholicism do stand out, however: Lawrence Taylor's *Occasions of Faith: An Anthropology of Irish Catholicism* (Philadelphia: University of Pennsylvania Press, 1995); John M. Ingham's *Mary, Michael, and Lucifer: Folk Catholicism in Central Mexico*, (Austin: University of Texas Press, 1986); R.L. Stirrat's *Power and Religiosity in a Post-Colonial Setting: Sinhala Catholics in Contemporary Sri Lanka*, Cambridge Studies in Social and Cultural Anthropology (Cambridge: Cambridge University Press, 1992); Mart Bax's *Medjugorje: Religion, Politics, and Violence in Rural Bosnia, Anthropological Studies, Vol. 16* (Amsterdam: University Press of Amsterdam, 1995); Leslie Desmangles's *The Faces of the Gods: Vodou and Roman Catholicism in Haiti* (Chapel Hill: University of North Carolina Press, 1993); David Kertzer's *Comrades and Christians: Religion and Political Struggle in Communist Italy* (Cambridge: Cambridge University Press, 1980); Thomas J. Csordas' *Language, Charisma and Creativity: the Ritual Life of a Religious Movement* (Berkeley: University of California Press, 1997); Michael J. Sallnow's *Pilgrims of the Andes: Regional Cults in Cusco* (Washington, DC: Smithsonian Institution Press, 1987) and Timothy Mitchell's *Passional Culture: Emotion, Religion and Society in Southern Spain* (Philadelphia: University of Pennsylvania Press, 1990).

    Many seminal articles in the anthropology of Catholicism have appeared in general collections on Christianity and on the varied religious traditions of particular areas of the world. The interaction of Catholicism with these other religious traditions (including competing visions of Christianity) is a focus of investigation in many of these compilations: George Saunders' (ed.), *Culture and Christianity: The Dialectics of Transformation* (Westport, CT.: Greenwood Press, 1988); Jane Schneider and Shirley Lindenbaum's (eds.), "Frontiers of Christian Evangelism: Essays in Honor of Joyce Rigelhaupt," a special issue of *American Ethnologist* 14(1), 1987; Wendy James and Douglas H. Johnson's (eds.), *Vernacular Christianity: Essays in the Anthropology of Religion Presented to Godfrey Lienhardt*, JASO Occasional Papers, No. 7 (Oxford: JASO, 1988); Eric R. Wolf's (ed.), *Religion, Power, and Protest in Local Communities: The Northern Shore of the Mediterranean* (Berlin: Mouton, 1984); Eric R. Wolf's (ed.), *Religious Regimes and State Formation: Perspectives from European Ethnology* (Albany: SUNY Press, 1991); John Barker's (ed.), *Christianity in Oceania: Ethnographic Perspectives* (Lanham, MD: University Press of America, 1990); Daniel J. Hughes and Sharon W. Tiffany's (eds.), *Mission, Church and Sect in Oceania* (Ann Arbor: University of Michigan Press, 1978) Gary Gossen's (ed.), *South and Meso-American Native Spirituality: From the Cult of the Feathered Serpent to the Theology of Liberation* (New York: Crossroad, 1993).

7. See Diana Brown's *Umbanda Religion and Politics in Urban Brazil* (Ann Arbor: University of Michigan Press, 1986).

8. See George Saunders' "The Magic of the South: Popular Religion and Elite Catholicism in Italian Ethnology," in Jane Schneider's (ed.), *Italy's "Southern Question": Orientalism in One Country* (Oxford: Berg, 1998), pp. 177–202.

9. The Catholic Church has long been characterized both by meticulous record keeping and by a very high level of scholarship and self-analysis. The statistics, historical background, and depictions of matters of "official" belief and practice provided in this chapter are drawn principally from the following sources: *The Catholic Encyclopedia* (New York: Encyclopedia Press, 1913); *The New Catholic Encyclopedia* (New York: McGraw Hill, 1967); Richard P. McBrien's (ed.), *The HarperCollins Encyclopedia of Catholicism* (New York: HarperCollins, 1995); the excellent set of articles on "Roman Catholicism" in *The New Encyclopedia Britannica*. 15th ed., vol. 26, pp. 877–913, 1997; and the articles on Christianity in Peter Bishop and Michael Darton's (eds.) *The Encyclopedia of World Faiths* (London: Macdonald Orbis, 1987).

10. Much of the anthropological literature on Catholic priests focuses on their role in the missionization process. See, for example, Peter Black's "The Teachings of Father Marino," in *Mission, Church and Sect in Oceania* (Ann Arbor: University of Michigan Press, 1978), pp. 307–354, 1978.

11. See Gerald A. Arbuckle's "The Impact of Vatican II on the Marists in Oceania," in *Mission, Church and Sect in Oceania* pp. 275–299, 1978; Peter McDonogh's "Metamorphoses of the Jesuits," *Comparative Studies in Society and History* 32: 778–90, 1991.

12. See Max Bax's "Marian Apparitions in Medjugorge: Rivaling Religious Regimes and State Formation in Yugoslavia," in Eric Wolf's (ed.) *Religious Regimes and State Formation: Perspectives from European Ethnology* (Albany: SUNY Press, 1991), pp. 29–53. Max Bax's *Medjugorje: Religion, Politics and Violence in Rural Bosnia.* (Amsterdam: VU Uitgeverij, 1995).

13. For excellent discussions of how Catholicism interacts with other religious traditions under colonialist conditions, see Godfrey Lienhardt's, "The Dinka and Catholicism," in John Davis (ed.), *Religious Organization and Religious Experience* (London: Academic Press, 1982) pp. 185–198; Peter Black's "Domestication of Catholicism on Tobi," *Pacific Studies* 17: 1–28, 1994; Robert M. Baum's "Emergence of a Diola Christianity," *Africa* 60: 370–398, 1990.

14. See David D. Gilmore's "Andalusian Anti-Clericalism," *Anthropology* 8:31–44, 1984.

15. See William Christian, Jr.'s *Visionaries: The Spanish Republic and the Reign of Christ* (Berkeley: University of California Press, 1996).

16. See Robin and Jill Nagle's *Claiming the Virgin: The Broken Promise of Liberation Theology in Brazil* (London: Routledge, 1997).

17. George Saunders' "Political Religion and Religious Politics in an Alpine Italian Village," in *Culture and Christianity: The Dialectics of Transformation* (Westport, CT: Greenwood Press, 1988), pp. 159–178; David Kertzer's *Comrades and Christians: Religion and Political Struggle in Communist Italy* (Cambridge: Cambridge University Press, 1980).

18. Michael Angrosino, "Culture Concept and the Mission of the Roman Catholic Church," *American Anthropologist* 96: 824–832, 1994.

19. For psychological treatments of the cult of Mary, see Anne Parsons' *Belief, Magic and Anomie* (New York: The Free Press, 1969); George R. Saunders' "Men and Women in Southern Europe: A Review of Some Aspects of Cultural Complexity," *The Journal of Psychoanalytic Anthropology* 4: 435–66, 1981; Michael P. Carroll's *The Cult of the Virgin Mary* (Princeton: Princeton University Press, 1986); Nancy Frey Breunner's "The Cult of the Virgin Mary in Southern Italy and Spain," *Ethos* 20: 66–95, 1992. For sociopolitical analyses of marianism, see Eric Wolf's "The Virgin of Guadalupe: A Mexican National Symbol," *Journal of American Folklore* 71: 34–39, 1958; Jane Collier's "From Mary to Modern Woman: The Material Basis of Marianismo and Its Transformation in a Spanish Village," *American Ethnologist* 13: 600–17, 1986; Max Bax's, "The Seers of Medjugorje," *Ethnologia Europea* 20: 167–176, 1990; Libbet Crandon-Malamud's "Blessings of the Virgin in Capitalist Society," *American Anthropologist* 95: 574–96, 1993; Michael Dean Murphy's "Class, Community and Costume in an Andalusian Pilgrimage," *Anthropological Quarterly* 67: 49–61, 1994.

20. See Candace Slater's *Trail of Miracles: Stories From a Pilgrimage in Northeast Brazil* (Berkeley: University of California Press, 1986) and her *City Steeple, City Streets: Saints' Tales from Granada and a Changing Spain* (Berkeley: University of California Press, 1990).

21. Christopher McKevitt "San Giovanni Rotondo and the Shrine of Padre Pio," in John Eade and Michael Sallnow's (eds.) *Contesting the Sacred: The Anthropology of Christian Pilgrimage* (London: Routledge, 1991), pp. 77–97.

22. Michael Taussig, *The Devil and Commodity Fetishism in South America* (Chapel Hill: University of North Carolina Press, 1980); Ingham, *Mary, Michael, and Lucifer.*

23. Taylor, *Occasions of Faith,* 1995.

24. The anthropological literature on Catholic pilgrimage is large and growing. Among the most important works are Victor and Edith Turner's *Image and Pilgrimage in Christian Culture: Anthropological Perspectives* (New York: Columbia University Press, 1978); Mary Lee and Sidney Nolan's *Christian Pilgrimage in Modern Western Europe* (Chapel Hill: University of North Carolina Press, 1989); N. Ross Crumrine and Alan Morinis' (eds.) *Pilgrimage in Latin America* (Westport, CT: Greenwood, 1991); John Eade and Michael Sallnow's (eds.) *Contesting the Sacred: The Anthropology of Christian Pilgrimage,* 1991; Alan Morinis' (ed.) *Sacred Journeys: The Anthropology of Pilgrimage* (Westport, CT: Greenwood, 1992).

25. See Michael P. Carroll's *Catholic Cults & Devotions: A Psychological Inquiry.* (Kingston, Canada: McGill-Queen's University Press, 1989).

26. George Foster's *Culture and Conquest: America's Spanish Heritage* (New York: Wenner-Gren Foundation for Anthropological Research, 1960).

27. Michael D. Murphy's "The Culture of Spontaneity and the Politics of Enthusiasm: Catholic Pentecostalism in a California Parish," in George Saunder's (ed.) *Culture and Christianity: The Dialectics of Transformation* (Westport, CT: Greenwood Press, 1988).

28. William Christian A. Jr.'s *Person and God in a Spanish Valley,* new rev. ed. (Princeton, NJ: Princeton University Press, 1989).

29. Michael P. Carroll notes a similar phenomenon in Italy in his book *Veiled Threats: The Logic of Popular Catholicism in Italy* (Baltimore, MD: The Johns Hopkins University Press, 1996).

30. See p. 145 in John Barker's "Christianity in Western Melanesian Ethnography," in James G. Carrier's (ed.) *History and Tradition in Melanesian Anthropology* (Berkeley: University of California Press, 1992) pp. 144–173.

31. See Mary Taylor Huber, "Constituting the Church: Catholic Missionaries on the Sepik Frontier," *American Ethnologist,* 1994, 14:107–125.

32. Michael French Smith's *Hard Times on Kairiru Island: Poverty, Development, and Morality in a Papua New Guinea Village* (Honolulu: University of Hawaii Press, 1994).

33. A *catechist* is usually a lay person who has been instructed in the task of teaching others (children, potential converts, etc.) the doctrines and observances of the Catholic faith.

Eighteen

Protestantism

Andrew Buckser

Purdue University

When Americans think of anthropology, they usually think of something exotic—Margaret Mead in the South Seas, Franz Boas among the Eskimo, Indiana Jones in the jungles of South America. Yet anthropology often produces its most striking insights when we apply it to things closer to home. Anthropological analysis can reveal a depth of complexity in familiar customs and institutions, which we assume lack the drama and excitement of faraway cultures. In religion, for example, many Americans take Protestantism for granted. The cluster of church spires at the center of most American towns excites little comment or reflection; Protestantism is a bland fact of everyday life, an unremarkable institution far removed from the dramatic rituals and colorful cosmologies of "primitive" religion". Yet a closer look reveals Protestantism as anything but bland. It constitutes today one of the most diverse and widespread religious movements in the world, comprising thousands of denominations in hundreds of countries. Its rituals range from the staid formality of the Anglican Church to the ecstatic exuberance of the Assemblies of God; its beliefs encompass both the rigorous rationalism of Calvinist Puritanism and the syncretistic spiritualism of many non-Western groups. Protestantism offers one of the world's richest contexts for exploring processes like culture change, spiritual innovation, and the impact of religion on political struggle. The anthropology of Protestantism, therefore, represents one of the most exciting and expanding areas of the anthropology of religion.

This chapter will discuss some of the basic features of Protestantism, as well as some of the approaches anthropologists have taken to studying it. It will summarize the history of the religion , note some dimensions of diversity within it, and present six cases of anthropological work on it. Let us begin, however, where Protestantism itself begins: with the question of belief.

BELIEFS

Protestant churches, as we will see, vary tremendously in the details of their theologies; this capacity for variation gives Protestantism both its striking dynamism and its equally striking fractiousness. But most Protestants adhere to a number of basic beliefs about the universe and the supernatural, built on the foundation of Catholic Christian theology. They begin by affirming Jewish beliefs in a single supreme deity, whose creation of the world and whose interaction with human beings are detailed in the Jewish scriptures. In addition, like all Christians, they affirm the divinity of Jesus Christ, a first-century Jewish messianic leader in Palestine. Jesus, they say, was the son of God, sent to earth to sacrifice himself for the sake of human beings. Those who believe in his divinity will be saved from death and be resurrected like him to an eternal life in heaven. Protestants also affirm the existence of the Holy Spirit, a being with the power to communicate divine favor and energy to believers. Like Catholics, most Protestants contend that these three entities—Father, Son, and Holy Spirit—comprise a single supreme being, a belief known as the doctrine of the Trinity. Many Protestants also posit the existence of another supernatural being: Satan, a fallen angel who rules over Hell and tempts human beings into sin. God and Satan may be served in their kingdoms by angels and devils; Protestantism tends to downplay these figures, however, and it admits the possibility of no other supernatural beings or forces.

With the prospects of eternal life or eternal damnation awaiting them after death, Protestants regard the achievement of salvation as the most essential task of human life. They cannot do this by themselves. Humans are imbued with sin, they are constantly acting in ways offensive to God, and not even the most conscientiously well-meaning person can deserve God's favor on his own merits. But through his death by crucifixion, Jesus has offered to take human sin on his shoulders, to grant forgiveness to human beings. To obtain this forgiveness, human beings must merely believe in it; faith in the divinity and forgiveness of Jesus is the only necessary condition for salvation. It is also the only sufficient condition. While Protestantism expects a high standard of moral behavior from believers, such behavior is a consequence, not a cause, of divine grace. No actions, however praiseworthy, can gain salvation for an unbeliever, nor can any crime, however reprehensible, bar a truly repentant believer from forgiveness. Not even the church can intercede on behalf of believers. Protestant sacraments, while important, are essentially symbolic actions, signs of belief and forgiveness which do not have effects in themselves.

Protestantism traces these beliefs almost exclusively to the Bible, a collection of ancient texts regarded as the revealed word of God. Part of this collection, the Old Testament, consists of the Jewish holy scriptures. The other part, the New Testament, contains several accounts of Jesus's life as well as letters and histories from his early followers. Protestantism takes the Bible as its ultimate source of legitimacy; all rules, rituals, and beliefs are valid only insofar as they have grounding in the scriptures. Protestants have translated the scriptures into hundreds of languages, making them accessible to virtually all literate believers. Their truths are understandable to all, requiring no initiation or special status, and studying them makes up an essential part of any Protestant's religious devotion. This reliance on scripture has tended to give Protestant churches a simpler system of rituals than other Christian churches. One of the first acts of the early Protestants, for example, was the abolition of such Catholic traditions as confession and clerical celibacy, neither of which were called for in the scriptures. The requirement of scriptural justification touches moral and social regulations as well. The apostle Paul's letters to the early Christian congregations frequently touch on social issues, and many Protestants look to them as a guide to family and community organization. Questions about marriage, family, business, government, and other issues can be adjudicated to some extent by referring them to scriptural recommendations.

These basic beliefs run through almost all Protestant groups, and they give Protestantism as a whole a distinctive character. Its focus on individual belief, for example, tends to produce individualism and a level of anti-authoritarianism throughout the Protestant world. At the same time, these beliefs allow considerable room for disagreements, and they provide little institutional structure for resolving them. As a result, a basic element of Protestant belief is its particularity. No one belongs to "the Protestant church;" Protestants invariably belong to specific denominations, each of which holds a distinct interpretation of scripture and church organization. These differences affect their ritual and liturgical structures, leading to striking diversity among the various Protestant churches. To get a sense of this diversity, we must first understand how it came about.

THE DEVELOPMENT OF PROTESTANTISM

Protestantism began as a reform movement in the Catholic Church in the early sixteenth century. Such reform movements had come and gone in the Church for a millennium; some had been suppressed by the Catholic hierarchy, while others had been incorporated as new teachings or monastic movements. In the sixteenth century, however, a combination of political and ecclesiastical developments led the reformers to break from the Church outright. The crisis began in 1517, when a German theologian named Martin Luther publicly objected to a practice known as the sale of indulgences. Indulgences, which allowed the wealthy essentially to buy forgiveness from their sins, were already a focus of criticism throughout Europe. In his complaint, however, Luther also questioned the doctrine of transubstantiation, the celibacy of priests, and a variety of other basic points of Church belief and practice. The Church reacted harshly, excommunicating Luther in 1521 and declaring him a political outlaw. His case became a cause celebre, as sympathetic rulers in various parts of northern Europe refused to enforce the decree. The church proved politically incapable of enforcement itself, and Luther became the leader of a powerful reform movement that spread throughout the continent. Its success varied with the level of political support it received. Where powerful monarchs endorsed it, as in Scandinavia and England, Protestantism took the form of a state church; where they opposed it, as in France, Protestantism was largely repressed. In some areas, like Switzerland and Germany, cities and principalities fostered either Protestantism or Catholicism depending on local sympathies. The close connection between religious and secular authority meant that the dispute over reform involved political and often military battles. The end result was that by the end of the sixteenth century, Protestant churches dominated most of northern Europe, and the Catholic church most of the south.

Unlike Catholicism, however, Protestantism had no uniform creed or structure. Most Protestant churches agreed with Luther's central theses: That sinners could achieve salvation only by faith, not by good works, and that the Bible, not any church organization, held the final authority on Christian doctrine. But Protestant theologians disagreed on many subsidiary points, and Protestant politicians found varying ways of applying these ideas to the social world. As a result, Protestantism quickly split into a number of doctrinal and geographical branches. As early as the 1520s, for example, a Zurich theologian named Ulrich Zwingli disputed Luther's interpretation of the Eucharist. While both denied the Catholic doctrine of transubstantiation, Luther argued that Christ was physically present in the bread and wine, whereas Zwingli argued that Christ's presence was spiritual. The disagreement split the early Protestant movement, with Zwingli dominating Switzerland and Luther most of Germany. Zwingli's successors, notably Geneva's John Calvin, promoted a deeper revision of Christianity that eventually became the Reformed branch of Protestantism. Even as they argued these issues, a number of Zwingli's own followers decried *his* reforms as superficial. They called for an even deeper rethinking of the religion, one that divorced itself from worldly politics and placed an intense emphasis on personal faith. Known as the Anabaptists for their belief in adult baptism, they developed into a powerful and even revolutionary movement in Germany in the 1530s. In the centuries to come, disputes and schisms of this kind became a basic and characteristic part of the Protestant world. Protestantism generated sectarian and denominational movements at a startling rate, often leading to conflict and even bloodshed among its members. Yet this tendency gave Protestantism a tremendous flexibility, allowing individual communities to tailor its doctrines to their own experiences, and thereby ensuring that its members felt an unusually powerful tie to the faith.

These different churches varied greatly in their connection to political authorities. Some became integral parts of the state, with the ruler serving as head of the church. Monarchs headed up national churches in England and Scandinavia, for example, while small-scale theocracies existed in various European cities; in the 1540s, for example, John Calvin achieved near dictatorial control for the Reform movement in Geneva. Others, like the Anabaptists, shunned worldly politics; after a disastrous attempt to govern the city of Munster in 1534, the Anabaptists firmly renounced both violence and temporal power. Still others sought to influence politics and society within the context of existing established churches. In England, the Puritan movement of the sixteenth and seventeenth centuries sought repeatedly to purge both the Anglican church and English society of what it saw as the vestiges of Catholicism. Such movements posed an implicit threat to existing power structures, and they often endured severe repression by established national churches. By the seventeenth century, the religious world of Protestant Europe included a dizzying array of official and unofficial churches, related in a complex web of dominance, subordination, resistance, and renunciation.

All of these strands found abundant room for expression during the colonial expansion of the seventeenth and eighteenth centuries. As European powers spread their influence across the globe, Protestants founded colonies and missions in radically new settings. For minority religious groups, these settings offered an unheard-of freedom for expansion, power, and further schism. North America became the site for much of this activity. Persecuted sects saw the continent as a refuge from the repressive policies of the powerful European churches, a place where believers could build pure societies unhampered by old beliefs and institutions. English Congregationalists, for example, harassed by the authorities at home, founded the Massachusetts Bay Colony in 1630. They regarded their creation as a "city on a hill," an example of true Christianity for the entire world, and for nearly a century they organized it as a theocratic state. Other religious groups found freedom elsewhere, many of them in the conspicuously tolerant colony of Rhode Island. Without the unifying force of persecution, however, the Protestant tendency toward schism accelerated. Within a few decades of their arrival in Rhode Island, the Baptist community split into Calvinist, Arminian, and Seventh Day factions. A century later, when the American Revolution established religious freedom in the new United States, the opportunities for Protestant variation became practically limitless.

Several common themes ran throughout this varied picture, including Luther's stress on the importance of individual faith. Protestants of all stripes regarded the personal experience of the individual as the key setting for religion; salvation came only through personal faith, an explicit individual awareness of the magnitude of Christ's benevolence. As their churches became increasingly established, however, that awareness became more difficult to maintain. Churches achieved an integration into the larger community, and the fervid devotion that filled their original members generally gave way to a looser and more complacent style of worship. That complacency led to a recurring feature of Protestantism: its tendency toward revivals, waves of revitalization and reformulation that have swept periodically through Protestant regions. In the mid-1720s, for example, charismatic preachers like Jonathan Edwards and T.J. Frelinghuysen ignited a powerful revival movement in New England and the mid-Atlantic colonies; lasting until the 1760s, the "Great Awakening" emphasized themes like the horrors of hell, the joys of heaven, and the importance of a direct emotional tie to the divine. It brought thousands of new members into the churches, and it split many established churches into opposed wings. Thirty years later, a "Second Great Awakening" swept across the entire United States, including the sparsely settled areas on the western frontier. Leaders of this movement preached not only in regular churches, but also in huge "camp meetings," which brought thousands of listeners together for thunderous sermons and calls for repentance. Such movements, of varying size and intensity, have occurred periodically in almost all Protestant areas since the eighteenth century. In some cases, they have achieved an international scale; the Pentecostal revival of the early twentieth century, for example, spawned churches throughout the United States, Scandinavia, Western Europe, and even parts of Eastern Europe in less than 20 years. In the United States, revivalism has sometimes become institutionalized in its own right. Figures like Dwight Moody, Billy Sunday, and Billy Graham have developed national institutions to promote ongoing revivalism throughout the nation and the world.

Until the twentieth century, most of this activity remained within a limited area; Protestants lived mainly in northern Europe or in the parts of America dominated by northern Europeans. Lutherans had sent missionaries elsewhere as early as 1706, and the Church of England had been active throughout the British Empire, but their results had been relatively modest. At the end of the nineteenth century, however, powerful missionary movements developed in a variety of Protestant churches, and Protestantism soon became active throughout the developing world. By the middle of the twentieth century, these missions had developed into independent churches, making Protestantism for the first time a truly worldwide phenomenon. Some of these new churches adhered strictly to the creeds and practices imported from the West. Many others, however, adapted the faith to accord with indigenous customs and beliefs, producing syncretic versions of Protestantism that Martin Luther might not have recognized. Pentecostalism, with its use of trance, possession, and healing by the Holy Spirit, proved particularly compatible with spirit-based and shamanistic religious systems. At the close of the twentieth century, these churches make up a tremendously dynamic and increasingly influential branch of the Protestant world.

DIMENSIONS OF PROTESTANT DIVERSITY

Protestantism began as a rejection of Catholic authority, and it incorporated the power of the individual conscience into the basis of its philosophy. This insistence on independence and freedom of thought has made Protestantism an unusually creative religious tradition. New ideas spring up constantly in all religions, but in Protestantism they have a striking tendency to develop into new theologies and church organizations. There is, therefore, no single Protestant theology, Protestant church organization, or Protestant ritual. The movement is less a religion than a patchwork of religions, a diverse array of churches united by a common history and a few core beliefs. New churches are constantly forming, and old ones are constantly dissolving or reformulating themselves. Any understanding of Protestantism's strengths and weaknesses must incorporate this diversity as a basic element of the faith.

The scale of that diversity is staggering. Protestantism includes over 17,000 separate denominations worldwide, each with a distinct history and ideological stance. They include both massive institutional state churches and tiny separatist congregations; some with stately formal ceremonies and others with ecstatic trance and faith healing; many with deeply ingrained traditions and many with recent and spontaneously evolving structures; some steeped in European culture and others far removed from it. We cannot hope to encompass this range of difference here. To get a sense of it, however, let us consider a few subjects on which Protestants have differed, to get a taste of the forms and reasons of Protestant diversity.

RELATION TO THE TEMPORAL WORLD

One issue that has divided Protestants concerns the relationship of believers to the temporal world. Most of the movement's theology, of course, focuses on the next world and how to enter it. Protestant churches try to guide their followers to heavenly salvation, ensuring them an eternal life of bliss after leaving this existence. For the time being, however, their members live in this world, a place filled with imperfection, sin, venality, and need. They need the guidance of their churches to tell them how to do this, how to balance the demands of the faith with the demands of the society around them. This fact requires Protestantism to take some position on the relationship of its churches to the temporal world. How should Protestants orient themselves to the society around them? To what extent should the requirements of daily living influence the conduct of believers? To what extent is an accommodation with the larger world necessary or even possible? Protestant groups have found a number of ways to answer such questions.

One response has advocated an active engagement with the world. In this view, worldly activities offer a number of opportunities for active Christians; by trying to change the societies they live in, Christians can emulate Jesus's life, they can attract more converts, and they can produce a world more pleasing to God. Politically powerful Protestants have often used the resources of the state to this end. During the Puritan ascendancy in seventeenth century England, for example, the Cromwell government tried to use social and moral reforms to transform England into a godly commonwealth. Elsewhere in Europe, Pietist-dominated states have at times required church attendance, forbidden various sinful amusements, and required Jews and other nonbelievers to meet with Protestant proselytizers. In some cases, like sixteenth-century Geneva and seventeenth-century Massachusetts, Protestant theocracies have attempted to forcibly impose strict standards of morality on all citizens. Such regimes have proved difficult to maintain, however, and opponents have argued that they conflict with the freedom of choice implicit in Luther's theory of conversion. More commonly, therefore, Protestants have focused their political activities on the abolition of practices they find offensive to religious principles. In the United States, for example, Protestants have participated actively on both sides of the debates over slavery, prohibition, homosexual rights, and abortion.

At the other extreme, some Protestant groups have rejected any engagement with worldly society, arguing that the world's corruption makes it a pointless danger for believing Christians. Instead, they have said, Christians should make societies of their own, removed from the larger culture, where they can live exclusively by their interpretation of divine law. The Amish of the United States and Canada, for example, have deliberately severed as many connections as possible between themselves and the larger society. Descendants of a Swiss Anabaptist sect, the Amish have rejected technologies and economic benefits that might tie them to their neighbors. They do not accept Social Security or Medicare, for example, nor do they send their children to non-Amish schools. They refuse to incorporate electricity, natural gas lines, telephones, mass media, automobiles, birth control, and other modern technologies into their culture; when they do adopt new technology, as some have recently with kerosene refrigerators, they do so with extreme caution. Within the group, members who stray too far from the correct path may be "shunned," cut off permanently from all social contact with their family and friends. In these ways the Amish maintain a wall of separation between themselves and the sinful world, protecting God's faithful from the distraction and temptation of the larger society. Other Baptist and Anabaptist sects, known by such names as Mennonites, Hutterites, and German Baptists, have taken similar approaches to separating themselves from the world. Similar intentions, though less rigidly implemented, have often characterized Protestant revival movements outside the Anabaptist wing.

Between these extremes, many Protestant groups have found a middle ground—engagement with the world in the limited form of charity. Charity allows churches to take an active interest in the world around them, without risking the dangers and divisions implicit in explicitly political activity. It aids the process of proselytization, by exposing its recipients to the beneficent face of the churches; at the same time, it provides a form of active participation for members that tends to heighten belief and church solidarity. It also emulates the activities of Jesus, who exalted the poor and drew much of his following from their ranks. For many Protestant churches, charity and social welfare activities represent the most important group functions outside of the worship service.

GOVERNANCE

Churches are not only sites of worship; they are also social institutions, which face the problems of organization, finance, and politics that characterize any collective enterprise. How should these be solved? Who should make decisions about which priest to hire, where to build churches, and when to borrow money? Protestants have taken several approaches to such issues of governance, and their choices have often played important roles in their history.

Protestantism developed out of Catholicism, and many Protestant churches continue to use a form of the Catholic *episcopal* system of governance. This system assigns individual congregations to larger regional groups, known as dioceses, each of which is governed by a bishop. The dioceses, in turn, belong to larger archdioceses, governed by archbishops, which are in turn governed by a senior archbishop or governing council. This system found particular favor in Northern Europe after the Reformation, when a number of countries incorporated the Church into their state structure. By adopting the episcopal structure, the monarch could exert control over the church merely by replacing the bishops with his own appointees. These churches and their descendants continue to use this system, although the selection of bishops now tends to be much more democratic. Episcopally governed churches include the Anglican Church, the Danish and Norwegian Lutheran Churches, the Lutheran and Episcopal churches in the United States, and the Methodist Church.

This system came under attack early on, however, particularly by John Calvin and the Reform wing of Protestantism. Calvin argued that the episcopal system lent itself to abuse by placing too much power in the hands of individual bishops. He favored a system that would allow individual members a greater say in church affairs, and he therefore developed an elaborate representational system of governance. This system, known as *presbyterian*, calls for each congregation to elect a board of elders to run local affairs. On a regional level, each congregation sends a small number of its elders to sit on a regional board, or presbytery; this board oversees the actions of individual congregations and resolves disputes between them. Presbyteries are gathered in turn into synods, and synods into a general assembly, each composed of representatives from the lower regional bodies. Through this ascending series of councils, presbyterian government allows democratic participation while maintaining systematic control of the church. The Reform branch of Protestantism, including the Presbyterian and Methodist churches, continues to use Calvin's system today.

A *congregationalist* approach takes Calvin's democratic reforms even further, by limiting or eliminating the authority of regional bodies to control local churches. The essence of Protestant worship, it argues, lies in the activities of individual groups of believers. Insofar as such groups follow their own consciences, no bishop or synod has a legitimate authority to stop them. Denominational councils have their uses, primarily in promoting interchurch communication and furnishing religious instruction, but they should have little or no coercive power over their member churches. Congregationalism has found its strongest support among groups with histories of repression or persecution, like the Anabaptists, the Baptists, and the English Congregationalists. Familiar with the abuses of large power structures, such groups have limited the ability of distant leaders to impose their will on local communities.

These different governance structures imply very different social, political, and theological dynamics within churches. Congregational churches, for example, have more freedom for both organizational and doctrinal innovation than episcopal or presbyterian churches; they also, however, have more difficulty maintaining their unity and political integrity. Disputes tend to produce schisms very quickly, since it is often easier to form a new church than to resolve disagreements within an existing one. The Baptist movement in the United States, for example, has resisted over a century of efforts to bring its members into a single denominational fold. Episcopal organization has proved far more effective in maintaining church unity, but it has imposed a price of its own. With their central control and emphasis on doctrinal unity, episcopal churches have tended to lose touch with individual members, and many have seen steady declines in membership and participation. In Scandinavia, for example, where episcopally organized Lutheran churches have established a near monopoly on religious activity, only a small fraction of the population participates actively in church affairs. Within Protestantism, organization of church polities has had powerful effects on doctrine and history.

BIBLICAL LITERALISM

As noted earlier, Protestantism places an enormous weight on its holy scriptures. The books of the New Testament, especially, are believed to contain firsthand accounts of the teachings of Jesus and his closest associates. The Old Testament, though less central to Protestant teaching, still contains the authoritative history of God and his relationship to his followers. Protestantism regards these scriptures as the key to the divine will, one that overrides such temporal sources of authority as government and tradition. How to use that key, however, raises some difficult questions. Many parts of the scriptures, for example, describe events that seem impossible on their face—Moses parting the Red Sea, or Jesus turning water into wine. Should Protestants understand such events as having actually happened, or should they see them as symbolic expressions of more abstract ideas? The scriptures also contain some disagreements— Genesis reports two different numbers of animals in the ark, for example, and the events of the creation are recounted in two different orders. How should Protestants explain such apparent contradictions, and what do they tell us about the texts themselves? Furthermore, the Bible includes rules and practices that often seem discordant with contemporary society, such as dietary prohibitions, polygamy, and speaking in tongues. To what extent are Christians obliged to follow these Biblical models? As with other questions, the answers to these are plentiful and often divisive.

The oldest and most established Protestant denominations have tended to take a liberal view of scripture, arguing that the complexity of the Biblical texts makes a literal interpretation impossible. They have subjected the Bible to a limited degree of historical criticism, and they have de-emphasized aspects that conflict sharply with current social practice. This trend has perhaps gone farthest in Unitarianism, which denies the Trinity of God, raises serious doubts about the divinity of Jesus, and values social action on a par with spiritual growth. In part, these positions reflect the older denominations' embeddedness in the larger social system. With deep roots in their communities, including large congregations and sometimes government ties, such churches need the flexibility to adapt scripture to local needs. This approach also reflects the older groups' reliance on seminary education for their leaders. Priesthood in the Episcopal church, for example, requires years of advanced study, including extensive education on the development and interpretation of the scriptures. This sort of education highlights the complexities and ambiguities of the Biblical texts; the more a denomination educates its ministers, therefore, the less literal its treatment of the scriptures tends to be.

Newer and less established Protestant groups, by contrast, such as the Pentecostal denominations, non-Western denominations, and some Baptists, tend to rely much more on lay clergy. They exalt the vigor of the plain believer "called" to the ministry over the detached intellectualism of a professional priesthood. While some have seminaries, the majority of their preachers have relatively little theological education. Such churches tend to advance more literal interpretations of scripture than the older groups. Many hold to the position of "biblical inerrancy," arguing that apparent mistakes or contradictions in the Bible actually represent only misinterpretations on the part of its readers. They adhere strongly, for example, to Biblical stories of the creation, and they actively dispute geological and evolutionary theories that conflict with it. The rigidity of these positions has occasionally led to conflicts with the larger society, particularly on issues surrounding public education, gender roles, and family policy. In the United States, Protestant fundamentalists have challenged the teaching of evolution in the public schools; instead, they have proposed a "creation science" that reconciles geological observations with Biblical teachings. They have also participated actively in debates over school prayer, abortion, and homosexual rights. The parallels between their positions and those of political conservatives has made them politically visible, and fundamentalists have become an influential part of the political process throughout the Western world.

A related question concerns the stability of scripture. Most Protestants accept the Bible as essentially complete; while they differ on how to interpret it, they agree on the basic canon of texts. Calvin rejected magic in part because it implied a different source of divine inspiration than the established scriptures. At least one group, however, has added another book to the canon: the Church of Jesus Christ of the Latter Day Saints, known generally as the Mormons. Mormonism's founder, Joseph Smith, claimed in the 1830s to have received a divine revelation, which culminated in his discovery of a new scripture he called the Book of Mormon. Based on this text, Smith's followers built a Mormon colony in the deserts of Utah in 1846, and their church has become one of the fastest-growing Christian movements of the twentieth century. Mormonism has flourished on Protestant soil, and its theology and spirit draw heavily on a Protestant tradition. Even so, its use of a different version of the scriptures conflicts deeply with most Protestant attitudes toward the Bible, and many groups dispute Mormonism's place in the Protestant fold.

THE SUPERNATURAL

On one level, all Protestants believe in the supernatural; the God who is central to the faith exists above and outside the visible natural world, and he is capable of descending into it as he pleases. The miracles of Jesus, including his resurrection, attest to the supernatural powers of the divine. But to what extent does this power manifest itself in contemporary life? Does God intervene in human affairs through miracles and signs? Does he confer on his followers any supernatural abilities? Is it possible for human beings to call forth and use any of the supernatural power implicit in the Protestant conception of the deity? These questions have animated a considerable debate since the early days of Protestantism, and they underlie some basic divisions in the faith today.

The oldest branches of Protestantism have generally rejected supernatural intervention, particularly the Reform-influenced groups. Early on, for example, Luther and his followers rejected the magical significance of church sacraments. Such events as baptism and the mass did not involve any physical transformation of reality, they said, but rather a symbolic expression of the participants' spiritual state. Likewise, Puritans aggressively denounced practices like faith healing and popular magic in seventeenth-century England. God, they said, has created the physical world as part of his divine plan, and human beings are charged to live within it. To conduct magic, to pray for miracles, even to forecast future events imply that one can improve upon God's handiwork, and perhaps even control God's actions. Puritan clergy in early Massachusetts tried hard to eradicate such popular magic, though with limited success. In this sense, Protestantism can involve a radical worldliness, which reserves religious activity for the spiritual realm and denies it any physical effects. Such an approach has at times made it unusually compatible with studies in the natural sciences.

For some Protestants, on the other hand, divine intervention lies at the very core of everyday religious practice. Pentecostal churches and their relatives argue that the New Testament explicitly sanctions supernatural manifestations. Such manifestations are "gifts of the spirit," evidence for believer and nonbeliever alike of the power of God. They point to the book of Acts, which reports that Jesus's apostles spoke in tongues when touched by the Holy Spirit. They also note Mark 16:17–18, which states that followers of Jesus will receive certain powers as a sign of their salvation: They will "cast out demons; they will speak in new tongues; they will pick up serpents, and if they drink any deadly thing, it will not hurt them; they will lay hands on the sick, and they will recover." Holiness churches sometimes take this passage at face value; in some parts of the United States, notably in Appalachia, Holiness congregations handle poisonous snakes and drink poisons during the course of their services. More commonly, Pentecostal churches incorporate faith healing and speaking in tongues (also called *glossolalia*) into their ritual. For Pentecostalists, the value of religious services lies not so much in their symbolic expression, as in the opportunity they provide for members to come in contact with the Holy Spirit. A Sunday service may include a variety of supernatural manifestations: members entering trance and speaking in tongues; ministers and members uttering prophecies inspired by the Holy Spirit; ecstatic dancing, visions, and trance; the healing of sick members through common prayer. Such manifestations may occur outside church as well, and the supernatural forces may represent Satan as well as the Holy Spirit. The dramatic character of these events has attracted the ridicule of other Protestants, who have dubbed their practitioners "holy rollers." At the same time, however, they provide an intense experience for members, one which gives participants a deep experiential tie to their churches and their coreligionists.

It would be easy to see all these disagreements as a sign of Protestant weakness. After all, if the Protestants can't convince each other of the power of their beliefs, how can they expect to convince outsiders? And indeed, the variation in Protestant belief has led to schism and infighting throughout its history. At the same time, however, this variation also gives Protestantism its greatest strength. More than in most religious traditions, Protestants can mold their faith to express their own experiences. They can easily amend its principles and rituals to reflect ideas that fit in with local culture and history. As a result, Protestantism has spread around the world with astonishing speed, and it has provided a medium for widely different societies to express their ideas about people, communities, and the divine.

THE ANTHROPOLOGY OF PROTESTANTISM

Despite its size and cultural complexity, Protestantism has drawn little attention from anthropologists until quite recently. In large part, this neglect has resulted from anthropology's focus on non-Western cultures. As the dominant religion of the modern West—and the native religion of many anthropologists!—Protestantism long seemed an unlikely subject for anthropological study. In addition, studying Protestantism inevitably means studying its history, and for a long time anthropology lacked the conceptual tools to incorporate history. As a result, anthropologists have left Protestantism largely to sociologists and historians, focusing their energies instead on more apparently remote religions. Of the 56 articles in Lessa and Vogt's classic *Reader in Comparative Religion,* for example, not one touches on Protestantism.[1]

Over the past three decades, however, some anthropologists have begun to explore Protestantism in depth. Their interest has reflected a general concern throughout anthropology with studying modernity, with subjecting Western cultures to the same kinds of scrutiny that has been applied to the rest of the world. Questions of history, of diversity, and of change have become central to the discipline. In this context, Protestantism makes a particularly appropriate subject of study. Not only do diversity and change play central roles in Protestantism, but Protestant cultures often have the kinds of documentary records that make detailed historical analyses possible. Protestantism has emerged as an unusually rich source of data for contemporary anthropological concerns.

To conclude our examination of Protestantism, therefore, let us now turn to a few examples of anthropological studies of the religion. The case studies that follow are neither comprehensive nor necessarily representative of anthropological work on Protestantism; they do give a sense, however, of the breadth and the variety of approaches that anthropologists have taken to the subject.

PROTESTANTISM AND ECONOMIC BEHAVIOR

A common theme in the anthropology of religion concerns the interaction between economic and religious activities. To what extent do religious beliefs shape the way people value and exchange material goods? Conversely, to what extent do economic, material interests influence the sorts of religious beliefs and affiliations that people hold? Protestantism, with its broad spread over a range of Western and non-Western economies, offers a fertile field for studying these issues. Indeed, perhaps the best-known study of Protestantism and culture examined the religion's influence on the development of modern capitalism.

In *The Protestant Ethic and the Spirit of Capitalism,* first published in 1904–1905, Max Weber tries to explain the origins of the capitalist ethos.[2] Modern rational capitalism, he says, involves a distinct and in many ways peculiar view of wealth. Capitalists see wealth as an end in itself; they do not make money in order to satisfy needs, but simply to acquire more of it. At the same time, he says, classic rational capitalists decline to make much use of the money they accumulate. The ideal businessman, following the example of Benjamin Franklin, combines a ceaseless quest for riches with personal frugality, renouncing luxury as moral weakness. Where, Weber asks, do these attitudes come from? Of all the ways in which capitalism could have come to conceive the relationship between people and material goods, why did it choose this one?

Weber argues that this ethos developed out of Calvinist Protestantism, the religious system that dominated the Western European merchant classes in the "heroic days" of seventeenth- and eighteenth-century capitalism. Calvinism, he says, preaches a radical form of predestination. God is conceived as so powerful and so omniscient that the eternal fate of each human soul has already been decided. God has chosen to save a favored few, the "elect"; the majority of humankind is condemned to eternal death, and no intercession by priests, kin, or sacraments can save them. Weber argues that such a theology places a tremendous psychological burden on its adherents. It imposes on them a crippling anxiety about their fate, as well as a deep isolation from others around them. To change their fate is impossible—how can a mere human presume to alter the decrees of God? Yet the anxiety and loneliness implied by the creed demand some sort of action. The solution, says Weber, came in the form of worldly activity. Calvin taught that the form of the world was ordained by God; the maintenance of God's church and commandments was the duty even of the damned, and the elect were expected to show a unique zeal in moral worldly activity. This zeal could serve as a sign of election for worshipers. Since those God intended to save would naturally behave most morally, rigidly moral conduct could reassure believers that they were destined for grace. Moral conduct included not only the avoidance of sin, but also an active engagement in the occupation to which one had been called. For a merchant, it meant a single-minded devotion to the expansion of his capital—not in order to enjoy its fruits, but for the sake of fulfilling a calling which God had ordained. The result was a "worldly asceticism," which combined the unending pursuit of wealth with an almost monastic rejection of luxury and pleasure. This combination made for a singularly effective economic system, one which increasingly dominated world trade in the centuries that followed.

Weber's analysis was not intended to explain the rise of capitalism itself; as he acknowledges, not all early capitalists were Calvinists, nor were all Calvinists capitalists. Capitalism would likely have transformed the West whether Protestantism had developed or not. But the particular ethos that dominated it, and the way in which Western Europeans conceived it, drew heavily on Protestant models of faith and action. Weber's study shows the complexity of the interaction between religious, economic, social, and political structures, an interaction which characterizes the modern West as much as any other time or place in human history.

PROTESTANTISM AND SOCIAL ACTION

A broader way of looking at Weber's subject is to consider the effects of Protestantism not just on economic activity, but on social action generally. Protestantism relates the actions of human beings to their destiny after death; while good deeds cannot bring salvation, those who are saved should feel a special duty to behave morally. Their gratitude to God should incline them to do good works, and their status as God's people requires them to set an example for others. A number of anthropologists have explored how these obligations shape the social interaction of Protestants. To what extent do the requirements of faith produce actual changes in the way Protestants behave?

Carol Greenhouse looks at one aspect of social action, that of dispute resolution, in her study of Baptists in the Atlanta suburb of Hopewell, Georgia.[3] Hopewell is an affluent town, composed almost entirely of middle-class whites, with a population divided mainly between Baptists and Methodists. The Baptists belong to a single church, and they take participation in church activities very seriously. Many attend not only the weekly Sunday service, but also Bible study groups and church social activities. Church members study scripture daily from an early age, and biblical references crop up constantly in conversation. This intense involvement with the church gives the Baptist community a distinctive identity, and its members perceive a sharp boundary between themselves and the larger, sinful world. Joining the church, for example, requires an emotional experience of conversion, involving personal contact with the Holy Spirit; this conversion is consecrated by a full-immersion baptism under the eyes of the congregation. Conversion assures members of a place in heaven after death, and they relate this salvation to all aspects of life. Christians, they say, have a different way of being parents, of being workers, of being citizens—their relationship to Jesus lies at the heart of all their activity in the earthly realm.

One aspect of this activity is the way they deal with disputes. Like all other people in all societies, the Baptists of Hopewell sometimes find themselves at odds with others. Sometimes they may dislike the way family members are treating them; sometimes they may disapprove of the morality of others' actions. At times, they may be the victims of crimes or accidents. Yet Greenhouse observes that the Baptists almost never come into open conflict. Differences within the community almost never lead to arguments or fights, and legal action by community members is almost unheard of. Greenhouse could not find a single Baptist name in the courthouse records for the preceding decade. Members refused to sue motorists who had damaged their cars in accidents, and they praised a family which had refused to press charges after the kidnapping of the wife and daughter. In a notoriously litigious society like the United States, this approach to social action is striking. Where, Greenhouse asks, does it come from?

She finds the answer in the Baptists' ideas about person, God, and conflict. In keeping with their individualistic notion of salvation, she says, Hopewell Baptists define their social identities in terms of roles, not relationships. Being a wife, for example, consists in occupying a distinct social position within a defined family structure, rather than in holding a relationship to a particular husband. Being a good wife, then, is not a matter of relating well to the husband, but of living up to the qualities which a good wife ought to have. Just as a person can only save his or her own soul, a person can only be good by attending to his or her own role. That role, in turn, is determined by Jesus. God has a plan for each human being, one which will assure each person the greatest happiness in the long term—if not in this life, then in the next. The challenge for Christians is to trust in God's wisdom, to accept that troubles which appear overwhelming are in fact gifts from Jesus. After all, even the most dire problems of the present are trivial in the context of salvation and eternal life. The forces that motivate conflict, therefore, should be unimportant to true Christians. Believers should be indifferent to such selfish concerns as material wealth and status. Rather, they should attend to their own social roles and spread the gospel, trusting in the plan of life that Jesus has chosen for them, and leaving conflict to the doomed souls in the world outside.

How, then, do Hopewell Baptists deal with conflict when it arises? Conflicts with people outside the congregation, in most cases, are resolved simply by giving in. Members justify this approach through such scriptural sentiments as "turn the other cheek" and "vengeance belongs to God." Any injustices that result will be more than made up for in the life to come, when the outsiders will go to hell and the insiders to heaven. Within the congregation, members deal with conflict in large part by denying it. They assert that God's plan takes the best interests of all Christians into account; if two members find themselves at odds, it is only because they do not fully see the divine plan which gives both exactly what they need. The solution is not to impose a settlement, but for both members to pray for the wisdom to see God's purposes, trusting God to work matters out. In matters that call for criticism, the community has developed a series of techniques for expressing opinions without confrontation. If a member disapproves of another's behavior, for example, she may tell a story to the offender that expresses her disapproval. The story, however, will refer to the problem only indirectly; she will tell of a person she once heard of, in a similar situation, who came to a bad end with similar behavior. She will phrase it, moreover, not as a criticism but as gossip, and she will slip it naturally into conversation without drawing attention to it. People may also disagree through joking, quoting Bible verses at one another that support their positions; since both are drawing on the infallible scripture, neither can actually be wrong. Such mechanisms allow members to express differing opinions without compromising the individual sovereignty that lies at the heart of the faith. The result is a self-reinforcing social dynamic: The community's beliefs rule out conflict, and the process of avoiding conflict reinforces the community's beliefs.

This form of Protestantism, taken all together, does more than simply provide a mechanism for resolving disputes between members. By establishing particular understandings of person, salvation, and community, it reconceives relationships in such a way that true conflict between members becomes virtually impossible. Disagreements stem not from real conflicts of interest, but from the limited human knowledge of the divine plan. Hardships are not true impositions, but gifts from God presented in hidden forms. As a result, the basic assumptions and motivations which lie behind human social action are different for the Baptists of Hopewell than for their neighbors. This accounts for the community's striking distinctiveness in its legal and other conflict-related actions. The different varieties of Protestantism, in other words, produce different ways of thinking about and behaving in the social world.

PROTESTANTISM'S ENCOUNTER WITH THE OTHER

Religions give their believers a system for understanding themselves; in doing so, they also provide a framework for understanding others. People evaluate strangers according to the categories and types of explanation which their religious systems supply for them. This function of religion has proved particularly important within Protestantism, which has had a high degree of contact with other groups throughout its history. In large part, this contact has taken place through colonization. Beginning in the seventeenth century, the Northern European countries which embraced Protestantism became some of the most aggressive and successful colonizing nations in human history. Britain created a Protestant empire that encircled the globe; the Netherlands, Germany, and some Scandinavian countries also built extensive colonial dominions. As they did so, they came into contact with radically different cultures, whose customs and appearance contrasted profoundly their own. In most cases, they made sense of these customs in the terms which their Protestant backgrounds provided. They attributed seemingly bizarre native customs to the same forces which explained deviance among themselves—such forces as sin, Satan, ignorance, and evil. The cultural conflicts and misunderstandings that resulted have been the subject of a number of anthropological studies.

William Simmons, for example, has examined the ways in which Puritan colonists in early New England perceived the Indians they encountered there.[4] The Puritans of the Massachusetts Bay Colony adhered to a stringent Reform tradition, based on the teachings of John Calvin; the Colony was intended in large part to provide an example for the world of an ideal holy society. One key point in Calvin's theology, as mentioned earlier, concerned the limited role of the supernatural in human life. God had set up the world for humanity, and he had chosen a certain number of "saints" for redemption, but beyond that he seldom manifested his powers on earth. God did not give supernatural help to individuals, according to Calvin, and he certainly did not endow any humans with supernatural powers. Insofar as magic intruded into the physical world, therefore, it did so through Satan. The devil would indeed help individuals, and he would give them occult powers, as long as they gave him control of their souls. As a result, only actual witches, who had consciously made a compact with the devil, were capable of practicing magic. This made witches profoundly evil beings, who had vast powers and who were sometimes possessed by devilish spirits. This understanding of the supernatural led Puritan ministers to preach vividly against magic, and to attempt to eradicate all folk magical practices among their followers. In the Massachusetts Bay Colony, magical practitioners were sometimes tried and executed as witches.

For their Indian neighbors, by contrast, supernatural spirits and forces were a basic part of everyday experience. Native beliefs involved a broad variety of spiritual beings, each of which could intrude in various ways on human life. The spirits of the dead, for example, known as Hobbamock, could reappear in the forms of humans or animals; at times they would take possession of a *powwow*, or shaman, giving him such powers as the ability to heal, the ability to cast spells, the ability to see the future, or the ability to change the weather. Native cosmology included a number of gods, or *manitos*, including a creator, spirits of the various animal and plant species, spirits of the compass points, and spirits of the heavenly bodies. *Manitos* often appeared and communicated to people in dreams. These manifestations played an important part in both ritual and practical matters, including warfare. During the conflict with the colonists known as King Philip's War, leaders consulted shamanic prophecies when determining military strategy.

What were the colonists to make of such practices? From a Calvinist standpoint, occult powers could only originate with Satan, and spirits and visions could only represent agents of the devil. If the powwows became possessed by spirits, the colonists could only explain them as witches; if the society revered and valued the powwows, then the society must be in thrall to Satan. Puritans could differ in the reasons they gave for this situation. Some attributed it to ignorance and tried to counter it by encouraging conversion to Christianity. Others regarded the Indians as beyond salvation, inherently diabolical beings who could only be exterminated. In either case, however, the colonists equated the Indians with witches, the most supremely evil and frighteningly dangerous figures in the Protestant imagination. This conception justified the most extreme measures in combating the Indians, including the massacre of 400 Pequots at Mystic in 1637. Long-term co-existence was clearly impossible, and by 1676 the Puritans had destroyed all of the autonomous Indian groups in southern New England. Looking at the Other through the categories of their religious system, the colonists saw this outcome as both pious and unavoidable.

This scenario has played itself out in a variety of forms all over the world, as Protestants have interpreted their encounters with other cultures in the terms with which they have understood themselves. Their own hostility to magic and the supernatural has made it difficult for Protestants to accept practices that lie at the heart of many other religious systems. In addition, the stark dualism of the Reform vision, which divides the world rigidly into saints and sinners, saved and damned, has often permitted a demonization of the Other. Any understanding of the patterns and outcomes of Northern European colonialism must include the religious vision that the colonists have brought with them.

PROTESTANTISM AND ANTHROPOLOGICAL THEORY

Anthropologists study Protestantism not only to find out about Protestants themselves, but also to shed light on larger issues in anthropological theory. In recent years, for example, many anthropologists have reconsidered some of the discipline's old assumptions about the uniformity and stability of human culture. Early anthropologists tended to assume that the cultures they studied were almost immune to history; they depicted "primitive" cultures as simple and unchanging, untouched by the sorts of conflicts and dynamics that characterize modern societies. Later studies, however, have decisively rejected this idea, demonstrating that change, disagreement, and disputes over power occur in virtually every human group. If this is the case, however, anthropologists need new ways of understanding how human groups function. If people don't simply follow preexisting patterns, as we once thought they did, how do cultures retain any kind of coherence? How does a cohesive social system evolve out of the whirlwind of conflicting interests, motives, and powers that characterize human interaction? Protestantism offers an ideal context for exploring these sorts of questions. Dissent has been central to Protestantism since its beginnings; perhaps more than any other religious tradition, Protestantism has celebrated the individual's ability to dispute and diverge from the dominant opinions of his or her environment. Each believer has both the right and the duty to formulate an individual connection to the principles of the faith. This individualism poses problems for the creation of stable church communities. The problems echo those of human culture generally, and the way that Protestants have solved them can shed light on the way that complete cultures—especially in the modern world—emerge and endure.

Peter Stromberg, for example, has used an analysis of an independent church in Sweden to reconsider the notion of "culture as consensus."[5] When anthropologists think of culture, he says, they tend to give it a double role. On the one hand, culture is a body of patterns that anthropologists describe, based on observing the behavior of their subjects. On the other hand, it is a force that makes people within a culture behave in patterned ways. Stromberg argues that this double usage is illogical, that culture cannot act as both cause and effect of human behavior. Moreover, he says, anthropologists tend to be vague about the actual mechanisms by which culture, through its symbols, affects behavior. Even though a culture may provide a common body of symbols, individuals within the group invariably have different ways of understanding and experiencing those symbols. It would be wrong, then, to suggest that the symbols automatically force people to act and think in particular ways. But then why is culture shared? What makes people unite around a common culture, if they are not mechanically forced to do so? Stromberg suggests that anthropology needs to find a way of explaining more precisely how human behavior and shared symbolic systems relate to one another.

To do so, he focuses on what he calls "commitment systems"—systems like religions or ideologies, in which the beliefs of members are strongly and consciously held. Such systems, he argues, appeal to their members in an almost physical way; members do not merely think about the group's symbols, they feel and experience them emotionally. One such system forms the focus of his study: the Immanuel Church in Stockholm, a large and active Lutheran congregation in the capital of one of the world's most prosperous nations. The Immanuel Church represents a strain of Protestantism known as pietism, a movement which emphasizes the emotional dimension of Christian belief. A key part of members' attachment to the church is the experience of "grace." Members encounter grace when some aspect of their religion becomes intensely meaningful, when it seems suddenly to expand their understanding of themselves and the world around them. They experience it as a direct contact with God, whose touch can transcend the narrowness of vision and self-absorption that ordinarily limits human consciousness. At such times, says Stromberg, members become profoundly committed to the group's symbols, not because of what the symbols mean semantically, but because of the effect they produce physically.

Interestingly, these effects differ sharply from one member to another. For one of Stromberg's informants, grace amounted to a surrender of control of his life to God. When this man encountered difficulties, he would meditate intensively on the words of scripture. Some of those words would jump out at him, and he would realize that God was telling him what to do. At such times, the words held a powerful meaningfulness that transcended his conscious understanding. Another member felt grace on those rare occasions when she connected well socially with other people; when she felt warmth and closeness with another person, she felt intensely the presence of God. A third member felt God's presence when she spoke in tongues, a fourth when he helped other people. Stromberg's study explores how these experiences related to the backgrounds of the particular individuals involved. For each of them, he concludes, grace occurs when the symbols of the community echo the emotional and cognitive dispositions of the individual, when a person's own unique experience finds a precise expression in a concept or figure from the collective culture. At such times the person does not merely make sense of the symbol, but also forms a relationship to it—the symbol becomes something almost human, which can be attached to and which can be used to give shape to the believer's self. The power of the symbol lies in its ability to connect with each member's separate personality.

In that case, says Stromberg, people need not think alike to share a common culture. The power of commitment systems lies not in their semantic meanings, but in their capacity to connect with believers' experiences. What matters is not whether all members interpret symbols the same way, but whether all members can find meaning in their own interpretations of the symbols. Stromberg contends that this approach provides an alternative to the "culture as consensus" model, one which can explain group unity without assuming group uniformity. This approach might prove especially useful in studying modern societies, where diversity, change, and individualism are central parts of the social world. The power of other symbolic systems in modern society—including popular ones like literature and theater—may stem from the same sources as that of grace in Immanuel Church, in their ability to provide a common frame of reference for interpreting individual experience. Studying the individualist ethic of Protestantism, in other words, may help us understand the individualism of our society as a whole.

PROTESTANTISM AND POWER

Another focus of anthropological work on Protestantism is its relation to power, to structures of authority and dominance in the social world. In part, this is because Protestantism has often been associated with the powerful. State Protestant churches, for example, have often supported the political establishment in Europe, while in the United States, positions of political and economic leadership were reserved mainly for Protestants until quite recently. At the same time, however, Protestantism has a long association with the poor and weak as well. The Anabaptist movement emerged among some of Europe's poorest populations, and groups like the Baptists, the Pentecostals, and the Holiness churches have thrived among the poor of America. The flexibility of Protestantism in this regard came vividly to light during the American debate over slavery, when all sides in the conflict—Southern slavery advocates, Northern abolitionists, and even the slaves themselves—expressed their views through the language of Protestant theology. The role of Protestantism in power relations, therefore, both as a force for reinforcing power and as a means of contesting it, has interested many anthropologists.

Jean Comaroff offers a particularly complex analysis in her discussion of Protestantism among the Tshidi of South Africa.[6] The Tshidi, a branch of the Tswana culture of southern Africa, first encountered Protestantism through Methodist missionaries in the beginning of the nineteenth century. At the time, the Tshidi were an autonomous political group, with a complex social and religious life built around kin-based clans and social networks. The Tshidi leaders initially found the Methodists quite valuable; the missionaries wanted to establish a base in the area, and they helped them negotiate with Dutch, British, and Zulu groups that were threatening to infringe Tshidi territory. Methodist religion at first had little appeal for the chiefs, and conversion occurred mainly around the fringes of Tshidi society. Over time, however, due to both external pressures from the Boers and British and internal political dynamics among the Tshidi, leaders gradually embraced Methodism, and by the end of the century it had become the official religion of the group. The status of Protestantism was reinforced as the Tshidi became subjugated by the British state in the twentieth century and turned from independent farmers and herders into poverty-stricken wage laborers.

Comaroff analyzes the ways in which traditional Tswana religion and Methodism expressed and reinforced power relationships within the society. Indigenous initiation rituals, for example, highlighted some of the contradictions that existed within the traditional order. The competition between the patrilineally based political groups and the matrilineally based social networks was underlined in the rituals that accompanied the transition to adulthood. In addition to reinforcing the social structure, therefore, Tswana ritual provided a framework for criticizing its weaknesses. Likewise, Methodism, a denomination that first arose among industrial laborers in England, incorporated potent ideas about power and resistance in a capitalist system. On the one hand, it glorified the working classes by proclaiming the importance of individual participation and the equality of all work. God, it said, spoke not only to the wealthy and well educated, but also to the common man, and the emotional experience of Christ that it promoted placed the poor in a position of unusual power within the religion. As the Tshidi became increasingly proletarianized under South African rule, Methodism expressed their distress, proclaiming the importance of people whom the capitalist system abused and ignored. At the same time, however, the Protestant separation between spirit and flesh, between church and state, made it difficult to actually challenge the institutions of power. Methodism sought justice in the next life, not this one, and it told its members to respect and submit to the worldly authorities which were oppressing them. Likewise, the organization of the church gave power to the affluent and literate and respected the authority of the British leaders of the church. While Methodism in some ways challenged the system, then, it also reinforced it, giving little ideological justification for challenges to the apartheid regime.

In the first decades of the twentieth century, however, and especially after World War II, a second Protestant movement became a major competitor to Methodism among the Tshidi. This movement was known as Zionism, and it derived from an American utopian sect led by John Alexander Dowie. In the late 1800s, Dowie established a church in Chicago called the Christian Catholic Apostolic Church in Zion; centered around faith healing and energetic worship, the church gained a large following among the city's poor. The church promised to heal not only its members' bodies, but also their social world, by building a new city full of piety, social order, and material plenty. In 1904 evangelists from the movement went to South Africa, where they began to incorporate Pentecostal elements into their preaching. The movement spread rapidly, accumulating new elements as it went, and it built an impressive base among the Tshidi. While Zionist churches held some things in common—glossolalia, for example, as well as healing, purification ceremonies, and strict behavioral rules—they tended to split into new groups very quickly, often picking up some elements of the local culture and indigenous religious system. By the late 1960s, when Comaroff arrived, the Tshidi city of Mafeking had more than 30 Zionist churches. Almost all of their followers were poor and illiterate, the lowest classes in an economically devastated region.

Why did these poor Tshidi embrace the Zionist movement? Comaroff says that they did so in part to express their dissatisfaction with society. The South African state ruthlessly suppressed most forms of political expression; those who dared to speak out against its injustices risked imprisonment, torture, and murder. Religion, however, was largely unsupervised, and it offered a forum for symbolic statements of dissent. Comaroff examines rituals in two of these churches, and she finds messages of resistance throughout them. The stress on faith healing, for example, denies the split between mind and body so central to Methodism. Like the indigenous Tswana rituals, Zionist healing implies that the spiritual world is inseparable from the physical one, and thus that the power that the poor receive from their religion can translate into power on earth. Consequently, the ability of these poor illiterates to lead services, purify water, and make direct contact with the Holy Spirit suggests that they can and should have power in the world at large. One church directly calls for the liberation of its people, and it has even built its own independent town. The language and ritual of the Zionist movement, Comaroff argues, is a form of symbolic resistance to the domination of a racist capitalist social order.

Comaroff's analysis shows the subtlety through which systems of resistance operate. One can oppose oppression not only by shouting for its overthrow, but also by challenging and reversing the language of symbols through which it acts. She also demonstrates the tremendous power of Protestantism within political processes. With the vast range of variation available to them, Protestants can shape their churches to represent political positions as well as theological ones, and they can cast potentially explosive political disputes in the protected language of religious devotion. The variation in Protestantism, so central to its history, places it at the center of political discourse wherever it travels.

PROTESTANTISM AND GENDER ROLES

Another area of interest within studies of Protestantism focuses on gender. In recent decades, anthropologists have devoted a great deal of research to understanding gender in different societies. How do cultures create, maintain, and sometimes change their understandings of what men and women should be and do? This question has particular importance for the anthropology of religion, since most religions promote a distinct vision of male and female roles. As they do on so many issues, Protestant groups vary considerably in their understandings of masculinity and femininity. Some scholars have regarded Protestantism as a force for gender inequality, since it often reinforces European social structures that define men's and women's roles hierarchically. At the same time, however, Protestant movements have often provided positions of leadership for women unavailable to them elsewhere in society, and some churches have campaigned actively for women's rights. The construction of gender in individual Protestant movements reflects both the ideologies of the movements and the particular cultural settings in which they exist.

Elizabeth Brusco has explored the relationship between Protestantism and gender in Latin America, an area which has seen explosive Protestant growth over the past half century. The region today has about 45 million Protestants, roughly 10 percent of the total population. While these Protestants represent a range of denominations, Pentecostalism holds a dominant position; over half of the Protestants in some Latin American countries are Pentecostalists, and Pentecostalism is growing at a startling rate. Many of the Pentecostal churches have roots in North American or European missionary work, but an increasing number have distanced themselves from groups outside Latin America. This surge of Pentecostalism in a region dominated by Catholicism has surprised many observers, including anthropologists.

How will this Pentecostal awakening affect traditional gender roles? Many observers have assumed that it will reinforce them; after all, Pentecostalists and other evangelicals in the United States have identified themselves heavily with traditional gender and family structures. They have advocated a paternalistic family structure, in which wives defer to the authority of their husbands in both spiritual and temporal matters. Latin American Pentecostals, many of whose churches have roots in North America, have often echoed such themes of family and patriarchy. But as Brusco argues, such similarities have different implications in the distinctive culture of Latin America. Traditional attitudes toward male and female behavior take very different forms from those in the United States; accordingly, what can seem conservative and male-centered in the north can, in Latin America, prove innovative and even revolutionary.

Brusco's own study examines the effects of religious involvement on Pentecostal families in Colombia.[7] Gender relationships in communities she studied, one of them rural and one urban, followed a pattern common in Latin American Pentecostalism; while men held most of the formal authority positions, women made up a substantial majority of the members. Women also held a number of less visible leadership positions, some of which had a practical importance far greater than many of the men's positions. Beyond issues of official power, the churches also placed constraints on male behavior that provided concrete benefits to women. Pentecostal prohibitions against drinking and gambling, for example, put a stop to a male activity that drained away up to 40 percent of many families' income. The Pentecostal opposition to infidelity, likewise, kept husbands from spending family resources to maintain mistresses. Taken together, the Pentecostal moral codes restricted male behavior in ways that substantially improved women's standards of living. It also gave them the resources to educate their children, giving their families long-term prospects for social mobility.

On a deeper level, moreover, Pentecostalism restructured male ideals in a way that had profound consequences for male-female relationships. Gender roles in Colombia, as in much of Latin America, are largely defined in terms of machismo, an ethic that calls for sharp differences in male and female behavior. Machismo values aggression, virility, and power in men while stressing submission and chastity for women. The Pentecostal value system, Brusco argues, requires something very different; it condemns violence, pride and self-indulgence, and it does so for both men and women. When men experience conversion, they must renounce the individualism implicit in machismo. They redefine the boundaries of their lives, emphasizing the domestic and church spheres over their traditional place in the public arena.

As a result, men and women in Pentecostal families share a common, collectivist value system almost antithetical to that of machismo. This change tends to improve women's political position—not because it puts women formally in charge, but because it redefines male interests in a way that echoes and supports female interests.

Brusco's analysis suggests a powerful role for religion in structuring gender relationships. Religion can bring about changes in private behavior that few other social forces can. Feminist political movements, for example, have found the domestic realm a difficult place to achieve change; while women in the United States have gained increasing access to prestigious jobs and political positions, for example, they have had little success in convincing men to take over domestic tasks. As a result, feminist successes in the public realm have often failed to produce tangible benefits for most women. Pentecostalism is certainly not feminism, and its effects vary from culture to culture. But in societies of tremendous male dominance like Colombia's, where public politics has seldom promoted women's interests, the reformation of gender roles implicit in Pentecostalism may ultimately have a more profound effect on gender equality than deliberate political action.

PROTESTANTISM AND SECULARIZATION

Over its four and a half centuries of existence, Protestantism has experienced enormous growth, changing from a small collection of Catholic dissidents to a religious tradition with millions of followers around the globe. In the past century, however, it has experienced a less positive trend—a growing disenchantment and disinterest among some of its core constituencies. Throughout Scandinavia, for example, where the overwhelming majority of the population belongs to Lutheran churches, only a tiny minority ever attends weekly services. Few people profess an active faith in God, and concepts like heaven and hell hold little meaning for most Lutherans. In the United States, mainline Protestant denominations like the Congregationalists, the Presbyterians, and the Methodists have reported steadily falling memberships for decades. Other Protestant strongholds in Western Europe and America have seen similar patterns. Western Protestantism seems to many observers to be undergoing a decline, one produced not by competition from other religions but by a general disenchantment with religion itself. This phenomenon is not unique to Protestantism, but it has occurred most noticeably in Protestant areas. This process of religious decline is often referred to as secularization, and it has attracted considerable attention from the social sciences.

Within sociology and anthropology, secularization has often been portrayed as an inevitable consequence of modernity. The modern world contains a number of elements that many theorists argue must undermine religion. The development of science, for example, replaces the supernatural theories of religion with logical, provable, naturalistic explanations of the world. The spread of capitalism also attacks religion, intruding rational bureaucracy and marketing into areas once dominated by religious belief. Moreover, the increasing fragmentation of modern society makes it difficult to retain the communal experiences that lie at the heart of religion. As a result, say many authors, the inevitable spread of modernity implies the inevitable extinction of religion. The very forces that Protestantism helped create—capitalism and science—will eventually destroy it. While one can find occasional resurgences of religion, some of which may last for decades, in the long run religion must fade and die.

My own research among Danish Protestants sought to test this theory, particularly the opposition it implies between religion and science.[8] Is science in fact incompatible with religion? When religious groups decline in Western society, do they do so because they have lost a competition with scientific explanations of the world? To find out, I studied three religious groups on a rural island in Denmark, one of the most self-consciously modern societies in the world. These three groups all developed from a pietist awakening that swept through Denmark in the nineteenth century. They included the Mors Island Free Congregation, an independent Lutheran church; the Inner Mission Society, a revival movement that operates through mission houses and prayer groups; and the Apostolic Church, a Pentecostal group with a small church in the island's market town. Each of these movements has deep roots in the local community, and each has a distinctive theological outlook. The Free Congregation links Christianity to Danish folk culture; it is only by exploring one's history and traditions, they say, that one can reach the level of self-awareness necessary for true Christian conversion. The Inner Mission, by contrast, rejects worldly culture as a realm of sin and temptation. It imposes strict moral rules on its members, who should maintain close communities of believers and keep their attention focused on the world to come. The Apostolic Church centers its approach on direct contact with the Holy Spirit. Through ecstatic religious worship, manifest in glossolalia and faith healing, individuals can feel God's presence and be assured of salvation. My research focused on the rise and development of these three groups, particularly as it touched on their interaction with modernity.

Some of the patterns that I found did fit with secularization theory. The use of supernatural explanations for events, for example, had virtually disappeared, and relatively few of the people I interviewed stated a firm belief in God. Other patterns, however, failed to follow the model. The Free Congregation had not declined in any observable way; in terms of membership, participation, and finances, it showed all the symptoms of a thriving church community. The Apostolic Church had neither prospered nor declined. It remained at the close of the century as it had been at the beginning, a small nonconformist group on the fringes of island society. The only group to have declined was the Inner Mission, which was indeed on the verge of collapse. Even there, however, there were no indications that it had expired in the face of scientific competition. Members had no difficulty picking and choosing those elements of scientific thought that fitted their doctrines. Indeed, many felt that science had in fact proven some of their theological positions correct. Their decline stemmed not from a loss of faith, but from the decline of the farming villages in which the movement was based. The mechanisms invoked by secularization theory did not seem to explain the patterns of rise and fall that characterized the religious system of the island.

A better explanation seemed to lie in the ways that the different groups thought about community. The differences in their basic theologies, after all, were relatively small, but their recipes for earthly life differed radically. The Free Congregation, with its focus on Danish rural tradition and personal freedom, had gained a large following among the rising class of free farmers in the nineteenth century; its focus on creativity and community also appealed to the growing professional class since 1960.

The Inner Mission, by contrast, had built its organization on small, ascetic local communities in farming villages. When changes in the economy broke up many of these villages after World War II, the basis of the Mission organization collapsed. The Apostolic Church drew its membership from the fringes of island life, welding alienated individuals into a tight ecstatic community. With the island neither growing nor shrinking, the size of that fringe seemed likely to be stable. The changes among these religious groups, in other words, seemed to stem not from processes of secularization or modernization, but from the constructions of person and community that shape the appeal of religious movements throughout the world.

Other research on secularization has tended to support this conclusion. Recent studies of American religion, for example, have disputed the idea of a Protestant decline; while some of the older denominations have lost membership, Baptist and Pentecostal churches have largely made up the difference. Likewise, dramatic religious revivals have swept through much of the world in the last decade, from the Middle East to East Asia to the old Warsaw Pact. Social scientists have increasingly criticized both the logic and the data that support secularization theory. Even as they do so, however, the central question of the theory remains important. Why have the old strongholds of Protestantism lost so much of their religious fervor? Why have so many people in Germany, England and Denmark, countries once ablaze with Protestant awakenings, come to regard their churches as lifeless relics? If anthropology rejects secularization theory, as it arguably should, it must still find a reason for the loss of Protestant belief in so much of the Protestant world.

NOTES

1. William Lessa and Evon Z. Vogt, eds., *Reader in Comparative Religion: An Anthropological Approach* (New York: Harper and Row, 1979).
2. Max Weber, *The Protestant Ethic and the Spirit of Capitalism* (New York: Charles Scribner's Sons, 1958).
3. Carol Greenhouse, *Praying for Justice: Faith, Order, and Community in an American Town* (Ithaca, NY: Cornell University Press, 1986).
4. William Simmons, "Cultural Bias in the New England Puritans' Perception of Indians," *William and Mary Quarterly* 38:1 (January 1981):56–72.
5. Peter Stromberg, *Symbols of Community: The Cultural System of a Swedish Church* (Tucson: University of Arizona Press, 1986).
6. Jean Comaroff, *Body of Power, Spirit of Resistance: The Culture and History of a South African People* (Chicago: University of Chicago Press, 1985).
7. Elizabeth Brusco, *The Reformation of Machismo* (Austin: University of Texas Press, 1994).
8. Andrew Buckser, *Communities of Faith: Sectarianism, Identity, and Social Change on a Danish Island* (Providence, R.I.: Berghahn, 1996).

Nineteen

Islam

Raymond Scupin

Lindenwood University

From the Western media we gain conflicting images and stereotypes of Islamic societies and Muslim peoples. Islamic societies are portrayed as extremely turbulent, precarious, and violent societies with strange bearded men, veiled women who could be stoned for adultery, and sinister billionaire sheiks in Arab countries who try to drive up the price of oil for the West. These images and stereotypes have a long history in the West, stemming from the time of the crusades in the medieval period, when Western Christians were engaged in religious and political wars against Muslims in order to reconquer the "Holy Lands." At that time Muslims were viewed as fearless fanatics who hated Christians and infidels, and who would terrorize communities in order to spread the Islamic faith by the sword. Later, as Western scholars began to translate the religious texts of Islam, they produced generalizations and conclusions about the inherent characteristics of Muslim peoples and their societies. This type of Western scholarship based on textual interpretation is usually referred to as "Orientalist" scholarship.[1] One of the most common assumptions promoted by these early Orientalist scholars about Islam is that it is an inherently violent tradition, which called for holy wars in order to force people to accept their religious tradition.

More recently with the political difficulties of the Middle East, the oil boycotts, and the Iranian revolution of the 1970s, these early Orientalist generalizations and essentialist descriptions of Islamic societies and Muslims were seized upon to reproduce images of a culturally backward religious tradition driven by terrorists and violent fanatics who want to restore ancient codes of behavior to suppress freedom and dissent within their countries. Despite these stereotypical images, Islam is the fastest growing of the world's major religious traditions, consisting of nearly 1 billion people, one-fifth of the world's population. Through numerous ethnographic studies these stereotyped essentialist descriptions of Islamic societies have been found to be inadequate and superficial. Ethnographers have penetrated beyond the surface appearances of Islam presented in the Western media and textual scholarship to comprehend a religious tradition which has many variations depending on the cultural region in which it is found and has many different social, political, and religious manifestations.

THE ORIGINS OF ISLAM

The Islamic tradition dates to the life of Muhammad, who was born in 570 C.E. in the city of Mecca, in what is now Saudi Arabia. He was born as a member of the Querysh ethnic group, who maintained political and economic control over Mecca. At that time Mecca was an important trading entrepot and spiritual center for animistic and polytheistic traditions. The Querysh were originally a nomadic group in the desert but became involved in organizing trading caravans across the Arabian desert to cities such as Damascus and Jerusalem. Bedouins, pastoralist tribes of the Arabian peninsula who maintained camels, transported goods across the deserts to these cities from Mecca. Historically, the Querysh group themselves had been bedouins before becoming dominant in the trading activities of Mecca. Up until the age of 40 Muhammad was a successful trader within the Querysh group. He had married a woman named Khadijah, who was head of a wealthy trading family, and had four daughters including Fatima. Muhammad had gained a reputation of being a businessman known as *al-Amin*, the trusted one.

At about the age of 40 Muhammad began to seek out more spiritual satisfaction and went to a serene cave on Mt. Hira, an area near Mecca, where he fasted and began to meditate. Muslims believe that it was at Mt. Hira that Muhammad began to receive revelations from God, *Allah* (the Arabic term for God), through the intermediary of the angel Gabriel, *Jibral.* After consulting his wife and other family members, Muhammad realized and others began to believe that he was indeed receiving revelations from God. He continued receiving these revelations for some 23 years. According to the Islamic tradition the most important of the revelations received was that there was only one God, *Allah,* and that Muhammad was the prophet of God. Muslims believe that Muhammad is the final prophet in the long line of prophets including Noah, Moses, and Jesus who are referred to in the Bible. Muslims share with Christians and Jews the faith that Abraham was the founder and first Prophet of their tradition. However, Muslims believe that Jews and Christians had strayed from the faith, and that before Muhammad's revelations, people were living in an age of religious ignorance, known as the *Jahilliyah.* In fact, Muslims do not believe that Muhammad founded a new religion, but instead was a religious reformer who was trying to restore the faith for all people, including Jews and Christians.

After receiving his initial revelations, Muhammad began to preach in Mecca of the universalistic, transcendent deity—*Allah.* These teachings are believed to have threatened the economic and political interests and religious beliefs of the Querysh families. Consequently, Muhammad was shunned and persecuted and had to move to the city of Yathrib, (later called *Medina,* the "City of the Prophet"), a city about 200 miles north of Mecca, with some of his followers. This move to Medina took place in the year 622 C.E. and is known as the *Hijra* (the emigration) and it marks the first year in the Islamic calendar. In Medina, Muhammad continued as religious leader but also ruled as supreme judge and political ruler of the earliest Islamic state and society, which incorporated many of the bedouin groups in the Arabian peninsula. Following the consolidation of his authority, he returned to take control of Mecca, which became the center of a vast Islamic empire. Muhammad died in 632 C.E., at the age of 72 but is believed by all Muslims to have led an exemplary life, and through his revelations and activities left behind a rich cultural and religious tradition, which would have an enormous influence on the world.[2]

RELIGIOUS TEXTS OF ISLAM

There are several bodies of texts that have become important within the Islamic tradition. The central text of Islam is the Qu'ran ("recitation"), which consists of the revelations received for 23 years by Muhammad. In the Qu'ran the term *al-Islam* means "submission and peace," and *Muslim* refers to "one who submits." The Qu'ran is considered the supreme glory of the Arabic language, which is divided into 114 chapters (*surahs*) with some 6,000 verses (*ayahs*). It is about the length of the New Testament of Christianity and is often memorized by Muslims. The Qu'ran is not a sustained narrative as is the Torah of Judaism. Instead, it consists of poetic and spiritual *surahs*, each beginning with the beautiful Arabic phrase *bismillah al rahman-al rahim* (in the Name of God, the Compassionate, the Merciful) and continues with moral teachings. One part of the Qu'ran deals with the pre*hijra* revelations received in Mecca and emphasizes other-worldly concerns emphasizing an extreme form of monotheism with a belief in the transcendent being and spiritual unity (*tauhid*) of Allah. The other portion of the Qu'ran are from the revelations received in post*hijra* life of Medina and reflect a concern with more worldly and pedestrian issues such as how to organize a political and economic system, take care of the poor and handicapped, and deal with crime.

A Jew or Christian reading the Qu'ran will recognize various religious teachings such as the narrative of Adam and Eve, the story of Noah and the flood, the various names of the prophets such as Abraham and Moses, and references to Jesus and his mother Mary, the only woman called in the Qu'ran by name, and mentioned more times than in the New Testament. The Qu'ranic conception of the universe includes a heaven, an earth, and a hell, with humans as God's representatives on earth who are ultimately going to be measured and judged according to their deeds. There are also angels such as *Jibril* and an evil adversary of the prophets and Allah, known as *Iblis*, or *Shaytan*. The root of Islamic ethics is that God ordains humans to implement his will, leaving individuals completely responsible to follow the path of righteousness or evil. Humans are depicted as limited, weak, and subject to temptation, but through repentance humans can return to the path of righteousness. The Qu'ran refers to a day of reckoning, where all humans will be judged according to their deeds and the righteous will go to heaven, while the evil ones will be condemned to eternal fires.

Another set of texts within Islam are known as the *hadith*, which are composed of the words and deeds of the prophet Muhammad's reported by his early followers. After his death, his companions collected reports of what he had said or done and preserved them for subsequent generations. Though the reports were first transmitted orally, some were recorded in writing eventually becoming a large voluminous *hadith* literature. After some two centuries of collecting, transmitting, and teaching *hadith*, various Muslim religious scholars began to compile and codify the literature and examine the authenticity of these various *hadith*. Throughout the history of Islam the Qu'ran and the *hadith* have functioned together to shape the life of the Muslim communities in the world.

One other body of religious texts that developed in the Islamic world is known as the *Sharia,* or Islamic law. The *Sharia* texts evolved gradually from the foundations of the Qu'ran and *hadith.* The *Sharia* became the basis of political rule for the various Islamic states as well as a normative code defining criminal laws, and family and marital relationships. As Islam spread beyond Mecca and the Arabian peninsula, the Qu'ran and *hadith* were often vague or silent about new circumstances and differing cultural conditions. Consequently, the *Sharia* developed to deal with these new conditions. But because of poor transportation and communications among different regions, four different schools of Islamic law emerged within a period of some two centuries. These schools, named after Muslim theologians, are known as the Maliki, Hanifa, Al-Shafi, and Hanbali. These schools of Islamic law reflected more conservative or liberal legal traditions depending on the political and cultural context of different countries. Eventually religious judges, *qadi,* and *mufti,* (one who issues *fatwa,* or religious rulings) came to oversee the various forms of *Sharia* in different civilizations of the Islamic world.

THE SPREAD OF ISLAMIC CIVILIZATION

One misconception regarding the spread of Islam into various regions of the world was that as Muslims conquered different areas, people were compelled to convert to the tradition. Undoubtedly, this occurred in some areas (as it did sometimes with many other religious traditions including Christianity and Buddhism). However, for the most part, Muslims took seriously the admonition from the Qu'ran (Surah 2:256, "There is no compulsion in religion"). In other words, no one can be forced to convert to accept Islam, and an individual must come to Islam by free choice. Aside from the Middle Eastern Arabic areas, Islam spread across the regions of North Africa and Spain (known as *Al-Andalus*), and eastward to south, central, and southeast Asia. In all of these regions the Qu'ran and the *Sharia* provided the ecclesiastical charter for the formation and extension of political, social, and religious authority.

In the initial stages of conversion to Islam, new converts would become familiar with what are known as the "Five Pillars of Islam," or *ibadat,* ("acts of service"). The Qu'ran's first pillar specifies that all Muslims must profess faith in Allah, and Muhammad as Allah's prophet. This is known as the *shahada,* or confession of faith. Secondly, Muslims must pray five times a day (*salat*), facing the sacred city of Mecca. Third, they must fast (*sawm*) during the month of Ramadan, the ninth month of the Islamic calendar. During Ramadan Muslims cannot eat or drink between sunrise and sunset, must refrain from smoking, and sexual intercourse, and maintain a spiritual state of mind. Fourth, they must give alms (*zakat*) to support the poor, orphans, and handicapped within their communities. And finally, they are obliged to make a pilgrimage (*hajj*) to Mecca at least once in one's lifetime (if they are financially and physically able). The *hajj* takes place in the twelfth month of the Islamic calendar. During the *hajj* pilgrims participate in various rituals such as circumambulating the *Kaaba* ("cube"), the site of the earliest mosque believed to be built by Abraham. As Muslim converts became more familiar with these rituals and prayers, they gradually learned more about the *Sharia* and other complex theological matters.

As Islam diffused throughout various regions from the time of its emergence, various Islamic civilizations such as the Ummayad dynasty (661–750 C.E.) based in

Damascus and the Abbasid dynasty (750–1258 C.E.) based in Baghdad were established. Within these civilizations there were major cultural achievements. The considerable economic prosperity of these civilizations enabled the rulers and nobles to serve as patrons of scholarship in the arts and sciences. Major universities were established that focused on the translation of texts from the Greeks, Romans, Hindus, and Persians into the Arabic language. Through these efforts Muslims developed such disciplines as algebra, improved on mathematics such as geometry and trigonometry, refined physics and astronomy, rationalistic philosophy, and art and architecture, in addition to introducing many medical techniques. Islamic philosophers such as Ibn Rushd and Ibn Sina (known as Averroes and Avicenna in the West), Al-Ghazali, and Omar Al-Khayyam contributed creative syntheses of Greek, Roman, Persian, Hindu, and Arabic intellectual achievements that provided stimuli for later developments in the West. During the period of about 700–1300 C.E., the cultural centers in Cairo, Cordoba (in southern Spain), and Palermo (in Sicily) were far more developed than the equivalent cultural centers of non-Islamic Europe; and Arabic was the major intellectual and scientific language of the world.

DIVERSITY WITHIN ISLAM

After Muhammad's death in 632 C.E., rivalries developed within the Islamic community, ultimately leading to a schism. The immediate cause of this schism was a dispute over the choice of a *caliph* or Islamic ruler. Muhammad did not have a son to become the *caliph*. Consequently, one faction of the Islamic community believed that the *caliph* should be the closest male relative of the prophet. This was the husband of the prophet's daughter Fatima, a man named Ali. However, other people within the Islamic community believed that the *caliph* should be Abu Bakr, a very close disciple of the prophet. Eventually, the majority within the community selected Abu Bakr. The result was a conflict between the majority group, the *Sunni*, and a minority sect known as the *Shia Ali*, (the partisans of Ali) which persists to this day.

Although there are minor differences with respect to ritual practices, the major doctrinal difference between the Sunni and Shia has to do with religious leadership. The Shia believe that the earthly Islamic community needs to be led by a charismatic, religious leader, and ideally a direct lineal male descendant of Ali, who acts as an intermediary between the human and the divine world. These Shia religious leaders, or Imams, were believed to have a spiritual power, *baraka*, which enabled them to lead the Islamic community. Ali did become the *caliph* for a brief period of time (656–661 C.E.), but was not able to sustain leadership for the Muslim majority. Ali had two sons, Hasan and Husayn who became religious martyrs, dying in a struggle with the Sunni majority to establish the Shia. Over the years there have been schisms within the Shia sect which resulted in more variation within the Islamic community in different regions of the world. For example, different Shia sects recognize different numbers of Imams after Husayn. One sect is known as the "Seveners," who acknowledge seven Imams after Husayn, while the majority of Shia recognize twelve Imams. All of the Shia, however, believe that eventually an Imam will return as the *Mahdi* ("the guided one") to lead the Islamic community. Presently, the Shia constitute about 10-15 percent of the worldwide Muslim population, while the Sunni make up the other 85-90 percent.

Another development within Islam has produced other alternative forms of the faith. In some areas of the Islamic world a search for a more direct form of spirituality led to what is referred to as Sufism. Sufism emerged as mystical and ascetic spiritual practices representing a withdrawal from the more orthodox religious and political forms of Islam based on the *Sharia*. It began with individual spiritual teachers variously known as *shayks, pirs, walis,* or *marabouts* who were believed to have achieved a level of spiritual consciousness, *baraka,* to enable them to have a direct spiritual union with *Allah*. These Sufi spiritual masters attracted followers into *tariqas*, religious brotherhoods or lodges. The *tariqas* would pray, chant from the Qu'ran, sometimes accompanied by music and dancing, and fast in order to obtain a purified, interior spiritual transcendence, or annihilation of the self and union with God. Specific Sufi masters were sometimes revered after their death as "saints," and shrines were established as pilgrimage sites for these saints. During various periods of Islamic history and within different regions Sufism evolved into mass movements that attracted large populations. In addition, Sufi missionaries brought Islam to different areas of the world such as Southeast Asia.

At different periods within Islamic history various revivalistic or renewal movements, referred to as *tajdid* movements calling for a return to a pristine or puritanical form of Islam, have also led to variation within the religious tradition. For example, in the eighteenth century in the Arabian peninsula a religious leader known as Ibn Abd al-Wahhabi (1703–1792 C.E.) tried to restore and purify the Islamic faith from what were believed to be all forms of *shirk* ("idolatry"). These forms of *shirk* were believed to be associated with beliefs of the Sufi, such as the veneration of saints, the use of music in ritual, or other practices which were deemed as unwarranted innovations. Al-Wahhab denounced these beliefs and practices and believed that they weakened the Islamic social, political, moral, and spiritual life of Muslims. Eventually, this religious leader consolidated his *tajdid* movement and joined with another bedouin tribal leader named Muhammad ibn Saud, and they subdued large areas of the Arabian peninsula, including the city of Mecca. The Wahhabis or *Muwahhidun* ("unitarians" who uphold monotheism) destroyed all shrines associated with Sufism in various areas of Arabia. This religious and political movement has influenced other revivalistic movements in the Islamic world and has shaped the form of the orthodox tradition within countries such as modern Saudi Arabia.

THE WEST AND THE ISLAMIC WORLD

The Middle East historically has served as a crossroads among the cultural areas of Europe, Asia, and Africa. European civilizations had been in contact with some of the Middle Eastern cultures during the medieval period. After the extension of the Islamic empire throughout North Africa and Spain, Western European rulers became apprehensive. Charles Martel, ruler of the Frankish kingdom in what is now France, defeated the Muslims in Tours in 732, thereby confining them to Spain. Beginning in the eleventh century, European leaders launched a series of military expeditions, known as the Crusades, to defeat the Islamic dynasties and return the Holy Land to Christian rule.

During the Crusades, Europeans became familiar with some of the goods and luxuries that were available in the Middle East and Asia. The Islamic civilizations were producing a variety of agricultural products, handicrafts, and goods that were relatively unknown to Western Europe. In addition, the Muslims controlled trade routes that brought commodities such as spices and silk from China and cotton goods from India. Thus, European rulers sought not only to recapture the Holy Land, but also to take over the trade and commerce that crisscrossed the Islamic world. This economic impulse continued into the fifteenth century, when the Portuguese established ports throughout the Islamic world from Arabia to Southeast Asia, eventually taking control of the lucrative commerce in spices and luxuries.

Aside from the Portuguese, most Europeans did not have much direct contact with Muslims until after the 1800s. As European countries industrialized, they came to view the Middle East and other Islamic countries as an area ripe for imperial control. In the European view the Middle East could supply raw materials and serve as markets for manufactured goods. Napoleon Bonaparte led an expedition to Egypt in 1798 and brought it under French rule for a brief period. He planned to incorporate Egypt as a colony that would complement French economic interests. Because of British rivalry following the Napoleonic Wars, the French had to evacuate Egypt, but Europeans gradually attained more influence in the region. Although Egypt was not colonized directly until 1882 by the British, various European advisors influenced Egyptian rulers to develop specific products for the world market. Egyptian rulers and the upper classes cooperated with Western interests in these activities to induce economic growth. Factories were built for processing sugar, and cotton became the most important agricultural commodity in the country. The most important development project that affected ties between the Islamic world and the West was the Suez Canal, which connects the Mediterranean Sea with the Gulf of Suez. Completed in 1869, the Suez Canal was financed through capital supplied by French and British interests. The canal shortened the distance between East and West, thereby drawing the Islamic world into the orbit of the West's political economy.

To offset British expansion in the Middle East, the French began to build a North African empire, taking control of Algeria, Tunisia, and Morocco. Morocco was considered the most "perfect" French colony. Through indirect rule, the French devised a "scientific colony" that required only a small number of French officials to supervise a vast territory. The French ruled through urban elites, rural leaders, and Moroccan religious officials. They developed large commercial enterprises such as railroads and mining, as well as various agricultural operations. These commercial enterprises enabled the colony to pay for itself, a definite asset for the French. European expansion continued throughout the nineteenth and early twentieth centuries. Turkey, which was then part of the Ottoman Empire, came under economic and financial control of Western interests. To reduce the disparity in economic development between their country and Europe, Turkish rulers gave concessions to French and British interests to develop industries and services in Turkey. However, these enterprises produced cheap goods that undermined indigenous Turkish businesses. Although not directly colonized, by the end of the nineteenth century Turkey had become a peripheral society exporting raw materials, providing cheap labor, and dependent on core societies for manufactured goods.

Although not as industrialized as many other European countries, Russia began to expand toward the Islamic world during the mid-1800s and eventually assumed control over various regions of central Asia, absorbing the Muslim populations of

Samarkand, Tashkent, and Turkestan. To attempt to secure access to the warm waters of the Persian Gulf, Russia also moved into Iran (formerly Persia), taking control of the northern half of the country. The British, who through their naval fleet maintained control of commerce in the Persian Gulf, were thus threatened by Russian expansion. As a countermeasure, the British moved into southern Iran and funneled capital into the region. They developed a tobacco monopoly and financed other economic projects. Eventually, in 1907 the British and Russians agreed to divide Iran into three spheres, with northern and central Iran, including Tehran, in the Russian sphere; southeast Iran in the British sphere; and an area in between as a neutral zone. The Iranians were neither consulted nor informed about the terms of this agreement.

In another part of the Islamic world, in Southeast Asia, the Dutch expanded into the East Indies, eventually incorporating the region—now known as Indonesia—into their colonial empire. By the nineteenth century, the Dutch had developed what they referred to as the "Kultur-System," which lasted until 1917. Through this system Indonesian peasants were allowed to grow only certain cash crops such as sugar, coffee, tobacco, and indigo for the world market. The British established control over the area of Malaysia and developed tin mining and rubber plantations and imported many Chinese to work in these industries along side the native Malay populace.

Following World War I, the European powers divided the Islamic world into different spheres of influence. In addition to the North African empire, the French gained the countries of Lebanon and Syria as direct colonies. Other areas such as Turkey and the Arabian peninsula remained politically independent but became dependent on the colonial economies. The British took Egypt, Iraq, and Palestine as direct colonies. They also allowed the immigration of European Jews, who had faced discrimination and persecution for centuries in European society, into Palestine. This British policy, which led to the immigration of thousands of Jews into Palestine, had dramatic consequences for the Middle East and the Islamic world. Most Muslim areas of South and Southeast Asia remained under British and Dutch colonial rule.

The economies of the colonized countries of the Islamic world were directed toward the production of agricultural commodities such as tea, coffee, sugar, tobacco, cotton, and opium for export. Prices of these commodities were subject to fluctuations in the world market. Land that had been converted to these export crops could no longer support peasant villages. Indigenous handicrafts declined dramatically in importance in comparison with export-oriented commodity production. In addition, as in other colonized areas of the world, imported Western manufactured goods flowed into the Islamic world.

With the penetration of the Western industrial economy into the Islamic world came new forms of education. Most Muslim countries had traditional Islamic schools, *madrasas*, with a religiously oriented curriculum. The *madrasas* taught the traditional Islamic sciences based on the cultural achievements of various Muslim civilizations. Western educators introduced secular forms of education in the languages of the imperial powers. In these new schools, indigenous dialects such as Arabic were taught as foreign languages. Along with new languages, Western ideas stemming from the Enlightenment and revolutions in America and France percolated into these colonies of the Islamic world—ideas regarding political liberty and nationalism.

REFORMIST, NATIONALIST, AND ISLAMIC MOVEMENTS

The extension of Western power into the Islamic world from the time of the nineteenth century elicited a number of responses, ranging from native reformist activities to nationalist independence movements. Because most people in these regions were Muslims, many of the anticolonial responses reflected a religious orientation. As these areas became dominated by the West, many Muslims came to view their traditions as under siege by the Christian West. In response, Muslim leaders called for a rethinking of Islamic traditions to accommodate pressures from the West. Reformers such as Muhammad Abduh in Egypt argued that Islam was compatible with Western ideas and institutions, whether they be rationality, science, technology, democracy, or capitalism. These reformists emphasized that the sources of Western strength—reason, science, and technology—evolved in part from early Muslim contributions to science, medicine, and scholarship. Thus, the reformists exhorted the believers to look to their own Islamic traditions as a source of inspiration to overcome Western domination. These reformist movements spread throughout the Muslim world, especially among the urban, educated classes, and they paved the way for later nationalist and independence movements throughout the region.

Various nationalist movements developed in Algeria, Morocco, Egypt, Turkey, Iran, Indonesia, Malaysia, and other Islamic countries. Like the Islamic reformists, these nationalist leaders called for an end to the European concessions and direct control over the economy. Many nationalist leaders had been educated in Western schools and had become familiar with the democratic ideals of the Enlightenment. Generally, the nationalists were more secular in orientation than the Muslim reformers. These activists participated in protests demanding complete independence from colonial domination. For example, nationalist leaders such as Gamal Nasser, who freed Egypt (and the Suez Canal) in the 1950s from British domination, stimulated other nationalist movements. Nasser called for the establishment of a pan-Arabic socialist regime that would unify all the Arab countries.

By the 1960s, most North African, Middle Eastern, and South and Southeast Asian countries had achieved independence from the Europeans. In the Middle East the French had been driven out of Lebanon and Syria, and they eventually withdrew from their other colonies in North Africa. Through internal resistance and rebellions the British were pushed out of Egypt and Iraq. Rather than producing a pan-Arab civilization, however, these nationalist movements led to the emergence of a number of nation-states, including Morocco, Algeria, Tunisia, Lebanon, Syria, Jordan, Iraq, and Kuwait. Nationalism also continues to be the most potent political force in the Islamic countries of South and Southeast Asia.

THE ANTHROPOLOGY OF ISLAM

One of the first anthropological studies that attempted to demonstrate the complexities of the Islamic tradition with a comparative focus was Clifford Geertz's *Islam Observed* (1968). Geertz had done extensive ethnographic field work in Indonesia and had written a number of books on political economy and religion in that region. Later, he turned to do ethnographic work in Morocco and found a very different configuration of the Islamic tradition. In *Islam Observed* he compared the forms of Islam in these two different countries and was one of the first ethnographers to question the essentialist images and stereotypes regarding religious traditions. Instead of understanding a religious tradition through primary textual sources, Geertz immersed himself in the cultures of these countries and emphasized the variation and contrasting forms of Islam based on differing histories, economies, social structure, and political conditions. Though both countries had mystical forms of Islam, influenced by Sufism, Geertz found significant differences between these traditions. This work engendered many other substantive contributions of ethnographers who continue to examine the Islamic tradition.[3]

In *Islam Observed* Geertz compared the forms of Islam in Morocco and Indonesia by examining three major aspects of these societies: the classical-mythological features of the Islamic tradition, the sociopolitical characteristics of Islam, and the reconfiguration of Islam following Western colonialism in these areas. Both of these countries lay on the extreme boundaries of the Islamic world, with Morocco, a country of North Africa, located in the most western portion of the Arabic cultural region, and Indonesia the most eastern region of the Muslim world and distant from Arabia, but containing the largest population of Muslims in any country. Morocco is a rugged country with various mountain ranges, including the Rif and Atlas ranges, with a population traditionally divided between camel-riding nomadic tribes known as *berbers* in the countryside, and Arabic-speaking town and city dwellers. Indonesia is a country consisting of a series of islands spreading out over some three thousand miles. The islands consist of ethnic groups with varying languages and cultures influenced by early animist, Hindu, and Buddhist traditions, including city dwellers in various trading port towns, interior tribal peoples that practice horticulture, and large-scale agricultural settlements connected to traditional centers of state authority, with princes, peasants, and merchants. As noted above, Morocco was eventually absorbed into the French colonial empire in the nineteenth century, whereas Indonesia became a Dutch colony beginning in the eighteenth century.

Morocco is a much older Islamic country than that of Indonesia. The Ummayad dynasty had expanded into Morocco some 50 years after the prophet Muhammad's death. An Islamic state was founded in Morocco by Idris II who in 800 C.E. founded the city of Fez, the first Moroccan capital. Idris II is believed to be a descendant of the prophet Muhammad, a *sharifian*, which gave his political authority a specific religious dimension, which has influenced Moroccan society up to the present. However, throughout Moroccan history, there was a continuing struggle between the rural nomadic tribes and the settled dynastic states based in the cities. This tension resulted in the rise and fall of various dynasties in Morocco, some of which were established by fierce camel-riding nomads organized on the basis of puritanical forms of Islam. On the other hand, Sufism, the mystical form of Islam, has had a widespread influence in Moroccan religious culture, and Sufi movements and practices are led by local holy men, known as *marabouts*—derived from the Arabic word *murabit,* "lashed" or "shackled" to God, some of whom also claimed to be descendants of the prophet Muhammad. Some of these Sufi leaders who had organized brotherhoods lodges or *tariqas*, were venerated as saints, and various shrines around the tombs of dead *marabouts* became the centers of worship for many Moroccans.

In examining the classical-mythological aspects of Islamic culture in Morocco, Geertz concentrates on the biography of a Muslim leader popularly known as Sidi

Lahsen Lyusi, who was a *berber* from the Atlas mountains and lived from 1631–1691 C.E.. He is believed to be a descendant of Idris II and therefore a *sharifian*, or lineal descendant of the prophet Muhammad. According to tradition, when Lyusi was about 20 years old, it is believed he left the mountains to become a pilgrim wandering from one city to another including Fez and Marrakesh. Eventually, he became a disciple of a Sufi leader and was able to gain *baraka* ("a spiritual charisma") through participation within the *tariqa*. After a period of some 30 years as a Sufi, he managed to become the spiritual advisor to the Sultan Mulay Ismail, the political ruler of Morocco. According to Moroccan mythology, while Lyusi was staying in the royal grounds, a wall around the city was being built by slave labor and other workers who were being treated cruelly. One man had fallen ill and was sealed into the wall. Some of the workers complained to Lyusi about this treatment of slaves and workers. Lyusi did not mention these complaints to the Sultan, but instead began to break dishes in protest, until all the dishes were broken. The Sultan believed he had been insulted, and expelled Lyusi from the city, but Lyusi pitched a tent near the wall of the city, which further enraged the Sultan. Lyusi fled back to the countryside and began to preach to the *berber* nomads denouncing the Sultan. Eventually, through some miraculous experiences the Sultan recognized the spiritual power, or *baraka* of Lyusi. After Lyusi died he was transformed into a saint, wherein a cult developed centered on his tomb, which became a major place of worship in Morocco.

Geertz describes this traditional mythology to illustrate the tension between the miraculous and mystical forms of Sufism and *baraka* and the legitimacy for the religious-political dynasties based on genealogical connections to the prophet Muhammad. The Sultans claimed descent from the prophet and this undoubtedly legitimized their religious and political authority. Alternatively, local forms of religious expression emphasized maraboutic Sufi beliefs and practices. Lyusi had both *baraka* and also had a genealogical connection to the prophet, or was a *sharif*. This powerful symbolic combination reinforced the twin poles of religious and political legitimacy, which persists within the culture of Moroccan Islam presently.

In *Islam Observed* Geertz discusses the sociopolitical institutions of Morocco to examine the relationship between politics and Islam. In Morocco there are three sociopolitical institutions: the *sayyid* complex, the *zawiya* complex, and the Sultanate itself. The *sayyid* complex is based on the Sufi maraboutic cults of important saints. The saints have become important spiritual intermediaries in popular Moroccan Islam. The *sayyid* cult consists of rituals such as animal sacrifice, devout displays of emotion near the tombs of saints, curing practices, and soothsaying. The *zawiya* complex involves the organizations of the Sufi lodges or brotherhood *tariqas*, large and small, that many male Moroccans have belonged to throughout the centuries. The *zawiyas* are led by pious men who organize the gatherings in which males come together to chant from the Qu'ran, especially repeating the names for God, and sometimes using ecstatic rituals in order to achieve a mystical union with God. The Sultanate complex embodies the royal cult of the Moroccan king who is believed to combine both the *baraka* of the saints, and the sacred authority based on the geneological connections to the prophet Muhammad. The royal cult of Morocco includes the celebrations of Muslim holidays officiated by the king and his control over appointments of religious clerics including judges within the state bureaucracy. Geertz describes these sociopolitical institutions as a context for the development of a form of Islam that is based on "activism," "toughness," "moralism," and "self-assertion." The force of Islam in Morocco is an extremely intense, all-consuming experience that affects the individual believer.

The local mythology that Geertz draws on to illustrate the form of Islam that exists within Indonesia is a narrative about a man by the name of Sunan Kalidjaga. Kalidjaga was a son of a royal official in the last major Hindu-Buddhist kingdom of Madjapahit in Indonesia during the sixteenth century. This period marked the decline of the Hindu-Buddhist traditions in Indonesia, and the spread of Islam into the region. Kalidjaga left his home town in the interior of Java to move to a harbor port city, where Islamic religious ideas and practices were beginning to filter into the populace. According to Geertz's informant, Kalidjaga had a scandalous past and had been a thief, a drunk, a gambler, and even stole from his own mother. When he went to Demak, the port city, he saw a Muslim, perhaps an Arab, named Bonang who was dressed in an aristocratic manner with expensive jewelry, carrying a gold cane. Kalidjaga tried to rob him with a dagger, but Bonang laughed at him and called him by name, and told him that attachment to worldly goods and desires is pointless. Bonang demonstrated a miracle to Kalidjaga, by showing him a tree of gold jewelry, while emphasizing that spiritual power is more important than worldly material goods. Astounded by this miracle, Kalidjaga told Bonang that he wanted to renounce his earlier life, become a Muslim and gain spiritual knowledge. Bonang let Kalidjaga know that it is a difficult spiritual path to become a Muslim, and that he needed to develop patience and should wait by a river until Bonang appeared again. The narrative goes on to relate how Kalidjaga waited by the river in a trancelike state for 10, 20, 30, and then 40 years until Bonang reappeared. Bonang let him know that now he has a deep spiritual knowledge and can begin to teach Islam to others. Eventually, Kalidjaga established a new royal city at Mataram and used his high royal position to promote Islam.

Through this local narrative, Geertz describes how the form of Islam has developed as a synthesis between the earlier Hindu-Buddhist religious tradition of Indonesia, which was based on spiritual practices such as long-term meditation and psychic discipline and the new ideals of Islam coming from the outside. Geertz notes that in this local narrative Kalidjaga had converted to Islam without seeing the Qu'ran, or entering a mosque, or hearing a prayer. The conversion to Islam was based on a willed, inner-state of consciousness, which involved a spiritual trance-induced form of long-term meditation. Kalidjaga, because of his royal birth, represented a symbolic condensation or synthesis of the earlier Hindu-Buddhist spiritual conceptions and practices with that of the new Islamic tradition, which has influenced Indonesian Islam up to the present.

Traditional Indonesian sociopolitical institutions were quite different than those of Morocco since they consisted of doctrinal worldviews stemming from early Hindu-Buddhist religious ideals that reinforced conceptions of divine rulers, spiritual inequalities among people, and a ritually based state or what Geertz refers to as a "theater-state." The king's court in the capital was presumed to be an exemplary center that served as a moral and spiritual model for the various kingdoms in traditional Indonesia. The king was considered a divine ruler imbued with supernatural powers. The Hindu-Buddhist doctrine of *karma* not only gave the rulers their sacred authority but also resulted in the spiritual inequality among people in the kingdoms and sanctioned sociopolitical inequalities. The theater state as described by Geertz was based on the elaborate ceremonies, high art, and mass spectacles organized by the court to induce loyalty to the exemplary center. For example, a funeral for a member of the royal family would be an occasion when everyone in the kingdom would be indirectly participating in sacred ceremonies, which mobilized the entire populace. Thus, in traditional Indonesian society, according to Geertz, the theater state was able to produce its religious and political legitimacy through these amplified theatrical performances.

When Islam spread to Indonesia, mainly through traders from the Middle East and South Asia in the fifteenth century, the Hindu-Buddhist states were declining. However, Islam diffused first within the trading centers and markets, while the traditional bureaucracy continued to be influenced by the earlier conceptions of divine royalty, spiritual and political inequality, and the theater state. Geertz maintains that fusion of Islam and earlier Indic conceptions gave Indonesia its own unique form of Islamic culture. The Islam of Indonesia is a more passive, meditative mystical tradition with an emphasis on "inwardness," "patience," "poise," "sensibility," "aestheticism," and an "obsessive self-effacement." The Indonesian experience of Islam is not as individually assertive as it is in Morocco, although, as Geertz notes, the scope of the religious experience in Indonesia is more extensive and pervasive.

The consequences of colonialism also have resulted in variations of the Islamic tradition in Morocco and Indonesia as described by Geertz. As the French colonized Morocco, various Islamic movements developed. One of the major developments was what Geertz discusses as "scripturalist" Islam, or schoolmaster Islam. Moroccan religious scholars began to develop a modern reformist Islamic movement based on the views of Muhammad Abduh of Egypt (discussed above). The reformers intended to modernize Islam and help improve the educational literacy of the populace, along with a better understanding of the scriptures. This Moroccan reformist movement was highly critical of the Sufi and maraboutic traditions. This has produced tensions between the modernist and traditional Muslims in Morocco.

In Indonesia, as the Dutch colonized the region, a similar form of reformist Islamic movement emerged, influenced by Middle Eastern religious trends. As a result of this reformist movement, Geertz depicts the development of two major types of Muslims who comprised Indonesian society: the *santri*, and the *abangan*. The *santri* are the educated Muslims who are associated with the reformist movement, and who want to eliminate the animist, Hindu, and Buddhist beliefs and practices in Indonesian culture. However, the majority of the population consisted of the *abangan* who are nominally Muslims but also maintain traditional beliefs and communal rituals based on animist, Hindu, and Buddhist beliefs. In both countries the scripturalist form of Islam was instrumental in bringing about the struggle for national independence from Western colonialism. It mobilized the educated Muslims who perceived a renewal of their tradition as an alternative to modern forms of secularism coming from the West.

Drawing on his ethnographic work and immersion into the societies of Morocco and Indonesia, Geertz was able to explore the complex interweaving of Islam into the everyday fabric of economic, social, and political culture. At a time when many Western economists and political scientists were suggesting that societies such as Morocco and Indonesia were headed in the direction of secularization, Geertz underscored the persistence of the Islamic tradition in these areas. He describes how modernization—the process of social change resulting from the adoption of industrial technology—led to improvements in communication and contacts with outsiders, and new types of political consciousness. In turn, this process has been accompanied by the reformulation of the Islamic tradition as a means of reassessing one's Muslim identity in the modern world. These new reformulations of Islam were cultivated within the context of former cultural heritages with their own unique histories and specific political economies. Consequently, with these new modernizing rapid changes, Islamic developments have ushered in new tensions and uncertainties within these Muslim countries.

Many other ethnographers have continued to study both Morocco and Indonesia to refine the findings and conclusions of Clifford Geertz. A number of ethnographers have done further research on the social structure of Moroccan society.[4] This research has had implications for understanding the empirical realities of the Islamic world. For example, one important concept that is emphasized in Islamic teachings is God's will (*qudrat Allah*), which is expressed in the most common expression in Arabic (*in sha Allah*) "if God wills." Generally within the Islamic world, any reference to the future actions is usually prefaced by the phrase *in sha Allah*. Early Western scholars interpreted this Arabic expression to suggest that Muslims were extremely fatalistic in comparison with Westerners. However, ethnographers such as Dale Eickelman in Morocco discovered that individuals develop relationships with one another based on dyadic (two-way) patron-client contracts through their own personal free choices, negotiations, and bargaining. This research demonstrates that Moroccans are not fatalistic in their attitudes or action and will construct their patron-client relationships on the basis of free choice and individual autonomy. Individual autonomy and personal choice are vital aspects of Moroccan culture. On the other hand, Moroccans do tend to believe that "God's will" has consequences for the distribution of wealth, power, and status in these dyadic and hierarchical relationships at any moment in time. Thus, in the Moroccan worldview human actions and the construction of social relationships are based on freedom of action and choice, but the religious and cultural meanings of these hierarchical relations are viewed as justifications of God's will. Hence, in some cases, religious beliefs may provide a meaningful way of explaining sociopolitical and economic inequalities.

One ethnographic study of Morocco by Henry Munson, *The House of Si Abd Allah: The Oral History of a Moroccan Family* (1984), illustrates some of the new tensions that have developed in Islamic societies through in-depth biographies of two Muslims. In this study, Munson concentrates on a life history of one family in northwestern Morocco. The life history of this family is interpreted through the voices of two grandchildren of Si Abd Allah: al-Hajj Muhammad, a traditional Muslim "fundamentalist" peddler, and Fatima Zohra, a "modern" Westernized young woman who lives with her husband and children in the United States. Through these different perspectives, Munson highlights the conflicts and tensions between Islamic fundamentalism and modernity. Al-Hajj Muhammad who often uses quotations from the Qu'ran and is a deeply religious Muslim, condemns the Christians and Jews as infidels who are doomed to eternal punishment. He perceives these other religious groups as using devious means in order to destroy the Islamic faith. Fatima, a modernist Muslim, accepts a universalist form of Islam that asserts that all good people will go to heaven despite their particular beliefs. Modernist Muslims, for example, will often cite the following verse from the Qu'ran:

> verily all those who believe
> Jews, Christians, and the Sabians
> all those who believe in God
> and the last day
> and who do good deeds
> they shall have their reward
> with their Lord
> and there shall be no fear upon them
> nor shall they grieve
>
> *[Qu'ran II: 62]*

Through the biographies and voices of these two very different Moroccans, one can understand how a fundamentalist form of Islam can offer meaning and purpose to a traditional Muslim man, whereas this type of fundamentalism is looked upon with disdain by a modern Muslim woman. It also illustrates how differences in social class and gender can influence various Islamic perspectives. These different strains of Islamic interpretation between the modernist-reformist educated classes, and more traditional-fundamentalist exist in Morocco as well as in other areas of the Islamic world.

Ethnographic studies of Indonesia have also amplified the understanding of Islam initiated by Geertz.[5] Recent ethnographic accounts of Indonesia indicate that the rural forms of Islam referred to by Geertz as a syncretic *abangan* Islam with animist, Hindu, and Buddhist elements is rapidly changing. Ethnographers such as Robert Hefner have shown that as rural villages have been opening to new global economic and political changes in Indonesia, older village *abangan* communal traditions and values are disappearing. New forms of consumption including the purchase of motorcycles, televisions, and other consumer goods that have created class differences in the village areas have undermined traditional communal ties and rituals. However, these new developments have also resulted in a new emphasis on identifying with national political interests beyond the village. This new national identity is interrelated with an Islamic identity, which is continuing to grow. A new form of Islamic identity is being forged in the village areas emphasizing attention to the basic beliefs and practices of Muslims, and a need to do away with older communal beliefs and practices. The older *santri-abangan* (orthodox versus syncretic) differences among Muslims is giving way to a new national form of Islamic identity combining a religious and political consciousness.

As more people are becoming educated and literate in both Morocco and Indonesia, ethnographers are paying more attention to how Islamic texts are used and interpreted in these societies. In *Knowledge and Power in Morocco: the Education of a Twentieth-Century Notable* (1985), Dale Eickelman focuses on the Moroccan scholarly tradition to understand how cultural and religious textual knowledge is transmitted and interpreted from one generation to another. This ethnographic study concentrates on a traditional rural *qadi*, an Islamic judge and scholar, in order to gain insights into this process of transmitting religious knowledge. In Morocco, as in most other Islamic areas, the symbolic, moral, and political authority of religious scholars is held to be superior to that of a student or disciple. In a religious education context, the use of *qal* or "reason" is not emphasized as a critical skeptical attitude, but rather as a disciplined means of discerning the meaning of the Qu'ran and code of conduct laid down by God. Thus, as religious knowledge is transmitted from teacher to students, it acquires both rhetorical and moral authority and can be used to justify and legitimize social relationships and political power. On the other hand, as indicated in the ethnographic studies of John Bowen of an ethnic group known as the Gayo on the island of Sumatra, Indonesia, Muslims will dispute among themselves and interpret the ambiguities in Islamic texts as social, economic, and political changes affect their lives. Instead of viewing Islamic texts as reinforcing universal doctrines, these ethnographers are demonstrating how Islamic texts are transmitted and interpreted within the context of new cultural changes in these developing societies.

FAMILY AND MARRIAGE IN ISLAMIC SOCIETIES

A voluminous amount of ethnographic research has become available on family, marriage, and gender in Islamic societies. In many of the early descriptions of Islamic societies the Muslim form of the family was depicted as always being based on tribal blood ties and was patrilineal, patriarchal, polygynous, (marriage between one male and two or more females), and endogamous (marriages arranged between cousins). These early discussions were based on interpretations of the Islamic religious texts, principally the Qu'ran and the *Sharia*. Ethnographers have discovered, however, that the ideas expressed in these religious texts regarding the Muslim family do not always coincide with the complex realities of economic, social, political, and cultural life in different areas of the Islamic world.

In some cases, early Orientalist scholarship tended to suggest that Islamic societies were blood-based, and therefore could not develop social or political institutions beyond that of tribal societies. For example, in some areas of the Middle Eastern Arab world, the term *hamula* is used to refer to an idealized patrilineal descent group that members view as a kinship group based on a male ancestor. The *hamula* is associated with a patronymn, the name of a particular male who is thought to be a paternal ancestor. In some rural areas the typical *hamula* is a number of patrilineages headed by a male referred to as a *shayk*. Traditionally, the *shayk* would resolve disputes among members of the *hamula* and encourage cooperation within this kin grouping. In Afghanistan, a similar form of kin group is referred to as a *qawm*. The *qawm* organizes groups within different territories who speak of themselves as sharing a male ancestor in the past. Despite the descriptions of the *hamula* or *qawm* as patrilineal descent groupings and its association with a particular patronymn, ethnographers find that it is frequently a loosely structured group combining patrilineal, affinal, matrilineal, and territorial relations. In addition, ethnographers find that Islam can exist in societies that have strong matrilineal or bilateral forms of social organization.[6] Anthropologists have concluded from their ethnographic research that Muslims, like people elsewhere in the world, may refer to the concepts of kinship and family to coordinate their affairs, but often economic, political, and other social circumstances influence their actual behavior.

Islamic societies are well known for condoning the marriage practice of polygyny, marriage between one male and two or more females. Polygyny is mentioned once in the Qu'ran:

> Marry of the women, who seem good to you,
> two, three, or four, and if ye fear that ye cannot
> do justice [to so many] the one [only].

(Qu'ran IV:3)

Although polygynous marriage is permitted and represents the traditional ideal norm within Muslim societies, ethnographers find that most marriages are actually monogamous. For example, less than 10 percent of married Kuwaiti males and about 0.05 percent of married Egyptian males are involved in polygynous marriages.[7] The major rationales for taking a second wife were either infertility or poor health of the first wife or the desire of wealthy males to demonstrate their high status. Usually polygynous marriages are contracted by wealthy males in both urban and rural areas. Polygyny is found among the new elite in some of the wealthy, oil-producing countries. However, economic limitations and the fact that the Islamic tradition prescribes equal justice for all wives encourage monogamous marriages among the majority of Muslims.

As in many other non-Western societies, arranged marriages based on parental decision making remains the predominant form within Islamic societies. Until recently, for example, Saudi Arabian males did not even view their wives until their wedding day. Yet, ethnographic research from Kuwait in the mid-1980s indicates that an individual's freedom to select a spouse varies according to education, socioeconomic status, age, and sex.[8] As people become more educated and achieve greater economic independence from their parents, they enjoy greater freedom in mate selection. At the same time Muslim parents and senior relatives are involved to some extent in consulting with the prospective groom and bride. Sometimes a matchmaker, a *khatbeh*, is utilized in establishing a relationship between a man and woman for a possible marriage.

Another traditional norm regarding marriage in the Arab-Islamic world, and mentioned within the Qu'ran, is the form of cousin marriage known as *bint amm*. *Bint amm* is a marriage between a male and his father's brother's daughter. Again, ethnographers find a good deal of flexibility and variation among these so-called prescribed Arab marriage practices. For example, in some cases marriages are also contracted outside the *bint amm*. The actual rate of cousin marriage varies from urban to rural regions, from village to village, and among different social classes within the same villages. In some villages, the *bint amm* is associated with the upper classes and is less common among other groups. This suggests that endogamous marital patterns are closely tied to specific economic exchanges and resources. In addition, there is considerable flexibility in who can be classified as a father's brother's daughter. Factors such as fertility, genealogy, class background, inheritance, exchanges of valuables, the values of family honor and prestige—all play a role in influencing *bint amm* marriages. Thus, ethnographic research has confirmed that both family and marriage practices are not associated with rigid norms inferred from religious texts but rather must be understood in the context of exchanges that entail economic, social, political, and cultural factors.

GENDER IN ISLAMIC SOCIETIES

The Western image of the Muslim woman is frequently that of a female hidden behind a veil and completely dominated by the demands of an oppressive patriarchal society. Early Orientalist scholars painted a grim and unwholesome portrait of the female in the Muslim household. Ethnographers find that this image obscures the complexity of gender relations in the Islamic world. The patriarchal ideal and the status of the female in the Muslim world cannot be understood without reference to two views that are developed within the Qu'ran itself. Prior to the origins of Islam, females were treated negatively. For example, in the pre-Islamic period the Bedouins practiced female infanticide by burying the unwanted child in sand. The Qu'ran explicitly forbids this practice. Along with other reforms that came with the origins of Islam, most Muslims view their tradition as having had a progressive influence on the role of women. Second, Islam condemns all sexual immorality, prescribing severe penalties for adultery. The Qu'ran enjoins both males and females to be chaste and modest.

The Islamic religious texts prescribe a specific set of statuses and corresponding roles for females to play within the Muslim family as daughter, sister, wife, and mother. Each of these statuses carries certain obligations, rights, privileges, and duties. These statuses are influenced by the patriarchal ideals of the Islamic texts, as they were also emphasized within the Biblical text. One passage of the Qu'ran is often cited when referring to the role of women:

> Men are in charge of women,
> because God hath made the one of them to excel the other,
> and because they spend of their property (for the support of women).
> So good women are the obedient
>
> *(Qu'ran IV: 34)*

This passage provides the context for the development of various laws that have influenced the status of Muslim women. For example, traditionally a woman could inherit only one-half of her parents' estate, compared to her brothers, who inherited full shares. This law assumed that a woman is fully cared for by her family and, when she marries, her husband's family will provide for her material needs. Thus, a Muslim woman does not need the full share of inheritance. Another traditional code in the *Sharia* indicates the patriarchal attitudes toward women in respect to political and legal issues. In legal cases a woman is granted half the legal status of a man. For example, if a crime is committed, two women (as opposed to one man) are needed as legal witnesses for testimony. This legal equation of "two females equals one male" reflects the traditional Islamic image of women as less experienced and less capable than men in political and legal affairs.

Ethnographic research since the 1960s has demonstrated that the actualities of male-female relations in these societies are far more complex than the religious texts might imply. By focusing exclusively on Islamic texts and laws, early researchers distorted and misunderstood the actual practices and interrelations between males and females, just as they were blind to regional variations of Islam itself. In addition, prior to the 1970s most of the ethnographic research in Muslim societies was done by males. This resulted in a skewed understanding of the position of women, because male ethnographers did not have the same access to the female informants as did female ethnographers. Eventually, female ethnographers such as Lois Beck, Elizabeth Fernea, Fadwa El-Guindi, Nancy Tapper, Lila Abu-Lughod, Christine Eickelman, Lila Ahmed, Margaret Gulick, Soraya Altorki, and others began to penetrate and study the Muslim female world.

Female ethnographers discovered that the position of Muslim women cannot be categorized uniformly. One major reason for variation is the extent to which Muslim countries have been exposed to Islamic reform movements. Some like Tunisia, Egypt, and Turkey have adopted legal reforms that have improved the status of women. Egyptian women have had access to secondary education since the early 1900s and have had career opportunities in medicine, law, engineering, management, and government. The Egyptian constitution accords women full equality with men, and—ideally—sexual discrimination in career opportunities is prohibited. Muslim feminist reform movements dedicated to improving the status of women have emerged. For example, traditionally, a Muslim wife did not have the same rights to obtain a divorce as her husband. Women could only divorce their husbands for reasons such as impotence, insanity, and lack of economic support. To prove these accusations, however, a wife needed a very sympathetic judge. However, in countries such as Egypt, Turkey, and Tunisia divorce laws for women have become liberalized. These countries have educated middle classes that support reform. In conjunction with these reform movements, along with the modification of divorce laws, some Muslim feminists have called for the abolition of polygyny. Certain countries—for example, Tunisia and Turkey—have prohibited this practice, and others have placed restrictions on it.

In contrast to these countries, the religiously conservative country of Saudi Arabia has highly restrictive cultural norms regarding women. Soraya Altorki, an ethnographer and one of the first Saudi females to receive a doctoral degree, conducted extensive research on the Saudi female.[9] The Saudi Arabian government, influenced by the Wahhabi fundamentalist tradition, calls for strict application of the Sharia to declare that any mingling of the sexes is morally wrong. Saudi women are segregated from males. They attend separate schools and upon finishing their education can seek employment only in exclusively female institutions such as women's hospitals, schools, and banks. Saudi women are forbidden by law to drive cars, and when riding on public buses they have to sit in special closed sections. All Saudi public buildings must have separate entrances and elevators for males and females.

Altorki describes how Saudi women do not openly challenge these patriarchal norms that inhibit full participation in the society or economy. In her book she admits to the limitations of her study because of her gender. However, she does indicate that some Saudi women have been able to produce some minor changes in women's education and the timing of marriage. In addition, among the elite families studied by Altorki, there is a shift from extended to nuclear families, and a change from patrilocal residence (where the wife goes to live with the husband's family) to neolocal residence (where the married couple establishes their own residence). These changes have resulted from internal social and economic trends for the elite in Saudi Arabia, and influences from the outside world. This has resulted in a little more independence for some women in Saudi society. Altorki concludes her study by emphasizing how women are able to resist authority and achieve some minor changes to enhance their autonomy in a society that is explicitly male dominated and reinforced through a coercive political and legal system.

THE VEIL AND SECLUSION

To many Westerners the most visible sign of the patriarchal order of the Islamic societies is the veil and the other enveloping garments worn by Muslim women. The veil, sometimes known as the *hijab*, has a long history in the Middle East. Veiling was known among the Mesopotamian, Persian, Jewish, Christian, and Byzantine societies prior to the origins of the Islamic tradition. Apparently, this tradition of the wearing of the *hijab* was associated with upper-class women among the elite in these societies. In Muslim society, the notion of *hijab* refers to a sacred divide between males and females. Traditionally, as a Muslim female approaches puberty, she is supposed to be restricted and kept from contact with males. The veil is an outward manifestation of this cultural understanding of separation, but it also has connections with modesty and morality. The wearing of the veil and the enforced seclusion of the Muslim female is known as *purdah* and is found in a number of Islamic countries. These practices reinforced a separation between the domestic private sphere of women and the male-dominated public sphere. Veiling and *purdah* tend to be associated with urban Muslim women. Many peasant (or Bedouin) women in the Middle East and North Africa do not wear the veil and generally have more freedom to associate with males than do Muslim women who reside in towns and cities. Practical circumstances for agricultural workers and rural women make strict seclusion impossible. But in the rapidly urbanizing areas of the Islamic world, some Muslim females report that the veil and accompanying garments offer practical protection from strangers and that they feel naked and self-conscious without these garments on public streets.

In addition, in countries such as Egypt, Turkey, and Malaysia that had formerly abandoned traditional dress codes, many educated, middle-class college-age women have opted to wear the veil and the all-enveloping garments. To some extent this return to traditional dress reflects the revival movements now occurring throughout the Islamic world (discussed below). Many women have adopted the traditional dress as an expression of their faith. The change in clothing, however, also has a political dimension. For many Muslim women, returning to the veil is both a religious and a political gesture aimed at Western colonialism and domination, which they view as an attack on Islamic cultural identity. One way in which Muslim women can affirm their Islamic religious and cultural identity and make a political statement of resistance to Western power and influence is to dress in the traditional manner.

Also, ethnographers find that many modern Muslim women deliberately adopt the *hijab* to adapt to modern social realities. As professional working women are carving out spaces for themselves in new arenas, the wearing of the *hijab* is a practical means for coping with a new social climate in which males are unaccustomed to working with women. The Islamic clothing desexualizes the atmosphere of this new female-male public social arena. Thus, modern Muslim women often adopt the *hijab* to reaffirm their religious and political identity and to renew their modesty in dress and etiquette as a practical strategy in dealing with males. Thus, the veil symbolizes conceptions of modesty and morality, as well as Islamic identity and resistance to Western economic, political, and cultural dominance.

The ethnographic studies of gender in the Islamic world indicate that male and female status and autonomy are influenced not by religious texts such as the Qu'ran and Sharia alone, but by the historical, economic, political, and global conditions that effect a specific locale or country. Undeniably though, in many respects the patriarchal family remains the central ideal of Islamic social organization. Hence, in some cases, attempts to reform women's status have been perceived as heretical assaults on the Islamic family and morality. Some of the recent Islamic revival movements have attempted to reactivate conservative, patriarchal cultural norms.

ISLAMIC REVITALIZATION

One pervasive trend reported in the Western media since the 1970s is sometimes referred to as Islamic fundamentalism. Generally the term "fundamentalism" when applied to Islam tends to imply terrorist and militant activities within the Muslim world. The depictions of Islamic fundamentalism reinforce the stereotypes of Muslims as violent and fanatical. Again, ethnographers find a wide variety of expressions of Islamic fundamentalism or revitalization throughout the Muslim world. Most contemporary fundamentalist movements had their roots in earlier reformist movements that sought to combine Islam with Western values as a means of coping with colonialism and industrialism. In some countries, however, fundamentalist groups have rejected reform in favor of the total elimination of secular, Western influences. These movements encouraged the reestablishment of an Islamic society based on the Qu'ran and *Sharia*. Some groups sought to bring about these changes peacefully, whereas others believed that an Islamic state could only be established through violent revolution.

Ethnographic studies have contributed to a better understanding of the sources of Islamic revival movements. Some generalizations can be developed from the ethnographic studies and interviews with various Muslim groups on the reasons why Islamic resurgent movements have recently developed. One critical factor was the 1967 Arab-Israeli war, which resulted in the crushing defeat of the Arab states and the loss of Arab territories to Israel. This event symbolized the economic and political weakness of the Islamic nations and inspired many Muslims to turn toward their faith as a source of communal bonds and political strength. Another significant factor was the oil boom. Many fundamentalists believed that by bestowing these societies with rich oil reserves, *Allah* was shifting power from the materialist and secular civilizations of the West to the Islamic world. Also, oil revenues in countries such as Libya, Iran, and Saudi Arabia were used to support fundamentalist movements throughout the Muslim world. In addition, Islamic countries were becoming more disillusioned with the Western forms of governments and economic systems, both capitalist and socialist, that were influencing their own societies. They began to seek an Islamic solution for organizing the political economy. Another factor was the success of the Islamic revolution in Iran that demonstrated how a Western-influenced secular regime could be overthrown by opposition forces organized under Islamic leadership and clergy.

THE IRANIAN ISLAMIC REVOLUTION: A CASE STUDY

Many Western social scientists and government officials were surprised by the Islamic revivalistic movements in the Middle East, especially Iran. They assumed that with modernization these societies would become increasingly secularized, and that the role of religion in economic, social, and political affairs would be reduced. Instead, many Muslim countries have experienced Islamic movements that were linked to national political and economic issues. One of the regions of the Middle East most affected by Islamic fundamentalist tendencies is Iran. Anthropologists Mary Hegland, Michael Fischer, William Beeman, Philip Salzman, and others have contributed through their ethnographic, historical, and comparative research toward an understanding of the Islamic revival in Iran.[10] They cite a number of factors that converged to produce this revival and subsequent Islamic revolution.

The Shia religious tradition spread to several areas of the Islamic world. It had particular appeal to the non-Arab populations of the Middle East such as the Iranians. In the sixteenth century, the Shia tradition became the official state religion of Iran, and today the vast majority of the population—some 90 percent—are Shia. The Shia religious leadership in Iran comprises village preachers, the *mullahs*, religious judges, the *mujtahids*, and at the apex of the religious hierarchy, the religious scholars, the *ayatollahs*. The term *ayatollah* is translated as "sign of God," and these religious specialists are perceived to be the most knowledgeable scholars and leaders of their age. The Shia religious tradition has always emphasized the importance of the religious clergy not only as the moral leaders, but also as the political leaders of the society. However, as Iranian society evolved, the political rulers—the shahs—competed with or tried to control the religious clergy.

During the nineteenth century as the Russians and British began to enter Iran, the shahs offered a large number of concessions to British and Russian bankers and private companies. Many Iranians believed that the shahs were giving control of Iranian economic resources to foreigners, who were gaining more political control of Iran. The religious clergy were critical of the shah's policies, and this resulted in intense competition between the shahs and the Shia clergy. In trying to maximize their political power, the shahs were also modernizing Iran's economy, military, and educational system along Western lines. These modernization policies generated internal opposition. The newly educated classes, who had acquired Western ideals of democracy and representative government, opposed the shahs' absolute power. In addition, the clergy opposed secularization and Western education, which interfered with the traditional religious education that they controlled. The Shia clergy accused the shah of allowing the West to undermine Islam.

In 1925 the Pahlavi dynasty came to power in Iran. Reza Shah Pahlavi viewed the Shia religious leaders as obstacles to his plans for rapid modernization. He attempted to reduce the power of the religious leadership by appropriating their lands, thus depriving them of income. Reza Shah decreed that secular laws would replace the *Sharia* and that women would no longer have to wear the veil. These policies led to more opposition from the religious clergy. During World War II Muhammad Reza Pahlavi, supported by Russian and Western interests, replaced his father as ruler. The new shah continued the modernization and secularization policies of his father.

By the 1960s he had centralized all political authority in his hands. Many Western multinationals were attracted to Iran because of its vast oil reserves and increasing incentives for business interests. The Iranian economy became increasingly dependent on Western imported goods, while internally, aside from oil production, few indigenous industries were developed.

In 1963 the Shah Pahlavi announced the "White Revolution," which included the commercialization of agriculture through land reforms and the expansion of capitalism. It also included public ownership of companies and voting rights for women. The land reforms disrupted the traditional peasant economy, creating a class of landless people. As these peasants were displaced from their land, they flocked to Iranian cities in search of scarce opportunities. The White Revolution further mobilized the opposition of the religious clergy. The shah was perceived as a puppet of United States (the "Great Satan") and Western imperialism. One of the major critics was the Ayatollah Khomeini, who was arrested and exiled in 1963.

In addition to the religious clerics, the shah's policies alienated many other sectors of Iranian society. To buttress his power, the shah, along with his secret police, the SAVAK, brutally crushed any opposition to his regime. The Westernized middle classes, the university students, the merchants in the bazaars, and the urban poor began to sympathize with any opposition to the shah's regime. These groups began to ally themselves with the Muslim clergy and their call for an Islamic revolution. For 15 years Khomeini continued to attack the shah in pamphlets and cassette-taped sermons smuggled into Iran.

Although united in their opposition to the shah, diverse segments of Iranian society viewed the Islamic revolution in different terms. The rural migrants who flooded into the Iranian cities steadfastly supported the Islamic clergy. The Westernized middle class viewed the Islamic revolution in terms of its own democratic aspirations. The middle class believed that the religious leaders would play a secondary role in the actual administration of the Iranian state. Many university students had been influenced by the writings of Ali Shariati, who interpreted Shia Islam as a form of liberation theology that would free their society from foreign domination. These elements within Iranian society formed a coalition that encouraged the social and political revolution led by Khomeini and the religious clerics. A cycle of demonstrations, violent protests, and religious fervor led to the downfall of the shah. In 1979, Khomeini returned to Iran to lead the revolution.

Since the overthrow of the shah, the religious clerics assumed nearly all of the important political positions. Khomeini announced the establishment of the Islamic Republic of Iran, a theocratic state ruled by the Shia clergy. The Shia clergy utilized the mosques as the basic building blocks of political power by forcing all Iranians to register at a mosque, which functioned as an amalgam of a government office, a place of worship, and a local police force. A systematic campaign was waged to purge Iranian society of its Western influences. Alcohol, gambling, prostitution, and pornography were strictly forbidden. Women were required to wear head scarves, and those who refused were sent to "reeducation centers." The Family Protection Act put into effect under the Shah Pahlavi in 1975, which gave the spouses equal rights to divorce, raised the minimum age for marriage, and placed the decision for child custody on the discretion of the courts, was abolished. One of Khomeini's first acts on coming to power in 1979 was to lower the minimum age for marriage from 18 to 13, gave fathers complete control in child custody cases, and he also gave husbands the right to polygyny and divorce at will.

The Shia regime believed it had a religious duty to export its revolution to other areas of the Islamic world. Since the Islamic revolution, most ethnographic research has been forbidden in Iran. Thus, it has been difficult to collect ethnographic data to analyze recent trends. From press reports it is clear that the revolution has radically changed the nature of Iranian society. The revolution was not only political but also a total social and cultural transformation of society. Iran is, however, racked with internal conflicts among different classes, religious factions, and generations. Economic problems exacerbated by the reduction in oil prices and a ten-year war against Iraq have led to infighting among radical militants, conservative fundamentalists, and moderates.

In May 1997, Mohammad Khatami, a moderate Muslim cleric, won Iran's presidential election in a landslide victory over more conservative candidates. Khatami attracted a broad coalition of centrists, women, youth of both genders, and middle-class intellectuals to his cause. He is believed to be a direct descendant of the Prophet Muhammad, which helped him consolidate support. While Khatami's victory is unlikely to result in immediate changes in the country's Islamic fundamentalist path, his election will most likely restrain the more conservative factions of the clergy who has ruled the country since 1979. One leading Ayatollah, Hussein Ali Montazeri, has been questioning openly the legitimacy of Iran's clerical rule. Only time will tell whether Iran will be able to overcome factionalism and resolve its political and economic problems.

One conclusion resulting from the many ethnographic studies of Islam is that this religious tradition, like all other religious traditions, can have varying interpretations in different contexts. The Islamic religion can be combined with diverse types of political and ideological activity. It can provide ideological support for Islamic fundamentalism and revolutionary change, as the case of Iran suggests. Thus, the Islamic fundamentalist trends in countries such as Afghanistan, Algeria, or Iran are interconnected with conditions that have resulted from colonialism from the West and internal factional, sectarian, and class differences. Islamic texts and scriptures are then drawn upon and interpreted to stimulate revivalistic and fundamentalist activities directed against the status quo.

In contrast, the Islamic traditions can be interpreted to help sustain a specific socioeconomic and political order, as in contemporary Saudi Arabia where some 2,000 princes control the entire political economy. Thus, Islam can be utilized and reformulated to justify political oppression and the domination of an elite. Or, the traditions can be used by moderate and progressive factions within the Islamic world to advance social justice, the rights of women and minorities, and democratic political reform. Anthropological research has demonstrated that Islam (or any other religious tradition) has a multiplicity of forms and interpretations in both rural and urban areas and must be understood with respect to local cultural contexts. Instead of attempting to locate an essential "Islamic tradition," most modern ethnographers view this tradition as highly variable, and responsive to the particular demands of Muslims as they adjust and cope with their own specific contingencies of life.

NOTES

1. The classic work on Orientalism is Edward Said's *Orientalism* (New York: Vintage, 1979). This book illustrates the misconceptions of Islam by early Western scholars. Although not in agreement with all of Said's criticisms, most Western scholars including anthropologists have become sensitive to the critique of Orientalism.

2. A number of anthropologists have attempted historical analyses of the origins of Islam. Eric Wolf's "The Social Organization of Mecca and the Origins of Islam," *Southwestern Journal of Anthropology* 7(4): 329–356 (Winter 1951), emphasizes the development of the political economy in early Meccan society. Barbara Aswad, "Social and Ecological Aspects in the Formation of Islam," reprinted in Louise E. Sweet, ed., *Peoples and Cultures of the Middle East*, Vol. 1. (New York: Natural History Press, 1970) also focuses on the economic and social evolution of the early Meccan Islamic history. Dale Eickelman's "Musaylima: An Approach to the Social Anthropology of Seventh Century Arabia," *Journal of the Economic and Social History of the Orient* 10, pt. 1 (July 1967), discusses the various competing claims for prophetic authority during the life of Muhammad. More recently, Elaine Combs-Shilling offers a symbolic analysis of the origins of Islam in her *Sacred Performances: Islam, Sexuality and Sacrifice* (New York: Columbia University Press. 1989). One broad overview of the Islamic world with an historical approach by an anthropologist is Charles Lindholm's *The Islamic Middle East: An Historical Anthropology* (Oxford: Blackwell, 1996). Other broad historical surveys of the Islamic tradition include John Esposito's *Islam: The Straight Path* (Oxford: Oxford University Press, 1991) and Frederick Denny's *An Introduction to Islam* (New York: Macmillan, 1985).

3. In Edward Said's critique of Orientalist scholarship (above), he notes how Geertz's *Islam Observed* represents a new form of comparative scholarship and is not based on stereotypical Orientalist images of Islam.

4. Ethnographies on Islam in Morocco include Clifford Geertz, Hildred Geertz, and Lawrence Rosen, eds., *Meaning and Order in Moroccan Society* (Cambridge: Cambridge University Press, 1979); Lawrence Rosen, *Bargaining for Reality: The Construction of Social Relations in a Muslim Community* (Chicago: University of Chicago, 1984); Ernest Gellner's *Saints of the Atlas* (Chicago: University of Chicago Press) and *Muslim Society* (Cambridge: Cambridge University Press, 1981); Dale Eickelman's *Moroccan Islam: Tradition and Society in a Pilgrimage Center* (Austin: University of Texas Press, 1976), and *Knowledge and Power in Morocco: The Education of a Twentieth Century Notable* (Princeton: Princeton University Press, 1985); and Henry Munson's *The House of Si Abd Allah: The Oral History of a Moroccan Family* (New Haven: Yale University Press, 1984); and *Religion and Power in Morocco* (New Haven: Yale University Press, 1993), Elaine Combs-Shilling, *Sacred Performances: Islam, Sexuality and Sacrifice* (New York: Columbia University Press, 1989); and Vanessa Maher, *Women and Property in Morocco* (Cambridge: Cambridge University Press, 1974).

5. Ethnographies on Islam in Indonesia include Mark Woodward's *Islam in Java: Normative Piety and Mysticism in the Sultanate of Yogyakarta* (Tucson: University of Arizona Press, 1989); John R. Bowen's *Sumatran Politics and Poetics: Gayo History, 1900–1989* (New Haven: Yale University Press, 1991) and *Muslims Through Discourse* (Princeton: Princeton University Press, 1993); Rita Kipp and Susan Rodgers, eds., *Indonesian Religion in Transition* (Tucson: University of Arizona Press, 1987); and Robert Hefner's *The Political Economy of Mountain Java: An Interpretive History* (Berkeley: University of California Press, 1990). Early works include Clifford Geertz's *The Religion of Java* (Chicago: University of Chicago Press, 1960), and Robert R. Jay's *Religion and Politics in Rural Central Java* (New Haven: Yale University, 1963).

6. An essay by Aihwa Ong "State versus Islam: Malay Families, Women's Bodies, and the Body Politic in Malaysia," *American Ethnologist* 17 (2): 258–276, 1990, deals with how Islam can be developed in a society with bilateral descent (tracing descent through both male and female sides of the family), and Susan Rasmussen "Accounting for Belief: Causation, Evil and Misfortune in Tuareg Systems of Thought," *Man*, n.s., 24: 124–144, 1989, shows how Islam can correspond to a society that emphasizes matrilineal rules of descent (tracing descent through the female line).

7. See Fahad Al-Thakeb "The Arab Family and Modernity: Evidence from Kuwait," *Current Anthropology* 25 (5): 575–580, 1985, for patterns of polygyny in Kuwait. Afaf Lutfi al-Sayyid Marsot, "The Revolutionary Gentlewomen in Egypt," in Lois Beck and Nikki Keddie, eds., *Women in the Muslim World* (Cambridge, MA: Harvard University Press, 1978) reports on a low rate of polygyny in Egypt. Ahmed Akbar notes that only 0.02 percent of males were polygynous in an Islamic tribal group described in his *Pukhtun Economy and Society: Traditional Structure and Economic Development in a Tribal Society* (London: Routledge, 1980).

8. Fahad Al-Thakeb notes new patterns of marital choice for Muslims in his "The Arab Family and Modernity: Evidence from Kuwait," *Current Anthropology* 25 (5): 575–580, 1985. An earlier ethnography by Hani Fakhouri titled *Kafr El-Elow: An Egyptian Village in Transition* (New York: Holt, Rinehart, and Winston, 1972) describes some typical arrangements for marriage among Egyptian Muslims.

9. Ethnographies dealing with the role of women in the Islamic world include Soraya Altorki, *Women in Saudi Arabia: Ideology and Behavior Among the Elite* (New York: Columbia University Press, 1986); Lila Abu-Lughod, *Writing Women's Worlds: Bedouin Stories* (Berkeley: University of California Press, 1993); Carol Delaney, *The Seed and the Soil: Gender and Cosmology in Turkish Village Society* (Berkeley: University of California Press, 1991); Fadwa el-Guindi "Veiling Infitah with Muslim Ethic: Egypt's Contemporary Islamic Movement," *Social Problems* 28: 465–485, 1981; Elizabeth Fernea, *Women and the Family in the Middle East: New Voices of Change* (Austin: University of Texas Press, 1985); Elizabeth Fernea, *In Search of Islamic Feminism* (New York: Doubleday Press, 1998); Christine Eickelman, *Women and Community in Oman* (New York University Press, 1984); Lois Beck and

Nikki Keddie, eds., *Women in the Muslim World* (Cambridge, MA: Harvard University Press, 1978); Nancy Tapper, "Gender and Religion in a Turkish Town: A Comparison of Two Types of Formal Women's Gatherings," in P. Holden, ed., *Women's Religious Experience* (London: Croom Helm, 1983); Cynthia Nelson, "Public and Private Politics: Women in the Middle Eastern World," *American Ethnologist* 1, (3): 551–563, 1974; Suzanne Brenner, "Reconstructing Self and Society: Javanese Muslim Women and 'the veil.' *American Ethnologist* 23, (4): 673–697, 1996; and Leila Ahmed, *Women and Gender in Islam: Historical Roots of a Modern Debate* (New Haven: Yale University Press, 1992).

10. Historical and ethnographic analyses by anthropologically informed scholars of the Iranian revolution include Nikki Keddie, ed., *Religion and Politics in Iran* (New Haven: Yale University Press, 1983); and her *Roots of Revolution: An Interpretative History of Modern Iran* (New Haven: Yale University Press, 1981); Mary Hegland, "Ritual and Revolution in Iran," in Myron Aronoff, ed., *Political Anthropology*. Vol. 2 (New York: Transaction Books, 1983); Michael Fischer, *Iran: From Religious Dispute to Revolution* (Cambridge, MA: Harvard University Press, 1980); William Beeman, "Images of the Great Satan: Representations of the United States in the Iranian Revolution," in Nikki Keddie, ed., *Religion and Politics in Iran* (New Haven: Yale University Press, 1983).

Twenty

The New Age and Related Forms of Contemporary Spirituality

Michael F. Brown

Williams College

One of the most colorful expressions of contemporary grass-roots religiosity is a loosely organized movement known as the New Age. Drawing freely from many traditions, the New Age offers a constantly changing panorama of techniques directed to the exploration of divinity within the individual. Key features of the New Age movement include a focus on self-development, rejection of rigid moral rules, skepticism about organized religion, and a willingness to seek inspiration in non-Western forms of religious understanding. The movement encompasses a wide range of spiritual practices, some of considerable antiquity, others of recent invention. These include dowsing, astrology, neo-shamanism, crystal healing, channeling, past-life therapy, Westernized forms of meditation, and the worship of nature spirits. Some scholars also group with the New Age a range of new religious movements that have taken on the characteristics of organized denominations, including the Church of Scientology and ISKCON, the International Society of Krishna Consciousness.[1]

The New Age has sparked controversy since its birth, and it continues to do so today. Some critics dismiss it as antirational and narcissistic. Others denounce its apparent commercialism, citing the proliferation of workshops that promise enlightenment for a fee. Evangelical Christians voice dismay at the movement's revival of "satanic" practices such as channeling. American communities have occasionally found themselves in conflict with New Age groups whose practices challenge local values. Although these skirmishes are rare, they tend to attract considerable attention from the national news media, leading to public hand wringing about "the cult problem" and "the rise of irrationality in our society." In 1997, the mass suicide of 39 members of Heaven's Gate, a group whose belief in the divine origin of UFOs is by no means unusual in the New Age movement, galvanized popular interest for several weeks before the nation's collective attention shifted to other matters.

Because New Age beliefs are flexible, it is hard to determine precisely how many people identify with them. Nevertheless, there is ample evidence that New Age perspectives influence a significant number of Americans and, increasingly, people in places as diverse as Japan, Brazil, the United Kingdom, Mexico, Italy, Germany, and Australia. Consultants and motivational trainers with philosophical roots in the New

Age regularly present workshops for the employees of Fortune 500 corporations, surely a sign that at least some elements of the movement have achieved respectability. The business-oriented magazine *Forbes* recently estimated that annual personal spending associated with the New Age had reached nearly $14 billion by 1996, suggesting that adherents number in the millions.[2]

HISTORICAL BACKGROUND

The term *New Age* first came into general public use in the 1970s, although the social currents that spawned it originated in the utopian politics of the late 1960s. To many young people in the United States and Europe it seemed that modern industrial society was on the verge of collapse, soon to be followed by a spiritual revolution that would usher in an era of self-awareness, social harmony, and ecological balance. The source of this transformation was not to be mainstream religions such as Christianity or Islam, which were closely identified with materialism and authoritarian politics. Far more attractive to the emerging New Age movement were spiritual traditions thought to emphasize personal insight and harmonious relationships with the natural world—notably, the religions of Asia (e.g., Hinduism and Taoism), native North and South America, and pre-Christian Europe. A prominent example of an early New Age experiment was Findhorn, a small farming community in Scotland that became famous for its use of spiritual principles to yield spectacularly large garden plants. Residents of Findhorn insisted that they were uncovering "new laws of manifestation" that would project human beings into higher states of consciousness and allow the production of food crops without the use of harmful fertilizers or pesticides.[3] The millenarian tone of experiments such as Findhorn—the belief, that is, that humanity had come to a major spiritual turning point—gave rise to the term New Age, a label that has persisted even though many of those involved in alternative spirituality dislike it.

A common theme of these explorations is a desire to transform the self by realizing the individual's full potential as a spiritual being, usually by casting off the multiple masks that family life places on us in childhood. The underlying assumption is that our "real" selves are both more authentic and closer to the divine than are the false selves shaped by social convention. Closely tied to this core belief is the conviction that we should be free to search for spiritual truth wherever it lies, ignoring the artificial doctrinal boundaries characteristic of organized religion. If important spiritual practices can be found among American Indians, Asian Buddhists, or Aboriginal Australians, then all these bits of wisdom should be used to craft each individual's personal version of divine truth. Underlying this vision is deep-seated suspicion of institutionalized religion, which New Agers reject as dogmatic and committed to the privileging of the congregation's needs over those of individual members.

These themes have roots in American history that far predate the rise of the New Age movement, leading scholars to argue that the New Age is not particularly new.[4] At the deepest level, New Age thinking draws heavily on the ancient tradition of Gnosticism, usually defined as the search for the divine through self-understanding. Virtually all major religions have produced Gnostic offshoots that stress mysticism, occult knowledge, and rejection of the worldly tendencies of those in power. (Because of these anti-institutional views, Gnostic groups are often considered heretical by religious authorities.) Another major current in New Age thinking is what theologians call monism, that is, the conviction that human beings can achieve oneness with the Godhead. Theological monism contrasts with the dualism characteristic of mainstream Christianity, which envisions God as superior to humanity in terms of power and moral authority.

Other elements of New Age thought draw on more distinctively American traditions. The United States has a long history of religious sectarianism driven by a desire for direct access to spiritual understanding, without an elaborate hierarchy of priests, ministers, or bishops. This search for unmediated contact with God has given rise to countless new religions and social movements since the nation's earliest days, a situation that has long amazed Europeans, who are far more comfortable with the authority of established churches.

Also characteristic of American values is a firm belief in the possibility of self-perfection. Many immigrants came to North America to break away from the traditions of their home countries in the hope that they could improve themselves. This created an environment favorable to philosophies that promised to develop various aspects of the self. The so-called New Thought movement of the late nineteenth and early twentieth centuries, for instance, helped to lay the groundwork for the New Age by stressing the ability of individuals to "think their way to wealth and happiness" through the powers of the mind. These ideas assumed a religious form in the revelations of Mary Baker Eddy, who founded Christian Science in 1879. Eddy took emerging ideas of "mind cure," the belief that illness is largely an illusion that can be countered by faith in God's essential goodness, and turned them into a new religion. The principles of New Thought live on in the contemporary best-seller *A Course in Miracles*, the text of which came to the psychologist Helen Schucman in a series of dreams from the late 1960s to the early 1970s. The *Course*, as it is sometimes known, argues that human pain and suffering are largely inventions of our wounded imaginations—in particular, our feelings of fear, guilt, and separation from the divine. The book has sold more than a million copies and continues to be studied by small groups across the United States and around the world.

Finally, the New Age elaborates religious themes made popular by the spiritualist movement of the mid-nineteenth century. Spiritualists claimed to communicate directly with the souls of the dead during sèances. Beginning in 1848, when Kate and Margaret Fox, two young sisters from Hydesville, New York, were believed to have established contact with a range of spirits, spiritualism became the focus of intense popular interest. Although the reputation of spiritualists was soon clouded by evidence of fraud, thousands of people, many of them from the highest levels of society, believed in its validity. The movement was especially attractive to educated women who felt that they had no legitimate role in mainstream Christian churches, which were overwhelmingly controlled by men. Spiritualism allowed women to take center stage in the pursuit of religious insight and to demonstrate spiritual mastery in public performances, which helps to explain why it was attractive to the earliest feminists and suffragettes.[5] Today women continue to be disproportionately represented in the New Age movement for many of the same reasons that drew their great-grandmothers to spiritualism a century ago. Anthropological research in other parts of the world has demonstrated that spirit-mediumship typically offers women an alternative source of religious power in male-dominated communities. In this sense, American women share much in common with their counterparts in Brazil or Bali.

CASE STUDIES

The most straightforward way to approach the New Age and related forms of alternative spirituality is to examine a representative range of practices associated with the movement. The following case studies illustrate variations in New Age beliefs while foregrounding common themes and concerns.

Channeling

In the early 1960s, Jane Roberts, a writer from Elmira, New York, began to transcribe the words of an "energy personality essence" named Seth, who spoke through her while she was in a trance state. When published in books such as *The Seth Material* (1970) and *Seth Speaks: The Eternal Validity of the Soul* (1972), Seth's messages found a wide public audience and helped to revive popular interest in spirit-mediumship. To distinguish contemporary mediums from the spiritualists of the nineteenth century, those involved in spirit communication began to refer to themselves as "channelers" or "channels" and to their activity as "channeling." Unlike their spiritualist forebears, who mostly confined themselves to communicating with the souls of the dead, New Age mediums were more likely to seek spiritual guidance from beings originating in other times, planets, or dimensions.[6]

Throughout the 1970s, others followed Jane Roberts's example by developing their ability to channel free-flowing speech, usually in a state of deep trance. Several emerged as charismatic leaders with a significant public audience. Prominent among them was JZ Knight, a former housewife from Tacoma, Washington, who claimed to channel an ancient warrior from Atlantis named Ramtha.[7] Ramtha's message, Knight explains in one of her commercially distributed videotapes, "allows us the vision, the hope, the desire to become all that we can become." At various times since first appearing to Knight in 1977, Ramtha has warned of impending disasters, including floods, earthquakes, and the collapse of the world economic system. But in general his messages emphasize self-affirmation and humanity's divine destiny. After more than a decade as a high-profile guru whose followers included the rich and famous, Knight began to focus her energies on the development of an educational institution called Ramtha's School of Enlightenment in Yelm, Washington, where she continues to channel Ramtha and to disseminate his teachings to an international audience.

Although Knight and other prominent channelers insist that their sources are uniquely authentic and insightful, channeling is shaped by democratic undercurrents that tend to undermine claims that any medium, however charismatic, holds a monopoly on truth. Many of those drawn to channeling insist that its goal should be to help everyone learn to communicate with spiritual allies or with the "higher self"—that is, an eternal aspect of each person, much like the concept of soul, that represents a source of deep wisdom and a link to the collective unconscious. The nation's growing network of New Age conference centers regularly offer workshops that provide instruction in "contacting spirit guides and allies" or "getting in touch with your higher powers." The ultimate goal of these classes is spiritual sovereignty—freedom from the hierarchy, guilt, and dependency that New Agers associate with established churches. From this perspective, everyone must acquire the tools to develop his or her own religious vision.

A channeling session that I attended in Santa Fe, New Mexico, in 1993 illustrates many of channeling's themes and preoccupations. The channeler, Jon Lockwood (a pseudonym), is an interior designer raised in western Maryland. Although a few famous mediums can fill the ballrooms of resort hotels with affluent clients, most channeling takes place in more modest circumstances, and Jon's channeling session was no exception. Eight people, mostly acquaintances, gathered in a friend's living room as Jon attempted to contact his spiritual ally, Ariel, whom Jon describes as a "seventh-dimensional energy" from a distant galaxy.

After sitting with his eyes closed for a few minutes, Jon twitched repeatedly and began to speak loudly in a vaguely British accent. "Hello, my friends. I'm very excited to be in the body again, actually. Yes. So! It's interesting what's happening on your planet in these times, yes?" As he spoke, Jon gesticulated energetically. His audience seemed relaxed and engaged. The general atmosphere was playful. Ariel's jokes prompted laughter and, after his opening monologue, a flurry of questions about spiritual matters. In response to a question about how one can choose between one channeled teaching or another, Ariel declared:

> There are many channeled teachings, there are many written teachings, there many religious teachings, there are teachings all over your planet. What you must do first is begin to honor *yourself.* Then you begin to read and you begin to hear and you begin to see teachings that hold part of the key to that which is you. My friends, at this time of transition, in these times of change, there is always confusion. And there is always one person who thinks they've got it right and that they understand the most. But as true change happens, one key is only the most evolved for a moment. That key then becomes a steppingstone to the next, and the next, and the next. That's what's so important for each of you to keep in mind. As you as an individual evolve, so does all of life on your planet. You see?

After answering questions for about an hour, Ariel said goodbye and promised to return soon. A few moments later, Jon emerged from his altered state. Although the most flamboyant varieties of channeling occur while channelers are deep in trance, a growing number practice what they call "conscious" or "light-trance" channeling, meaning that they remain conscious of their own thoughts even as they provide a conduit for the words of their spiritual ally. The entities that they channel often communicate in an informal, everyday style, and a first-time observer might not even realize that channeling is taking place.

Ariel's message stressed the importance of holding particular beliefs not out of fear or even habit, but because they offer personally meaningful insight. Ariel's words can also be heard as a caution against religious leaders who claim absolute authority over truth. From the New Age perspective, every teacher holds important pieces of information but not the entire picture. As greater numbers of individuals achieve their own spiritual understanding, it is believed, the world will experience a collective "evolution" in the direction of higher consciousness.

The relentless focus on self-affirmation—expressed clearly in Ariel's declaration, "What you must do first is begin to honor *yourself*"—has given rise to accusations that New Age thought is shallow and narcissistic, stressing selfishness at the expense of social responsibility. Even to a sympathetic observer, there are moments when the messages offered by channelers seem alternately self-absorbed, amoral, and absurd. For instance, a group of channelers from Colorado who claim to be "walk-ins" (people whose bodies have been taken over by an extraterrestrial consciousness) insist that all human suffering is an illusion and that evil cannot possibly exist. In 1993, they told a small Santa Fe audience that because we are manifestations of "God-All-That-Is," we cannot do harm to one another and therefore shouldn't concern ourselves with conventional morality or laws, which are based on negative emotions such as fear. In fairness, it should be pointed out that some members of the audience seemed to regard these claims as doubtful. Yet they also appeared to enjoy exploring outrageous ideas even when they could not embrace them wholeheartedly. "We all construct our own personal reality," I was told on many occasions, the implication being that exposure to unusual beliefs can be useful in broadening our vision of the world and disrupting habitual attitudes that stand in the way of personal fulfillment.

In interviews, female channelers, who outnumber males by about two to one, report that they feel empowered by the experience of channeling male spirits or energies. One woman, for example, reported that channeling a male being helped her to "achieve male-female integration" by "filling in the gaps" created by her identity as a woman. Others claim that channeling opens them to forms of consciousness that have moved beyond male and female identities altogether. Male channelers are less likely to cross the gender divide in their performances, although most argue that channeling is in itself a feminine activity because it forces men to assume a passive role in relation to their spirit guides. Clearly one of the attractions of channeling is that it allows people to try out new ways of experiencing gender in an era when Americans are struggling to redefine ideas of masculinity and femininity. An extreme expression of this idea can be seen in the revelation that some male members of the Heaven's Gate group had been surgically castrated to prepare themselves for the spiritual transformation that they anticipated after their mass suicide.

Harmonic Convergence

Although the Harmonic Convergence is an event rather than an ongoing form of religious expression, it illustrates a key theme in New Age thought, the conviction that humankind has reached a critical turning point in its spiritual evolution. The event itself occurred on August 16–17, 1987, a date identified by the writer Josè Arguelles as a critical conjunction of cosmic forces foreseen by the Maya calendar. According to Arguelles, the Harmonic Convergence would cause the return of "long-dormant archetypal memories and impressions," leading to the beginnings of a major spiritual renaissance that will be completed at a second and more important Harmonic Convergence episode in 2012.[8] In anticipation of the event, people gathered at sacred sites around the world, including such places as Mt. Shasta in California, Chaco Canyon National Monument in New Mexico, and Machu Picchu in the Peruvian Andes. There they meditated, offered blessings, and focused their thoughts on world harmony—often to the accompaniment of television cameras and tape recorders wielded by curious journalists, who turned the event into a media carnival.

The Harmonic Convergence set the tone for other less publicized events based on astrological conjunctions or exotic calendrical systems. Organizers of these fixed-date encounters sometimes predict catastrophic "earth changes," including earthquakes, floods, and asteroid showers. More often they anticipate an instantaneous revolution in human consciousness, a claim that took center stage in the "12:12 event" of December 12, 1994, advertised as the "gateway to freedom" that would mark the beginning of a new Golden Age of spirituality. Interviews with people who have participated in these events suggest a wide spectrum of personal commitment. Some clearly believed that their lives would change dramatically on the date in question, and they grappled with disillusionment when it passed without incident. (In describing her sense of betrayal when the major earthquake predicted by a famous channeler failed to occur, a New Mexico woman told me, "It was a transition point in my life. I learned, very much the hard way, that channeled information isn't all valid.") Most, however, seemed to have approached the Harmonic Convergence as a welcome opportunity to share in a collective outpouring of spiritual energy, regardless of the outcome.

Events such as the Harmonic Convergence increasingly incorporate geographical features defined as "power spots" or "vortexes." The number of recognized power spots is growing, and some have generated significant tourist traffic. Vortex sites in Sedona, Arizona, receive more than 5,000 visitors a month during the summer tourist season, and the number continues to grow annually. Business has been so good, in fact, that several local companies now offer specialized vortex tours in pink jeeps.[9] The notion that astronomical bodies, cosmic energies, sacred geographical sites, and human consciousness are integrated into a single system exemplifies the New Age quest for holism.

Neo-paganism

Neo-paganism is an informal network of people devoted to Wicca, the Craft, Goddess-focused spirituality, and other ritual practices inspired by the religions of pagan Europe and the Mediterranean. (Most neo-pagans are careful to distinguish themselves from satanists, who emphasize dark, occult powers rather than the life-affirming natural forces central to neo-paganism.) Neo-pagans attempt to re-create a religious sensibility that they believe existed in many parts of the world before it was forced underground by Christianity, a religion that in the words of Starhawk, a prominent advocate of feminist neo-paganism, imposed a "Father God-ruled patriarchy" that denied the feminine aspects of life and subordinated the life of the flesh to that of the spirit. "The symbol of the Goddess," she argues, "conveys the spiritual power both to challenge systems of oppression and to create new, life-oriented cultures."[10]

Although neo-pagans divide themselves into a bewildering array of groups, each with its own traditions and rituals, they share several common features. All are polytheistic, acknowledging multiple spirits and forms of consciousness. They seek union with nature rather than dominion over it, a principle that makes neo-pagan worship particularly attractive to people holding passionate environmentalist views. They are committed to a balance of masculine and feminine principles in ritual practice. Above all, they celebrate the sensual, embodied quality of life and reject religious perspectives that deny the reality of the flesh.

Neo-pagans can be just as critical of New Age practices as they are of Christianity. "Paganism rejects the Gnostic denigration of matter and darkness prevalent in New Age, and celebrates the world as real and as given," writes one observer of neo-pagan beliefs.[11] Channelers in particular are dismissed as insipid optimists by many neo-pagans, who pride themselves on a willingness to grapple with the dangerous and destructive side of the world as well as with its beauty. The emotional tone of neo-pagan events differs significantly from that of typical New Age gatherings, especially in the former's emphasis on earthiness and long-term commitment. Nevertheless, from a more distanced perspective, neo-pagan and New Age practices exhibit more similarities than differences. Both, for instance, seek direct personal engagement with the sacred, and they reject the male-dominated organizational structures of monotheistic religion. Like other manifestations of the New Age, neo-paganism says more about modern anxieties—related to gender, personal identity, and our ambivalent relationship with nature—than it does about the religious practices of pre-Christian peoples.

Scientology

Scientology, now organized as the Church of Scientology, is a formally structured religious and therapeutic sect based on the teachings of the science-fiction writer L. Ron Hubbard, whose book *Dianetics: The Modern Science of Mental Health* (1950) represents the church's foundational text. The Church of Scientology's role as a provider of therapeutic services has long generated controversy, including countless lawsuits and denunciations from former church members, as well as extravagant praise from those who insist that Scientology has changed their lives for the better. There is little question that the church's business practices set it apart from other New Age groups, and many scholars would resist linking it to the movement at all. Yet if we look past the church's organizational structure and instead concentrate on its *message*, Scientology's affinities to the New Age become apparent.

L. Ron Hubbard first presented Scientology, then called Dianetics, as a new technology of personal liberation vaguely resembling psychotherapy. His original revelation was that human limitations and neuroses are the products of negative memories or images ("engrams") that must be dislodged if we are to achieve our full potential. Engrams can be eliminated through a form of spiritual counseling called "auditing," which requires precise interview protocols and the strategic use of an electronic tool called the "E-meter."

By the late 1950s, this scientific-sounding therapy started to take on explicitly religious overtones. Hubbard and his followers began to speculate that people could acquire engrams in past lives, for example. The accumulating engrams made it difficult to see our true nature as "thetans," that is, immortal forms of consciousness that can bring matter and energy into being at will. A contemporary Scientology document explains:

> The thetan is the spiritual being . . . that which animates the body and uses the mind. One of the most basic tenets of Scientology is that man is an immortal spiritual being

whose experience extends well beyond a single lifetime and whose capabilities are unlimited, even if not presently realized.[12]

If we strip away Scientology's exotic terminology—"engram," "thetan," and "auditing," and so forth—these concepts differ only slightly from those applied elsewhere in the New Age movement. Channelers, for instance, routinely help clients to identify traumatic past-life experiences that create unconscious sources of anxiety. Channeling itself is described by many practitioners as a process of connection to their higher self, a concept similar to the "thetan." The Church of Scientology declares that its goal is "to bring one to a new state where he can reach his own conclusions concerning the nature of God or a Supreme Being. . . . [S]alvation in Scientology is attained through personal spiritual enlightenment."[13] Few people involved in other facets of New Age spirituality, even those unsympathetic to Scientology's financial practices, would object to this statement of purpose.

THE NEW AGE AS POSTMODERN RELIGION

The case studies illustrate several prominent characteristics of New Age beliefs and practices:

Eclecticism. People involved in the New Age movement are strongly attracted to the improvisational blending of religious concepts originating in many different places. Eclecticism allows everyone to customize a religious perspective that is right for them. Equally important, a mixture of spiritual concepts from different places and times is thought to reflect universal truths rather than local ones. "Look," one channeler told me, "we are really trying to become global citizens. We are looking to become less identified with our culture, sex, or race, and more identified with the universal sense of human nature." By this she implied that local views are intrinsically small-minded and negative, whereas global perspectives are better able to transcend the petty interests of individual communities. Paul Heelas, a sociologist who has studied the New Age movement, refers to this process as "detraditionalization," the rejection of a self defined by local interests and loyalties. Detraditionalized persons see their "true selves" as existing independently of any particular moral framework or set of values. They feel free to choose among all available options—whether of lifestyles, beliefs, or religious practices—in order to satisfy personal needs.[14] Neo-pagans, who by most accounts tend to be deeply committed to small-group process and the intimacy of shared community, are less detraditionalized than other groups we have considered, yet even they do not hesitate to borrow from many different cultures in search of spiritual meaning.

The native peoples whose religious practices are subject to this borrowing are sometimes outraged by what they see as a cavalier attitude toward their sacred traditions. American Indians in particular continue to denounce the imitation of their religious practices by outsiders searching for personal transformation. The commercialism and insensitivity that they condemn can be seen in a recent issue of a magazine published in Sedona that advertised custom-made "power shields" which "awaken a new level of understanding of Sun Bear's vision of the Medicine Wheel and Native American teachings," beginning at only $200. Assessing this tendency to decontexualize other people's religious practices, one critic has called the contemporary West a "cannibal culture" because of its willingness to treat the entire world as a giant supermarket from which it can take pieces of other people's heritage.[15] When confronted by such objections, New Agers are likely to reply that religion is the common property of humanity, not of any particular group or culture.

Self-multiplicity. To varying degrees, the case studies show a preoccupation with the increasingly fragmented identities characteristic of modern life. Channelers experiment with their own multiplicity by serving as the vehicle for various spiritual entities, some of whom may provide information about the channeler's own prior incarnations. Scientologists try to recover their thetan identity by clearing the negative experiences acquired during many past lives. Neo-pagans explore their masculine and feminine identities in an attempt to bring them into greater harmony. All of these groups seek inner unity at some level (e.g., the "higher self"), but their search for holism is pursued precisely because of a growing awareness of inner contradiction or dissonance.

Preoccupation With the Moral Significance of Technology. A disconcerting feature of New Age practices is their oscillation between a fascination with what might be called "technologies of transcendence" and the total rejection of technology in favor of a nostalgic return to oneness with the natural world. Interest in the spiritual potential of new technologies can be seen in the Church of Scientology's use of the E-meter. More extreme examples include so-called UFO cults whose members await transportation to other planets or dimensions by technologically superior aliens. In contrast, some neo-pagans extol the virtues of returning to a pretechnological lifestyle that they believe can restore the planet's ecological balance and revive "true" spiritual values among the earth's many peoples.

Resistance to Formal Institutions and Master Narratives. People attracted to New Age practices express skepticism about science, government, organized religion, and other key social institutions. They are equally wary of formal belief systems, preferring instead to invent their own moral codes and versions of the truth. (Scientologists, who join a complex international organization and participate in a standardized self-development process, contradict this generalization. Even they, however, refuse to define God or the sacred in any specific way, believing this to be a matter of personal choice.) Morality, New Agers often say, depends on negative judgments that perpetuate unhappiness and a profound sense of separation from others. One of the paradoxes of New Age groups, of course, is that without some kind of shared framework they have no reason to stay together. Only sects that decide upon a set of collective assumptions and procedures are likely to survive the centrifugal tendencies of New Age thought.

Eclecticism, self-fragmentation, and the rejection of master narratives are characteristic of *postmodernity*, a diffuse set of attitudes and social arrangements that some theorists see emerging from the conflicting demands of contemporary life. Whereas modernity has been based on faith in progress and in the inevitable triumph of rationalism, postmodernity rejects these dominant narratives in favor of idiosyncratic and individualistic ones. Modernity values intention and purpose; postmodernity celebrates an attitude of playfulness. Modernity holds out the promise of ultimate truth; postmodernity offers skepticism or ironic distance from truth.[16] Theorists disagree about whether, or to what extent, American society is "becoming postmodern," but there is little question that postmodern attitudes flourish in many quarters. We can hardly find better evidence of this than in the rise of New Age spirituality.

It is important to keep the scale of the New Age movement in perspective when considering the present and future status of religion. On the world scene, major religions such as Islam and Christianity continue to attract converts in significant numbers. More than 85 percent of Americans identify themselves as Christians, and there is little evidence that this pattern is likely to change any time soon. The fastest-growing sector of American religion is not the New Age but independent Christian churches, many espousing a conservative, evangelical philosophy far removed from the ideas discussed in this chapter. Nevertheless, surveys of religious affiliation fail to capture the impact that New Age ideas have had on religious sensibilities worldwide. In the United States, the influential—and aging—Baby Boom generation is beginning to confront its own mortality, a situation sure to intensify popular interest in unconventional forms of spirituality. Affordable airline travel and global communications networks now make it possible for middle-class religious seekers in all corners of the world to indulge their curiosity about the spiritual practices of American Indian healers, Tibetan diviners, or Amazonian shamans. These factors suggest that the New Age will continue to exercise a subtle but pervasive influence on religious attitudes and practices well into the twenty-first century.

NOTES

1. Important surveys of the New Age and related trends in contemporary religion include Catherine L. Albanese, *Nature Religion in America: From the Algonkian Indians to the New Age* (Chicago: University of Chicago Press, 1990); Paul Heelas, *The New Age Movement: The Celebration of Self and the Sacralization of Modernity* (Cambridge, MA: Blackwell, 1996); and Michael York, *The Emerging Network: A Sociology of the New Age and Neo-Pagan Movements* (Lanham, MD: Rowman & Littlefield, 1995). Works sharply critical of the movement include Douglas R. Groothius, *Unmasking the New Age* (Downers Grove, IL: InterVarsity Press, 1986); Wendy Kaminer, *Sleeping with Extra-Terrestrials* (New York: Pantheon, 1999); and Melanie McGrath, *Motel Nirvana: Dreaming of the New Age in the American Desert* (New York: Picador, 1996).

2. Tim W. Ferguson and Josephine Lee, "Coin of the New Age," *Forbes*, September 9, 1996, pp. 86–87.

3. For a brief summary of Findhorn's history and philosophy, see Stephen M. Clark, "Myth, Metaphor, and Manifestation: The Negotiation of Belief in a New Age Community," in James R. Lewis and J. Gordon Melton, eds., *Perspectives on the New Age* (Albany, NY: State University of New York Press, 1992), pp. 97–104.

4. See, for example, Robert Ellwood, "How New Is the New Age?" in Lewis and Melton, eds., *Perspectives on the New Age*, pp. 59–67.

5. The feminist roots of spiritualism are assessed in Ann Braude, *Radical Spirits: Spiritualism and Women's Rights in Nineteenth-century America*(Boston: Beacon Press, 1989).

6. Sources on the history and social significance of channeling include Michael F. Brown, *The Channeling Zone: American Spirituality in an Anxious Age* (Cambridge, MA: Harvard University Press, 1997); Joel Bjorling, *Channeling: A Bibliographic Exploration*, Sects and Cults in America, Bibliographic Guide No. 15 (New York: Garland Publishing, 1992); Dureen J. Hughes, "Blending with an Other: An Analysis of Trance Channeling in the United States," *Ethos* 19 (1991): 161–184; and Suzanne Riordan, "Channeling: A New Revelation?" in Lewis and Melton, eds., *Perspectives on the New Age*, pp. 105–126.

7. For details on the career of JZ Knight, see J. Gordon Melton, *Finding Enlightenment: Ramtha's School of Ancient Wisdom* (Hillsboro, OR: Beyond Words Publishing, 1997). A skeptical assessment of the revelations of Knight and other prominent channelers is offered in Henry Gordon, *Channeling Into the New Age: The "Teachings" of Shirley MacLaine and Other Such Gurus* (Buffalo, NY: Prometheus Books, 1988).

8. Quoted in Phillip C. Lucas, "The New Age Movement and the Pentecostal/Charismatic Revival," in Lewis and Melton, eds., *Perspectives on the New Age*, p. 205. For additional information on the Harmonic Convergence and similar events, see J. Gordon Melton, Jerome Clark, and Aidan A. Kelly, *New Age Encyclopedia* (Detroit, MI: Gale Research, 1990) pp. 204–205; and Charles B. Strozier, *Apocalypse: On the Psychology of Fundamentalism in America* (Boston: Beacon, 1994), pp. 228–234.

9. "Wheels of Misfortune," *Newsweek*, July 10, 1991, p. 28.

10. Starhawk, *The Spiral Dance: A Rebirth of the Ancient Religion of the Great Goddess* (San Francisco: HarperSanFrancisco, 1989), pp. 24–25. Other useful works on contemporary neo-paganism include Margot Adler, *Drawing Down the Moon: Witches, Druids, Goddess-Worshippers, and Other Pagans in America Today*, rev. ed. (Boston: Beacon Press, 1986); Graham Harvey, *Contemporary Paganism: Listening People, Speaking Earth* (New York: New York University Press, 1997); James R. Lewis, ed., *Magical Religion and Modern Witchcraft* (Albany, NY: State University of New York Press, 1996); and T. M. Luhrmann, *Persuasions of the Witches' Craft: Ritual Magic in Contemporary England* (Cambridge: Harvard University Press, 1989). A recent issue of *Gnosis Magazine* (No. 48, Summer 1998) offers several essays that question the antiquity and authenticity of contemporary neo-paganism.

11. Graham Harvey, *Contemporary Paganism*, p. 220. See note 10.

12. "What Is the True Story of Scientology?" <http://faq.scientology.org/ref_1.htm>, accessed 12 April 1998, unpaginated. Other helpful sources on Scientology include Robert S. Ellwood and Harry B. Partin, *Religious and Spiritual Groups in Modern America*, 2nd ed. (Englewood Cliffs, NJ: Prentice Hall, 1988), pp. 140–146; and Harriet Whitehead, *Renunciation and Reformulation: A Study of Conversion in an American Sect* (Ithaca, NY: Cornell University Press, 1987).

13. "What Is the True Story of Scientology?" unpaginated. See note 12.

14. Paul Heelas, *The New Age Movement*, pp. 155–157. See note 1.

15. Deborah Root, *Cannibal Culture: Art, Appropriation, and the Commodification of Difference* (Boulder, CO: Westview, 1996).

16. For a cogent discussion of these issues, see David Harvey, *The Condition of Postmodernity* (Cambridge, MA: Blackwell, 1989).

Twenty-One

Future Trends in Religion

Raymond Scupin

Lindenwood University

We began this textbook with a brief overview of some of the predictions about religion in the future by various writers and social theorists of the 1960s. Some of these social theorists were convinced that religion had seen its last days in the evolution of humanity. They assumed that as modern industrial society was developing in a more scientific direction, religion would decline and eventually disappear completely. They envisioned the future as a completely secular world dependent upon scientific and rational explanations of all phenomena, including the nature of human existence, the relationship between humans and society, and solutions to fundamental moral issues. As we saw in Chapter Two, many of the social theorists of the nineteenth century including Emile Durkheim, Karl Marx, Max Weber, E.B. Tylor, and James Frazier held similar views. These nineteenth-century theorists predicted a wholly secular world devoid of religion and faith, based on scientific and rationalist explanations. As we have seen, however, trends ranging from revivals of aboriginal religion to the resurgence of traditional forms of religion and the emergence of development of New Age religious movements, the social theorists of the nineteenth century and the 1960s were mistaken. As we enter the twenty-first century, religion has become remarkably active, vital, and is ever more important. What, then, can anthropologists say about future trends, and what will be their role in the study of religion in this future?

One of the fundamental assumptions of most anthropologists and other social theorists at the end of the nineteenth century, which up until recently has had a major influence within twentieth-century social theory, was "secularization theory." Developed by social theorists during the Enlightenment in the West and espoused by Weber, Durkheim, Marx, or anthropologists such as E.B. Tylor or Frazer, secularization theory assumed that religion was going to decline or disappear. These scholars noted that since the early developments of the modernization of society, beginning in the 1600s in the West, other institutions emerged which took over many of the functions the religious institutions had carried on in earlier societies. They emphasized that civil laws, the public universities, social welfare, health care, and governments developed their own structures which wholly or partially replaced the religiously based churches. The emergence of the nation-state, the expansion of industrial capitalism, the rise of science, and the unfolding of the Protestant Reformation, which fragmented church authority, were all factors that led to increasing secularization. This secularization theory arose concurrently with the rise of social science, including anthropology, and was linked to the enlightenment and to revolutionary ideologies of the eighteenth and nineteenth centuries. It predicted that as the modern world developed, increasing rationality and greater individualization would produce a progressive diminution of the authority and legitimacy of religious institutions. In the twentieth century people would place their faith, their money, and their political support increasingly with science and secular institutions, rather than with religion and religious institutions.

The studies assembled for this textbook show that these assumptions are highly questionable. Contemporary anthropologists agree that secularization theory is fraught with and hampered by ambiguities as we attempt to understand religious trends in the twenty-first century. What ethnographic research has made clear is that different societies have had very different experiences with secularization processes. Near the end of the twentieth century a number of religious trends emerged, including the re-emergence of orthodox religious vitality after the downfall of the former Soviet Union and the Eastern bloc countries such as Poland in the 1990s, the rise of religious fundamentalist tendencies in most of the major world religions including Hinduism, Buddhism, Judaism, Christianity, and Islam, and the increasing role of religion in public institutions, political, economic, and social in most societies throughout the world. Instead of "withering away" and becoming marginal in modern society, religion appears to be resurfacing and is becoming revitalized at the beginning of the twenty-first century. Contrary to the expectations of the secularization theorists, the increasing technological and scientific revolutions that have dramatically transformed our world, religious experience appears to be more important than ever for constructing a meaningful world in the midst of these global processes.

Thus, presently, most anthropologists agree that the secularization model is neither a good descriptive account of what is happening regarding religious evolution, nor does it appear to be a good predictive model as many social theorists believed it was. The premises and predictions of secularization theory have not born fruit for anthropological studies. In contrast to secularization theory predictions, many recent religious revivals have occurred in those societies that have been most affected by modernization. As twentieth- and twenty-first century global processes introduce sweeping technological, economic, political, social, and ideological changes, many traditional beliefs and values are challenged. To cope with these destabilizing transformations, many people are reemphasizing traditional cultural values, including religion. For example, the fundamentalist movements in North America, whether Catholic, Jewish, or Protestant, can be partially understood as a reaction against the perceived threat of secularization processes and modernization. The same can be said of Buddhist, Hindu, and Islamic resurgence in other parts of the world.

A more modest claim of the secularization thesis promoted by a number of social scientists is that as modernization takes place, religion would become a private affair disentangled from public institutions within society. In a recent essay called

"A Pinch of Destiny: Religion as Experience, Meaning, Identity, Power," Clifford Geertz reflects on the difference between religion in the beginning of the twentieth century and at the end of the twentieth century. He focuses on the text *The Varieties of Religious Experience: A Study in Human Nature* by William James published in 1902 to indicate how scholars thought about religion earlier in this century. Geertz notes how, in James's' conclusion, he describes religious feelings and sentiments as "the individual pinch of destiny," faith as the individual feels it. His focus in on the individual. Then, however, Geertz writes that at the end of the twentieth century,

> We see it [religion] in other terms because the ground has shifted under our feet; we have other extremes to examine, other fates to forestall. The pinch is still there, sharp and nagging. But it feels, for some reason, somehow different. Less private, perhaps, or harder to locate, more difficult exactly to put one's finger on not so surely a reliable indicator or a revelatory sign, not so surely a metaphysical ache.

Geertz goes on to say:

> When the phrase "religious struggle" appears, as it does so often these days, in the media, in scholarly writing, even in churchly harangues and homilies, it tends not to refer to private wrestlings with inner demons. These days, "religious struggle" mostly refers to quite outdoor occurences, plein air proceedings in the public square—alleyway encounters, high court holdings. Yugoslavia, Algeria, India, Ireland. Immigration policies, minority problems, school curricula, sabbath observations, head scarves, abortion debates. Riots, terrorism, fatwas, Aum Supreme Truth, Kach, Waco, Santeria, the storming of the Golden Temple. Political monks in Sri Lanka, born-again power-brokers in the United States, warrior saints in Afghanistan. Anglican nobelist, Desmond Tutu, works to get South Africans to confront their past; Roman nobelist, Carlos Ximenes Belo, works to encourage East Timorese to resist their present. The Dalai Lama haunts the world's capitals to keep the Tibetan cause alive. Nothing particularly private—covert perhaps, or surreptitious, but hardly private—about all that."

In these passages, Geertz is pointing out that religion has, once again, become an extremely public affair in many different types of societies at the end of the twentieth century. In many respects, religion has become "deprivatized."[1] The world has confounded the theorists' expectations. Despite this deprivatization of religion, as many of the essays in this textbook have demonstrated, though religion has become more public, it has had profound consequences for an individual's private life. The various fundamentalist movements have all called upon individuals to reassess personal morality as it pertains to one's private and personal concerns. In addition, it appears that in the highly industrialized societies such as the United States and Europe, individuals have much more personal choice regarding their own religious "experience." Michael Brown's essay in this text on the New Age movements shows how people in the United States change their faith readily based on their own personal and private needs.

As discussed in Chapter Three, starting with Franz Boas and Bronislaw Malinowski, anthropologists have abandoned the grand social evolutionary theories of the nineteenth century when assessing the development of religion. Instead we have emphasized the importance of gathering empirical data about the particular cultural background that shapes the specific forms that religious belief and practice take in different times and places. More than any other discipline, we assert that theoretical speculation without sound ethnographic data is sterile. The anthropologists of the twenty-first century will have to reaffirm this lesson. As the pioneers of anthropology in the early twentieth century emphasized, there is no substitute for long-term exposure in the field for those attempting to analyze religion. Future anthropologists will continue to immerse themselves in the different cultural environments of the world to produce rigorous, in-depth, richer, and thicker ethnographies to establish a context for opening the door for valid comparative studies of religious phenomena. These ethnographic studies of the twenty-first century will be marked by both sensitive methodological and theoretically approaches.

Predictions about global evolutionary trends of religion will have to be set aside. The only confident prediction that anthropologists can make about religion in the twenty-first century is that religion will persist as an integral and dynamic element in human affairs around the world. Its forms may change, but the underlying human needs and social dynamics that support it will not. What people will hold sacred may change, but religion will continue to be a vital component. Instead of secularization resulting in the demise of religion, anthropologists expect the religious and the secular to coexist indefinitely into the future.

Anthropologists of the twenty-first century will have to refocus on how religious associations give structure and meaning to human relations and create communities and enable action. They will have to describe how religions provide the language, symbols, motives, and meaning for both cooperation within communities or cultural conflict between and within societies. More than ever, anthropologists who study religion in this new century are committed to in-depth ethnographic reporting and description. Our aim is to provide more robust and accurate representations of religious beliefs and practices, to provide the richly detailed ethnographic descriptions without which theory remains abstract, too detached from the lives it purports to explain. There is a renewed attention to continue to examine ethnographic practices to ensure more unbiased qualitative approaches in comprehending religious phenomena. Ethnographic methods will resume their role of interpreting meanings of religious belief and practice attempting to understand action from the perspective of the actor, and providing substantial narratives about myth, folklore, and symbols. The mission of anthropologists of the twenty-first century will involve gaining access to other religious ways of life in order to represent what it is like to be a human being in another cultural and religious milieu. Anthropologists will continue to ask questions about what it is like for another human being who may have different preferences, values, goals, tastes, desires, and may be constrained or enabled by different economic, social, and political institutions. Twenty-first century anthropologists are devoted to the construction of valid, plausible, and intelligible accounts of religious beliefs and practices in multiple contexts around the world.

You may wonder about the practical importance of anthropologists' research on religion. Anthropologists are actively involved in documenting the local responses to global, political, and religious trends of people in the regions of Latin America, Africa, the Middle East, Asia, as well as in the United States and Europe. We record the dislocations caused by global economic and political trends influencing religious processes in these societies and the ways in which people have attempted to cope with these changes. The continuing agony of religious conflicts in Ireland, Bosnia, Sri Lanka, and elsewhere threatens people throughout the world, and existing institutions have not been able to resolve them.

With greater understanding of the religious aspirations specific to these different peoples, national governments and the international community will be better able to respond to their diverse needs and interests. As anthropologists identify the cultural and religious variations that can block international coordination, they may help to contribute to the reduction of ethnic and religious tensions worldwide. If hopes for peace depend on greater mutual understanding, there is still much for anthropologists to do.[2]

NOTES

1. Clifford Geertz's essay "A Pinch of Destiny: Religion as Experience, Meaning, Identity, Power" was read as the William James Lecture at Harvard University, 1997. One sociological theorist who has emphasized the "de-privatization" of religion and criticized the traditional approach of secularization theory is Jose Casanova. See his book *Public Religions in the Modern World* (Chicago: University of Chicago Press, 1994).

2. I would like to thank Wade Tarzia, Andrew Buckser, and Michael Brown for giving me their advice on this concluding chapter. John McCreery helped me clarify some of my thoughts through an extensive rewriting and editing of my first draft of this conclusion.